The

International
Dictionary

The

International
Dictionary
THE WORDS YOU NEED
IN **21** LANGUAGES

COMPILED BY H. L. OUSEG

A Citadel Press Book
Published by Carol Publishing Group

Carol Publishing Group Edition, 1995

Previously published as *21–Language Dictionary*

A Citadel Press Book
Published by Carol Publishing Group
Citadel Press is a registered trademark of Carol Communications, Inc.

Editorial Offices: 600 Madison Avenue, New York, NY 10022
Sales & Distribution Offices: 120 Enterprise Avenue, Secaucus, NJ 07094
In Canada: Canadian Manda Group, One Atlantic Avenue, Suite 105
Toronto, Ontario, M6K 3E7

Queries regarding rights and permissions should be addressed to:
Carol Publishing Group, 600 Madison Avenue, New York, NY 10022

Manufactured in the United States of America
10 9 8 7 6 5 4 3 2 1

Carol Publishing Group books are available at special discounts
for bulk purchases, sales promotions, fund raising, or
educational purposes. Special editions can also be created to
specifications. For details contact: Special Sales Department,
Carol Publishing Group, 120 Enterprise Ave., Secaucus, NJ 07094

Library of Congress Cataloging-in-Publication Data

Ouseg, H. L.
    The international dictionary : the words you need in 21 languages
    / compiled by H. L. Ouseg.
        p. cm.
    "A Citadel Press book."
    ISBN 0-8065-1677-1 (pbk.)
    1. Dictionaries, Polyglot. I. Title.
    P361.086 1995
    413—dc20   95-19916
                                                        CIP

The International Dictionary

TO THE

HONORABLE

FRANCIS E. WALTER,
United States Congressman,

This book is inscribed as a modest token of
sincere and profound esteem,
by the
Author.

FOREWORD

THIS INTERNATIONAL DICTIONARY is useful not only to all tourists traveling in any part of the world, but also to interpreters, translators, stewards, journalists, teachers, students, —as well as to all in Army-, Navy-, Air Force-, Radio-, Press-, Consular-, Diplomatic- services, etc. In this book can be found 420 possible bilingual dictionaries. All you have to do is: locate the word or phrase in the main dictionary (if you speak English) or in the alphabetical word list of the language from which you want to translate by a system of numbering. You then have it in front of you in twenty foreign languages at the same time!

CONTENTS

PRONUNCIATION RULES

For practical purposes, the *PRONUNCIATION* will be explained by comparison with English sounds. It must never be forgotten, however, that the sound-systems of no two languages are exactly identical.

CZECH

is a phonetic language—pronounced as it is written:

a as a in daft
á as a in father (long)
b as b in bell
c as ts in hats
č as ch in chin
ḋ as d in day
d' as d in dew or duke
e as e in nest
é as a in fast (long)
f as f in fifty
g as g in gum
h as h in hallow
ch as ch in the Scottish loch
i as i in pink
í as i in machine (long)
j as y in yesterday
k as k in kind
l as l in load
m as m in mister
n as n in never
ň as ni in opinion
o as o in oracular
ó as o in or (long)
p as p in people
r as r in red
ř similar to rsh: Pershing
s as s in salt
š as sh in shoe
t as t in tea
t' as t in tune
u as u in put
ú *or* ů— as in rule
v as v in veal
y as y in hardly
ý as ee in heel
z as z in zero
ž as z in azure

DANISH

a like a in father
b like b in bell
c like c in cigarette
d like d in day; often silent before s or after e, u, r or between l, u, r
e like e in nest or ai in aisle, ice
f like f in five
g like g in go; silent after i and u
h like h in hallow; silent before j and **v**
ch like sh in shoe
i like i in pink
j like y in yes
k like k in kind
l like l in load
m like m in mister
n like n in never
o like o in or
p like p in people
r like r in red
s like s in salad
sj like sh in shoe
t like t in tea
u like u in put
v like v in veal silent after l
y like ee in fee with **pursed lips**
z like s in salt
ae like a in fat
ø like e in her with **rounded lips**
å (aa) like o in or

DUTCH

a like a in father
b like b in barber
c like c in cent
ch like ch in the Scottish loch
d like d in day
e like e in nest
f like f in far
g like h in hallow
h like h in hair
i like i in pink
k like k in kind
l like l in leave
m like m in mister
n like n in name
o like o in or
p like p in paper
q like q in quarter
r like r in rain
s like s in salt
t like t in ten
u like e in her with pursed lips
w often like v in veal
v often like f in five
z like z in zero, but very often as s in salt

FINNISH

a like a in daft
aa like a in far (long pron.)
d like d in day
e like e in nest
ee like ee in née
g like g in give
h like h in horse
i like i in pink
j like y in yes
k like k in kind
l like l in leave
m like m in mister
n like n in never
o like o in oracular
oo like o in or (long)
p like p in paper
r like r in rain
s like s in salt
t like t in ten
u like u in put
v like w in water
y like i in big
ä like a in fat
ää the same, but long
ö like e in her with pursed lips
öö the same, but long

In the foreign words:

b like b in boy
c like ts in hats
f like f in five
z like z in zero

FRENCH

Vowels and diphthongs:

a like a in father
e, ai, ei — like e in bed or like a in care;
    e is silent at the end of a word
i, y like i in big
o, au, eau — like o in ore
u — like ee in fee with pursed lips
ui — the same sound as described above —
    quite rapidly, but the following vowel
    must sound as clearly as possible,
    e.g. nuit (night) : nee*i*
ou — like oo in look
eu, oeu — like e in her or ea in learn
oi — wa in ward
y — very often like y in you

Consonants:

c — like s in glass before i and e
c — like k in kind before a, o, u and before a consonant
g — like g in gold
g, j — like s in measure
h is always quite mute. When it is said to be
    "aspire" (we write a (') before word), it merely
    means that no liaison should be made.
p — p in English, but often mute at the end of words.
All other consonants sound like in English.

The *nasal sounds:* am, an, em, en, un, in, ain, ein . . .
    are uttered while keeping the passage between
    throat and nose closely shut; in linking, the
    n of the nasal sounds is carried over to the
    following vowel.

The sound of French *gn* is pronounced like ni in Union.

The French language has three accents, which
principally belong to the e; the acute accent é, the
grave accent è, the circumflex accent ê. If the e is
without the accent it either sounds short or not
at all,—if with the accent it is always pronounced.

In the case, when a word begins with a vowel (or a
mute h), it is joined with the last consonant of the
preceding word, also, when the consonant is
followed by a mute e.

GERMAN

Simple vowels:

a — like a in father
e — like e in bed, better
i — like i in pink
o — like o in ore, order
u — like u in put

Compound vowels:

ä — like a in fat
ö — like e in her with pursed lips
ü — like ee in fee with pursed lips

Diphthongs:

au — like ow in cow
eu — like oi in toil, oil
ei, ai, ay — like i in ice
ie — like ee in need

Consonants:

c — like k in kind — if before a, o, u, a consonant or when final
g — like g in go; or like s in measure (before e, i)
h — like h in horse
ch—like guttural ch in the Scotch and Irish word loch
j — like y in yes
s — like z in zebra
s — like s in miss, when final, doubled or next to
       a voiceless consonant
sch — like sh in ship
sp — like shp with p
st — like sht with t
v — like f in far
w — like v in very
z — like ts in tse-tse fly

All other consonants are pronounced like in English.

HUNGARIAN

a like o in or
á like a in father
b like b in boy
c like ts in tse-tse fly
cs like ch in church
d like d in day
e like e in bed
f like f in far
g like g in gold
h like h in hallow
i like i in pink
í like i in machine
j like y in yes
k like k in kind
l like l in long
m like m in mister
n like n in never
ny like ni in union
o like o in order
ö like e in her with **pursed lips**
p like p in pink
r like rr in Perry
s like sh in ship
sz like ss in miss
t like t in tea
u like u in put
ü like ee in fee with **pursed lips**
v like v in very
z like s in rose or like z in zero
zs like s in measure, vision

ITALIAN

a like a in father
b like b in boy
c after e or i like ch in chill, in all other cases
     like k in kind
d like d in day
e as a in late (close) or as e in let (open)
f like f in far
g before e or i as g in general,
     in all other cases as g in go
h is always silent
i like i in machine
l like l in long
m approximately as m in mister
n like n in never
o like o in rope (close) or as o in soft (open)
p like p in pink
r like r in Perry (trilled)
s like s in sand (unvoiced) or as s in rose (voiced)
t like t in tea
u like u in put
v like v in very
z like ts in hats (unvoiced) or like a prolonged dz

Double consonants always represent a single
prolonged sound. ch (before e or i) like k in
kilometer
gh before e or i as g in go
gli like lli in billiard or million

But: When no vowel follows gli, the i is pronounced.
gn like ni in onion
sc like sh before e or i, or like sk in any other cases

In the groups scia, scio, sciu the vowel i (unless it
is stressed) is not sounded, serving only to indicate
that sc must be pronounced sh.

CROATIAN

a like a in dark
b like b in boy
c like ts in hats
č like ch in chin
ć like tj in tube
d like in day
dž like g in general
e like in nest
f like f in five
g like g in go
h like ch in loch
i like i in pink
j like y in yes
k like k in kind
l like l in load
m like m in mister
n like n in never
nj like nu in numeral (softly)
o like o in or
p like p in people
r like rr in Perry
s like s in son
š like sh in ship
t like t in tea
u like u in put
v like v in veal
z like z in zero
ž like z in azure

NORWEGIAN

a like a in father
b like b in boy
c like ts in hats
d like d in day
e like e in nest
f like f in five
g like g in go
h like h in hallow
i like i in ink
j like y in yes
k like ch in the Scott. loch
l like l in load
m like m in mister
n like n in never
o like o in or
p like p in pink
r like r in red
s like s in salt
t like t in tea
u as u in put (softly with **pursed lips**)
v like v in veal
z like z in zero
ae like a in fat
ø like e in her with **pursed lips**
ä like a in hare
kj, tj like ch in the Scott. loch
sj, sk, skj like sh in ship
hv, hj, v like v in veal

POLISH

a like a in daft (short)
ą like English "om"
b like b in boy
c like ts in hats
ć, cz like ch in church
d like d in day
e like e in pet
ę like English "en"
f like in five
g like g in go
h like h in hallow
ch is strongly aspirated h—as in loch
i like i in pink
j like y in yes
k like k in kind
l hard as l in lily
ł in Western Poland pronounced as English "w",
      in the east like l in ill
m like in mister
n like n in never
ń like ni in union
o as o in or (short)
ó like oo in moon, but always very short
p like p in pink
r like r in red—hard, unless followed by z
rz like si in vision
s like s in salt unless followed by i or z
ś like sh in ship
t like t in tea
u like oo in moon, but short
w like v in veal
y like y in yes
z like z in zero, unless preceded by "c", r, or s—
      or followed by i
ź like si in vision
zi like zhee, short
ci like chee very short
dz like j in jet (d+zh)
si like shee, short
sz like sh in shoe
szcz like shch in Ashchurch

PORTUGUESE

(Pronunciation as spoken in Rio de Janeiro)

a, á and *à* like a in father (open)
â like u in cut (closed)
ã the nasalized vowel as u in rung
b like b in boy
c before a, o, u like k in kind
c before e, i like c in cigarette
ç like s in see
ch like sh in ship
d like d in day
e, ê (close) like ey in they
e, é, è (open) like e in met
e in an unstressed syllable not final or initial
      like u in cut
e in an unstressed final syllable or monosyllable—
      like y in city
e in an unstressed initial syllable when followed
      by sh, or zh, lh, nh—like i in perish
e before m or n in an unstressed init. syllable—
      like ee in see, but nasalized
ei like ayi in playing
f like f in five
g before a, o, u like g in go
g before vowels or after a vowel and before r—like gh
g before e, i—like s in measure
h is silent unless it is part of the combinations ch, lh, nh
i like i in machine
i before m or n like ee in see, nasalized
j like s in measure
k like k in kilometer (in foreign words only)
l like l in load
lh like lli in million but made as a single sound
m like m in mister, except at end of a word,
      when it is ng
n like n in never, except in ns at end of a word,
      when it is ngsh
n before qu or ca like n in bank
nh like ni in companion
o as in note
o as aw in saw
o and *ô* as o in note (closed)
o, ó and *ò* as aw in saw (open)
õ the nasalized vowel pronounced "ong"
o always in unstressed syllables like oo in moon
p like p in pink
qu followed by a, o—like qu in quick
qu followed by e, i—like k in kick
r like rr in Perry
s like s in see
s between two vowels like s in rose
s at the end of a sentence like sh in push
t like t in tea
u like oo in boot
u in gua, guo, qua, quo—like w in wet
v like v in valve
w only in foreign words like w in wet
x like sh in she or z in zero s in see and
      x in fix (between vowels)
z like z in zero except at end of a word wen it is zh,
      like s in occasion

RUMANIAN

a approx. as e in her
â as ee with pursed lips
b like b in boy
c before a, o, u as k in kind
c before e, i like ch in cherry
d like in day
e like e in neck
f like f in five
g before a, o, u like g in go
g before e, i as j in journal
h like h in hallow
che, chi before e i—like k in kind
i like i in pink
j like j in journal
k like k in kind
l like l in like
m like m in mister
n like n in never
o like o in or
p like p in pink
r like r in Perry
s like s in salt
ş like sh in shoe
t like t in tea
ţ like z in zero
u like u in put
v like v in veal
y like ee with pursed lips
z like z in zero

SLOVAK

a like in father
ä like a in fat
á very long
b like b in boy
c like ts in hats
č like ch in child
d like d in day
ď like du in duration
e like e in nest
é very long
f like f in five
g like g in go
h like h in hallow
ch like ch in the Scottish loch
i like i in pink
í like i in machine
j like y in yes
k like k in kind
l like l in load
ľ softly as in Battalion
m like m in mister
n like n in nest
ň as gn in cognac
o, ô, ó as in no
p like p in pink
r like r in red
ř like rsh in Pershing (approx.)
s like s in salt
s like sh in shoe
t like t in tea
ť like tu in Tudor
u like u in put
ú the same, but long
v like v in veal
y like ee in fee with pursed lips
z like z in zero
ž like ge in orange

SPANISH

Vowels:

a like a in father
e like e in bed
i like i in pink
o like o in ore
u like u in put
y like e in me; The y at the beginning of the word
      is pronounced like y in yes

The combination of two vowels is called diphthong:
ai, ia, au, ua, ei, ie, eu, ue, iu, ui, io, uo ... they are
never pronounced by a simple impulse of the voice,
but always separately: piano (peeano)

Three vowels (triphtongs) : eai, eei, uai, etc.—are also
pronounced separately.

Consonants:

c like ts in hats—before i and e
c like k in cross before a, o, u, l, r and when it is
      at the end of a syllable
ch like ch in charity
d like d in day—except at the end of words, where
      it sounds very soft
g before a, o, u and a consonant like g in give, go
g before e, i like strongly aspirated h in "hat" or
      like ch in loch
If the g stands before n—the letters are separately
pronounced
gu before e and i is pronounced like g in game
      (the u is mute)
h is never pronounced
j like ch in loch, but softer
j — when it comes at the end of a word, sounds
      slightly aspirated
ll is pronounced separately as in billiard
ñ like ni in opinion, union
que sounds like k in key
r like rr in Perry
s like a sharp hissing s in sister
z like z in zone
All other consonants sound like in English.

The Spanish language has only one accent (called
      acento agudo).

SWEDISH

a like a in father
b like b in boy
c before *a, o, u* or a consonant like *k* in kind
c before *e, i, y* like s in see
d like d in day
e like e in tell, (when short),—like i in machine,
     (when long)
f like f in five
g before e, i, y, ä, ö like g in gem
g before a, o, u or a consonant like g in go
h like h in hallow
i like i in pink
j like y in you
k like ch in chair before e, i, y, ä, ö
k like k in kind before a, o, u, or a consonant
l like l in load
m like m in mister
n like n in never
o like oo in soon
p like p in pink
r like r in red
s like s in salt
t like t in tea
u like u in under
v like v in veal
w like v in vest; used only in proper nouns
x like x in fox
y like y in system
z like an English s
å like o in old
ä like a in fat
ö like e in her with pursed lips

TURKISH

a like a in daft
á like a in father (long)
b like b in boy
c like g in gentleman
ç like ch in church
d like d in day
e like e in pet
f like f in five
g as y in yes, often silent
h like h in hallow
i like i in pink
ī like i in machine
j like g in gendarme
k like k in kid
l like l in low
m like m in mister
n like n in never
o like o in or
ö like e in her with pursed lips
p like p in pink
r like r in Perry
s like ss in Miss
ş like sh in ship
t like t in tea
u like u in put
ü like y in system
v like v in veal
y like y in yes
z like z in zero

RUSSIAN

а as a in father
б as b in boy
в as v in vast
г as g in get
д as d in dark
е as e in nest
ж as s in pleasure
з as z in zero
и as ee in meet or i in machine
й as i in pink
к as k in kind
л as l in load
м as m in mister
н as n in nest
о as o in or
п as p in pen
р as r in red
с as s in salt
т as t in tea
у as u in put
ф as f in father
х as ch in loch
ц as ts in nuts
ч as ch in chin
ш as sh in sharp
щ as shch e.g. in fresh-cheeks
ы as y in system
э as a in fat
ю as you
я as ya in royal
ь a sign softening the following consonants:
дь like d in duke
зь like z in azure
ль like l in Luke
нь like n in new
сь like s in sure
ть like t in tune
дзь like j in Joseph
ць like ch in much

SERBIAN

а as a in father
б as b in boy
в as v in vast
г as g in get
д as d in dark
ђ as d in duke
е as e in yet
ж as s in pleasure
з as z in zero
и as i in pink
ј as y in year
к as k in kid
л as l in load
Љ as lu in Luke
м as m in mister
н as n in never
Њ as n in new
о as o in or
п as p in pen
р as r in red
с as s in salt
т as t in tea
ђ as t in tune
у as u in put
ф as f in five
х as ch in loch
ц as ts in nuts
ч as ch in chin
Џ as j in Joseph
ш as sh in sharp

UKRAINIAN

а as a in father
б as b in boy
в as v in vast
г as g in get
г as h in hen
д as d in dark
е as a in hat
э as e in yet
ж as s in pleasure
з as z in zero
и as i in pink
i as ee in meet
ï as y in year
й as y in boy
к as k in kid
л as l in load
м as m in mister
н as n in never
о as o in or
п as p in pen
р as r in red
с as s in salt
т as t in tea
у as u in put
ф as f in five
х as ch in loch
ц as ts in nuts
ч as ch in chin
ш as sh in sharp
щ as shch e.g. in fresh-cheeks
ю as you
я as ya in royal
ь a sign softening the following consonants:
дь like d in duke
зь like z in azure
ль like l in Luke
нь like n in new
сь like s in sure
ть like t in tune
дзь like j in Joseph
ць like ch in much

GRAMMATICAL ABREVIATIONS

adj. adjective
adv. adverb
c. genus communis
conj. conjunction
dem. demonstrative
f. femininum
inf. infinitive
int. interjection
m. masculinum
n. neuter
pl. plural
pron. pronoun
prep. preposition
s. substantivum
v. verb

1 ABLE *adj.*

Czech	: schopný; schopen 1
Danish	: duclig 1
Dutch	: bekwaam 1
Finnish	: kykenevä 1
French	: capable 1
German	: fähig 1
Hungarian	: képes 1
Italian	: abile 1
Croatian	: sposoban 1
Norwegian	: skikket 1
Polish	: zdolny 1
Portuguese	: hábil, capaz 1
Rumanian	: capabil 1
Slovak	: schopný 1
Spanish	: hábil, capaz 1
Swedish	: duktig 1
Turkish	: salik, ehil 1
Russian	: способний 1
Serbian	: способан 1
Ukrainian	: здібний; здатний 1

2 ACCORDION *s.*

Czech	: (tahací) harmonika, *f.* 2
Danish	: Träkharmonika, *m./c.* 2
Dutch	: de harmonika 2
Finnish	: hanuri; harmonika 2
French	: accordéon, *m.* 2
German	: die Ziehharmonika 2
Hungarian	: harmonika 2
Italian	: fisarmonica, *f.* 2
Croatian	: harmonika, *f.* 2
Norwegian	: trekkspill, *n.* 2
Polish	: harmonika ręczna, *f.* 2
Portuguese	: concertina, *a* 2
Rumanian	: armonică, *f.* 2
Slovak	: t'ahacia harmonika, *f.* 2
Spanish	: acordeón, *m.* 2
Swedish	: dragspel-et 2
Turkish	: çekilen armonika 2
Russian	: гармонь, *f.* 2
Serbian	: хармоника, *f.* 2
Ukrainian	: гармонія, *f.* 2

3 ACRES *s. pl.*

Czech	: pole, *n.* 3
Danish	: Ager, *m./c.* 3
Dutch	: de akker 3
Finnish	: pelto 3
French	: champ, *m.* 3
German	: der Acker 3
Hungarian	: szántóföld 3
Italian	: campo, *m.* 3
Croatian	: njiva, *f.* 3
Norwegian	: åker, *m.* 3
Polish	: rola, *f.*; pole, *n.* 3
Portuguese	: campo, *o* 3
Rumanian	: ogorul 3
Slovak	: rol'a, *f.* 3
Spanish	: campo, *m.* 3
Swedish	: åker-n 3
Turkish	: tarla 3
Russian	: поле, *n.* 3
Serbian	: њива, *f.* 3
Ukrainian	: ріля, *f.*; поле, *n.*; нива, *f.* 3

4 ADDRESS *s.*

Czech	: adresa, *f.* 4
Danish	: adresse, *c.* 4
Dutch	: adres 4
Finnish	: osoite 4
French	: adresse, *f.* 4
German	: die Adresse 4
Hungarian	: cím 4
Italian	: indirizzo, *m.* 4
Croatian	: naslov, *m.* 4
Norwegian	: adresse, *c.* 4
Polish	: adres, *m.* 4
Portuguese	: endereço, *m.* 4
Rumanian	: adresă, *f.* 4
Slovak	: adresa, *f.* 4
Spanish	: dirección, *f.* 4
Swedish	: adress-en 4
Turkish	: adres 4
Russian	: адрес, *m.* 4
Serbian	: наслов, *m.* 4
Ukrainian	: адреса, *f.* 4

5 AEROPLANE *s.*

Czech	: letadlo, *n.* 5
Danish	: Flyvemaskine, *c.* 5
Dutch	: de vlieg machine 5
Finnish	: lentokone 5
French	: avion, *m.* 5
German	: das Flugzeug 5
Hungarian	: repülőgép 5
Italian	: aeroplano, *m.* 5
Croatian	: zrakoplov, *m.* 5
Norwegian	: fly, *n.* 5
Polish	: aeroplan, *m.* 5
Portuguese	: avião, *o* 5
Rumanian	: avionul 5
Slovak	: lietadlo, *n.* 5
Spanish	: avión, *m.* 5
Swedish	: flygplan-et 5
Turkish	: tayyare 5
Russian	: самолет, *m.* 5
Serbian	: авијон, *m.* 5
Ukrainian	: літак, *m.* 5

6 AFTERNOON *s.*

Czech	: odpoledne, *n.* 6
Danish	: Eftermiddag, *m.* 6
Dutch	: de namiddag 6
Finnish	: iltapäivä 6
French	: après-midi, *f.* 6
German	: der Nachmittag 6
Hungarian	: délután 6
Italian	: pomeriggio, *m.* 6
Croatian	: popodne, *n.* 6
Norwegian	: ettermiddag, *m.* 6
Polish	: popołudnie, *n.* 6
Portuguese	: tarde, *a* 6
Rumanian	: după amiază, *f.* 6
Slovak	: popoludnie, *n.* 6
Spanish	: la tarde 6
Swedish	: eftermiddagen 6
Turkish	: ikindi 6
Russian	: послеобеда, *n.* 6
Serbian	: поподне, *n.* 6
Ukrainian	: пополудне, *n.* 6

7 AID see **455 HELP**

8 AIR-FIELD s. (AIRPORT)
Czech	: letiště, n.	8
Danish	: Flyveplads, m.	8
Dutch	: het vliegveld	8
Finnish	: lentokenttä	8
French	: terrain d'atterrissage, m.	8
German	: der Flugplatz	8
Hungarian	: repülötér	8
Italian	: aeroporto, m.	8
Croatian	: zrakoplovno pristanište, n.	8
Norwegian	: flyplass, m.	8
Polish	: lotnisko, n.	8
Portuguese	: campo de aviação, o	8
Rumanian	: aerodromul	8
Slovak	: letište, n.	8
Spanish	: puerto aéreo, m.	8
Swedish	: flygplats-en	8
Turkish	: tayyare meydani	8
Russian	: аэродром, m.	8
Serbian	: аеродром, m.	8
Ukrainian	: летуиський майдан, m.	8

9 AIRPLANE see **5 AEROPLANE**

10 AIR-RAID SHELTER s.
Czech	: (protiletecký) kryt, m.	10
Danish	: Beskyttelsesrum, n.	10
Dutch	: de schuilkelder	10
Finnish	: suojakellari	10
French	: cave-abris, f.	10
German	: der Luftschutzkeller	10
Hungarian	: a légvédelmi óvóhely	10
Italian	: rifugio antiaereo, m.	10
Croatian	: sklonište protiv napadaja iz zraka	10
Norwegian	: tilfluktsrom, n.	10
Polish	: schron przeciwlotniczy, m.	10
Portuguese	: abrigo contra ataques aéreos, o	10
Rumanian	: adapostul antiaerian	10
Slovak	: protiletecký kryt, m.	10
Spanish	: refugio antiaéreo, m.	10
Swedish	: skyddsrumm-et	10
Turkish	: sıginak	10
Russian	: подвал для защиты от воздушных налетов, m.	10
Serbian	: склониште, n.	10
Ukrainian	: протилетунске схоронище, n.	10

11 ALE s. see **81 BEER**

12 ALLOWED see **714 PERMITTED**

13 ALONE see **885 SINGLE**

14 AND conj.
Czech	: a	14
Danish	: og	14
Dutch	: en	14
Finnish	: ja	14
French	: et	14
German	: und	14
Hungarian	: es; meg	14
Italian	: e; ed	14
Croatian	: i; te	14
Norwegian	: og	14
Polish	: i	14
Portuguese	: e	14
Rumanian	: si; iar	14
Slovak	: a; aj	14
Spanish	: y	14
Swedish	: och	14
Turkish	: ve	14
Russian	: и; а	14
Serbian	: ог	14
Ukrainian	: i; а	14

15 ALUMINIUM s.
Czech	: aluminium, n.	15
Danish	: Aluminium, n.	15
Dutch	: het aluminium	15
Finnish	: aluminium	15
French	: l'aluminium, m.	15
German	: das Aluminium	15
Hungarian	: az aluminium	15
Italian	: alluminio, m.	15
Croatian	: aluminij, m.	15
Norwegian	: aluminium, n.	15
Polish	: aluminijum, n.	15
Portuguese	: alumínio, o	15
Rumanian	: aluminiu, n.	15
Slovak	: alumínium, n.	15
Spanish	: el aluminio	15
Swedish	: aluminium-et	15
Turkish	: alüminyom	15
Russian	: алюминий, m.	15
Serbian	: алуминијум, m.	15
Ukrainian	: алюміній, m.	15

16 ANANAS s.
Czech	: ananas, m.	16
Danish	: Ananas, m./c.	16
Dutch	: de ananas	16
Finnish	: ananas	16
French	: l'ananas, m.	16
German	: die Ananas	16
Hungarian	: ananász	16
Italian	: ananas, m.	16
Croatian	: ananas, m.	16
Norwegian	: ananas, m.	16
Polish	: ananas, m.	16
Portuguese	: ananás, o	16
Rumanian	: ananasul	16
Slovak	: ananas, m.	16
Spanish	: ananá, m.	
Swedish	: ananas-en	16
Turkish	: ananas	16
Russian	: ананас, m.	16
Serbian	: ананас, m.	16
Ukrainian	: ананас, m.	16

17 ANCHOR s.

Czech	:	kotva, f. 17
Danish	:	Anker, n. 17
Dutch	:	het anker 17
Finnish	:	ankkuri 17
French	:	ancre, f. 17
German	:	der Anker 17
Hungarian	:	horgony 17
Italian	:	ancora, m. 17
Croatian	:	sidro, n. 17
Norwegian	:	anker, n. 17
Polish	:	kotwica, f. 17
Portuguese	:	âncora, a 17
Rumanian	:	ancoră, f. ·17
Slovak	:	kotva, f. 17
Spanish	:	ancla, f. 17
Swedish	:	ankare-t 17
Turkish	:	çapa 17
Russian	:	якорь, m. 17
Serbian	:	сидро, n. 17
Ukrainian	:	якір, m. 17

18 ANGLE s. (fishing)

Czech	:	udice, f. 18
Danish	:	Fiskestang, c. 18
Dutch	:	de hengel 18
Finnish	:	onki 18
French	:	ligne de pêche, f. 18
German	:	die Angel 18
Hungarian	:	horog 18
Italian	:	amo, m. 18
Croatian	:	udica, f. 18
Norwegian	:	fiskekrok, m. 18
Polish	:	wędka, f. 18
Portuguese	:	anzól, o 18
Rumanian	:	undiţa, f. 18
Slovak	:	udica, f. 18
Spanish	:	anzuelo, m. 18
Swedish	:	fiskpö-et 18
Turkish	:	olta 18
Russian	:	удочка, f. 18
Serbian	:	удица, f. 18
Ukrainian	:	вудка, f. 18

19 ANIMAL s.

Czech	:	zvíře 19
Danish	:	Dyr, n. 19
Dutch	:	het dier 19
Finnish	:	eläin 19
French	:	l'animal 19
German	:	das Tier 19
Hungarian	:	állat 19
Italian	:	animale, m. 19
Croatian	:	životinja, f. 19
Norwegian	:	dyr, n. 19
Polish	:	zwierzę n. 19
Portuguese	:	animal, o 19
Rumanian	:	animalul 19
Slovak	:	zwiera, n. 19
Spanish	:	animal, m. 19
Swedish	:	djur-et 19
Turkish	:	hayvan 19
Russian	:	животное, n. 19
Serbian	:	животиньа, f. 19
Ukrainian	:	звіря, f. 19

20 ANKLE s.

Czech	:	kotník, m. (na noze) 20
Danish	:	Ankel, s. 20
Dutch	:	de enkel 20
Finnish	:	nilkkanivel 20
French	:	cheville, f. 20
German	:	das Fussgelenk 20
Hungarian	:	boka 20
Italian	:	articolazione del piede, f. 20
Croatian	:	·zglob, m. 20
Norwegian	:	ankelled, n. 20
Polish	:	staw napiętkowy 20
Portuguese	:	articulação do pé, a 20
Rumanian	:	glezna, f. 20
Slovak	:	členok, m. 20
Spanish	:	articulación, f. 20
Swedish	:	fotled-en 20
Turkish	:	ayak mifsali 20
Russian	:	сустав ноги, m. 20
Serbian	:	зглоб, m. 20
Ukrainian	:	напятковий сустав, m. 20

21 ANSWER v.

Czech	:	odpověděti 21
Danish	:	svare 21
Dutch	:	antwoorden 21
Finnish	:	vastata 21
French	:	répondre 21
German	:	antworten 21
Hungarian	:	felelni 21
Italian	:	rispondere 21
Croatian	:	odgovarati 21
Norwegian	:	svare 21
Polish	:	odpowiadać 21
Portuguese	:	responder 21
Rumanian	:	a räspunde 21
Slovak	:	odpovedat' 21
Spanish	:	contestar 21
Swedish	:	svara 21
Turkish	:	cevap vermek 21
Russian	:	отвечать 21
Serbian	:	одговорити 21
Ukrainian	:	віповідати 21

22 ANVIL s.

Czech	:	kovadlina, f. 22
Danish	:	Ambolt, m. 22
Dutch	:	het aambeeld 22
Finnish	:	alasin 22
French	:	enclume, f. 22
German	:	der Amboss 22
Hungarian	:	üllö 22
Italian	:	incudine, f. 22
Croatian	:	nakovanj, m. 22
Norwegian	:	ambolt, m. 22
Polish	:	kowadlo, n. 22
Portuguese	:	bigorna, a 22
Rumanian	:	nicovală, f. 22
Slovak	:	nákova, f. 22
Spanish	:	yunque, m. 22
Swedish	:	städ-et 22
Turkish	:	örs 22
Russian	:	наковальня, f. 22
Serbian	:	наковань, m. 22
Ukrainian	:	ковало, n. 22

23 APARTMENT see 356 FLAT

'24 APOLOGIZE see 318 EXCUSE

25 APPARATUS see 560 MACHINE

26 APPLE s.

Czech	: jablko, n.	26
Danish	: Äble, n.	26
Dutch	: de appel	26
Finnish	: omena	26
French	: pomme, f.	26
German	: der Apfel	26
Hungarian	: alma	26
Italian	: mela, f.	26
Croatian	: jabuka, f.	26
Norwegian	: eple, n.	26
Polish	: jabłko, n.	26
Portuguese	: maçã, a	26
Rumanian	: mărul	26
Slovak	: jablko, n.	26
Spanish	: manzana, f.	26
Swedish	: äpple-t	26
Turkish	: elma	26
Russian	: яблоко, n.	26
Serbian	: jaбука, f.	26
Ukrainian	: яблуко. n.	26

27 APPROACH see 229 COME

28 APRICOT s.

Czech	: merunka, f.	28
Danish	: Abrikos, c.	28
Dutch	: de abrikoos	28
Finnish	: aprikoosi	28
French	: abrikot, m.	28
German	: die Aprikose	28
Hungarian	: kajszi barack	28
Italian	: albicocca, f.	28
Croatian	: kajsija, f.	28
Norwegian	: aprikos, m.	28
Polish	: morela, f.	28
Portuguese	: damasco, o	28
Rumanian	: caisa	28
Slovak	: marhuľa, f.	28
Spanish	: albaricoque	28
Swedish	: aprikos-en	28
Turkish	: kaysı	28
Russian	: абрикос, m.	28
Serbian	: кajсиja, f.	28
Ukrainian	: мореля, f.	28

29 APRIL s.

Czech	: duben, m.	29
Danish	: April	29
Dutch	: April	29
Finnish	: huhtikuu	29
French	: avril, m.	29
German	: der April	29
Hungarian	: április	29
Italian	: aprile, m.	29
Croatian	: travanj, m.	29
Norwegian	: april	29
Polish	: kwiecień, m.	29
Portuguese	: abril, o	29
Rumanian	: aprilie, m.	29
Slovak	: april, m.	29
Spanish	: abril	29
Swedish	: april	29
Turkish	: nisan	29
Russian	: апрель, m.	29
Serbian	: Април, m.	29
Ukrainian	: Квітень, m.	29

30 APRON s.

Czech	: zástěra, f.	30
Danish	: Forkläde, n.	30
Dutch	: de schort	30
Finnish	: esiliina	30
French	: tablier, m.	30
German	: die Schürze	30
Hungarian	: kötény	30
Italian	: grembiale, m.	30
Croatian	: pregača, f.	30
Norwegian	: forklä, n,	30
Polish	: fartuch, m.	30
Portuguese	: aventale, o	30
Rumanian	: sorțul	30
Slovak	: zástera, f.	30
Spanish	: delantal, m.	30
Swedish	: förkläde-t	30
Turkish	: önlük	30
Russian	: передник, m.	30
Serbian	: прегача, f.	30
Ukrainian	: фартушок, m.	30

31 ARM-CHAIR s.

Czech	: křeslo, n.	31
Danish	: Länestol, m./c.	31
Dutch	: de leuningstoel	31
Finnish	: nojatuoli	31
French	: fauteuil, m.	31
German	: der Lehnstuhl	31
Hungarian	: fotel	31
Italian	: poltrona, f.	31
Croatian	: stolac, m.	31
Norwegian	: lenestol, m.	31
Polish	: fotel, m.	31
Portuguese	: poltrona, a	31
Rumanian	: jilțul	31
Slovak	: stolička, f.	31
Spanish	: sillón, m.	31
Swedish	: länstol-en	31
Turkish	: koltuk	31
Russian	: кресло, n.	31
Serbian	: столац, m.	31
Ukrainian	: фотель, m.	31

32 ARMY s.

Czech	: vojsko, n.; armáda, f. 32
Danish	: Militär, n. 32
Dutch	: het militair 32
Finnish	: sotaväki 32
French	: militaire, m. 32
German	: das Militär 32
Hungarian	: a katonaság 32
Italian	: militare, m. 32
Croatian	: vojska, pl. 32
Norwegian	: militär, pl. 32
Polish	: wojsko, n. 32
Portuguese	: fôrças armadas, as 32
Rumanian	: militariă, f. 32
Slovak	: vojsko, n. 32
Spanish	: ejército, m. 32
Swedish	: det militära 32
Turkish	: asker 32
Russian	: военные; войско, n. 32
Serbian	: војска, pl. 32
Ukrainian	: військо, n. 32

33 ARRIVAL s.

Czech	: příjezd, příchod, m. 33
Danish	: Indrejse 33
Dutch	: de inreis 33
Finnish	: maahantulo 33
French	: l'entrée, l'entry 33
German	: die Einreise 33
Hungarian	: beutazás 33
Italian	: l'entrata, f. 33
Croatian	: ulaz u državu, m. 33
Norwegian	: innreise, f. 33
Polish	: wjazd, m. 33
Portuguese	: viagem de entrada 33
Rumanian	: intrarea in tară, f. 33
Slovak	: vcestovanie, n. 33
Spanish	: entrada, f. 33
Swedish	: inresa, ankomst-en 33
Turkish	: avdet 33
Russian	: в'езд, m. 33
Serbian	: улас; путованье у, m. 33
Ukrainian	: візд, m. 33

34 ARRIVE see 229 COME

35 ARTIFICIAL SILK s.

Czech	: umělé hedvábí, n. 35
Danish	: Kunstsilke, m./c. 35
Dutch	: de kunstzijde 35
Finnish	: tekosilkki 35
French	: soie artificielle, f. 35
German	: die Kunstseide 35
Hungarian	: müselyem 35
Italian	: seta artificiale, f. 35
Croatian	: vještacka jedwab, m. 35
Norwegian	: kunstsilke, m. 35
Polish	: sztuczny jedwab, m. 35
Portuguese	: sêda artificial, a 35
Rumanian	: matasa artificială, f. 35
Slovak	: umely hodváb, m. 35
Spanish	: seda artificial, f. 35
Swedish	: konstsilke-t 35
Turkish	: suni ipek 35
Russian	: искуственный шелк, m. 35
Serbian	: вештачка свила, f. 35
Ukrainian	: штучний шовк, m. 35

36 ASK v.

Czech	: tázati se, žádati 36
Danish	: spörge 36
Dutch	: vragen 36
Finnish	: kysyä 36
French	: demander 36
German	: fragen 36
Hungarian	: kérdezni 36
Italian	: domandare 36
Croatian	: pitati 36
Norwegian	: spörre 36
Polish	: pytać 36
Portuguese	: perguntar 36
Rumanian	: a intreba 36
Slovak	: pytat' sa 36
Spanish	: preguntar 36
Swedish	: fråga 36
Turkish	: sormak 36
Russian	: спрашивать 36
Serbian	: питати 36
Ukrainian	: питати 36

37 ASPARAGUS s.

Czech	: chřest, m. 37
Danish	: Asparges, pl. 37
Dutch	: de asperge 37
Finnish	: parsa 37
French	: asperge, f. 37
German	: der Spargel 37
Hungarian	: spárga 37
Italian	: asparago, m. 37
Croatian	: šparoga, f. 37
Norwegian	: asparges, c. 37
Polish	: szparag, m. 37
Portuguese	: espargo, o 37
Rumanian	: sparanghelul 37
Slovak	: špargl'a, f. 37
Spanish	: espárrago, m. 37
Swedish	: sparris-en 37
Turkish	: kuş konmaz 37
Russian	: спаржа, f. 37
Serbian	: шпарога, f. 37
Ukrainian	: шпараг, m. 37

38 ASSEMBLE see 584 Meet

39 ASSIST see 455 HELP

40 ASTER s.

Czech	: astra, f. 40
Danish	: Asters, pl. 40
Dutch	: de aster 40
Finnish	: asteri 40
French	: aster, m. 40
German	: die Aster 40
Hungarian	: az öszirózsa 40
Italian	: astero, m. 40
Croatian	: astra, f. 40
Norwegian	: asters, pl. 40
Polish	: astra, f. 40
Portuguese	: sécia, a 40
Rumanian	: ochiul boului, m. 40
Slovak	: astra, f. 40
Spanish	: aster, m. 40
Swedish	: aster-n 40
Turkish	: pat 40
Russian	: астра, f. 40
Serbian	: астра, f. 40
Ukrainian	: айстра, f. 40

6

41 ATTEMPT   v. see 1035 TRY

45 AUTOMOBILE see 612 MOTORCAR (car)

42 ATTIC s.

Czech	:	půda, *f.* 42
Danish	:	Spiskammer, *n.* 42
Dutch	:	de zolder 42
Finnish	:	aitta 42
French	:	grenier, *m.* 42
German	:	der Speicher 42
Hungarian	:	padlás 42
Italian	:	granaio, *m.* 42
Croatian	:	žitnica, *f.* 42
Norwegian	:	loft, *n.* 42
Polish	:	śpichlerz, *m.* 42
Portuguese	:	depósito, *o* 42
Rumanian	:	pod, *n.* 42
Slovak	:	pôjd, *n.* 42
Spanish	:	desván, *m.* 42
Swedish	:	vind-en 42
Turkish	:	dam alti 42
Russian	:	чердак, *m.* 42
Serbian	:	житница, *f.* 42
Ukrainian	:	шпихлір, *m.* 42

46 AUTUMN (FALL) s.

Czech	:	podzim, *m.* 46
Danish	:	Efteraar 46
Dutch	:	de herfst 46
Finnish	:	syksy 46
French	:	automne, *m.* 46
German	:	der Herbst 46
Hungarian	:	ösz 46
Italian	:	autunno, *m.* 46
Croatian	:	jesen, *f.* 46
Norwegian	:	höst, *m.* 46
Polish	:	jesień, *f.* 46
Portuguese	:	outono, *o* 46
Rumanian	:	toamnă, *f.* 46
Slovak	:	jeseň, *f.* 46
Spanish	:	otoño, *m.* 46
Swedish	:	höst-en 46
Turkish	:	sonbahar 46
Russian	:	осень, *f.* 46
Serbian	:	jесен, *f.* 46
Ukrainian	:	осінь, *f.* 46

43 AUGUST s.

Czech	:	srpen, *m.* 43
Danish	:	August 43
Dutch	:	Augustus 43
Finnish	:	elokuu 43
French	:	août, *m.* 43
German	:	der August 43
Hungarian	:	augusztus 43
Italian	:	agosto 43
Croatian	:	kolovoz, *m.* 43
Norwegian	:	august 43
Polish	:	sierpień 43
Portuguese	:	agosto 43
Rumanian	:	August 43
Slovak	:	august 43
Spanish	:	agosto 43
Swedish	:	augusti 43
Turkish	:	ağustos 43
Russian	:	август 43
Serbian	:	Август 43
Ukrainian	:	Серпень, 43

47 AVIATOR s. (a flier, airman)

Czech	:	letec, *m.*; pilot, *m.* 47
Danish	:	Flyver, *m.* 47
Dutch	:	de vliegenier 47
Finnish	:	lentäjä 47
French	:	aviateur, *m.* 47
German	:	der Flieger 47
Hungarian	:	pilóta 47
Italian	:	aviatore, *m.* 47
Croatian	:	zrakoplovac, *m.* 47
Norwegian	:	flyver, *m.* 47
Polish	:	lotnik, *m.* 47
Portuguese	:	aviador, *o* 47
Rumanian	:	aviatorul 47
Slovak	:	letec, *m.* 47
Spanish	:	aviador, *m.* 47
Swedish	:	flygare-n 47
Turkish	:	tayyareci 47
Russian	:	летчик, *m.* 47
Serbian	:	авиjатичар, *m.* 47
Ukrainian	:	(летун), авіатор, *m.* 47

44 AUNT s.

Czech	:	teta, *f.* 44
Danish	:	tante, *f.* 44
Dutch	:	tante, f. 44
Finnish	:	täti 44
French	:	tante, *f.* 44
German	:	die Tante 44
Hungarian	:	néne 44
Italian	:	zia, *f.* 44
Croatian	:	strina; tetka, *f.* 44
Norwegian	:	tante, *f.* 44
Polish	:	ciotka, *f.* 44
Portuguese	:	tía, *f.* 44
Rumanian	:	mătusă, *f.* 44
Slovak	:	teta, *f.* 44
Spanish	:	tía, *f.* 44
Swedish	:	tant-en 44
Turkish	:	hala 44
Russian	:	тетка; тетя, *f.* 44
Serbian	:	стрина; тетка, *f.* 44
Ukrainian	:	тітка, *f.* 44

48 AXE s. (AX)

Czech	:	sekera, *f.* 48
Danish	:	Ökse, *m./c.* 48
Dutch	:	de bijl 48
Finnish	:	kirves 48
French	:	hache, *f.* 48
German	:	das Beil 48
Hungarian	:	fejsze 48
Italian	:	scure, *f.* 48
Croatian	:	sjekira, *f.* 48
Norwegian	:	öks, *f.* 48
Polish	:	topór, *m.* 48
Portuguese	:	machado, *o* 48
Rumanian	:	toporul 48
Slovak	:	sekera, *f.* 48
Spanish	:	hacha, *f.* 48
Swedish	:	yxa-n 48
Turkish	:	balta 48
Russian	:	топор, *m.* 48
Serbian	:	брадва, *f.* 48
Ukrainian	:	топір *m.*; сокира, *f.* 48

49 BABY s.

Czech	:	nemluvně; malé dítě n. 49
Danish	:	pattebarn, n. 49
Dutch	:	klein kind 49
Finnish	:	lapsi 49
French	:	bébé; enfant, m. 49
German	:	kleines Kind 49
Hungarian	:	gyermek 49
Italian	:	bambino, m. 49
Croatian	:	dijete; čedo, n. 49
Norwegian	:	barn, n. 49
Polish	:	dziecko, n. 49
Portuguese	:	nené, m.; criancinha, f. 49
Rumanian	:	copil, m. 49
Slovak	:	dieťa, n.; dieťatko, n. 49
Spanish	:	nene; bebé 49
Swedish	:	spädbarn 49
Turkish	:	cocuk 49
Russian	:	дитя; ребенок, n. 49
Serbian	:	дијете; чедо, n. 49
Ukrainian	:	немовля, n. 49

52 BACON s.

Czech	:	slanina, f. 52
Danish	:	Fläsk, n. 52
Dutch	:	het spek 52
Finnish	:	silava 52
French	:	lard, m. 52
German	:	der Speck 52
Hungarian	:	szalonna 52
Italian	:	lardo, m. 52
Croatian	:	slanina, f. 52
Norwegian	:	flesk, n. 52
Polish	:	słonina, f. 52
Portuguese	:	toucinho, o 52
Rumanian	:	slănina, f. 52
Slovak	:	slanina, f. 52
Spanish	:	tocino, m. 52
Swedish	:	späck-et 52
Turkish	:	domuz yaği 52
Russian	:	сало, n. 52
Serbian	:	сланина, f. 52
Ukrainian	:	солонина, f. 52

50 BACK s. (the part of the human body)

Czech	:	záda, pl. 50
Danish	:	Ryg, m./c. 50
Dutch	:	de rug 50
Finnish	:	selkä 50
French	:	dos, m. 50
German	:	der Rücken 50
Hungarian	:	hát 50
Italian	:	schiena, f. 50
Croatian	:	ledja, f. 50
Norwegian	:	rygg, m. 50
Polish	:	grzbiet, m. 50
Portuguese	:	costas, as 50
Rumanian	:	spatele; dos 50
Slovak	:	chrbát, m. 50
Spanish	:	espalda, f. 50
Swedish	:	rygg-en 50
Turkish	:	arka 50
Russian	:	спина, f. 50
Serbian	:	леħа, f. 50
Ukrainian	:	хребет, m.; спина, f. 50

53 BAD adj.

Czech	:	špatný 53
Danish	:	slet 53
Dutch	:	slecht 53
Finnish	:	huono 53
French	:	mauvais; mal 53
German	:	schlecht 53
Hungarian	:	rossz 53
Italian	:	cattivo; male 53
Croatian	:	loš 53
Norwegian	:	dårlig 53
Polish	:	źle 53
Portuguese	:	mal 53
Rumanian	:	rău 53
Slovak	:	zlý 53
Spanish	:	malo 53
Swedish	:	dålig 53
Turkish	:	fena 53
Russian	:	плохой 53
Serbian	:	слабо 53
Ukrainian	:	злий; поганий 53

51 BACK s. (the rear part)

Czech	:	zadní strana; záda 51
Danish	:	Bagside, m. 51
Dutch	:	de achtergevel 51
Finnish	:	nurja puoli; tausta 51
French	:	l'arrière, f.; dos m. 51
German	:	die Rückseite 51
Hungarian	:	hátrész 51
Italian	:	la parte posteriore 51
Croatian	:	stražnja strana, f. 51
Norwegian	:	bakside, f. 51
Polish	:	strona odwrotna, f. 51
Portuguese	:	parte de trás, a 51
Rumanian	:	dosul casei 51
Slovak	:	zadná strana, f. 51
Spanish	:	parte trasera, f. 51
Swedish	:	baksida-n 51
Turkish	:	arka taraf, f. 51
Russian	:	задняя сторона, f. 51
Serbian	:	задња страна, f. 51
Ukrainian	:	задня сторона, f. 51

54 BAG s. (handbag)

Czech	:	kabelka, f.; kufřík 54
Danish	:	Haandtaske, c. 54
Dutch	:	de handtasch 54
Finnish	:	käsilaukku 54
French	:	sac à mains, m. 54
German	:	die Handtasche 54
Hungarian	:	kézi táska 54
Italian	:	borsetta, f. 54
Croatian	:	ručna torba, f. 54
Norwegian	:	håndveske, f. 54
Polish	:	torebka, f. 54
Portuguese	:	malinha da mão, a 54
Rumanian	:	poseta, f. 54
Slovak	:	kabelka, f. 54
Spanish	:	bolsa, f. 54
Swedish	:	(hand) väska-n 54
Turkish	:	el çantası 54
Russian	:	сумочка, f. 54
Serbian	:	ручaа торба, f. 54
Ukrainian	:	торбинка, f. 54

8

55 BAGGAGE see 555 LUGGAGE

56 BAKE v.

Czech : péci 56
Danish : bage 56
Dutch : bakken 56
Finnish : leipoa 56
French : cuire au four 56
German : backen 56
Hungarian : süti 56
Italian : cuocere al forno 56
Croatian : peći 56
Norwegian : bake 56
Polish : piec 56
Portuguese : fritai 56
Rumanian : a coace 56
Slovak : piect', smažit' 56
Spanish : cocer (en el horno) 56
Swedish : grädda 56
Turkish : ekmek pişimerk 56
Russian : жарить 56
Serbian : пећи 56
Ukrainian : пекти 56

57 BAKER s.

Czech : pekař, m. 57
Danish : Bager, m./c. 57
Dutch : de bakker 57
Finnish : leipuri 57
French : boulanger, m. 57
German : der Bäcker 57
Hungarian : pék 57
Italian : panettiere, m. 57
Croatian : pekar, m. 57
Norwegian : baker, m. 57
Polish : piekarz, m. 57
Portuguese : padeiro, o 57
Rumanian : brutarul 57
Slovak : pekár, m. 57
Spanish : panadero, m. 57
Swedish : bagare-n 57
Turkish : firinei 57
Russian : пекарь; булочник, m. 57
Serbian : пекар, m. 57
Ukrainian : пекар, m. 57

58 BALCONY s.

Czech : balkon, m. 58
Danish : Balkon, m./c. 58
Dutch : het balkon 58
Finnish : parveke 58
French : balcon, m. 58
German : der Balkon 58
Hungarian : erkély 58
Italian : balcone, m. 58
Croatian : balkon, m. 58
Norwegian : balkon, m. 58
Polish : balkon, m. 58
Portuguese : balcão, o 58
Rumanian : balconul 58
Slovak : balkón, m. 58
Spanish : balcón, m. 58
Swedish : balkong-en 58
Turkish : balkon 58
Russian : балкон, m. 58
Serbian : балкон, m. 58
Ukrainian : балкон, m. 58

59 BANANA s.

Czech : banán, m. 59
Danish : Banan, c. 59
Dutch : de banaan 59
Finnish : banaani 59
French : banane, f. 59
German : die Banane 59
Hungarian. : banán 59
Italian : banana, f. 59
Croatian : banana, f. 59
Norwegian : banan, m. 59
Polish : banany, pl. 59
Portuguese : banana, a 59
Rumanian : banana, f. 59
Slovak : banán, m. 59
Spanish : banana, f. 59
Swedish : banan-en 59
Turkish : muz 59
Russian : банан, m. 59
Serbian : банана, f. 59
Ukrainian : банани, pl. 59

60 BANDAGE s.

Czech : obvaz, m. 60
Danish : Bind, n.; Bandage 60
Dutch : het verband 60
Finnish : side 60
French : pansement, m. 60
German : die Binde 60
Hungarian : kötés 60
Italian : fascia f. 60
Croatian : zavoj, m. 60
Norwegian : forbinding, m. 60
Polish : opaska, n. 60
Portuguese : atadura, a 60
Rumanian : bandajul 60
Slovak : obväz, m. 60
Spanish : venda, f. 60
Swedish : binda-n 60
Turkish : bag 60
Russian : бинт, m. 60
Serbian : лревоj, m. 60
Ukrainian : опаска, f.; бандаж, m. 60

61 BARLEY s.

Czech : ječmen, m. 61
Danish : Byg, m./c. 61
Dutch : de gerst 61
Finnish : ohra 61
French : orge, f. 61
German : die Gerste 61
Hungarian : árpa 61
Italian : orzo, m. 61
Croatian : ječam, m. 61
Norwegian : bygg, m. 61
Polish : jeęzmień, m. 61
Portuguese : cevada, a 61
Rumanian : orzul 61
Slovak : jačmen, m. 61
Spanish : cebada, f. 61
Swedish : korn-et 61
Turkish : arpa 61
Russian : ячмень, m. 61
Serbian : jечам, m. 61
Ukrainian : ячмінь, m. 61

62 BARN s.

Czech	:	stodola, *f.* 62
Danish	:	Lade, *m./c.* 62
Dutch	:	de schuur 62
Finnish	:	lato; riihi 62
French	:	grange, *f.* 62
German	:	die Scheune 62
Hungarian	:	csür 62
Italian	:	capanna, *f.* 62
Croatian	:	žitnica, *f.* 62
Norwegian	:	låve, *m.* 62
Polish	:	stodoła, *f.* 62
Portuguese	:	palheiro, *o* 62
Rumanian	:	sopronul 62
Slovak	:	stodola, *f.* 62
Spanish	:	granero, *m.* 62
Swedish	:	lada-n 62
Turkish	:	samanlik 62
Russian	:	сарай, *m.* 62
Serbian	:	житница, *f.* 62
Ukrainian	:	клуня; стодола, *f.* 62

63 BARREL s.

Czech	:	sud, *m.* 63
Danish	:	Tönde, *m./c.* 63
Dutch	:	de ton 63
Finnish	:	astia 63
French	:	tonneau, *m.* 63
German	:	das Fass 63
Hungarian	:	hordó 63
Italian	:	botte, *f.* 63
Croatian	:	bačva, *f.* 63
Norwegian	:	tönne, *f.* 63
Polish	:	beczka, *f.* 63
Portuguese	:	barril, *o* 63
Rumanian	:	butoiul 63
Slovak	:	sud, *m.* 63
Spanish	:	tonel, *m.* 63
Swedish	:	fat-et 63
Turkish	:	fıçı 63
Russian	:	бочка, *f.* 63
Serbian	:	буре, *n.* 63
Ukrainian	:	бочка, *f.* 63

64 BASEMENT (CELLAR) s.

Czech	:	sklep, *m.* 64
Danish	:	Kälder, *m./c.* 64
Dutch	:	de kelder 64
Finnish	:	kellari 64
French	:	cave, *f.* 64
German	:	der Keller 64
Hungarian	:	pince 64
Italian	:	cantina, *f.* 64
Croatian	:	podrum, *m.* 64
Norwegian	:	kjeller, *m.* 64
Polish	:	piwnica, *f.* 64
Portuguese	:	cave, *a* 64
Rumanian	:	pivniță, *f.* 64
Slovak	:	pivnica, *f.* 64
Spanish	:	bodega, *f.* 64
Swedish	:	källare-n 64
Turkish	:	kiler 64
Russian	:	погреб, *m.* 64
Serbian	:	подрум, *m.* 64
Ukrainian	:	пивниця, *f.*; льох, *m.* 64

65 BASKET s.

Czech	:	koš, *m.* 65
Danish	:	Kurv, *m./c.* 65
Dutch	:	de mand 65
Finnish	:	kori; koppa 65
French	:	corbeille, *f.* 65
German	:	der Korb 65
Hungarian	:	kosár 65
Italian	:	cesta, *f.* 65
Croatian	:	koš, m.; košarica, *f.* 65
Norwegian	:	kurv, *m.* 65
Polish	:	kosz, *m.* 65
Portuguese	:	cêsto, *o* 65
Rumanian	:	coşul 65
Slovak	:	kôš, *m.* 65
Spanish	:	canasto, *m.* 65
Swedish	:	korg-en 65
Turkish	:	sepet 65
Russian	:	корзина, *f.* 65
Serbian	:	кошарица, *f.* 65
Ukrainian	:	кіш; кошик, *m.* 65

66 BATHING-DRESS s.

Czech	:	koupací oblek, *m.* 66
Danish	:	Badedragt, *c.* 66
Dutch	:	het badpak 66
Finnish	:	uimapuku 66
French	:	maillot de bain, *m.* 66
German	:	der Badeanzug 66
Hungarian	:	fürdöruha 66
Italian	:	costume da bagno, *m.* 66
Croatian	:	kupaći kostim, *m.* 66
Norwegian	:	badedrakt, *m./c.* 66
Polish	:	strój kąpielowy 66
Portuguese	:	maillot, *o* 66
Rumanian	:	costumul de baie 66
Slovak	:	kúpaci oblek, *m.* 66
Spanish	:	traje de baño 66
Swedish	:	baddräkt-en 66
Turkish	:	mayo 66
Russian	:	купальный костюм, *m.* 66
Serbian	:	купаћи костим, *m.* 66
Ukrainian	:	купелевий стрій, *m.* 66

67 BATHE v.

Czech	:	koupati (se) 67
Danish	:	bade 67
Dutch	:	baden 67
Finnish	:	kylpeä 67
French	:	baigner 67
German	:	baden 67
Hungarian	:	fürödni 67
Italian	:	fare il bagno 67
Croatian	:	kupati se 67
Norwegian	:	bade 67
Polish	:	kapać się 67
Portuguese	:	tomar banho 67
Rumanian	:	a face baie 67
Slovak	:	kúpat' sa 67
Spanish	:	bañar 67
Swedish	:	bada 67
Turkish	:	hamamde yikanmak 67
Russian	:	купатся 67
Serbian	:	купати се 67
Ukrainian	:	купатися 67

68 BATH-ROBE (GOWN) s.

Czech	: koupací plášt', m.	68
Danish	: Badekaabe, c. 68	
Dutch	: de badmantel 68	
Finnish	: kylpyviitta 68	
French	: le peignoir 68	
German	: der Bademantel 68	
Hungarian	: fürdököpeny 68	
Italian	: accappatoio, m. 68	
Croatian	: kupaći ogrtač, m. 68	
Norwegian	: badekåpe, f. 68	
Polish	: plaszcz kapielowy, m.	68
Portuguese	: roupão, o 68	
Rumanian	: halatul de baie 68	
Slovak	: plášt' na kúpanie, m.	68
Spanish	: bata de baño, f. 68	
Swedish	: badkappa-n 68	
Turkish	: bornos 68	
Russian	: купальный халат, m.	68
Serbian	: купаћи огртач, m. 68	
Ukrainian	: купальний плащ, m.	68

69 BATH-TOWEL s.

Czech	: koupací utěrka, f. 69
Danish	: Badehaandkläde, n. 69
Dutch	: het badlaken 69
Finnish	: kylpyliina 69
French	: serviette de bain, f. 69
German	: das Badetuch 69
Hungarian	: fürdölepedö 69
Italian	: asciugatoio, m. 69
Croatian	: peškir za kupanje, m. 69
Norwegian	: badehåndklä, n. 69
Polish	: chustka kąpielowa, f. 69
Portuguese	: toalha de banho, a 69
Rumanian	: prosupul de baie 69
Slovak	: uterák na kúpanie, m. 69
Spanish	: frazada de baño, f. 69
Swedish	: badlakan-et 69
Turkish	: banyo hav lusu 69
Russian	: купальная простыня, f. 69
Serbian	: пешкир за купање, m. 69
Ukrainian	: купальне рядно, n. 69

70 BATH-TUB s.

Czech	: koupací vana, f. 70
Danish	: Badekar, n. 70
Dutch	: de badkuip 70
Finnish	: kylpyamme 70
French	: baignoire, f. 70
German	: die Badewanne 70
Hungarian	: fürdökád 70
Italian	: vasca da bagno, f. 70
Croatian	: kada za kupanje, f. 70
Norwegian	: badekar, n. 70
Polish	: wanna do kąpania, f. 70
Portuguese	: banheira, a 70
Rumanian	: cadă, f. 70
Slovak	: vaňa, f. 70
Spanish	: bañera, f. 70
Swedish	: badkar-et 70
Turkish	: kurna 70
Russian	: ванна, f. 70
Serbian	: када за купање, f. 70
Ukrainian	: ванна, f. 70

71 BATTERY s. (POCKET LAMP, FLASHLIGHT)

Czech	: baterka, f.; kapesní svítilna, f.	71
Danish	: Lommelygte 71	
Dutch	: de zaklamp 71	
Finnish	: taskulamppu 71	
French	: lampe de poche, f. 71	
German	: die Taschenlampe 71	
Hungarian	: zseblámpa, f. 71	
Italian	: lampada tascabile, f. 71	
Croatian	: džepna lampa, f. 71	
Norwegian	: lommelykt, f. 71	
Polish	: latarka, f. 71	
Portuguese	: lâmpada de algibeira, a 71	
Rumanian	: lampa de buzunar, f. 71	
Slovak	: vrecková lampa, f. 71	
Spanish	: lámpara de bolsillo, f. 71	
Swedish	: ficklampa-n 71	
Turkish	: cep lâmbası 71	
Russian	: карманная лампа, f. 71	
Serbian	: ћепиа лампа, f. 71	
Ukrainian	: кишенкова лампочка, f. 71	

72 BE v.

Czech	: býti; existovati 72
Danish	: väre; blive 72
Dutch	: zijn; leven 72
Finnish	: olla 72
French	: être 72
German	: sein 72
Hungarian	: van; lenni 72
Italian	: essere 72
Croatian	: biti; bivati 72
Norwegian	: vaere 72
Polish	: być 72
Portuguese	: ser; estar 72
Rumanian	: a fi; a exista 72
Slovak	: byt' 72
Spanish	: ser; estar 72
Swedish	: vara; blive 72
Turkish	: olmak 72
Russian	: быть 72
Serbian	: бити; пивати 72
Ukrainian	: бути 72

73 BEANS s. pl.

Czech	: fazole, f. 73
Danish	: Bönner, pl. 73
Dutch	: de boon 73
Finnish	: papuja pavut 73
French	: haricot, m. 73
German	: die Bohne 73
Hungarian	: bab 73
Italian	: fagiuolo, m. 73
Croatian	: pasulj, m. 73
Norwegian	: bönne, f. 73
Polish	: fasola, f. 73
Portuguese	: feijão, o 73
Rumanian	: fasolea, f. 73
Slovak	: fazul'a, f. 73
Spanish	: habas, f. 73
Swedish	: bönorna 73
Turkish	: fasulye 73
Russian	: фасоль, f. 73
Serbian	: пасуль, m. 73
Ukrainian	: фасоля, f. 73

74 BEAUTIFUL adj.

Czech	:	krásný 74
Danish	:	skön 74
Dutch	:	schoon 74
Finnish	:	kaunis 74
French	:	beau 74
German	:	schön 74
Hungarian	:	szép 74
Italian	:	bello 74
Croatian	:	lijep 74
Norwegian	:	vakker 74
Polish	:	pieknie 74
Portuguese	:	bonito 74
Rumanian	:	frumos 74
Slovak	:	krásný 74
Spanish	:	bello 74
Swedish	:	skön 74
Turkish	:	güzel 74
Russian	:	красиво; -ый 74
Serbian	:	лепо 74
Ukrainian	:	гарний, преквасний 74

75 BED s.

Czech	:	postel, f. 75
Danish	:	Seng, m./c. 75
Dutch	:	het bed 75
Finnish	:	sänky; vuode 75
French	:	lit, m. 75
German	:	das Bett 75
Hungarian	:	ágy 75
Italian	:	letto, m. 75
Croatian	:	krevet, m. 75
Norwegian	:	seng, f. 75
Polish	:	lóžko, n. 75
Portuguese	:	cama, a 75
Rumanian	:	patul 75
Slovak	:	posteľ, f. 75
Spanish	:	cama, f. 75
Swedish	:	säng-en 75
Turkish	:	yatak 75
Russian	:	кровать, f. 75
Serbian	:	кревет, m. 75
Ukrainian	:	ліжко, n. 75

76 BED-ROOM s.

Czech	:	ložnice, f. 76
Danish	:	Sovekammer, n. 76
Dutch	:	de slaapkamer 76
Finnish	:	makuuhuone 76
French	:	chambre à coucher 76
German	:	das Schlafzimmer 76
Hungarian	:	hálószoba 76
Italian	:	camera, f. 76
Croatian	:	spavaonica, f. 76
Norwegian	:	sovevärelse, n. 76
Polish	:	sypialnia, f. 76
Portuguese	:	quarto de dormir, o 76
Rumanian	:	camera de culcare 76
Slovak	:	spalňa, f. 76
Spanish	:	dormitorio, m. 76
Swedish	:	sobrumm-et 76
Turkish	:	yatak odasi 76
Russian	:	спальня, f. 76
Serbian	:	спаваоница, f. 76
Ukrainian	:	спальня, f. 76

77 BEE s.

Czech	:	včela, f. 77
Danish	:	Bi, f./c. 77
Dutch	:	de bij 77
Finnish	:	mehiläinen 77
French	:	abeille, f. 77
German	:	die Biene 77
Hungarian	:	méh 77
Italian	:	ape, f. 77
Croatian	:	pčela, f. 77
Norwegian	:	bi, f. 77
Polish	:	pszcola, f. 77
Portuguese	:	abelha, a 77
Rumanian	:	albinä, f. 77
Slovak	:	včela, f. 77
Spanish	:	abeja, f. 77
Swedish	:	bi-et 77
Turkish	:	arı 77
Russian	:	пчела, f. 77
Serbian	:	пчела, f. 77
Ukrainian	:	бджола, f. 77

78 BEECH s.

Czech	:	buk, m. 78
Danish	:	Bög, m./c. 78
Dutch	:	de beuk 78
Finnish	:	pyökki 78
French	:	hêtre, m. 78
German	:	die Buche 78
Hungarian	:	a bükkfa 78
Italian	:	faggio, m. 78
Croatian	:	bukva, f. 78
Norwegian	:	bök, m. 78
Polish	:	buk, m. 78
Portuguese	:	faia, a 78
Rumanian	:	fagul 78
Slovak	:	buk, m. 78
Spanish	:	haya, m. 78
Swedish	:	bok-en 78
Turkish	:	kain ağaci 78
Russian	:	бук, m. 78
Serbian	:	буква, f. 78
Ukrainian	:	бук, m. 78

79 BEEF s.

Czech	:	hovězí maso, n. 79
Danish	:	Okseköd, n. 79
Dutch	:	het ossevlees 79
Finnish	:	naudanliha 79
French	:	boeuf, m. 79
German	:	das Rindfleisch 79
Hungarian	:	marhahús 79
Italian	:	carne di manzo f. 79
Croatian	:	govedina, f. 79
Norwegian	:	oksekjött, n. 79
Polish	:	mięso wolowe, n. 79
Portuguese	:	carne de vaca, a 79
Rumanian	:	carnea de vacä 79
Slovak	:	hovädzie mäso, n. 79
Spanish	:	carne de vaca 79
Swedish	:	nötkött-et 79
Turkish	:	sigir eti 79
Russian	:	говядина, f. 79
Serbian	:	говеђје месо, n. 79
Ukrainian	:	волове мясо, n.; яловичина, f. 79

80 BEEFSTEAK s.

Czech	: hovězí řízek, m.	80
Danish	: Bófsteg, m./c.	80
Dutch	: de beefsteak	80
Finnish	: pihvi 80	
French	: bifteck, m.	80
German	: das Beefsteak	80
Hungarian	: rostélyos 80	
Italian	: bistecca, f.	80
Croatian	: bifstek, m.	80
Norwegian	: biff, m.	80
Polish	: befsztyk, m.	80
Portuguese	: bife, o 80	
Rumanian	: biftecul 80	
Slovak	: biftek, m.	80
Spanish	: biftec, m.	80
Swedish	: biffstek-en	80
Turkish	: bıfstik 80	
Russian	: бифштекс, m.	80
Serbian	: бифстек, m.	80
Ukrainian	: біфштик, m.	80

81 BEER s.

Czech	: pivo, n.	81
Danish	: Öl, n.	81
Dutch	: het bier	81
Finnish	: olut 81	
French	: bière, f.	81
German	: das Bier	81
Hungarian	: sör 81	
Italian	: birra, f.	81
Croatian	: pivo, n.	81
Norwegian	: öl, n.	81
Polish	: piwo, n.	81
Portuguese	: cerveja, a	81
Rumanian	: bereă, f.	81
Slovak	: pivo, n.	81
Spanish	: cerveza, f.	81
Swedish	: vitt vin	81
Turkish	: bira 81	
Russian	: пиво, n.	81
Serbian	: пиво, n.	81
Ukrainian	: пиво, n.	81

82 BEET-ROOT s.

Czech	: červená řepa, f.	82
Danish	: Rödbeder, c.	82
Dutch	: de roode biet	82
Finnish	: punaJuuria 82	
French	: betterave, f.	82
German	: die rote Rübe	82
Hungarian	: cékla 82	
Italian	: barbabietola rossa, f.	82
Croatian	: cvekla 82	
Norwegian	: rödbete, m.	82
Polish	: czerwone buraki, pl.	82
Portuguese	: beterraba, a	82
Rumanian	: sfecla roşie	82
Slovak	: cvikla, f.	82
Spanish	: remolacha, f.	82
Swedish	: rödbeta-n	82
Turkish	: kirmigi turp	82
Russian	: бурак 82	
Serbian	: црвена репа, f.	82
Ukrainian	: червоний буряк, m.	82

83 BEGIN v.

Czech	: začíti; začínati	83
Danish	: begynde 83	
Dutch	: beginnen 83	
Finnish	: alkaa 83	
French	: commencer 83	
German	: beginnen 83	
Hungarian	: megelkezd 83	
Italian	: cominciare 83	
Croatian	: počinjati; početi	83
Norwegian	: begynne 83	
Polish	: zacząć 83	
Portuguese	: começar 83	
Rumanian	: a începe 83	
Slovak	: začať' 83	
Spanish	: comenzar 83	
Swedish	: börja 83	
Turkish	: baslamak 83	
Russian	: начать 83	
Serbian	: починјати 83	
Ukrainian	: починати 83	

84 BEGINNING see 936 START

85 BELLY s.

Czech	: břicho, n.	85
Danish	: Legeme, n.	85
Dutch	: de buik; het lichaam	85
Finnish	: ruumis 85	
French	: ventre; estomac m.	85
German	: der Leib; der Bauch	85
Hungarian	: törzs 85	
Italian	: ventre, m.	85
Croatian	: tjelo, n.	85
Norwegian	: liv, n.; underliv, n.	85
Polish	: brzuch, m.	85
Portuguese	: ventre, o	85
Rumanian	: trupul, n.	85
Slovak	: telo, n.	85
Spanish	: vientre, f.	85
Swedish	: buk-en 85	
Turkish	: karın 85	
Russian	: бюшина, f.	85
Serbian	: тело, n.	85
Ukrainian	: тіло, живіт, m.	85

86 BELT s.

Czech	: řemen, m.; opasek, m.	86
Danish	: Bälte, m. 86	
Dutch	: de ceintuur	86
Finnish	: vyö 86	
French	: ceinture, f.	86
German	: der Gürtel,	86
Hungarian	: öv 86	
Italian	: cintura, f.	86
Croatian	: pojas, m.	86
Norwegian	: belte, n.	86
Polish	: pas, m.	86
Portuguese	: cinto, o	86
Rumanian	: cingătoarea, f.	86
Slovak	: opasok, m.	86
Spanish	: cinturón, m.	86
Swedish	: bälte-t 86	
Turkish	: kemer 86	
Russian	: пояс, m.	86
Serbian	: појас, m.	86
Ukrainian	: пасок; пояс. m.	86

87 BENCH s.

Czech	:	lavice, f. 87
Danish	:	Bänk, m./c. 87
Dutch	:	de bank 87
Finnish	:	penkki 87
French	:	banc, m. 87
German	:	die Bank 87
Hungarian	:	pad 87
Italian	:	banca, f. 87
Croatian	:	klupa, f. 87
Norwegian	:	benk, m. 87
Polish	:	ławka, f. 87
Portuguese	:	banco, o 87
Rumanian	:	bancă, f. 87
Slovak	:	lavica, f. 87
Spanish	:	banco, m. 87
Swedish	:	bänk-en 87
Turkish	:	kanape 87
Russian	:	скамья, f. 87
Serbian	:	клупа, f. 87
Ukrainian	:	лавка, f. 87

88 BENEVOLENT see 499 KIND

89 BICYCLE s.

Czech	:	jízdní kolo, n. 89
Danish	:	Cykel, m./c. 89
Dutch	:	de fiets 89
Finnish	:	polkupyörä 89
French	:	bicyclette, f. 89
German	:	das Fahrrad 89
Hungarian	:	kerékpár 89
Italian	:	bicicletta, f. 89
Croatian	:	točak; bicikel, m. 89
Norwegian	:	sykkel, m. 89
Polish	:	rower, m. 89
Portuguese	:	bicicleta, a 89
Rumanian	:	bicicletă, f. 89
Slovak	:	bicykel, m. 89
Spanish	:	bicicleta, f. 89
Swedish	:	cykel-n 89
Turkish	:	bisiklet 89
Russian	:	велосипед, m. 89
Serbian	:	велосипед, m. 89
Ukrainian	:	колесо, n.; велосипед, m. 89

90 BILL s.

Czech	:	účet, m. 90
Danish	:	Regning, m. 90
Dutch	:	De rekening 90
Finnish	:	lasku 90
French	:	addition, f.; facture f. 90
German	:	die Rechnung 90
Hungarian	:	számla 90
Italian	:	Il conto 90
Croatian	:	račun, m. 90
Norwegian	:	regning, f. 90
Polish	:	rachunek, m. 90
Portuguese	:	conta, a 90
Rumanian	:	socoteală, f. 90
Slovak	:	účet, m. 90
Spanish	:	cuenta, f. 90
Swedish	:	räkning-en 90
Turkish	:	herap 90
Russian	:	счет m. 90
Serbian	:	рачук, m. 90
Ukrainian	:	рахунок, m. 90

91 BILLIARD s.

Czech	:	kulečník, m. 91
Danish	:	Billard, m./c. 91
Dutch	:	het billard 91
Finnish	:	biljaardi 91
French	:	billard, m. 91
German	:	das Billard 91
Hungarian	:	billiárd 91
Italian	:	bigliardo, m. 91
Croatian	:	biliard, m. 91
Norwegian	:	billjard, m. 91
Polish	:	bilard, m. 91
Portuguese	:	bilhar, o 91
Rumanian	:	biliardul 91
Slovak	:	biliard, m. 91
Spanish	:	billar, m. 91
Swedish	:	biljard 91
Turkish	:	billard 91
Russian	:	биллиард, m. 91
Serbian	:	биллард, m. 91
Ukrainian	:	білярд, m. 91

92 BIRD s.

Czech	:	pták, m. 92
Danish	:	Fugl, m./c. 92
Dutch	:	de vogel 92
Finnish	:	lintu 92
French	:	oiseau, m. 92
German	:	der Vogel 92
Hungarian	:	madár 92
Italian	:	uccello, m. 92
Croatian	:	ptica, f. 92
Norwegian	:	fugl, m. 92
Polish	:	ptak, m. 92
Portuguese	:	pássaro, o 92
Rumanian	:	pasăreă, f. 92
Slovak	:	vták, m. 92
Spanish	:	ave, m. 92
Swedish	:	fågel-n 92
Turkish	:	kuş 92
Russian	:	птица, f. 92
Serbian	:	птица, f. 92
Ukrainian	:	птах, m.; птиця, f. 92

93 BIRTH s.

Czech	:	narození, n. 93
Danish	:	Födsel, m. 93
Dutch	:	de geboorte 93
Finnish	:	syntymä 93
French	:	naissance, f. 93
German	:	die Geburt 93
Hungarian	:	születés 93
Italian	:	nascita, f. 93
Croatian	:	rodjenje, n. 93
Norwegian	:	födsel, m. 93
Polish	:	poród, m.; urodzenie, n. 93
Portuguese	:	nascimento, o 93
Rumanian	:	naşterea, f. 93
Slovak	:	narodzenie, n.; pôrod, m. 93
Spanish	:	nacimiento, m. 93
Swedish	:	födelse-n 93
Turkish	:	dogis 93
Russian	:	рождение, n. 93
Serbian	:	рођенье, n. 93
Ukrainian	:	порід, m.; народження, n. 93

94 BIRTH-DAY s.

Czech	: narozeniny, *pl.*	94
Danish	: Födselsdag, *m.*	94
Dutch	: de verjaardag	94
Finnish	: syntymäpäivä	94
French	: anniversaire, *m.*	94
German	: der Geburtstag	94
Hungarian	: születésnap	94
Italian	: giorno natalizio, *m.*	94
Croatian	: rodjendan, *m.*	94
Norwegian	: födselsdag, *m.*	94
Polish	: urodziny, *pl.*	94
Portuguese	: aniversário, *o*	94
Rumanian	: ziuă de naştere, *f.*	94
Slovak	: narodeniny, *pl.*	94
Spanish	: cumpleaños, *m.*	94
Swedish	: födelsedag-en	94
Turkish	: doğum günü	94
Russian	: день рождения, *m.*	94
Serbian	: рођен дан, *m.*	94
Ukrainian	: уродини; день народженна, .*m.*	94

95 BISCUIT s.

Czech	: suchar, *m.*	95
Danish	: Tvebak, *m./c.*	95
Dutch	: het beschuit	95
Finnish	: korppu	95
French	: biscotte, *f.*	95
German	: der Zwieback	95
Hungarian	: kétszersült	95
Italian	: biscotto, *m.*	95
Croatian	: dvopek, *m.*	95
Norwegian	: kavring, *m.*	95
Polish	: suchar, *m.*	95
Portuguese	: biscoito, *o*	95
Rumanian	: pesmetii, *pl.*	95
Slovak	: suchár, *m.*	95
Spanish	: bizcocho, *m.*	95
Swedish	: skorpa-n	95
Turkish	: peksımet	95
Russian	: сухарь, *m.*	95
Serbian	: двопек, *m.*	95
Ukrainian	: сухар, *m.*	95

96 BITTER adj.

Czech	: hořký	96
Danish	: bitter	96
Dutch	: bitter	96
Finnish	: typeä	96
French	: amer	96
German	: bitter	96
Hungarian	: keserü	96
Italian	: amaro	96
Croatian	: gorak	96
Norwegian	: bitter	96
Polish	: gozki	96
Portuguese	: amargo	96
Rumanian	: amar	96
Slovak	: horký	96
Spanish	: amargo	96
Swedish	: bitter	96
Turkish	: aci	96
Russian	: горький	96
Serbian	: горак	96
Ukrainian	: гіркий.	96

97 BLACK adj.

Czech	: černý	97
Danish	: sort	97
Dutch	: zwart	97
Finnish	: musta	97
French	: noir	97
German	: schwarz	97
Hungarian	: fekete	97
Italian	: nero	97
Croatian	: crn	97
Norwegian	: svart	97
Polish	: czarny	97
Portuguese	: prêto	97
Rumanian	: negru	97
Slovak	: čierny	97
Spanish	: negro	97
Swedish	: svart	97
Turkish	: kara, siyah	97
Russian	: черный	97
Serbian	: црн	97
Ukrainian	: чорний	97

98 BLAME v.

Czech	: haniti	98
Danish	: dadle	98
Dutch	: afkeuren	98
Finnish	: moittia	98
French	: réprimander	98
German	: tadeln	98
Hungarian	: rosszalni	98
Italian	: biasimare	98
Croatian	: koriti	98
Norwegian	: dadle	98
Polish	: ganić	98
Portuguese	: censurar	98
Rumanian	: a dojeni	98
Slovak	: karhat'	98
Spanish	: vituperar	98
Swedish	: klandra	98
Turkish	: aiplamak	98
Russian	: порицать	98
Serbian	: корити	98
Ukrainian	: докоряти; ганити,	98

99 BLANKET s.

Czech	: (vlněná) přikrývka, *f.*	99
Danish	: ultäppe, *n.*	99
Dutch	: deken	99
Finnish	: peite	99
French	: couverture, *f.*	99
German	: die (wollene) Decke	99
Hungarian	: takaró	99
Italian	: coperta da letto, *f.*	99
Croatian	: pokrivač, *m.*	99
Norwegian	: teppe, *n.*	99
Polish	: pane	99
Portuguese	: cobertor, *m.*	99
Rumanian	: plapomă, *f.*	99
Slovak	: pokrývka, *f.*	99
Spanish	: cobija, *f.*	99
Swedish	: (ylle) filt-et	99
Turkish	: örtü	99
Russian	: покрывало, *n.*	99
Serbian	: покривач, *m.*	99
Ukrainian	: покришка, *f.*	99

100 BLOTTER *s.* (a piece of blotting paper)

Czech	:	ssací papír, *m.* 100
Danish	:	Klatpapir, *c.* 100
Dutch	:	de vloeier 100
Finnish	:	imuri 100
French	:	buvard, *m.* 100
German	:	der Löscher 100
Hungarian	:	itatós 100
Italian	:	carta assorbente, *f.* 100
Croatian	:	upijač za mastilo, *m.* 100
Norwegian	:	löscher, *m.* 100
Polish	:	bibularz, *m.* 100
Portuguese	:	mata-borrão, *o* 100
Rumanian	:	sugativă, *f.* 100
Slovak	:	pijak, *m.* 100
Spanish	:	secatintas, *m.* 100
Swedish	:	dokument-skåp-et 100
Turkish	:	murakkap silgisi 100
Russian	:	промакательная бумага, **f.** 100
Serbian	:	упијач за мастило, *m.* 100
Ukrainian	:	промокальниця, *f.* 100

103 BLUEBERRY *s.*

Czech	:	borůvka, *f.* 103
Danish	:	Blaabär, *m./c.* 103
Dutch	:	de boschbes 103
Finnish	:	mustikat, *pl.* 103
French	:	myrtille, *f.* 103
German	:	die Heidelbeere 103
Hungarian	:	áfonya 103
Italian	:	bacca di mirtillo, *f.* 103
Croatian	:	borovnica, *f.* 103
Norwegian	:	blåbär, *n.* 103
Polish	:	borówka, *f.* 103
Portuguese	:	airela, *a* 103
Rumanian	:	afina, *f.* 103
Slovak	:	čučoriedka, *f.* 103
Spanish	:	baya del arándano 103
Swedish	:	blåbär-et 103
Turkish	:	yaban mersini 103
Russian	:	черника, *f.* 103
Serbian	:	боровница, *f.* 103
Ukrainian	:	чорниця, *f.* 103

101 BLOUSE *s.*

Czech	:	bluza, *f.*; halenka, *f.* 101
Danish	:	Bluse, *m./c.* 101
Dutch	:	de blouse 101
Finnish	:	pusero 101
French	:	blouse, *f.* 101
German	:	die Bluse 101
Hungarian	:	blúz 101
Italian	:	camicietta, *f.* 101
Croatian	:	bluza, *f.* 101
Norwegian	:	bluse, *m.* 101
Polish	:	bluza, *f.* 101
Portuguese	:	blusa, *a* 101
Rumanian	:	bluza, *f.* 101
Slovak	:	halienka, *f.* 101
Spanish	:	blusa, *f.* 101
Swedish	:	blus-en 101
Turkish	:	bluz 101
Russian	:	блузка, *f.* 101
Serbian	:	блуза, *f.* 101
Ukrainian	:	блюзка, *f.* 101

104 BLUNT *adj.*

Czech	:	tupý 104
Danish	:	stump 104
Dutch	:	stomp 104
Finnish	:	tylsä 104
French	:	émoussé 104
German	:	stumpf 104
Hungarian	:	tompa 104
Italian	:	smussato 104
Croatian	:	tup 104
Norwegian	:	stump 104
Polish	:	tepy 104
Portuguese	:	embotado 104
Rumanian	:	tocit 104
Slovak	:	tupý 104
Spanish	:	obtuso 104
Swedish	:	trubbig 104
Turkish	:	yassi 104
Russian	:	тупой 104
Serbian	:	туп 104
Ukrainian	:	тупий 104

102 BLUE *adj.*

Czech	:	modrý 102
Danish	:	blaa 102
Dutch	:	blauw 102
Finnish	:	sininen 102
French	:	bleu 102
German	:	blau 102
Hungarian	:	kék 102
Italian	:	azzurro 102
Croatian	:	plav 102
Norwegian	:	blå 102
Polish	:	błękitny 102
Portuguese	:	azul 102
Rumanian	:	albastru 102
Slovak	:	modrý 102
Spanish	:	azul 102
Swedish	:	blå 102
Turkish	:	mari 102
Russian	:	синий 102
Serbian	:	плав 102
Ukrainian	:	блакитний; синій 102

105 BOAT *s.*

Czech	:	člun, *m.*; lod'ka, *f.* 105
Danish	:	Baad, *m./c.* 105
Dutch	:	de boot 105
Finnish	:	vene; pursi 105
French	:	canot, *m.* 105
German	:	das Boot 105
Hungarian	:	csónak 105
Italian	:	barca, *f.* 105
Croatian	:	čamac, *m.* 105
Norwegian	:	båt, *m.* 105
Polish	:	czółno, *n.* 105
Portuguese	:	bote, *o* 105
Rumanian	:	barcă, *f.* 105
Slovak	:	čl'n, *m.* 105
Spanish	:	bote, *m.* 105
Swedish	:	båt-en 105
Turkish	:	kayik 105
Russian	:	лодка, *f.* 105
Serbian	:	чамац, *m.* 105
Ukrainian	:	човен, *m.* 105

16

106 BOIL v.

Czech	:	vařiti 106
Danish	:	koge 106
Dutch	:	kooken 106
Finnish	:	keittää 106
French	:	cuire 106
German	:	kochen 106
Hungarian	:	főzni 106
Italian	:	cuocere 106
Croatian	:	kuhati 106
Norwegian	:	koke 106
Polish	:	gotowac 106
Portuguese	:	cozinhar, ferver 106
Rumanian	:	a fierbe 106
Slovak	:	varit' 106
Spanish	:	hervir; cocer 106
Swedish	:	koka 106
Turkish	:	pişmek 106
Russian	:	варить 106
Serbian	:	кувати 106
Ukrainian	:	варити 106

107 BOILED EGG s.

Czech	:	vařené vejce, n. 107
Danish	:	kogt Äg, c. 107
Dutch	:	het gekookte ei 107
Finnish	:	keitetty muna 107
French	:	oeuf cuit, m. 107
German	:	das gekochte Ei 107
Hungarian	:	főtt tojás 107
Italian	:	uovo cotto, m. 107
Croatian	:	kuhano jaje, n. 107
Norwegian	:	kokt egg, c. 107
Polish	:	zgotowane jajo 107
Portuguese	:	ôvo cozido, o 107
Rumanian	:	oul fiert 107
Slovak	:	varené vajce, n. 107
Spanish	:	huevo hervido, m. 107
Swedish	:	kokt ägg 107
Turkish	:	pismis yumurta 107
Russian	:	варенное яйцо, n. 107
Serbian	:	кивано jaje, n. 107
Ukrainian	:	варене яице, n. 107

108 BOILED FISH s.

Czech	:	vařená ryba, f. 108
Danish	:	kogt Fisk, m./c. 108
Dutch	:	de gekookte vis 108
Finnish	:	keitetty kala 108
French	:	poisson cuit, m. 108
German	:	der gekochte Fisch 108
Hungarian	:	főtt hal 108
Italian	:	pesce cotto, m. 108
Croatian	:	kuhana riba, f. 108
Norwegian	:	kokt fisk, m. 108
Polish	:	gotowana ryba, f. 108
Portuguese	:	peixe cozido, o 108
Rumanian	:	peştele rasol 108
Slovak	:	varená ryba, f. 108
Spanish	:	pescado hervido 108
Swedish	:	kokt fisk 108
Turkish	:	pişmiş balık 108
Russian	:	варенная рыба, f. 108
Serbian	:	кувана риба, f. 108
Ukrainian	:	варена риба f. 108

109 BOILER s.

Czech	:	kotlík, m.; kotel na vodu, m. 109
Danish	:	Vand-kedel, m. 109
Dutch	:	de waterketel 109
Finnish	:	vesikattila 109
French	:	chaudron, m. 109
German	:	der Wasserkessel 109
Hungarian	:	üst 109
Italian	:	caldaia, f. 109
Croatian	:	kotao za vodu, m. 109
Norwegian	:	vankjel, m. 109
Polish	:	kocioł, m. 109
Portuguese	:	chaleira, a 109
Rumanian	:	cazanul de apă 109
Slovak	:	kotlík na vodu, m. 109
Spanish	:	caldera, f. 109
Swedish	:	vattenkittel-n 109
Turkish	:	so ihriğı 109
Russian	:	котел для водь m. 109
Serbian	:	котао за воду, n. 109
Ukrainian	:	котел на воду, m. 109

110 BOMB s.

Czech	:	bomba, f. 110
Danish	:	Bombe, m./c. 110
Dutch	:	de bom 110
Finnish	:	pommi 110
French	:	bombe, f. 110
German	:	die Bombe 110
Hungarian	:	bomba 110
Italian	:	bomba, f. 110
Croatian	:	bomba, f. 110
Norwegian	:	bombe, f. 110
Polish	:	bomba, f. 110
Portuguese	:	bomba, a 110
Rumanian	:	bombă, f. 110
Slovak	:	bomba, f. 110
Spanish	:	bomba, f. 110
Swedish	:	bomb-en 110
Turkish	:	bamba 110
Russian	:	бомба, f. 110
Serbian	:	бомба, f. 110
Ukrainian	:	бомба, f. 110

111 BOOK s.

Czech	:	kniha, f. 111
Danish	:	Bog, m./c. 111
Dutch	:	het boek 111
Finnish	:	kirja 111
French	:	livre, m. 111
German	:	das Buch 111
Hungarian	:	könyv 111
Italian	:	libro, m. 111
Croatian	:	knjiga, f. 111
Norwegian	:	bok, f. 111
Polish	:	książka, f. 111
Portuguese	:	livro, o 111
Rumanian	:	carteă, f. 111
Slovak	:	kniha, f. 111
Spanish	:	libro, m. 111
Swedish	:	bok-en 111
Turkish	:	kitap 111
Russian	:	книга, f. 111
Serbian	:	кньига, f. 111
Ukrainian	:	книжка, f. 111

112 BOOK-CASE s.

Czech	:	knihovna (příruční), f.	112
Danish	:	Bogskab, n.	112
Dutch	:	de boekenkast	112
Finnish	:	kirjakaappi	112
French	:	bibliothéque, f.	112
German	:	der Bücherschrank	112
Hungarian	:	könyvszekrény	112
Italian	:	scafale per i libri, m.	112
Croatian	:	ormar za knjige, m.	112
Norwegian	:	bokskap, n.	112
Polish	:	szafa na książki	112
Portuguese	:	estante para livros, a	112
Rumanian	:	bibliotecă, f.	112
Slovak	:	knihovna, f.	112
Spanish	:	armario para libros, m.	112
Swedish	:	bokhyllan	112
Turkish	:	kitap dolabi	112
Russian	:	шкаф для книг, m.	112
Serbian	:	ормар за књиге, m.	112
Ukrainian	:	шафка на книжки, f.	112

113 BOOKING OFFICE s.

Czech	:	výdejna jízdenek, f.	113
Danish	:	Billethul, n.	113
Dutch	:	het loket	113
Finnish	:	lippumyynti	113
French	:	guichet, m.	113
German	:	der Schalter	113
Hungarian	:	jegykiadóablak	113
Italian	:	sportello, m.	113
Croatian	:	šalter, m.	113
Norwegian	:	luke; billettluke, f.	113
Polish	:	okienko, n.	113
Portuguese	:	guichet, o	113
Rumanian	:	ghişeul	113
Slovak	:	okienko, n.	113
Spanish	:	el despacho de billetes	113
Swedish	:	biljettlucka-n	113
Turkish	:	bilet kişesi	113
Russian	:	билетная касса, f.	113
Serbian	:	шалтер, m.	113
Ukrainian	:	віконце, n.	113

114 BOOKKEEPER s.

Czech	:	účetní, m.	114
Danish	:	Bogholder, m./c.	114
Dutch	:	de boekhoulder	114
Finnish	:	kirjanpitäjä	114
French	:	comptable, m.	114
German	:	der Buchhalter	114
Hungarian	:	a könyvelö	114
Italian	:	contabile, m.	114
Croatian	:	knjigovodja, m.	114
Norwegian	:	bokholder, m.	114
Polish	:	buhalter, m.	114
Portuguese	:	guarda-livros, o	114
Rumanian	:	contabilul	114
Slovak	:	účtovník, m.	114
Spanish	:	el tenedor de libros	114
Swedish	:	bokhållare-n	114
Turkish	:	defter tutan	114
Russian	:	бухгалтер, m.	114
Serbian	:	књиговоћа, m.	114
Ukrainian	:	книговід; рахівник, m.	114

115 BOOK SHOP s.

Czech	:	knihkupectví, n.	115
Danish	:	Boghandel, m./c.	115
Dutch	:	de boekwinkel	115
Finnish	:	kirjakauppa	115
French	:	librairie, m.	115
German	:	der Buchladen	115
Hungarian	:	könyvkereskedés	115
Italian	:	libreria, f.	115
Croatian	:	knjižara, f.	115
Norwegian	:	bokhandel, m.	115
Polish	:	księgarnia, f.	115
Portuguese	:	livraria, a	115
Rumanian	:	librăriă, f.	115
Slovak	:	knihkupectvo, n.	115
Spanish	:	librería, f.	115
Swedish	:	bokhandel-n	115
Turkish	:	kitap dukâni	115
Russian	:	книжный магазин, m.	115
Serbian	:	књижара, f.	115
Ukrainian	:	книгарня, f.	115

116 BOOT s.

Czech	:	bota (vysoká), f.	116
Danish	:	Ridestóvle, pl.	116
Dutch	:	de laars	116
Finnish	:	saappaat	116
French	:	botte, f.	116
German	:	der Stiefel	116
Hungarian	:	csizma	116
Italian	:	stivale, m.	116
Croatian	:	čizma, f.	116
Norwegian	:	stövel, m.	116
Polish	:	buty, pl.	116
Portuguese	:	bota de cano alto, a	116
Rumanian	:	cisma, f.	116
Slovak	:	čižma, f.	116
Spanish	:	bota, f.	116
Swedish	:	stövel-n	116
Turkish	:	çizme	116
Russian	:	сапог, pl.	116
Serbian	:	чизма, f.	116
Ukrainian	:	чоботи, pl.	116

117 BORER s.

Czech	:	vrták, m.	117
Danish	:	Bor, m./c.	117
Dutch	:	de boor	117
Finnish	:	pora; kaira	117
French	:	vrille, f.	117
German	:	der Bohrer	117
Hungarian	:	fúró	117
Italian	:	trapane, m.	117
Croatian	:	svrdlo, n.; bušač, m.	117
Norwegian	:	bor, m.	117
Polish	:	świderek, m.	117
Portuguese	:	broca, a	117
Rumanian	:	burghiul	117
Slovak	:	vrták, m.	117
Spanish	:	atornillador, m.	117
Swedish	:	borr-en	117
Turkish	:	burgu	117
Russian	:	бурав, m.	117
Serbian	:	бушач, m.	117
Ukrainian	:	сверлел; сверлик, m.	117

18

118 BOW s. (music.)

Czech	: smyčec, m. (houslový)	118
Danish	: Violinbue, m./c.	118
Dutch	: de strijkstok	118
Finnish	: jousi	118
French	: l'archer, m.	118
German	: der Bogen	118
Hungarian	: vonó	118
Italian	: arco, m.	118
Croatian	: gudalo, n.	118
Norwegian	: fiolinbue, m.	118
Polish	: smyczek, m.	118
Portuguese	: arco para o violino, o	118
Rumanian	: arcuşul	118
Slovak	: sláčik, m.	118
Spanish	: arco, m.	118
Swedish	: stråke-n	118
Turkish	: kemer	118
Russian	: смычек, m.	118
Serbian	: гудало, n.	118
Ukrainian	: смик; смичок, m.	118

119 BOW s. (slips)

Czech	: motýlek, m.	119
Danish	: Slips; Butterfly	119
Dutch	: de das	119
Finnish	: solmuke	119
French	: le noeud	119
German	: die Schleife	119
Hungarian	: csokor; nyakkendö	119
Italian	: gravatta, f.	119
Croatian	: leptir kravata, f.	119
Norwegian	: slöyfe, c., f.	119
Polish	: krawat	119
Portuguese	: gravata para traje de rigor, a	119
Rumanian	: cravata, f.	119
Slovak	: maśl'a	119
Spanish	: lazo, m.	119
Swedish	: rosett-en	119
Turkish	: papillon	119
Russian	: галстук -бабочка, m.	119
Serbian	: петља, f.	119
Ukrainian	: метелик, m.	119

120 BOWL s. (deep dish)

Czech	: mísa, f.	120
Danish	: Fad, n.	120
Dutch	: de schotel	120
Finnish	: vati	120
French	: plat, m.	120
German	: die Schüssel	120
Hungarian	: tál	120
Italian	: scodella f.	120
Croatian	: zdela, f.	120
Norwegian	: fat, n.	120
Polish	: miska, f.	120
Portuguese	: tigela, a	120
Rumanian	: castronul	120
Slovak	: misa, f.	120
Spanish	: fuente, f.	120
Swedish	: skål-en	120
Turkish	: kâse	120
Russian	: миска, f.	120
Serbian	: чинија, f.	120
Ukrainian	: полумисок, m.; миска, f.	120

121 BOY s.

Czech	: chlapec; hoch, m.	121
Danish	: Dreng, m.	121
Dutch	: de jongen	121
Finnish	: poika	121
French	: garçon, m.	121
German	: der Knabe	121
Hungarian	: fiú	121
Italian	: ragazzo, m.	121
Croatian	: dječak, m.	121
Norwegian	: gutt, m.	121
Polish	: chłopiec, m.	121
Portuguese	: menino, o	121
Rumanian	: băiatul	121
Slovak	: chlapec, m.	121
Spanish	: niño, m.	121
Swedish	: gosse-n	121
Turkish	: oğlan	121
Russian	: мальчик, m.	121
Serbian	: дечак, m.	121
Ukrainian	: хлопець, m.	121

122 BOX see 175 CASE

123 BRACELET s.

Czech	: náramek, m.	123
Danish	: Armbaand, n.	123
Dutch	: de armband	123
Finnish	: rannerengas	123
French	: bracelet, m.	123
German	: das Armband	123
Hungarian	: karkötö	123
Italian	: braccialetto, m.	123
Croatian	: narukvica, f.	123
Norwegian	: armbånd, n.	123
Polish	: bransoleta, f.	123
Portuguese	: pulseira, a	123
Rumanian	: brătară	123
Slovak	: náramok, m.	123
Spanish	: pulsera, f.	123
Swedish	: armband-et	123
Turkish	: bilezik	123
Russian	: браслет, m.	123
Serbian	: наруквица, f.	123
Ukrainian	: обручка; браслет, m.	123

124 BRACES s.

Czech	: šle, pl.	124
Danish	: Seler, c.	124
Dutch	: de bretels	124
Finnish	: (housunkannatimet); olkaimet	124
French	: bretelles, f. pl.	124
German	: der Hosenträger	124
Hungarian	: nadrágtartó	124
Italian	: le bretelle	124
Croatian	: naramenice, pl.	124
Norwegian	: bukseseler, pl.	124
Polish	: szelki, pl.	124
Portuguese	: suspensórios, os	124
Rumanian	: breteaua	124
Slovak	: traky, pl.	124
Spanish	: tirantes, pl.	124
Swedish	: hängslen-a	124
Turkish	: pantalon askilari	124
Russian	: подтяжки, pl.	124
Serbian	: ораменице, pl.	124
Ukrainian	: підтяжки, pl.	124

125 BRASS s.

Czech	:	mosaz, *f.* 125
Danish	:	Messing, *n.* 125
Dutch	:	het messing 125
Finnish	:	messinki 125
French	:	laiton, *m.* 125
German	:	das Messing 125
Hungarian	:	sárgaréz 125
Italian	:	ottone, *m.* 125
Croatian	:	mjed, *f.* 125
Norwegian	:	messing, *m.* 125
Polish	:	mosiądz, *m.* 125
Portuguese	:	latão, *o* 125
Rumanian	:	alamă, *f.* 125
Slovak	:	mosadz, *f.* 125
Spanish	:	latón 125
Swedish	:	mässing-en 125
Turkish	:	jarı bakır 125
Russian	:	латунь, *f.* 125
Serbian	:	мед, *m.* 125,
Ukrainian	:	мосяж, *m.* 125

126 BREAD s.

Czech	:	chléb, *m.* 126
Danish	:	Bröd, *n.* 126
Dutch	:	het brood 126
Finnish	:	leipä 126
French	:	pain, *m.* 126
German	:	das Brot 126
Hungarian	:	kenyér 126
Italian	:	pane, *m.* 126
Croatian	:	kruh, *m.* 126
Norwegian	:	bröd, *n.* 126
Polish	:	chleb, *m.* 126
Portuguese	:	pão, *o* 126
Rumanian	:	pâinea, *f.* 126
Slovak	:	chlieb, *m.* 126
Spanish	:	pan, *m.* 126
Swedish	:	bröd-et 126
Turkish	:	ekmek 126
Russian	:	хлеб, *m.* 126
Serbian	:	хлеб, *m.* 126
Ukrainian	:	хліб, *m.* 126

127 BREAKFAST s.

Czech	:	snídaně, *f.* 127
Danish	:	Morgenmad, *c.* 127
Dutch	:	het ontbijt 127
Finnish	:	aamiainen 127
French	:	petit déjeuner, *m.* 127
German	:	das Frühstück 127
Hungarian	:	reggeli 127
Italian	:	colazione, *m.* 127
Croatian	:	doručak, *m.* 127
Norwegian	:	frokost, *m.* 127
Polish	:	śniadanie, *n.* 127
Portuguese	:	primeiro almôço, *o* 127
Rumanian	:	dejunul 127
Slovak	:	raňajky, *pl.* 127
Spanish	:	desayuno, *m.* 127
Swedish	:	frukost-en 127
Turkish	:	kahvaltı 127
Russian	:	завтрак, *m.* 127
Serbian	:	доручак, *m.* 127
Ukrainian	:	сніданок, *m.* 127

128 BRICK s.

Czech	:	cihla, *f.* 128
Danish	:	Mursten, *c.* 128
Dutch	:	de baksteen 128
Finnish	:	kivi 128
French	:	brique, *f.* 128
German	:	der Ziegelstein 128
Hungarian	:	tégla 128
Italian	:	mattone, *m.* 128
Croatian	:	opeka, *f.* 128
Norwegian	:	teglsten, *m.* 128
Polish	:	cegla, *f.* 128
Portuguese	:	tijolo, *o* 128
Rumanian	:	cărămidă, *f.* 128
Slovak	:	tehla, *f.* 128
Spanish	:	ladrillo, *m.* 128
Swedish	:	tegelsten-en 128
Turkish	:	tuğla 128
Russian	:	кирпичъ, *m.* 128
Serbian	:	опека, *f.* 128
Ukrainian	:	цегла, *f.* 128

129 BRICK-LAYER s.

Czech	:	zedník, *m.* 129
Danish	:	Murer, *m.* 129
Dutch	:	de metselaar 129
Finnish	:	muurari 129
French	:	maçon, *m.* 129
German	:	der Maurer 129
Hungarian	:	a kömüves 129
Italian	:	muratore, *m.* 129
Croatian	:	zidar, *m.* 129
Norwegian	:	murer, *m.* 129
Polish	:	murarz, *m.* 129
Portuguese	:	pedreiro, *o* 129
Rumanian	:	zidarul 129
Slovak	:	murár, *m.* 129
Spanish	:	albañil, *m.* 129
Swedish	:	murare-n 129
Turkish	:	divarci 129
Russian	:	каменщик, *m.* 129
Serbian	:	зидар, *m.* 129
Ukrainian	:	муляр, *m.* 129

130 BRIDGE s.

Czech	:	most, *m.* 130
Danish	:	Bro, *m./c.* 130
Dutch	:	de brug 130
Finnish	:	silta;laituri 130
French	:	pont, *m.* 130
German	:	die Brücke 130
Hungarian	:	hid 130
Italian	:	ponte, *m.* 130
Croatian	:	most, *m.* 130
Norwegian	:	bro, *m.*; bru, *f.* 130
Polish	:	most, *m.* 130
Portuguese	:	ponte, *a* 130
Rumanian	:	podul 130
Slovak	:	most, *m.* 130
Spanish	:	puente, *f.* 130
Swedish	:	bro-n 130
Turkish	:	köprü 130
Russian	:	мост, *m.* 130
Serbian	:	мост, *m.* 130
Ukrainian	:	міст, *m.* 130

131 BRIEF see 877 SHORT

132 BRING v.

Czech	: nésti; přinésti	132
Danish	: bringe	132
Dutch	: brengen	132
Finnish	: tuoda	132
French	: apporter	132
German	: bringen	132
Hungarian	: hoz	132
Italian	: portare	132
Croatian	: donositi	132
Norwegian	: bringe	132
Polish	: przynieść	132
Portuguese	: trazer	132
Rumanian	: a aduce	132
Slovak	: doniesť	132
Spanish	: traer	132
Swedish	: bära	132
Turkish	: getirmek	132
Russian	: при-носить	132
Serbian	: доносити	132
Ukrainian	: приносити	132

133 BROOCH s.

Czech	: brož, f.	133
Danish	: Broche, m./c.	133
Dutch	: de broche	133
Finnish	: rintasolki	133
French	: broche, f.	133
German	: die Brosche	133
Hungarian	: melltü	133
Italian	: spillo, m.	133
Croatian	: broš, m.	133
Norwegian	: brosje, f. c.	133
Polish	: broszka, f.	133
Portuguese	: broche, o	133
Rumanian	: broşa, f.	133
Slovak	: brošňa, f.	133
Spanish	: prendedor, m.	133
Swedish	: brosch-en	133
Turkish	: broş	133
Russian	: брошка, f.	133
Serbian	: брош	133
Ukrainian	: брошка, f.	133

134 BROOK s.

Czech	: potok, m.	134
Danish	: Bäk, m./c.	134
Dutch	: de beek	134
Finnish	: puro	134
French	: ruisseau, m.	134
German	: der Bach	134
Hungarian	: patak	134
Italian	: ruscello, m.	134
Croatian	: potok, m.	134
Norwegian	: bekk, m.	134
Polish	: strumyk, m.	134
Portuguese	: ribeiro, o	134
Rumanian	: pârâul	134
Slovak	: potok, m.	134
Spanish	: arroyo, m.	134
Swedish	: bäck-en	134
Turkish	: dere	134
Russian	: ручей, m.	134
Serbian	: поток, m.	134
Ukrainian	: ручай, m.	134

135 BROOM s.

Czech	: smeták, m.	135
Danish	: Fejekost, m./c.	135
Dutch	: de bezem	135
Finnish	: luuta	135
French	: balai, m.	135
German	: der Besen	135
Hungarian	: seprü	135
Italian	: scopa, f.	135
Croatian	: metla, f.	135
Norwegian	: kost, m.	135
Polish	: miotła, f.	135
Portuguese	: vassoura, a	135
Rumanian	: mătură, f.	135
Slovak	: metla, f.	135
Spanish	: escoba, f.	135
Swedish	: kvast-en	135
Turkish	: süpurga	135
Russian	: метла, f.	135
Serbian	: метла, f.	135
Ukrainian	: вiник, m.	135

136 BROWN adj.

Czech	: hnědý	136
Danish	: brun	136
Dutch	: bruin	136
Finnish	: ruskea	136
French	: brun	136
German	: braun	136
Hungarian	: barna	136
Italian	: marrone	136
Croatian	: smedj	136
Norwegian	: brun	136
Polish	: brunatny	136
Portuguese	: castanho	136
Rumanian	: brun	136
Slovak	: hnedý	136
Spanish	: pardo	136
Swedish	: brun	136
Turkish	: esmer	136
Russian	: коричневый	136
Serbian	: црноманьаст	136
Ukrainian	: бурий; брунатний	136

137 BRUSH s. (for painting)

Czech	: štětec, m.	137
Danish	: Pensel, m./c.	137
Dutch	: de kwast	137
Finnish	: pensseli	137
French	: pinceau, m.	137
German	: der Pinsel	137
Hungarian	: ecset	137
Italian	: pennello, m.	137
Croatian	: kičica, f.	137
Norwegian	: pensel, m.	137
Polish	: pędzel, m.	137
Portuguese	: pincel, o	137
Rumanian	: pensulă, f.	137
Slovak	: štetec, m.	137
Spanish	: brocha, f.	137
Swedish	: pensel-n	137
Turkish	: fırça	137
Russian	: кисть, f.	137
Serbian	: кичица, f.	137
Ukrainian	: кистка, f.	137

138 BRUSH v.

Czech	:	kartáčovati 138
Danish	:	börste 138
Dutch	:	borstelen 138
Finnish	:	harjata 138
French	:	brosser 138
German	:	bürsten 138
Hungarian	:	kefélni 138
Italian	:	spazzolare 138
Croatian	:	četkati 138
Norwegian	:	börste 138
Polish	:	czyścić szczotką 138
Portuguese	:	escovar 138
Rumanian	:	a peria 138
Slovak	:	kefovat' 138
Spanish	:	cepillar 138
Swedish	:	borsta 138
Turkish	:	firçalamak 138
Russian	:	чистить щеткой 138
Serbian	:	четкати 138
Ukrainian	:	чистити 138

139 BUG s. (bedbug)

Czech	:	štěnice, f. 139
Danish	:	Väggetöj, c. 139
Dutch	:	de wandluis 139
Finnish	:	lude 139
French	:	punaise, f. 139
German	:	die Wanze 139
Hungarian	:	poloska 139
Italian	:	cimice, f. 139
Croatian	:	stjenica, f. 139
Norwegian	:	veggelus, f. 139
Polish	:	pluskwa, f. 139
Portuguese	:	percevejo, o 139
Rumanian	:	pioşniţa 139
Slovak	:	ploštica, f. 139
Spanish	:	chinche, f. 139
Swedish	:	vägglus-en 139
Turkish	:	tahta kurusu 139
Russian	:	клоп, m. 139
Serbian	:	стеница, f. 139
Ukrainian	:	блощиця, f. 139

140 BULB see 308 electric-light bulb

141 BUNCH (of flowers) s.

Czech	:	kytice, f. 141
Danish	:	Buket, m./c. 141
Dutch	:	de bouquet 141
Finnish	:	kukkavihko 141
French	:	bouquet, m. 141
German	:	der Blumenstrauss 141
Hungarian	:	virágcsokor 141
Italian	:	mazzo di fiori, m. 141
Croatian	:	kita svijeća, f. 141
Norwegian	:	blomster-bukett, m. 141
Polish	:	bukiet, m. 141
Portuguese	:	ramo de flores, o 141
Rumanian	:	buchetul de flori 141
Slovak	:	kytica, f. 141
Spanish	:	ramo de flores, m. 141
Swedish	:	blombukett-en 141
Turkish	:	çiçek demeti 141
Russian	:	букет цветов, m. 141
Serbian	:	кита цвећа f. 141
Ukrainian	:	китиця, f. 141

142 BUS see 611 (MOTOR) BUS

143 BUSINESS s.

Czech	:	obchod; obchodní záležitost 143
Danish	:	forretning, c. 143
Dutch	:	bedrij, f. 143
Finnish	:	asia, (liike) asia 143
French	:	commerce, m. 143
German	:	das Geschäft 143
Hungarian	:	ügy; üzlet 143
Italian	:	negozio, m. 143
Croatian	:	posao; trgovina, f. 143
Norwegian	:	forretning, c. 143
Polish	:	handel, m. 143
Portuguese	:	negócio, m. 143
Rumanian	:	afacere, f.; treabă, f. 143
Slovak	:	obchod, podnik, m. 143
Spanish	:	negocio; comercio, m. 143
Swedish	:	ärende-n; handeln 143
Turkish	:	iş; dükkân 143
Russian	:	дело, n. 143
Serbian	:	посао; трговина 143
Ukrainian	:	справа; діловитість 143

144 BUTCHER s.

Czech	:	řezník, m. 144
Danish	:	Slagter, m. 144
Dutch	:	de slager 144
Finnish	:	teurastaja 144
French	:	boucher, m. 144
German	:	der Fleischer 144
Hungarian	:	hentes 144
Italian	:	macellaio m. 144
Croatian	:	mesar, m. 144
Norwegian	:	slakter, m. 144
Polish	:	rzeźnik, m. 144
Portuguese	:	carniceiro, m. 144
Rumanian	:	macelarul 144
Slovak	:	mäsiar, m. 144
Spanish	:	carnicero, m. 144
Swedish	:	slaktare-n 144
Turkish	:	kasap 144
Russian	:	мясник, m. 144
Serbian	:	месар, m. 144
Ukrainian	:	різник, m. 144

145 BUTTER s.

Czech	:	máslo, n. 145
Danish	:	Smör, n. 145
Dutch	:	de boter 145
Finnish	:	voi 145
French	:	beurre, m. 145
German	:	die Butter 145
Hungarian	:	vaj 145
Italian	:	burro, m. 145
Croatian	:	maslac, m. 145
Norwegian	:	smör, n. 145
Polish	:	masło, n. 145
Portuguese	:	manteiga, a 145
Rumanian	:	untul 145
Slovak	:	maslo, n. 145
Spanish	:	manteca, f. 145
Swedish	:	smör-et 145
Turkish	:	sadeyağ
Russian	:	масло, n. 145
Serbian	:	маслац, m. 145
Ukrainian	:	масло, n. 145

146 BUTTERFLY s.		
Czech	: motýl, m.	146
Danish	: Sommerfugl, m./c.	146
Dutch	: de vlinder	146
Finnish	: perhonen	146
French	: papillon, m.	146
German	: der Schmetterling	146
Hungarian	: pillangó	146
Italian	: farfalla, f.	146
Croatian	: leptir, m.	146
Norwegian	: sommerfugl, m.	146
Polish	: motyl, m.	146
Portuguese	: borboleta, a	146
Rumanian	: fluturele	146
Slovak	: motýľ', m.	146
Spanish	: mariposa, f.	146
Swedish	: fjäril-en	146
Turkish	: kelebek	146
Russian	: бабочка, f.	146
Serbian	: лептир, m.	146
Ukrainian	: метелик, m.	146

147 BUTTON s.		
Czech	: knoflík, m.	147
Danish	: Knap, m./c.	147
Dutch	: de knoop	147
Finnish	: nappi	147
French	: bouton, m.	147
German	: der Knopf	147
Hungarian	: gomb	147
Italian	: bottone, m.	147
Croatian	: dügme	147
Norwegian	: knapp, m.	147
Polish	: guzik, f.	147
Portuguese	: batão, o	147
Rumanian	: nasturele, m.	147
Slovak	: gombík, m.	147
Spanish	: botón, m.	147
Swedish	: knapp-en	147
Turkish	: dügme	147
Russian	: пуговица, f.	147
Serbian	: дугме, n.	147
Ukrainian	: гудзик, m.	147

148 BUY v.	
Czech	: koupiti	148
Danish	: köbe	148
Dutch	: koopen	148
Finnish	: ostaa	148
French	: acheter	148
German	: kaufen	148
Hungarian	: venni	148
Italian	: comprare	148
Croatian	: kupiti	148
Norwegian	: kjöpe	148
Polish	: kupować	148
Portuguese	: comprar	148
Rumanian	: a cumpăra	148
Slovak	: kupovat'	148
Spanish	: comprar	148
Swedish	: köpa	148
Turkish	: satin almak	148
Russian	: покупать	148
Serbian	: купити	148
Ukrainian	: купувати	148

149 CABARET s.		
Czech	: kabaret, m.	149
Danish	: Kabaret, m.	149
Dutch	: het cabaret	149
Finnish	: kapakka	149
French	: cabaret, m.	149
German	: das Kabarett	149
Hungarian	: kabaré	149
Italian	: cabaret, m.	149
Croatian	: kabaret, m.	149
Norwegian	: kabaret, m.	149
Polish	: kabaret, m.	149
Portuguese	: cabaret, o	149
Rumanian	: cabaretul	149
Slovak	: kabaret, m.	149
Spanish	: cabaret, m.	149
Swedish	: kabarett-en	149
Turkish	: kabaret	149
Russian	: кабарэ, с.	149
Serbian	: кабарет, m.	149
Ukrainian	: кабарет, m.	149

150 CABBAGE s.		
Czech	: zelí, n.	150
Danish	: Hvidkaal, m./c.	150
Dutch	: de witte kool	150
Finnish	: valkokaali	150
French	: chou blanc, m.	150
German	: der Weisskohl	150
Hungarian	: kelkáposzta	150
Italian	: cavolo bianco, m.	150
Croatian	: bijeli kupus, m.	150
Norwegian	: hvitkål, m.	150
Polish	: biała kapusta, f.	150
Portuguese	: couve branca, a	150
Rumanian	: varza albă	150
Slovak	: kapusta, f.	150
Spanish	: repollo, m.	150
Swedish	: vitkål-en	150
Turkish	: lahana	150
Russian	: капуста, f.	150
Serbian	: бели кулус, m.	150
Ukrainian	: біла капуста, f.	150

151 CABIN s.		
Czech	: kajuta, f.	151
Danish	: Kahyt, m.	151
Dutch	: de kajuit	151
Finnish	: kajuutta	151
French	: cabine, f.	151
German	: die Kajüte	151
Hungarian	: kajüt	151
Italian	: cabina, f.	151
Croatian	: kabina, f.	151
Norwegian	: kahytt, m.	151
Polish	: kajuta, f.	151
Portuguese	: camarote, o	151
Rumanian	: cabină, f.	151
Slovak	: kajuta, f.	151
Spanish	: camarote, m.	151
Swedish	: kajuta-n	151
Turkish	: kayuta	151
Russian	: каюта, f.	151
Serbian	: кајита, f.	151
Ukrainian	: каюта, f.	151

152 CAFÉ s.

Czech	:	kavárna, f. 152
Danish	:	Cafe, m./c. 152
Dutch	:	het café 152
Finnish	:	kahvila 152
French	:	café, m. 152
German	:	das Caféhaus 152
Hungarian	:	kávéház 152
Italian	:	caffè, m. 152
Croatian	:	kavana, f. 152
Norwegian	:	kafé, m. 152
Polish	:	kawiarnia, f. 152
Portuguese	:	café, o 152
Rumanian	:	cafeneă, f. 152
Slovak	:	kaviareň, f. 152
Spanish	:	café, m. 152
Swedish	:	café-t 152
Turkish	:	kahvehane 152
Russian	:	кафе, n. 152
Serbian	:	кафана, f. 152
Ukrainian	:	каварня, f. 152

153 CALL v.

Czech	:	volati; zavolati 153
Danish	:	kalde 153
Dutch	:	roep 153
Finnish	:	huutaa 153
French	:	appeler 153
German	:	rufen 153
Hungarian	:	kiált 153
Italian	:	chiamare 153
Croatian	:	zvati; pozivati 153
Norwegian	:	rope; kalle 153
Polish	:	wołać 153
Portuguese	:	chamar 153
Rumanian	:	a striga 153
Slovak	:	volat'; zavolat' 153
Spanish	:	llamar; gritar 153
Swedish	:	kalla 153
Turkish	:	çağirmak 153
Russian	:	кричать; позвать 153
Serbian	:	звати; позивати 153
Ukrainian	:	кликати; звати 153

154 CAKE s.

Czech	:	pečivo, n.; koláč, m. 154
Danish	:	Kage, m./c. 154
Dutch	:	de koek 154
Finnish	:	kakku 154
French	:	gâteau, m. 154
German	:	der Kuchen 154
Hungarian	:	tészta 154
Italian	:	torta, f. 154
Croatian	:	kolač, m. 154
Norwegian	:	kake, m. 154
Polish	:	ciastko, n. 154
Portuguese	:	bôlo, o 154
Rumanian	:	cozonacul 154
Slovak	:	koláč, m. 154
Spanish	:	pasteles, pl. 154
Swedish	:	kaka-n 154
Turkish	:	pasta 154
Russian	:	пирог, m. 154
Serbian	:	колач, m. 154
Ukrainian	:	тістечко, n.; торт, m. 154

155 CALF s. (the young of the cow, etc)

Czech	:	tele, n. 155
Danish	:	Kalv, m./c. 155
Dutch	:	het kalf 155
Finnish	:	vasikka 155
French	:	veau, m. 155
German	:	das Kalb 155
Hungarian	:	borjú 155
Italian	:	vitello, m. 155
Croatian	:	tele, n. 155
Norwegian	:	kalv, m. 155
Polish	:	cielę, n. 155
Portuguese	:	vitela, a 155
Rumanian	:	vițelul 155
Slovak	:	tel'a, n. 155
Spanish	:	ternero, m. 155
Swedish	:	kalv-en 155
Turkish	:	buzaği 155
Russian	:	теленок, m. 155
Serbian	:	теле, n. 155
Ukrainian	:	теля, n. 155

156 CALF s. (the part of the human leg)

Czech	:	lýtko, n. 156
Danish	:	Läg 156
Dutch	:	de kuit 156
Finnish	:	pohje 156
French	:	mollet, m. 156
German	:	die Wade 156
Hungarian	:	lábikra 156
Italian	:	polpaccio, m. 156
Croatian	:	list, m. 156
Norwegian	:	legg, m. 156
Polish	:	łydka, f. 156
Portuguese	:	barriga da perna, a 156
Rumanian	:	pulpa, f. 156
Slovak	:	lýtko, n. 156
Spanish	:	pantorrilla, f. 156
Swedish	:	vad-en 156
Turkish	:	baldır 156
Russian	:	икра, f. 156
Serbian	:	лист, m 156
Ukrainian	:	литка, f. 156

157 CAMEL s.

Czech	:	velbloud, m. 157
Danish	:	Kamel, m. 157
Dutch	:	het kameel 157
Finnish	:	kameli 157
French	:	chameau, m. 157
German	:	das Kamel 157
Hungarian	:	teve 157
Italian	:	cammello, m. 157
Croatian	:	deva, f. 157
Norwegian	:	kamel 157
Polish	:	wielbłąd, m. 157
Portuguese	:	camelo, o 157
Rumanian	:	cămila, f. 157
Slovak	:	t'ava, f. 157
Spanish	:	camello, m. 157
Swedish	:	kamel-en 157
Turkish	:	deve 157
Russian	:	верблюд, m. 157
Serbian	:	дева, f. 157
Ukrainian	:	верблюд, m. 157

158 CAMERA s.

Czech	:	fotografický aparát, m. 158
Danish	:	Fotografiapparat, c. 158
Dutch	:	het fototoestel 158
Finnish	:	valokuvauskone 158
French	:	appareil photographique, m. 158
German	:	der Photoapparat 158
Hungarian	:	fényképezögép 158
Italian	:	apparecchio, m. 158
Croatian	:	fotografski aparat, m. 158
Norwegian	:	fotografiapparat, m. 158
Polish	:	aparat fotograficzny, m. 158
Portuguese	:	aparelho fotográfico, o 158
Rumanian	:	aparatul de fotografiat 158
Slovak	:	fotografický aparat, m. 158
Spanish	:	cámara, f. 158
Swedish	:	kamara-n 158
Turkish	:	fotograf aleji 158
Russian	:	фотоапарат, m. 158
Serbian	:	фотографски апарат, m. 158
Ukrainian	:	фотографічний апарат, m. 158

159 CAMP s.

Czech	:	tábor, m. 159
Danish	:	lejr, c. 159
Dutch	:	kamp 159
Finnish	:	varasto 159
French	:	camp, m. 159
German	:	der Lager 159
Hungarian	:	tanya 159
Italian	:	campo, m. 159
Croatian	:	logor; tabor, m. 159
Norwegian	:	leie; leir, c. 159
Polish	:	obóz, m. 159
Portuguese	:	campo, m. 159
Rumanian	:	pat, c. 159
Slovak	:	láper, m.; tábor, m. 159
Spanish	:	campo, m. 159
Swedish	:	läger-n 159
Turkish	:	yatak 159
Russian	:	лагерь, m. 159
Serbian	:	лагор, m. 159
Ukrainian	:	табір. m. 159

160 CAMPING OUT see 159 CAMP

161 CANDLE s.

Czech	:	svíce, f. 161
Danish	:	Vokslys, n. 161
Dutch	:	de kaars 161
Finnish	:	kynttilä 161
French	:	bougie, f. 161
German	:	die Kerze 161
Hungarian	:	gyertya 161
Italian	:	candela, f. 161
Croatian	:	sveća, f. 161
Norwegian	:	vokslys, n. 161
Polish	:	świeca, f. 161
Portuguese	:	vela, a 161
Rumanian	:	lumânarea, f: 161
Slovak	:	svieca, f. 161
Spanish	:	vela, f. 161
Swedish	:	ljus-et 161
Turkish	:	mum 161
Russian	:	свеча, f. 161
Serbian	:	свећа, f. 161
Ukrainian	:	свічка, f. 161

162 CANNON s. (gun)

Czech	:	dělo, n. 162
Danish	:	Skyts, n. 162
Dutch	:	het geschut 162
Finnish	:	tykki 162
French	:	canon, m. 162
German	:	das Geschütz 162
Hungarian	:	löveg 162
Italian	:	cannone, m. 162
Croatian	:	top, m. 162
Norwegian	:	skyts, m. 162
Polish	:	działo, n. 162
Portuguese	:	peça de artilharia, a 162
Rumanian	:	tunul 162
Slovak	:	delo, n. 162
Spanish	:	cañón, m. 162
Swedish	:	artilleripjäs-en 162
Turkish	:	top 162
Russian	:	пушка, f. 162
Serbian	:	топ, m. 162
Ukrainian	:	гармата, f. 162

163 CANTEEN s.

Czech	:	kantina, f. 163
Danish	:	Marketenderi, c. 163
Dutch	:	de cantine 163
Finnish	:	kantiini 163
French	:	cantine, f. 163
German	:	die Kantine 163
Hungarian	:	kantin 163
Italian	:	cantina, f. 163
Croatian	:	kantina, f. 163
Norwegian	:	kantine, m. 163
Polish	:	kantyna, f. 163
Portuguese	:	cantin, f. 163
Rumanian	:	cantină, f. 163
Slovak	:	kantína, f. 163
Spanish	:	cantina, f. 163
Swedish	:	matsal-en 163
Turkish	:	kantin 163
Russian	:	кантина. f. 163
Serbian	:	кантина, f. 163
Ukrainian	:	кантина, f. 163

164 CAP s.

Czech	:	čepice, f. 164
Danish	:	Hue, m./c. 164
Dutch	:	de pet 164
Finnish	:	lakki 164
French	:	casquette, f. 164
German	:	die Mütze 164
Hungarian	:	sapka 164
Italian	:	berretto, m. 164
Croatian	:	kapa, f. 164
Norwegian	:	lue, f. 164
Polish	:	czapka, f. 164
Portuguese	:	boné, o 164
Rumanian	:	sapca, f. 164
Slovak	:	čiapka, f. 164
Spanish	:	gorra, f. 164
Swedish	:	mössa-n 164
Turkish	:	kasket 164
Russian	:	шапка, f. 164
Serbian	:	капа, f. 164
Ukrainian	:	шапка, f. 164

165 CAPE s. (a garment)

Czech	: plášténka, f. 165
Danish	: Slag, n. 165
Dutch	: de cape 165
Finnish	: viitta 165
French	: cape, f. 165
German	: der Umhang 165
Hungarian	: köpeny 165
Italian	: mantellina, f. 165
Croatian	: ogrtač, m. 165
Norwegian	: kappe, c. 165
Polish	: zarzutka, f. 165
Portuguese	: chale-manta, o 165
Rumanian	: pelerină, f. 165
Slovak	: pelerína, f. 165
Spanish	: capa, f. 165
Swedish	: cape-n 165
Turkish	: kadın pelerini 165
Russian	: накидка, f. 165
Serbian	: обесак, m. 165
Ukrainian	: накидка; пелзрина, f. 165

166 CAPTAIN s.

Czech	: kapitán, m. 166
Danish	: Kaptajn, m./c. 166
Dutch	: de kapitein 166
Finnish	: kapteeni 166
French	: capitaine, m. 166
German	: der Kapitän 166
Hungarian	: kapitány 166
Italian	: capitano, m. 166
Croatian	: kapetan, m. 166
Norwegian	: kaptein, m. 166
Polish	: kapitan, m. 166
Portuguese	: comandante, o 166
Rumanian	: capitanul 166
Slovak	: kapitán m. 166
Spanish	: capitán, m. 166
Swedish	: kapten-en 166
Turkish	: kaptan 166
Russian	: капитан, m. 166
Serbian	: калетан, m. 166
Ukrainian	: капітан, m. 166

167 CAPTURE v. see **178 CATCH**

168 CAR s. see **612 (MOTOR) CAR**

169 CARAWAY s. (seeds)

Czech	: kmín, m. 169
Danish	: Kommen, m./c. 169
Dutch	: de kummel 169
Finnish	: kumina 169
French	: kummel, m. 169
German	: der Kümmel 169
Hungarian	: kömény 169
Italian	: comino, m. 169
Croatian	: kim, m. 169
Norwegian	: karve, m. 169
Polish	: kminek, m. 169
Portuguese	: cominho, o 169
Rumanian	: cuişoara, f. 169
Slovak	: rasca, f. 169
Spanish	: comino, m. 169
Swedish	: kummin-en 169
Turkish	: kimiyun 169
Russian	: тмин, m. 169
Serbian	: ким, m. 169
Ukrainian	: кмин, m. 169

170 CARNATION s.

Czech	: karafiát, m. 170
Danish	: Nellike, m./c. 170
Dutch	: de anjelier 170
Finnish	: neilikka 170
French	: oeillet, m. 170
German	: die Nelke 170
Hungarian	: szegfü 170
Italian	: garofano, m. 170
Croatian	: karanfil, m. 170
Norwegian	: nellik, m. 170
Polish	: gwoździk, m. 170
Portuguese	: cravo, o 170
Rumanian	: garoafă, f. 170
Slovak	: klinček, m. 170
Spanish	: clavel, m. 170
Swedish	: nejlika-n 170
Turkish	: karenfil 170
Russian	: гвоздика, f. 170
Serbian	: каранфил, m. 170
Ukrainian	: гвоздик, m. 170

171 CARPENTER s.

Czech	: truhlář, m. 171
Danish	: Snedker, m. 171
Dutch	: de timmerman 171
Finnish	: puuseppä 171
French	: menuisier, m. 171
German	: der Schreiner 171
Hungarian	: asztalos 171
Italian	: falegname, m. 171
Croatian	: stolar, m. 171
Norwegian	: snekker, m. 171
Polish	: stolarz, m. 171
Portuguese	: marceneiro, o 171
Rumanian	: tămplarul 171
Slovak	: truhlár, m. 171
Spanish	: ebanista, m. 171
Swedish	: snickare-n 171
Turkish	: mavangoz 171
Russian	: столяр, m. 171
Serbian	: столар, m. 171
Ukrainian	: столяр, m. 171

172 CARPET s.

Czech	: koberec, m. 172
Danish	: Gulvtäppe, c. 172
Dutch	: het tapijt 172
Finnish	: matto 172
French	: tapis, m. 172
German	: der Teppich 172
Hungarian	: szönyeg 172
Italian	: tappeto, m. 172
Croatian	: ćilim, m. 172
Norwegian	: gulvteppe, n. 172
Polish	: kobierzec, m. 172
Portuguese	: tapête, o 172
Rumanian	: covorul 172
Slovak	: koberec, m. 172
Spanish	: alfombra, f. 172
Swedish	: matta-n 172
Turkish	: halı 172
Russian	: ковер, m. 172
Serbian	: ћилим, m. 172
Ukrainian	: килим, m. 172

173 CARROTS s. pl.

Czech	:	mrkev, *f.* 173
Danish	:	Gulerödder, *pl.* 173
Dutch	:	het peentje 173
Finnish	:	porkkanoita 173
French	:	carottes, *pl. f.* 173
German	:	die Möhre 173
Hungarian	:	sárgarépa 173
Italian	:	carote, *f. pl.* 173
Croatian	:	mrkva, *f.* 173
Norwegian	:	gulerot, *f.* 173
Polish	:	marchew, *f.* 173
Portuguese	:	cenoura, *a* 173
Rumanian	:	morcovul 173
Slovak	:	mrkva, *f.* 173
Spanish	:	zanahorias, *pl.* 173
Swedish	:	morötter-na, *pl.* 173
Turkish	:	havuç 173
Russian	:	морковь, *f.* 173
Serbian	:	мркве, *pl.* 173
Ukrainian	:	морква, *f.* 173

174 CART s.

Czech	:	vůz, *m.* 174
Danish	:	Traekvogn, *c.* 174
Dutch	:	de kar 174
Finnish	:	kärryt 174
French	:	brouette, *f.* 174
German	:	die Karre 174
Hungarian	:	taliga 174
Italian	:	carriola, *f.* 174
Croatian	:	kola, *pl.* 174
Norwegian	:	kjerre, *f.* 174
Polish	:	taczki, *pl.* 174
Portuguese	:	carro, *o* 174
Rumanian	:	roaba 174
Slovak	:	vozík, *m.* 174
Spanish	:	carreta, *f.* 174
Swedish	:	skottkärra-n 174
Turkish	:	el arabasi 174
Russian	:	тачка, *f.* 174
Serbian	:	кола, *f.* 174
Ukrainian	:	тачка, *f.* 174

175 CASE s. (a box)

Czech	:	bedna, *f.* 175
Danish	:	Kasse, *f./c.* 175
Dutch	:	de kist 175
Finnish	:	kirstu 175
French	:	boîte, *f.* 175
German	:	die Kiste 175
Hungarian	:	láda 175
Italian	:	cassetta, *f.* 175
Croatian	:	sanduk, *m.* 175
Norwegian	:	kiste, *f.*; kasse, *f.* 175
Polish	:	skrzynia, *f.* 175
Portuguese	:	caixa, *a* 175
Rumanian	:	ladă, *f.* 175
Slovak	:	debna, *f.* 175
Spanish	:	rastro, *m.* 175
Swedish	:	lår-en 175
Turkish	:	sandık 175
Russian	:	ящик, *m.* 175
Serbian	:	сандук, *m.* 175
Ukrainian	:	скриня, *f.* 175

176 CASTLE s.

Czech	:	zámek, *m.* 176
Danish	:	Slot, *n.* 176
Dutch	:	het slot 176
Finnish	:	linna 176
French	:	château, *m.* 176
German	:	das Schloss 176
Hungarian	:	kastély 176
Italian	:	castello, *m.* 176
Croatian	:	dvor, *m.* 176
Norwegian	:	slott, *n.* 176
Polish	:	zamek, *m.* 176
Portuguese	:	palácio, *o* 176
Rumanian	:	palatul 176
Slovak	:	zámok, *m.* 176
Spanish	:	castillo, *m.* 176
Swedish	:	slott-et 176
Turkish	:	saray 176
Russian	:	замок, *m.* 176
Serbian	:	двор, *m.* 176
Ukrainian	:	замок, *m.* 176

177 CAT s.

Czech	:	kočka, *f.* 177
Danish	:	Kat, *f./c.* 177
Dutch	:	de kat 177
Finnish	:	kissa 177
French	:	chat, *m.* 177
German	:	die Katze 177
Hungarian	:	macska 177
Italian	:	gatto, *m.* 177
Croatian	:	mačka, *f.* 177
Norwegian	:	katt, *f.* 177
Polish	:	kot, *m.* 177
Portuguese	:	gato, *o* 177
Rumanian	:	pisică, *f.* 177
Slovak	:	mačka, *f.* 177
Spanish	:	gato, *m.* 177
Swedish	:	katt-en 177
Turkish	:	kedi 177
Russian	:	кошка, *f.* 177
Serbian	:	мачка, *f.* 177
Ukrainian	:	кітка; кішка, *f.* 177

178 CATCH v.

Czech	:	chytati; chytnouti 178
Danish	:	fange 178
Dutch	:	vangen 178
Finnish	:	ottaa 178
French	:	attraper 178
German	:	fangen 178
Hungarian	:	fogni 178
Italian	:	acchiappare 178
Croatian	:	hvatati 178
Norwegian	:	fange 178
Polish	:	łapać 178
Portuguese	:	capturar 178
Rumanian	:	a prinde 178
Slovak	:	chytat' 178
Spanish	:	coger 178
Swedish	:	fånga 178
Turkish	:	yakalamak 178
Russian	:	ловить 178
Serbian	:	хватати 178
Ukrainian	:	ловити 178

179 CATHEDRAL s.

Czech	:	chrám, m. 179
Danish	:	Domkirke, m. 179
Dutch	:	de dom 179
Finnish	:	tuomiokirkko 179
French	:	cathédrale, f. 179
German	:	der Dom 179
Hungarian	:	székesegyház 179
Italian	:	duomo, m. 179
Croatian	:	stolna crkva, f. 179
Norwegian	:	domkirke, m. 179
Polish	:	katedra, f. 179
Portuguese	:	catedral, a 179
Rumanian	:	catedrală, f. 179
Slovak	:	dom, m. 179
Spanish	:	catedral, f. 179
Swedish	:	domkyrka-n 179
Turkish	:	büyük kelisa 179
Russian	:	собор m. 179
Serbian	:	саборна црква, f. 179
Ukrainian	:	собор, m. 179

180 CATTLE s. (Brit. animals)

Czech	:	dobytek, m. 180
Danish	:	Kväg, c.; Okse, m. 180
Dutch	:	het rund 180
Finnish	:	nauta 180
French	:	boeuf, m. 180
German	:	das Rind 180
Hungarian	:	marha 180
Italian	:	manzo, m. 180
Croatian	:	govedo, n. 180
Norwegian	:	storfe, n.; buskap, m. 180
Polish	:	bydło, pl. 180
Portuguese	:	gado bovino, o 180
Rumanian	:	vita 180
Slovak	:	rožný dobytok m. 180
Spanish	:	res 180
Swedish	:	nötkreatur-et 180
Turkish	:	sığir 180
Russian	:	скотина, f. 180
Serbian	:	говедо, n. 180
Ukrainian	:	худоба; скот 180

181 CAULIFLOWER s.

Czech	:	květák, m. 181
Danish	:	Blomkaal, c. 181
Dutch	:	de bloemkool 181
Finnish	:	kukkakaali 181
French	:	choufleur, m. 181
German	:	der Blumenkohl 181
Hungarian	:	karfiol 181
Italian	:	cavolo fiore, m. 181
Croatian	:	karfiol, m. 181
Norwegian	:	blomkål, m. 181
Polish	:	kalafjor, m. 181
Portuguese	:	couve-flor, a 181
Rumanian	:	varza creață 181
Slovak	:	karfiol, m. 181
Spanish	:	coliflor, m. 181
Swedish	:	blomkål-en 181
Turkish	:	karnabit 181
Russian	:	цветная капуста, f. 181
Serbian	:	карфиол, m. 181
Ukrainian	:	кучерява капуста, f. 181

182 CELLAR s. see 64 BASEMENT

183 CEILING-LAMP s.

Czech	:	lustr, m. 183
Danish	:	Lampe, c. 183
Dutch	:	de plafondlamp 183
Finnish	:	lapiolamppu 183
French	:	lampe plafond, m. 183
German	:	die Deckenlampe 183
Hungarian	:	menyezetlámpa 183
Italian	:	lampada per il soffitto, f. 183
Croatian	:	svjetilka na tavanici, f. 183
Norwegian	:	taklampe, f. 183
Polish	:	lampa z umbra, f. 183
Portuguese	:	lustre, o 183
Rumanian	:	lampă, f. 183
Slovak	:	luster, m. 183
Spanish	:	lámpara de techo 183
Swedish	:	taklampa-n 183
Turkish	:	tavan lambasi 183
Russian	:	висячая лампа, f. 183
Serbian	:	лампа на таваници, f. 183
Ukrainian	:	звисаюча лямпа, f. 183

184 CHAIR s.

Czech	:	židle, f. 184
Danish	:	Stol, m./c. 184
Dutch	:	de stoel 184
Finnish	:	tuoli 184
French	:	chaise, f. 184
German	:	der Stuhl 184
Hungarian	:	szék 184
Italian	:	sedia, f. 184
Croatian	:	stolica, f. 184
Norwegian	:	stol, m. 184
Polish	:	krzeslo, n. 184
Portuguese	:	cadeira, a 184
Rumanian	:	scaunul 184
Slovak	:	stolička, f. 184
Spanish	:	silla, f. 184
Swedish	:	stol-en 184
Turkish	:	sandaliye 184
Russian	:	стул, m. 184
Serbian	:	столица, f. 184
Ukrainian	:	крісло, n. 184

185 CHAMBER-MAID s.

Czech	:	pokojská, f. 185
Danish	:	Stuepige, f. 185
Dutch	:	het kamermeisje 185
Finnish	:	siivooja 185
French	:	femme de chambre, f. 185
German	:	das Zimmermädchen 185
Hungarian	:	szobalány 185
Italian	:	cameriera, f. 185
Croatian	:	sobarica, f. 185
Norwegian	:	varelsepike, f. 185
Polish	:	pokojówka, f. 185
Portuguese	:	criada de quarto, a 185
Rumanian	:	fata in casă 185
Slovak	:	chyžná, f. 185
Spanish	:	camarera, f. 185
Swedish	:	jungiru-n 185
Turkish	:	oda kizi 185
Russian	:	горничная, f. 185
Serbian	:	слушкиньа, f. 185
Ukrainian	:	покоївка; служниця, f. 185

28

---

186 CHAMOIS s.
(a goatlike antelope of Europe)

Czech	: kamzík, *m.*	186
Danish	: Gemze, *m./c.*	186
Dutch	: de gems 186	
Finnish	: vuorikauris 186	
French	: cha͘mois, *m.*	186
German	: die Gemse 186	
Hungarian	: zerge 186	
Italian	: camoscio, *m.*	186
Croatian	: divokoza, *f.*	186
Norwegian	: gemse, *m.*	186
Polish	: kozica, *f.*	186
Portuguese	: cabra montesa, *a*	186
Rumanian	: ciută, *f.*	186
Slovak	: kamzík, *m.*	186
Spanish	: gamuza, *f.*	186
Swedish	: stenget-en 186	
Turkish	: yaban geçisi 186	
Russian	: серна, *f.*	186
Serbian	: дивокоза, *f.*	186
Ukrainian	: гірська коза, *f*	186

187 CHAMPAGNE s.

Czech	: šampaňské(víno), *n.*	187
Danish	: Champagne, *c.*	187
Dutch	: de champagne	187
Finnish	: samppanja 187	
French	: vin mousseux, *m.*	187
German	: der Sekt 187	
Hungarian	: pezsgö 187	
Italian	: spumante, *m.*	187
Croatian	: pjenušac, *m.*	187
Norwegian	: sekt, *m.*	187
Polish	: szampan, *m.*	187
Portuguese	: champanhe, *o*	187
Rumanian	: şampanie, *f.*	187
Slovak	: šampaňské, *n.*	187
Spanish	: champán, *m.*	187
Swedish	: champagne-n 187	
Turkish	: şampanya şarabi 187	
Russian	: шампанское, *n.*	187
Serbian	: сект, *m.*	187
Ukrainian	: шампан, *m.*	187

188 CHEAP adj.

Czech	: levný 188	
Danish	: billigt 188	
Dutch	: goedkoop 188	
Finnish	: halpa 188	
French	: bon marché 188	
German	: billig 188	
Hungarian	: olcsó(n) 188	
Italian	: a buon mercato	188
Croatian	: jeftin 188	
Norwegian	: billig 188	
Polish	: tanie 188	
Portuguese	: barato 188	
Rumanian	: eftin 188	
Slovak	: lacný 188	
Spanish	: barato 188	
Swedish	: billig 188	
Turkish	: hakşinas 188	
Russian	: дешевый 188	
Serbian	: јефтин 188	
Ukrainian	: дешевий 188	

189 CHEEK s.

Czech	: líce, *n.*; tvář, *f.*	189
Danish	: Kind, *n.*	189
Dutch	: de wang 189	
Finnish	: poski 189	
French	: joue, *f.*	189
German	: die Wange 189	
Hungarian	: arc 189	
Italian	: guancia, *f.*	189
Croatian	: obraz, *m.*	189
Norwegian	: kinn, *n.*	189
Polish	: lica, twarz, *f.*	189
Portuguese	: bochecha, *a*	189
Rumanian	: obrazul 189	
Slovak	: líce, *n.*	189
Spanish	: mejilla, *f.*	189
Swedish	: kind-en 189	
Turkish	: yanak 189	
Russian	: щека, *f.*	189
Serbian	: образ, *m.*	189
Ukrainian	: щока, *f.*	189

190 CHEESE s.

Czech	: sýr, *m.*	190
Danish	: Ost, *m./c.*	190
Dutch	: de kaas 190	
Finnish	: juusto 190	
French	: fromage, *m.*	190
German	: der Käse 190	
Hungarian	: sajt 190	
Italian	: formaggio, *m.*	190
Croatian	: sir, *m.*	190
Norwegian	: ost, *m.*	190
Polish	: ser, *m.*	190
Portuguese	: queijo, *o*	190
Rumanian	: brînză, *f.*	190
Slovak	: syr, *m.*	190
Spanish	: queso, *m.*	190
Swedish	: ost-en 190	
Turkish	: peynir 190	
Russian	: сыр, *m.*	190
Serbian	: сир, *m.*	190
Ukrainian	: сир, *m.*	190

191 CHEMISE s.

Czech	: dámská košilka, *f.*	191
Danish	: Understróje, *f./c.*	191
Dutch	: het dameshemd	191
Finnish	: naistenpaita 191	
French	: chemise, *f.*	191
German	: das Damenhemd	191
Hungarian	: nöi ing 191	
Italian	: camicia per signora, *f.*	191
Croatian	: ženska košulja, *f.*	191
Norwegian	: dametröie, *f.*	191
Polish	: koszula damska, *f.*	191
Portuguese	: camisa para senhoras, *a*	191
Rumanian	: camaşa de doamnă, *f.*	191
Slovak	: dámska košel'a, *f.*	191
Spanish	: camisa de día para mujeres	191
Swedish	: linne-t 191	
Turkish	: kadin gömleği 191	
Russian	: женская сорочка, *f.*	191
Serbian	: женска кошуља, *f.*	191
Ukrainian	: жіноча сорочка, *f.*	191

192 CHERRY *s.*

Czech : třešně, *f.* 192
Danish : Kirsebär, *pl.* 192
Dutch : de kers 192
Finnish : kirsikat 192
French : cerise, *f.* 192
German : die Kirsche 192
Hungarian : cseresznye 192
Italian : ciliege, *f.* 192
Croatian : trešnja, *f.* 192
Norwegian : kirsebär, *n.* 192
Polish : czereśnia, *f.* 192
Portuguese : cereja, *a* 192
Rumanian : cireaşa, *f.* 192
Slovak : čerešňa, *f.* 192
Spanish : cerezas, *pl.* 192
Swedish : körsbär-en 192
Turkish : keras 192
Russian : вишни; черешни, *pl.* 192
Serbian : трешньа, *f.* 192
Ukrainian : черешні, *pl.* 192

193 CHESS *s.* (a game)

Czech : šachy, *pl.* 193
Danish : Skak, *m./c.* 193
Dutch : het schakspel 193
Finnish : shakki 193
French : échecs, *m. pl.* 193
German : das Schach 193
Hungarian : sakk 193
Italian : scacchi, *m. pl.* 193
Croatian : šah, *m.* 193
Norwegian : sjakk, *m.* 193
Polish : szachy, *pl.* 193
Portuguese : xadrez, *o* 193
Rumanian : şahul 193
Slovak : šach, *m.* 193
Spanish : ajedrez, *m.* 193
Swedish : schack-et 193
Turkish : şatrenc 193
Russian : шахматы, *pl.* 193
Serbian : шах, *m.* 193
Ukrainian : шахи, *pl.* 193

194 CHEST *s.* (a part of the human body)

Czech : hrud', *f.*; prsa, *pl.* 194
Danish : Bryst, *n.* 194
Dutch : de borst 194
Finnish : rinta 194
French : poitrine, *f.* 194
German : die Brust 194
Hungarian : mell 194
Italian : petto, *m.* 194
Croatian : prsa, *pl.* 194
Norwegian : bryst, *n.* 194
Polish : piersi, *pl.* 194
Portuguese : peito, *o* 194
Rumanian : pieptul 194
Slovak : prsia, *pl.* 194
Spanish : pecho, *m.* 194
Swedish : bröst-et 194
Turkish : göğus 194
Russian : грудь, *f.* 194
Serbian : прса, *f.* 194
Ukrainian : груди, *pl.* 194

195 CHEST *s.* (a trunk) see 175 CASE, BOX

196 CHEST OF DRAWERS *s.*

Czech : prádelník, *m.* 196
Danish : Kommode, *m./c.* 196
Dutch : de commode 196
Finnish : vaatekaappi 196
French : commode, *f.* 196
German : die Kommode 196
Hungarian : a fiókos szekrény 196
Italian : cassettone, *m.* 196
Croatian : ormar, *m.* 196
Norwegian : kommode, *m.* 196
Polish : komoda, *f.* 196
Portuguese : cómoda, *a* 196
Rumanian : scrinul 196
Slovak : bielizník, *m.* 196
Spanish : la cómoda 196
Swedish : byrå-n 196
Turkish : çamasir ve elbise dolabi 196
Russian : комод, *m.* 196
Serbian : комода, *f.* 196
Ukrainian : комода, *f.* 196

197 CHICKEN *s.*

Czech : kuře, *n.* 197
Danish : Höne, *n.* 197
Dutch : de kip 197
Finnish : kana 197
French : poule 197
German : das Huhn 197
Hungarian : tyúk 197
Italian : pollo, *m.* 197
Croatian : kokoš, *f.* 197
Norwegian : hone, *f.* 197
Polish : kura, *f.* 197
Portuguese : galinha, *a* 197
Rumanian : gäina, *f.* 197
Slovak : sliepka, *f.*; kura, *f.* 197
Spanish : gallina 197
Swedish : höna-n 197
Turkish : tavuk 197
Russian : курица, *f.* 197
Serbian : кокош, *f.* 197
Ukrainian : курка, *f.* 197

198 CHIN *s.*

Czech : brada, *f.* 198
Danish : Hage, *f./c.* 198
Dutch : de kin 198
Finnish : leuka 198
French : menton, *m.* 198
German : das Kinn 198
Hungarian : áll 198
Italian : mente, *m.* 198
Croatian : brada, *f.* 198
Norwegian : hake, *f.* 198
Polish : broda, *f.* 198
Portuguese : queixo, *o* 198
Rumanian : bärbia 198
Slovak : brada, *f.* 198
Spanish : barba *f.* 198
Swedish : haka-n 198
Turkish : çene 198
Russian : подбородок, *m.* 198
Serbian : брада, *f,* 198
Ukrainian : борода, *f.* 198

199 CHISEL s.

Czech	:	dláto, *n.* 199
Danish	:	Mejsel, *m./c.* 199
Dutch	:	de beitel 199
Finnish	:	meisseli 199
French	:	ciseau, *m.* 199
German	:	der Meissel 199
Hungarian	:	vésö 199
Italian	:	scalpello, *m.* 199
Croatian	:	dlijeto, *n.* 199
Norwegian	:	meisel, *m.* 199
Polish	:	dłóto, *n.* 199
Portuguese	:	cinzel, *o* 199
Rumanian	:	daltă, *f.* 199
Slovak	:	dláto, *n.* 199
Spanish	:	cincel, *m.* 199
Swedish	:	mejsel-n 199
Turkish	:	minkaş 199
Russian	:	зубило, *n.* 199
Serbian	:	длето, *n.* 199
Ukrainian	:	долото, *n.* 199

200 CHIVE s.

Czech	:	pažitka, *f.* 200
Danish	:	Purlög, *c.* 200
Dutch	:	de bieslook 200
Finnish	:	sipuli 200
French	:	la ciboulette 200
German	:	der Schnittlauch 200
Hungarian	:	metélöhagyma 200
Italian	:	foglie di cipolline, *f. pl.* 200
Croatian	:	luk vlasac, *m.* 200
Norwegian	:	graslök, *m.* 200
Polish	:	szczypiorek, *m.* 200
Portuguese	:	cebolinha, *a* 200
Rumanian	:	ceapa, *f.* 200
Slovak	:	pažítka, *f.* 200
Spanish	:	puerro, *f.* 200
Swedish	:	gräslök-en 200
Turkish	:	sarmusak yapraği 200
Russian	:	зелзный лук, *m.* 200
Serbian	:	лук власац, *m.* 200
Ukrainian	:	тримбулька, *f.* 200

201 CHOCOLATE s.

Czech	:	čokoláda, *f.* 201
Danish	:	Chokolade, *m./c.* 201
Dutch	:	de chocolade 201
Finnish	:	suklaa 201
French	:	chocolat, *m.* 201
German	:	die Schokolade 201
Hungarian	:	csokoládé 201
Italian	:	cioccolata, *f.* 201
Croatian	:	čokolada, *f.* 201
Norwegian	:	sjokolade, *m.* 201
Polish	:	czekolada, *f.* 201
Portuguese	:	chocolate, *o* 201
Rumanian	:	şocolată, *f.* 201
Slovak	:	čokoláda, *f.* 201
Spanish	:	chocolate, *m.* 201
Swedish	:	schoklad 201
Turkish	:	çikolata 201
Russian	:	шоколад, *m.* 201
Serbian	:	чоколада, *f.* 201
Ukrainian	:	чоколада, *f.* 201

202 CHURCH s.

Czech	:	kostel, *m.* 202
Danish	:	Kirke, *m./c.* 202
Dutch	:	de kerk 202
Finnish	:	kirkko 202
French	:	église, *f.* 202
German	:	die Kirche 202
Hungarian	:	templom 202
Italian	:	chiesa, *f.* 202
Croatian	:	crkva, *f.* 202
Norwegian	:	kirke, *f.* 202
Polish	:	kościol, *m.* 202
Portuguese	:	igreja, *a* 202
Rumanian	:	biserică, *f.* 202
Slovak	:	kostol, *m.* 202
Spanish	:	iglesia, *m.* 202
Swedish	:	kyrka-n 202
Turkish	:	kelisa 202
Russian	:	церковь, *f.* 202
Serbian	:	црква, *f.* 202
Ukrainian	:	церква, *f.* 202

203 CIGAR s.

Czech	:	doutník, *m.* 203
Danish	:	Cigar, *m./c.* 203
Dutch	:	de sigaar 203
Finnish	:	sikari 203
French	:	cigare, *m.* 203
German	:	die Zigarre 203
Hungarian	:	szivar 203
Italian	:	sigaro, *m.* 203
Croatian	:	cigara, *f.* 203
Norwegian	:	sigar, *m.* 203
Polish	:	cygaro, *n.* 203
Portuguese	:	charuto, *o* 203
Rumanian	:	tigară de foi 203
Slovak	:	cigara, *f.* 203
Spanish	:	cigarro, *m.* 203
Swedish	:	cigarr-en 203
Turkish	:	sigar 203
Russian	:	сигара, *f.* 203
Serbian	:	цигара, *f.* 203
Ukrainian	:	цигара, *f.* 203

204 CIGARETTE s.

Czech	:	cigareta, *f.* 204
Danish	:	Cigaret, *m./c.* 204
Dutch	:	de cigaret 204
Finnish	:	savuke 204
French	:	cigarette, *f.* 204
German	:	die Zigarette, *f.* 204
Hungarian	:	cigaretta 204
Italian	:	sigaretta, *f.* 204
Croatian	:	cigareta, *f.* 204
Norwegian	:	sigarett, *m.* 204
Polish	:	papieros, *m.* 204
Portuguese	:	cigarro, *o* 204
Rumanian	:	ţigară, *f.* 204
Slovak	:	cigareta, *f.* 204
Spanish	:	pitillo, *m.* 204
Swedish	:	cigarett-en 204
Turkish	:	sigara 204
Russian	:	папироса, *f.* 204
Serbian	:	цигарета, *f.* 204
Ukrainian	:	цигарка, *f.* 204

205 CITY s. see 1022 TOWN

206 CITY-HALL s. see 1023 TOWN-HALL

207 CLARINET s.

Czech	:	klarinet, *m.* 207
Danish	:	Klarinet, *m./c.* 207
Dutch	:	de clarinet 207
Finnish	:	klarinetti 207
French	:	clarinette, *f.* 207
German	:	die Klarinette 207
Hungarian	:	klarinét 207
Italian	:	clarinetto, *m.* 207
Croatian	:	klarinet, *m.* 207
Norwegian	:	klarinett, *m.* 207
Polish	:	klarnet, *m.* 207
Portuguese	:	clarinete, *o* 207
Rumanian	:	clarinetă, *f.* 207
Slovak	:	klarinet, *m.* 207
Spanish	:	clarinete, *m.* 207
Swedish	:	klarinett-en 207
Turkish	:	klarinet 207
Russian	:	кларнет, *m.* 207
Serbian	:	кларинет, *m.* 207
Ukrainian	:	клярнет, *m.* 207

208 CLASP s. see 211 CLIP

209 CLEAN adj.

Czech	:	čistý 209
Danish	:	ren 209
Dutch	:	schoon 209
Finnish	:	puhdas 209
French	:	propre; pur 209
German	:	rein 209
Hungarian	:	tizzta 209
Italian	:	puro 209
Croatian	:	čist 209
Norwegian	:	ren 209
Polish	:	czysty 209
Portuguese	:	limpo 209
Rumanian	:	curat 209
Slovak	:	čistý 209
Spanish	:	limpio; puro 209
Swedish	:	ren 209
Turkish	:	pâk 209
Russian	:	чистый 209
Serbian	:	чист 209
Ukrainian	:	чистий 209

210 CLINICAL THERMOMETER s.

Czech	:	teploměr, *m.* 210
Danish	:	Sygetermometer, *c.* 210
Dutch	:	de thermometer 210
Finnish	:	lämpömittari 210
French	:	thermomètre médical, *m.* 210
German	:	das Thermometer 210
Hungarian	:	lázmérö 210
Italian	:	termometro per la febbre, *m.* 210
Croatian	:	toplomer, *m.* 210
Norwegian	:	febertermometer, *n.* 210
Polish	:	termometr, *m.* 210
Portuguese	:	termómetro, *o* 210
Rumanian	:	termometrul 210
Slovak	:	teplomer, *m.* 210
Spanish	:	termómetro clínico, *m.* 210
Swedish	:	febertermometer-n 210
Turkish	:	sitma termometrosi 210
Russian	:	термометр, *m.* 210
Serbian	:	топломер, *m.* 210
Ukrainian	:	тепломір, *m.* 210

211 CLIP s. (a clasp)

Czech	:	sponka, *f.*; svorka, *f.* 211
Danish	:	Clips, *c.* 211
Dutch	:	de clip 211
Finnish	:	sinkilä 211
French	:	attache de bureau, *f.* 211
German	:	die Büroklammer 211
Hungarian	:	iratkapoes 211
Italian	:	grappette, *f. pl.* 211
Croatian	:	spojka za spise, *f.* 211
Norwegian	:	binders, *pl.* 211
Polish	:	spinacz, *m.* 211
Portuguese	:	gancho, *o* 211
Rumanian	:	clama de birou 211
Slovak	:	sponka na spisy, *f.* 211
Spanish	:	prendedor de escritorio 211
Swedish	:	pappers-klämma-n 211
Turkish	:	perçin çivisi 211
Russian	:	скобки дпя бумаги, *pl.* 211
Serbian	:	канцеларийски ексерчичи, *pl.* 211
Ukrainian	:	споювач, *m.* 211

212 CLOCK s.

Czech	:	hodiny 212
Danish	:	Uret 212
Dutch	:	de klok 212
Finnish	:	kello 212
French	:	montre pendule 212
German	:	die Uhr 212
Hungarian	:	óra 212
Italian	:	orologio 212
Croatian	:	sat 212
Norwegian	:	klokke, *f.* 212
Polish	:	godzina, *f.* 212
Portuguese	:	relojo, *o* 212
Rumanian	:	ceasul 212
Slovak	:	hodiny 212
Spanish	:	el reloj 212
Swedish	:	klocka-n 212
Turkish	:	saat 212
Russian	:	часы 212
Serbian	:	часовник, *m.* 212
Ukrainian	:	година, *f.*; годинник, *m.* 212

213 CLOSED adj.

Czech	:	zavřený 213
Danish	:	lukket 213
Dutch	:	gesloten 213
Finnish	:	suljettu 213
French	:	fermé 213
German	:	geschlossen 213
Hungarian	:	zárva 213 *
Italian	:	chiuso 213
Croatian	:	zatvoren 213
Norwegian	:	lukket 213
Polish	:	zamknięty 213
Portuguese	:	fechado 213
Rumanian	:	inchis 213
Slovak	:	zavretý 213
Spanish	:	cerrado 213
Swedish	:	stängd 213
Turkish	:	kapalı 213
Russian	:	закрытый 213
Serbian	:	затворен 213
Ukrainian	:	замкнений 213

214 CLOTHING s. (gentlemen's)

Czech	: oděv, *m.* (mužský)	214
Danish	: Herretój	214
Dutch	: de kleeding	214
Finnish	: vaatteet	214
French	: les vêtements de l'homme	214
German	: die Kleidung (männl.)	214
Hungarian	: ruházat (férfi)	214
Italian	: indumenti (maschili), *m. pl.*	**214**
Croatian	: odijelo (muško), *n.*	214
Norwegian	: herrekledning, *n.*	214
Polish	: odzienie męskie, *n.*	214
Portuguese	: imbrăcăminteabărbăteasc	214
Rumanian	: a roupa para homens	214
Slovak	: odev (mužský), *m.*	214
Spanish	: indumentaria (masculina)	**214**
Swedish	: klädedräkt (manlig)	214
Turkish	: erkek elbisesi	214
Russian	: одежда, *f.*	214
Serbian	: одело, *n.*	214
Ukrainian	: одяг, *m.*	214

215 CLOUD s.

Czech	: mrak, *m.* 215
Danish	: Sky, *m./c.* 215
Dutch	: de wolk 215
Finnish	: pilvi 215
French	: nuage, *m.* 215
German	: die Wolke 215
Hungarian	: felhö 215
Italian	: nuvola, *f.* 215
Croatian	: oblak, *m.* 215
Norwegian	: sky, *m.* 215
Polish	: chmura, *f.* 215
Portuguese	: nuvem, *a* 215
Rumanian	: norul 215
Slovak	: oblak, *m.* 215
Spanish	: nube, *f.* 215
Swedish	: moln-et 215
Turkish	: bulut 215
Russian	: облако, *n.* 215
Serbian	: облак, *m.* 215
Ukrainian	: хмара, *f.* 215

216 CLOVE s.

Czech	: hřebíček (koření), *m.*	216
Danish	: Nelliker, *c.*	216
Dutch	: de kruidnagel	216
Finnish	: mausteneilikka	216
French	: clous de girofle, *m. pl.*	216
German	: die Gewürznelke	216
Hungarian	: szegfüszeg	216
Italian	: garofani, *m. pl.*	216
Croatian	: karanfil, *m.*	216
Norwegian	: nellikspiker, *pl.*	216
Polish	: goździki, *pl.*	216
Portuguese	: cravo da India, *o*	216
Rumanian	: nucşoara, *f.*	216
Slovak	: hrebíček, *m.*	216
Spanish	: clavo de especia	216
Swedish	: kryddnejlikorna	216
Turkish	: bahar karanfili	216
Russian	: гвоздика, *f.*	216
Serbian	: клинчић, *m.*	216
Ukrainian	: гвоздики, *pl.*	216

217 CLOVER s.

Czech	: jetel, *m.* 217
Danish	: Klöver, *n.* 217
Dutch	: de klaver 217
Finnish	: apila 217
French	: trèfle, *m.* 217
German	: der Klee 217
Hungarian	: a lóhere 217
Italian	: trifoglio, *m.* 217
Croatian	: djetelina, *f.* 217
Norwegian	: klöver, *n.* 217
Polish	: koniczyna, *f.* 217
Portuguese	: trevo, *o* 217
Rumanian	: trifoiul 217
Slovak	: d'atelina, *f.* 217
Spanish	: trébol, *m.* 217
Swedish	: klöver-n 217
Turkish	: kepek 217
Russian	: клевер, *m.* 217
Serbian	: детелина, *f.* 217
Ukrainian	: конюшина, *f.* 217

218 COCK s.

Czech	: kohout, *m.* 218
Danish	: Hane, *m.* 218
Dutch	: de haan 218
Finnish	: kukko 218
French	: coq, *m.* 218
German	: der Hahn 218
Hungarian	: kakas 218
Italian	: gallo, *m.* 218
Croatian	: pjetao, *m.* 218
Norwegian	: hane, *m.* 218
Polish	: kogut, *m.* 218
Portuguese	: galo, *o* 218
Rumanian	: cocoşul 218
Slovak	: kohút, *m.* 218
Spanish	: gallo, *m.* 218
Swedish	: tupp-en 218
Turkish	: horos 218
Russian	: петух, *m.* 218
Serbian	: петао, *m.* 218
Ukrainian	: когут, *m.* 218

219 COAL-SHOVEL s.

Czech	: lopata na uhlí, *f.*	219
Danish	: Kulskuffe, *m./c.*	219
Dutch	: de kolenschep	219
Finnish	: hiililapio	219
French	: pèle à feu, *f.*	219
German	: die Kohlenschaufel	219
Hungarian	: a szeneslapát	219
Italian	: para per il carbone, *f.*	219
Croatian	: lopata za ugljen, *f.*	219
Norwegian	: kullskuffe, *m.*	219
Polish	: szufla do wegla, *f.*	219
Portuguese	: pá para carvão, *a*	219
Rumanian	: vătraiu, *n.*	219
Slovak	: lopatka na uhlie, *f.*	219
Spanish	: badila para carbón	219
Swedish	: kolskyffel-n	219
Turkish	: kömur küregi	219
Russian	: совок, *m.*	219
Serbian	: лопата	219
Ukrainian	: лопатка, *f.*	219

220 COCOA s.

Czech	: kakao, n. 220
Danish	: Chocolade, c. 220
Dutch	: de cacao 220
Finnish	: kaakkao 220
French	: cacao, m. 220
German	: der Kakao 220
Hungarian	: kakaó 220
Italian	: cacao, m. 220
Croatian	: kakao, m. 220
Norwegian	: kakao, 220
Polish	: kakao, n. 220
Portuguese	: cacau, a 220
Rumanian	: cacauă, f. 220
Slovak	: kakao, n. 220
Spanish	: cacao, n. 220
Swedish	: kakao 220
Turkish	: kakao 220
Russian	: какао,, n. 220
Serbian	: какао, m. 220
Ukrainian	: какао, n. 220

221 COFFEE s.

Czech	: káva, f. 221
Danish	: Kaffee, m./c. 221
Dutch	: de koffie 221
Finnish	: kahvi 221
French	: café, m. 221
German	: der Kaffee 221
Hungarian	: kávé 221
Italian	: caffè, m. 221
Croatian	: kava, f. 221
Norwegian	: kaffe, m. 221
Polish	: kawa, f. 221
Portuguese	: café, o 221
Rumanian	: cafeă, f. 221
Slovak	: káva, f. 221
Spanish	: café, m. 221
Swedish	: kaffe-t 221
Turkish	: kahve 221
Russian	: кафе, n. 221
Serbian	: кафа, f. 221
Ukrainian	: кава, f. 221

222 COGNAC s.

Czech	: koňak, m. 222
Danish	: Kognak, m. 222
Dutch	: de cognac 222
Finnish	: konjakki 222
French	: cognac, m. 222
German	: der Kognak 222
Hungarian	: konyak 222
Italian	: cognac, m. 222
Croatian	: konjak, m. 222
Norwegian	: konjak, m. 222
Polish	: koniak, m. 222
Portuguese	: conhaque, o 222
Rumanian	: cognacul 222
Slovak	: koňak, m. 222
Spanish	: coñak, m. 222
Swedish	: konjak-en 222
Turkish	: konyak 222
Russian	: коньяк, m. 222
Serbian	: коньак, m. 222
Ukrainian	: коняк, m. 222

223 COLD adj.

Czech	: studený 223
Danish	: kold 223
Dutch	: koud 223
Finnish	: kylmä 223
French	: froid 223
German	: kalt 223
Hungarian	: hideg 223
Italian	: freddo 223
Croatian	: hladan 223
Norwegian	: kald 223
Polish	: chłodny 223
Portuguese	: frio 223
Rumanian	: frig 223
Slovak	: studený 223
Spanish	: frío 223
Swedish	: kall 223
Turkish	: soğuk 223
Russian	: холодно; -ый 223
Serbian	: хладан 223
Ukrainian	: хлодний 223

224 COLLAR s.

Czech	: límec, m. 224
Danish	: Flip, m./c. 224
Dutch	: de boord 224
Finnish	: kaulus 224
French	: col, m. 224
German	: der Kragen . 224
Hungarian	: gallér 224
Italian	: colletto, m. 224
Croatian	: ogrlica, f. 224
Norwegian	: krave, m.; snipp, m. 224
Polish	: kołnierz, m. 224
Portuguese	: colarinho, o 224
Rumanian	: gulerul 224
Slovak	: golier, m. 224
Spanish	: cuello, m. 224
Swedish	: krage-n 224
Turkish	: yaka 224
Russian	: воротник, m. 224
Serbian	: крагна, f. 224
Ukrainian	: ковнірець, m. 224

225 COLONIAL SOLDIER s.

Czech	: koloniální voják, m. 225
Danish	: Kolonialsoldat, m. 225
Dutch	: de kolonial-soldaat 225
Finnish	: siirtomaasotilas 225
French	: le soldat colonial 225
German	: der Kolonialsoldat 225
Hungarian	: gyarmatikatona 225
Italian	: soldato coloniale 225
Croatian	: kolonijalni vojnik 225
Norwegian	: kolonisoldat, m. 225
Polish	: żolnierz kolonialny, m. 225
Portuguese	: soldado colonial, o 225
Rumanian	: soldatul colonial 225
Slovak	: koloniálny vojak, m. 225
Spanish	: soldado de colonia, m. 225
Swedish	: kolonisoldat-en 225
Turkish	: mustemlikat askeri 225
Russian	: колониальный солдат, m. 225
Serbian	: колонијални војник, m. 225
Ukrainian	: колоніяльний жовнір, m. 225

226 COLOR s. (Brit. colour)

Czech	:	barva, *f.* 226
Danish	:	Farve, *m./c.* 226
Dutch	:	de kleur 226
Finnish	:	värri(t) 226
French	:	couleur, *f.* 226
German	:	die Farbe 226
Hungarian	:	szín 226
Italian	:	colore, *m.* 226
Croatian	:	boja, *f.* 226
Norwegian	:	farve, *m.* 226
Polish	:	kolor, *m.* 226
Portuguese	:	côr, *a* 226
Rumanian	:	culorile, *f. pl.* 226
Slovak	:	farba, *f.* 226
Spanish	:	color; colorido, *m.* 226
Swedish	:	färg-er 226
Turkish	:	renkler 226
Russian	:	цвет, *m.* 226
Serbian	:	боja, *f.* 226
Ukrainian	:	краска, *f.*; колір; фарба, *f.* 226

227 COLOUR s. chiefly Brit. see **226 COLOR**

228 COMB s.

Czech	:	hřeben, *m.* 228
Danish	:	Kam, *m./c.* 228
Dutch	:	de kam 228
Finnish	:	kampa 228
French	:	peigne, *m.* 228
German	:	der Kamm 228
Hungarian	:	fésü 228
Italian	:	pettine, *m.* 228
Croatian	:	češalj, *m.* 228
Norwegian	:	kam, *m.* 228
Polish	:	grzebień, *m.* 228
Portuguese	:	pente, *o* 228
Rumanian	:	pieptenele 228
Slovak	:	hrebeň, *m.* 228
Spanish	:	peine, *m.* 228
Swedish	:	kamm-en 228
Turkish	:	tarak 228
Russian	:	гребень, *m.* 228
Serbian	:	чешаљ, *m.* 228
Ukrainian	:	гребінець, *m.* 228

229 COME v.

Czech	:	přijíti; přicházeti 229
Danish	:	komme 229
Dutch	:	komen 229
Finnish	:	tulla 229
French	:	venir; arriver 229
German	:	kommen 229
Hungarian	:	jön 229
Italian	:	venire; arrivare 229
Croatian	:	dolaziti 229
Norwegian	:	komme 229
Polish	:	chodzić 229
Portuguese	:	vir 229
Rumanian	:	a veni 229
Slovak	:	prísť' 229
Spanish	:	venir 229
Swedish	:	(an) komma 229
Turkish	:	gelmek 229
Russian	:	приходить 229
Serbian	:	доћи 229
Ukrainian	:	приходити 229

230 COMPARTMENT s.

Czech	:	oddělení, *n.* 230
Danish	:	Kupe, *m./c.* 230
Dutch	:	de coupé 230
Finnish	:	osasto 230
French	:	compartiment, *m.* 230
German	:	das Abteil 230
Hungarian	:	szakasz 230
Italian	:	scompartimento, *m.* 230
Croatian	:	odjelenje, *n.* 230
Norwegian	:	kupe, *m.* 230
Polish	:	przedzial, *m.* 230
Portuguese	:	compartimento, *o* 230
Rumanian	:	compartimentul 230
Slovak	:	kupé, *n.* 230
Spanish	:	departamento, *m.* 230
Swedish	:	kupé-n 230
Turkish	:	merki 230
Russian	:	отделение, *n.* 230
Serbian	:	оделење, *n.* 230
Ukrainian	:	переділ, *m.* 230

231 COMPASS s.

Czech	:	kompas, *m.* 231
Danish	:	Kompas, *n./c.* 231
Dutch	:	het kompas 231
Finnish	:	kompassi 231
French	:	boussole, *f.* 231
German	:	der Kompass 231
Hungarian	:	iránytü 231
Italian	:	bussola, *m.* 231
Croatian	:	kompas, *m.* 231
Norwegian	:	kompass, *n.* 231
Polish	:	kompas, *m.* 231
Portuguese	:	bússola, *a* 231
Rumanian	:	busolă, *f.* 231
Slovak	:	kompas, *m.* 321
Spanish	:	brújula, *f.* 231
Swedish	:	kompass-en 231
Turkish	:	pusula 231
Russian	:	компас, *m.* 231
Serbian	:	компас, *m.*. 231
Ukrainian	:	бусоля, *f.*; компас, *m.* 231

232 CONSULATE s.

Czech	:	konsulát, *m.* 232
Danish	:	Konsulat, *n.* 232
Dutch	:	het consulaat 232
Finnish	:	konsulaatti 232
French	:	consulat, *m.* 232
German	:	das Konsulat 232
Hungarian	:	a konzulátus 232
Italian	:	consolato, *m.* 232
Croatian	:	konzulat, *m.* 232
Norwegian	:	konsulat, *m.* 232
Polish	:	konsulat, *m.* 232
Portuguese	:	consulado, *o* 232
Rumanian	:	consulatul 232
Slovak	:	konzulát, *m.* 232
Spanish	:	el consulado 232
Swedish	:	konsulat-et 232
Turkish	:	konsolosluk 232
Russian	:	консульство, *n.* 232
Serbian	:	конзулат, *m.* 232
Ukrainian	:	конзулят, *m.* 232

233 CONSULTING HOUR s.

Czech	: ordinační hodina, f.	233
Danish	: Konsultationstid	233
Dutch	: het spreekuur	233
Finnish	: vastaanotto	233
French	: heure de visite	233
German	: die Sprechstunde	233
Hungarian	: fogadóóra	233
Italian	: orario delle visite, m.	233
Croatian	: sat za primanje	233
Norwegian	: kontortid, m.	233
Polish	: godzina przyjęć, f.	233
Portuguese	: hora de consultas, a	233
Rumanian	: consultaţie	233
Slovak	: prijímacie hodiny, pl.	233
Spanish	: hora de consulta	233
Swedish	: mottagningstid-en	233
Turkish	: kabul saati	233
Russian	: приемное время, n,	233
Serbian	: час приманьа,	233
Ukrainian	: година принять, f.	233

234 CONTROL s.

Czech	: kontrola, f.	234
Danish	: kontrol, c.	234
Dutch	: controle	234
Finnish	: tarkastus	234
French	: contrôle, m.	234
German	: Kontrolle, f.	234
Hungarian	: ellenörzés	234
Italian	: registro, m.	234
Croatian	: nadzor; pregledba, f.	234
Norwegian	: kontroll, c.	234
Polish	: rewizja, f.	234
Portuguese	: autoridade, f.; verificação, m.	234
Rumanian	: control, c.	234
Slovak	: kontrola, f.	234
Spanish	: control, m.	234
Swedish	: kontroll-en	234
Turkish	: kontrol	234
Russian	: контроль, m.	234
Serbian	: надзор, m.	234
Ukrainian	: контроль, m.	234

235 COOK v.

Czech	: vařiti	235
Danish	: koge	235
Dutch	: kooken	235
Finnish	: keittää	235
French	: cuire	235
German	: kochen	235
Hungarian	: fözni	235
Italian	: cuocere	235
Croatian	: kuhati	235
Norwegian	: koke	235
Polish	: gotowac	235
Portuguese	: cozinhar, ferver	235
Rumanian	: a fierbe	235
Slovak	: varit'	235
Spanish	: hervir; cocer	235
Swedish	: koka	235
Turkish	: pişmek	235
Russian	: варить	235
Serbian	: кувати	235
Ukrainian	: варити	235

236 COPPER s.

Czech	: měd', f.	236
Danish	: Kobber, n.	236
Dutch	: het koper	236
Finnish	: kupari	236
French	: cuivre, m.	236
German	: das Kupfer	236
Hungarian	: réz	236
Italian	: rame, m.	236
Croatian	: bakar, m.	236
Norwegian	: kopper, n.	236
Polish	: miedź, f.	236
Portuguese	: cobre, a	236
Rumanian	: aramă, f.	236
Slovak	: med,' f.	236
Spanish	: cobre, m.	236
Swedish	: koppar-n	236
Turkish	: bakır	236
Russian	: медь, f.	236
Serbian	: бакар, m.	236
Ukrainian	: мідь, f.	236

237 CORK-SCREW s.

Czech	: vývrtka, f.	237
Danish	: Propträkker, m./c.	237
Dutch	: de kurktrekker	237
Finnish	: korkkiruuvi	237
French	: tire-bouchon, m.	237
German	: der Korkzieher	237
Hungarian	: dugóhúzó	237
Italian	: cavataraccioli, m.	237
Croatian	: vadičep, m.	237
Norwegian	: korketrekker, m.	237
Polish	: korkociag, m.	237
Portuguese	: saccarolhas, o	237
Rumanian	: tirbişonul	237
Slovak	: vývrtka, f.	237
Spanish	: sacacorchos, m.	237
Swedish	: korkskruv-en	237
Turkish	: tirbuşon	237
Russian	: штопор, m.	237
Serbian	: вадичеп, m.	237
Ukrainian	: коркотяг; штопор, m.	237

238 CORN s. (on the toes)

Czech	: kuří oko, n.	238
Danish	: Ligtorn, m.	238
Dutch	: het eksteroog	238
Finnish	: liikavarvas	238
French	: cor, m.	238
German	: das Hühnerauge	238
Hungarian	: tyúkszem	238
Italian	: callo, m.	238
Croatian	: kurje oko, n.	238
Norwegian	: liktorn, m.	238
Polish	: nagniotek, m.	238
Portuguese	: calo, o	238
Rumanian	: bătătura, f.	238
Slovak	: kurie oko, n.	238
Spanish	: callo, m.	238
Swedish	: liktå-n	238
Turkish	: nasır	238
Russian	: мозоль, m.	238
Serbian	: курје око, n.	238
Ukrainian	: нагніток, m.	238

239 CORRESPOND v. see 21 ANSWER

240 CORSET s.

Czech	:	korset, m.	240
Danish	:	Korset, c.	240
Dutch	:	het corset	240
Finnish	:	korsetti	240
French	:	corset, m.	240
German	:	das Korsett	240
Hungarian	:	füzö	240
Italian	:	corsetto, m.	240
Croatian	:	korzet, m.	240
Norwegian	:	korsett, m.	240
Polish	:	gorset, m.	240
Portuguese	:	espartilho, o	240
Rumanian	:	corsetul	240
Slovak	:	šnurovačka, f.	240
Spanish	:	corsé, m.	240
Swedish	:	korsett-en	240
Turkish	:	korse	240
Russian	:	корсет, m.	240
Serbian	:	корзет, m.	240
Ukrainian	:	корсет, m.	240

241 COSTLY see 323 EXPENSIVE

242 COSTUME s.

Czech	:	kostým, m.	242
Danish	:	Spadseredragt, c.	242
Dutch	:	het mantelpak	242
Finnish	:	saketti	242
French	:	tailleur, m.	242
German	:	das Jackenkleid	242
Hungarian	:	kosztüm	242
Italian	:	costume m.	242
Croatian	:	kostim, m.	242
Norwegian	:	drakt, m.	242
Polish	:	żakiet, .m.	242
Portuguese	:	trajo, o	242
Rumanian	:	taiorul	242
Slovak	:	kostým, m.	242
Spanish	:	vestido de sastre, m.	242
Swedish	:	dräkt-en	242
Turkish	:	çakett	242
Russian	:	костюм, m.	242
Serbian	:	костим, m.	242
Ukrainian	:	жакет; костюм,m.	242

243 COTTON s.

Czech	:	bavlna, f.	243
Danish	:	Bomuld, m./c.	243
Dutch	:	het katoen	243
Finnish	:	puuvilla	243
French	:	coton, m.	243
German	:	die Baumwolle	243
Hungarian	:	gyapot	243
Italian	:	cotone, m.	243
Croatian	:	pamuk, m.	243
Norwegian	:	bomull, m.	243
Polish	:	bawełna, f.	243
Portuguese	:	algodão, o	243
Rumanian	:	bumbacul	243
Slovak	:	bavlna, f.	243
Spanish	:	algodón, m.	243
Swedish	:	bomull-en	243
Turkish	:	pamuk	243
Russian	:	хлопок, m.	243
Serbian	:	памук, m.	243
Ukrainian	:	бабовна, f.	243

244 COUCH s. see 907 SOFA

245 COW s.

Czech	:	kráva, f.	245
Danish	:	Ko, f.	245
Dutch	:	de koe	245
Finnish	:	lehmä	245
French	:	vache, f.	245
German	:	die Kuh	245
Hungarian	:	tehén	245
Italian	:	vacca	245
Croatian	:	krava, f.	245
Norwegian	:	ku, f.	245
Polish	:	krowa, f.	245
Portuguese	:	vaca, a	245
Rumanian	:	vacă, f.	245
Slovak	:	krava, f.	245
Spanish	:	vaca, f.	245
Swedish	:	ko-n	245
Turkish	:	inek	245
Russian	:	корова, f.	245
Serbian	:	крава, f.	245
Ukrainian	:	корова, f.	245

246 COWBERRY s.

Czech	:	brusinka, f.	246
Danish	:	Tyttebär, m./c.	246
Dutch	:	de roode boschbes	246
Finnish	:	puolukka	246
French	:	airelle rouge, f.	246
German	:	die Preisselbeere	246
Hungarian	:	verés áfonya	246
Italian	:	bacca di mirtillo, f.	246
Croatian	:	brusnica, f.	246
Norwegian	:	tyttebär, m.	246
Polish	:	borówka czerwona, f.	246
Portuguese	:	airela encarnada, a	246
Rumanian	:	merişoara, f.	246
Slovak	:	brusnica, f.	246
Spanish	:	arándano encarnado	246
Swedish	:	lingon-et	246
Turkish	:	kirmizi yaban mersini	246
Russian	:	брусника, f.	246
Serbian	:	брусница, f.	246
Ukrainian	:	брусничка, f.	246

247 CRACKER s.

Czech	:	keks, m.	247
Danish	:	Kiks, n.	247
Dutch	:	de cakes	247
Finnish	:	keksi	247
French	:	le biscuit	247
German	:	der Keks	247
Hungarian	:	keksz	247
Italian	:	pasticcino, m.	247
Croatian	:	keks, m.	247
Norwegian	:	kjeks, c.	247
Polish	:	piernik; keks, m.	247
Portuguese	:	bolacha, a	247
Rumanian	:	biscuiţii, pl.	247
Slovak	:	keks, m.	247
Spanish	:	galletas, pl.	247
Swedish	:	kex-en	247
Turkish	:	keks	247
Russian	:	печенье, n.	247
Serbian	:	кекс, m.	247
Ukrainian	:	кекс, m.	247

248 CRANE   s. (a device)
Czech   : jeřáb, m.   248
Danish   : Kran, m./c.   248
Dutch   : de kraan   248
Finnish   : nosturi   248
French   : grue, f.   248
German   : der Kran   248
Hungarian   : daru   248
Italian   : gru, f.   248
Croatian   : dizalica, f.   248
Norwegian   : kran, m.   248
Polish   : kran, m.   248
Portuguese : guindaste, o   248
Rumanian   : macară, f.   248
Slovak   : zorav, m.   248
Spanish   : grúa, f.   248
Swedish   : lyftkran-en   248
Turkish   : maçuna   248
Russian   : кран подемный, m.   248
Serbian   : чекрк, m.   248
Ukrainian   : підойма, m.   248

251 CUCUMBER   s.
Czech   : okurka, f.   251
Danish   : Agurk, m./c.   251
Dutch   : de komkommer   251
Finnish   : kurkku   251
French   : concombre; cornichon, m.   251
German   : die Gurke   251
Hungarian   : uborka   251
Italian   : il citriolo   251
Croatian   : krastavac, m.   251
Norwegian   : agurk, m.   251
Polish   : ogórek, m.   251
Portuguese : pepino, o   251
Rumanian   : castravete   251
Slovak   : uhorka, pl.   251
Spanish   : pepino, m.   251
Swedish   : gurka-n   251
Turkish   : higar   251
Russian   : огурец, m.   251
Serbian   : краставац, m.   251
Ukrainian   : огірок, m.   251

249 CREAM   s.   (a part of milk)
Czech   : smetana, f.   249
Danish   : Flöde, m./c.   249
Dutch   : de room   249
Finnish   : kerma   249
French   : crème, f.   249
German   : die Sahne   249
Hungarian   : tejszin   249
Italian   : panna, f.   249
Croatian   : skorup, m.   249
Norwegian   : flöte, m.   249
Polish   : śmietana, f.   249
Portuguese : nata, a   249
Rumanian   : frişcă, f.   249
Slovak   : smotana, f.   249
Spanish   : crema, f.   249
Swedish   : grädde-n   249
Turkish   : kaymak   249
Russian   : сливки, pl.   249
Serbian   : скоруп, m.   249
Ukrainian   : сметана, f.   249

252 CUP   s.
Czech   : šálek, m.   252
Danish   : Kop, c.   252
Dutch   : de kop   252
Finnish   : kuppi   252
French   : tasse, f.   252
German   : die Tasse   252
Hungarian   : csésze   252
Italian   : tazza, f.   252
Croatian   : šalica, f.   252
Norwegian   : kopp, m.   252
Polish   : filiżanka, f.   252
Portuguese : chávena, a   252
Rumanian   : ceaşca, f.   252
Slovak   : šálka, f.   252
Spanish   : taza, f.   252
Swedish   : kopp-en   252
Turkish   : bardak   252
Russian   : чашка, f.   252
Serbian   : шоља, f.   252
Ukrainian   : чашка, f.   252

250 CRIB   s.
Czech   : jesle, pl.   250
Danish   : Krybbe, m./c.   250
Dutch   : de krib   250
Finnish   : seimi   250
French   : crèche, f.   250
German   : die Krippe   250
Hungarian   : jászol   250
Italian   : mangiatoa, f.   250
Croatian   : jasle, pl.   250
Norwegian   : krybbe, f.   250
Polish   : żłób, m.   250
Portuguese : manjedoura, a   250
Rumanian   : jesleă, f.   250
Slovak   : jasle, pl.   250
Spanish   : comedero, m.   250
Swedish   : krubba-n   250
Turkish   : yemlik   250
Russian   : ясли, pl.   250
Serbian   : јасле, pl.   250
Ukrainian   : (жолоб), m.; дитяче ліжко, n.   250

253 CURTAIN   s.
Czech   : záclona, f.   253
Danish   : Gardin, c.   253
Dutch   : het gordijn   253
Finnish   : verho   253
French   : le rideau   253
German   : der Vorhang   253
Hungarian   : függöny   253
Italian   : tendina, f.   253
Croatian   : zavjesa, f.   253
Norwegian   : gardin, m.; forheng, n.   253
Polish   : firanka, f.   253
Portuguese : cortina, a   253
Rumanian   : perdeă, f.   253
Slovak   : záclona, f.   253
Spanish   : cortina, f.   253
Swedish   : gardin-en   253
Turkish   : perde   253
Russian   : занавеска, f.   253
Serbian   : завеса, f.   253
Ukrainian   : занавіси, pl.   253

38

254 CUT v.

Czech	: řezati; stříhati	254
Danish	: skäre	254
Dutch	: snede	254
Finnish	: leikata	254
French	: couper; séparer	254
German	: schneiden	254
Hungarian	: elválaszt	254
Italian	: tagliare; separare	254
Croatian	.: rezati	254
Norwegian	: skille	254
Polish	: rzezać	254·
Portuguese	: ferir; cortar	254
Rumanian	: a tăia	254
Slovak	: rezat'; strihat'	254
Spanish	: cortar; tajar	254
Swedish	: skära; hugga	254
Turkish	: kesmek	254
Russian	: резать	254
Serbian	: резати	254
Ukrainian	: різати	254

255 CUTLET s.

Czech	: kotleta, f.	255
Danish	: 'Kotelet, c.	255
Dutch	: dè carbonade	255
Finnish	: kotletti	255
French	: côtelette, f.	255
German	: das Kotelett	255
Hungarian	: a bordasült	255
Italian	: cotoletta, f.	255
Croatian	: kotlet, m.	255
Norwegian	: kotelett, m.	255
Polish	: kotlet, m.	255
Portuguese	: costeleta, a	255
Rumanian	: cotletul	255
Slovak	: rebierko, n.	255
Spanish	: la chuleta	255
Swedish	: kotlett-en	255
Turkish	: kotlet	255
Russian	: котлета, f.	255
Serbian	: котлет, m.	255
Ukrainian	: котлет, m.	255

256 CYPRESS s.

Czech	: cypriš, m.	256
Danish	: Cypres, m./c.	256
Dutch	: de cypres	256
Finnish	: sypressi	256
French	: cyprès, m.	256
German	: die Zypresse	256
Hungarian	: ciprus	256
Italian	: cipresso, m.	256
Croatian	: cipresa, m.	256
Norwegian	: cypres, f.	256
Polish	: cypres, m.	256
Portuguese	: cipreste, o	256
Rumanian	: chiparosul	256
Slovak	: cyprus, m.	256
Spanish	: ciprés, m.	256
Swedish	: cypress-en	256
Turkish	: servi ağaci	256
Russian	: кипарис, m.	256
Serbian	: ципреса, f.	256
Ukrainian	: кипарис, m.	256

257 DANCE s.

Czech	: tanec, m.	257
Danish	· : Dansen, c.	257
Dutch	: de dans	257
Finnish	: tanssi	257
French	: danse, f.	257
German	: der Tanz	257
Hungarian	: tánc	257
Italian	: danza, f.	257
Croatian	: ples, m.	257
Norwegian	: dans, m.	257
Polish	: tanecz, m.	257
Portuguese	: dansa, a	257
Rumanian	: dansul	257
Slovak	: tanec, m.	257
Spanish	: baile; danza, f.	257
Swedish	: dans-en	257
Turkish	: dans	257
Russian	: танец, m.	257
Serbian	: игра, f.	257
Ukrainian	: танець, m.	257

258 DANGER s.

Czech	: nebezpečí, n.	258
Danish	: Fare, c.	258
Dutch	: Gevaar	258
Finnish	: vaara	258
French	: danger, m.	258
German	: die Gefahr	258
Hungarian	: veszedalem	258
Italian	: pericolo, m.	258
Croatian	: opasnost, f.	258
Norwegian	: fare, c.	258
Polish	: opasnost, f.	258
Portuguese	: perigo, m.	258
Rumanian	: pericol, c.	258
Slovak	: nebezpečenstvo, n.	258
Spanish	: peligro, m.	258
Swedish	: fara	258
Turkish	: tehlike	258
Russian	: опасность, f.	258
Serbian	: опасность, f.	258
Ukrainian	: небезпека, n.	258

259 DARK adj.

Czech	: tmavý	259
Danish	: mörk	259
Dutch	: donker	259
Finnish	: tumma	259
French	: foncé	259
German	: dunkel	259
Hungarian	: sötét	259
Italian	: oscuro	259
Croatian	: taman	259
Norwegian	: mörk	259
Polish	: ciemny	259
Portuguese	: escuro	259
Rumanian	: intunecos	259
Slovak	: tmavý	259
Spanish	: oscuro	259
Swedish	: mörk	259
Turkish	: koyu renkli	259
Russian	: темно; -ый	259
Serbian	: таман	259
Ukrainian	: темний	259

260 DATE s. (fruit of the date palm)

Czech	:	datle, f. 260
Danish	:	Dattel, c. 260
Dutch	:	de dadel 260
Finnish	:	taateli 260
French	:	datte, f. 260
German	:	die Dattel 260
Hungarian	:	datolya 260
Italian	:	dattero, m. 260
Croatian	:	datulja, f. 260
Norwegian	:	daddel, m. 260
Polish	:	daktyl, n. 260
Portuguese	:	tâmara, a 260
Rumanian	:	curmala, f. 260
Slovak	:	datľa, f. 260
Spanish	:	dátil, m. 260
Swedish	:	dadel-n 260
Turkish	:	hurma 260
Russian	:	финик, m. 260
Serbian	:	датуља, f. 260
Ukrainian	:	дактиль, m. 260

261 DAUGHTER s.

Czech	:	dcera, f. 261
Danish	:	datter, c. 261
Dutch	:	dochter 261
Finnish	:	tytär 261
French	:	fille, f. 261
German	:	die Tochter 261
Hungarian	:	leány 261
Italian	:	figlia, f. 261
Croatian	:	kći, f. 261
Norwegian	:	datter, f. 261
Polish	:	córka, f. 261
Portuguese	:	filha, f. 261
Rumanian	:	fiică, f. 261
Slovak	:	dcéra, f. 261
Spanish	:	hija, f. 261
Swedish	:	dotter, f. 261
Turkish	:	kiz 261
Russian	:	дочь, f. 261
Serbian	:	кћи, f. 261
Ukrainian	:	дочка, f. 261

262 DAY s.

Czech	:	den, m. 262
Danish	:	Dag, m. 262
Dutch	:	de dag 262
Finnish	:	päivä 262
French	:	jour, m. 262
German	:	der Tag 262
Hungarian	:	nap 262
Italian	:	giorno, m. 262
Croatian	:	dan, m. 262
Norwegian	:	dag, m. 262
Polish	:	dzień, m. 262
Portuguese	:	dia, o 262
Rumanian	:	zi, f. 262
Slovak	:	deň, m. 262
Spanish	:	día, m. 262
Swedish	:	dag-en 262
Turkish	:	gün 262
Russian	:	день, m. 262
Serbian	:	дан, m. 262
Ukrainian	:	день, m. 262

263 THE DAY AFTER TOMORROW adv.

Czech	:	pozítří 263
Danish	:	i Overmorgen 263
Dutch	:	overmorgen 263
Finnish	:	ylihuomenna 263
French	:	après-demain 263
German	:	übermorgen 263
Hungarian	:	holnapután 263
Italian	:	dopodomani 263
Croatian	:	prekosutra 263
Norwegian	:	iovermorgen 263
Polish	:	pojutrze 263
Portuguese	:	depois de amanhã 263
Rumanian	:	poimâne 263
Slovak	:	pozajtre 263
Spanish	:	pasado mañana 263
Swedish	:	i övermorgon 263
Turkish	:	yarin obirgün 263
Russian	:	послезавтра 263
Serbian	:	прекеутра 263
Ukrainian	:	позавтра 263

264 THE DAY BEFORE YESTERDAY adv.

Czech	:	předevčerem 264
Danish	:	i Forgaars 264
Dutch	:	eergisteren 264
Finnish	:	toissa päivänä 264
French	:	avant-hier 264
German	:	vorgestern 264
Hungarian	:	tegnapelött 264
Italian	:	ieri l'altro 264
Croatian	:	prekjučer 264
Norwegian	:	i forgärs 264
Polish	:	przedwczoraj 264
Portuguese	:	anteontem 264
Rumanian	:	alaltăieri 264
Slovak	:	predvčerom 264
Spanish	:	anteayer 264
Swedish	:	i förrgår 264
Turkish	:	evvelsi gün 264
Russian	:	позавчера 264
Serbian	:	прекјуче 264
Ukrainian	:	передвчора 264

265 DEAL-TREE s.

Czech	:	borovice, f. 265
Danish	:	Tyrvetrae, n. 265
Dutch	:	de denneboom 265
Finnish	:	mänty 265
French	:	melèze, m. 265
German	:	die Kiefer 265
Hungarian	:	erdeifenyö 265
Italian	:	pino, m. 265
Croatian	:	bor, m. 265
Norwegian	:	furu, f. 265
Polish	:	sosna, f. 265
Portuguese	:	pinheiro, bravo, o 265
Rumanian	:	pinul 265
Slovak	:	borovica, f. 265
Spanish	:	pino rodeno, m. 265
Swedish	:	fura-n 265
Turkish	:	çam ağaci 265
Russian	:	сосна, f. 265
Serbian	:	бор, m. 265
Ukrainian	:	сосна, f. 265

266 DEATH *s.*

Czech	:	smrt, *f.* 266
Danish	:	Död, *m./c.* 266
Dutch	:	de dood 266
Finnish	:	kuolema 266
French	:	mort, *f.* 266
German	:	der Tod 266
Hungarian	:	halál 266
Italian	:	morte, *f.* 266
Croatian	:	smrt, *f.* 266
Norwegian	:	död, *m.* 266
Polish	:	śmierć, *f.* 266
Portuguese	:	morte, *a* 266
Rumanian	:	moartea 266
Slovak	:	smrt, *f.* 266
Spanish	:	muerte, *f.* 266
Swedish	:	död-en 266
Turkish	:	ölüm 266
Russian	:	смерть, *f.* 266
Serbian	:	смрт, *f.* 266
Ukrainian	:	смерть, *f.* 266

267 DECEMBER *s.*

Czech	:	prosinec, *m.* 267
Danish	:	December 267
Dutch	:	December 267
Finnish	:	joulukuu 267
French	:	décembre, *m.* 267
German	:	der Dezember 267
Hungarian	:	december 267
Italian	:	dicembre 267
Croatian	:	prosinac, *m.* 267
Norwegian	:	desember 267
Polish	:	grudzień 267
Portuguese	:	dezembro 267
Rumanian	:	Decembrie 267
Slovak	:	december 267
Spanish	:	diciembre 267
Swedish	:	december 267
Turkish	:	birici känun 267
Russian	:	декабрь 267
Serbian	:	Децембар 267
Ukrainian	:	Грудень 267

268 DEER *s.* (roe)

Czech	:	srnec, *m.*; srnka, *f.* 268
Danish	:	Raadyr, *n.* 268
Dutch	:	het ree 268
Finnish	:	metsäkauris 268
French	:	chevreuil, *m.* 268
German	:	das Reh 268
Hungarian	:	öz 268
Italian	:	capriolo, *m.* 268
Croatian	:	srna, *f.* 268
Norwegian	:	rådyr, *n.* 268
Polish	:	sarna, *f.* 268
Portuguese	:	corço, *o* 268
Rumanian	:	căprioară, *f.* 268
Slovak	:	srnec, *m.* 268
Spanish	:	corzo, *m.* 268
Swedish	:	rådjur-et 268
Turkish	:	karace 268
Russian	:	козуля, *f.* 268
Serbian	:	срна 268
Ukrainian	:	серна, *f.* 268

269 DEFECTIVE *adj.* see 53 BAD

270 DELIGHTED *adj.* see 406 GLAD

271 DEMAND *v.* see 36 ASK

272 DEPART *v.* see 522 LEAVE

273 DEPARTURE *s.* see 322 EXIT

274 DESK *s.*

Czech	:	psací stůl, *m.* 274
Danish	:	Skrivebord, *n.* 274
Dutch	:	de schrijftafel 274
Finnish	:	kirjoituspytä 274
French	:	bureau, *m.* 274
German	:	der Schreibtisch 274
Hungarian	:	iróasztal 274
Italian	:	scrivania, *f.* 274
Croatian	:	pisaći sto, *m.* 274
Norwegian	:	skrivebord, *n.* 274
Polish	:	biurko, *n.* 274
Portuguese	:	secretária, *a* 274
Rumanian	:	biroul; masa de scris 274
Slovak	:	písací stôl, *m.* 274
Spanish	:	mesa de despacho, *f.* 274
Swedish	:	skrivbord-et 274
Turkish	:	yazi masasi 274
Russian	:	письменный стол, *m.* 274
Serbian	:	писаћи сто, *m.* 274
Ukrainian	:	стіл до писання, *m.* 274

275 DIE *s.* (a small cube)

Czech	:	kostka, *f.* 275
Danish	:	Terning, *c.* 275
Dutch	:	de dobbelsteen 275
Finnish	:	noppa; kuutio 275
French	:	cornet, *m.* 275
German	:	der Würfel 275
Hungarian	:	kocka 275
Italian	:	dado, *m.* 275
Croatian	:	kocka, *f.* 275
Norwegian	:	terning, *m.* 275
Polish	:	kostka, *f.* 275
Portuguese	:	dado, *o* 275
Rumanian	:	zarul 275
Slovak	:	kocka, *f.* 275
Spanish	:	dado, *m.* 275
Swedish	:	tärning-en 275
Turkish	:	zar 275
Russian	:	костяшки, *pl.* 275
Serbian	:	коцка, *f.* 275
Ukrainian	:	кістка, *f.* 275

276 DINING-CAR s.

Czech	:	jídelní vůz, *m.* 276
Danish	:	Spisevogn, *m./c.* 276
Dutch	:	de restauratiewagen 276
Finnish	:	ravintolavaunu 276
French	:	wagon-restaurant, *m.* 276
German	:	der Speisewagen 276
Hungarian	:	étkezökocsi 276
Italian	:	carrozza ristorante, *f.* 276
Croatian	:	jedaća kola, *pl.* 276
Norwegian	:	spisevogn, *m.* 276 .
Polish	:	wóz restauracyjny, *m.* 276
Portuguese	:	vagão-restaurante, *o* 276
Rumanian	:	vagonul restaurant 276
Slovak	:	jedálny vozeň, *m.* 276
Spanish	:	coche-restaurant, *m.* 276
Swedish	:	restaurang-vagn-en 276
Turkish	:	yemek arabasi 276
Russian	:	столоввагон-ресторан, *m.* 276
Serbian	:	ресторан вагон, *m.* 276
Ukrainian	:	вагон-ресторан, *m.* 276

277 DINING-ROOM s.

Czech	:	jídelna, *f.* 277
Danish	:	Spisestue, *m./c.* 277
Dutch	:	de eetkamer 277
Finnish	:	ruokasali 277
French	:	salle à manger, *f.* 277
German	:	das Esszimmer 277
Hungarian	:	ebédlö 277
Italian	:	sala da pranzo, *f.* 277
Croatian	:	blagovaonica, *f.* 277
Norwegian	:	spisestue, *m.* 277
Polish	:	jadalnia, *f.* 277
Portuguese	:	sala de jantar, *a* 277
Rumanian	:	sufrageriă, *f.* 277
Slovak	:	jedáleň, *f.* 277
Spanish	:	comedor, *m.* 277
Swedish	:	matsal-en 277
Turkish	:	yemek odası 277
Russian	:	столовая, *f.* 277
Serbian	:	трпезарија, *f.* 277
Ukrainian	:	їдальня, *f.* 277

278 DINNER s. (lunch)

Czech	:	oběd, *m.* 278
Danish	:	Middagsmad, *m./c.* 278
Dutch	:	het middageten 278
Finnish	:	lounas 278
French	:	déjeuner; dîner, *m.* 278
German	:	das Mittagessen 278
Hungarian	:	ebéd 278
Italian	:	pranzo, *m.* 278
Croatian	:	ručak, *m.* 278
Norwegian	:	middagsmat, *m.* 278
Polish	:	obiad, *m.* 278
Portuguese	:	almôço, *o* 278
Rumanian	:	masa de prănz 278
Slovak	:	obed, *m.* 278
Spanish	:	comida, *f.* 278
Swedish	:	middag-en 278
Turkish	:	öğle yemegi 278
Russian	:	обед, *m.* 278
Serbian	:	ручак, *m.* 278
Ukrainian	:	обід, *m.* 278

279 DIRTY adj.

Czech	:	špinavý 279
Danish	:	smudsig 279
Dutch	:	vuil 279
Finnish	:	likainen 279
French	:	sale 279
German	:	schmutzig 279
Hungarian	:	piszkos 279
Italian	:	sporco 279
Croatian	:	nečist 279
Norwegian	:	smussig 279
Polish	:	brudny 279
Portuguese	:	sujo 279
Rumanian	:	murdar 279
Slovak	:	špinavý 279
Spanish	:	sucio 279
Swedish	:	smutsig 279
Turkish	:	kirli 279
Russian	:	грязный 279
Serbian	:	нечист 279
Ukrainian	:	брудний 279

280 DISTRESS see 1031 TROUBLE

281 DO v. see 564 MAKE

282 DO AGAIN see 798 REPEAT

283 DOCUMENT s.

Czech	:	doklad, *m.*; spis, *m.* 283
Danish	:	Dokument, *c.* 283
Dutch	:	de acte 283
Finnish	:	asiakirja 283
French	:	document, *m.* 283
German	:	die Urkunde 283
Hungarian	:	ügyirat 283
Italian	:	documento, *m.* 283
Croatian	:	spis, *m.*; dokument, *m.* 283
Norwegian	:	aktstykke, *n.* 283
Polish	:	dokument, *m.* 283
Portuguese	:	documento, *o* 283
Rumanian	:	dosarul 283
Slovak	:	doklad, *m.*; spis, *m.* 283
Spanish	:	documento, *m.* 283
Swedish	:	aktstycke-t 283
Turkish	:	evrak 283
Russian	:	дело; акт, *m.* 283
Serbian	:	спис, *m.* 283
Ukrainian	:	документ, *m.* 283

42

284 DOG s.

Czech	: pes, m. 284
Danish	: Hund, m./c. 284
Dutch	: de hond 284
Finnish	: koira 284
French	: chien, m. 284
German	: der Hund 284
Hungarian	: kutya 284
Italian	: cane, m. 284
Croatian	: pas, m. 284
Norwegian	: hund, m. 284
Polish	: pies, m. 284
Portuguese	: cão, o 284
Rumanian	: cîinele, m. 284
Slovak	: pes, m. 284
Spanish	: perro, m. 284
Swedish	: hund-en 284
Turkish	: köpek 284
Russian	: собака, f; пес, m. 284
Serbian	: пас. m. 284
Ukrainian	: пес, m. 284

285 DONKEY s.

Czech	: osel, m. 285
Danish	: Äsel, c. 285
Dutch	: de ezel 285
Finnish	: aasi 285
French	: âne, m. 285
German	: der Esel 285
Hungarian	: szamár 285
Italian	: asino, m. 285
Croatian	: magarac, m. 285
Norwegian	: esel, n. 285
Polish	: osioł, m. 285
Portuguese	: burro, o 285
Rumanian	: măgarul 285
Slovak	: somár, m. 285
Spanish	: burro, m. 285
Swedish	: asna-n 285
Turkish	: eşek 285
Russian	: осел, m. 285
Serbian	: магарац, m. 285
Ukrainian	: осел, m. 285

286 DOOR s.

Czech	: dveře, pl. 286
Danish	: Dör, m./c. 286
Dutch	: de deur 286
Finnish	: ovi 286
French	: porte, f. 286
German	: die Türe 286
Hungarian	: ajtó 286
Italian	: porta, f. 286
Croatian	: vrata, f., pl. 286
Norwegian	: dör, f. 286
Polish	: drzwi, pl. 286
Portuguese	: porta, a 286
Rumanian	: uşă, f. 286
Slovak	: dvere, pl. 286
Spanish	: puerta, f. 286
Swedish	: dörren 286
Turkish	: kapi 286
Russian	: дверь, f. 286
Serbian	: врата, f. 286
Ukrainian	: двері, pl. 286

287 DRAWERS s. (am. TROUSERS OR PANTS)

Czech	: spodní kalhoty, pl. 287
Danish	: Underbukser, pl. 287
Dutch	: de onderbroek 287
Finnish	: alushousut 287
French	: caleçon, m. 287
German	: die Unterhose 287
Hungarian	: alsónadrág 287
Italian	: mutande, pl. f. 287
Croatian	: gaće, pl. 287
Norwegian	: underbukse, f. 287
Polish	: kalesony, pl. 287
Portuguese	: ceroulas, as 287
Rumanian	: ismenele, pl. 287
Slovak	: spodné nohavice, pl. 287
Spanish	: calzoncillos, pl. 287
Swedish	: kalsonger-na, pl. 287
Turkish	: iç pantalonu 287
Russian	: подштанники, pl. 287
Serbian	: raħe, pl. 287
Ukrainian	: підштанці, pl.; панталони, pl. 287

288 DRESS s.

Czech	: šaty (dámské), pl. 288
Danish	: Kjole, m./c. 288
Dutch	: de jurk; japon 288
Finnish	: leninki 288
French	: robe, f. 288
German	: das Kleid 288
Hungarian	: ruha 288
Italian	: vestito, m. 288
Croatian	: haljina, f. 288
Norwegian	: kjole, m. 288
Polish	: ubranie; suknia 288
Portuguese	: vestido, o 288
Rumanian	: rochia, f. 288
Slovak	: šaty, pl. 288
Spanish	: vestido, m. 288
Swedish	: klänning-en 288
Turkish	: elbise 288
Russian	: платье, n. 288
Serbian	: хаљина, f. 288
Ukrainian	: одяг, m. 288

289 DRESSING s. (an application for a wound)

Czech	: obvaz, m. 289
Danish	: Vorbinding, m./c. 289
Dutch	: het verband 289
Finnish	: side 289
French	: bandage, m. 289
German	: der Verband 289
Hungarian	: kötés 289
Italian	: fasciatura, f. 289
Croatian	: ovoj, m. 289
Norwegian	: forbinding, m. 289
Polish	: przewiazka, f. 289
Portuguese	: ligadura, a 289
Rumanian	: pansamentul 289
Slovak	: obväz, m. 289
Spanish	: vendaje, m. 289
Swedish	: förband-et 289
Turkish	: sarği 289
Russian	: перевязка, f. 289
Serbian	: превоj, m. 289
Ukrainian	: перевязь, f. 289

290 DRESSING-ROBE s. (gown)

Czech	:	župan, *m.* 290
Danish	:	Morgenkjole. *c.* 290
Dutch	:	de peignoir 290
Finnish	:	aamunuttu 290
French	:	peignoir, *m.* 290
German	:	der Morgenrock 290
Hungarian	:	pongyola 290
Italian	:	vestaglia, *f.* 290
Croatian	:	jutarnja halina, *f.* 290
Norwegian	:	slåbrok,*m.*; morgenkjole, *m.* 290
Polish	:	ubior ranny, *m.* 290
Portuguese	:	roupão, *o* 290
Rumanian	:	capotul 290
Slovak	:	župan, *m.* 290
Spanish	:	bata, *f.* 290
Swedish	:	morgonrock-en 290
Turkish	:	sabah entarisi 290
Russian	:	утренний халат, *m.* 290
Serbian	:	јутарња хаљина, *f.* 290
Ukrainian	:	ранній одяг, *m.* 290

291 DRINK v.

Czech	:	píti 291
Danish	:	drikke 291
Dutch	:	drinken 291
Finnish	:	juoda 291
French	:	boire 291
German	:	trinken 291
Hungarian	:	inni 291
Italian	:	bere 291
Croatian	:	piti 291
Norwegian	:	drikke 291
Polish	:	pić 291
Portuguese	:	beber 291
Rumanian	:	a bea 291
Slovak	:	pit' 291
Spanish	:	beber 291
Swedish	:	dricka 291
Turkish	:	içmek 291
Russian	:	пить 291
Serbian	:	пити 291
Ukrainian	:	пити 291

292 DRIVE v.

Czech	:	jeti; jezditi 292
Danish	:	køre 292
Dutch	:	rijden 292
Finnish	:	kulkea 292
French	:	aller en voiture 292
German	:	fahren 292
Hungarian	:	utazni 292
Italian	:	andare 292
Croatian	:	voziti 292
Norwegian	:	kjøre 292
Polish	:	jechać 292
Portuguese	:	andar de 292
Rumanian	:	a merge cu 292
Slovak	:	jazdit' 292
Spanish	:	ir en coche 292
Swedish	:	köra 292
Turkish	:	gitmek 292
Russian	:	ехать 292
Serbian	:	возити 292
Ukrainian	:	їхати 292

293 DRIVER s.

Czech	:	šofér, *m.* 293
Danish	:	Chauffeur, *m.* 293
Dutch	:	de chauffeur 293
Finnish	:	shoffööri 293
French	:	chauffeur, *m.* 293
German	:	der Chauffeur 293
Hungarian	:	gépkocsivezető 293
Italian	:	autista, *m.* 293
Croatian	:	šofer, *m.* 293
Norwegian	:	sjåför, *m.* 293
Polish	:	szofer, *m.* 293
Portuguese	:	motorista, *o* 293
Rumanian	:	şoferul 293
Slovak	:	vodič, *m.* 293
Spanish	:	chofer, *m.* 293
Swedish	:	chaufför-en 293
Turkish	:	şofer 293
Russian	:	шофер, *m.* 293
Serbian	:	шофер, *m.* 293
Ukrainian	:	шофер, *m.* 293

294 DRUG s. see 971 TABLET

295 DRUM s.

Czech	:	buben, *m.* 295
Danish	:	Tromme, *m./c.* 295
Dutch	:	de trommel 295
Finnish	:	rumpu 295
French	:	tambour, *m.* 295
German	:	die Trommel 295
Hungarian	:	dob 295
Italian	:	tamburo, *m.* 295
Croatian	:	bubajn, *m.* 295
Norwegian	:	tromme, *f.* 295
Polish	:	bęben, *m.* 295
Portuguese	:	tambor, *o* 295
Rumanian	:	tobă, *f.* 295
Slovak	:	bubon, *m.* 295
Spanish	:	pandereta, *f.* 295
Swedish	:	trumman 295
Turkish	:	davul 295
Russian	:	барабан, *m.* 295
Serbian	:	бубањ, *m.* 295
Ukrainian	:	барабан, *m.* 295

296 DUCK s.

Czech	:	kachna, *f.* 296
Danish	:	And, *m./c.* 296
Dutch	:	de eend 296
Finnish	:	sorsa; ankka 296
French	:	canard, *m.* 296
German	:	die Ente 296
Hungarian	:	kacsa 296
Italian	:	anitra, *f.* 296
Croatian	:	patka, *f.* 296
Norwegian	:	and, *f.* 296
Polish	:	kaczka, *f.* 296
Portuguese	:	pato, *o* 296
Rumanian	:	raţa, *f.* 296
Slovak	:	kačica, *f.* 296
Spanish	:	pato, *m.* 296
Swedish	:	anka-n 296
Turkish	:	ördek 296
Russian	:	утка, *f.* 296
Serbian	:	патка, *f.* 296
Ukrainian	:	качка, *f.* 296

297 EAR s.

Czech	:	ucho, *n.*; uši, *pl.* 297
Danish	:	Öre, *n.* 297
Dutch	:	het oor 297
Finnish	:	korva 297
French	:	oreille, *m.* 297
German	:	das Ohr 297
Hungarian	:	fül 297
Italian	:	orecchio, *m.* 297
Croatian	:	uho, *n.* 297
Norwegian	:	öre, *n.* 297
Polish	:	ucho, *n.* 297
Portuguese	:	orelha, *a* 297
Rumanian	:	urechea 297
Slovak	:	ucho, *n.* 297
Spanish	:	oreja, *f.* 297
Swedish	:	öra-t; öron-en, *pl.* 297
Turkish	:	kulak 297
Russian	:	ухо, *n.* 297
Serbian	:	ухо, *n.* 297
Ukrainian	:	вухо, *n.* 297

298 EAR-PROTECTOR s.

Czech	:	chránítko na uši, *n.* 298
Danish	:	Örebeskytter, *m./c.* 298
Dutch	:	de oorkleppen 298
Finnish	:	korvalappu 298
French	:	protège-oreille 298
German	:	der Ohrenschützer 298
Hungarian	:	fülvédő 298
Italian	:	proteggiorecchi 298
Croatian	:	štitnik za uši, *m.* 298
Norwegian	:	örebeskytter, *m.* 298
Polish	:	ochraniacze na ucha 298
Portuguese	:	protector das orelhas, *o* 298
Rumanian	:	aparatoarea de urechi 298
Slovak	:	chránítko na uši, *n.* 298
Spanish	:	orejera, *f.* 298
Swedish	:	öronvärmare-n 298
Turkish	:	kulak saklayan 298
Russian	:	ушегейки, *pl.* 298
Serbian	:	штит за уши, *m.* 298
Ukrainian	:	наушники, *pl.* 298

299 EAR-RING s.

Czech	:	naušnice, *f.* 299
Danish	:	Örering, *m./c.* 299
Dutch	:	de oorknop 299
Finnish	:	korvakoriste 299
French	:	boucle d'oreille, *f.* 299
German	:	der Ohrring 299
Hungarian	:	fülbevaló 299
Italian	:	orecchino, *m.* 299
Croatian	:	naušnica, *f.* 299
Norwegian	:	örering, *m.* 299
Polish	:	kólczyk, *m.* 299
Portuguese	:	brinco, *o* 299
Rumanian	:	cercelul 299
Slovak	:	náušnica, *f.* 299
Spanish	:	pendiente, *f.* 299
Swedish	:	örhänge-t 299
Turkish	:	küpe 299
Russian	:	серьга, *f.* 299
Serbian	:	минђуша, *m.* 299
Ukrainian	:	кульчик, *m.*; сережка, *f.* 299

300 EAST s.

Czech	:	východ, *m.* 300
Danish	:	öst, *c.* 300
Dutch	:	oosten 300
Finnish	:	itä 300
French	:	est; orient, *m.* 300
German	:	der Osten 300
Hungarian	:	kelet 300
Italian	:	levante; oriente; est, *m.* 300
Croatian	:	istok, *m.* 300
Norwegian	:	öst, *c.* 300
Polish	:	wschod, *m.* 300
Portuguese	:	éste, *m.*; oriental 300
Rumanian	:	est, *c.* 300
Slovak	:	východ, *m.* 300
Spanish	:	este; oriente, *m.* 300
Swedish	:	öster-n 300
Turkish	:	şark 300
Russian	:	восток, *m.* 300
Serbian	:	исток, *m.* 300
Ukrainian	:	схід, *m.* 300

301 EAT v.

Czech	:	jísti 301
Danish	:	spise 301
Dutch	:	eten 301
Finnish	:	syödä 301
French	:	manger 301
German	:	essen 301
Hungarian	:	enni 301
Italian	:	mangiare 301
Croatian	:	jesti 301
Norwegian	:	spise 301
Polish	:	jeść 301
Portuguese	:	comer 301
Rumanian	:	a mânca 301
Slovak	:	jest' 301
Spanish	:	comer 301
Swedish	:	äta 301
Turkish	:	yemek 301
Russian	:	есть 301
Serbian	:	јести 301
Ukrainian	:	їсти 301

302 EEL s.

Czech	:	úhoř, *m.* 302
Danish	:	Aal, *m./c.* 302
Dutch	:	de paling 302
Finnish	:	ankerias 302
French	:	l'anguille, *f.* 302
German	:	der Aal 302
Hungarian	:	angolna 302
Italian	:	Anguilla,*f.* 302
Croatian	:	jegulja, *f.* 302
Norwegian	:	ål, *c.* 302
Polish	:	węgorz, *m.* 302
Portuguese	:	enguia, *a* 302
Rumanian	:	tiparul 302
Slovak	:	úhoř, *m.* 302
Spanish	:	anguila, *f.* 302
Swedish	:	ål-en 302
Turkish	:	yilan baliği 302
Russian	:	угорь, *m.* 302
Serbian	:	јегуља, *f.* 302
Ukrainian	:	вугор, *m.* 302

303 EGG *s.*

Czech	:	vejce, *n.* 303
Danish	:	Äg, *c.* 303
Dutch	:	het ei 303
Finnish	:	muna 303
French	:	oeuf, *m.* 303
German	:	das Ei 303
Hungarian	:	tojás 303
Italian	:	uovo, *m.* 303
Croatian	:	jaje, *n.* 303
Norwegian	:	egg, *n.* 303
Polish	:	jajo, *n.* 303
Portuguese	:	ôvo, *o* 303
Rumanian	:	oul, *c.* 303
Slovak	:	vajce, *n.* 303
Spanish	:	huevo, *m.* 303
Swedish	:	ägg-et 303
Turkish	:	yumurta 303
Russian	:	яйцо, *n.* 303
Serbian	:	jaje, *n.* 303
Ukrainian	:	яйце, *n.* 303

304 EIGHT

Czech	:	osm 304
Danish	:	otte 304
Dutch	:	acht 304
Finnish	:	kahdeksan 304
French	:	huit 304
German	:	acht 304
Hungarian	:	nyole 304
Italian	:	otto 304
Croatian	:	osam 304
Norwegian	:	åtte 304
Polish	:	osiem 304
Portuguese	:	oito 304
Rumanian	:	opt 304
Slovak	:	osem 304
Spanish	:	ocho 304
Swedish	:	atta 304
Turkish	:	sekiz 304
Russian	:	восемь 304
Serbian	:	осам 304
Ukrainian	:	вісім 304

305 EIGHTEEN

Czech	:	osmnáct 305
Danish	:	atten 305
Dutch	:	achttien 305
Finnish	:	kahdeksantoista 305
French	:	dix-huit 305
German	:	achtzehn 305
Hungarian	:	tizennyolc 305
Italian	:	diciótto 305
Croatian	:	osamnaest 305
Norwegian	:	atten 305
Polish	:	osicmnascie 305
Portuguese	:	dezóito 305
Rumanian	:	optsprezece 305
Slovak	:	osemnást' 305
Spanish	:	diez y ocho 305
Swedish	:	åderton 305
Turkish	:	on sekiz 305
Russian	:	восемнадцать 305
Serbian	:	осамнаест 305
Ukrainian	:	вісімнадцять 305

306 EIGHTY

Czech	:	osmdesát 306
Danish	:	firs 306
Dutch	:	tachtig 306
Finnish	:	kahdeksankymmentä 306
French	:	quatre-vingt 306
German	:	achtzig 306
Hungarian	:	nyolcvan 306
Italian	:	ottanta 306
Croatian	:	osamdeset 306
Norwegian	:	åtti 306
Polish	:	osiemdziesiąt 306
Portuguese	:	iotenta 306
Rumanian	:	optzeci 306
Slovak	:	osemdesiat 306
Spanish	:	ochenta 306
Swedish	:	åttio 306
Turkish	:	seksen 306
Russian	:	восемьдесят 306
Serbian	:	осемдесет 306
Ukrainian	:	вісімдесять 306

307 ELBOW *s.*

Czech	:	loket, *m.* 307
Danish	:	Albue, *m./c.* 307
Dutch	:	de elboog 307
Finnish	:	kyynärpää 307
French	:	coude, *m.* 307
German	:	der Ellbogen 307
Hungarian	:	könyök 307
Italian	:	gomito, *m.* 307
Croatian	:	lakat, *m.* 307
Norwegian	:	albue, *m.* 307
Polish	:	łokieć, *m.* 307
Portuguese	:	cotovêlo, *o* 307
Rumanian	:	cotul 307
Slovak	:	laket', *m.* 307
Spanish	:	codo, *m.* 307
Swedish	:	armbåge-n 307
Turkish	:	dirsek 307
Russian	:	локоть, *m.* 307
Serbian	:	лакат, *m.* 307
Ukrainian	:	лікоть, *m.* 307

308 ELECTRIC-LIGHT BULB *s.*

Czech	:	elektrická žárovka, *f.* 308
Danish	:	Lyspäre, *m./c.* 308
Dutch	:	de peer 308
Finnish	:	hehkulamppu 308
French	:	ampoule électrique, *f.* 308
German	:	die Glühbirne 308
Hungarian	:	villanykörte 308
Italian	:	lampadina, *f.* 308
Croatian	:	sijalica, *f.* 308
Norwegian	:	lyspäre, *c.* 308
Polish	:	żarówka, *f.* 308
Portuguese	:	lâmpada eléctrica, *f.* 308
Rumanian	:	becul 308
Slovak	:	žiarovka, *f.* 308
Spanish	:	bombilla, *f.* 308
Swedish	:	glödlampa-n 308
Turkish	:	elektrik ampulu 308
Russian	:	электрическая лампочки, *f.* 308
Serbian	:	сијалица, *f.* 308
Ukrainian	:	жарівка, *f.* 308

46

309 ELEVATOR *s.*

Czech	: zdviž, *f.*; výtah, *m.*	309
Danish	: Elevator, *c.*	309
Dutch	: de lift	309
Finnish	: hissi	309
French	: ascenseur, *m.*	309
German	: der Fahrstuhl	309
Hungarian	: felvenó	309
Italian	: ascensore, *m.*	309
Croatian	: lift, *m.*	309
Norwegian	: heis, *m.*; elevator, *m.*	309
Polish	: winda, *f.*	309
Portuguese	: elevador, *o*	309
Rumanian	: ascensorul	309
Slovak	: výt'ah, *m.*	309
Spanish	: ascensor, *m.*	309
Swedish	: hiss-en	309
Turkish	: asansör	309
Russian	: лифт, *m.*	309
Serbian	: лифт, *m.*	309
Ukrainian	: ліфт, *m.*; підвижня, *f.*	309

310 ELEVEN

Czech	: jedenáct	310
Danish	: elleve	310
Dutch	: elf	310
Finnish	: yksitoista	310
French	: onze	310
German	: elf	310
Hungarian	: tizenegy	310
Italian	: úndici	310
Croatian	: jedanaest	310
Norwegian	: elleve	310
Polish	: jedenaście	310
Portuguese	: onze	310
Rumanian	: unsprezece	310
Slovak	: jedenást'	310
Spanish	: once	310
Swedish	: elfva	310
Turkish	: on bir	310
Russian	: одиннадцать	310
Serbian	: jеданаест	310
Ukrainian	: одинадять	310

311 ENGINE *s.*

Czech	: lokomotiva, *f.*	311
Danish	: Lokomotiv, *n.*	311
Dutch	: de locomotief	311
Finnish	: veturi	311
French	: locomotive, *f.*	311
German	: die Lokomotive	311
Hungarian	: mozdony	311
Italian	: locomotiva, *f.*	311
Croatian	: lokomotiva, *f.*	311
Norwegian	: lokomotiv, *n.*	311
Polish	: lokomotywa, *f.*	311
Portuguese	: locomotiva, *a*	311
Rumanian	: locomotiva, *a.*	311
Slovak	: lokomotíva, *f.*	311
Spanish	: locomotora, *f.*	311
Swedish	: lokomotiv-et	311
Turkish	: lokomotiv	311
Russian	: локомотив, *m.*; паравоз	311
Serbian	: локомотива, *f.*	311
Ukrainian	: льокомотива, *f.*	311

312 ENGLISH *adj.*

Czech	: anglický	312
Danish	: engelsk	312
Dutch	: Engels	312
Finnish	: engelsk	312
French	: anglais	312
German	: englisch	312
Hungarian	: angol (ul)	312
Italian	: inglese	312
Croatian	: engleski	312
Norwegian	: engelsk	312
Polish	: angielski	312
Portuguese	: inglés	312
Rumanian	: englez	312
Slovak	: anglický	312
Spanish	: inglés	312
Swedish	: engels	312
Turkish	: ingiliz	312
Russian	: англиский	312
Serbian	: енглески	312
Ukrainian	: англійський	312

313 ENROLL *v.* see **793 REGISTER**

314 ENTRANCE *s.*

Czech	: vchod, *m.*	314
Danish	: Indgang, *m./c.*	314
Dutch	: de ingang	314
Finnish	: sisänkäytävä	314
French	: entrée, *f.*	314
German	: der Eingang	314
Hungarian	: bejárat	314
Italian	: ingresso, *m.*	314
Croatian	: ulaz, *m.*	314
Norwegian	: inngang, *m.*	314
Polish	: wejscie, *n.*	314
Portuguese	: entrada, *a*	314
Rumanian	: intrarea	314
Slovak	: vchod, *m.*	314
Spanish	: entrada, *f.*	314
Swedish	: ingång-en	314
Turkish	: giriş	314
Russian	: вход, *m.*	314
Serbian	: улаз, *m.*	314
Ukrainian	: вхід, *m.*	314

315 ENTRAP *v.* see **178 CATCH**

316 EVENING *s.*

Czech	: večer, *m.*	316
Danish	: Aften, *m.*	316
Dutch	: de avond	316
Finnish	: ilta	316
French	: soir, *m.*	316
German	: der Abend	316
Hungarian	: este	316
Italian	: sera, *f.*	316
Croatian	: veće, *n.*	316
Norwegian	: aften, *m.*	316
Polish	: wieczór, *m.*	316
Portuguese	: noite, *a*	316
Rumanian	: seară, *f.*	316
Slovak	: večer, *m.*	316
Spanish	: noche, *f.*	316
Swedish	: afton-en; kväll-en	316
Turkish	: ekşam	316
Russian	: вечер, *m.*	316
Serbian	: вече, *n.*	316
Ukrainian	: вечір, *m.*	316

317 EXCHANGE-OFFICE s.

Czech : směnárna, f. 317
Danish : Vekselerer-kontor, n. 317
Dutch : het wissel kantor 317
Finnish : rahanvaihtokonttori 317
French : le bureau de change 317
German : die Wechselstube 317
Hungarian : pénzváltóhely 317
Italian : ufficio cambiavalute, m. 317
Croatian : mjenjačnica, f. 317
Norwegian : vekselérkontor, n. 317
Polish : kantor wymiany, m. 317
Portuguese : casa de câmbio, a 317
Rumanian : biroul de schimb 317
Slovak : zmenáreň, f. 317
Spanish : oficina de cambio, f. 317
Swedish : växelkontor-et 317
Turkish : sarrâf dükkâni 317
Russian : меняльная лавка, f. 317
Serbian : мењачница, f. 317
Ukrainian : розмінна контора, f. 317

318 EXCUSE v.

Czech : prominouti; odpustiti 318
Danish : undskylde 318
Dutch : verontschuldigen 318
Finnish : antaa anteeksi 318
French : excuser 318
German : entschuldigen 318
Hungarian : menteget 318
Italian : scusare 318
Croatian : ispričati (se) 318
Norwegian : unnskylde 318
Polish : przebatrzyć 318
Portuguese : dá me licença! 318
Rumanian : a scuza 318
Slovak : odpustit' 318
Spanish : excusa 318
Swedish : ursäkta 318
Turkish : affetmek 318
Russian : извинять(ся) 318
Serbian : испричати се 318
Ukrainian : звільняти 318

319 EXERCISES see 430 GYMNASTICS

320 EXHAUSTED see 1007 TIRED

321 EXIST v. see 72 BE

322 EXIT s.

Czech : východ, m. 322
Danish : Udgang, m. 322
Dutch : de uitgang 322
Finnish : uloskäytävä 322
French : sortie, f. 322
German : der Ausgang 322
Hungarian : kijárat 322
Italian : uscita, f. 322
Croatian : izlaz, m. 322
Norwegian : utgang, m. 322
Polish : wyjscie, n. 322
Portuguese : saída, a 322
Rumanian : eşirea 322
Slovak : východ, m. 322
Spanish : salida, f. 322
Swedish : utgång-en 322
Turkish : çikis 322
Russian : выход, m. 322
Serbian : излаз, m. 322
Ukrainian : вихід, m. 322

323 EXPENSIVE adj.

Czech : drahý; nákladný 323
Danish : udvidelig 323
Dutch : duur 323
Finnish : kallis 323
French : cher; coûteux 323
German : teuer 323
Hungarian : drága 323
Italian : dispendioso 323
Croatian : skup 323
Norwegian : dyr 323
Polish : drogy 323
Portuguese : caro 323
Rumanian : scump 323
Slovak : drahý 323
Spanish : costoso 323
Swedish : dyr; kostsam 323
Turkish : pahali 323
Russian : дорогой 323
Serbian : скуп 323
Ukrainian : дорогий 323

324 EXTENSIVE see 518 LARGE

325 EXTREMELY see 1057 VERY

326 EYE s.

Czech : oko, n.; oči, pl. 326
Danish : Öje, n. 326
Dutch : het oog 326
Finnish : silmä(t) 326
French : oeil, m.; yeux, m. pl. 326
German : das Auge 326
Hungarian : szem 326
Italian : occhi, m. pl. 326
Croatian : oko, n. 326
Norwegian : öye, n. 326
Polish : oko, m.; oczy, pl. 326
Portuguese : ôlho, o 326
Rumanian : ochiul 326
Slovak : oko, n. 326
Spanish : ojo, m. 326
Swedish : öga-t, ögon-en 326
Turkish : gözler 326
Russian : глаза, pl. 326
Serbian : око, n. 326
Ukrainian : око, n. 326

327 EYE GLASSES s. (spectacles)

Czech : brýle, pl. 327
Danish : Briller, pl. 327
Dutch : de bril 327
Finnish : silmälasit 327
French : lunettes, f. pl. 327
German : die Brille 327
Hungarian : szemüveg 327
Italian : occhiali, m. pl. 327
Croatian : naočari, pl. 327
Norwegian : briller, pl. 327
Polish : okulary, pl. 327
Portuguese : óculos, os 327
Rumanian : ochelarii, pl. 327
Slovak : okuliare, pl. 327
Spanish : anteojos, pl. 327
Swedish : glasögon-en 327
Turkish : gözluk 327
Russian : очки, pl. 327
Serbian : наочари, pl. 327
Ukrainian : окуляри, pl. 327

328 FACE s.

Czech	:	obličej, m. 328
Danish	:	Ansigt, n. 328
Dutch	:	het gezicht 328
Finnish	:	kasvot 328
French	:	visage, m. 328
German	:	das Gesicht 328
Hungarian	:	arc 328
Italian	:	faccia, f. 328
Croatian	:	lice, n. 328
Norwegian	:	ansikt, n. 328
Polish	:	twarz, f. 328
Portuguese	:	rosto, o 328
Rumanian	:	fată, f. 328
Slovak	:	obličaj, m. 328
Spanish	:	cara, f. 328
Swedish	:	ansikte-t 328
Turkish	:	yüz 328
Russian	:	лицо, n. 328
Serbian	:	лице, n. 328
Ukrainian	:	лице, n. 328

331 FAR adv.

Czech	:	daleko 331
Danish	:	fjern 331
Dutch	:	ver 331
Finnish	:	pitkä 331
French	:	loin 331
German	:	weit 331
Hungarian	:	széles 331
Italian	:	lontano 331
Croatian	:	dalek 331
Norwegian	:	vidt 331
Polish	:	daleko 331
Portuguese	:	distante; longe 331
Rumanian	:	departe 331
Slovak	:	d'aleko 331
Spanish	:	lejos 331
Swedish	:	fjärran 331
Turkish	:	uzak 331
Russian	:	далеко 331
Serbian	:	далек 331
Ukrainian	:	далеко 331

329 FACTORY s.

Czech	:	tovární, f. 329
Danish	:	Fabrik, c. 329
Dutch	:	de fabriek 329
Finnish	:	tehdas 329
French	:	usine, f. 329
German	:	die Fabrik 329
Hungarian	:	gyár 329
Italian	:	fabbrica, f. 329
Croatian	:	tvornica, f. 329
Norwegian	:	fabrikk, m. 329
Polish	:	fabryka, f. 329
Portuguese	:	fábrica, a 329
Rumanian	:	fabrică, f. 329
Slovak	:	továreň, f. 329
Spanish	:	fábrica, f. 329
Swedish	:	fabrik-en 329
Turkish	:	fabrika 329
Russian	:	фабрика, f. 329
Serbian	:	творница, f. 329
Ukrainian	:	фабрика, f. 329

332 FARM s.

Czech	:	selský dvůr, m.; farma, f. 332
Danish	:	Bondegaard, m./c. 332
Dutch	:	de boerenhoeve 332
Finnish	:	talonpoikaiskartano 332
French	:	ferme, f. 332
German	:	der Bauernhof 332
Hungarian	:	a tanya 332
Italian	:	podere, m. 332
Croatian	:	seljački posjed, m. 332
Norwegian	:	bondegård, m. 332
Polish	:	gospodarstwo wiejskie, n. 332
Portuguese	:	herdade, a 332
Rumanian	:	curtea tăăneasca, f. 332
Slovak	:	sedliacky dvor, m. 332
Spanish	:	granja, f. 332
Swedish	:	bondgård-en 332
Turkish	:	çiftlik 332
Russian	:	хутор, m. 332
Serbian	:	сельачко газдинство, n. 332
Ukrainian	:	хутір, m.; обійстя, n; ферма, f. 332

330 FALL s. (Autumn)

Czech	:	podzim, m. 330
Danish	:	Efteraar 330
Dutch	:	de herfst 330
Finnish	:	syksy 330
French	:	automne, m. 330
German	:	der Herbst 330
Hungarian	:	ösz 330
Italian	:	autunno, m. 330
Croatian	:	jesen, f. 330
Norwegian	:	höst, m. 330
Polish	:	jesień, f. 330
Portuguese	:	outono, o 330
Rumanian	:	toamnă, f. 330
Slovak	:	jeseň, f. 330
Spanish	:	otoño, m. 330
Swedish	:	höst-en 330
Turkish	:	sonbahar 330
Russian	:	осень, f. 330
Serbian	:	јесен, f. 330
Ukrainian	:	осінь, f. 330

333 FARM-HOUSE s.

Czech	:	statek, m.; selské stavení, n. 333
Danish	:	Bondehus, n. 333
Dutch	:	het boerenhuis 333
Finnish	:	talonpoikaistalo 333
French	:	ferme, f. 333
German	:	das Bauernhaus 333
Hungarian	:	parasztház 333
Italian	:	casa del contadino, f. 333
Croatian	:	seljačka kuća, f. 333
Norwegian	:	bondegård, m. 333
Polish	:	chata, f. 333
Portuguese	:	casa de campo, a 333
Rumanian	:	ırı вѕаѕ ıneasca, f. 333
Slovak	:	sedliacky dom, m. 333
Spanish	:	casería, f. 333
Swedish	:	bondgård-en 333
Turkish	:	köyevi 333
Russian	:	крестьянский дом, m. 333
Serbian	:	сельачка куħа, f. 333
Ukrainian	:	селянська хата, f. 333

334 FATHER s.

Czech	:	otec, *m.* 334
Danish	:	fader, *m.* 334
Dutch	:	vader, m. 334
Finnish	:	isä 334
French	:	père, *m.* 334
German	:	Vater, *m.* 334
Hungarian	:	atya; apa 334
Italian	:	padre, *m.* 334
Croatian	:	otac, *m.* 334
Norwegian	:	far, *c./m.* 334
Polish	:	ojciec, *m.* 334
Portuguese	:	pal, *m.* 334
Rumanian	:	tată, *m.* 334
Slovak	:	otec, *m.* 334
Spanish	:	padre, *m.* 334
Swedish	:	fader-en 334
Turkish	:	peder; baba 334
Russian	:	отец, *m.* 334
Serbian	:	отач, *m.* 334
Ukrainian	:	батько, *m.* 334

335 FATIGUED see 1007 TIRED

336 FEBRUARY s.

Czech	:	únor, *m.* 336
Danish	:	Februar 336
Dutch	:	Februari 336
Finnish	:	helmikuu 336
French	:	février, *m.* 336
German	:	der Februar 336
Hungarian	:	február 336
Italian	:	febbraio, *m.* 336
Croatian	:	veljača, *f.* 336
Norwegian	:	februar 336
Polish	:	luty, *m.* 336
Portuguese	:	fevereiro, *m.* 336
Rumanian	:	Februari, *m.* 336
Slovak	:	február, *m.* 336
Spanish	:	febrero 336
Swedish	:	februari 336
Turkish	:	subat 336
Russian	:	февраль 336
Serbian	:	фебруар 336
Ukrainian	:	Лютень 336

337 FEED v.

Czech	:	krmiti 337
Danish	:	fodre 337
Dutch	:	voederen 337
Finnish	:	ruokkia 337
French	:	nourrir 337
German	:	füttern 337
Hungarian	:	etetni 337
Italian	:	dar da mangiare 337
Croatian	:	krmiti 337
Norwegian	:	fore 337
Polish	:	karmić 337
Portuguese	:	dar de comer 337
Rumanian	:	a da de mîncare 337
Slovak	:	krmit' 337
Spanish	:	alimentar 337
Swedish	:	göda 337
Turkish	:	yem vermek 337
Russian	:	кормить 337
Serbian	:	хранити 337
Ukrainian	:	кормити 337

338 FERRY s.

Czech	:	převoz, *m.* 338
Danish	:	Färge, *f./c.* 338
Dutch	:	de veer 338
Finnish	:	lautta 338
French	:	bac, *m.* 338
German	:	die Fähre 338
Hungarian	:	komp 338
Italian	:	chiatta, *m.* 338
Croatian	:	skela, *f.* 338
Norwegian	:	ferje, *f.* 338
Polish	:	prom, *m.* 338
Portuguese	:	balsa, *a* 338
Rumanian	:	luntra de trecere 338
Slovak	:	prievoz, *m.* 338
Spanish	:	barca, *f.* 338
Swedish	:	färja-n 338
Turkish	:	sal 338
Russian	:	паром, *m.* 338
Serbian	:	скела, *f.* 338
Ukrainian	:	порон, *m.* 338

339 FEW adv. (little)

Czech	:	málo 339
Danish	:	få; lille 339
Dutch	:	weinig 339
Finnish	:	vähä 339
French	:	peu; petit 339
German	:	wenig 339
Hungarian	:	kevés 339
Italian	:	poco 339
Croatian	:	malo 339
Norwegian	:	lite 339
Polish	:	troche 339
Portuguese	:	alguns 339
Rumanian	:	putin 339
Slovak	:	málo; trocha 339
Spanish	:	pocos 339
Swedish	:	och; några 3339
Turkish	:	az; birkaç 339
Russian	:	мало 339
Serbian	:	мало 339
Ukrainian	:	мало 339

340 FIELD see 3 ACRES

341 FIFTEEN

Czech	:	patnáct 341
Danish	:	femten 341
Dutch	:	vijftien 341
Finnish	:	viisitoista 341
French	:	quinze 341
German	:	fünfzehn 341
Hungarian	:	tizenöt 341
Italian	:	quindici 341
Croatian	:	petnaest 341
Norwegian	:	femten 341
Polish	:	pietnaśćie 341
Portuguese	:	quinze 341
Rumanian	:	cincisprezece 341
Slovak	:	pätnást' 341
Spanish	:	quince 341
Swedish	:	femton 341
Turkish	:	on beş 341
Russian	:	пятнадцать 341
Serbian	:	петнаест 341
Ukrainian	:	пятнадцать 341

50

342 FIFTY

Czech	:	padesát 342
Danish	:	halvtres 342
Dutch	:	vijftig 342
Finnish	:	viisikymmentä 342
French	:	cinquante 342
German	:	fünfzig 342
Hungarian	:	ötven 342
Italian	:	cinquanta 342
Croatian	:	pedeset 342
Norwegian	:	femti 342
Polish	:	piędziesiąt 342
Portuguese	:	cinqüenta 342
Rumanian	:	cincizeci 342
Slovak	:	pätdesiat 342
Spanish	:	cincuenta 342
Swedish	:	femtio 342
Turkish	:	elli 342
Russian	:	пятьдесят 342
Serbian	:	педесет 342
Ukrainian	:	пятьдесять 342

343 FIG s.

Czech	:	fík, m. 343
Danish	:	Figen, m./c. 343
Dutch	:	de vijg 343
Finnish	:	viikuna 343
French	:	figue, f. 343
German	:	die Feige 343
Hungarian	:	füge 343
Italian	:	fico, m. 343
Croatian	:	smokva, f. 343
Norwegian	:	fiken, m. 343
Polish	:	figa, f. 343
Portuguese	:	figo, o 343
Rumanian	:	smochină, f. 343
Slovak	:	figa, f. 343
Spanish	:	higo, m. 343
Swedish	:	fikon-et 343
Turkish	:	incir 343
Russian	:	фига, f. 343
Serbian	:	смоква, f. 343
Ukrainian	:	фіга, f. 343

344 FILE s. (a metal tool)

Czech	:	pilník, m. 344
Danish	:	Fil, m./c. 344
Dutch	:	de vijl 344
Finnish	:	viila 344
French	:	lime, f. 344
German	:	die Feile 344
Hungarian	:	reszelö 344
Italian	:	lima, f. 344
Croatian	:	pila, f. 344
Norwegian	:	fil, m. 344
Polish	:	pilnik, m. 344
Portuguese	:	lima, a 344
Rumanian	:	pilă, f. 344
Slovak	:	pilník, m. 344
Spanish	:	lima, f. 344
Swedish	:	fil-en 344
Turkish	:	eğe 344
Russian	:	напильник, m. 344
Serbian	:	пила, f. 344
Ukrainian	:	пильник, m. 344

345 FILLING STATION s.

Czech	:	čerpací stanice, f.; benzinová pumpa, f. 345
Danish	:	Tank (station), m./c. 345
Dutch	:	de benzinepomp 345
Finnish	:	bensiiniasema 345
French	:	poste d'essence, m. 345
German	:	die Tankstelle 345
Hungarian	:	a benzintank 345
Italian	:	posto rifornimento 345
Croatian	:	benzinska stanica, f. 345
Norwegian	:	bensin-stasjon, m. 345
Polish	:	stacja benzynowa, f. 345
Portuguese	:	pôsto de abastecimento, o 345
Rumanian	:	depozitul de benzină 345
Slovak	:	benzínová pumpa, f. 345
Spanish	:	el depósito de gasolina 345
Swedish	:	bensin-station-en 345
Turkish	:	tank yeri 345
Russian	:	бензиновая помпа, f. 345
Serbian	:	бензинска станица, f. 345
Ukrainian	:	бензинова станица, f. 345

346 FILM s.

Czech	:	film, m. 346
Danish	:	Film, m./c. 346
Dutch	:	de film 346
Finnish	:	filmi 346
French	:	film, m. 346
German	:	der Film 346
Hungarian	:	a film 346
Italian	:	pellicola, f. 346
Croatian	:	film, m. 346
Norwegian	:	film, m. 346
Polish	:	film, m. 346
Portuguese	:	filme, o 346
Rumanian	:	filmul 346
Slovak	:	film, m. 346
Spanish	:	película, f. 346
Swedish	:	film-en 346
Turkish	:	filim 346
Russian	:	фильм, m. 346
Serbian	:	филм, m. 346
Ukrainian	:	фільм, m. 346

347 FIND v.

Czech	:	nalézti; nalézati 347
Danish	:	finde 347
Dutch	:	vinden 347
Finnish	:	löytää 347
French	:	trouver 347
German	:	finden 347
Hungarian	:	talál; lel 347
Italian	:	trovare 347
Croatian	:	nalaziti 347
Norwegian	:	finne 347
Polish	:	nalazić 347
Portuguese	:	achar 347
Rumanian	:	a găsi 347
Slovak	:	nájst' 347
Spanish	:	hallar; encontrar 347
Swedish	:	finna 347
Turkish	:	bulmak 347
Russian	:	находить 347
Serbian	:	налазити 347
Ukrainian	:	находити 347

348 FINGER s. (fingers)

Czech	:	prst, *m.*; prsty, *pl.* 348
Danish	:	Finger, *m./c.* 348
Dutch	:	de vinger 348
Finnish	:	sormi 348
French	:	doigt, *m.* 348
German	:	der Finger 348
Hungarian	:	ujj 348
Italian	:	dito,*f.*; dita, *f. pl.* 348
Croatian	:	prst, *m.* 348
Norwegian	:	finger, *m.* 348
Polish	:	palec, *m.*; palce, *pl.* 348
Portuguese	:	dedo, *o* 348
Rumanian	:	degetul 348
Slovak	:	prst, *m.* 348
Spanish	:	dedo, *m.* 348
Swedish	:	finger, fingret; **fingrar-na**, *pl.* 348
Turkish	:	parmaklar 348
Russian	:	палец, *m.* 348
Serbian	:	прст, *m.* 348
Ukrainian	:	пальці, *pl.* 348

349 FINGER-NAIL s.

Czech	:	nehet, *m.* 349
Danish	:	Fingernegl, *m./c.* 349
Dutch	:	de nagel 349
Finnish	:	kynsi 349
French	:	ongle, *m.* 349
German	:	der Fingernagel 349
Hungarian	:	köröm 349
Italian	:	unghia,*f.* 349
Croatian	:	nokat, *m.* 349
Norwegian	:	negl, *m.* 349
Polish	:	paznokć, *m.* 349
Portuguese	:	unha, *a* 349
Rumanian	:	unghia degetului 349
Slovak	:	necht, *m.* 349
Spanish	:	uña, *f.* 349
Swedish	:	nagel-n 349
Turkish	:	tirnak 349
Russian	:	ноготь, *m.* 349
Serbian	:	накат, *m.* 349
Ukrainian	:	ніготь, *m.* 349

350 FIRE s.

Czech	:	oheň, *m.* 350
Danish	:	Ild, *m./c.* 350
Dutch	:	het vuur 350
Finnish	:	tuli 350
French	:	feu, *m.* 350
German	:	das Feuer 350
Hungarian	:	tüz 350
Italian	:	fuoco, *m.* 350
Croatian	:	vatra, *f.* 350
Norwegian	:	ild, *m.* 350
Polish	:	ogień, *m.* 350
Portuguese	:	fogo, *o* 350
Rumanian	:	focul 350
Slovak	:	oheň, *m.* 350
Spanish	:	fuego, *m.* 350
Swedish	:	eld-en 350
Turkish	:	ateş 350
Russian	:	огонь, *m.* 350
Serbian	:	ватра, *f.* 350
Ukrainian	:	вогонь, *m.* 350

351 FIRST FLOOR s. (Am. second floor)

Czech	:	první poschodí, *n.* 351
Danish	:	förste Sal 351
Dutch	:	de eerste verdieping 351
Finnish	:	ensimmäinen kerros 351
French	:	premier étage, *m.* 351
German	:	der erste Stock 351
Hungarian	:	elsö emelet 351
Italian	:	primo piano, *m.* 351
Croatian	:	prvi sprat, *m.* 351
Norwegian	:	annen etasje 351
Polish	:	pierwsze piętro 351
Portuguese	:	primeiro andar, *o* 351
Rumanian	:	etajul intâiu 351
Slovak	:	prvé poschodie, *n.* 351
Spanish	:	piso primero 351
Swedish	:	en trappa upp 351
Turkish	:	birnci kat 351
Russian	:	второй этаж, *m.* 351
Serbian	:	први спрат, *m.* 351
Ukrainian	:	перший поверх, *m.* 351

352 FIR-TREE s.

Czech	:	jedle, *f.* 352
Danish	:	Ädelgran; Gran, *f./c.* 352
Dutch	:	de den 352
Finnish	:	hopeakuusi 352
French	:	sapin, *m.* 352
German	:	die Tanne 352
Hungarian	:	fenyö 352
Italian	:	abete, *m.* 352
Croatian	:	jela, *f.* 352
Norwegian	:	gran, *f.* 352
Polish	:	jodła, *f.* 352
Portuguese	:	abeto, *o* 352
Rumanian	:	bradul 352
Slovak	:	jedl'a, *f.* 352
Spanish	:	abeto, *m.* 352
Swedish	:	tall-en 352
Turkish	:	çirca ağaci 352
Russian	:	пихта, f. 352
Serbian	:	јела, *f.* 352
Ukrainian	:	ялина, *f.* 352

353 FISH s.

Czech	:	ryba, *f.* 353
Danish	:	Fisk, *c.* 353
Dutch	:	de vis 353
Finnish	:	kala 353
French	:	poisson, *m.* 353
German	:	der Fisch 353
Hungarian	:	hal 353
Italian	:	pesce, *m.* 353
Croatian	:	riba, *f.* 353
Norwegian	:	fisk, *m.* 353
Polish	:	ryba, *f.* 353
Portuguese	:	peixe, *o* 353
Rumanian	:	peştele 353
Slovak	:	ryba, *f.* 353
Spanish	:	pez, *m.* 353
Swedish	:	fisk-en 353
Turkish	:	balik 353
Russian	:	рыба, *f.* 353
Serbian	:	риба, *f.* 353
Ukrainian	:	риба, *f.* 353

354 FIST *s.*

Czech	: pěst, *f.* 354
Danish	: knyttet Haand 354
Dutch	: de vuist 354
Finnish	: nyrkki 354
French	: poing, *m.* 354
German	: die Faust 354
Hungarian	: ököl 354
Italian	: pugno, *m.* 354
Croatian	: šaka, *f.* 354
Norwegian	: neve, *m.* 354
Polish	: pieść, *f.* 354
Portuguese	: punho, *o* 354
Rumanian	: pumnul 354
Slovak	: päst, *f.* 354
Spanish	: puño, *m.* 354
Swedish	: knytnäve-n 354
Turkish	: yumruk 354
Russian	: кулак, *m.* 354
Serbian	: шака, *f.* 354
Ukrainian	: пястук, *m.* 354

357 FLAX *s.*

Czech	: len, *m.* 357
Danish	: Hör, *c.* 357
Dutch	: het vlas 357
Finnish	: pellava 357
French	: lin, *m.* 357
German	: der Flachs 357
Hungarian	: a kender 357
Italian	: lino, *m.* 357
Croatian	: lan, *m.* 357
Norwegian	: lin, *n.* 357
Polish	: len, *m.* 357
Portuguese	: linho, *o* 357
Rumanian	: inul 357
Slovak	: ľan, *m.* 357
Spanish	: lino, *m.* 357
Swedish	: lin-et 357
Turkish	: keten 357
Russian	: лен, *m.* 357
Serbian	: лан, *m.* 357
Ukrainian	: льон, *m.* 357

355 FIVE

Czech	: pět 355
Danish	: fem 355
Dutch	: vijf 355
Finnish	: viisi 355
French	: cinq 355
German	: fünf 355
Hungarian	: öt 355
Italian	: cinque 355
Croatian	: pet 355
Norwegian	: fem 355
Polish	: pięć 355
Portuguese	: cinco 355
Rumanian	: cinci 355
Slovak	: pät 355
Spanish	: cinco 355
Swedish	: fem 355
Turkish	: beş 355
Russian	: пять 355
Serbian	: пет 355
Ukrainian	: пять 355

358 FLEA *s.*

Czech	: blecha, *f.* 358
Danish	: Loppe, *m./c.* 358
Dutch	: de vloo 358
Finnish	: kirppu 358
French	: puce, *f.* 358
German	: der Floh 358
Hungarian	: bolha 358
Italian	: pulce, *f.* 358
Croatian	: buha, *f.* 358
Norwegian	: loppe, *f.* 358
Polish	: pchła, *f.* 358
Portuguese	: pulga, *a* 358
Rumanian	: puricele, *m.* 358
Slovak	: blcha, *f.* 358
Spanish	: pulga, *f.* 358
Swedish	: loppa-n 358
Turkish	: pire 358
Russian	: блоха, *f.* 358
Serbian	: буха, *f.* 358
Ukrainian	: блоха, *f.* 358

FLASHLIGHT see 71 BATTERY

356 FLAT *s.* (a residence)

Czech	: byt, *m.* 356
Danish	: Bolig; Lejlighed 356
Dutch	: woning, de 356
Finnish	: asunto 356
French	: L'appartement, *m.* 356
German	: die Wohnung 356
Hungarian	: lakás 356
Italian	: l'appartamento, *m.* 356
Croatian	: stan, *m.* 356
Norwegian	: leiligheten, *c.* 356
Polish	: mieszkanie, *n.* 356
Portuguese	: habitaçâo, *a* 356
Rumanian	: locuinţă, *f.* 356
Slovak	: byt, *m.* 356
Spanish	: la habitación 356
Swedish	: vaning-en 356
Turkish	: ikametgiâh 356
Russian	: квартира, *f.* 356
Serbian	: стан, *m.* 356
Ukrainian	: помешкання; квартира, *f.* 356

359 FLOUR *s.*

Czech	: mouka, *f.* 359
Danish	: Mel, *n.* 359
Dutch	: het meel 359
Finnish	: jauho 359
French	: farine, *f.* 359
German	: das Mehl 359
Hungarian	: liszt 359
Italian	: farina, *f.* 359
Croatian	: brašno, *n.* 359
Norwegian	: mel, *n.* 359
Polish	: mąka, *f.* 359
Portuguese	: farinha, *a* 359
Rumanian	: fäina, *f.* 359
Slovak	: múka, *f.* 359
Spanish	: harina, *f.* 359
Swedish	: mjöl-et 359
Turkish	: un 359
Russian	: мука, *f.* 359
Serbian	: брашно, *n.* 359
Ukrainian	: мука, *f.* 359

360 FLOWER s.

Czech	:	květina, f. 360
Danish	:	Blomst, m/c. 360
Dutch	:	de bloem 360
Finnish	:	kukka 360
French	:	fleur, f. 360
German	:	die Blume 360
Hungarian	:	a virág 360
Italian	:	flore, m. 360
Croatian	:	cvijet, m. 360
Norwegian	:	blomst, m. 360
Polish	:	kwiat, m. 360
Portuguese	:	flôr, a 360
Rumanian	:	boareă, f. 360
Slovak	:	kvet, m. 360
Spanish	:	flor, f. 360
Swedish	:	blomma-n 360
Turkish	:	çicek 360
Russian	:	цветок, m. 360
Serbian	:	цвет, m. 360
Ukrainian	:	цвіт, m. 360

361 FLUTE s.

Czech	:	flétna, f. 361
Danish	:	Flöjte, c. 361
Dutch	:	de fluit 361
Finnish	:	huilu 361
French	:	flûte, f. 361
German	:	die Flöte 361
Hungarian	:	fuvola 361
Italian	:	flauto, m. 361
Croatian	:	frula, f. 361
Norwegian	:	flöyte, f. 361
Polish	:	flet, m. 361
Portuguese	:	flauta, a 361
Rumanian	:	flautul 361
Slovak	:	flauta, f. 361
Spanish	:	flauta, f. 361
Swedish	:	flöjt-en 361
Turkish	:	flüt 361
Russian	:	флейта, f. 361
Serbian	:	фрула, f. 361
Ukrainian	:	флояра, f. 361

362 FLY s.

Czech	:	moucha, f. 362
Danish	:	Flue, m./c. 362
Dutch	:	de vlieg 362
Finnish	:	kärpänen 362
French	:	mouche, f. 362
German	:	die Fliege 362
Hungarian	:	légy 362
Italian	:	mosca, f. 362
Croatian	:	muha, f. 362
Norwegian	:	flue, f. 362
Polish	:	mucha, f. 362
Portuguese	:	môsca, a 362
Rumanian	:	muscă, f. 362
Slovak	:	mucha, f. 362
Spanish	:	mosca, f. 362
Swedish	:	fluga-n 362
Turkish	:	sinek 362
Russian	:	муха, f. 362
Serbian	:	муха, f. 362
Ukrainian	:	муха, f. 362

363 FOOT s.

Czech	:	noha, f. 363
Danish	:	Fod. m. 363
Dutch	:	de voet 363
Finnish	:	jalka 363
French	:	pied, m. 363
German	:	der Fuss 363
Hungarian	:	lábfej 363
Italian	:	piede, m. 363
Croatian	:	noga, f. 363
Norwegian	:	fot, m. 363
Polish	:	stopa, f. 363
Portuguese	:	pé, o 363
Rumanian	:	piciorul 363
Slovak	:	chodidlo, n. 363
Spanish	:	pie, m. 363
Swedish	:	fot-en 363
Turkish	:	ayak 363
Russian	:	нога, f. 363
Serbian	:	нога, f. 363
Ukrainian	:	стопа, f. 363

364 FOOTBALL s. (the game)

Czech	:	kopaná, f. 364
Danish	:	Fodboldspil, c. 364
Dutch	:	het voetbalspel 364
Finnish	:	potkupallopeli 364
French	:	jeu de football, m. 364
German	:	das Fussballspiel 364
Hungarian	:	a labdarugás 364
Italian	:	giuocco del calcio, m. 364
Croatian	:	nogomet, m. 364
Norwegian	:	fothallspill, n. 364
Polish	:	zawody piłki nóżnej, pl. 364
Portuguese	:	jôgo de futebol, o 364
Rumanian	:	footballul 364
Slovak	:	futbal, m. 364
Spanish	:	juego de fútbol 364
Swedish	:	fotboll 364
Turkish	:	futbol 364
Russian	:	футбольная игра, f. 364
Serbian	:	ногомет, m. 364
Ukrainian	:	змагання в копаний мяч, f. 364

365 FORBIDDEN see 758 PROHIBITED

366 FOREFINGER s.

Czech	:	ukazováček, m. 366
Danish	:	Pegefinger, m./c. 366
Dutch	:	de wijsvinger 366
Finnish	:	etusormi 366
French	:	index, m. 366
German	:	der Zeigefinger 366
Hungarian	:	mutatóujj 366
Italian	:	indice, m. 366
Croatian	:	kažiprst, m. 366
Norwegian	:	pekefinger, m. 366
Polish	:	palec vskazujący, m. 366
Portuguese	:	dedo indicador, o 366
Rumanian	:	degetul arătător 366
Slovak	:	ukazovák, m. 366
Spanish	:	índice, m. 366
Swedish	:	pekfinger, (-gret) 366
Turkish	:	işaret parmaği 366
Russian	:	указательный палец, m. 366
Serbian	:	кажипрст, m. 366
Ukrainian	:	вказуючий палець, m. 366

367 FOREHEAD s.

Czech	:	čelo, n. 367
Danish	:	Pande, m./c. 367
Dutch	:	het voorhoofd 367
Finnish	:	otsa 367
French	:	front, m. 367
German	:	die Stirn 367
Hungarian	:	homlok 367
Italian	:	fronte, f. 367
Croatian	:	čelo, n. 367
Norwegian	:	panne, f. 367
Polish	:	czolo, n. 367
Portuguese	:	testa, a 367
Rumanian	:	fruntea 367
Slovak	:	čelo n. 367
Spanish	:	frente, f. 367
Swedish	:	panna-n 367
Turkish	:	alın 367
Russian	:	лоб, m. 367
Serbian	:	чело, n. 367
Ukrainian	:	чоло, n. 367

368 FOREST s. see 1106 WOOD

369 FORGET v.

Czech	:	zapomenouti; zapomněti 369
Danish	:	gleme 369
Dutch	:	vergeten 369
Finnish	:	unohtaa 369
French	:	oublier 369
German	:	vergessen 369
Hungarian	:	elfelejt 369
Italian	:	dimenticare 369
Croatian	:	zaboraviti 369
Norwegian	:	glemme 369
Polish	:	zapomnieć 369
Portuguese	:	esquecer 369
Rumanian	:	a uita 369
Slovak	:	zabudnút' 369
Spanish	:	olvidar 369
Swedish	:	glömma 369
Turkish	:	unutmak 369
Russian	:	забивать 369
Serbian	:	заворавити 369
Ukrainian	:	забувати 369

370 FORGET-ME-NOT s.

Czech	:	pomněnka, f. 370
Danish	:	Forglemmigej 370
Dutch	:	het vergeet-mij-nietje 370
Finnish	:	lemmikki 370
French	:	myosotis, m. 370
German	:	das Vergissmeinnicht 370
Hungarian	:	a nefelejts 370
Italian	:	non-ti-scordardi-me, m. 370
Croatian	:	potočnica, f. 370
Norwegian	:	forglemmegei 370
Polish	:	niezapominajka, f. 370
Portuguese	:	miosótis, o 370
Rumanian	:	nu-mă-uita, f. 370
Slovak	:	nezabúdka, f. 370
Spanish	:	miosota, f. 370
Swedish	:	förgätmigej-en 370
Turkish	:	siçan kulagi 370
Russian	:	незабудка, f. 370
Serbian	:	незаборавак, m. 370
Ukrainian	:	незабудька, f. 370

371 FORK s.

Czech	:	vidlička, f. 371
Danish	:	Gaffel, m./c. 371
Dutch	:	de vork 371
Finnish	:	haarukka 371
French	:	fourchette, f. 371
German	:	die Gabel 371
Hungarian	:	villa 371
Italian	:	forchetta, f. 371
Croatian	:	viljuška, f. 371
Norwegian	:	gaffel, m. 371
Polish	:	widelce, pl. 371
Portuguese	:	garfo, o 371
Rumanian	:	furculiţă, f. 371
Slovak	:	vidlička, f. 371
Spanish	:	tenedor, m. 371
Swedish	:	gaffel-n 371
Turkish	:	çatal 371
Russian	:	вилка, f. 371
Serbian	:	вильушка, f. 371
Ukrainian	:	вилки, pl. 371

372 FORM s. (a paper)

Czech	:	formulář, m. 372
Danish	:	Formular, n. 372
Dutch	:	het formulier 372
Finnish	:	kaavake 372
French	:	formulaire, m. 372
German	:	das Formular 372
Hungarian	:	ürlap 372
Italian	:	modulo, m. 372
Croatian	:	primerak, m. 372
Norwegian	:	formular, n. 372
Polish	:	formularz, m. 372
Portuguese	:	formulário, o 372
Rumanian	:	formularul 372
Slovak	:	formulár, m. 372
Spanish	:	formulario, m. 372
Swedish	:	formulär-et 372
Turkish	:	dosya 372
Russian	:	формуляр, m. 372
Serbian	:	примерак, m. 372
Ukrainian	:	формуляр, m. 372

373 FOURTEEN

Czech	:	čtrnaćt 373
Danish	:	fjorten 373
Dutch	:	veertien 373
Finnish	:	neljätoista 373
French	:	quatorze 373
German	:	vierzehn 373
Hungarian	:	tizennégy 373
Italian	:	quattórdici 373
Croatian	:	četrnaest 373
Norwegian	:	fjorten 373
Polish	:	tczternaśćie 373
Portuguese	:	quatorze 373
Rumanian	:	paisprezece 373
Slovak	:	štrnást' 373
Spanish	:	catorce 373
Swedish	:	fiorton 373
Turkish	:	on dört 373
Russian	:	четырнадцать 373
Serbian	:	четрнаест 373
Ukrainian	:	чотирнадчть 373

374 FORTY

Czech	: čtyřicet 374
Danish	: fyrre 374
Dutch	: veertig 374
Finnish	: neljäkymmentä 374
French	: quarante 374
German	: vierzig 374
Hungarian	: negyven 374
Italian	: quaranta 374
Croatian	: četrdeset 374
Norwegian	: förti 374
Polish	: czterdzieści 374
Portuguese	: quarenta 374
Rumanian	: patruzeci 374
Slovak	: štyridsat' 374
Spanish	: cuarenta 374
Swedish	: fyrtio 374
Turkish	: kirk 374
Russian	: сорок 374
Serbian	: четрдесет 374
Ukrainian	: сорок 374

377 FOUR

Czech	: čtyri 377
Danish	: fire 377
Dutch	: vier 377
Finnish	: neljä 377
French	: quatre 377
German	: vier 377
Hungarian	: négy 377
Italian	: quattro 377
Croatian	: četiri 377
Norwegian	: fire 377
Polish	: cztery 377
Portuguese	: quatro 377
Rumanian	: patru 377
Slovak	: štyri 377
Spanish	: cuatro 377
Swedish	: fyra 377
Turkish	: dört 377
Russian	: четыре 377
Serbian	: четири 377
Ukrainian	: чотири 377

375 FOUNTAIN s.

Czech	: fontána, f.; vodotrysk, m. 375
Danish	: Springvand, n. 375
Dutch	: het fontein 375
Finnish	: suihkukaivo 375
French	: fontaine, f. 375
German	: der Springbrunnen 375
Hungarian	: szókökút 375
Italian	: fontana, f. 375
Croatian	: vodoskok, m. 375
Norwegian	: springvann, n. 375
Polish	: wodotrysk, m. 375
Portuguese	: fonte, a 375
Rumanian	: fântâna arteziană, f. 375
Slovak	: vodomet, m. 375
Spanish	: fuente, f. 375
Swedish	: springbrunn-en 375
Turkish	: fiskiye 375
Russian	: фонтан, m. 375
Serbian	: водоскок, m. 375
Ukrainian	: водограй, m. 375

378 FOX s.

Czech	: liška, f. 378
Danish	: Räv, m/c. 378
Dutch	: de vos 378
Finnish	: kettu 378
French	: renard, m. 378
German	: der Fuchs 378
Hungarian	: róka 378
Italian	: volpe, f. 378
Croatian	: lisica, f. 378
Norwegian	: rev, m. 378
Polish	: lis, m. 378
Portuguese	: raposo, o 378
Rumanian	: vulpeă, f. 378
Slovak	: líška, f. 378
Spanish	: zorro, m. 378
Swedish	: rav-en 378
Turkish	: tilki 378
Russian	: лисица, f. 378
Serbian	: лисица, f. 378
Ukrainian	: лис, m. 378

376 FOUNTAIN-PEN s.

Czech	: plnicí pero, m. 376
Danish	: Fyldepen, m/c. 376
Dutch	: de vulpenhouder 376
Finnish	: täytekynä 376
French	: stylo(graph), m. 375
German	: der Füllhalter 376
Hungarian	: töltötoll 376
Italian	: penna stilografica f. 376
Croatian	: nalivpero, n. 376
Norwegian	: fyllepenn, m. 376
Polish	: wieczne pióro, n. 376
Portuguese	: caneta de tinta permanente, a 376
Rumanian	: stiloul 376
Slovak	: plniace pero, n. 376
Spanish	: pluma estilográfica 376
Swedish	: reservoar penna-n 376
Turkish	: dolma kalem 376
Russian	: самопишущяя ручка, f. 376
Serbian	: наливперо, n. 376
Ukrainian	: вічне перо, n. 376

379 FREE adj.

Czech	: volný(-o) 379
Danish	: fri 379
Dutch	: vrij 379
Finnish	: vapaa 379
French	: libre 379
German	: frei 379
Hungarian	: szabad 379
Italian	: libero 379
Croatian	: slobodan (-dno) 379
Norwegian	: fri, ledig 379
Polish	: wolny 379
Portuguese	: livre 379
Rumanian	: liber 379
Slovak	: vol'ný 379
Spanish	: libre 379
Swedish	: fri 379
Turkish	: serbest 379
Russian	: свободный 379
Serbian	: слободан 379
Ukrainian	: вільний 379

380 FRIDAY s.

Czech	:	pátek, m. 380
Danish	:	Fredag, m. 380
Dutch	:	de vrijdag 380
Finnish	:	perjantai 380
French	:	vendredi, m. 380
German	:	der Freitag 380
Hungarian	:	péntek 380
Italian	:	venerdi, m. 380
Croatian	:	petak, m. 380
Norwegian	:	fredag, m. 380
Polish	:	piątek, m. 380
Portuguese	:	sexta-feira, a 380
Rumanian	:	Vineri, f. 380
Slovak	:	piatok, m. 380
Spanish	:	viernes, m. 380
Swedish	:	fredag-en 380
Turkish	:	cuma 380
Russian	:	пятница, f. 380
Serbian	:	петак, m. 380
Ukrainian	:	пятниця, f. 380

381 FRIED FISH s.

Czech	:	pečená ryba, f. 381
Danish	:	Stegt Fisk, m/c. 381
Dutch	:	de gebakken vis 381
Finnish	:	paistettu kala 381
French	:	poisson frit, m. 381
German	:	der gebackene Fisch 381
Hungarian	:	sült hal 381
Italian	:	pesce fritto, m. 381
Croatian	:	pečena riba, f. 381
Norwegian	:	stekt fisk, m. 381
Polish	:	pieczona ryba, f. 381
Portuguese	:	peixe frito, o 381
Rumanian	:	peştele prăjit 381
Slovak	:	smažená ryba, f. 381
Spanish	:	pescado frito, m. 381
Swedish	:	stekt fisk 381
Turkish	:	kizartilmis balik 381
Russian	:	жаренная рыба, f. 381
Serbian	:	печена риба, f. 381
Ukrainian	:	печена риба, f. 381

382 FRIED POTATOES s.

Czech	:	pečené brambóry, pl. 382
Danish	:	stegte Kartoffler, pl. 382
Dutch	:	de gebakken aardappel, pl. 382
Finnish	:	paistettuja perunoita 382
French	:	pomme sautée, f. 382
German	:	die Bratkartoffel 382
Hungarian	:	sült burgonya 382
Italian	:	patate fritte, pl. 382
Croatian	:	pečeni krumpir, m. 382
Norwegian	:	stekte poteter 382
Polish	:	smażone kartofie, pl. 382
Portuguese	:	batata frita, a 382
Rumanian	:	cartoful prăjit 382
Slovak	:	pečené zemiaky, pl. 382
Spanish	:	patatas fritas, pl. 382
Swedish	:	stekt potatis 382
Turkish	:	kizartmiş patates, pl. 382
Russian	:	жаренная картофель, f. 382
Serbian	:	печени кромпир, m. 382
Ukrainian	:	печені бараболі, pl. 382

383 FRIEND s.

Czech	:	přítel, m. 383
Danish	:	ven, c. 383
Dutch	:	vriend 383
Finnish	:	ystävä 383
French	:	ami, m.; amie, f. 383
German	:	der Freund; die Freundin 383
Hungarian	:	barát 383
Italian	:	amico, m. 383
Croatian	:	prijatelj, m. 383
Norwegian	:	venn, c. 383
Polish	:	prijatel 383
Portuguese	:	amigo, m. 383
Rumanian	:	prieten, m. 383
Slovak	:	priatel', m. 383
Spanish	:	amigo, m.; amiga, f. 383
Swedish	:	vän, c. 383
Turkish	:	dost; muhip 383
Russian	:	друг; приятель, m. 383
Serbian	:	приятелj, m. 383
Ukrainian	:	друг, m. 383

384 FROCK s. (a dress)

Czech	:	sukně, f. 384
Danish	:	Frakke, m. 384
Dutch	:	de rok 384
Finnish	:	hame 384
French	:	jupe, f. 384
German	:	der Rock 384
Hungarian	:	szoknya 384
Italian	:	gonna, f. 384
Croatian	:	suknja, f. 384
Norwegian	:	frakk, m.;skjört, n. 384
Polish	:	suknia, f. 384
Portuguese	:	saia, a 384
Rumanian	:	fusta, f. 384
Slovak	:	sukňa, f. 384
Spanish	:	falda, f. 384
Swedish	:	kjol-en 384
Turkish	:	eteklik 384
Russian	:	юбка, f. 384
Serbian	:	сукња, f. 384
Ukrainian	:	суконка, f. 384

385 FRONT s. (the foremost part)

Czech	:	popředí; průčelí, n. 385
Danish	:	Forside, m. 385
Dutch	:	de voorgevel 385
Finnish	:	etupuoli 385
French	:	façade, f. 385
German	:	die Vorderseite 385
Hungarian	:	homlokzat 385
Italian	:	la facciata 385
Croatian	:	pročelje, n. 385
Norwegian	:	forside, f. 385
Polish	:	fasada, f. 385
Portuguese	:	fachada, a 385
Rumanian	:	fată, f. 385
Slovak	:	predná strana, f. 385
Spanish	:	fachada, f. 385
Swedish	:	framsida-n 385
Turkish	:	ön taraf 385
Russian	:	передняя сторона, f. 385
Serbian	:	прочелье, n. 385
Ukrainian	:	передня сторона, f. 385

386 FRUIT s.

Czech	:	ovoce, n. 386
Danish	:	Frugt, m. 386
Dutch	:	het fruit 386
Finnish	:	hedelmät, pl. 386
French	:	fruit, m. 386
German	:	das Obst 386
Hungarian	:	gyümölcs 386
Italian	· :	frutta, f. 386
Croatian	:	voće, m. 386
Norwegian	:	frukt, m. 386
Polish	:	owoc, m. 386
Portuguese	:	fruta, a 386
Rumanian	:	fructă, f. 386
Slovak	:	ovocie, n. 386
Spanish	:	fruto, m. 386
Swedish	:	frukt-en 386
Turkish	:	meyve 386
Russian	:	фрукты, pl. 386
Serbian	:	воће, n. 386
Ukrainian	:	овоч, m. 386

387 FRYING-PAN s.

Czech	:	pánev, f. 387
Danish	:	Stegepande, c. 387
Dutch	:	de braadpan 387
Finnish	:	paistinpannu 387
French	:	poêle à frire, f. 387
German	:	die Bratpfanne 387
Hungarian	:	sütöserpenyö 387
Italian	:	padella, f. 387
Croatian	:	tava, f. 387
Norwegian	:	stekepanne, f. 387
Polish	:	patelnia, m. 387
Portuguese	:	frigideira, a 387
Rumanian	:	tigaiă, f. 387
Slovak	:	paňva, f. 387
Spanish	:	sartén, f. 387
Swedish	:	stekpanna-n 387
Turkish	:	tava 387
Russian	:	сковорода, f. 387
Serbian	:	тигань, f. 387
Ukrainian	:	сковородка, f. 387

388 FUNNEL s.

Czech	:	nálevka, f. 388
Danish	:	Tragt, m./c.
Dutch	:	de trechter 388
Finnish	:	suppilo 388
French	:	entonnoir, m. 388
German	:	der Trichter 388
Hungarian	:	tölcsér 388
Italian	:	l'imbuto, m. 388
Croatian	:	lijevak, m. 388
Norwegian	:	trakt, m. 388
Polish	:	lejek, m. 388
Portuguese	:	funil, o 388
Rumanian	:	pîlnia, f. 388
Slovak	:	lievik, m. 388
Spanish	:	embudo, m. 388
Swedish	:	tratt-en 388
Turkish	:	honi 388
Russian	:	воронка, f. 388
Serbian	:	левак, m. 388
Ukrainian	:	лійка, f. 388

389 FUR-COAT s.

Czech	:	kožich, m. 389
Danish	:	Pels, c. 389
Dutch	:	de bontmantel 389
Finnish	:	turkki 389
French	:	le mateau de fourrure 389
German	:	der Pelzmantel 389
Hungarian	:	bunda 389
Italian	:	pelliccia, f. 389
Croatian	:	plast od krzna, m. 389
Norwegian	:	pelskåpe, f. 389
Polish	:	futro, n. 389
Portuguese	:	casaco de peles, o 389
Rumanian	:	haina de blană, f. 389
Slovak	:	kožuch, m. 389
Spanish	:	abrigo de pieles, m. 389
Swedish	:	päls-en 389
Turkish	:	kürk 389
Russian	:	меховое пальто, n.; шуба, f. 389
Serbian	:	капут од крзна, m. 389
Ukrainian	:	шуба, f. 389

390 FUR-COLLAR s.

Czech	:	kožešinový límec, m. 390
Danish	:	Pelskrave, m./c. 390
Dutch	:	de bontkraag 390
Finnish	:	turkiskaulus 390
French	:	col de fourrure 390
German	:	der Pelzkragen 390
Hungarian	:	prémgallér 390
Italian	:	bavero di pelliccia, m. 390
Croatian	:	krznena ogrlica, f. 390
Norwegian	:	pelskrave, m. 390
Polish	:	kolnierz futrzany, m. 390
Portuguese	:	cabeçâo de peles, o 390
Rumanian	:	gulerul de blană 390
Slovak	:	kožušinový golier, m. 390
Spanish	:	cuello de piel, m. 390
Swedish	:	pälskrage-n 390
Turkish	:	kürk yaka 390
Russian	:	воротник меховой, m. 390
Serbian	:	крагна од крзна, f. 390
Ukrainian	:	хутуяний ковнір, m. 390

391 FURRIER s.

Czech	:	kožešník, m. 391
Danish	:	Buntmager, m. 391
Dutch	:	de bontwerker 391
Finnish	:	turkkuri 391
French	:	fourreur, m. 391
German	:	der Kürschner 391
Hungarian	:	szücs 391
Italian	:	pellicciaio, m. 391
Croatian	:	krznar, m. 391
Norwegian	:	buntmaker, m. 391
Polish	:	kuśnierz, m. 391
Portuguese	:	peleiro, o 391
Rumanian	:	blănarul 391
Slovak	:	kožušník, m. 391
Spanish	:	peletero, m. 391
Swedish	:	körsnär-en 391
Turkish	:	kürkcü 391
Russian	:	скорняк, m. 391
Serbian	:	крзнар, m. 391
Ukrainian	:	кушнір, m. 391

58

392 GALLERY see 58 BALCONY

393 GAME s. (wild animals)

Czech	:	zvěřina, f. 393
Danish	:	Vildt, m. 393
Dutch	:	het wild 393
Finnish	:	paistettu metsänriista 393
French	:	rôti de gibier, m. 393
German	:	der Wildbraten 393
Hungarian	:	vad 393
Italian	:	cacciagone, f. 393
Croatian	:	divljač, f. 393
Norwegian	:	viltstek, m. 393
Polish	:	dziczyzna, f. 393
Portuguese	:	(assado de) caça, o. 393
Rumanian	:	vânatul 393
Slovak	:	divina, f. 393
Spanish	:	caza, f. 393
Swedish	:	vilt-et 393
Turkish	:	av eti 393
Russian	:	дичь, f. 393
Serbian	:	дивљач, f. 393
Ukrainian	:	дичина, f. 393

394 GARAGE s.

Czech	:	garáž, f. 394
Danish	:	Garage, m. 394
Dutch	:	de garage 394
Finnish	:	autovaja 394
French	:	garage, m. 394
German	:	die Garage 394
Hungarian	:	a garázs 394
Italian	:	rimessa, f. 394
Croatian	:	spremište, m. 394
Norwegian	:	garasje, m. 394
Polish	:	garaż, m. 394
Portuguese	:	garage, a. 394
Rumanian	:	garajul 394
Slovak	:	garáž, f. 394
Spanish	:	el garaje 394
Swedish	:	garage-t 394
Turkish	:	garage 394
Russian	:	гараж, m. 394
Serbian	:	гаража, f. 394
Ukrainian	:	гараж, m. 394

395 GARDEN s.

Czech	:	zahrada, f. 395
Danish	:	Have, m./c. 395
Dutch	:	de tuin 395
Finnish	:	puutarha 395
French	:	jardin, m. 395
German	:	der Garten 395
Hungarian	:	kert 395
Italian	:	giardino, m. 395
Croatian	:	vrt, m. 395
Norwegian	:	have, m. 395
Polish	:	ogród, m. 395
Portuguese	:	jardim, o 395
Rumanian	:	grădina, f. 395
Slovak	:	záhrada, f. 395
Spanish	:	jardín, m. 395
Swedish	:	tradgård-en 395
Turkish	:	bahce 395
Russian	:	сад, m. 395
Serbian	:	врт, m. 395
Ukrainian	:	город, m. 395

396 GARLIC s.

Czech	:	česnek, m. 396
Danish	:	Hvidlög, m./c. 396
Dutch	:	het knoflook 396
Finnish	:	valkolaukka 396
French	:	ail, m. 396
German	:	der Knoblauch 396
Hungarian	:	fokhagyma 396
Italian	:	aglio, m. 396
Croatian	:	češnjak, m. 396
Norwegian	:	hvitlök, m. 396
Polish	:	czosnek, m. 396
Portuguese	:	alho, o 396
Rumanian	:	usturoi, c. 396
Slovak	:	česnak, m. 396
Spanish	:	ajo, m. 396
Swedish	:	vitlök-en 396
Turkish	:	sarzmusak 396
Russian	:	чеснок, m. 396
Serbian	:	чешњак, m. 396
Ukrainian	:	часник, m. 396

397 GARRET s.

Czech	:	podkroví, n. 397
Danish	:	Kvistkammer, n. 397
Dutch	:	de zolderkamer 397
Finnish	:	kattokamari 397
French	:	mansarde, f. 397
German	:	die Dachkammer 397
Hungarian	:	padlásszoba 397
Italian	:	soffitta, f. 397
Croatian	:	soba na tavanu, f. 397
Norwegian	:	kvistvärelse, n. 397
Polish	:	mansarda, m. 397
Portuguese	:	âguas-furtadas, as 397
Rumanian	:	mansardă, f. 397
Slovak	:	mazarda, f. 397
Spanish	:	guardilla, f. 397
Swedish	:	vindskammare-n 397
Turkish	:	damodasi 397
Russian	:	чердачная комната, f. 397
Serbian	:	соба на табану, f. 397
Ukrainian	:	комірка, на даху, f. 397

398 GAS s.

Czech	:	plyn, m. 398
Danish	:	gas, c. 398
Dutch	:	gas 398
Finnish	:	kaasu 398
French	:	gaz, m. 398
German	:	das Gas 398
Hungarian	:	gáz 398
Italian	:	gas, m. 398
Croatian	:	plin, m. 398
Norwegian	:	gass c. 398
Polish	:	gaz 398
Portuguese	:	gâs, m. 398
Rumanian	:	gaz, c. 398
Slovak	:	plyn, m. 398
Spanish	:	gas, m. 398
Swedish	:	gas 398
Turkish	:	gaz 398
Russian	:	газ, m. 398
Serbian	:	плин, m. 398
Ukrainian	:	газ, m. 398

399 GASOLINE s. (Brit. PETROL)

Czech	: benzin, m. 399
Danish	: Benzin, m./c. 399
Dutch	: de benzine 399
Finnish	: bensiini 399
French	: essence, f. 399
German	: das Benzin 399
Hungarian	: benzin 399
Italian	: benzina, f. 399
Croatian	: benzin, m. 399
Norwegian	: bensin, m. 399
Polish	: benzyna, f. 399
Portuguese	: gasolina, a 399
Rumanian	: benzină, f. 399
Slovak	: benzín, m. 399
Spanish	: bencina, f. 399
Swedish	: bensin-en 399
Turkish	: benzin 399
Russian	: бензин, m. 399
Serbian	: бензин, m. 399
Ukrainian	: беизина, f. 399

400 GATE s.

Czech	: vrata, pl. 400
Danish	: Port, m./c. 400
Dutch	: de poort 400
Finnish	: portti 400
French	: portail, m. 400
German	: das Tor 400
Hungarian	: kapu 400
Italian	: portone, m. 400
Croatian	: kapija, f. 400
Norwegian	: port, m. 400
Polish	: brama, f. 400
Portuguese	: portão, o 400
Rumanian	: poartă, f. 400
Slovak	: brána, f. 400
Spanish	: portal, m. 400
Swedish	: port-en 400
Turkish	: büyük bahçe kapisi 400
Russian	: ворота, pl. 400
Serbian	: капија, f. 400
Ukrainian	: брама, f. 400

401 GATHER v. see **444 HARVEST**

402 GET v. see **973 TAKE**

403 GIFT s.

Czech	: dar, m. 403
Danish	: gave, c. 403
Dutch	: gave 403
Finnish	: lahja 403
French	: don, m. 403
German	: das Geschenk 403
Hungarian	: ajándék 403
Italian	: dono, m. 403
Croatian	: dar, m. 403
Norwegian	: gave, c./f. 403
Polish	: dar, m. 403
Portuguese	: dom, m. 403
Rumanian	: dar, c. 403
Slovak	: dar, m. 403
Spanish	: don, m.; regalo, m. 403
Swedish	: gåva-n 403
Turkish	: hediye 403
Russian	: дар, m. 403
Serbian	: дар, m. 403
Ukrainian	: подарунок, m 403

404 GIRL s.

Czech	: dívka, f. 404
Danish	: Pige, f. 404
Dutch	: het meisje 404
Finnish	: tyttö 404
French	: fille, f. 404
German	: das Mädchen 404
Hungarian	: leány 404
Italian	: ragazza, f. 404
Croatian	: djevojka, f. 404
Norwegian	: pike, f. 404
Polish	: dziewczyna, f. 404
Portuguese	: menina, a 404
Rumanian	: fata, f. 404
Slovak	: dievča, n. 404
Spanish	: niña, f. 404
Swedish	: flicka-n 404
Turkish	: kiz 404
Russian	: девочка, f. 404
Serbian	: девојка, f. 404
Ukrainian	: дівчина, f. 404

405 GIVE v.

Czech	: dáti 405
Danish	: give 405
Dutch	: geven 405
Finnish	: antaa 405
French	: donner 405
German	: geben 405
Hungarian	: ad 405
Italian	: dare; donare 405
Croatian	: dati 405
Norwegian	: gi 405
Polish	: dać 405
Portuguese	: dar 405
Rumanian	: a da 405
Slovak	: dat'; dávat' 405
Spanish	: dar; ceder 405
Swedish	: giva 405
Turkish	: vermek 405
Russian	: дать; давать 405
Serbian	: дати 405
Ukrainian	: давати 405

406 GLAD adj.

Czech	: rád; potěšen 406
Danish	: glad 406
Dutch	: vrolijk 406
Finnish	: iloinen 406
French	: heureux; content 406
German	: froh; gern 406
Hungarian	: vidám 406
Italian	: contento; allegro 406
Croatian	: veseo 406
Norwegian	: glad 406
Polish	: rad 406
Portuguese	: contento; alegrar-se 406
Rumanian	: vestl; voios 406
Slovak	: rád; veselý 406
Spanish	: contento 406
Swedish	: glad 406
Turkish	: hoşnut 406
Russian	: веселый 406
Serbian	: весело 406
Ukrainian	: радий 406

407 GLASS s.

Czech	:	sklenice, f. 407
Danish	:	Glas, n. 407
Dutch	:	het glas 407
Finnish	:	lasi 407
French	:	verre, m. 407
German	:	das Glas 407
Hungarian	:	pohár 407
Italian	:	bicchiere, m. 407
Croatian	:	čaša, f. 407
Norwegian	:	glass, n. 407
Polish	:	szklanka, f. 407
Portuguese	:	copo, o 407
Rumanian	:	paharul 407
Slovak	:	pohár, m. 407
Spanish	:	vaso, m. 407
Swedish	:	glas-et 407
Turkish	:	pardak 407
Russian	:	стакан, m. 407
Serbian	:	чаша, f. 407
Ukrainian	:	склянка, f. 407

408 GLASSES see 327 EYE GLASSES

409 GLOVE s.

Czech	:	rukavice, f. 409
Danish	:	Handsker, pl. 409
Dutch	:	de handschoen 409
Finnish	:	käsineet 409
French	:	gant, m. 409
German	:	der Handschuh 409
Hungarian	:	keztyü 409
Italian	:	guanto, m. 409
Croatian	:	rukavica, f. 409
Norwegian	:	hanske, m. 409
Polish	:	rękawiczki, pl. 409
Portuguese	:	luva, a 409
Rumanian	:	manuşa, f. 409
Slovak	:	rukavica, f. 409
Spanish	:	guantes, pl. 409
Swedish	:	handskar-na, pl. 409
Turkish	:	eldiven 409
Russian	:	перчатки, pl. 409
Serbian	:	рукавица, f. 409
Ukrainian	:	дукавички, pl. 409

410 GLUE s.

Czech	:	lepidlo, n. 410
Danish	:	Lim, c. 410
Dutch	:	de lijm 410
Finnish	:	liima 410
French	:	co'le, f. 410
German	:	der Klebstoff 410
Hungarian	:	ragasztószer 410
Italian	:	colla, f. 410
Croatian	:	lepak, m. 410
Norwegian	:	lim, klebestoff, c. 410
Polish	:	klej, m. 410
Portuguese	:	cola, a 410
Rumanian	:	lipiciul 410
Slovak	:	lepidlo, n. 410
Spanish	:	aglutinante, m. 410
Swedish	:	klistr-et 410
Turkish	:	yapişici mevad 410
Russian	:	клей, m. 410
Serbian	:	лепак, m. 410
Ukrainian	:	клей, m. 410

411 GO v. see 1070 WALK

412 GOAT s.

Czech	:	koza, f. 412
Danish	:	Ged, m./c. 412
Dutch	:	de geit 412
Finnish	:	kuttu 412
French	:	chèvre, f. 412
German	:	die Ziege 412
Hungarian	:	kecske 412
Italian	:	capra, f. 412
Croatian	:	koza, f. 412
Norwegian	:	geit, f. 412
Polish	:	koza, f. 412
Portuguese	:	cabra, a 412
Rumanian	:	capra 412
Slovak	:	koza, f. 412
Spanish	:	cabra, f. 412
Swedish	:	get-en 412
Turkish	:	keçi 412
Russian	:	коза, f. 412
Serbian	:	коза, f. 412
Ukrainian	:	коза, f. 412

413 GO AWAY see 522 LEAVE

414 GOD s.

Czech	:	Bůh, m. 414
Danish	:	gud, c. 414
Dutch	:	God, m. 414
Finnish	:	Jumala 414
French	:	Dieu, m. 414
German	:	Gott, m. 414
Hungarian	:	isten 414
Italian	:	Dio, m. 414
Croatian	:	bog, m. 414
Norwegian	:	Gud, c. 414
Polish	:	Bóg, m. 414
Portuguese	:	Deus. m. 414
Rumanian	:	Dumnezen, m.; zeu, m. 414
Slovak	:	Boh, m. 414
Spanish	:	Dios 414
Swedish	:	Gud, m. 414
Turkish	:	Allah 414
Russian	:	бог, m. 414
Serbian	:	бог, m. 414
Ukrainian	:	бог, m. 414

415 GOOD adj.

Czech	:	dobrý 415
Danish	:	god 415
Dutch	:	goed 415
Finnish	:	hyvä 415
French	:	bon, bien 415
German	:	gut 415
Hungarian	:	jó 415
Italian	:	buono, bene 415
Croatian	:	dobro 415
Norwegian	:	god 415
Polish	:	dobrze 415
Portuguese	:	bom 415
Rumanian	:	bun, bine 415
Slovak	:	dobrý 415
Spanish	:	bueno 415
Swedish	:	god 415
Turkish	:	iyi 415
Russian	:	хорошо; ладно 415
Serbian	:	добро 415
Ukrainian	:	добрий 415

416 GOOD-BYE

Czech : Sbohem; žijte blaze 416
Danish : farvel, n. 416
Dutch : tot ziens 416
Finnish : jäähyväiset, pl. 416
French : adieu 416
German : Lebewohl, n. 416
Hungarian : búcsúszó 416
Italian : addio 416
Croatian : zbogom 416
Norwegian : farvel 416
Polish : do widzenia 416
Portuguese : adeus 416
Rumanian : rămas bun! 416
Slovak : s Bohom 416
Spanish : adiós 416
Swedish : farväl; adjö 416
Turkish : veda 416
Russian : прощай 416
Serbian : збогом 416
Ukrainian : прощайте! 416

417 GOOSE s.

Czech : husa, f. 417
Danish : Gaas, m. 417
Dutch : de gans 417
Finnish : hanhi 417
French : oie, f. 417
German : die Gans 417
Hungarian : liba 417
Italian : oca, f. 417
Croatian : guska, f. 417
Norwegian : gås, f. 417
Polish : geś, f. 417
Portuguese : ganso, o 417
Rumanian : gâscă, f. 417
Slovak : hus, f. 417
Spanish : ganso, m. 417
Swedish : gås-en 417
Turkish : kaz 417
Russian : гусь, m. 417
Serbian : гуска, f. 417
Ukrainian : гуска, f. 417

418 GOOSEBERRY s.

Czech : angrešt, m. 418
Danish : Stikkelsbär, c. 418
Dutch : de kruisbes 418
Finnish : karviaismarja 418
French : groseille à maquereau, f. 418
German : die Stachelbeere 418
Hungarian : egres 418
Italian : uva spina, f. 418
Croatian : ogrozd, m. 418
Norwegian : stikkelsbär, m. 418
Polish : agrest, f. 418
Portuguese : uva do norte, a 418
Rumanian : agrisa, f. 418
Slovak : agreš, m. 418
Spanish : uva espina, f. 418
Swedish : krusbär-et 418
Turkish : büyürtlen 418
Russian : крыжовник, m. 418
Serbian : кулина, f. 418
Ukrainian : агрест, m. 418

419 GO QUICKLY see 826 RUN

420 GOWN s. see 290 DRESSING-ROBE

421 GRAND adj. see 518 LARGE

422 GRAND PIANO s.

Czech : piano, n.; klavír, m. 422
Danish : Flygel, n. 422
Dutch : de vleugel 422
Finnish : konserttipiano 422
French : le piano è queue 422
German : das Klavier 422
Hungarian : zongora 422
Italian : piano a coda, m. 422
Croatian : glasovir, m. 422
Norwegian : piano, flygel 422
Polish : fortepian trójkątny, m. 422
Portuguese : piano de cauda, o 422
Rumanian : pianul 422
Slovak : klavír, m. 422
Spanish : piano de cola, m. 422
Swedish : flugel-n 422
Turkish : kanat şeklinde piyano 422
Russian : рояль, m. 422
Serbian : гласовир, m. 422
Ukrainian : фортепян криловий, m. 422

423 GRAPE s.

Czech : hroznové víno, n. 423
Danish : Vindrue, m/c. 423
Dutch : de druif 423
Finnish : viinirypäle 423
French : raisin, m. 423
German : die Weintraube 423
Hungarian : szöllö 423
Italian : uva, f. 423
Croatian : grožđje, n. 423
Norwegian : vindrue, m. 423
Polish : winogrona, f. 423
Portuguese : cacho de uvas, o 423
Rumanian : strugurele, n. 423
Slovak : hrozno, n. 423
Spanish : uva, f. 423
Swedish : vindruva-n 423
Turkish : üzüm 423
Russian : виноград, m. 423
Serbian : грожħе, n. 423
Ukrainian : виноград, m. 423

424 GRAVY s.

Czech : omáčka, f. 424
Danish : Sauce, m./c. 424
Dutch : de jus 424
Finnish : kastike 424
French : sauce, f. 424
German : die Tunke 424
Hungarian : mártás 424
Italian : salsa, f. 424
Croatian : umok, m. 424
Norwegian : saus, m. 424
Polish : sos, m. 424
Portuguese : môlho, o 424
Rumanian : sosul 424
Slovak : omáčka, f. 424
Spanish : salsa, f. 424
Swedish : sås-en 424
Turkish : salça 424
Russian : соус, m.; подлива, f. 424
Serbian : умок, m. 424
Ukrainian : підлива, f.; cоc, m. 424

62

425 GREATLY see 626 MUCH

426 GREEN adj.

Czech	:	zelený 426
Danish	:	grön 426
Dutch	:	groen 426
Finnish	:	vihreä 426
French	:	vert 426
German	:	grün 426
Hungarian	:	zöld 426
Italian	:	verde 426
Croatian	:	zelen 426
Norwegian	:	grönn 426
Polish	:	zielony 426
Portuguese	:	verde 426
Rumanian	:	verde 426
Slovak	:	zelený 426
Spanish	:	verde 426
Swedish	:	grön 426
Turkish	:	yeşil 426
Russian	:	зеленый 426
Serbian	:	зелен 426
Ukrainian	:	зелений 426

427 GREY adj.

Czech	:	šedý 427
Danish	:	graa 427
Dutch	:	grijs 427
Finnish	:	harmaa 427
French	:	gris 427
German	:	grau 427
Hungarian	:	szürke 427
Italian	:	grigio 427
Croatian	:	siv 427
Norwegian	:	grå 427
Polish	:	szary 427
Portuguese	:	cinzento 427
Rumanian	:	gri 427
Slovak	:	sivý 427
Spanish	:	gris 427
Swedish	:	grå 427
Turkish	:	kir 427
Russian	:	серый 427
Serbian	:	сив 427
Ukrainian	:	сірий; сивий 427

428 GROUND-FLOOR s. (Am. the first floor)

Czech	:	přízemí, n. 428
Danish	:	Stuln, c. 428
Dutch	:	het parterre 428
Finnish	:	pohjakerros 428
French	:	rez-dechaussée 428
German	:	das Erdgeschoss 428
Hungarian	:	földszint 428
Italian	:	pianterreno, m. 428
Croatian	:	prizemlje, n. 428
Norwegian	:	förste etasje, n. 428
Polish	:	parter, n. 428
Portuguese	:	rés-do-chão, o 428
Rumanian	:	parterul 428
Slovak	:	prizemie, n. 428
Spanish	:	piso bajo, m. 428
Swedish	:	nedre botten 428
Turkish	:	zeminkati 428
Russian	:	первыи этаж, m. 428
Serbian	:	приземље, n. 428
Ukrainian	:	повал; партер, m. 428

429 GUITAR s.

Czech	:	kytara, f. 429
Danish	:	Guitar, m./c. 429
Dutch	:	de gitaar 429
Finnish	:	kitarri; kitara 429
French	:	guitare, f. 429
German	:	die Gitarre 429
Hungarian	:	gitár 429
Italian	:	chitarra, f. 429
Croatian	:	kitara, f. 429
Norwegian	:	gitar, m. 429
Polish	:	gitara, f. 429
Portuguese	:	guitarra, a 429
Rumanian	:	ghitară, f. 429
Slovak	:	gitara, f. 429
Spanish	:	guitarra, f. 429
Swedish	:	gitarr-en 429
Turkish	:	kitara 429
Russian	:	гитара, f. 429
Serbian	:	гитара, f. 429
Ukrainian	:	гітара, f. 429

430 GYMNASTICS s.

Czech	:	tělocvik, m. 430
Danish	:	Gymnastik, c. 430
Dutch	:	de gymnastiek 430
Finnish	:	voimistelu 430
French	:	gymnastique, f. 430
German	:	das Turnen 430
Hungarian	:	a torna 430
Italian	:	ginnastica, f. 430
Croatian	:	gimnastyka, f. 430
Norwegian	:	turning, m. 430
Polish	:	gimnastyka, f. 430
Portuguese	:	fazer gimnástica, o 430
Rumanian	:	gimnastică, f. 430
Slovak	:	cvičenie, n. 430
Spanish	:	hacer gimnasia 430
Swedish	:	gymnastik-en 430
Turkish	:	cimnastik 430
Russian	:	гимнастика, f. 430
Serbian	:	гимнастика, f. 430
Ukrainian	:	руханка, f. 430

431 HAIL s.

Czech	:	kroupy, pl. 431
Danish	:	Hagl, n. 431
Dutch	:	de hagel 431
Finnish	:	rakeet 431
French	:	grêle, f. 431
German	:	der Hagel 431
Hungarian	:	jégesö 431
Italian	:	grandine, f. 431
Croatian	:	tuča, f. 431
Norwegian	:	hagl, n. 431
Polish	:	grad, m. 431
Portuguese	:	granizo, o 431
Rumanian	:	grindină, f. 431
Slovak	:	krupobitie, n. 431
Spanish	:	granizo, m. 431
Swedish	:	haglet 431
Turkish	:	doln 431
Russian	:	град, m. 431
Serbian	:	град, m. 431
Ukrainian	:	град, m. 431

432 HAIR s.

Czech	:	vlas, *m.*; vlasy, *pl.* 432
Danish	:	Haar, *n.* 432
Dutch	:	het haar 432
Finnish	:	tukka; hiukset 432
French	:	cheveux, *m. pl.* 432
German	:	das Haar 432
Hungarian	:	haj 432
Italian	:	capelli, *m. pl.* 432
Croatian	:	kosa, *f.* 432
Norwegian	:	hår, *n.* 432
Polish	:	włosy, *pl.* 432
Portuguese	:	cabelo, *o* 432
Rumanian	:	părul 432
Slovak	:	vlasy, *m. pl.* 432
Spanish	:	cabello, pelo 432
Swedish	:	har-et 432
Turkish	:	sac 432
Russian	:	волосы, *pl.* 432
Serbian	:	коса, *f.* 432
Ukrainian	:	волосся, *pl.* 432

435 HALF s.

Czech	:	půl; polovina, *f.* 435
Danish	:	en halv 435
Dutch	:	een half 435
Finnish	:	puoli 435
French	:	un demi 435
German	:	einhalb 435
Hungarian	:	fél 435
Italian	:	una metà 435
Croatian	:	polovina 435
Norwegian	:	en halv 435
Polish	:	połowa 435
Portuguese	:	um meio 435
Rumanian	:	o jumătate 435
Slovak	:	jedna polovica 435
Spanish	:	medio 435
Swedish	:	en halv 435
Turkish	:	yarim 435
Russian	:	половина 435
Serbian	:	половина 435
Ukrainian	:	половина 435

433 HAIR-BRUSH s.

Czech	:	kartáč na vlasy, *m.* 433
Danish	:	Haarbörste, *m./c.* 433
Dutch	:	de haarborstel 433
Finnish	:	hiusharja 433
French	:	brosse à cheveux 433
German	:	die Haarbürste 433
Hungarian	:	hajkefe 433
Italian	:	spazzola per i capelli, *f.* 433
Croatian	:	četka za kosu, *f.* 433
Norwegian	:	hårbörste, *m.* 433
Polish	:	szczotka do włosów, *f.* 433
Portuguese	:	escova para o cabelo, *a* 433
Rumanian	:	periä de cap, *f.* 433
Slovak	:	kafa na vlasy, *f.* 433
Spanish	:	cepillo para el cabello 433
Swedish	:	hårborste-n 433
Turkish	:	saç firçasi 433
Russian	:	щетка для волос, *f.* 433
Serbian	:	четка за косу, *f.* 433
Ukrainian	:	щітка до волосся, *f.* 433

436 HALL PORTER s. (janitor)

Czech	:	vrátný, *m.* 436
Danish	:	Portier, *m.* 436
Dutch	:	de portier 436
Finnish	:	vahtimestari 436
French	:	portier, *m.* 436
German	:	der Portier 436
Hungarian	:	kapus 436
Italian	:	portiere, *m.* 436
Croatian	:	vratar, *m.* 436
Norwegian	:	portier, *m.*; portner, *m.* 436
Polish	:	portjer, *m.* 436
Portuguese	:	porteiro, *o* 436
Rumanian	:	portarul 436
Slovak	:	vrátnik, *m.* 436
Spanish	:	portero, *m.* 436
Swedish	:	portier-en 436
Turkish	:	kapuci 436
Russian	:	швейцар, *m.* 436
Serbian	:	вратар, *m.* 436
Ukrainian	:	дверник, *m.* 436

434 HAIR-DRESSER s.

Czech	:	holič. *m.* 434
Danish	:	Friseur, *m./c.* 434
Dutch	:	de kapper 434
Finnish	:	parturi 434
French	:	coiffeur, *m.* 434
German	:	der Friseur 434
Hungarian	:	fodrász 434
Italian	:	parrucchiere, *m.* 434
Croatian	:	brijač, *m.* 434
Norwegian	:	frisör, *m.* 434
Polish	:	fryzjer, *m.* 434
Portuguese	:	cabeleireiro, *o* 434
Rumanian	:	frizerul 434
Slovak	:	holič, *m.* 434
Spanish	:	peluquero, *m.* 434
Swedish	:	frisör-en 434
Turkish	:	berber 434
Russian	:	парикмахер, *m.* 434
Serbian	:	чеслар, *m.* 434
Ukrainian	:	фризіэр, *m.* 434

437 HAM s.

Czech	:	šunka, *f.* 437
Danish	:	Skinke, *m./c.* 437
Dutch	:	de ham 437
Finnish	:	kinkku 437
French	:	jambon, *m.* 437
German	:	der Schinken 437
Hungarian	:	sonka 437
Italian	:	prosciutto, *m.* 437
Croatian	:	šunka, *f.* 437
Norwegian	:	skinke, *m.* 437
Polish	:	szynka, *f.* 437
Portuguese	:	presunto, *o* 437
Rumanian	:	şuncă, *f.* 437
Slovak	:	šunka, *f.* 437
Spanish	:	jamón 437
Swedish	:	skinka-n 437
Turkish	:	domuz butu 437
Russian	:	ветчина, *f.* 437
Serbian	:	шунка, *f.* 437
Ukrainian	:	шинка, *f.* 437

438 HAMMER s.

Czech	:	kladivo, n. 438
Danish	:	Hammer, m./c. 438
Dutch	:	de hamer 438
Finnish	:	vasara 438
French	:	marteau, m. 438
German	:	der Hammer 438
Hungarian	:	kalapács 438
Italian	:	martello, m. 438
Croatian	:	čekič, m. 438
Norwegian	:	hammer, m. 438
Polish	:	młot, m. 438
Portuguese	:	martelo, o 438
Rumanian	:	ciocanul 438
Slovak	:	kladivo, n. 438
Spanish	:	martillo, m. 438
Swedish	:	hammar-en 438
Turkish	:	çekiç 438
Russian	:	молотокъ, m. 438
Serbian	:	чекиħ, m. 438
Ukrainiun	:	молот. m. 438

439 HAND s.

Czech	:	ruka, f.; ruce, pl. 439
Danish	:	Haand, m./c. 439
Dutch	:	de hand 439
Finnish	:	käsi 439
French	:	main, f. 439
German	:	die Hand 439
Hungarian	:	kéz 439
Italian	:	mano, f. 439
Croatian	:	ruka, f. 439
Norwegian	:	hånd, f. 439
Polish	:	ręka, f. 439
Portuguese	:	mão, a 439
Rumanian	:	mâna, f. 439
Slovak	:	ruka f. 439
Spanish	:	mano, f. 439
Swedish	:	hand-en 439
Turkish	:	el 439
Russian	:	рука, f. 439
Serbian	:	рука, f. 439
Ukrainian	:	рука, f. 439

440 HAND-GRENADE s.

Czech	:	ruční granát, m. 440
Danish	:	Haandgranat, m./c. 440
Dutch	:	de handgranaat, m. 440
Finnish	:	käsikranaati 440
French	:	grenade à main, f. 440
German	:	die Handgranate 440
Hungarian	:	kézigránát 440
Italian	:	bomba a mano, f. 440
Croatian	:	ručna granata, f. 440
Norwegian	:	handgranat, m. 440
Polish	:	granata ręczna, f. 440
Portuguese	:	granada de mão, a 440
Rumanian	:	granata de mâna, f. 440
Slovak	:	ručný granát, m. 440
Spanish	:	bomba de mano 440
Swedish	:	handgranat-en 440
Turkish	:	el bombasi 440
Russian	:	ручная граната, f. 440
Serbian	:	ручна граната, f. 440
Ukrainian	:	ручна граната, f. 440

441 HANDKERCHIEF s.

Czech	:	kapesník, m. 441
Danish	:	Lommetørkläde, n. 441
Dutch	:	de zakdoek 441
Finnish	:	nenäliina 441
French	:	mouchoir, m. 441
German	:	das Taschentuch 441
Hungarian	:	zsebkendö 441
Italian	:	fazzoletto, m. 441
Croatian	:	džepna maramica, f. 441
Norwegian	:	lommetörklä, n. 441
Polish	:	chusteczka do nosa 441
Portuguese	:	lenço, o 441
Rumanian	:	batista, f. 441
Slovak	:	vreckovka, f. 441
Spanish	:	pañuelo, m. 441
Swedish	:	näsduk-en 441
Turkish	:	mendil 441
Russian	:	носовой платок, m. 441
Serbian	:	ħепна марамица, f. 441
Ukrainian	:	хусточка до носа, f. 441

442 HARE s.

Czech	:	zajíc, m. 442
Danish	:	Hare, m. 442
Dutch	:	de haas 442
Finnish	:	jänis 442
French	:	lièvre, m. 442
German	:	der Hase 442
Hungarian	:	vadnyúl 442
Italian	:	lepre, f. 442
Croatian	:	zec, m. 442
Norwegiar.	:	hare, m. 442
Polish	:	zając, m. 442
Portuguese	:	lebre, a 442
Rumanian	:	iepurele 442
Slovak	:	zajac, m. 442
Spanish	:	liebre, f. 442
Swedish	:	hare-n 442
Turkish	:	tavşan 442
Russian	:	заяц, m. 442
Serbian	:	зец, m. 442
Ukrainian	:	заяць, m. 442

443 HARMONICA see 619 MOUTH ORGAN

444 HARVEST v.

Czech	:	sklízeti 444
Danish	:	höste 444
Finnish	:	leikata 444
French	:	récolter 444
German	:	ernten 444
Hungarian	:	aratni 444
Italian	:	raccogliere 444
Croatian	:	žeti 444
Norwegian	:	höste 444
Polish	:	żnąć 444
Portuguese	:	colher 444
Rumanian	:	a strânge recolta 444
Slovak	:	žat' 444
Spanish	:	cosechar 444
Swedish	:	skörda 444
Turkish	:	ekin toplamak 444
Russian	:	жать; собирать 444
Serbian	:	жети 444
Ukrainian	:	жати 444

445 HASTEN v.

Czech	: spěchati 445
Danish	: haste 445
Dutch	: zich haasten 445
Finnish	: kiirehtiä 445
French	: hâter: accélérér 445
German	: eilen 445
Hungarian	: siet 445
Italian	: affrettare 445
Croatian	: žuriti se 445
Norwegian	: ile; haste 445
Polish	: pospieczić 445
Portuguese	: apressar-se 445
Rumanian	: a se grăbi; a fi urgent 445
Slovak	: ponáhľaťʼ sa 445
Spanish	: apresurar (se) 445
Swedish	: skynda 445
Turkish	: aceleetmek 445
Russian	: (по)спешить 445
Serbian	: журити се 445
Ukrainian	: поспішати 445

446 HAT s.

Czech	: klobouk, m. 446
Danish	: Hat, m./c. 446
Dutch	: de hoed 446
Finnish	: hattu 446
French	: chapeau, m. 446
German	: der Hut 446
Hungarian	: kalap 446
Italian	: cappello, m. 446
Croatian	: šešir, m. 446
Norwegian	: hatt, c. 446
Polish	: kapelusz, m. 446
Portuguese	: chapéu, o 446
Rumanian	: pălăria, f. 446
Slovak	: klobúk, m. 446
Spanish	: sombrero, m. 446
Swedish	: hatt-en 446
Turkish	: şapka 446
Russian	: шляпа, f. 446
Serbian	: шешир, m. 446
Ukrainian	: капелюх, m. 446

447 HAVE v.

Czech	: míti; vlastniti 447
Danish	: have 447
Dutch	: hebben 447
Finnish	: omata 447
French	: avoir 447
German	: haben 447
Hungarian	: van vmije; bir vmivel 447
Italian	: avere 447
Croatian	: imati 447
Norwegian	: ha, eie 447
Polish	: mieć 447
Portuguese	: ter; tomar 447
Rumanian	: a avea 447
Slovak	: mať'; držať' 447
Spanish	: tener; haber; poseer 447
Swedish	: hava 447
Turkish	: tutmak; malik olmak 447
Russian	: иметь 447
Serbian	: имати 447
Ukrainian	: мати 447

448 HAZELNUT s.

Czech	: liskový ořech, m. 448
Danish	: Hasselnöd 448
Dutch	: de hazelnoot 448
Finnish	: pähkinä 448
French	: noisette, f. 448
German	: die Haselnuss 448
Hungarian	: mogyoró 448
Italian	: nocella, f. 448
Croatian	: lješnjak, m. 448
Norwegian	: haselnött, f. 448
Polish	: orzech laskowy, m. 448
Portuguese	: avelã, a 448
Rumanian	: aluna, f. 448
Slovak	: lieskový oriešok, m. 448
Spanish	: avellana, f. 448
Swedish	: hasselnöt-en 448
Turkish	: findik 448
Russian	: мелкий орешек, m. 448
Serbian	: лешњак, m. 448
Ukrainian	: лісковий горіх, m. 448

449 HEAD s.

Czech	: hlava, f. 449
Danish	: Hovede, c. 449
Dutch	: het hoofd 449
Finnish	: pää 449
French	: tête, f. 449
German	: der Kopf 449
Hungarian	: fej 449
Italian	: testa. f. 449
Croatian	: glava, f. 449
Norwegian	: hode, n. 449
Polish	: głowa, f. 449
Portuguese	: cabeça, a 449
Rumanian	: capul 449
Slovak	: hlava, f. 449
Spanish	: cabeza, f. 449
Swedish	: huvud-et 449
Turkish	: baş 449
Russian	: голова, f. 449
Serbian	: глава, f. 449
Ukrainian	: голова, f. 449

450 HEAD-CLERK s.

Czech	: přednosta úřadu, m. 450
Danish	: Kontorchef, m./c. 450
Dutch	: het hoofd van het kantoor 450
Finnish	: toimiston päällikkö 450
French	: chef de bureau, m. 450
German	: der Bürovorsteher 450
Hungarian	: irodavezetö 450
Italian	: capufficio, m. 450
Croatian	: šef, m. 450
Norwegian	: kontorchef, m. 450
Polish	: kierownik biura, m. 450
Portuguese	: chefe do escritório, o 450
Rumanian	: şeful de birou 450
Slovak	: prednosta úradu, m. 450
Spanish	: jefe de oficina, m. 450
Swedish	: kontorschef-en 450
Turkish	: yazihane reisı 450
Russian	: начальник канцелярии, m. 450
Serbian	: шеф, m. 450
Ukrainian	: начальник бюра, m. 450

451 HEAD-CLOTH s.

Czech	:	šátek na hlavu, m. 451
Danish	:	Hovedtörkläde 451
Dutch	:	de hoofddoek 451
Finnish	:	päähuivi 451
French	:	foulard, m. 451
German	:	das Kopftuch 451
Hungarian	:	fejkendö 451
Italian	:	fazzoletto per il capo, m. 451
Croatian	:	rubac, m. 451
Norwegian	:	hodetörklä, n. 451
Polish	:	chustka, f. 451
Portuguese	:	lenço de cabeça, o 451
Rumanian	:	basmaua, f. 451
Slovak	:	šatka na hlavu, f. 451
Spanish	:	pañuelo de cabeza 451
Swedish	:	schalett-en 451
Turkish	:	baş bezi 451
Russian	:	платок головной, m. 451
Serbian	:	рубац, m. 451
Ukrainian	:	хустина, f. 451

452 HEART s.

Czech	:	srdce, n. 452
Danish	:	Hjerte, n. 452
Dutch	:	het hart 452
Finnish	:	sydän 452
French	:	coeur, m. 452
German	:	das Herz 452
Hungarian	:	sziv 452
Italian	:	cuore, m. 452
Croatian	:	srce, n. 452
Norwegian	:	hjerte, n. 452
Polish	:	serce, n. 452
Portuguese	:	coração, o 452
Rumanian	:	inima, f. 452
Slovak	:	srdce, n. 452
Spanish	:	corazón, m. 452
Swedish	:	hjärta-t 452
Turkish	:	yürek 452
Russian	:	сердце, n. 452
Serbian	:	срце, n. 452
Ukrainian	:	сердце, n. 452

453 HEEL s. (the back part of the foot)

Czech	:	pata, f. 453
Danish	:	Hal, m./c. 453
Dutch	:	de hiel 453
Finnish	:	kantapää 453
French	:	talon, m. 453
German	:	die Ferse 453
Hungarian	:	sarok 453
Italian	:	calcagno, m. 453
Croatian	:	peta, f. 453
Norwegian	:	häl, m. 453
Polish	:	pięta, f. 453
Portuguese	:	calcanhar, o 453
Rumanian	:	călcâiul 453
Slovak	:	päta, f. 453
Spanish	:	tobillo, m. 453
Swedish	:	häl-en 453
Turkish	:	ökçe 453
Russian	:	пятка, f. 453
Serbian	:	пета, f. 453
Ukrainian	:	пята, f. 453

454 HEEL s. (a part of a shoe)

Czech	:	podpatek, m. 454
Danish	:	Häl, m. 454
Dutch	:	de hak 454
Finnish	:	korko 454
French	:	talon, m. 454
German	:	der Absatz 454
Hungarian	:	sarok 454
Italian	:	tacco, m. 454
Croatian	:	peta, f. 454
Norwegian	:	häl, m. 454
Polish	:	obcas, m. 454
Portuguese	:	salto, o 454
Rumanian	:	tocul 454
Slovak	:	podpätok, m. 454
Spanish	:	tacón, m. 454
Swedish	:	klack-en 454
Turkish	:	ökçe 454
Russian	:	каблук, m. 454
Serbian	:	пета, f. 454
Ukrainian	:	закаблук, m. 454

455 HELP v.

Czech	:	pomoci 455
Danish	:	hjälpe 455
Dutch	:	helpen 455
Finnish	:	auttaa 455
French	:	aider 455
German	:	helfen 455
Hungarian	:	segít 455
Italian	:	aiutare 455
Croatian	:	pomagati 455
Norwegian	:	hjelpe 455
Polish	:	pomoc 455
Portuguese	:	ajuda, f. 455
Rumanian	:	a ajuta 455
Slovak	:	pomôct' 455
Spanish	:	ayudar 455
Swedish	:	hjälp 455
Turkish	:	yardim etm. 455
Russian	:	помогать 455
Serbian	:	помагати 455
Ukrainian	:	допомагати 455

456 HERE adv.

Czech	:	zde 456
Danish	:	her 456
Dutch	:	hier 456
Finnish	:	täällä 456
French	:	ici 456
German	:	hier 456
Hungarian	:	itt 456
Italian	:	qui 456
Croatian	:	ovdje 456
Norwegian	:	her 456
Polish	:	tutaj 456
Portuguese	:	aqui 456
Rumanian	:	aici 456
Slovak	:	tu 456
Spanish	:	aquí 456
Swedish	:	här 456
Turkish	:	burada 456
Russian	:	здесь 456
Serbian	:	овде 456
Ukrainian	:	тут 456

457 HERRING s.

Czech	: slaneček, *m.*	457
Danish	: Sild, *m./c.*	457
Dutch	: de haring	457
Finnish	: silli	457
French	: hareng, *m.*	457
German	: der Hering	457
Hungarian	: hering	457
Italian	: arringa, *f.*	457
Croatian	: sledj, m.	457
Norwegian	: sild, *f.*	457
Polish	: śledź, *m.*	457
Portuguese	: arenque, *o*	457
Rumanian	: scrumbia, *f.*	457
Slovak	: haring, *m.*	457
Spanish	: arenque, *m.*	457
Swedish	: sill-en	457
Turkish	: ringa baligi	457
Russian	: селедка, *f.*	457
Serbian	: слеђ, *m.*	457
Ukrainian	: оселедець, *m.*	457

460 HOE s.

Czech	: motyka, *f.*	460
Danish	: Hakke, *c.*	460
Dutch	: het houweel	460
Finnish	: piilu	460
French	: pioche, *f.*	460
German	: die Hacke	460
Hungarian	: kapa	460
Italian	: piccozza, *f.*	460
Croatian	: sjekira, *f.*	460
Norwegian	: grew, *n.*; hakke, *f.* 460
Polish	: motyka, *f.*	460
Portuguese	: enxada, *a*	460
Rumanian	: târnàcopul	460
Slovak	: čakan, *m.*	460
Spanish	: azada, *f.*	460
Swedish	: hacka-n	460
Turkish	: kazma	460
Russian	: топор, *m.*	460
Serbian	: секира, *f.*	460
Ukrainian	: копаниця, *f.*	460

458 HEY s.

Czech	: seno, *n.*	458
Danish	: Hö, *n.*	458
Dutch	: het hooi	458
Finnish	: heinä	458
French	: foin, *m.*	458
German	: das Heu	458
Hungarian	: széna	458
Italian	: fieno, *m.*	458
Croatian	: sijeno, *n.*	458
Norwegian	: höy, *n.*	458
Polish	: siano, *n.*	458
Portuguese	: feno, *o*	458
Rumanian	: fânul	458
Slovak	: seno, *n.*	458
Spanish	: heno, *m.*	458
Swedish	: hö-et	458
Turkish	: kuru ot	458
Russian	: сено, *n.*	458
Serbian	: сено, *n.*	458
Ukrainian	: сіно, *n.*	458

461 HONEY s.

Czech	: med, *m.*	461
Danish	: Honning, *c.*	461
Dutch	: de honig	461
Finnish	: hunaja	461
French	: miel, *m.*	461
German	: der Honig	461
Hungarian	: méz	461
Italian	: miele, *m.*	461
Croatian	: med, *m.*	461
Norwegian	: honning, *m.*	461
Polish	: miód, *m.*	461
Portuguese	: mel, *o*	461
Rumanian	: mierea de stup	461
Slovak	: med, *m.*	461
Spanish	: miel, *f.*	461
Swedish	: honung-en	461
Turkish	: bal	461
Russian	: мед, *m.*	461
Serbian	: мед, *m.*	461
Ukrainian	: мед, *m.*	461

459 HIGHWAY s.

Czech	: silnice, *f.*	459
Danish	: Landevej, *m./c.*	459
Dutch	: de landstraat	459
Finnish	: maantie	459
French	: route, *f.*	459
German	: die Landstrasse	459
Hungarian	: az országút	459
Italian	: strada di campagna, *f.*	459
Croatian	: seoska cesta, *f.*	459
Norwegian	: landevei, *m.*	459
Polish	: droga krajowa, *f.*	459
Portuguese	: estrada de rodagem, *a*	459
Rumanian	: soseaua, *f.*	459
Slovak	: hradská, *f.*	459
Spanish	: carretera, *f.*	459
Swedish	: landsväg-en	459
Turkish	: büyük yol	459
Russian	: шоссейная дорога, *f.*	459
Serbian	: друм, *m.*	459
Ukrainian	: шлях, *m.*	459

462 HOOF s.

Czech	: kopyto, *n.*	462
Danish	: Hov, *m/c.*	462
Dutch	: de hoef	462
Finnish	: kavio	462
French	: sabot, *m.*	462
German	: der Huf	462
Hungarian	: pata	462
Italian	: zoccolo, *f.*	462
Croatian	: kopito, *n.*	462
Norwegian	: hov, *n.*	462
Polish	: kopyto, *n.*	462
Portuguese	: casco, *m.*	462
Rumanian	: copita, *f.*	462
Slovak	: kopyto, *n.*	462
Spanish	: casco, *m.*	462
Swedish	: hov-en	462
Turkish	: nal	462
Russian	: копыто, *n.*	462
Serbian	: копито, *n.*	462
Ukrainian	: копито, *n.*	462

463 HORSE s.

Czech	: kůň, *m.* 463
Danish	: Hest, *m.* 463
Dutch	: het paard 463
Finnish	: hevonen 463
French	: cheval, *m.* 463
German	: das Pferd 463
Hungarian	: ló 463
Italian	: cavallo, *m.* 463
Croatian	: konj, *m.* 463
Norwegian	: hest, *m.* 463
Polish	: kon, *m.* 463
Portuguese	: cavalo, *o* 463
Rumanian	: calul 463
Slovak	: kôň, *m.* 463
Spanish	: caballo, *m.* 463
Swedish	: häst-en 463
Turkish	: at 463
Russian	: лошадь, f.; конь, *m.* 463
Serbian	: конь, *m.* 463
Ukrainian	: кінь, *m.* 463

464 HORSE-RACE s.

Czech	: koňské dostihy, *pl.* 464
Danish	: Hesteväddelöb, *n.* 464
Dutch	: het paardenrennen 464
Finnish	: ratsastuskilpailu 464
French	: course de chevaux, *f.* 464
German	: das Pferderennen 464
Hungarian	: a lóverseny 464
Italian	: corsa di cavalli 464
Croatian	: konjske trke, *pl.* 464
Norwegian	: hesteveddelöp, *n.* 464
Polish	: wyścigi konne 464
Portuguese	: corrida de cavalos, *a* 464
Rumanian	: alergarea de cai 464
Slovak	: koňské dostihy, *pl.* 464
Spanish	: carrera de caballos 464
Swedish	: ridtävling-en 464
Turkish	: yariş 464
Russian	: скачки, *pl.* 464
Serbian	: коньска грка, *f.* 464
Ukrainian	: кінні перегони, *pl.* 464

465 HORSE-SHOE s.

Czech	: podkova *f.* 465
Danish	: Hestesko, *m./c.* 465
Dutch	: het hoefijzer 465
Finnish	: hevosenkenkä 465
French	: fer à cheval, *m.* 465
German	: das Hufeisen 465
Hungarian	: patkó 465
Italian	: ferro, *m.* 465
Croatian	: potkova, *f.* 465
Norwegian	: hestesko, *m.* 465
Polish	: podkowa, *f.* 465
Portuguese	: ferradura, *a* 465
Rumanian	: potcoavă, *f.* 465
Slovak	: podkova, *f.* 465
Spanish	: herradura, *f.* 465
Swedish	: hästsko-n 465
Turkish	: nal 465
Russian	: подкова, *f.* 465
Serbian	: потковица, *f.* 465
Ukrainian	: підкова, *f.* 465

466 HOSPITAL s.

Czech	: nemocnice, *f.* 466
Danish	: Sygehus, *n.* 466
Dutch	: het ziekenhuis 466
Finnish	: sairaala 466
French	: hôpital, *m.* 466
German	: das Krankenhaus 466
Hungarian	: kórház 466
Italian	: ospedale, *m.* 466
Croatian	: bolnica, *f.* 466
Norwegian	: sykehus, *n.* 466
Polish	: szpital, *m.* 466
Portuguese	: hospital, *o* 466
Rumanian	: spitalul 466
Slovak	: nemocnica, *f.* 466
Spanish	: hospital, *m.* 466
Swedish	: sjukhus-et 466
Turkish	: hastane 466
Russian	: больница, *f.* 466
Serbian	: болница, *f.* 466
Ukrainian	: лічниця, *f.* 466

467 HOTEL s.

Czech	: hotel, *m.* 467
Danish	: Hotel, *n.* 467
Dutch	: het hotel 467
Finnish	: hotelli 467
French	: hôtel, *m.* 467
German	: das Hotel 467
Hungarian	: szálloda 467
Italian	: albergo, *m.* 467
Croatian	: hotel, *m.* 467
Norwegian	: hotell, *n.* 467
Polish	: hotel, *m.* 467
Portuguese	: hotel, *o* 467
Rumanian	: hotelul 467
Slovak	: hotel, *m.* 467
Spanish	: hotel, *m.* 467
Swedish	: hotell-et 467
Turkish	: otel 467
Russian	: отель, *m.* 467
Serbian	: хотел, *m.* 467
Ukrainian	: гостинниця, *f.* 467

468 HOUR s.

Czech	: hodina, *f.* 468
Danish	: Time, *n.* 468
Dutch	: het uur 468
Finnish	: tunti 468
French	: heure, *f.* 468
German	: die Stunde 468
Hungarian	: óra 468
Italian	: ora, *f.* 468
Croatian	: sat, *m.* 468
Norwegian	: time, *m.* 468
Polish	: godzina, *f.* 468
Portuguese	: hora, *a* 468
Rumanian	: oră, *f.* 468
Slovak	: hodina, *f.* 468
Spanish	: hora, *f.* 468
Swedish	: timme-n 468
Turkish	: saat 468
Russian	: час, *m.* 468
Serbian	: сат, *m.* 468
Ukrainian	: година, *f.* 468

469 HOUSE s.

Czech	: dům, m.	469
Danish	: Huset, n.	469
Dutch	: het huis	469
Finnish	: talo	469
French	: la maison	469
German	: das Haus	469
Hungarian	: ház	469
Italian	: casa, f.	469
Croatian	: kuća, f.	469
Norwegian	: hus, n.	469
Polish	: dom, m.	469
Portuguese	: a casa	469
Rumanian	: casă, f.	469
Slovak	: dom, m.	469
Spanish	: casa, f.	469
Swedish	: hus-et	469
Turkish	: ev	469
Russian	: дом, m.	469
Serbian	: куħa, f.	469
Ukrainian	: дім, m.	469

470 HUNDRED

Czech	: sto	470
Danish	: Hundrede	470
Dutch	: honderd	470
Finnish	: sata	470
French	: cent	470
German	: hundert	470
Hungarian	: száz	470
Italian	: cento	470
Croatian	: sto	470
Norwegian	: hundre	470
Polish	: sto	470
Portuguese	: cem	470
Rumanian	: una sută	470
Slovak	: sto	470
Spanish	: cien	470
Swedish	: hundra	470
Turkish	: yüz	470
Russian	: сто	470
Serbian	: сто	470
Ukrainian	: сто	470

471 HUNGRY adj.

Czech	: hladový	471
Danish	: sulten	471
Dutch	: honger	471
Finnish	: nälkäinen	471
French	: affame	471
German	: hungrig	471
Hungarian	: éhes (en)	471
Italian	: affamato	471
Croatian	: gladan	471
Norwegian	: sulten	471
Polish	: głodny	471
Portuguese	: estomeado	471
Rumanian	: flămînd	471
Slovak	: hladny	471
Spanish	: hambriento	471
Swedish	: hungrig	471
Turkish	: aç	471
Russian	: голодный	471
Serbian	: гладан	471
Ukrainian	: голодний	471

472 HURT s. see 688 PAIN

473 HUSBAND see 566 MAN

474 ICE-CREAM s.

Czech	: zmrzlina, f.	474
Danish	: Is, m./c.	474
Dutch	: het ijs	474
Finnish	: jäätelö	474
French	: glace, f.	474
German	: das Eis	474
Hungarian	: fagylalt	474
Italian	: gelato, m.	474
Croatian	: sladoled, m.	474
Norwegian	: is, m.	474
Polish	: lody, pl.	474
Portuguese	: sorvete, o	474
Rumanian	: inghețată, f.	474
Slovak	: zmrzlina, f.	474
Spanish	: helado, m.	474
Swedish	: glass-en	474
Turkish	: dondurma	474
Russian	: мороженное, n.	474
Serbian	: сладолед, m.	474
Ukrainian	: морозиво, n.	474

475 ILL adj. (sick)

Czech	: nemocný	475
Danish	: syg	475
Dutch	: ziek	475
Finnish	: sairas	475
French	: malade	475
German	: krank	475
Hungarian	: beteg	475
Italian	: ammalato	475
Croatian	: bolestan	475
Norwegian	: syk	475
Polish	: chory	475
Portuguese	: doente	475
Rumanian	: bolnav	475
Slovak	: chorý	475
Spanish	: enfermo	475
Swedish	: sjuk	475
Turkish	: hasta	475
Russian	: больной	475
Serbian	: болестан	475
Ukrainian	: хворий	475

476 IMMEDIATE see 771 QUICK

477 INCENDIARY BOMB s.

Czech	: zápalná bomba, f.	477
Danish	: Brandbombe, c.	477
Dutch	: de brandbomb	477
Finnish	: palopommi	477
French	: la bombe à incendie	477
German	: die Brandbombe	477
Hungarian	: gyujtóbomba	477
Italian	: bomba incendiaria, f.	477
Croatian	: zapaljivačka bomba. f.	477
Norwegian	: brandbombe, f.	477
Polish	: bomba zapalająca, f.	477
Portuguese	: bomba incendiária, a	477
Rumanian	: bomba incendiară, f.	477
Slovak	: bomba zápalná, f.	477
Spanish	: bomba incendiaria, f.	477
Swedish	: brandbomb-en	477
Turkish	: yakici bomba	477
Russian	: зажигательная бомба, f.	477
Serbian	: запаљивачка бомба, f.	477
Ukrainian	: запальна бомба, f.	477

478 INCORRECT see 53 BAD

479 INDIA-RUBBER *s.*

Czech	:	guma, *f.* 479
Danish	:	Viskeläder, *c.* 479
Dutch	:	het gom 479
Finnish	:	raapekumi 479
French	:	gomme, *f.* 479
German	:	der Radiergummi 479
Hungarian	:	radir 479
Italian	:	gomma da cancellare, *f.* 479
Croatian	:	guma za brisanje, *f.* 479
Norwegian	:	viskelär, *c.* 479
Polish	:	radyrka, *f.* 479
Portuguese	:	borracha, *a* 479
Rumanian	:	guma de sters, *f.* 479
Slovak	:	guma, *f.* 479
Spanish	:	goma de borrar 479
Swedish	:	radergummi-t 479
Turkish	:	lastik 479
Russian	:	резинка, *f.* 479
Serbian	:	гума за брисање, *f.* 479
Ukrainian	:	радирка, *f.* 479

480 INDIVIDUAL see 885 SINGLE

481 INFANTRY-MAN *s.*

Czech	:	pěšák, *m.* 481
Danish	:	Infanterist, *m.* 481
Dutch	:	de grenadier 481
Finnish	:	jalkasotamies 481
French	:	fantassin, *m.* 481
German	:	der Grenadier 481
Hungarian	:	gyalogos 481
Italian	:	fante, *m.* 481
Croatian	:	pješak, *m.* 481
Norwegian	:	infanterist, *m.* 481
Polish	:	piechur, *m.* 481
Portuguese	:	soldado de infanteria, *o* 481
Rumanian	:	infanteristul 481
Slovak	:	pešiak, *m.* 481
Spanish	:	soldado de infantería, *m.* 481
Swedish	:	infanterist-en 481
Turkish	:	piyade askeri 481
Russian	:	пехотинец, *m.* 481
Serbian	:	пешак, *m.* 481
Ukrainian	:	піхотинець, *m.* 481

482 INFORM *v.* see 981 TELL

483 INFORMATION OFFICE *s.*

Czech	:	informační kancelář, *f.* 483
Danish	:	Oplysningsbureau, *c.* 483
Dutch	:	het inlichtingbureau 483
Finnish	:	tietotoimisto 483
French	:	bureau de renseignements, *m.* 483
German	:	die Auskunftsstelle 483
Hungarian	:	felvilágositó iroda 483
Italian	:	ufficio informazioni, *m.* 483
Croatian	:	izvještajni ured, *m.* 483
Norwegian	:	opplysnings byrå 483
Polish	:	informacje, *pl.* 483
Portuguese	:	secçao de informações, *a* 483
Rumanian	:	biroul de informaţii 483
Slovak	:	informačná kancelaria, *f.* 483
Spanish	:	oficina de información 483
Swedish	:	upplysningsbyrån-n 483
Turkish	:	malumat yeri 483
Russian	:	справочное бюро, *n.* 483
Serbian	:	извештајни биро, *m.* 483
Ukrainian	:	інформаційна станиця, *f.* 483

484 INK-STAND *s.*

Czech	:	kalamář, *m.* 484
Danish	:	Bläkhus, *n.* 484
Dutch	:	de inkpot 484
Finnish	:	mustepullo 484
French	:	encrier, *m.* 484
German	:	das Tintefass 484
Hungarian	:	tintatartó 484
Italian	:	calamaio, *m.* 484
Croatian	:	mastionica, *f.* 484
Norwegian	:	blekkhus, *n.* 484
Polish	:	kałamarz, *m.* 484
Portuguese	:	tinteiro, *o* 484
Rumanian	:	călimară, *f.* 484
Slovak	:	kalamár *m.* 484
Spanish	:	tintero, *m.* 484
Swedish	:	bläckhorn-et 484
Turkish	:	mürekkep hokkasi 484
Russian	:	чернильница, *f.* 484
Serbian	:	мастионица, *f.* 484
Ukrainian	:	каламар, *m.* 484

485 INN *s.*

Czech	:	hostinec, *m.* 485
Danish	:	Restauration, *c.* 485
Dutch	:	het restaurant 485
Finnish	:	ravintola 485
French	:	auberge, *f.* 485
German	:	das Gasthaus 485
Hungarian	:	vendéglö 485
Italian	:	locanda, *f.* 485
Croatian	:	gostiona, *f.* 485
Norwegian	:	gjestgiveri, *n.* 485
Polish	:	restauracja, *f.* 485
Portuguese	:	restaurante, *o* 485
Rumanian	:	restaurantul 485
Slovak	:	hostinec, *m.* 485
Spanish	:	fonda, *f.* 485
Swedish	:	restaurant-en 485
Turkish	:	lokanta 485
Russian	:	ресторан, *m.* 485
Serbian	:	гостиона, *f.* 485
Ukrainian	:	ресторан, *m.* 485

486 INQUIRE *v.* see 36 ASK

487 INTERPRETER *s.*

Czech	:	tlumočník, *m.*; tlumočnice, *f.* 487
Danish	:	fortolker, *c.* 487
Dutch	:	tolk, m. 487
Finnish	:	tulkki 487
French	:	interprète *m.* 487
German	:	Dolmetcher, *m.* 487
Hungarian	:	tolmács 487
Italian	:	interprete, *m.* 487
Croatian	:	tumač, *m.* 487
Norwegian	:	tolk, *c.* 487
Polish	:	tlumatcz, *m.* 487
Portuguese	:	intérpretar, *m.* 487
Rumanian	:	interpret, *m.* 487
Slovak	:	tlmočník, *m.* 487
Spanish	:	intérprete, *m.* 487
Swedish	:	tolk-en 487
Turkish	:	tercüman 487
Russian	:	переводник, *m.* 487
Serbian	:	тумач, *m.* 487
Ukrainian	:	перекладач, *m.* 487

488 IRON s. (a metallic element)

Czech	:	železo, n. 488
Danish	:	Jern, c. 488
Dutch	:	het ijzer 488
Finnish	:	rauta 488
French	:	fer, m. 488
German	:	das Eisen 488
Hungarian	:	vas 488
Italian	:	ferro, m. 488
Croatian	:	željezo, n. 488
Norwegian	:	jern, c. 488
Polish	:	żelazo, n. 488
Portuguese	:	ferro, m. 488
Rumanian	:	ficrul 488
Slovak	:	železo, n. 488
Spanish	:	hierro, m. 488
Swedish	:	järn-et 488
Turkish	:	demir 488
Russian	:	железо, n. 488
Serbian	:	гвожђе, n. 488
Ukrainian	:	залізо, n. 488

489 IRON s. (for pressing cloth)

Czech	:	žehlička, f. 489
Danish	:	Strygejern, n. 489
Dutch	:	het strijkijzer 489
Finnish	:	silitysranta 489
French	:	fer à repasser, m. 489
German	:	das Bügeleisen 489
Hungarian	:	vasaló 489
Italian	:	ferro da stiro, m. 489
Croatian	:	glačalo, n. 489
Norwegian	:	strykejern, n. 489
Polish	:	żelazko do prasowania 489
Portuguese	:	ferro eléctrico, o 489
Rumanian	:	fierul de călcat, m. 489
Slovak	:	hladidlo, n. 489
Spanish	:	plancha, f. 489
Swedish	:	strykjärn-et 489
Turkish	:	ütü 489
Russian	:	утюг, m. 489
Serbian	:	утија, f. 489
Ukrainian	:	залізко, n. 489

490 IRONING-BOARD s.

Czech	:	prkno na žehlení, n. 490
Danish	:	Strygebrät, c. 490
Dutch	:	de strijkplank 490
Finnish	:	silityslauta 490
French	:	planche à repasser, f. 490
German	:	das Bügelbrett 490
Hungarian	:	a vasalódeszka 490
Italian	:	asse per stirare, f. 490
Croatian	:	daska za glačanje, f. 490
Norwegian	:	strykefjel, m. 490
Polish	:	deska do prasowania, f. 490
Portuguese	:	tábua de engomar, a 490
Rumanian	:	scândura de frecat 490
Slovak	:	doska na hladenie, f. 490
Spanish	:	la tabla de planchar 490
Swedish	:	strykbräde-t 490
Turkish	:	ötü tahtasi 490
Russian	:	гладильная доска, f. 490
Serbian	:	даска за пегланье, f. 490
Ukrainian	:	дошка до прасуваня, f. 490

491 JACKET s.

Czech	:	kabát, m.; sako, n. 491
Danish	:	Jakke, m./c. 491
Dutch	:	het colbert 491
Finnish	:	takki 491
French	:	veston, m. 491
German	:	der Rock 491
Hungarian	:	kabát 491
Italian	:	giacca, f. 491
Croatian	:	kaput, m. 491
Norwegian	:	frakk, m.; jakke, m. 491
Polish	:	surdut, m. 491
Portuguese	:	casaco, o 491
Rumanian	:	haina, f. 491
Slovak	:	kabát, m. 491
Spanish	:	americana, f. 491
Swedish	:	rock-en 491
Turkish	:	caket 491
Russian	:	пиджак, m. 491
Serbian	:	капут, m. 491
Ukrainian	:	блюзка, f. 491

492 JANUARY s.

Czech	:	leden, m. 492
Danish	:	Januar, m. 492
Dutch	:	Januari 492
Finnish	:	tammikuu 492
French	:	janvier, m. 492
German	:	der Januar 492
Hungarian	:	januar 492
Italian	:	gennaio 492
Croatian	:	sijecanj, m. 492
Norwegian	:	januar, m., c. 492
Polish	:	styczeń, m. 492
Portuguese	:	janeiro, o 492
Rumanian	:	Januarie 492
Slovak	:	január, m. 492
Spanish	:	enero 492
Swedish	:	Januari 492
Turkish	:	ikinci kânun; kânunusani 492
Russian	:	январь, m. 492
Serbian	:	јануар, m. 492
Ukrainian	:	Січень, m. 492

493 JOINER s.

Czech	:	tesař, m. 493
Danish	:	Tömmermand, m. 493
Dutch	:	de timmerman 493
Finnish	:	puuseppä 493
French	:	charpentier, m. 493
German	:	der Zimmermann 493
Hungarian	:	ácz 493
Italian	:	carpentiere, m. 493
Croatian	:	tesar, m. 493
Norwegian	:	tömmermann, m. 493
Polish	:	cieśla, m. 493
Portuguese	:	carpinteiro, o 493
Rumanian	:	dulgherul 493
Slovak	:	tesár, m. 493
Spanish	:	carpintero, m. 493
Swedish	:	timmerman-en 493
Turkish	:	dülger 493
Russian	:	плотник, m. 493
Serbian	:	тесар, m. 493
Ukrainian	:	тесля, m. 493

494 JULY s.

Czech	: červenec, m.	494
Danish	: Juli 494	
Dutch	: Juli 494	
Finnish	: heinäkuu 494	
French	: juillet, m.	494
German	: der Juli 494	
Hungarian	: július 494	
Italian	: luglio, m.	494
Croatian	: srpanj, m.	494
Norwegian	: juli 494	
Polish	: lipiec, m.	494
Portuguese	: julho, o 494	
Rumanian	: Iulie, m.	494
Slovak	: júl 494	
Spanish	: julio 494	
Swedish	: juli 494	
Turkish	: temuz 494	
Russian	: июль 494	
Serbian	: Јули 494	
Ukrainian	: Липень 494	

495 JUNE s.

Czech	: červen, m.	495
Danish	: Juni 495	
Dutch	: Juni 495	
Finnish	: kesäkuu 495	
French	: juin, m.	495
German	: der Juni 495	
Hungarian	: június 495	
Italian	: giugno, m.	495
Croatian	: lipanj, m.	495
Norwegian	: juni 495	
Polish	: czerwiec, m.	495
Portuguese	: junho, o 495	
Rumanian	: Iunie, m.	495
Slovak	: jún 495	
Spanish	: junio 495	
Swedish	: juni 495	
Turkish	: haziran 495	
Russian	: июнь, m.	495
Serbian	: Јуни, m.	495
Ukrainian	: Червень, m.	495

496 KEY s.

Czech	: klíč, m.	496
Danish	: Nögle, m./c.	496
Dutch	: de sleutel	496
Finnish	: avain 496	
French	: clé, f.	496
German	: der Schlüssel	496
Hungarian	: kulcs 496	
Italian	: chiave, f.	496
Croatian	: ključ, m.	496
Norwegian	: nökkel, m.	496
Polish	: klucz, m.	496
Portuguese	: chave, a 496	
Rumanian	: cheiă, f.	496
Slovak	: kľúč, m.	496
Spanish	: llave, f.	496
Swedish	: nyckel-n 496	
Turkish	: anahtar 496	
Russian	: ключ, m.	496
Serbian	: ключ, m.	496
Ukrainian	: ключ, m.	496

497 KIDNEY s.

Czech	: ledvina, f.	497
Danish	: Nyre, n.	497
Dutch	: de nier	497
Finnish	: munuainen 497	
French	: rognons, m. pl.	497
German	: die Niere	497
Hungarian	: vese 497	
Italian	: arnione, m.	497
Croatian	: bubreg, m.	497
Norwegian	: nyre, n.	497
Polish	: nerka, f.	497
Portuguese	: rim, o 497	
Rumanian	: rinichiul, m.	497
Slovak	: l'advina, f.	497
Spanish	: riñón, m.	497
Swedish	: njure-n 497	
Turkish	: bübrek	497
Russian	: почка, f.	497
Serbian	: буброг, m.	497
Ukrainian	: нирка, f.	497

498 KILOGRAM s. (kilo)

Czech	: kilo, n.; kilogram, m.	498
Danish	: Kilo, n.; Kilogram, n.	498
Dutch	: een kilo	498
Finnish	: kilo-gramma	498
French	: un kilogramme	498
German	: das Kilogramm	498
Hungarian	: egy kiló	498
Italian	: un chilogramma	498
Croatian	: željezo, n.	488
Norwegian	: kilogram, n.	498
Polish	: jeden kilogram, m.	498
Portuguese	: um kilo	498
Rumanian	: un kilogram	498
Slovak	: kilogram, m.	498
Spanish	: un kilogramo	498
Swedish	: ett kilo-gramm	498
Turkish	: bir kilogram	498
Russian	: килограм, m.	498
Serbian	: килограм, m.	498
Ukrainian	: одно кіло, n.	498

499 KIND adj.

Czech	: laskavý; přátelsky; milý;	499
Danish	: venlig 499	
Dutch	: vrindelijk	499
Finnish	: hyvänsuopa; ystävällinen	499
French	: genre; bon	499
German	: gütig; freundlich	499
Hungarian	: barátságos	499
Italian	: benevolo; grazioso	499
Croatian	: dobrostiv	499
Norwegian	: god 499	
Polish	: łaskawy	499
Portuguese	: bon; amável	499
Rumanian	: bun 499	
Slovak	: láskavý; láskave	499
Spanish	: benévolo; bondadoso	499
Swedish	: god; vänlig	499
Turkish	: sulhen; sevimli	499
Russian	: любезный	499
Serbian	: добростив	499
Ukrainian	: добрий; милий	499

500 KING s.

Czech	:	král, *m.* 500
Danish	:	konge, *m.* 500
Dutch	:	koning, m. 500
Finnish	:	kuningas 500
French	:	roı, *m.* 500
German	:	der König 500
Hungarian	:	kiraly 500
Italian	:	re, *m.* 500
Croatian	:	kralj, *m.* 500
Norwegian	:	konge, *m.* 500
Polish	:	král, *m.* 500
Portuguese	:	rei, *m.* 500
Rumanian	:	rege, *m.* 500
Slovak	:	král', *m.* 500
Spanish	:	rey, *m.* 500
Swedish	:	konung-en 500
Turkish	:	kiral 500
Russian	:	король, *m.* 500
Serbian	:	краљ, *m.* 500
Ukrainian	:	король, *m.* 500

501 KISS s.

Czech	:	polibek, *m.* 501
Danish	:	kys, *n.* 501
Dutch	:	kus, n. 501
Finnish	:	suudelma 501
French	:	baiser, *m.* 501
German	:	der Kuss 501
Hungarian	:	csök 501
Italian	:	bacio, *m.* 501
Croatian	:	poljubac, *m.* 501
Norwegian	:	kyss, *c./m.* 501
Polish	:	ljubacz, *m.* 501
Portuguese	:	beijo, *m.* 501
Rumanian	:	săturare, *f.* 501
Slovak	:	pol'ubok, *m.*; bozk, *m.* 501
Spanish	:	beso, *m.* 501
Swedish	:	kyss-en 501
Turkish	:	pusej; opücük 501
Russian	:	поцелуй, *m.* 501
Serbian	:	пољубац, *m.* 501
Ukrainian	:	поцілунок, *m.* 501

502 KITCHEN s.

Czech	:	kuchyně, *f.* 502
Danish	:	Kökken, *n.* 502
Dutch	:	de keuken 502
Finnish	:	keittiö 502
French	:	cuisine, *f.* 502
German	:	die Küche 502
Hungarian	:	konyha 502
Italian	:	cucina, *f.* 502
Croatian	:	kuhinja, *f.* 502
Norwegian	:	kjökken, *n.* 502
Polish	:	kuchnia, *f.* 502
Portuguese	:	cozinha, *a* 502
Rumanian	:	bucätäria, *f.* 502
Slovak	:	kuchyňa, *f.* 502
Spanish	:	cocina, *f.* 502
Swedish	:	kök-et 502
Turkish	:	mutbah 502
Russian	:	кухня, *f..* 502
Serbian	:	кухиньа, *f.* 502
Ukrainian	:	кухня, *f.* 502

503 KNEE s.

Czech	:	koleno, *n.* 503
Danish	:	Knä, *m.* 503
Dutch	:	de knie 503
Finnish	:	polvi 503
French	:	genou, *m.* 503
German	:	das Knie 503
Hungarian	:	térd 503
Italian	:	ginocchio, *m.* 503
Croatian	:	koljeno, *n.* 503
Norwegian	:	kne, *n.* 503
Polish	:	kolano, *n.* 503
Portuguese	:	jòelho, *o* 503
Rumanian	:	genunchiul 503
Slovak	:	koleno, *n.* 503
Spanish	:	rodilla, *f.* 503
Swedish	:	knä-t 503
Turkish	:	diz 503
Russian	:	надколенье, *n.* 503
Serbian	:	колено, *n.* 503
Ukrainian	:	коліно, *n.* 503

504 KNIFE s.

Czech	:	nůž, *m.* 504
Danish	:	Kniv, *m./c.* 504
Dutch	:	het mes 504
Finnish	:	veitsi 504
French	:	couteau, *m.* 504
German	:	das Messer 504
Hungarian	:	kés 504
Italian	:	coltello, *m.* 504
Croatian	:	nož. *m.* 504
Norwegian	:	kniv, *m.* 504
Polish	:	nóż, *m.* 504
Portuguese	:	faca, *a* 504
Rumanian	:	catitul 504
Slovak	:	nôž, *m.* 504
Spanish	:	cuchillo, *m.* 504
Swedish	:	kniv-en 504
Turkish	:	biçak 504
Russian	:	нож, *m.* .504
Serbian	:	нож, *m.* 504
Ukrainian	:	ніж, *m.* 504

505 KOHLRABI s.

Czech	:	kedluben, *m.* 505
Danish	:	Kaalrabi, *m./c.* 505
Dutch	:	het koolraapje 505
Finnish	:	kaalirapi 505
French	:	chou-rave, *m.* 505
German	:	der Kohlrabi 505
Hungarian	:	karalábé 505
Italian	:	cavolo rapa, *m.* 505
Croatian	:	keleraba, *f.* 505
Norwegian	:	kålrabi, *m.* 505
Polish	:	kalarepa, *f.* 505
Portuguese	:	rábano, *o* 505
Rumanian	:	gulia, *f.* 505
Slovak	:	kaleráb, *m.* 505
Spanish	:	colinabo, *m.* 505
Swedish	:	kalrabi-n 505
Turkish	:	kara karğa 505
Russian	:	кольраби, *n.* 505
Serbian	:	келераба, *f.* 505
Ukrainian	:	калярепа, *f.* 505

506 LACE *s.* (dress of lace)

Czech	:	krajka, *f.* 506
Danish	:	Blonder, *pl.* 506
Dutch	:	de kant 506
Finnish	:	terä 506
French	:	dentelle, *f.* 506
German	:	die Spitze 506
Hungarian	:	a csipke 506
Italian	:	merletto, *m.* 506
Croatian	:	čipka, *f.* 506
Norwegian	:	knipling, *m.* 506
Polish	:	koronka, *f.* 506
Portuguese	:	vestido de rendas, *o* 506
Rumanian	:	dantelă, *f.* 506
Slovak	:	čipka, *f.* 506
Spanish	:	encaje 506
Swedish	:	spets-en 506
Turkish	:	dantela 506
Russian	:	кружева, *n.* 506
Serbian	:	чипка, *f.* 506
Ukrainian	:	мережка, *f.* 506

507 LADDER *s.*

Czech	:	žebřík, *m.* 507
Danish	:	Stige, *m./c.* 507
Dutch	:	de ladder 507
Finnish	:	tikapuut 507
French	:	échelle, *f.* 507
German	:	die Leiter 507
Hungarian	:	létra 507
Italian	:	scala a mano, *f.* 507
Croatian	:	ljestve, *pl.* 507
Norwegian	:	stige, *m.* 507
Polish	:	drabina, *f.* 507
Portuguese	:	escada, *a* 507
Rumanian	:	scară, *f.* 507
Slovak	:	rebrík, *m.* 507
Spanish	:	escalera, *f.* 507
Swedish	:	stege-n 507
Turkish	:	mutehairik merdiven 507
Russian	:	лестница, *f.* 507
Serbian	:	лества, *f.* 507
Ukrainian	:	драбина, *f.* 507

508 LADIES' HAT *s.*

Czech	:	dámský klobouk, *m.* 508
Danish	:	Damehat, *m.* 508
Dutch	:	de dameshoed 508
Finnish	:	naistenhattu 508
French	:	chapeau, *m.* 508
German	:	der Damenhut 508
Hungarian	:	nöi kalap 508
Italian	:	cappelino, *m.* 508
Croatian	:	ženski šešir, *m.* 508
Norwegian	:	damehatt, *m.* 508
Polish	:	kapelusz damski, *m.* 508
Portuguese	:	chapéu de senhora, *o* 508
Rumanian	:	pălăria de damă, *f.* 508
Slovak	:	dámský klobúk, *m.* 508
Spanish	:	sombrero de señora, *m.* 508
Swedish	:	damhatt-en 508
Turkish	:	kadin şapkasi 508
Russian	:	шляпа дамская, *f.* 508
Serbian	:	женски шешир, *m.* 508
Ukrainian	:	жіночий капелюх, *m.* 508

509 LADIES' SHOE *s.*

Czech	:	dámské střevíce, *pl.* 509
Danish	:	Damesko, *pl.* 509
Dutch	:	de damesschoer 509
Finnish	:	naistenkengät 509
French	:	chaussures, *f. pl.* 509
German	:	der Damenschuh 509
Hungarian	:	nöi cipö 509
Italian	:	scarpe per signora, *f. pl.* 509
Croatian	:	ženska cipela, *f.* 509
Norwegian	:	damesko, *m.* 509
Polish	:	trzewiki, *pl.* 509
Portuguese	:	sapato para senhora, *o* 509
Rumanian	:	pantoful de damă 509
Slovak	:	dámska topánka, *f.* 509
Spanish	:	zapatos de señora, *pl.* 509
Swedish	:	damsko-n 509
Turkish	:	kadin ayak kaplari 509
Russian	:	дамские туфли, *n.* 509
Serbian	:	женска ципела, *f.* 509
Ukrainian	:	жіночі черевики, *pl.* 509

510 LADY *s.*
see 625 Mrs.

511 LADY'S CLOTHES *s.*

Czech	:	dámské šatstvo, *n.* 511
Danish	:	Dametój 511
Dutch	:	de kleeding 511
Finnish	:	puku 511
French	:	vêtements de la femme 511
German	:	die Damenkleidung 511
Hungarian	:	ruházat (nöi) 511
Italian	:	indumenti femminili, *f. pl.* 511
Croatian	:	odijelo žensko, *n.* 511
Norwegian	:	dameklädning, *f.* 511
Polish	:	odzienie kobiece, *n.* 511
Portuguese	:	roupa de senhoras, *a* 511
Rumanian	:	imbrăcămintea femeiască 511
Slovak	:	ženský odev, *m.* 511
Spanish	:	indumentaria femenina, *f.* 511
Swedish	:	klädedräkt kvinnlig 511
Turkish	:	kadin elbisesi 511
Russian	:	одежда, женская, *f.* 511
Serbian	:	одело женско, *n.* 511
Ukrainian	:	одяг жіночий, *m.* 511

512 LADY'S COAT *s.*

Czech	:	dámský plášť, *m.* 512
Danish	:	Kaabe, *c.* 512
Dutch	:	de mantel 512
Finnish	:	naistenviitta 512
French	:	manteau, *m.* 512
German	:	der Damenmantel 512
Hungarian	:	nöi kabát 512
Italian	:	soprabito per signora, *m.* 512
Croatian	:	damski ogrtač, *m.* 512
Norwegian	:	käpe, *m.* 512
Polish	:	plaszcz damski, *m.* 512
Portuguese	:	casaco de senhora, *o* 512
Rumanian	:	Pardesiul 512
Slovak	:	dámský plášť, *m.* 512
Spanish	:	abrigo de señora 512
Swedish	:	kappa-n 512
Turkish	:	manto 512
Russian	:	пальто дамское, *n.* 512
Serbian	:	огртач, *m.* 521
Ukrainian	:	жіночий плащ, *m.* 512

513 LADY'S SUSPENDERS s.

Czech	:	podvazkový pás, m. 513
Danish	:	Strömpeholder, c. 513
Dutch	:	de jarretière 513
Finnish	:	sukkanauha 513
French	:	jarretelle, f. 513
German	:	der Strumpfhalter 513
Hungarian	:	harisnyatartó 513
Italian	:	reggicalze, m. 513
Croatian	:	podvezica, f. 513
Norwegian	:	strömpeholder, c. 513
Polish	· :	podwiazki, pl. 513
Portuguese	:	liga, a 513
Rumanian	:	port-jartiera 513
Slovak	:	podväzkový pas, m. 513
Spanish	:	ligas, pl. 513
Swedish	:	strumpa-n 513
Turkish	:	çovap baği 513
Russian	:	подвазка, f. 513
Serbian	:	ластиш за чарапе, m. 513
Ukrainian	:	підвазка, f. 513

514 LAKE s.

Czech	:	jezero, n. 514
Danish	:	Sö, c. 514
Dutch	:	het meer 514
Finnish	:	jarvi 514
French	:	lac, m. 514
German	:	der See 514
Hungarian	:	a tó 514
Italian	:	lago, m. 514
Croatian	:	jezero, n. 514
Norwegian	:	innsjö; sjö, m. 514
Polish	:	jezioro, n. 514
Portuguese	:	lago, o 514
Rumanian	:	lacul 514
Slovak	:	jazero, n. 514
Spanish	:	lago, m. 514
Swedish	:	insjö-n 514
Turkish	:	göl 514
Russian	:	озеро, n. 514
Serbian	:	језеро, n. 514
Ukrainian	:	озеро, n. 514

515 LANDSCAPE s.

Czech	:	krajina, f. 515
Danish	:	Landskab, n. 515
Dutch	:	het landschap 515
Finnish	:	maisema 515
French	:	paysage, m. 515
German	:	die Landschaft 515
Hungarian	:	vidék 515
Italian	:	paesaggio, m. 515
Croatian	:	krajina, f. 515
Norwegian	:	landskap, n. 515
Polish	:	krajobraz, m. 515
Portuguese	:	paīsagem, a 515
Rumanian	:	peisajul 515
Slovak	:	kraj, m. 515
Spanish	:	paisaje, m. 515
Swedish	:	landskap-et 515
Turkish	:	manzara 515
Russian	:	ландшафт, m. 515
Serbian	:	крајина, f. 515
Ukrainian	:	краэвид, m. 515

516 LANTERN s.

Czech	:	lucerna, f.; lampa, f. 516
Danish	:	Lygte, f./c. 516
Dutch	:	de lantaarn 516
Finnish	:	lyhty 516
French	:	lanterne, f. 516
German	:	die Laterne 516
Hungarian	:	lámpás 516
Italian	:	lanterna, f. 516
Croatian	:	svjetijka, f. 516
Norwegian	:	lanterne, f. 516
Polish	:	latarnia, f. 516
Portuguese	:	lanterna, a 516
Rumanian	:	lanternä, f. 516
Slovak	:	lampáš, m. 516
Spanish	:	linterna, f. 516
Swedish	:	lykta-n 516
Turkish	:	fanar 516
Russian	:	фонарь, m. 516
Serbian	:	светилька, f. 516
Ukrainian	:	ліхтарня, f.; світило, n. 516

517 LARD s.

Czech	:	sádlo, n. 517
Danish	:	Klaret, c. 517
Dutch	:	het varkensvet 517
Finnish	:	rasva 517
French	:	saindoux, m. 517
German	:	das Schmalz 517
Hungarian	:	zsir 517
Italian	:	strutto, m. 517
Croatian	:	mast, f. 517
Norwegian	:	smult 517
Polish	:	smalec, m. 517
Portuguese	:	banha, a 517
Rumanian	:	untura, f. 517
Slovak	:	mast', f. 517
Spanish	:	grasa de cerdo 517
Swedish	:	fett-et 517
Turkish	:	eritilmiş domuz yaği 517
Russian	:	смалец, m. 517
Serbian	:	маст 517
Ukrainian	:	смалець 517

518 LARGE adj.

Czech	:	velký 518
Danish	:	stor 518
Dutch	:	groot 518
Finnish	:	suuri 518
French	:	grand 518
German	:	gross 518
Hungarian	:	nagy 518
Italian	:	grande 518
Croatian	:	velik 518
Norwegian	:	stor 518
Polish	:	wielki 518
Portuguese	:	grande 518
Rumanian	:	mare 518
Slovak	:	vel'ký 518
Spanish	:	grande 518
Swedish	:	stor 518
Turkish	:	büyük 518
Russian	:	большой 518
Ukrainian	:	великий 518
Serbian	:	велик 518

519 LAVATORY s.
see 1012 TOILET

520 LEAD s.

Czech	:	olovo *n.* 520
Danish	:	Bly, *n.* 520
Dutch	:	het lood 520
Finnish	:	lyijy 520
French	:	plomb, *m.* 520
German	:	das Blei 520
Hungarian	:	ólom 520
Italian	:	piombo, *m.* 520
Croatian	:	olovo, *n.* 520
Norwegian	:	bly, *n.* 520
Polish	:	ołów, *m.* 520
Portuguese	:	chumbo, *o* 520
Rumanian	:	plumbul 520
Slovak	:	olovo *n.* 520
Spanish	:	plomo, *m.* 520
Swedish	:	bly-et 520
Turkish	:	kurşun 520
Russian	:	свинец, *m.* 520
Serbian	:	олово, *n.* 520
Ukrainian	:	олово, *n.* 520

521 LEARN v.

Czech	:	učiti se 521
Danish	:	laere 521
Dutch	:	leren 521
Finnish	:	oppia 521
French	:	apprendre 521
German	:	lernen 521
Hungarian	:	tanul 521
Italian	:	insegnare 521
Croatian	:	učiti (se) 521
Norwegian	:	laere 521
Polish	:	utrzyćsię 521
Portuguese	:	aprender 521
Rumanian	:	a învăta 521
Slovak	:	učit sa 521
Spanish	:	aprender; saber 521
Swedish	:	lära sig; få veta 521
Turkish	:	ögrenmek 521
Russian	:	учиться 521
Serbian	:	учити се 521
Ukrainian	:	вчитися 521

522 LEAVE v.

Czech	:	odjeti; opustiti 522
Danish	:	forlade 522
Dutch	:	overlaten 522
Finnish	:	matkustaa 522
French	:	partir; laisser 522
German	:	abreisen; hinterlassen 522
Hungarian	:	elutazik 522
Italian	:	lasciare; abbandonare 522
Croatian	:	otputovati 522
Norwegian	:	rive av; lösrive 522
Polish	:	odjezdzać; odjechać 522
Portuguese	:	partir; deixar 522
Rumanian	:	a pleca- 522
Slovak	:	odcestovat' 522
Spanish	:	partir; dejar 522
Swedish	:	upphöra 522
Turkish	:	azimet etmek 522
Russian	:	уезжать 522
Serbian	:	отпутовати 522
Ukrainian	:	виїжджати 522

523 LEEK s.

Czech	:	pór, *m.* 523
Danish	:	Porre, *m.* 523
Dutch	:	de prei 523
Finnish	:	laukka 523
French	:	poireau, *m.* 523
German	:	der Lauch 523
Hungarian	:	hagyma 523
Italian	:	porro, *m.* 523
Croatian	:	mladi luk, *m.* 523
Norwegian	:	lök, *m.* 523
Polish	:	por, *m.* 523
Portuguese	:	alho-porro, *o* 523
Rumanian	:	arpagica, *f.* 523
Slovak	:	pór, *m.* 523
Spanish	:	puerro, *m.* 523
Swedish	:	lök-en 523
Turkish	:	prasa 523
Russian	:	лук-порей, *m.* 523
Serbian	:	зелени лукац, *m.* 523
Ukrainian	:	пора; прас, *f.* 523

524 LEG s.

Czech	:	noha, *f.* 524
Danish	:	Ben, *n.* 524
Dutch	:	het been 524
Finnish	:	sääri 524
French	:	jambe, *f.* 524
German	:	das Bein 524
Hungarian	:	láb 524
Italian	:	gamba, *f.* 524
Croatian	:	noga, *f.* 524
Norwegian	:	ben, *n.* 524
Polish	:	noga, *f.* 524
Portuguese	:	perna, *a* 524
Rumanian	:	piciorul 524
Slovak	:	noha, *f.* 524
Spanish	:	pierna, *f.* 524
Swedish	:	ben-et 524
Turkish	:	bacak 524
Russian	:	нога, *f.* 524
Serbian	:	нога, *f.* 524
Ukrainian	:	нога, *f.* 524

525 LEMON s.

Czech	:	citron, *m.* 525
Danish	:	Citron, *m./c.* 525
Dutch	:	de citroen 525
Finnish	:	sitruuna 525
French	:	citron, *m.* 525
German	:	die Zitrone 525
Hungarian	:	citrom 525
Italian	:	limone, *m.* 525
Croatian	:	limun, *m.* 525
Norwegian	:	citron, *m.* 525
Polish	:	cytryna, *f.* 525
Portuguese	:	limão, *o* 525
Rumanian	:	Lămîie, *f.* 525
Slovak	:	citrón, *m.* 525
Spanish	:	limón, *m.* 525
Swedish	:	citron-en 525
Turkish	:	leymon 525
Russian	:	лимон, *m.* 525
Serbian	:	лимун, *m.* 525
Ukrainian	:	цитрина, *f.* 525

526 LETTER *s.*

Czech	: dopis, *m.*; psaní, *n.*	526
Danish	: Brev, *n.*	526
Dutch	: de brief	526
Finnish	: kirje	526
French	: lettre, *f.*	526
German	: der Brief	526
Hungarian	: levél	526
Italian	: lettera, *f.*	526
Croatian	: pismo, *n.*	526
Norwegian	: brev, *n.*	526
Polish	: list, *m.*	526
Portuguese	: carta, *a*	526
Rumanian	: scrisoareă, *f.*	526
Slovak	: list, *m.*	526
Spanish	: carta, *f.*	526
Swedish	: brevet	526
Turkish	: mektup	526
Russian	: письмо, *n.*	526
Serbian	: писмо, *n.*	526
Ukrainian	: лист, *m.*	526

527 LIE *v.*

Czech	: ležeti	527
Danish	: ligge	527
Dutch	: liggen	527
Finnish	: maata	527
French	: ètre couché	527
German	: liegen	527
Hungarian	: feküdni	527
Italian	: giacere	527
Croatian	: ležati	527
Norwegian	: ligge	527
Polish	: leżeć	527
Portuguese	: estar deitado, jazer	527
Rumanian	: a sta culcat	527
Slovak	: ležať'	527
Spanish	: yacer	527
Swedish	: ligga	527
Turkish	: yatmak	527
Russian	: лежать	527
Serbian	: лежати	527
Ukrainian	: лежати	527

528 LIFE-BELT *s.*

Czech	: záchranný pás, *m.*	528
Danish	: Redningsbälte, *n.*	528
Dutch	: de reddingsboei	528
Finnish	: pelastusvyö	528
French	: ceinture de sauvetage, *f.*	528
German	: der Rettungsgürtel	528
Hungarian	: mentööv	528
Italian	: salvagente, *m.*	528
Croatian	: pojas za spasavanje. *m.*	528
Norwegian	: redningsbelte, *n.*	528
Polish	: pas ratunkowy, *m.*	528
Portuguese	: salva-vidas, *o*	528
Rumanian	: colacul de salvare	528
Slovak	: záchranný pás, *m.*	528
Spanish	: cinturón salvavidas	528
Swedish	: livbält-et	528
Turkish	: can kurtaran	528
Russian	: спасательный пояс, *m.*	528
Serbian	: појас за спасавање, *m.*	528
Ukrainian	: рятунковий пояс, *m.*	528

529 LIFT *s.*

see **309 ELEVATOR**

530 LIGHT *adj.* (color)

Czech	: světlý	530
Danish	: lys	530
Dutch	: licht	530
Finnish	: valoisa	530
French	: clair	530
German	: hell	530
Hungarian	: világos	530
Italian	: chiaro	530
Croatian	: jasan	530
Norwegian	: lys	530
Polish	: jasny	530
Portuguese	: claro	530
Rumanian	: luminos	530
Slovak	: jasný	530
Spanish	: claro	530
Swedish	: ljus	530
Turkish	: acik	530
Russian	: светло; -ый	530
Serbian	: јасан	530
Ukrainian	: ясний	530

531 LIGHT *s.* (e.g. daylight)

Czech	: světlo, *n.*	531
Danish	: Cykellygte, *c.*	531
Dutch	: het licht	531
Finnish	: valo	531
French	: lumière, *f.*	531
German	: das Licht	531
Hungarian	: a fény	531
Italian	: luce, *f.*	531
Croatian	: svjetlo, *n.*	531
Norwegian	: lys, *n.*	531
Polish	: światlo lampowe, *n.*	531
Portuguese	: luz, *a*	531
Rumanian	: lumină, *f.*	531
Slovak	: svetlo, *n.*	531
Spanish	: la luz	531
Swedish	: lykta-n	531
Turkish	: ziya	531
Russian	: свет, *m.*	531
Serbian	: светлост, *f.*	531
Ukrainian	: світло, *n.*	531

532 LIGHT METAL *s.* (of little weight)

Czech	: lehký kov, *m.*	532
Danish	: Letmétal, *n.*	532.
Dutch	: het lichtmetaal	532
Finnish	: kevytmetalli	532
French	: métal léger, *m.*	532
German	: das Leichtmetall	532
Hungarian	: a könnyü fém	532
Italian	: metallo leggero, *m.*	532
Croatian	: laka kovina, *f.*	532
Norwegian	: lettmetall, *n.*	532
Polish	: lekki metal, *m.*	532
Portuguese	: metal leve, *o*	532
Rumanian	: aluminiul	532
Slovak	: ľahký kov, *m.*	532
Spanish	: el metal ligero	532
Swedish	: lättmetal--en	532
Turkish	: hafif maden	532
Russian	: легкий металл, *m.*	532
Serbian	: лаки метал, *m.*	532
Ukrainian	: легкий металь *m.*	532

533 LIGHTNING *s.*

Czech	: blesk, *m.* 533
Danish	: Lyn, *n.* 533
Dutch	: de bliksem 533
Finnish	: salama 533
French	: éclair, *m.* 533
German	: der Blitz 533
Hungarian	: villám 533
Italian	: lampo, *m.*; fulmine, *m.* 533
Croatian	: bliesak, *m.* 533
Norwegian	: lyn, *n.* 533
Polish	: piorun, *m.* 533
Portuguese	: relâmpago, *o* 533
Rumanian	: fulgerul 533
Slovak	: blesk, *m.* 533
Spanish	: relámpago, *m.* 533
Swedish	: blixt-en 533
Turkish	: yıldırım 533
Russian	: молиня, *f.* 533
Serbian	: муньа, *f.* 533
Ukrainian	: блискавка, *f.* 533

534 LILAC *s.*

Czech	: bez, *m.* 534
Danish	: Syren, m.; Hyld, *m./c.* 534
Dutch	: de sering 534
Finnish	: syreeni 534
French	: lilas, *m.* 534
German	: der Flieder 534
Hungarian	: az orgona 534
Italian	: lillà, *m.* 534
Croatian	: jorgovan, *m.* 534
Norwegian	: syrin, *m.* 534
Polish	: bez, *m.* 534
Portuguese	: lalás, *o* 534
Rumanian	: liliacul 534
Slovak	: orgován, *m.* 534
Spanish	: sauco, *m.* 534
Swedish	: syren-en 534
Turkish	: lailak 534
Russian	: сирень *f.* 534
Serbian	: jopгован, *m.* 534
Ukrainian	: бузок; боз, *m.* 534

535 LILY OF THE VALLEY *s.*

Czech	: konvalinka, *f.* 535
Danish	: Liljekonval, *m./c.* 535
Dutch	: het lelietje-van-dalen 535
Finnish	: kielo 535
French	: muguet, *m.* 535
German	: das Maiglöckchen 535
Hungarian	: gyöngyvirág 535
Italian	: mughetto, *m.* 535
Croatian	: djurdjica, *f.* 535
Norwegian	: liljekonval, *m.* 535
Polish	: konwalja, *f.* 535
Portuguese	: lírio dos vales, *o* 535
Rumanian	: lăcrimoră, *f.* 535
Slovak	: konvalinka, *f.* 535
Spanish	: lirio de los valles, *m.* 535
Swedish	: liljekonvalje-n 535
Turkish	: inci çiçeği 535
Russian	: ландыш, *m.* 535
Serbian	: ђурчевак, *m.* 535
Ukrainian	: конвалія, *f.* 535

536 LIME-TREE *s.*

Czech	: lípa, *f.* 536
Danish	: Lindeträ, *n.* 536
Dutch	: de linde 536
Finnish	: lehmus 536
French	: tilleul, *m.* 536
German	: die Linde 536
Hungarian	: a hársfa 536
Italian	: tigho, *m.* 536
Croatian	: lipa, *f.* 536
Norwegian	: lind, *m.* 536
Polish	: lipa, *f.* 536
Portuguese	: tília, *a* 536
Rumanian	: teiul 536
Slovak	: lipa, *f.* 536
Spanish	: tilo, *m.* 536
Swedish	: lind-en 536
Turkish	: ahlamur ağaci 536
Russian	: липа, *f.* 536
Serbian	: липа, *f.* 536
Ukrainian	: липа, *f.* 536

537 LINEN *s.*

Czech	: plátno, *n.* 537
Danish	: Lärred, *n.* 537
Dutch	: het linnen 537
Finnish	: pellavakangas 537
French	: lin, *m.* 537
German	: das Leinen 537
Hungarian	: vászon 537
Italian	: lino, *m.* 537
Croatian	: platno, *n.* 537
Norwegian	: lin, *n.* 537
Polish	: płótno, *n.* 537
Portuguese	: linho, *o* 537
Rumanian	: pânză, *f.* 537
Slovak	: plátno, *n.* 537
Spanish	: lino, *m.* 537
Swedish	: linne-t 537
Turkish	: keten 537
Russian	: льняная материя, *f.* 537
Serbian	: платно, *n.* 537
Ukrainian	: полотно, *n.* 537

538 LINING *s.*

Czech	: podšívka, *f.* 538
Danish	: For, *c.* 538
Dutch	: de voering 538
Finnish	: vuorikangas 538
French	: étoffe à doublure, *f.* 538
German	: der Futterstoff 538
Hungarian	: bélésanyag 538
Italian	: fodera, *f.* 538
Croatian	: podstava, *f.* 538
Norwegian	: forstoff, *n.* 538
Polish	: material na podszwewki, *m.* 538
Portuguese	: fôrro, *o* 538
Rumanian	: captuşala 538
Slovak	: podšívka, *f.* 538
Spanish	: forro, *m.* 538
Swedish	: fodr-et 538
Turkish	: astar 538
Russian	: подкладка, *f.* 538
Serbian	: подстава, *f.* 538
Ukrainian	: підшивка, *f.* 538

539 LIP s. (lips)

Czech	: ret, *m.*; rty, *pl.*	539
Danish	: Läber, *pl.*	539
Dutch	: de lip	539
Finnish	: huuli	539
French	: lèvre, *f.*	539
German	: die Lippe	539
Hungarian	: ajak	539
Italian	: labbra, *f. pl.*	539
Croatian	: usna, *f.*	539
Norwegian	: leppe, *f.*; lebe, *m.*	539
Polish	: wargi, *pl.*	539
Portuguese	: lábio, *o*	539
Rumanian	: buza, *f.*	539
Slovak	: pera; pery, *pl.*	539
Spanish	: labios, *pl.*	539
Swedish	: läpp-en	539
Turkish	: dudaklar	539
Russian	: губы, *pl.*	539
Serbian	: усне, *pl.*	539
Ukrainian	: губи, *pl.*	539

540 LIP-STICK s.

Czech	: tyčinka na rty, *f.*	540
Danish	: Läbestift, *m./c.*	540
Dutch	: de lippenetift	540
Finnish	: huulipuikko	540
French	: bâton de rouge, *m.*	540
German	: der Lippenstift	540
Hungarian	: ajakrúzs	540
Italian	: rossetto, *m.*	540
Croatian	: crvenilo za usne, *n.*	540
Norwegian	: lebestift, *m.*	540
Polish	: szminka, *f.*	540
Portuguese	: baton, *o*	540
Rumanian	: roşul de buze	540
Slovak	: červeň na pery, *f.*	540
Spanish	: lapiz de carmín	540
Swedish	: läppstift-et	540
Turkish	: dudak boyasi	540
Russian	: губная помада, *f.*	540
Serbian	: црвенило за усне, *n.*	540
Ukrainian	: устна помадка, *f.*	540

541 LIQUEUR s.

Czech	: likér, *m.*	541
Danish	: Likör, *m./c.*	541
Dutch	: de liqueur	541
Finnish	: likööri	541
French	: liqueur, *f.*	541
German	: der Likör	541
Hungarian	: likör	541
Italian	: liquore, *m.*	541
Croatian	: liker, *m.*	541
Norwegian	: likör, *m.*	541
Polish	: likier, *m.*	541
Portuguese	: licôr, *o*	541
Rumanian	: licheorúl	541
Slovak	: likér, *m.*	541
Spanish	: licor, *m.*	541
Swedish	: likör-en	541
Turkish	: likör	541
Russian	: ликер, *m.*	541
Serbian	: ликер, *m.*	541
Ukrainian	: лікер, *m.*	541

542 LITTLE
see 339 FEW

543 LIVE v.
see 72 BE

544 LIVER s.

Czech	: játra, *pl.*	544
Danish	: Lever, *m./c.*	544
Dutch	: de lever	544
Finnish	: maksa	544
French	: foie, *m.*	544
German	: die Leber	544
Hungarian	: máj	544
Italian	: fegato, *m.*	544
Croatian	: džigerica, *f.*	544
Norwegian	: lever, *m.*	544
Polish	: wątroba, *f.*	544
Portuguese	: fígado, *o*	544
Rumanian	: ficatul, *m.*	544
Slovak	: jatrá	544
Spanish	: hígado, *m.*	544
Swedish	: lever-n	544
Turkish	: kara ciğer	544
Russian	: печенка, *f.*	544
Serbian	: ђигерица, *f.*	544
Ukrainian	: печінка, *f.*	544

545 LIVING-ROOM s.

Czech	: obývací pokoj, *m.*	545
Danish	: Dagligstue, *m./c.*	545
Dutch	: de huiskamer	545
Finnish	: asuinhuone	545
French	: salon, *m.*	545
German	: das Wohnzimmer	545
Hungarian	: lakószoba	545
Italian	: salotto, *m.*	545
Croatian	: soba, *f.*	545
Norwegian	: dagligstue, *f.*	545
Polish	: pokój mieszkalny, *m.*	545
Portuguese	: sala, *a*	545
Rumanian	: camera de locuit, *f.*	545
Slovak	: obývacia izba, *f.*	545
Spanish	: gabinete, *m.*	545
Swedish	: vardagsrum-et	545
Turkish	: oturmak odasi	545
Russian	: жилая комната, *f.*	545
Serbian	: соба, *f.*	545
Ukrainian	: кімната, *f.*	545

546 LOBSTER s.

Czech	: rak (mořský), *m.*	546
Danish	: Hummer, *m./c.*	546
Dutch	: de langouste	546
Finnish	: hummeri	546
French	: homard, *m.*	546
German	: der Hummer	546
Hungarian	: homár	546
Italian	: aragosta, *f.*	546
Croatian	: morski rak, *m.*	546
Norwegian	: hummer, *m.*	546
Polish	: homar, *m.*	546
Portuguese	: langosta, *a*	546
Rumanian	: langusta, *f.*	546
Slovak	: morský rak, *m.*	546
Spanish	: langosta, *f.*	546
Swedish	: hummer-n	546
Turkish	: astakoz	546
Russian	: омар, *m.*	546
Serbian	: морски рак, *m.*	546
Ukrainian	: гомар, *m.*	546

80

547 LOCK   s. (of a door)

Czech	: zámek, m. 547
Danish	: Laas, c. 547
Dutch	: het slot 547
Finnish	: lukko 547
French	: verrou, m. 547
German	: das Schloss 547
Hungarian	: lakat 547
Italian	: serratura, f. 547
Croatian	: dvorac, m. 547
Norwegian	: lås, c. 547
Polish	: kłódka, f.; zámek, m. 547
Portuguese	: cadeado, o 547
Rumanian	: lacâtul 547
Slovak	: zámka, f. 547
Spanish	: cerradura, f. 547
Swedish	: lås-et 547
Turkish	: asma kilid 547
Russian	: замок (подвесной), m. 547
Serbian	: катанац, m. 547
Ukrainian	: колодка, f. 547

548 LONG   adj.

Czech	: dlouhý 548
Danish	: lang 548
Dutch	: lang 548
Finnish	: pitkä 548
French	: long 548
German	: lang 548
Hungarian	: hosszu 548
Italian	: lungo 548
Croatian	: dug 548
Norwegian	: lang 548
Polish	: długi 548
Portuguese	: comprido 548
Rumanian	: lung 548
Slovak	: dlhý 548
Spanish	: largo 548
Swedish	: lång 548
Turkish	: uzun 548
Russian	: длинный 548
Serbian	: дуг 548
Ukrainian	: довгий 548

549 LOUSE   s.

Czech	: veš, f. 549
Danish	: Lus, m./c. 549
Dutch	: de luis 549
Finnish	: täi 549
French	: pou, m. 549
German	: die Laus 549
Hungarian	: tetü 549
Italian	: pidocchio, m. 549
Croatian	: uš, f. 549
Norwegian	: lus, f. 549
Polish	: wesz, f. 549
Portuguese	: piolho, o 549
Rumanian	: paduchele 549
Slovak	: voš, f. 549
Spanish	: piojo, m. 549
Swedish	: lus-en 549
Turkish	: bit 549
Russian	: вошь, f. 549
Serbian	: уш, f. 549
Ukrainian	: вош, f. 549

550 LOVE   v.

Czech	: milovati 550
Danish	: elske 550
Dutch	: liefhebben 550
Finnish	: rakastaa 550
French	: aimer 550
German	: lieben 550
Hungarian	: szeret 550
Italian	: amare 550
Croatian	: ljubiti 550
Norwegian	: elske 550
Polish	: ljubić 550
Portuguese	: amar 550
Rumanian	: a iubi 550
Slovak	: milovat'; l'ubit' 550
Spanish	: amar; querer 550
Swedish	: älska 550
Turkish	: sevmek 550
Russian	: любить 550
Serbian	: љубити 550
Ukrainian	: кохоння 550

551 LORD   see 414 GOD

552 LOW   adj.   see 877 SHORT

553 LOWER-ARM   s.

Czech	: předloktí, n. 553
Danish	: Underarm, m./c. 553
Dutch	: de onderarm 553
Finnish	: kyynärvarsi 553
French	: avant-bras, m. 553
German	: der Unterarm 553
Hungarian	: alsókar 553
Italian	: avambraccio, m. 553
Croatian	: podlaktica, f. 553
Norwegian	: underarm, m. 553
Polish	: przedramię, n. 553
Portuguese	: ante braço, o 553
Rumanian	: antebraț 553
Slovak	: predlaktie, n. 553
Spanish	: antebrazo, m. 553
Swedish	: underarm-en 553
Turkish	: kol 553
Russian	: нижняя часть руки, f. 553
Serbian	: подлактица, f. 553
Ukrainian	: долішне рамя, n. 553

554 LOW-SHOE   s.

Czech	: polobota, f.; -ky, pl. 554
Danish	: Sko, m./c. 554
Dutch	: de lage schoen 554
Finnish	: puolikenkä 554
French	: le soulier bas 554
German	: der Halbschuh 554
Hungarian	: félcipö 554
Italian	: scarpa scollata, f. 554
Croatian	: niska cipela, f. 554
Norwegian	: lav sko, c. 554
Polish	: trzewiki, pl. 554
Portuguese	: sapato, o 554
Rumanian	: pantoful, m. 554
Slovak	: poltopánka, f. 554
Spanish	: zapato, m. 554
Swedish	: sko, n.; 554
Turkish	: potin 554
Russian	: полуботинки, pl. 554
Serbian	: ниска зипела, f. 554
Ukrainian	: черевикі низькі, pl. 554

555 LUGGAGE *s.*

Czech	:	zavazadlo, *n.* 555
Danish	:	Bagage, *m./c.* 555
Dutch	:	de bagage 555
Finnish	:	matkatavara 555
French	:	bagages, *m. pl.* 555
German	:	das Gepäck 555
Hungarian	:	poggyász 555
Italian	:	bagagli, *m. pl.* 555
Croatian	:	prtljag, *m.* 555
Norwegian	:	bagasje, *m.* 555
Polish	:	bagaż, *f.* 555
Portuguese	:	begagem, *a* 555
Rumanian	:	bagajul 555
Slovak	:	batožina *f.* 555
Spanish	:	equipaje, *m.* 555
Swedish	:	resgods-et 555
Turkish	:	eşya 555
Russian	:	багаж, *m.* 555
Serbian	:	пртљаг, *m.* 555
Ukrainian	:	пакунок, *m.* 555

556 LUGGAGE OFFICE *s.*

Czech	:	úschovna zavazadel, *f.* 556
Danish	:	Garderobe, *c.* 556
Dutch	:	de bagage-bewaarplaats 556
Finnish	:	matkatavarain säilytys 556
French	:	consigne, *f.* 556
German	:	die Gepäckaufbewahrung 556
Hungarian	:	ruhatár 556
Italian	:	deposito bagagli, *m.* 556
Croatian	:	garderoba, *f.* 556
Norwegian	:	oppbevaring, *m.* 556
Polish	:	przechowalnia bagażu, *f.* 556
Portuguese	:	depósito para a begagem, *o* 556
Rumanian	:	garderobă, *f.* 556
Slovak	:	úschovňa batožiny, *f.* 556
Spanish	:	consigna, *f.* 556
Swedish	:	bagage-inlämningen 556
Turkish	:	eşya muhafazasi 556
Russian	:	хранение багажа, *n.* 556
Serbian	:	багажник, *m.* 556
Ukrainian	:	багажник, *m.* 556

557 LUNG *s.* (lungs pl.)

Czech	:	plíce, *pl.* 557
Danish	:	Lunge, *m.* 557
Dutch	:	de long 557
Finnish	:	keuhko(t) 557
French	:	poumon, *m.* 557
German	:	die Lunge 557
Hungarian	:	tüdö 557
Italian	:	polmene, *m.* 557
Croatian	:	pluća, *pl.* 557
Norwegian	:	lunge, *f.* 557
Polish	:	płuca, *pl.* 557
Portuguese	:	pulmões, os 557
Rumanian	:	plămâuul 557
Slovak	:	pl'úca, *pl.* 557
Spanish	:	pulmones, *pl.* 557
Swedish	:	lunga-n 557
Turkish	:	ciğer 557
Russian	:	легкое, *n.* 557
Serbian	:	плуħa, *f.* 557
Ukrainian	:	легені, *pl.* 557

558 LUNCH *s.*

see **278 DINNER**

559 MACARONI *pl.*

Czech	:	makarony, *pl.* 559
Danish	:	Makaroni, *pl.* 559
Dutch	:	de macaroni 559
Finnish	:	makarooneja 559
French	:	macaronis, *m. pl.* 559
German	:	die Makkaroni 559
Hungarian	:	makaroni 559
Italian	:	maccheroni, *m. pl.* 559
Croatian	:	makaroni, *pl.* 559
Norwegian	:	makkaroni, *pl.* 559
Polish	:	makaron, *m.* 559
Portuguese	:	macarrão, *o* 559
Rumanian	:	macaroanele, *pl.* 559
Slovak	:	makaróny, *pl.* 559
Spanish	:	macarrones, *pl.* 559
Swedish	:	makaroner-na 559
Turkish	:	makarna 559
Russian	:	макароны, *pl.* 559
Serbian	:	макарони, *pl.* 559
Ukrainian	:	макарон, *pl.* 559

560 MACHINE *s.*

Czech	:	stroj, *m.*; přítroj, *m.* 560
Danish	:	maskine, *c.* 560
Dutch	:	machine, c. 560
Finnish	:	kone 560
French	:	machine, *f.* 560
German	:	die Maschine 560
Hungarian	:	gép 560
Italian	:	macchina, *f.* 560
Croatian	:	stroj, *m.* 560
Norwegian	:	maskin, *c.* 560
Polish	:	maszyna, *f.* 560
Portuguese	:	máquina, *f.* 560
Rumanian	:	maşină, *f.* 560
Slovak	:	stroj, *m.* 560
Spanish	:	máquina, *f.* 560
Swedish	:	maskin-et 560
Turkish	:	makina 560
Russian	:	машина, *f.* 560
Serbian	:	строј, *m.* 560
Ukrainian	:	машина, *f.* 560

561 MACHINE-GUN *s.*

Czech	:	kulomet, *m.*; strojní puška, *f.* 561
Danish	:	Maskingevär, *n.* 561
Dutch	:	de mitrailleur 561
Finnish	:	konekivääri 561
French	:	mitrailleuse, *f.* 561
German	:	das Maschinengewehr 561
Hungarian	:	gépfegyver 561
Italian	:	mitragliatrice, *f.* 561
Croatian	:	mašinska puška, *f.* 561
Norwegian	:	maskingevär, *n.* 561
Polish	:	karabin maszynowy, *m.* 561
Portuguese	:	metralhadora, *a* 561
Rumanian	:	mitralieră, *f.* 561
Slovak	:	gul'omet, *m.* 561
Spanish	:	ametralladora, *f.* 561
Swedish	:	kulspruta-n 561
Turkish	:	makinali tufek 561
Russian	:	кулемет, *m.* 561
Serbian	:	митральез, *m.* 561
Ukrainian	:	скоростріл; кулемет, *m.* 561

562 MAID s. (a servant)

Czech	:	služebná, *f.* 562
Danish	:	Tjenestepige, *f.* 562
Dutch	:	de meid 562
Finnish	:	Stadt; tyttö 562
French	:	servante, *f.* 562
German	:	die Magd; das Dienstmädchen 562
Hungarian	:	cselédlány 562
Italian	:	serva, *f.* 562
Croatian	:	služavka, *f.* 562
Norwegian	:	tjenestepike, *f.* 562
Polish	:	dziewka, *f.* 562
Portuguese	:	criada, *a* 562
Rumanian	:	servitoareă, *f.* 562
Slovak	:	slúžka, *f.* 562
Spanish	:	criada, *f.* 562
Swedish	:	piga-n 562
Turkish	:	hizmetcikiz 562
Russian	:	батрачка, *f.* 562
Serbian	:	служавка, *f.* 562
Ukrainian	:	дівка, *f.* 562

565 MAN s. (the human race)

Czech	:	člověk, *m.* 565
Danish	:	Mennesket 565
Dutch	:	de mensch 565
Finnish	:	ihminen 565
French	:	l'homme 565
German	:	der Mensch 565
Hungarian	:	ember 565
Italian	:	uomo, *m.* 565
Croatian	:	čovjek, *m.* 565
Norwegian	:	menneske, *n.* 565
Polish	:	człowiek, *m.* 565
Portuguese	:	o homem 565
Rumanian	:	omul, *m.* 565
Slovak	:	človek, *m.* 565
Spanish	:	hombre, *m.* 565
Swedish	:	människa-n 565
Turkish	:	insan 565
Russian	:	человек, *m.* 565
Serbian	:	човек, *m.* 565
Ukrainian	:	чоловік, *m.* 565

563 MAIZE s.

Czech	:	kukuřice, *f.* 563
Danish	:	Majs, *m./c.* 563
Dutch	:	de mais 563
Finnish	:	maissi 563
French	:	maïs, *m.* 563
German	:	der Mais 563
Hungarian	:	kukorica 563
Italian	:	grano turco, *m.* 563
Croatian	:	kukuruz, *m.* 563
Norwegian	:	mais, *m.* 563
Polish	:	kukuruza, *f.* 563
Portuguese	:	milho, *o* 563
Rumanian	:	porumbul 563
Slovak	:	kukurica, *f.* 563
Spanish	:	maíz, *m.* 563
Swedish	:	majs-en 563
Turkish	:	misir 563
Russian	:	кукуруза, *f.* 563
Serbian	:	кукуруз, *m.* 563
Ukrainian	:	кукурудза, *f.* 563

566 MAN s. (a husband)

Czech	:	muž; manžel, *m.* 566
Danish	:	Mand, *m.* 566
Dutch	:	de man 566
Finnish	:	mies 566
French	:	homme, *m.* 566
German	:	der Mann, (Ehe-mann) 566
Hungarian	:	féril 566
Italian	:	uomo, *m.* 566
Croatian	:	muž, *m.* 566
Norwegian	:	mann, *m.* 566
Polish	:	mężczyzna, *m.* 566
Portuguese	:	homem, *o* 566
Rumanian	:	barbatul, *m.* 566
Slovak	:	muž, *m.* 566
Spanish	:	hombre, *m.* 566
Swedish	:	man-nen 566
Turkish	:	erkek 566
Russian	:	мужчина, *m.* 566
Serbian	:	муж, *m.* 566
Ukrainian	:	мущина, *m.* 566

564 MAKE v.

Czech	:	udělati; činiti 564
Danish	:	lave; göre 564
Dutch	:	maken 564
Finnish	:	tehdä 564
French	:	faire 564
German	:	machen 564
Hungarian	:	czinál 564
Italian	:	fare 564
Croatian	:	činiti 564
Norwegian	:	lage 564
Polish	:	zrobić; czynić 564
Portuguese	:	fazer 564
Rumanian	:	a face 564
Slovak	:	robit'; činit' 564
Spanish	:	hacer 564
Swedish	:	göra 564
Turkish	:	yapmak 564
Russian	:	делать 564
Serbian	:	лаге 564
Ukrainian	:	робити; творити 564

567 MANDOLIN s.

Czech	:	mandolina, *f.* 567
Danish	:	Mandolin, *m./c.* 567
Dutch	:	de mandoline 567
Finnish	:	mandoliini 567
French	:	mandoline, *f.* 567
German	:	die Mandoline 567
Hungarian	:	mandolin 567
Italian	:	mandolino, *m.* 567
Croatian	:	mandolina, *f.* 567
Norwegian	:	mandolin, *m.* 567
Polish	:	mandolina, *f.* 567
Portuguese	:	mandolim, *o* 567
Rumanian	:	mandolină, *f.* 567
Slovak	:	mandolína, *f.* 567
Spanish	:	mandolina, *f.* 567
Swedish	:	mandolin-en 567
Turkish	:	mandolin 567
Russian	:	мандолина, *f.* 567
Serbian	:	мандолина, *f.* 567
Ukrainian	:	мандоліна, *f.* 567

568 MAP s.

Czech	:	mapa, *f.* 568
Danish	:	Landkort, *n.* 568
Dutch	:	landkaart 568
Finnish	:	kartta 568
French	:	carte, *f.* 568
German	:	die Landkarte 568
Hungarian	:	térkép 568
Italian	:	carta geografica, *f.* 568
Croatian	:	zemljopisna karta; mapa, *f.* 568
Norwegian	:	kart, *n.* 568
Polish	·	mapa, *f.* 568
Portuguese	:	mapa, *c.* 568
Rumanian	:	hartă, *f.* 568
Slovak	:	mapa, *f.* 568
Spanish	:	mapa, *f.* 568
Swedish	:	karta, *f.* 568
Turkish	:	coğrafya haritasi 568
Russian	:	карта, *f.* 568
Serbian	:	карта; мапа, *f6.* 568
Ukrainian	:	карта, *f.* 568

571 MARKET s.

Czech	:	trh, *m.* 571
Danish	:	Torv, *n.* 571
Dutch	:	de markt 571
Finnish	:	tori 571
French	:	marché, *m.* 571
German	:	der Markt 571
Hungarian	:	a piac 571
Italian	?	mercato, *n.* 571
Croatian	:	sajam; trg; tržište, *n.* 571
Norwegian	:	torv, *n.*; markedsplass, *m.* 571
Polish	:	targowisko, *n.* 571
Portuguese	:	mercado, *o* 571
Rumanian	:	piaţă, *f.* 571
Slovak	:	trh, *m.* 571
Spanish	:	mercado, *m.* 571
Swedish	:	torg-et 571
Turkish	:	çarşi 571
Russian	:	рынок, *m.* 571
Serbian	:	трг; пијаца, *f.* 571
Ukrainian	:	торг; базар, *m.* 571

569 MARCH s.

Czech	:	březen, *m.* 569
Danish	:	Marts 569
Dutch	:	Maart 569
Finnish	:	maaliskuu 569
French	:	mars, *m.* 569
German	:	der März 569
Hungarian	:	március 569
Italian	:	marzo, *m.* 569
Croatian	:	ožujak, *m.* 569
Norwegian	:	mars 569
Polish	:	marzec, *m.* 569
Portuguese	:	março, *o* 569
Rumanian	:	Martie, *m.* 569
Slovak	:	marec, *m.* 569
Spanish	:	marzo 569
Swedish	:	mars 569
Turkish	:	mart 569
Russian	:	март, *m.* 569
Serbian	:	Март, *m.* 569
Ukrainian	:	Марець; Березень, *m.* 569

572 MARMALADE s.

Czech	:	marmeláda, *f.* 572
Danish	:	Marmelade, *m./c.* 572
Dutch	:	de jam 572
Finnish	:	marmelaadi 572
French	:	confiture, *f.* 572
German	:	die Marmelade 572
Hungarian	:	lekvár 572
Italian	?	marmellata, *f.* 572
Croatian	:	pekmez, *m.* 572
Norwegian	:	syltetöi, *n.* 572
Polish	:	marmelada, *f.* 572
Portuguese	:	marmelada, *a* 572
Rumanian	:	marmeladă, *f.* 572
Slovak	:	lekvár, *m.* 572
Spanish	:	mermelada, *f.* 572
Swedish	:	marmelad-en 572
Turkish	:	reçel 572
Russian	:	мармелад, *m.* 572
Serbian	:	пекмез, *m.* 572
Ukrainian	:	мармеляда,, *f.* 572

570 MARGARINE s.

Czech	:	margarin, *m.* 570
Danish	:	Margarine, *c.* 570
Dutch	:	de margarine 570
Finnish	:	margariini 570
French	:	margarine, *f.* 570
German	:	die Margarine 570
Hungarian	:	margarin 570
Italian	:	margarina, *f.* 570
Croatian	:	margarin, *m.* 570
Norwegian	:	margarin, *m.* 570
Polish	:	margaryna, *f.* 570
Portuguese	:	margarina, *a* 570
Rumanian	:	margarină, *f.* 570
Slovak	:	margarín, *m.* 570
Spanish	:	margarina, *f.* 570
Swedish	:	margarin-et, *f.* 570
Turkish	:	margarin 570
Russian	:	маргарин, *m.* 570
Serbian	:	маргарина, *f.* 570
Ukrainian	:	маргарин, *f.* 570

573 MAROON s.

Czech	:	kaštan, *m.* 573
Danish	:	Kastanie, *c.* 573
Dutch	:	de tamme kastanje 573
Finnish	:	kastanja 573
French	:	marron, *m.* 573
German	:	die Marone 573
Hungarian	:	gesztenye 573
Italian	:	castagna, *f.* 573
Croatian	:	talijanski kesten, *m.* 573
Norwegian	:	marone, *m.* 573
Polish	:	kasztan, *m.* 573
Portuguese	:	castanha, *a* 573
Rumanian	:	castana, *f.* 573
Slovak	:	gaštan, *m.* 573
Spanish	:	castaña, *f.* 573
Swedish	:	kastanj-en 573
Turkish	:	kestane 573
Russian	:	каштан, *m.* 573
Serbian	:	кестен, *m.* 573
Ukrainian	:	їстивний каштан, *m,* 573

574 MARRIAGE s.

Czech	: manželství, n. 574
Danish	: Ägteskab, n. 574
Dutch	: het huwelijk 574
Finnish	: avioliitto 574
French	: le mariage 574
German	: die Ehe 574
Hungarian	: házasság 574
Italian	: matrimonio, m. 574
Croatian	: brak, m. 574
Norwegian	: ekteskap, n. 574
Polish	: małżeństwo, n. 574
Portuguese	: matrimónio, o 574
Rumanian	: căsătorie, f. 574
Slovak	: manželstvo, n. 574
Spanish	: matrimonio, m. 574
Swedish	: äktenskap-et 574
Turkish	: evlenme 574
Russian	: супружество; брак 574
Serbian	: брак, m. 574
Ukrainian	: тупружитво, n.; шлюб, m. 574

577 MATTRESS s.

Czech	: matrace, f. 577
Danish	: madres, c. 577
Dutch	: matras 577
Finnish	: patja 577
French	: matelas, m. 577
German	: die Matratze 577
Hungarian	: matrac 577
Italian	: materassa, f. 577
Croatian	: madraca, f. 577
Norwegian	: madrass, c. 577
Polish	: matrac, f. 577
Portuguese	: colchão, m. 577
Rumanian	: saltea, f. 577
Slovak	: matrac, m. 577
Spanish	: colchón, m. 577
Swedish	: madres, m. 577
Turkish	: şilte; döşek 577
Russian	: матрац, m. 577
Serbian	: мадраца, f. 577
Ukrainian	: матрац, f. 577

575 MASTER s.

Czech	: mistr, m. 575
Danish	: Mester, m. 575
Dutch	: de meester 575
Finnish	: mestari 575
French	: maître, m. 575
German	: der Meister 575
Hungarian	: mester 575
Italian	: capo, m. 575
Croatian	: majstor, m. 575
Norwegian	: mester, m. 575
Polish	: majster, m. 575
Portuguese	: mestre, o 575
Rumanian	: maistrul 575
Slovak	: majster, m. 575
Spanish	: maestro, m. 575
Swedish	: mästare-n 575
Turkish	: usta 575
Russian	: мастер, m. 575
Serbian	: мајстар, m. 575
Ukrainian	: майстер m. 575

578 MAY s.

Czech	: květen, m. 578
Danish	: Maj 578
Dutch	: Mei 578
Finnish	: toukokuu 578
French	: mai, m. 578
German	: der Mai 578
Hungarian	: május 578
Italian	: maggio, m. 578
Croatian	: svibanj, m. 578
Norwegian	: mai 578
Polish	: maj, m. 578
Portuguese	: maio, o 578
Rumanian	: Mai, m. 578
Slovak	: máj, m. 578
Spanish	: mayo 578
Swedish	: maj 578
Turkish	: mais 578
Russian	: май, m. 578
Serbian	: Maj, m. 578
Ukrainian	: Май, m. 578

576 MATCH s.

Czech	: zápalka, f. 576
Danish	: Tändstik, c. 576
Dutch	: de lucifer 576
Finnish	: tulitikku 576
French	: allumette, f. 576
German	: das Streichholz 576
Hungarian	: gyufa 576
Italian	: flammifero, m. 576
Croatian	: šibica, f. 576
Norwegian	: fyrstikk, f. 576
Polish	: zapałki, pl. 576
Portuguese	: fósforo, o 576
Rumanian	: chibritul 576
Slovak	: zápalka, f. 576
Spanish	: fósforo, m. 576
Swedish	: tändsticksask-en 576
Turkish	: kibrit 576
Russian	: спички, pl. 576
Serbian	: шибица, f. 576
Ukrainian	: сірник, m. 576

579 MAYBE adv.

Czech	: snad; možná 579
Danish	: maaske 579
Dutch	: misschien 579
Finnish	: ehkä; kenties 579
French	: peut-être 579
German	: vielleicht 579
Hungarian	: talán 579
Italian	: forse 579
Croatian	: možda 579
Norwegian	: kanskje 579
Polish	: morze 579
Portuguese	: pode ser 579
Rumanian	: poate 579
Slovak	: možno 579
Spanish	: quizás 579
Swedish	: kanske 579
Turkish	: belki; ihtimalki 579
Russian	: может быть 579
Serbian	: можда 579
Ukrainian	: можливо 579

580 MEADOW s.

Czech	:	louka, f. 580
Danish	:	Eng, m./c. 580
Dutch	:	de wei 580
Finnish	:	niitty 580
French	:	prairie, f. 580
German	:	die Wiese 580
Hungarian	:	rét 580
Italian	:	prato, m. 580
Croatian	:	livada, f. 580
Norwegian	:	eng, f. 580
Polish	:	łąka, f. 580
Portuguese	:	prado, o 580
Rumanian	:	livadă, f. 580
Slovak	:	lúka, f. 580
Spanish	:	prado, m. 580
Swedish	:	äng-en 580
Turkish	:	çayir 580
Russian	:	луг, m. 580
Serbian	:	ливада, f. 580
Ukrainian	:	луг, m; лука; сіножать, f. 580

583 MEDICINE s.

Czech	:	lék, m. 583
Danish	:	Medicin, m./c. 583
Dutch	:	het medicijn 583
Finnish	:	lääke 583
French	:	médicament, m. 583
German	:	die Medizin 583
Hungarian	:	orvosság 585
Italian	:	medicina, f. 583
Croatian	:	lijek, m. 583
Norwegian	:	medisin, m. 583
Polish	:	lekarstwo, n. 583
Portuguese	:	remédio, o 583
Rumanian	:	medicamentul 583
Slovak	:	liek, m. 583
Spanish	:	medicina, f. 583
Swedish	:	medicin-en 583
Turkish	:	ilac 583
Russian	:	лекарство, n. 583
Serbian	:	лек, m. 583
Ukrainian	:	лекарство, n. 583

581 MEAL s.

Czech	:	jídlo, n. 581
Danish	:	Maaltid, n. 581
Dutch	:	de maaltijd 581
Finnish.	:	ruoka 581
French	:	repas, m. 581
German	a	die Mahlzeit 581
Hungarian	:	az étkezés 581
Italian	:	pasto, m. 581
Croatian	:	obrok; objed, m. 581
Norwegian	:	måltid, n. 581
Polish	:	obiad, m. 581
Portuguese	:	refeição, a 581
Rumanian	:	ora mesei 581
Slovak	:	čas k jedlu, m. 581
Spanish	:	comida, f. 581
Swedish	:	måltid-en 581
Turkish	:	yemek vakţi 581
Russian	:	обед, m. 581
Serbian	:	оброк, m. 581
Ukrainian	:	обід, ж. 581

584 MEET v.

Czech	:	setkati se; sejíti se; shromážditi 584
Danish	:	möde 584
Dutch	:	tegenkomen 584
Finnish	:	kohdata; sattua yhteen 584
French	:	rencontrer 584
German	:	begegnen; zusammentreffen 584
Hungarian	:	találkozik 584
Italian	:	incontrare 584
Croatian	:	sastajati se 584
Norwegian	:	treffe; möte 584
Polish	:	spotkać 584
Portuguese	:	encontrar-se 584
Rumanian	:	a întîlni 584
Slovak	:	stretnút' sa 584
Spanish	:	encontrar(se); reunirse 584
Swedish	:	möta; samman-träffa 584
Turkish	:	rasgelmek 584
Russian	:	встречать 584
Serbian	:	састајати се 584
Ukrainian	:	сходистия 584

582 MEAT s.

Czech	:	maso, n. 582
Danish	:	Köd, n. 582
Dutch	:	het vlees 582
Finnish	:	liha 582
French	:	viande, f. 582
German	:	das Fleisch 582
Hungarian	:	hús 582
Italian	:	carne, f. 582
Croatian	:	meso, n. 582
Norwegian	:	kjött, n. 582
Polish	:	mięso, n. 582
Portuguese	:	carne, a 582
Rumanian	:	carnea, f. 582
Slovak	:	mäso, n. 582
Spanish	:	carne, f. 582
Swedish	:	kött-et 582
Turkish	:	et 582
Russian	:	мясо,n. 582
Serbian	:	месо, n. 582
Ukrainian	:	мясо, n. 582

585 MELON s.

Czech	:	meloun, m. 585
Danish	:	Melon, m./c. 585
Dutch	:	de meloen 585
Finnish	:	melooni 585
French	:	melon, m. 585
German	:	die Melone 585
Hungarian	:	dinnye 585
Italian	:	melone, m. 585
Croatian	:	lubenica, f. 585
Norwegian	:	melon, m. 585
Polish	:	melon, m. 585
Portuguese	:	melão, o 585
Rumanian	:	pepenele 585
Slovak	:	melón, m. 585
Spanish	:	melón, m. 585
Swedish	:	melon-en 585
Turkish	:	kavun 585
Russian	:	дыня, f. 585
Serbian	:	лубеница, f. 585
Ukrainian	:	кавун; мельон, m. 585

586 MEND v.

Czech	:	látati; spravovati 586
Danish	:	stoppe 586
Dutch	:	stoppen 586
Finnish	:	parsia 586
French	:	repriser 586
German	:	stopfen 586 '
Hungarian	:	foltozni 586
Italian	:	rammendare 586
Croatian	:	krpati 586
Norwegian	:	stoppe 586
Polish	:	cerować 586
Portuguese	:	remendar 586
Rumanian	:	a cărpi 586
Slovak	:	štopkat' 586
Spanish	:	zurcir 586
Swedish	:	stoppa 586
Turkish	:	tikamak 586
Russian	:	штопать 586
Serbian	:	крпати 586
Ukrainian	:	латати, 586

587 MENU s. (bill of fare)

Czech	:	jídelní lístek, m. 587
Danish	:	Spisekort, m./c. 587
Dutch	:	het menu 587
Finnish	:	ruokalista 587
French	:	menu, m. 587
German	:	die Speisekarte 587
Hungarian	:	étlap 587
Italian	:	carta dei cibi, f. 587
Croatian	:	jelovnik, m. 587
Norwegian	:	spiseseddel, m. 587
Polish	:	spis potraw, m. 587
Portuguese	:	lista, a 587
Rumanian	:	lista de bucate 587
Slovak	:	jedálny lístok, m. 587
Spanish	:	lista de platos 587
Swedish	:	matsedel-n 587
Turkish	:	yemek listasi 587
Russian	:	меню, n. 587
Serbian	:	јеловник, m. 587
Ukrainian	:	стравоспис, m. 587

588 MERCHANT-SHIP s.

Czech	:	obchodní loď', f. 588
Danish	:	Handelsskib, n. 588
Dutch	:	het handelsschip 588
Finnish	:	kauppalaiva 588
French	:	navire de commerce, m. 588
German	:	das Handelsschif 588
Hungarian	:	kereskedelmi hajó 588
Italian	:	nave mercantile, f. 588
Croatian	:	trgovačka ladja, f. 588
Norwegian	:	handelsskip, n. 588
Polish	:	okręt handlowy, m. 588
Portuguese	:	navio mercante, o 588
Rumanian	:	vas de comerţ, c. 588
Slovak	:	obchodná loď', f. 588
Spanish	:	buque mercantil, m. 588
Swedish	:	handelsfartyg-et 588
Turkish	:	ticaret gemisi 588
Russian	:	торговое судно, n. 588
Serbian	:	трговачка ладја, f. 588
Ukrainian	:	торговельний корабель, m. 588

589 MERRY adj.

Czech	:	veselý; radostný 589
Danish	:	munter; lystig 589
Dutch	:	vrolijk 589
Finnish	:	iloinen 589
French	:	gai; plaisant 589
German	:	fröhlich; lustig 589
Hungarian	:	vidám 589
Italian	:	giocondo 589
Croatian	:	veseo 589
Norwegian	:	lystig 589
Polish	:	esoły 589
Portuguese	:	alegre 589
Rumanian	:	vesel 589
Slovak	:	veselý 589
Spanish	:	alegre; jovial 589
Swedish	:	munter; glad 589
Turkish	:	şen; hoş 589
Russian	:	веселый, 589
Serbian	:	весео 589
Ukrainian	:	веселий 589

590 METAL s.

Czech	:	kov, m. 590
Danish	:	Metal, n. 590
Dutch	:	het metaal 590
Finnish	:	metalli 590
French	:	metal, m. 590
German	:	das Metall 590
Hungarian	:	érc 590
Italian	:	metalli, m. pl. 590
Croatian	:	kovina, f. 590
Norwegian	:	metall, n. 590
Polish	:	metale, pl. 590
Portuguese	:	metal, o 590
Rumanian	:	metalul 590
Slovak	:	kov, m. 590
Spanish	:	metal, m. 590
Swedish	:	metaller-na, pl. 590
Turkish	:	mandeler 590
Russian	:	металл, m. 590
Serbian	:	ковина, f. 590
Ukrainian	:	метали, pl. 590

591 MILITARY HOSPITAL s.

Czech	:	vojenská nemocnice, f. 591
Danish	:	Lazaret, n. 591
Dutch	:	het lazaret 591
Finnish	:	sotillas-sairaala 591
French	:	hôpital militaire, m. 591
German	:	das Lazarett 591
Hungarian	:	hadi kórhaz 591
Italian	:	lazzaretto, m. 591
Croatian	:	vojnička bolnica, f. 591
Norwegian	:	lasarett, n. 591
Polish	:	szpital, m. 591
Portuguese	:	hospital militar, o 591
Rumanian	:	lazaretul 591
Slovak	:	vojenská nemocnica, f. 591
Spanish	:	hospital militar, m. 591
Swedish	:	krigslasarett-et 591
Turkish	:	seyyar hastane 591
Russian	:	лазарет, m. 591
Serbian	:	војничка болница, f. 591
Ukrainian	:	лазарет шпиталь, m, 591

592 MILK s.

Czech	: mléko, n. 592
Danish	: Mälk, m./c. 592
Dutch	: de melk 592
Finnish	: maito 592
French	: lait, m. 592
German	: die Milch 592
Hungarian	: tej 592
Italian	: latte, m. 592
Croatian	: mlijeko, m. 592
Norwegian	: melk, f. 592
Polish	: mleko, n. 592
Portuguese	: leite, o 592
Rumanian	: laptele 592
Slovak	: mlieko, n. 592
Spanish	: leche, f. 592
Swedish	: mjölk-en 592
Turkish	: süt 592
Russian	: молоко, n. 592
Serbian	: млеко, n. 592
Ukrainian	: молоко, n. 592

593 MILK v.

Czech	: dojiti 593
Danish	: malke 593
Dutch	: melken 593
Finnish	: lypsää 593
French	: traire 593
German	: melken 593
Hungarian	: fejni 593
Italian	: mungere 593
Croatian	: musti 593
Norwegian	: melke 593
Polish	: dojić 593
Portuguese	: ordenhar 593
Rumanian	: a mulge 593
Slovak	: dojit' 593
Spanish	: ordeñar 593
Swedish	: mjölka 593
Turkish	: sağmak 593
Russian	: доить 594
Serbian	: музати 593
Ukrainian	: лоїти 593

594 MINERAL WATER s.

Czech	: minerální voda, f. 594
Danish	: Mineralvand, n. 594
Dutch	: het mineraal water 594
Finnish	: kivennäisvesi 594
French	: eau minérale, f. 594
German	: das Mineralwasser 594
Hungarian	: ásványviz 594
Italian	: acqua minerale, f. 594
Croatian	: mineralna voda, f. 594
Norwegian	: mineralvann, n. 594
Polish	: woda mineralna, f. 594
Portuguese	: água mineral, a 594
Rumanian	: apa minerală, f. 594
Slovak	: minerálka, f. 594
Spanish	: agua mineral, f. 594
Swedish	: mineral vattnet 594
Turkish	: maden suyu 594
Russian	: минеральная вода, f. 594
Serbian	: минерална вода, f. 594
Ukrainian	: мінерална вода, f. 594

595 MINUTE s.

Czech	: minuta, f. 595
Danish	: Minut 595
Dutch	: de minuut 595
Finnish	: minuutti 595
French	: minute, f. 595
German	: die Minute, f. 595
Hungarian	: perc 595
Italian	: minuto, m. 595
Croatian	: minuta, f. 595
Norwegian	: minutt, n. 595
Polish	: minuta, f. 595
Portuguese	: minuto, o 595
Rumanian	: minuta, f. 595
Slovak	: minuta, f. 595
Spanish	: minuto, m. 595
Swedish	: minut-en 595
Turkish	: dakika 595
Russian	: минута, f. 595
Serbian	: минута, f. 595
Ukrainian	: хвилина, f. 595

596 MIRABELLE s.

Czech	: mirabelka, f. 596
Danish	: Mirabel, c. 596
Dutch	: de mirabelle 596
Finnish	: eräs luumulaji 596
French	: mirabelle, f. 596
German	: die Mirabelle 596
Hungarian	: móra-bóra szliva 596
Italian	: mirabella, f. 596
Croatian	: mirabela, f. 596
Norwegian	: mirabelle, m. 596
Polish	: mirabela, f. 596
Portuguese	: mirabela, a 596
Rumanian	: mirabela, f. 596
Slovak	: mirabelka, f. 596
Spanish	: ciruela amarilla, f. 596
Swedish	: bigarrå 596
Turkish	: sarierik 596
Russian	: слива, f. 596
Serbian	: мирабела, f. 596
Ukrainian	: мірабеля, f. 596

597 MISS s. (Young Lady)

Czech	: slečna, f. 597
Danish	: Fröken, c. 597
Dutch	: Mejuffrouw 597
Finnish	: neiti 597
French	: Mademoiselle, f. 597
German	: das Fräulein 597
Hungarian	: kisasszony 597
Italian	: Signorina, f. 597
Croatian	: gospodica, f. 597
Norwegian	: fröken, c./f. 597
Polish	: panna; Panno! 597
Portuguese	: menina, f. 597
Rumanian	: domnisoară f.; fată, f. 597
Slovak	: slečna, f. 597
Spanish	: señorita 597
Swedish	: fröken 597
Turkish	: bayan; küçük hamin 597
Russian	: госпожа, f. 597
Serbian	: господица, f. 597
Ukrainian	: люба, f. 597

88

598 MOLE s.

Czech	:	krtek, *m.* 598
Danish	:	Muldvarp, *m./c.* 598
Dutch	:	de mol 598
Finnish	:	maamyyrä 598
French	:	taupe, *f.* 598
German	:	der Maulwurf 598
Hungarian	:	vakondok 598
Italian	:	talpa, *f.* 598
Croatian	:	krtica, *f.* 598
Norwegian	:	mullvarp, *m.* 598
Polish	:	kret, *m.* 598
Portuguese	:	toupeira, *a* 598
Rumanian	:	cârtiţa, *f.* 598
Slovak	:	krt, *m.* 598
Spanish	:	topo, *m.* 598
Swedish	:	mullvad-en 598
Turkish	:	köstebek 598
Russian	:	крот, *m.* 598
Serbian	:	кртица, *f.* 598
Ukrainian	:	кріт, *m.* 598

599 MONDAY s.

Czech	:	pondělí, *n.* 599
Danish	:	Mandag, *m.* 599
Dutch	:	de maandag 599
Finnish	:	maanantai 599
French	:	lundi, *m.* 599
German	:	der Montag 599
Hungarian	:	hétfö 599
Italian	:	lunedi, *m.* 599
Croatian	:	ponedeljak, *m.* 599
Norwegian	:	mandag, *m.* 599
Polish	:	poniedzialek, *m.* 599
Portuguese	:	segunda feira, *a* 599
Rumanian	:	Luni, *f.* 599
Slovak	:	pondelok, *m.* 599
Spanish	:	lunes, *m.* 599
Swedish	:	måndagen 599
Turkish	:	pazarertesi 599
Russian	:	понедельник, *m.* 599
Serbian	:	понедельак, *m.* 599
Ukrainian	:	понеділок, *m.* 599

600 MONEY s.

Czech	:	peníze, *pl.* 600
Danish	:	Penge, *pl.* 600
Dutch	:	het geld 600
Finnish	:	raba 600
French	:	argent, *m.* 600
German	:	das Geld 600
Hungarian	:	pénz 600
Italian	:	denaro, *m.*; moneta, *f.* 600
Croatian	:	novac, *m.* 600
Norwegian	:	penger, *pl.* 600
Polish	:	pieniądze, *pl.* 600
Portuguese	:	dinheiro, *o* 600
Rumanian	:	bassul, bani 600
Slovak	:	peniaze, *pl.* 600
Spanish	:	dinero, *m.* 600
Swedish	:	pengar-na 600
Turkish	:	para 600
Russian	:	деньги, *pl.* 600
Serbian	:	новац, *m.* 600
Ukrainian	:	гроші, *pl.* 600

601 MONEY ORDER s.

Czech	:	poštovní poukázka, *f.* 601
Danish	:	Postanvisning, *c.* 601
Dutch	:	de postwissel 601
Finnish	:	postiosoitus 601
French	:	mandat-poste, *m.* 601
German	:	die Postanweisung 601
Hungarian	:	postautalvány 601
Italian	:	vaglia postale, *m.* 601
Croatian	:	poštanska doznačnica, *f.* 601
Norwegian	:	postanvisning, *c.* 601
Polish	:	przekaz pocztowy, *m.* 601
Portuguese	:	vale de correio, *o* 601
Rumanian	:	mandatul poştal 601
Slovak	:	poštová poukázka, *f.* 601
Spanish	:	giro postal 601
Swedish	:	postanvisning-en 601
Turkish	:	posta havale senedi 601
Russian	:	почтовый перевод, *m.* 601
Serbian	:	поштанска упутница, *f.* 601
Ukrainian	:	поштовий переказ, *m.* 601

602 MONTH v.

Czech	:	měsíc, *m.* 602
Danish	:	Maaned, *m.* 602
Dutch	:	de maand 602
Finnish	:	kuukausi 602
French	:	mois, *m.* 602
German	:	der Monat 602
Hungarian	:	hónap 602
Italian	:	mese, *m.* 602
Croatian	:	mjesec, *m.* 602
Norwegian	:	måned, *m.* 602
Polish	:	miesiąc, *m.* 602
Portuguese	:	mês, *o* 602
Rumanian	:	lună, *f.* 602
Slovak	:	mesiac, *m.* 602
Spanish	:	mes, *m.* 602
Swedish	:	månad-en 602
Turkish	:	ay 602
Russian	:	месяц, *m.* 602
Serbian	:	месец, *m.* 602
Ukrainian	:	місяць, *m.* 602

603 MONUMENT s.

Czech	:	pommík, *m.* 603
Danish	:	Mindesmärke, *m./c.* 603
Dutch	:	het standbeeld 603
Finnish	:	muistomerkki 603
French	:	monument, *m.* 603
German	:	das Denkmal 603
Hungarian	:	emlékmű 603
Italian	:	monomento, *m.* 603
Croatian	:	spomenik, *m.* 603
Norwegian	:	minnesmerke, *n.* 603
Polish	:	pamiętnik, *m.* 603
Portuguese	:	monumento, *o* 603
Rumanian	:	monumentul 603
Slovak	:	pomník, *m.* 603
Spanish	:	monumento, *m.* 603
Swedish	:	monument-et 603
Turkish	:	abide 603
Russian	:	памятник, *m.* 603
Serbian	:	споменик, *m.* 603
Ukrainian	:	памятник, *m.* 603

604 MOON s.

Czech	:	měsíc, *m.* 604
Danish	:	Maane, *m./c.* 604
Dutch	:	de maan 604
Finnish	:	kuu 604
French	:	lune, *f.* 604
German	:	der Mond 604
Hungarian	:	hold 604
Italian	:	luna, *f.* 604
Croatian	:	mjesec, *m.* 604
Norwegian	:	måne, *m.* 604
Polish	:	księżyc, *m.* 604
Portuguese	:	lua, *a* 604
Rumanian	:	luna, *f.* 604
Slovak	:	mesiac *m.* 604
Spanish	:	luna, *f.* 604
Swedish	:	måne-n 604
Turkish	:	ay 604
Russian	:	луна, *f.*; месяц, *m.* 604
Serbian	:	месец, *m.* 604
Ukrainian	:	місяць, *m.* 604

605 MORNING s.

Czech	:	ráno; jitro, *n.* 605
Danish	:	Morgen, *m.* 605
Dutch	:	de ochtend 605
Finnish	:	aamu 605
French	:	matin, *m.* 605
German	:	der Morgen 605
Hungarian	:	reggel 605
Italian	:	mattina, *f.* 605
Croatian	:	jutro, *n.* 605
Norwegian	:	morgen, *m.* 605
Polish	:	ranek, *m.* 605
Portuguese	:	manhã, *a* 605
Rumanian	:	dimineată. *f.* 605
Slovak	:	ráno, *n.* 605
Spanish	:	mañana, *f.* 605
Swedish	:	morgon-en 605
Turkish	:	sabah 605
Russian	:	утро, *n.* 605
Serbian	:	јутро, *n.* 605
Ukrainian	:	ранок, *m.* 605

606 MORTAR s.

Czech	:	malta, *f.* 606
Danish	:	Kalk, *c.* 606
Dutch	:	de mortel 606
Finnish	:	laasti 606
French	:	mortier, *m.* 606
German	:	der Mörtel 606
Hungarian	:	vakolat 606
Italian	:	calcina, *f.* 606
Croatian	:	mort, *m.* 606
Norwegian	:	murkalk, *m.* 606
Polish	:	zaprava, *f.* 606
Portuguese	:	argamassa, *a* 606
Rumanian	:	tencuiala; mortarul 606
Slovak	:	malta, *f.* 606
Spanish	:	argamasa, *f.* 606
Swedish	:	murbruk-et 606
Turkish	:	harç 606
Russian	:	известка *f.* 606
Serbian	:	морт, *m.* 606
Ukrainian	:	тинк, *m.*; ступка, *f.* 606

607 MOSQUITO s.

Czech	:	komár, *m.* 607
Danish	:	Myg, *m./c.* 607
Dutch	:	de mug 607
Finnish	:	pistokärpänen 607
French	:	moustique, *m.* 607
German	:	die Stechmücke 607
Hungarian	:	szúnyog 607
Italian	:	tafano, *m.* 607
Croatian	:	komarac, *m.* 607
Norwegian	:	mygg, *m.* 607
Polish	:	komar, *m.* 607
Portuguese	:	mosquito, *o* 607
Rumanian	:	tânţarul 607
Slovak	:	komár, *m.* 607
Spanish	:	mosquito, *m.* 607
Swedish	:	mygga-n 607
Turkish	:	sivri sinek 607
Russian	:	комар, *m.* 607
Serbian	:	комарац, *m.* 607
Ukrainian	:	комар, *m.* 607

608 MOTHER s.

Czech	:	matka, *f.* 608
Danish	:	moder, *f./c.* 608
Dutch	:	moeder, *f./c.* 608
Finnish	:	äiti 608
French	:	mère, *f.* 608
German	:	die Mutter 608
Hungarian	:	anya 608
Italian	:	madre, *f.* 608
Croatian	:	majka; mati 608
Norwegian	:	mor, *f./c.* 608
Polish	:	matka, *f.* 608
Portuguese	:	mãi, *f.* 608
Rumanian	:	mamă, *f.* 608
Slovak	:	matka, *f.* 608
Spanish	:	madre, *f.* 608
Swedish	:	moder, *f.* 608
Turkish	:	ana; anne; valide 608
Russian	:	мать, *f.* 608
Serbian	:	мајка; мати, *f.* 608
Ukrainian	:	мати, *f.* 608

609 MOTION PICTURE
see 622 MOVIE

610 MOTOR s.

Czech	:	motor, *m.* 610
Danish	:	Motor, *m./c.* 610
Dutch	:	de motor 610
Finnish	:	moottori 610
French	:	moteur, *m.* 610
German	:	der Motor 610
Hungarian	:	motor 610
Italian	:	motore, *m.* 610
Croatian	:	motor, *m.* 610
Norwegian	:	motor, *m.* 610
Polish	:	motor, *m.* 610
Portuguese	:	motor, *o* 610
Rumanian	:	motorul 610
Slovak	:	motor, *m.* 610
Spanish	:	motor, *m.* 610
Swedish	:	motor-n 610
Turkish	:	motor 610
Russian	:	мотор, *m.* 610
Serbian	:	мотор, *m.* 610
Ukrainian	:	мотор, *m.* 610

611 MOTORBUS *s.*

Czech	: autobus, *m.* 611
Danish	: Omnibus, *c.* 611
Dutch	: de autobus 611
Finnish	: linja-auto 611
French	: autobus, *m.* 611
German	: der Autobus 611
Hungarian	: autobusz 611
Italian	: autobus, *m.* 611
Croatian	: autobus, *m.* 611
Norwegian	: buss, *m.* 611
Polish	: autobus, *m.* 611
Portuguese	: auto-ónibus, *o* 611
Rumanian	: autobuzul 611
Slovak	: autobus, *m.* 611
Spanish	: autobús, *m.* 611
Swedish	: buss-en 611
Turkish	: otobus 611
Russian	: автобус, *m.* 611
Serbian	: аутобус, *m.* 611
Ukrainian	: автобус. *m.* 611

612 (MOTOR) CAR *s.*

Czech	: osobní auto, *n.* 612
Danish	: Bil, *m./c.* 612
Dutch	: de (personen) auto 612
Finnish	: henkilöauto 612
French	: voiture; auto(mobile), *f.* 612
German	: das Personenauto 612
Hungarian	: személy gépkocsi 612
Italian	: auto per personne 612
Croatian	: putnički automobil, *m.* 612
Norwegian	: personbil, *m.* 612
Polish	: taksówka, *f.* 612
Portuguese	: automóvel, *o* 612
Rumanian	: automobilul 612
Slovak	: osobné auto, *n.* 612
Spanish	: automóvil, *m.* 612·
Swedish	: bill-en 612
Turkish	: otomobil 612
Russian	: автомобиль, *m.* 612
Serbian	: путнички аутомобил, *m.* 612
Ukrainian	: особове авто, *n.* 612

613 MOTORCYCLE *s.*

Czech	: motocykl, *m.* 613
Danish	: Motorcykel, *c.* 613
Dutch	: de motorfiets 613
Finnish	: moottoripyörä 613
French	: la motocyclette 613
German	: das Motorrad 613
Hungarian	: motorkerékpár 613
Italian	: motocicletta, *f.* 613
Croatian	: motocikel, *m.* 613
Norwegian	: motorsykkel, *m.* 613
Polish	: rower motorowy, *m.* 613
Portuguese	: motocicletă, *f.* 613
Rumanian	: motocicleta, *a* 613
Slovak	: motocykel, *m.* 613
Spanish	: motocicleta, *f.* 613
Swedish	: motorcykel-n 613
Turkish	: motosiklet 613
Russian	: мотоцикл, *m.* 613
Serbian	: мотоцикл, *m.* 613
Ukrainian	: ровер моторовй, *m.* 613

614 MOTOR-TRUCK *s.*

Czech	: nákladní auto, *n.* 614
Danish	: Lastbil, *m./c.* 614
Dutch	: de vrachtauto 614
Finnish	: kuorma-auto 614
French	: camion, *m.* 614
German	: das Lastauto 614
Hungarian	: teherauto 614
Italian	: camione, *m.* 614
Croatian	: teretni auto, *m.* 614
Norwegian	: lastebil, *m.* 614
Polish	: auto ciężarowe, *n.* 614
Portuguese	: caminhão, *o* 614
Rumanian	: camionul 614
Slovak	: nákladné auto, *n.* 614
Spanish	: camión, *m.* 614
Swedish	: lastbíl-en 614
Turkish	: kamyon 614
Russian	: грузовой автомобиль, *m.* 614
Serbian	: теретни ауто, *m.* 614
Ukrainian	: вантажне авто, *n.* 614

615 MOUNTAIN *s.*

Czech	: hora, *f.* 615
Danish	: Bjerg, *n.* 615
Dutch	: de berg 615
Finnish	: vuori 615
French	: montagne, *f.* 615
German	: der Berg 615
Hungarian	: hegy 615
Italian	: monte, *m.* 615
Croatian	: brdo, *n.* 615
Norwegian	: fjell, *n.* 615
Polish	: góra, *f.* 615
Portuguese	: montanha, *a* 615
Rumanian	: muntele, *m.* 615
Slovak	: vrch, *m.* 615
Spanish	: monte, *m.* 615
Swedish	: berg-et 615
Turkish	: dağ 615
Russian	: гора, *f.* 615
Serbian	: брдо, *n.* 615
Ukrainian	: гора, *f.* 615

616 MOUNTAINS *s. pl.*

Czech	: pohoří, *n.*; hory, *f. pl.* 616
Danish	: Bjergkäde, *m./c.* 616
Dutch	: het gebergte 616
Finnish	: vuoristo 616
French	: montagne, *f.* 616
German	: das Gebirge 616
Hungarian	: hegység 616
Italian	: montagna, *f.* 616
Croatian	: planina, *f.* 616
Norwegian	: fiellkjede, *m.* 616
Polish	: góry, *pl.* 616
Portuguese	: serra, *a* 616
Rumanian	: munții, *pl.* 616
Slovak	: pohorie, *n.* 616
Spanish	: montaña, *f.* 616
Swedish	: bergskeda-n 616
Turkish	: dağlik 616
Russian	: горы, *pl.* 616
Serbian	: планина, *f.* 616
Ukrainian	: гори, *pl.* 616

91

617 MOUSE s.

Czech	:	myš, f. 617
Danish	:	Mus, m./c. 617
Dutch	:	de muis 617
Finnish	:	hiiri 617
French	:	souris, f. 617
German	:	die Maus 617
Hungarian	:	egér 617
Italian	:	topo, m. 617
Croatian	:	miš, f. 617
Norwegian	:	mus, f. 617
Polish	:	mysz, f. 617
Portuguese	:	ratinho, o 617
Rumanian	:	şoarecele 617
Slovak	:	myš, f. 617
Spanish	:	ratón, m. 617
Swedish	:	mus-en 617
Turkish	:	fare 617
Russian	:	мышь, f. 617
Serbian	:	миш, m. 617
Ukrainian	:	миш, f. 617

618 MOUTH s.

Czech	:	ústa, pl. 618
Danish	:	Mund, m. 618
Dutch	:	de mond 618
Finnish	:	suu 618
French	:	bouche, f. 618
German	:	der Mund 618
Hungarian	:	száj 618
Italian	:	bocca, f. 618
Croatian	:	usta, f. 518
Norwegian	:	munn, m. 618
Polish	:	usta 618
Portuguese	:	bôca, a 618
Rumanian	:	gura, f. 618
Slovak	:	ústa, pl. 618
Spanish	:	boca, f. 618
Swedish	:	mun-nen 618
Turkish	:	ağiz 618
Russian	:	рот, m. 618
Serbian	:	уста, f. 618
Ukrainian	:	уста, pl. 618

619 MOUTH ORGAN s.

Czech	:	foukací harmonika, f. 619
Danish	:	Mundharmonika, c. 619
Dutch	:	de mondharmonika 619
Finnish	:	huuliharppu 619
French	:	harmonica, m. 619
German	:	die Mundharmonika 619
Hungarian	:	szájharmonika 619
Italian	:	organetto per bocca, m. 619
Croatian	:	usna harmonika, f. 619
Norwegian	:	munnspill, n.; harmonikk, m. 619
Polish	:	ustna harmonika, f. 619
Portuguese	:	gaita, a 619
Rumanian	:	muzicuţă, f. 619
Slovak	:	fúkacia harmonika, f. 619
Spanish	:	armónica, f. 619
Swedish	:	munspel-et 619
Turkish	:	ağiz armonikasi 619
Russian	:	гармошка, губная, f. 619
Serbian	:	усна хармоника, f. 619
Ukrainian	:	усна гармонійка, f. 619

620 MOUTH-WASH s.

Czech	:	ústní voda, f. 620
Danish	:	Mundvand, n. 620
Dutch	:	het mondwater 620
Finnish	:	suuvesi 620
French	:	eau dentifrice. f. 620
German	:	das Mundwasser 620
Hungarian	:	szájvíz 620
Italian	:	acqua per la bocca, f. 620
Croatian	:	voda za usta, f. 620
Norwegian	:	munnvann, n. 620
Polish	:	woda do ust, f. 620
Portuguese	:	água dentifrica, a 620
Rumanian	:	apa de gură, f. 620
Slovak	:	ústna voda, f. 620
Spanish	:	enjuagatorio, m. 620
Swedish	:	munvattnet 620
Turkish	:	ağiz suyu 620
Russian	:	жидкость для полоскания рта, f. 620
Serbian	:	вода за зубе, f. 620
Ukrainian	:	вода до уст, f. 620

621 MOVE QUICKLY v.
see 826 RUN

622 MOVIE s.

Czech	:	biograf, m.; kino, n. 622
Danish	:	Biograf, c. 622
Dutch	:	de bioscoop 622
Finnish	:	elokuvat 622
French	:	cinéma, m. 622
German	:	das Kino 622
Hungarian	:	mozi 622
Italian	:	cinema, m. 622
Croatian	:	kino, n. 622
Norwegian	:	kino, n. 622
Polish	:	kino, n. 622
Portuguese	:	cinema, o 622
Rumanian	:	cinematograful 622
Slovak	:	kino, n. 622
Spanish	:	cine, m. 622
Swedish	:	bio-n 622
Turkish	:	sinema 622
Russian	:	кинематограф, m. 622
Serbian	:	кино, n. 622
Ukrainian	:	кіно, n. 622

623 MOW v.

Czech	:	kositi 623
Danish	:	slaa 623
Dutch	:	maaien 623
Finnish	:	niittää 623
French	:	faucher 623
German	:	mähen 623
Hungarian	:	kaszálni 623
Italian	:	falciare 623
Croatian	:	kositi 623
Norwegian	:	slå 623
Polish	:	kosić 623
Portuguese	:	ceifar 623
Rumanian	:	a cosi 623
Slovak	:	kosit' 623
Spanish	:	segar 623
Swedish	:	meja 623
Turkish	:	biçmek 623
Russian	:	косить 623
Serbian	:	косити 623
Ukrainian	:	косити 623

624 MR. (Mister)
   see 886 SIR

625 MRS. s. (Lady)

Czech	:	paní, f. 625
Danish	:	Fru 625
Dutch	:	Mevrouw 625
Finnish	:	rouva 625
French	:	dame; madame, f. 625
German	:	die Frau 625
Hungarian	:	asszony; nö 625
Italian	:	dama; signora, f. 625
Croatian	:	gospoda; žena, f. 625
Norwegian	:	kone; hustru, c.; fru 625
Polish	:	pani, f. 625
Portuguese	:	senhora, f. 625
Rumanian	:	femeie f.; doamnă 625
Slovak	:	pani, f. 625
Spanish	:	señora; dama 625
Swedish	:	dam; fru 625
Turkish	:	kadin; bayan 625
Russian	:	госпожа, f. 625
Serbian	:	господа, f. 625
Ukrainian	:	пані; дама, f. 625

626 MUCH adv. (many)

Czech	:	mnoho 626
Danish	:	megen; mange 626
Dutch	:	veel 626
Finnish	:	paljo; moni 626
French	:	beaucoup de 626
German	:	viel 626
Hungarian	:	sok 626
Italian	:	molto 626
Croatian	:	mnogo 626
Norwegian	:	megen; meget 626
Polish	:	durzo 626
Portuguese	:	muito 626
Rumanian	:	mult 626
Slovak	:	mnoho; vel'a 626
Spanish	:	mucho 626
Swedish	:	mycket 626
Turkish	:	çok; birçok 626
Russian	:	много, 626
Serbian	:	много 626
Ukrainian	:	багато 626

627 MULE s.

Czech	:	mezek, m.; soumar, m. 627
Danish	:	Muldyr, n. 627
Dutch	:	het muildier 627
Finnish	:	muuli 627
French	:	mulet, m. 627
German	:	das Maultier 627
Hungarian	:	öszvér 627
Italian	:	mulo, m. 627
Croatian	:	mazga, f. 627
Norwegian	:	muldyr, n. 627
Polish	:	muł, m. 627
Portuguese	:	mula, a 627
Rumanian	:	catărul 627
Slovak	:	mulica, f. 627
Spanish	:	mulo, m. 627
Swedish	:	mulasha-n 627
Turkish	:	katir 627
Russian	:	мул, m. 627
Serbian	:	мазга, f. 627
Ukrainian	:	мул, m. 627

628 MUSHROOM s.

Czech	:	houba, f.; hřib, m. 628
Danish	:	Svamp, m./c. 628
Dutch	:	de paddestoel 628
Finnish	:	sienet 628
French	:	champignon, m. 628
German	:	der Pilz 628
Hungarian	:	gomba 628
Italian	:	funghi, m. pl. 628
Croatian	:	gljiva, f. 628
Norwegian	:	sopp, m. 628
Polish	:	grzyby, m. pl. 628
Portuguese	:	cogumelo, o 628
Rumanian	:	ciuperca, f. 628
Slovak	:	hríb, m. 628
Spanish	:	boleto, m. 628
Swedish	:	svamp-en 628
Turkish	:	mantar 628
Russian	:	грибы, pl. 628
Serbian	:	гљива, f. 628
Ukrainian	:	гриби, pl. 628

629 MUSIC s.

Czech	:	hubda, f. 629
Danish	:	musik, c. 629
Dutch	:	muziek, c. 629
Finnish	:	musiikki 629
French	:	musique, f. 629
German	:	die Musik 629
Hungarian	:	zene 629
Italian	:	musica, f. 629
Croatian	:	glazba, f. 629
Norwegian	:	musikk, c. 629
Polish	:	muzyka, f. 629
Portuguese	:	música, f. 629
Rumanian	:	musică, f. 629
Slovak	:	hudba, f. 629
Spanish	:	música, f. 629
Swedish	:	musik 629
Turkish	:	misika; musiki 629
Russian	:	музыка, f. 629
Serbian	:	глазба, f. 629
Ukrainian	:	музика, f. 629

630 MUSIC s. (the printed score)

Czech	:	noty, pl. f. 630
Danish	:	Node, f./c. 630
Dutch	:	de noot 630
Finnish	:	nuottia 630
French	:	notes, pl. 630
German	:	die Note 630
Hungarian	:	hangjegy 630
Italian	:	note, f. pl. 630
Croatian	:	kajda; nota, f. 630
Norwegian	:	note, f. 630
Polish	:	nuty, pl. 630
Portuguese	:	nota de música, a 630
Rumanian	:	notele, pl. 630
Slovak	:	noty, pl. 630
Spanish	:	nota musical 630
Swedish	:	noter-na 630
Turkish	:	nota 630
Russian	:	ноты, pl. 630
Serbian	:	нота, f. 630
Ukrainian	:	ноти, pl. 630

631 MUSICAL INSTRUMENT s.

Czech : hudební nástroj, m. 631
Danish : Musikinstrument, c. 631
Dutch : het muziekinstrument 631
Finnish : soitin 631
French : l'instrument de musique 631
German : das Musikinstrument 631
Hungarian : hangszer 631
Italian : strumenti musicali, m. pl. 631
Croatian : muzički instrument, m. 631
Norwegian : musikk instrument, m. 631
Polish : instrument muzyczny, m. 631
Portuguese : o instrumento de musica 631
Rumanian : instrumentul muzical 631
Slovak : hudobný nástroj, m. 631
Spanish : instrumento de música, m. 631
Swedish : musikinstrument-et 631
Turkish : müzikaletleri 631
Russian : музикалень инстумент, m. 631
Serbian : музицки инструмент, m. 631
Ukrainian : музикални инструмент, m. 631

632 MUTTON s.

Czech : skopové maso, n. 632
Danish : Faarekód, n. 632
Dutch : het schapenvlees 632
Finnish : lampaanliha 632
French : mouton, m. 632
German : das Hammelfleisch 632
Hungarian : ürühús 632
Italian : la carne di montone 632
Croatian : ovnetina, f. 632
Norwegian : fårekjött, n. 632
Polish : baranina, f. 632
Portuguese : carne de carneiro, a 632
Rumanian : carnea de berbec, f. 632
Slovak : baranina f. 632
Spanish : carnero, m. 632
Swedish : fårkött-et 632
Turkish : koyun eti 632
Russian : баранина, f. 632
Serbian : овнетина, f. 632
Ukrainian : баранина, f. 632

633 MY pron.

Czech : můj, má, mé 633
Danish : min, mit, mine 633
Dutch : mijn 633
Finnish : minun 633
French : mon, ma, mes 633
German : mein, meine, mein; meine, pl. 633
Hungarian : enyém 633
Italian : mio, mia, mie 633
Croatian : moj 633
Norwegian : min 633
Polish : moj 633
Portuguese : minha(s) ; men(s) 633
Rumanian : meu 633
Slovak : môj, moja, moje 633
Spanish : mi, mía 633
Swedish : min 633
Turkish : benim 633
Russian : мой, моя, мое 633
Serbian : мой 633
Ukrainian : мій; моя; мое 633

634 NAIL s. (a piece of metal)

Czech : hřeb, m.; hřebík, m. 634
Danish : Söm, m./c. 634
Dutch : de spijker 634
Finnish : naula 634
French : clou, m. 634
German : der Nagel 634
Hungarian : szeg 634
Italian : chiodo, m. 634
Croatian : klin; čavao, m. 634
Norwegian : spiker, m. 634
Polish : gwóźdź, m. 634
Portuguese : prego, o 634
Rumanian : cuiul 634
Slovak : klinec, m. 634
Spanish : clavo, m. 634
Swedish : spik-en 634
Turkish : çivi 634
Russian : гвоздь, m. 634
Serbian : ексер, m. 634
Ukrainian : цьвях, m. 634

635 NAIL-FILE s.

Czech : pilník na nehty, m. 635
Danish : Neglefil, m./c. 635
Dutch : de nagelvijl 635
Finnish : kynsiviila 635
French : lime à angle, f. 635
German : die Nagelfeile 635
Hungarian : hörömreszelö 635
Italian : limetta per le unghie, f. 635
Croatian : turpijica za nokte 635
Norwegian : neglefil, m. 635
Polish : pilnik do paznokci, m. 635
Portuguese : lima para as unhas, a 635
Rumanian : pila de unghil 635
Slovak : pilník na nehty, m. 635
Spanish : lima para pulir las uñas 635
Swedish : nagelfil-en 635
Turkish : tirnak eğesi 635
Russian : пилка для ногтей, f. 635
Serbian : турпија за нокте, f. 635
Ukrainian : пильник до нігтів, m. 635

636 NAME s.

Czech : jméno, n.; název, m. 636
Danish : navn, n. 636
Dutch : nömen 636
Finnish : nimi 636
French : nom, m. 636
German : der Name 636
Hungarian : név 636
Italian : nome, m. 636
Croatian : ime, n. 636
Norwegian : navn, n. 636
Polish : nazvisko, n. 636
Portuguese : nome, m. 636
Rumanian : nume, c. 636
Slovak : meno, n. 636
Spanish : nombre, m. 636
Swedish : namn-et 636
Turkish : isim 636
Russian : имя, n. 636
Serbian : име, n. 636
Ukrainian : ім'я; імення, 636

637 NAME v. see 153 CALL

638 NAPE s.

Czech	:	šíje, *f.* 638
Danish	:	Nakke, *m./c.* 638
Dutch	:	de nek 638
Finnish	:	niska 638
French	:	nuque, *f.* 638
German	:	das Genick 638
Hungarian	:	nyakszirt 638
Italian	:	nuca, *f.* 638
Croatian	:	zatiljak, m.; šija, *f.* 638
Norwegian	:	nakke, *m.* 638
Polish	:	kark, *m.* 638
Portuguese	:	nuca, *a* 638
Rumanian	:	ceafă, *f.* 638
Slovak	:	šija, *f.* 638
Spanish	:	nuca, *f.* 638
Swedish	:	nacke-n 638
Turkish	:	ense 638
Russian	:	затылок, *m.* 638
Serbian	:	потиљак, *m.* 638
Ukrainian	:	потилиця, *f.* 638

639 NARRATE
see 981 TELL

640 NECK s.

Czech	:	krk, *m.* 640
Danish	:	Hals, *m./c.* 640
Dutch	:	de hals 640
Finnish	:	kaula 640
French	:	cou, *m.* 640
German	:	der Hals 640
Hungarian	:	nyak 640
Italian	:	collo, *m.* 640
Croatian	:	vrat, *m.* 640
Norwegian	:	hals, *m.* 640
Polish	:	szyja, *f.* 640
Portuguese	:	pescoço, *o* 640
Rumanian	:	gâtul 640
Slovak	:	krk, *m.* 640
Spanish	:	cuello, *m.* 640
Swedish	:	hals-en 640
Turkish	:	boyun 640
Russian	:	шея, *f.* 640
Serbian	:	врат, *m.* 640
Ukrainian	:	шия, *f.* 640

641 NECKLACE s.

Czech	:	náhrdelník, *m.* 641
Danish	:	Halskäde, *m./c.* 641
Dutch	:	de halsketting 641
Finnish	:	kaulakoriste 641
French	:	collier, *m.* 641
German	:	die Halskette 641
Hungarian	:	nyaklánc 641
Italian	:	collana, *f.* 641
Croatian	:	ogrlica, *f.* 641
Norwegian	:	halskjede, *m.* 641
Polish	:	naszyjnik, *m.* 641
Portuguese	:	colar, *o* 641
Rumanian	:	colierul 641
Slovak	:	náhrdelník, *m.* 641
Spanish	:	cadena, *f.* 641
Swedish	:	halsband-et 641
Turkish	:	kolye 641
Russian	:	ожерелье, *n.* 641
Serbian	:	огрлица, *f.* 641
Ukrainian	:	намисто, *n.*; коралі, *pl.* 641

642 NEEDLE s.

Czech	:	jehla, *f.* 642
Danish	:	Naal, *f./c.* 642
Dutch	:	de naaid 642
Finnish	:	neula 642
French	:	l'aiguille, *f.* 642
German	:	die Nadel 642
Hungarian	:	tü 642
Italian	:	ago, *m.* 642
Croatian	:	igla, *f.* 642
Norwegian	:	nål, *f.* 642
Polish	:	igla, *f.* 642
Portuguese	:	agulha, *a* 642
Rumanian	:	acul 642
Slovak	:	ihla, *f.* 642
Spanish	:	aguja, *f.* 642
Swedish	:	nål-en 642
Turkish	:	iğne 642
Russian	:	игла, *f.* 642
Serbian	:	игла, *f.* 642
Ukrainian	:	голка, *f.* 642

643 NET s.

Czech	:	sít', *f.* 643
Danish	:	Net, *n.* 643
Dutch	:	het net 643
Finnish	:	kalaverkko 643
French	:	filet, *m.* 643
German	:	das Netz 643
Hungarian	:	háló 643
Italian	:	rete, *f.* 643
Croatian	:	mreža, *f.* 643
Norwegian	:	nett, *n.*; garn, *n.* 643
Polish	:	sieć, *f.* 643
Portuguese	:	rêde, *a* 643
Rumanian	:	plasă, *f.* 643
Slovak	:	siet', *f.* 643
Spanish	:	red, *f.* 643
Swedish	:	nät-et 643
Turkish	:	ağ 643
Russian	:	сетка, *f.* 643
Serbian	:	мрежа, *f.* 643
Ukrainian	:	сітка, *f.* 643

644 NEW adj.

Czech	:	nový, nová, **nové** 644
Danish	:	ny 644
Dutch	:	vers 644
Finnish	:	uusi 644
French	:	neuf, neuve 644
German	:	neu, neue 644
Hungarian	:	új 644
Italian	:	nuovo 644
Croatian	:	nov 644
Norwegian	:	ny 644
Polish	:	nowy 644
Portuguese	:	novo 644
Rumanian	:	nou 644
Slovak	:	nový, nová, **nové** 644
Spanish	:	nuevo 644
Swedish	:	ny 644
Turkish	:	yeni 644
Russian	:	новый 644
Serbian	:	нов 644
Ukrainian	:	новий 644

645 NEWSPAPER s.

Czech	:	noviny, *pl.* 645
Danish	:	Avis, *m./c.* 645
Dutch	:	de krant 645
Finnish	:	lehti 645
French	:	journal, *m.* 645
German	:	die Zeitung 645
Hungarian	:	ujság 645
Italian	:	giornale, *m.* 645
Croatian	:	novine, *pl.* 645
Norwegian	:	avis, *f.* 645
Polish	:	gazeta, *f.* 645
Portuguese	:	carta para jogar, *a* 645
Rumanian	:	ziarul 645
Slovak	:	noviny, *pl.* 645
Spanish	:	periódico, *m.* 645
Swedish	:	tidning-en 645
Turkish	:	gazeta 645
Russian	:	газета, *f.* 645
Serbian	:	новина, *f.* 645
Ukrainian	:	часопись, *m.* 645

646 NICE adj.
see 499 KIND

647 NICKEL s.

Czech	:	nikl, *m.* 647
Danish	:	Nikkel, *n.* 647
Dutch	:	het nikkel 647
Finnish	:	nikkeli 647
French	:	nickel, *m.* 647
German	:	das Nickel 647
Hungarian	:	nikkel 647
Italian	:	nichelio, *m.* 647
Croatian	:	nikel, *m.* 647
Norwegian	:	nikkel, *n.* 647
Polish	:	nikel, *m.* 647
Portuguese	:	níquel, *o* 647
Rumanian	:	nikelul 647
Slovak	:	nikel, *m.* 647
Spanish	:	nickel, *m.* 647
Swedish	:	nicklet 647
Turkish	:	nikel 647
Russian	:	никель, *m.* 647
Serbian	:	никал, *m.* 647
Ukrainian	:	нікель, *m.* 647

648 NIGHT s.

Czech	:	noc, *f.* 648
Danish	:	Nat, *f.* 648
Dutch	:	de nacht 648
Finnish	:	yö 648
French	:	nuit, *f.* 648
German	:	die Nacht 648
Hungarian	:	éjszaka 648
Italian	:	notte, *f.* 648
Croatian	:	noč, *f.* 648
Norwegian	:	natt, *f.* 648
Polish	:	noc, *f.* 648
Portuguese	:	noite, *a* 648
Rumanian	:	noapte, *f.* 648
Slovak	:	noc, *f.* 648
Spanish	:	noche, *f.* 648
Swedish	:	natt-en 648
Turkish	:	gece 648
Russian	:	ночь, *f.* 648
Serbian	:	ноħ, *f.* 648
Ukrainian	:	ніч, *f.* 648

649 NIGHT SHIRT s.

Czech	:	noční košile, *f.* 649
Danish	:	Natskjorte, *m./c.* 649
Dutch	:	het nachthemd 649
Finnish	:	yöpaita 649
French	:	chemise de nuit, *f.* 649
German	:	das Nachthemd 649
Hungarian	:	hálóing 649
Italian	:	camicia da notte, *f.* 649
Croatian	:	noćna košulja, *f.* 649
Norwegian	:	nattskjorte, *f.* 649
Polish	:	nocna koszula, *f.* 649
Portuguese	:	camisa de dormir, *a* 649
Rumanian	:	camasa de noapte, *f.* 649
Slovak	:	nočná košel'a, *f.* 649
Spanish	:	camisa de noche, *f.* 649
Swedish	:	nattskjorta-n 649
Turkish	:	gecelik 649
Russian	:	ночная, рубаха, *f.* 649
Serbian	:	ноħна кошуља, *f.* 649
Ukrainian	:	нічна сорочка, *f.* 649

650 NIGHT-TABLE s.

Czech	:	noční stolek, *m.* 650
Danish	:	Natbord, *c.* 650
Dutch	:	het nachtkastje 650
Finnish	:	yöpöytä 650
French	:	table de nuit, *f.* 650
German	:	der Nachtisch 650
Hungarian	:	éjjeliszekrény 650
Italian	:	comodino, *m.* 650
Croatian	:	noćni ormarić, *m.* 650
Norwegian	:	nattbord, *n.* 650
Polish	:	szafka nocna, *f.* 650
Portuguese	:	mesa de cabeceira, *a* 650
Rumanian	:	noptierä, *f.* 650
Slovak	:	nočný stolík 650
Spanish	:	mesita de noche 650
Swedish	:	nattduksbord-et 650
Turkish	:	gece masasi 650
Russian	:	ночной, столик, *m.* 650
Serbian	:	ноħни орманчиħ, *m.* 650
Ukrainian	:	нічний столик, *m.* 650

651 NINE

Czech	:	devět 651
Danish	:	ni 651
Dutch	:	negen 651
Finnish	:	yhdeksän 651
French	:	neuf 651
German	:	neun 651
Hungarian	:	kilenc 651
Italian	:	nove 651
Croatian	:	devet 651
Norwegian	:	ni 651
Polish	:	dziewięć 651
Portuguese	:	nove 651
Rumanian	:	nouä 651
Slovak	:	devät 651
Spanish	:	nueve 651
Swedish	:	nio 651
Turkish	:	dokuz 651
Russian	:	девять 651
Serbian	:	девет 651
Ukrainian	:	девять 651

652 NINETEEN

Czech	:	devatenáct 652
Danish	:	nitten 652
Dutch	:	negentien 652
Finnish	:	yhdeksäntoista 652
French	:	dix-neuf 652
German	:	neunzehn 652
Hungarian	:	tizenkilenc 652
Italian	:	dicianove 652
Croatian	:	devetnaest 652
Norwegian	:	nitten 652
Polish	:	dziewietnaście 652
Portuguese	:	dezanove 652
Rumanian	:	nonăsprezece 652
Slovak	:	devätnást' 652
Spanish	:	diez y nueve 652
Swedish	:	nitton 652
Turkish	:	on dokuz 652
Russian	:	девятнадцать 652
Serbian	:	деветнаест 652
Ukrainian	:	дев'ятнадцять 652

653 NINETY

Czech	:	devadesát 653
Danish	:	halvfems 653
Dutch	:	negentig 653
Finnish	:	yhdeksänkymmentä 653
French	:	quatre-vingt-dix 653
German	:	neunzig 653
Hungarian	:	kilencven 653
Italian	:	novanta 653
Croatian	:	devedeset 653
Norwegian	:	nitti 653
Polish	:	dziewiędziesiąt 653
Portuguese	:	noventa 653
Rumanian	:	nouăzeci 653
Slovak	:	devätdesiat 653
Spanish	:	noventa 653
Swedish	:	nittio 653
Turkish	:	doksan 653
Russian	:	девяносто, 653
Serbian	:	деведесет 653
Ukrainian	:	дев'ятьдесять 653

654 NO

Czech	:	ne 654
Danish	:	nej 654
Dutch	:	neen 654
Finnish	:	ei 654
French	:	non 654
German	:	nein 654
Hungarian	:	nem 654
Italian	:	no 654
Croatian	:	ne 654
Norwegian	:	nei 654
Polish	:	nie 654
Portuguese	:	não 654
Rumanian	:	nu 654
Slovak	:	nie 654
Spanish	:	no 654
Swedish	:	nej 654
Turkish	:	hayir 654
Russian	:	нет 654
Serbian	:	не 654
Ukrainian	:	ні 654

655 NOODLES

Czech	:	nudle, f. pl. 655
Danish	:	Nudler, pl. 655
Dutch	:	de vermecelli 655
Finnish	:	makarooneia 655
French	:	nouilles, f. pl. 655
German	:	die Nudeln, pl. 655
Hungarian	:	metélt 655
Italian	:	pasta, f. 655
Croatian	:	rezanci, pl. 655
Norwegian	:	nude, pl. 655
Polish	:	kluski, pl. 655
Portuguese	:	massa, a 655
Rumanian	:	tăieţei, pl. 655
Slovak	:	rezance, pl. 655
Spanish	:	fideos, pl. 655
Swedish	:	nudel, pl. 655
Turkish	:	şehriye 655
Russian	:	лапша, f. 655
Serbian	:	резанци, pl. 655
Ukrainian	:	локшина, f. 655

656 NOON s.

Czech	:	poledne, n. 656
Danish	:	Middag, m. 656
Dutch	:	de middag 656
Finnish	:	puolipäivä 656
French	:	midi, m. 656
German	:	der Mittag 656
Hungarian	:	dél 656
Italian	:	mezzogiorno, m. 656
Croatian	:	podne, n. 656
Norwegian	:	middag, m. 656
Polish	:	południe, n. 656
Portuguese	:	meio-dia, o 656
Rumanian	:	amiază, f. 656
Slovak	:	poludnie, n. 656
Spanish	:	mediodía, m. 656
Swedish	:	middagstiden 656
Turkish	:	öğle 656
Russian	:	полдень 656
Serbian	:	подне, n. 656
Ukrainian	:	полудне, n. 656

657 NORTH s.

Czech	:	sever, m. 657
Danish	:	Nord, c. 657
Dutch	:	Noorden 657
Finnish	:	pohjoinen 657
French	:	nord, m. 657
German	:	der Norden 657
Hungarian	:	észak 657
Italian	:	settentrione, m. 657
Croatian	:	sjever, m. 657
Norwegian	:	nord, c. 657
Polish	:	północ 657
Portuguese	:	norte, m. 657
Rumanian	:	nord, c. 657
Slovak	:	sever, m. 657
Spanish	:	norte, m. 657
Swedish	:	nord-en 657
Turkish	:	şimal 657
Russian	:	север, m. 657
Serbian	:	сјевер, m. 657
Ukrainian	:	північ; норд, m. 657

658 NOSE s.

Czech	:	nos, m.	658
Danish	:	Näse, m./c.	658
Dutch	:	de neus	658
Finnish	:	nenä	658
French	:	nez, m.	658
German	:	die Nase	658
Hungarian	:	orr	658
Italian	- :	naso, m.	658
Croatian	:	nos, m.	658
Norwegian	:	nese, f.	658
Polish	:	nos, m.	658
Portuguese	:	nariz, o	658
Rumanian	:	nasul	658
Slovak	:	nos, m.	658
Spanish	:	nariz, m.	658
Swedish	:	näsa-n	658
Turkish	:	burun	658
Russian	:	нос,m.	658
Serbian	:	нос, m.	658
Ukrainian	:	ніс, m.	658

659 NOTIFY OF THE DEPARTURE

Czech	:	odhlásiti (se)	659
Danish	:	afmelde	659
Dutch	:	afmelden	659
Finnish	:	ilmoittaa pois	659
French	:	déclarer le départ	659
German	:	abmelden	659
Hungarian	:	kijelenteni	659
Italian	:	snotificare	659
Croatian	:	odjaviti	659
Norwegian	:	utmelde	659
Polish	:	wymeldować	659
Portuguese	:	anunciar a partida	659
Rumanian	:	a anunta plecarea	659
Slovak	:	odhlásit'	659
Spanish	:	declarar la salida	659
Swedish	:	avmäla	659
Turkish	:	evvelce resmen bildirmek	659
Russian	:	выписаться	659
Serbian	:	одјавити	659
Ukrainian	:	вимельдувати	659

660 NOVEMBER s.

Czech	:	listopad, m.	660
Danish	:	November	660
Dutch	:	November	660
Finnish	:	marraskuu	660
French	:	novembre	660
German	:	der November	660
Hungarian	:	november	660
Italian	:	novembre	660
Croatian	:	studeni, m.	660
Norwegian	:	november	660
Polish	:	listopad	660
Portuguese	:	novembro	660
Rumanian	:	Noembrie	660
Slovak	:	november	660
Spanish	:	noviembre	660
Swedish	:	november	660
Turkish	:	ikinci teşrin	660
Russian	:	ноябрь	660
Serbian	:	Новембар	660
Ukrainian	:	Падолист	660

661 NUMBER s.

Czech	:	číslo, n.	661
Danish	:	Tal, n.	661
Dutch	:	het getal	661
Finnish	:	numero	661
French	:	nombre, m.	661
German	:	die Zahl; die Nummer	661
Hungarian	:	szám	661
Italian	:	numero, m.	661
Croatian	:	broj	661
Norwegian	:	tall, n.	661
Polish	:	numer, m.	661
Portuguese	:	número, o	661
Rumanian	:	număr	661
Slovak	:	číslo, n.	661
Spanish	:	número, m.	661
Swedish	:	siffra-n	661
Turkish	:	sayiler	661
Russian	:	число, n.	661
Serbian	:	број, m.	661
Ukrainian	:	число, n.	661

662 NURSE s.

Czech	:	ošetřovatelka, f.; sestra, f.	662
Danish	:	Söster, f.	662
Dutch	:	de zuster	662
Finnish	:	sairaanhoitajatar	662
French	:	infirmière, f.	662
German	:	die Schwester	662
Hungarian	:	növer	662
Italian	:	suora, f.	662
Croatian	:	sestra, f.	62
Norwegian	:	söster, f.	662
Polish	:	siostra, f.	662
Portuguese	:	enfermeira, a	662
Rumanian	:	sora de caritate	662
Slovak	:	ošetrovateľka, f.	662
Spanish	:	enfermera, f.	662
Swedish	:	syster-n	662
Turkish	:	hasta bakici kadin	662
Russian	:	сиделка, f.	662
Serbian	:	сестра, f.	662
Ukrainian	:	сестра, f.	662

663 NUTMEG s.

Czech	:	muškát, m.	663
Danish	:	Muskatnöd, m./c.	663
Dutch	:	de nootmuskaat	663
Finnish	:	muskottipähkinä	663
French	:	noix de muscade, f.	663
German	:	die Muskatnuss	663
Hungarian	:	szerecsendió	663
Italian	:	noce moscata, f.	663
Croatian	:	muskat, m.	663
Norwegian	:	muskatnött, m.	663
Polish	:	gałka muszkatulowa, f.	663
Portuguese	:	noz moscada, a	663
Rumanian	:	untdelemnul	663
Slovak	:	muškátový oriešok, m.	663
Spanish	:	nuez moscada, f.	663
Swedish	:	muskatnöt-en	663
Turkish	:	hind cevizi	663
Russian	:	мушкатный орех, m.	663
Serbian	:	мускат, m.	663
Ukrainian	:	мускатний горіх, m.	663

664 OAK-TREE s.

Czech : dub, *m.* 664
Danish : Eg; Egetrae, *n.* 664
Dutch : ijk(eboom) 664
Finnish : tammi 664
French : chêne, *m.* 664
German : die Eiche 664
Hungarian : tölgy 664
Italian : quercia, *f.* 664
Croatian : hrast, *m.* 664
Norwegian : eik, *f.* 664
Polish : dab, *m.* 664
Portuguese : carvalho, *o* 664
Rumanian : stejarul 664
Slovak : dub, *m.* 664
Spanish : encina, *f.* 664
Swedish : ek-en 664
Turkish : mişe ağaci 664
Russian : дуб, *m.* 664
Serbian : храст, *m.* 664
Ukrainian : дуб, *m.* 664

665 OAR s. (for a boat)

Czech : veslo, *n.* 665
Danish : Aare, *m./c.* 665
Dutch : de roeispaan 665
Finnish : airo; peräsin 665
French : rame, *f.* 665
German : das Ruder 665
Hungarian : evezö 665
Italian : remo, *m.* 665
Croatian : veslo, *n.* 666
Norwegian : åre, *f.* 665
Polish : wiosło, *n.* 665
Portuguese : remo, *o* 665
Rumanian : vâsla, *f.* 665
Slovak : veslo, *n.* 665
Spanish : remo, *m.* 665
Swedish : åra-n 665
Turkish : kürek 665
Russian : весло, *n.* 665
Serbian : весло, *n.* 665
Ukrainian : весло, *n.* 665

666 OATS s. pl.

Czech : oves, *m.* 666
Danish : Havre, *m./c.* 666
Dutch : de haver 666
Finnish : kaura 666
French : avoine, *f.* 666
German : der Hafer 666
Hungarian : zab 666
Italian : avena, *f.* 666
Croatian : zob, *m.* 666
Norwegian : havre, *m.* 666
Polish : owies, *m.* 666
Portuguese : aveia, *a* 666
Rumanian : ovăzul 666
Slovak : ovos, *m.* 666
Spanish : avena, *f.* 666
Swedish : havre-n 666
Turkish : yulaf 666
Russian : овес, *m.* 666
Serbian : зоб, *m.* 666
Ukrainian : овес, *m.* 666

667 OBJECT s. **see 991 THING**

668 OCCUPY v. **see 973 TAKE**

669 OCTOBER s.

Czech : říjen, *m.* 669
Danish : October 669
Dutch : October 669
Finnish : lokakuu 669
French : octobre, *m.* 669
German : der Oktober 669
Hungarian : október 669
Italian : ottobre, *m.* 669
Croatian : listopad, *m.* 669
Norwegian : oktober 669
Polish : październik 669
Portuguese : outubro 669
Rumanian : Octombrie 669
Slovak : október 669
Spanish : octubre 669
Swedish : oktober 669
Turkish : birinci teşrin 669
Russian : октябрь 669
Serbian : Октобар 669
Ukrainian : жовтень 669

670 OFFICE s.

Czech : kancelář, *f.* 670
Danish : Kontor, *f./c.* 670
Dutch : het bureau 670
Finnish : toimisto 670
French : bureau, *m.* 670
German : das Büro 670
Hungarian : iroda 670
Italian : ufficio, *m.* 670
Croatian : kancelarija, *f.* 670
Norwegian : kontor, *f.* 670
Polish : kancelarja, *f.* 670
Portuguese : escritório, *o* 670
Rumanian : biroul 670
Slovak : pisáreň, *f.* 670
Spanish : despacho, *m.* 670
Swedish : kontor-et 670
Turkish : yazi odasi 670
Russian : канцелярия, *f.* 670
Serbian : канцеларија, *f.* 670
Ukrainian : канцелярия, *f.* 670

671 OFFICER s.

Czech : důstojník, *m.*; úředník, *m.* 671
Danish : Officer, *m.* 671
Dutch : de officier 671
Finnish : upseeri 671
French : officier 671
German : der Officier 671
Hungarian : tiszt 671
Italian : ufficiale, *m.* 671
Croatian : časnik, *m.* 671
Norwegian : offiser, *m.* 671
Polish : oficer, *m.* 671
Portuguese : oficial, *o* 671
Rumanian : ofiţerul 671
Slovak : dôstojník, *m.* 671
Spanish : oficial, *m.* 671
Swedish : officeren 671
Turkish : zâbit 671
Russian : офицер, *m.* 671
Serbian : официр, *m.* 671
Ukrainian : старшина, *m.* 671

99

672 OIL s.

Czech	: olej, *m.* 672
Danish	: Olje, *m./c.* 672
Dutch	: de olie 672
Finnish	: öljy 672
French	: huile, *f.* 672
German	: das Öl 672
Hungarian	: olaj 672
Italian⁻	: olio, *m.* 672
Croatian	: ulje, *n.* 672
Norwegian	: olje, *m.* 672
Polish	: oliwa, *f.* 672
Portuguese	: azeite, *o* 672
Rumanian	: oţetul 672
Slovak	: olej, *m.* 672
Spanish	: aceite, *m.* 672
Swedish	: olja-n 672
Turkish	: yağ 672
Russian	: масло постное, *n.* 672
Serbian	: улье, *n.* 672
Ukrainian	: олій, *m.* 672

673 OIL SARDINE s.

Czech	: olejové sardinky, *pl.* 673
Danish	: Sardiner ì Olie 673
Dutch	: de sardine in olie 673
Finnish	: sardiini 673
French	: sardine à l'huile, *f* 673
German	: die Ölsardine 673
Hungarian	: szardinia 673
Italian	: sardina nell'olio, *f.* 673
Croatian	: sardina, *f.* 673
Norwegian	: sardiner i olje, *pl.* 673
Polish	: sardynki na oliwie, *pl.* 673
Portuguese	: sardinha em azeite, *a* 673
Rumanian	: sardeaua, *f.* 673
Slovak	: sardinka, *f.* 673
Spanish	: sardina en aceite, *f.* 673
Swedish	: sardin i olja 673
Turkish	: savdalya baligi 673
Russian	: сардинка, *f.* 673
Serbian	: сардина у улу, *f.* 673
Ukrainian	: сардинка на оливі, *f.* 673

674 OINTMENT s.

Czech	: mast, *f.* 674
Danish	: Salve; Smorelse 674
Dutch	: de zalf 674
Finnish	: voide 674
French	: pommade, *f.*; onguent, *m.* 674
German	: die Salbe 674
Hungarian	: kenöcs 674
Italian	: pomata, *f.* 674
Croatian	: mast, *f.* 674
Norwegian	: salve, *f.* 674
Polish	: maść, *f.* 674
Portuguese	: ungüento, *o* 674
Rumanian	: alifiă, *f.* 674
Slovak	: mast', *f.* 674
Spanish	: ungüento, *m.* 674
Swedish	: salva-n 674
Turkish	: merhem 674
Russian	: мазь, *f.* 674
Serbian	: маст, *f.* 674
Ukrainian	: масть, *f.* 674

675 OLD adj.

Czech	: starý 675
Danish	: gammel 675
Dutch	: oud 675
Finnish	: altto 675
French	: vieux 675
German	: alt 675
Hungarian	: öreg 675
Italian	: vecchio 675
Croatian	: star 675
Norwegian	: gammel 675
Polish	: stare 675
Portuguese	: velho 675
Rumanian	: bătrîn; vechi 675
Slovak	: starý 675
Spanish	: viejo 675
Swedish	: gammal 675
Turkish	: ihtiyar; eski 675
Russian	: старый 675
Serbian	: стар 675
Ukrainian	: старий 675

676 OLIVE s.

Czech	: oliva, *f.* 676
Danish	: Oliven, *c.* 676
Dutch	: de olijf 676
Finnish	: öljyhedelmä 676
French	: L'olive, *f.* 676
German	: die Olive 676
Hungarian	: olajbogyó 676
Italian	: Oliva, *f.* 676
Croatian	: oliva, *f.* 676
Norwegian	: oliven 676
Polish	: oliwka, *f.* 676
Portuguese	: azeitona, *a* 676
Rumanian	: maslina, *f.* 676
Slovak	: oliva, *f.* 676
Spanish	: aceituna, *f.* 676
Swedish	: oliv-en 676
Turkish	: zeytin 676
Russian	: маслина, *f.* 676
Serbian	: олива, *f.* 676
Ukrainian	: оливка, *f.* 676

677 ONCE adv.

Czech	: jednou, jedenkrát 677
Danish	: een gange 677
Dutch	: eenmaal 677
Finnish	: (yksi) kerta 677
French	: une fois 677
German	: einmal 677
Hungarian	: egyszer 677
Italian	: polvere per 677
Croatian	: jedan puta 677
Norwegian	: en gang 677
Polish	: jeden raz 677
Portuguese	: uma vez 677
Rumanian	: odată 677
Slovak	: jedenkrát 677
Spanish	: una vez 677
Swedish	: en gång 677
Turkish	: bir kere 677
Russian	: один раз 677
Serbian	: један пут 677
Ukrainian	: один раз 677

678 ONE

Czech	:	jedna 678
Danish	:	een, eet 678
Dutch	:	één 678
Finnish	:	yksi 678
French	:	un 678
German	:	eins 678
Hungarian	:	egy 678
Italian	:	uno 678
Croatian	:	jedan 678
Norwegian	:	en 678
Polish	:	jeden 678
Portuguese	:	um 678
Rumanian	:	unu 678
Slovak	:	jedna 678
Spanish	:	uno 678
Swedish	:	ett 678
Turkish	:	bir 678
Russian	:	один 678
Serbian	:	један 678
Ukrainian	:	один 678

679 ONION s.

Czech	:	cibule, f. 679
Danish	:	Lög, m./c. 679
Dutch	:	de ui 679
Finnish	:	sipuli 679
French	:	oignon, m. 679
German	:	die Zwiebel 679
Hungarian	:	hagyma 679
Italian	:	cipolla, f. 679
Croatian	:	crveni luk, m. 679
Norwegian	:	blomsterlök, m. 679
Polish	:	cebula, f. 679
Portuguese	:	cebola, a 679
Rumanian	:	fructele, pl. 679
Slovak	:	cibul'a, f. 679
Spanish	:	cebolla, f. 679
Swedish	:	lök-en 679
Turkish	:	soğan 679
Russian	:	лук, m. 679
Serbian	:	црни лук, m. 679
Ukrainian	:	цибуля, f. 679

680 OPEN adj.

Czech	:	otevřený 680
Danish	:	aaben 680
Dutch	:	open 680
Finnish	:	auki 680
French	:	ouvert 680
German	:	offen 680
Hungarian	:	nyitva 680
Italian	:	aperto 680
Croatian	:	otvoren 680
Norwegian	:	åpen 680
Polish	:	otwarty 680
Portuguese	:	aberto 680
Rumanian	:	deschis 680
Slovak	:	otvorený 680
Spanish	:	abierto 680
Swedish	:	öppen 680
Turkish	:	açik 680
Russian	:	открыто; -ый 680
Serbian	:	отворен 680
Ukrainian	:	отворений 680

681 ORANGE s.

Czech	:	pomeranč, m. 681
Danish	:	Appelsin, m./c. 681
Dutch	:	de sinaasappel 681
Finnish	:	oranssi 681
French	:	orange, f. 681
German	:	die Orange 681
Hungarian	:	narancs 681
Italian	:	arancia, f. 681
Croatian	:	naranča, f. 681
Norwegian	:	appelsin, m. 681
Poiish	:	pomarancza, f. 681
Portuguese	:	laranja, a 681
Rumanian	:	portocala, f. 681
Slovak	:	pomaranč, m. 681
Spanish	:	naranja, f. 681
Swedish	:	apelsin-en 681
Turkish	:	portakal 681
Russian	:	апельсин, m. 681
Serbian	:	наранча, f. 681
Ukrainian	:	помаранча, f. 681

682 ORE s.

Czech	:	ruda, f. 682
Danish	:	Malm, c. 682
Dutch	:	het erts 682
Finnish	:	malmi 682
French	:	minerai, m. 682
German	:	das Erz 682
Hungarian	:	érc; fém 682
Italian	:	minerale, m. 682
Croatian	:	ruda, f. 682
Norwegian	:	erts, m. 682
Polish	:	ruda, f. 682
Portuguese	:	mineral, a 682
Rumanian	:	mineralul 682
Slovak	:	ruda, f. 682
Spanish	:	mineral, m. 682
Swedish	:	malm-en 682
Turkish	:	filiz maden 682
Russian	:	руда, f. 682
Serbian	:	руда, f. 682
Ukrainian	:	рула, f. 682

683 OVERCOAT s.

Czech	:	plášt', m. 683
Danish	:	Frakke, Kappe, m./c. 683
Dutch	:	de jas 683
Finnish	:	päällystakki 683
French	:	pardessus, m. 683
German	:	der Mantel 683
Hungarian	:	köpeny 683
Italian	:	soprabito, m. 683
Croatian	:	plašt, m. 683
Norwegian	:	frakk, m. 683
Polish	:	plaszcz, m. 683
Portuguese	:	sobretudo, o 683
Rumanian	:	mantauă, f. 683
Slovak	:	plást', m. 683
Spanish	:	abrigo, m. 683
Swedish	:	överrock-en 683
Turkish	:	manto 683
Russian	:	пальто, n. 683
Serbian	:	плашт, m. 683
Ukrainian	:	плащ, m. 683

101

684 OVERSHOE s.

Czech	:	přezuvka, f.; přezuvky *pl.* 684
Danish	:	Galoche, c. 684
Dutch	:	de overschoen 684
Finnish	:	päällyskenkiä;-kengät 684
French	:	la galoche 684
German	:	der Überschuh 684
Hungarian	:	sárcipö 684
Italian	:	soprascarpe, *m.* 684
Croatian	:	kaljača, f. 684
Norwegian	:	kalosje, c. 684
Polish	:	kalosze, *pl.* 684
Portuguese	:	galocha, *a* 684
Rumanian	:	galosii, *pl.* 684
Slovak	:	galoša, f. 684
Spanish	:	chanclos *pl.* 684
Swedish	:	galosch-en; galoscher-na, *pl.* 684
Turkish	:	kaloş 684
Russian	:	галоша, f. 684
Serbian	:	кальача, f. 684
Ukrainian	:	кальоша, f. 684

685 OWN v.
see 447 HAVE

686 OX s.

Czech	:	vůl, *m.* 686
Danish	:	Stud, *m.;* Okse, *m.* 686
Dutch	:	de os 686
Finnish	:	härkä 686
French	:	boeuf, *m.* 686
German	:	der Ochse 686
Hungarian	:	az ökör 686
Italian	:	bue, *m.* 686
Croatian	:	vol, *m.* 686
Norwegian	:	okse, *m.* 686
Polish	:	wól, *m.*; (byk) 686
Portuguese	:	boi, *o* 686
Rumanian	:	boul 686
Slovak	:	vôl, *m.* 686
Spanish	:	buey, *m.* 686
Swedish	:	oxe, *m.* 686
Turkish	:	oküz 686
Russian	:	вол; бык, *m.* 686
Serbian	:	во; бик, *m.* 686
Ukrainian	:	віл; бик, *m.* 686

687 OYSTER s.

Czech	:	ústřice, f. 687
Danish	:	Östers, *pl.* 687
Dutch	:	de oester 687
Finnish	:	osteri 687
French	:	huître, f. 687
German	:	die Auster 687
Hungarian	:	osztriga 687
Italian	:	ostrica, f. 687
Croatian	:	ostriga, f. 687
Norwegian	:	östers, *pl.* 687
Polish	:	ostryga, f. 687
Portuguese	:	ostra, *a* 687
Rumanian	:	stridia, f. 687
Slovak	:	ústrica, f. 687
Spanish	:	ostra, f. 687
Swedish	:	ostron-et 687
Turkish	:	istridiya 687
Russian	:	устрица, f. 687
Serbian	:	острига, f. 687
Ukrainian	:	устриця, f. 687

688 PAIN s.

Czech	:	bolest, f. 688
Danish	:	Smerte, m. 688
Dutch	:	de pijn 688
Finnish	:	kipu 688
French	:	douleur, f. 688
German	:	der Schmerz 688
Hungarian	:	fájdalom 688
Italian	:	dolore, m. 688
Croatian	:	bol, m. 688
Norwegian	:	smerte, m. 688
Polish	:	ból, m. 688
Portuguese	:	dôr a 688
Rumanian	:	durereă, f. 688
Slovak	:	bolest' f. 688
Spanish	:	dolor, m. 688
Swedish	:	smärta-n 688
Turkish	:	ağri 688
Russian	:	боль, f. 688
Serbian	:	бол, m. 688
Ukrainian	:	біль, f. 688

689 PAINTING s.

Czech	:	obraz, m.; malba, f. 689
Danish	:	Maleri, n. 689
Dutch	:	het schilderij 689
Finnish	:	taulu 689
French	:	tableau, m. 689
German	:	das Gemälde 689
Hungarian	:	a festmény 689
Italian	:	pittura, f. 689
Croatian	:	slika, f. 689
Norwegian	:	maleri, n. 689
Polish	:	malunek, m. 689
Portuguese	:	quadro, o 689
Rumanian	:	pictură, f. 689
Slovak	:	obraz, m. 689
Spanish	:	la pintura 689
Swedish	:	tavia-n 689
Turkish	:	resim 689
Russian	:	картина, f. 689
Serbian	:	слика, f. 689
Ukrainian	:	малюнок, m. 689

690 PALM-TREE s.

Czech	:	palma, f. 690
Danish	:	Palme, c. 690
Dutch	:	de palm 690
Finnish	:	palmu 690
French	:	palmier, m. 690
German	:	die Palme 690
Hungarian	:	pálma 690
Italian	:	palma, f. 690
Croatian	:	palma, f. 690
Norwegian	:	palme, f. 690
Polish	:	palma, f. 690
Portuguese	:	palmeira, a 690
Rumanian	:	palmierul 690
Slovak	:	palma, f. 690
Spanish	:	palma f. 690
Swedish	:	palm-en 690
Turkish	:	hurma ağaci 690
Russian	:	пальма, f. 690
Serbian	:	палма, f. 690
Ukrainian	:	пальма, f. 690

691 PAN s.
see 387 FRYING PAN

692 PANTS
see 287 drawers or 1032 trousers

693 PAPER s.

Czech	:	papír, m. 693
Danish	:	Papir, n. 693
Dutch	:	het papier 693
Finnish	:	paperi 693
French	:	papier, m. 693
German	:	das Papier 693
Hungarian	:	papir 693
Italian	:	carta, f. 693
Croatian	:	papir, m. 693
Norwegian	:	papir, n. 693
Polish	:	papier, m. 693
Portuguese	:	papel, o 693
Rumanian	:	hîrtie, f. 693
Slovak	:	papier, m. 693
Spanish	:	papel, m. 693
Swedish	:	papper-et 693
Turkish	:	kâğat 693
Russian	:	бумага, f. 693
Serbian	:	хартија, f. 693
Ukrainian	:	папір, m. 693

694 PAPRIKA s.

Czech	:	paprika, f. 694
Danish	:	Paprika, m./c. 694
Dutch	:	de paprica 694
Finnish	:	paprika 694
French	:	paprica, m. 694
German	:	der Paprika 694
Hungarian	:	paprika 694
Italian	:	peperone, m. 694
Croatian	:	paprika, f. 694
Norwegian	:	paprika, f. 694
Polish	:	papryka, f. 694
Portuguese	:	paprica, a 694
Rumanian	:	chimionul 694
Slovak	:	paprika, f. 694
Spanish	:	pimiento picante, m. 694
Swedish	:	paprika-n 694
Turkish	:	kirmizi biber 694
Russian	:	красный перец, m. 694
Serbian	:	паприка, f. 694
Ukrainian	:	паприка, f. 694

695 PARACHUTE s.

Czech	:	padák, m. 695
Danish	:	Faldskärm, m. 695
Dutch	:	de parachute 695
Finnish	:	laskuvarjo 695
French	:	parachute, m. 695
German	:	der Fallschirm 695
Hungarian	:	az ejtôernyö 695
Italian	:	paracadute, m. 695
Croatian	:	padobran, m. 695
Norwegian	:	falleskjerm, m. 695
Polish	:	spadochron, m. 695
Portuguese	:	pára-quedas, o 695
Rumanian	:	paraşută, f. 695
Slovak	:	padák, m. 695
Spanish	:	paracaídas, m. 695
Swedish	:	fallskärm-en 695
Turkish	:	paraşüt 695
Russian	:	парашют, m. 695
Serbian	:	падобран, m.695
Ukrainian	:	легкопад, m. 695

696 PARCEL s.

Czech	:	balík, m. 696
Danish	:	Pakke, m./c. 696
Dutch	:	het paket 696
Finnish	:	paketti 696
French	:	paquet, m. 696
German	:	das Paket 696
Hungarian	:	csomag 696
Italian	:	pacco, m. 696
Croatian	:	paket, m. 696
Norwegian	:	pakke, m. 696
Polish	:	pakunek, m. 696
Portuguese	:	pacote, o 696
Rumanian	:	pachetul 696
Slovak	:	balík, m. 696
Spanish	:	paquete, m. 696
Swedish	:	paket-et 696
Turkish	:	paket 696
Russian	:	пакет, m. 696
Serbian	:	пакет, m. 696
Ukrainian	:	пакунок; пакет, m. 696

697 PARDON v.
see 318 EXCUSE

698 PARENTS s. pl.

Czech	:	rodiče, m. pl. 698
Danish	:	foräldre, pl. 698
Dutch	:	ouders, pl. 698
Finnish	:	vanhemmat, pl. 698
French	:	parents, pl. 698
German	:	die Eltern, pl. 698
Hungarian	:	szülök 698
Italian	:	padre e madre 698
Croatian	:	roditelji, pl. 698
Norwegian	:	foreldre, pl. 698
Polish	:	rodzice, pl. 698
Portuguese	:	pais, m. pl. 698
Rumanian	:	părinti, m. pl. 698
Slovak	:	rodičia, pl. 698
Spanish	:	padres, pl. 698
Swedish	:	föräldrar, pl. 698
Turkish	:	ebeveyn 698
Russian	:	родители, m. pl. 698
Serbian	:	родитељи, m. pl. 698
Ukrainian	:	родители, m. pl. 698

699 PARK s.

Czech	:	sad, m.; sady, pl. 699
Danish	:	Park, m./c. 699
Dutch	:	het park 699
Finnish	:	puisto 699
French	:	parc, m. 699
German	:	der Park 699
Hungarian	:	park 699
Italian	:	parco, m. 699
Croatian	:	park, m. 699
Norwegian	:	park, m. 699
Polish	:	park, m. 699
Portuguese	:	parque, o 699
Rumanian	:	parcul 699
Slovak	:	park, m. 699
Spanish	:	parque, m. 699
Swedish	:	park-en 699
Turkish	:	park 699
Russian	:	парк; сад, m. 699
Serbian	:	парк, m. 699
Ukrainian	:	горол; парк, m. 699

700 PARSLEY s.

Czech	:	petržel, *f.* 700
Danish	:	Persille, *c.* 700
Dutch	:	de pieterselie 700
Finnish	:	persilja 700
French	:	persil, *m.* 700
German	:	die Petersilie 700
Hungarian	:	petrezselyem 700
Italian	:	prezzemolo, *m.* 700
Croatian	:	peršin, *m.* 700
Norwegian	:	persille, *m.* 700
Polish	:	pietruszka, *f.* 700
Portuguese	:	salsa, *a* 700
Rumanian	:	pătrunjel, *m.* 700
Slovak	:	petržlen, *m.; petruška, f.* 700
Spanish	:	perejil, *m.* 700
Swedish	:	persilja-n 700
Turkish	:	maydanoz 700
Russian	:	петрушка, *f.* 700
Serbian	:	першун, *m.* 700
Ukrainian	:	петрушка, *f.* 700

701 PARTRIDGE s.

Czech	:	koroptev, *f.* 701
Danish	:	Agerhöne, *f./c.* 701
Dutch	:	de patrijs 701
Finnish	:	peltopyy 701
French	:	perdrix, *f.* 701
German	:	das Rebhuhn 701
Hungarian	:	fogoly 701
Italian	:	pernice, *f.* 701
Croatian	:	jarebica, *f.* 701
Norwegian	:	rapphöne, *f.* 701
Polish	:	kuropatwa, *f.* 701
Portuguese	:	perdiz, *a* 701
Rumanian	:	potîrniche, *f.* 701
Slovak	:	prepelica, *f.* 701
Spanish	:	perdiz, *f.* 701
Swedish	:	rapphöna-n 701
Turkish	:	keklik 701
Russian	:	куропатка, *f.* 701
Serbian	:	јеребица, *f.* 701
Ukrainian	:	куріпка; куропатва, *f.* 701

702 PASSPORT s.

Czech	:	(cestovní) pas, *m.* 702
Danish	:	Pas, *n.* 702
Dutch	:	de pas 702
Finnish	:	passi 702
French	:	passe-port, *m.* 702
German	:	der Pass 702
Hungarian	:	útlevél 702
Italian	:	passaporto, *m.* 702
Croatian	:	pasoš, *m.* 702
Norwegian	:	pass, *n.* 702
Polish	:	paszport, *m.* 702
Portuguese	:	passa-porta, *o* 702
Rumanian	:	pașaportul 702
Slovak	:	cestovný pas 702
Spanish	:	pasaporte, *m.* 702
Swedish	:	pass-et 702
Turkish	:	pasaport 702
Russian	:	паспорт, *m.* 702
Serbian	:	пасош, *m.* 702
Ukrainian	:	пашпорт, *m.* 702

703 PAVEMENT s.

Czech	:	chodnik, *m.* 703
Danish	:	Fortov, *n.* 703
Dutch	:	het trottoir 703
Finnish	:	katukäytävä 703
French	:	trottoir, *m.* 703
German	:	der Bürgersteig 703
Hungarian	:	járda 703
Italian	:	marciapiede, *m.* 703
Croatian	:	trotoar, *m.* 703
Norwegian	:	fortau, *n.* 703
Polish	:	chodnik, *m.* 703
Portuguese	:	calçada, *a* 703
Rumanian	:	trotuarul 703
Slovak	:	chodník, *m.* 703
Spanish	:	acera, *f.* 703
Swedish	:	trottoar-en 703
Turkish	:	kaldırım 703
Russian	:	тротуар, *m.* 703
Serbian ·	:	тротоар, *m.* 703
Ukrainian	:	хідник, *m.* 703

704 PAY v.

Czech	:	platiti; zaplatiti 704
Danish	:	betale 704
Dutch	:	betalen 704
Finnish	:	maksaa 704
French	:	payer 704
German	:	zahlen 704
Hungarian	:	fizet 704
Italian	:	pagare 704
Croatian	:	platiti 704
Norwegian	:	betale 704
Polish	:	zapłacić 704
Portuguese	:	pagar 704
Rumanian	:	a plăti 704
Slovak	:	platit' 704
Spanish	:	pagar 704
Swedish	:	betala 704
Turkish	:	ödemek 704
Russian	:	платить 704
Serbian	:	платити 704
Ukrainian	:	платити 704

705 PEAR s.

Czech	:	hruška, *f.* 705
Danish	:	Päre, *m./c.* 705
Dutch	:	de peer 705
Finnish	:	päärynä 705
French	:	poire, *f.* 705
German	:	die Birne 705
Hungarian	:	körte 705
Italian	:	pera, *f.* 705
Croatian	:	kruška, *f.* 705
Norwegian	:	päre, *f.* 705
Polish	:	gruszka, *f.* 705
Portuguese	:	pêra, *a* 705
Rumanian	:	para, *f.* 705
Slovak	:	hruška, *f.* 705
Spanish	:	pera, *f.* 705
Swedish	:	päron-et 705
Turkish	:	armut 705
Russian	:	груша, *f.* 705
Serbian	:	крушка, *f.* 705
Ukrainian	:	грушка, *f.* 705

104

706 PEAS s. pl.

Czech	:	hrách, m. 706
Danish	:	Erter, pl. 706
Dutch	:	de erwt 706
Finnish	:	herneitä 706
French	:	petit pois, m. 706
German	:	die Erbse 706
Hungarian	:	borsó 706
Italian	:	piselli, pl. m. 706
Croatian	:	grašak, m. 706
Norwegian	:	ert, f. 706
Polish	:	groch, m. 706
Portuguese	:	ervilha, a 706
Rumanian	:	mazărea, f. 706
Slovak	:	hrach. m. 706
Spanish	:	guisantes, pl. 706
Swedish	:	ärter-na 706
Turkish	:	bizelya 706
Russian	:	горох, m. 706
Serbian	:	грашак, m. 706
Ukrainian	:	горох, m. 706

707 PEASANT s.

Czech	:	sedlák, m.; rolník, m. 707
Danish	:	Bonde, m. 707
Dutch	:	de boer 707
Finnish	:	talonpoika 707
French	:	paysan, m. 707
German	:	der Bauer 707
Hungarian	:	gazda 707
Italian	:	contadino, m. 707
Croatian	:	seljak, m. 707
Norwegian	:	bonde, m. 707
Polish	:	wieśniak, m. 707
Portuguese	:	camponês, o 707
Rumanian	:	ţăranul 707
Slovak	:	sedliak, m. 707
Spanish	:	aldeano, m. 707
Swedish	:	bonde-n 707
Turkish	:	köylü 707
Russian	:	крестьянин, m. 707
Serbian	:	сељак, m. 707
Ukrainian	:	селянин, m. 707

708 PEASANT-WOMAN s.

Czech	:	selka, f.; hospodyně, f. 708
Danish	:	Bondekone, f. 708
Dutch	:	de boerin 708
Finnish	:	talonpojan vaimo 708
French	:	paysanné, f. 708
German	:	die Bäuerin 708
Hungarian	:	gazdasszony 708
Italian	:	contadina, f. 708
Croatian	:	seljakinja, f. 708
Norwegian	:	bondekone, f. 708
Polish	:	wieśniaczka, f. 708
Portuguese	:	camponesa, a 708
Rumanian	:	ţăranca, f. 708
Slovak	:	sedliačka, f. 708
Spanish	:	aldeana, f. 708
Swedish	:	bondhustru-n 708
Turkish	:	köylu kadin 708
Russian	:	крестьянка, f. 708
Serbian	:	сељанка, f. 708
Ukrainian	:	селянка, f. 708

709 PEN s.

Czech	:	pero, n. 709
Danish	:	Pen, m./c. 709
Dutch	:	de pen 709
Finnish	:	kynä 709
French	:	plume, f. 709
German	:	die Feder 709
Hungarian	:	toll 709
Italian	:	penna, f. 709
Croatian	:	pero, n. 709
Norwegian	:	penn, f. 709
Polish	:	pióro, n. 709
Portuguese	:	pena, a 709
Rumanian	:	peuiţa, f. 709
Slovak	:	pero, n. 709
Spanish	:	pluma, f. 709
Swedish	:	penna-n 709
Turkish	:	kalem 709
Russian	:	перо, n. 709
Serbian	:	перо, n. 709
Ukrainian	:	перо, n. 709

710 PENCIL s.

Czech	:	tužka, f. 710
Danish	:	Blyant, m./c. 710
Dutch	:	het potlood 710
Finnish	:	lyijykynä 710
French	:	crayon, m. 710
German	:	der Bleistift 710
Hungarian	:	ceruza 710
Italian	:	matita, f. 710
Croatian	:	olovka, f. 710
Norwegian	:	blyant, m. 710
Polish	:	ołówek, m. 710
Portuguese	:	lápis, o 710
Rumanian	:	creionul 710
Slovak	:	ceruzka, f. 710
Spanish	:	lápiz, m. 710
Swedish	:	blyertspenna-n 710
Turkish	:	kurşun kalem 710
Russian	:	карандаш, m. 710
Serbian	:	оловка, f. 710
Ukrainian	:	олівець, m. 710

711 PEPPER s.

Czech	:	pepř, m. 711
Danish	:	Peber, c. 711
Dutch	:	de peper 711
Finnish	:	pippuri 711
French	:	poivre, m. 711
German	:	der Pfeffer 711
Hungarian	:	bors 711
Italian	:	pepe, m. 711
Croatian	:	papar, m. 711
Norwegian	:	pepper, n. 711
Polish	:	pieprz, m. 711
Portuguese	:	pimentão, o 711
Rumanian	:	piperul 711
Slovak	:	čierne korenie, n. 711
Spanish	:	pimienta, f. 711
Swedish	:	peppar 711
Turkish	:	biber 711
Russian	:	перец, m. 711
Serbian	:	бибер, m. 711
Ukrainian	:	перець, m. 711

712 PERHAPS see 579 MAYBE

713 PERIL s.   see 258 DANGER

714 PERMITTED

Czech	:	dovoleno 714
Danish	:	tilladt 714
Dutch	:	veroorloofd 714
Finnish	:	sallittu 714
French	:	permis 714
German	:	erlaubt 714
Hungarian	:	szabad 714
Italian	:	permesso 714
Croatian	:	dozvoljeno 714
Norwegian	:	tillatt 714
Polish	:	dozvolony, -o 714
Portuguese	:	permitido 714
Rumanian	:	permis 714
Slovak	:	dovolené 714
Spanish	:	permitido 714
Swedish	:	tillåtet 714
Turkish	:	caiz 714
Russian	:	разрешено 714
Serbian	:	дозвольено 714
Ukrainian	:	Дозволено 714

715 PETROL (Brit.)   see 399 GASOLINE

716 PHARMACY s.

Czech	:	lékárna, f. 716
Danish	:	Apotek, n. 716
Dutch	:	de apotheek 716
Finnish	:	apteekki 716
French	:	pharmacie, f. 716
German	:	die Apotheke 716
Hungarian	:	a gyógyszertár 716
Italian	:	farmacia, f. 716
Croatian	:	ljekarna, f. 716
Norwegian	:	apotek, n. 716
Polish	:	apteka, f. 716
Portuguese	:	farmácia, a 716
Rumanian	:	farmaciă, f. 716
Slovak	:	lekáreň, f. 716
Spanish	:	farmacia, f. 716
Swedish	:	apotek-et 716
Turkish	:	eczahane 716
Russian	:	аптека, f. 716
Serbian	:	апотека, f. 716
Ukrainian	:	аптика, f. 716

717 PHYSICIAN s.

Czech	:	lékař, m. 717
Danish	:	Läge, m. 717
Dutch	:	de dokter 717
Finnish	:	lääkäri 717
French	:	médecin, m. 717
German	:	der Arzt 717
Hungarian	:	orvos 717
Italian	:	medico, m. 717
Croatian	:	liječnik, m. 717
Norwegian	:	lege, m. 717
Polish	:	lekarz, m. 717
Portuguese	:	médico, o 717
Rumanian	:	medicul 717
Slovak	:	lekár, m. 717
Spanish	:	médico, m. 717
Swedish	:	läkare-n 717
Turkish	:	hekim 717
Russian	:	доктор, m. 717
Serbian	:	лекар, m. 717
Ukrainian	:	лікар, m. 717

718 PIANO s.

Czech	:	pianino, n. 718
Danish	:	Klaver; Fortepiano, n. 718
Dutch	:	de piano 718
Finnish	:	piano 718
French	:	piano, m. 718
German	:	das Klavier 718
Hungarian	:	zongora; piano 718
Italian	:	pianoforte, m. 718
Croatian	:	pianino, m. 718
Norwegian	:	piano; klaver, c. 718
Polish	:	fortepian zwykly, m. 718
Portuguese	:	piano, o 718
Rumanian	:	pianină, f. 718
Slovak	:	pianíno, n. 718
Spanish	:	piano, m. 718
Swedish	:	piano-t 718
Turkish	:	piyano 718
Russian	:	пианино, n. 718
Serbian	:	клавир. m. 718
Ukrainian	:	фортепян, m. 718

719 PICTURE s.
see 515 LANDSCAPE

720 PIG s.

Czech	:	prase, n. 720
Danish	:	Svin, n. 720
Dutch	:	het varken 720
Finnish	:	sika 720
French	:	porc, m. 720
German	:	das Schwein 720
Hungarian	:	sertés 720
Italian	:	maiale, m. 720
Croatian	:	svinja, f. 720
Norwegian	:	gris, m. 720
Polish	:	świnia, f. 720
Portuguese	:	poreo, o 720
Rumanian	:	porcul 720
Slovak	:	brav, m. 720
Spanish	:	cerdo, m. 720
Swedish	:	svin-et 720
Turkish	:	domuz 720
Russian	:	свиня, f. 720
Serbian	:	свиньа, f. 720
Ukrainian	:	свиня, f. 720

721 PIGEON s.

Czech	:	holub, m. 721
Danish	:	Due, m./c. 721
Dutch	:	de duif 721
Finnish	:	kyyhkynen 721
French	:	pigeon, m. 721
German	:	die Taube 721
Hungarian	:	galamb 721
Italian	:	piccione, m. 721
Croatian	:	golub, m. 721
Norwegian	:	due, f. 721
Polish	:	gołab, m. 721
Portuguese	:	pomba, a 721
Rumanian	:	porumbelul 721
Slovak	:	holub, m. 721
Spanish	:	paloma, f. 721
Swedish	:	duva-n 721
Turkish	:	güvercin 721
Russian	:	голубь, m. 721
Serbian	:	голуб, m. 721
Ukrainian	:	голуб, m. 721

722 PILLOW s.

Czech	: polštář, *m.*; poduška, *f.* 722
Danish	: pude, *c.* 722
Dutch	: kussen 722
Finnish	: korvatyyny 722
French	: oreiller, *m.* 722
German	: das Kopfkissen 722
Hungarian	: vánkos 722
Italian	: guanciale, *m.* 722
Croatian	: uzglavlje, *n.* 722
Norwegian	: hodepute, *f.* 722
Polish	: poduszka, *f.* 722
Portuguese	: almofada, *f.* 722
Rumanian	: căpătîi, *c.* 722
Slovak	: poduška, *f.* 722
Spanish	: almohada, *f.* 722
Swedish	: kudde-n 722
Turkish	: baş yastiği 722
Russian	: подушка, *f.* 722
Serbian	: узглавле 722
Ukrainian	: подушка, *f.* 722

723 PILOT s.
see 47 AVIATOR

724 PIN s.

Czech	: špendlík, *m.* 724
Danish	: Knappenaal, *m./c.* 724
Dutch	: de speld 724
Finnish	: nuppineula 724
French	: l'épingle, *f.* 724
German	: die Stecknadel 724
Hungarian	: gombostü 724
Italian	: spilla, *f.* 724
Croatian	: pribadača, *f.* 724
Norwegian	: knappenål, *m.* 724
Polish	: szpilka, *f.* 724
Portuguese	: alfinete, *o* 724
Rumanian	: acul de gămălie 724
Slovak	: špendlík, *m.* 724
Spanish	: alfiler, *m.* 724
Swedish	: knappnål-en 724
Turkish	: toplu iğne 724
Russian	: булавка, *f.* 724
Serbian	: игла, *f.* 724
Ukrainian	: шпилька, *f.* 724

725 PINE-TREE s.

Czech	: smrk, *m.* 725
Danish	: Gran; Rodgran, *f./c.* 725
Dutch	: de pijnboom 725
Finnish	: kuusi 725
French	: pin, *m.* 725
German	: die Fichte 725
Hungarian	: lúcfenyö 725
Italian	: abete rosso, *m.* 725
Croatian	: omorika, *f.* 725
Norwegian	: gran, *f.* 725
Polish	: jeł, *f.* 725
Portuguese	: pinheiro, *o* 725
Rumanian	: moliftul 725
Slovak	: smrek, *m.* 725
Spanish	: pino, *m.* 725
Swedish	: gran-en 725
Turkish	: çam ağaci 725
Russian	: сосна, *f.* 725
Serbian	: оморика, *f.* 725
Ukrainian	: смерека, хвоя, *f.* 725

726 PIPE s. (for smoking)

Czech	: dýmka, *f.* 726
Danish	: Pibe, *m./c.* 726
Dutch	: de pijp 726
Finnish	: piippu 726
French	: pipe, *f.* 726
German	: die Pfeife 726
Hungarian	: pipa 726
Italian	: pipa, *f.* 726
Croatian	: lula, *f.* 726
Norwegian	: pipe, *f.* 726
Polish	: fajka, *f.* 726
Portuguese	: cachimbo, *o* 726
Rumanian	: luleă. *f.* 726
Slovak	: fajka, *f.* 726
Spanish	: pipa, *f.* 726
Swedish	: pipa-n 726
Turkish	: pipo 726
Russian	: трубка, *f.* 726
Serbian	: лула, *f.* 726
Ukrainian	: люлька, *f.* 726

727 PISTOL s.

Czech	: pistole, *f.* 727
Danish	: Pistol, *m./c.* 727
Dutch	: de pistool 727
Finnish	: pistooli 727
French	: pistolet, *m.* 727
German	: die Pistole 727
Hungarian	: pisztoly 727
Italian	: pistola, *f.* 727
Croatian	: pištolja, *f.* 727
Norwegian	: pistol, *m.* 727
Polish	: pistolet, *m.* 727
Portuguese	: pistola, *a* 727
Rumanian	: pistolul 727
Slovak	: pištol'a, *f.* 727
Spanish	: pistola, *f.* 727
Swedish	: pistol-en 727
Turkish	: tabanca 727
Russian	: револвер; пистолет, *m.* 727
Serbian	: револвер, *m.* 727
Ukrainian	: пістоля, *f.* 727

728 PLANE s. (a tool)

Czech	: hoblík, *m.* 728
Danish	: Hövl, *m./c.* 728
Dutch	: de schaaf 728
Finnish	: höylä 728
French	: rabot, *m.* 728
German	: der Hobel 728
Hungarian	: gyalu 728
Italian	: pialla, *f.* 728
Croatian	: strug; blanja, *f.* 728
Norwegian	: hövel, *m.* 728
Polish	: hebel, *m.* 728
Portuguese	: plaina, *a* 728
Rumanian	: rindeă, *f.* 728
Slovak	: hoblík, *m.* 728
Spanish	: cepillo de carpintero, *m.* 728
Swedish	: hyvel-n 728
Turkish	: rende 728
Russian	: рубанок. *m.* 728
Serbian	: струг, *m.* 728
Ukrainian	: струг, *m.* 728

729 PLATE s.

Czech	:	talíř, *m.* 729
Danish	:	Tallerken, *m./c.* 729
Dutch	:	het bord 729
Finnish	:	lautanen 729
French	:	assiette, *f.* 729
German	:	der Teller 729
Hungarian	:	tányér 729
Italian	:	piatto, *m.* 729
Croatian	:	tanjir, *m.* 729
Norwegian	:	tallerken, *m.* 729
Polish	:	talerz, *m.* 729
Portuguese	:	prato, *o* 729
Rumanian	:	farfuria 729
Slovak	:	tanier, *m.* 729
Spanish	:	plato, *m.* 729
Swedish	:	tallrik-en 729
Turkish	:	tabak 729
Russian	:	тарелка, *f.* 729
Serbian	:	таньир, *m.* 729
Ukrainian	:	тарілка, *f.* 729

730 PLATFORM s.

Czech	:	nástupiště, *n.* 730
Danish	:	Perron, *m./c.* 730
Dutch	:	het perron 730
Finnish	:	asemasilta 730
French	:	quai, *m.* 730
German	:	der Bahnsteig 730
Hungarian	:	perron 730
Italian	:	pensilina, *f.* 730
Croatian	:	kolosjek, *m.* 730
Norwegian	:	perrong, *m.* 730
Polish	:	peron, *m.* 730
Portuguese	:	plataforma, *a* 730
Rumanian	:	peron, *n.* 730
Slovak	:	nástupište, *n.* 730
Spanish	:	andén, *m.* 730
Swedish	:	perrong-en 730
Turkish	:	demir yol medhali 730
Russian	:	перон, *m.* 730
Serbian	:	перон, *m.* 730
Ukrainian	:	перон, *m.*; пятформа, *f.* 730

731 PLAYING-CARD s.

Czech	:	hrací karty, *pl.* 731
Danish	:	Spillekort, *pl.* 731
Dutch	:	de speelkaart 731
Finnish	:	korttipeli 731
French	:	cartes à jouer, *f. pl.* 731
German	:	die Spielkarte 731
Hungarian	:	kártya 731
Italian	:	carte da giuoco, *f. pl.* 731
Croatian	:	igraća karta, *f.* 731
Norwegian	:	spillekort, *n.* 731
Polish	:	karty do gry, *pl.* 731
Portuguese	:	carta para jogar, *a* 731
Rumanian	:	cartea de joc, *f.* 731
Slovak	:	karty na hranie, *pl.* 731
Spanish	:	naipes, *pl.* 731
Swedish	:	spelkort-en 731
Turkish	:	oyun kâğidi 731
Russian	:	карты игральные, *pl.* 731
Serbian	:	играћа карта, *f.* 731
Ukrainian	:	карти до гри, *pl.* 731

732 PLEASE

Czech	:	prosím 732
Danish	:	vär saa god 732
Dutch	:	als't U belieft; alstublieft 732
Finnish	:	olkaa hyvä 732
French	:	s'il vous plaît 732
German	:	bitte 732
Hungarian	:	tessék 732
Italian	:	prego 732
Croatian	:	molim 732
Norwegian	:	vär så god 732
Polish	:	prosze 732
Portuguese	:	faça o favor 732
Rumanian	:	poftim 732
Slovak	:	prosím 732
Spanish	:	haga el favor 732
Swedish	:	var så god 732
Turkish	:	rica ederim; lûtfen 732
Russian	:	пожалуйста 732
Serbian	:	молим 732
Ukrainian	:	прошу 732

733 PLEASED see 406 GLAD

734 PLEASING see 499 KIND, GLAD

735 PLOUGH s.

Czech	:	pluh, *m.* 735
Danish	:	Plov, *m./c.* 735
Dutch	:	de ploeg 735
Finnish	:	aura 735
French	:	charrue, *f.* 735
German	:	der Pflug 735
Hungarian	:	eke 735
Italian	:	aratro, *m.* 735
Croatian	:	plug, *m.* 735
Norwegian	:	plog, *m.* 735
Polish	:	plug, *m.* 735
Portuguese	:	arado, *o* 735
Rumanian	:	plugul 735
Slovak	:	pluh, *m.* 735
Spanish	:	arado, *m.* 735
Swedish	:	plog-en 735
Turkish	:	sapan 735
Russian	:	плуг, *m.* 735
Serbian	:	плуг, *m.* 735
Ukrainian	:	плуг, *m.* 735

736 PLOUGH v.

Czech	:	orati 736
Danish	:	plöje 736
Dutch	:	ploegen 736
Finnish	:	kyntää 736
French	:	labourer 736
German	:	pflügen 736
Hungarian	:	szántani 736
Italian	:	arare 736
Croatian	:	orati 736
Norwegian	:	plöye 736
Polish	:	orać 736
Portuguese	:	arar 736
Rumanian	:	a ara 736
Slovak	:	orat' 736
Spanish	:	arar 736
Swedish	:	plöja 736
Turkish	:	çift sürmek 736
Russian	:	пахать 736
Serbian	:	орати 736
Ukrainian	:	орати 736

108

737 PLUG s.

Czech	: kontakt (do zásuvky), m.	737
Danish	: Stikkontakt, m./c.	737
Dutch	: het stopkontact 737	
Finnish	: pistokytkin 737	
French	: attacco, m.	737
German	: der Steckkontakt 737	
Hungarian	: falicsatlakozó 737	
Italian	: contatto, m.	737
Croatian	: štekontakt. m.	737
Norwegian	: stikkontakt, m.	737
Polish	: kontakt włącznikowy, m.	737
Portuguese	: tomada, a 737	
Rumanian	: priză, f.	737
Slovak	: zástrčka, f.	737
Spanish	: clavija de conexión 737	
Swedish	: väggkontakt-en 737	
Turkish	: priz 737	
Russian	: штепсель, m.	737
Serbian	: штеконтакт, m.	737
Ukrainian	: втичковий контакт, m.	737

740 POCKET KNIFE s.

Czech	: kapesní nůž, m.	740
Danish	: Lommekniv, m./c.	740
Dutch	: het zakmes 740	
Finnish	: taskuveitsi 740	
French	: canif, m.	740
German	: das Taschenmesser	740
Hungarian	: zsebkés 740	
Italian	: temperino, m.	740
Croatian	: džepni nož, m.	740
Norwegian	: lommekniv, m.	740
Polish	: scyzoryk, m.	740
Portuguese	: canivete, o 740	
Rumanian	: briceagul 740	
Slovak	: vreckový nôž, m.	740
Spanish	: navaja de bolsillo, f.	740
Swedish	: fickniv-en 740	
Turkish	: çaki 740	
Russian	: нож перочинный, m.	740
Serbian	: ћепни нож, m.	740
Ukrainian	: ножик, m.	740

738 PLUM s.

Czech	: švestka, f. 738	
Danish	: Blomme, c. 738	
Dutch	: de pruim 738	
Finnish	: luumu 738	
French	: prune, f. 738	
German	: die Pflaume 738	
Hungarian	: szilva 738	
Italian	: prugna, f. 738	
Croatian	: šljiva, f. 738	
Norwegian	: plomme, m. 738	
Polish	: śliwka, f. 738	
Portuguese	: ameixa, a 738	
Rumanian	: pruna, f. 738	
Slovak	: slivka, f. 738	
Spanish	: ciruela, f. 738	
Swedish	: plommom-et 738	
Turkish	: erik 738	
Russian	: слива, f. 738	
Serbian	: шљива, f. 738	
Ukrainian	: сливка, f. 738	

741 POINTED adj.

Czech	: špičatý 741
Danish	: spids 741
Dutch	: spits 741
Finnish	: terävä 741
French	: pointu 741
German	: spitz 741
Hungarian	: hegyes 741
Italian	: appunzito 741
Croatian	: šiljast 741
Norwegian	: spiss 741
Polish	: ostry 741
Portuguese	: agudo 741
Rumanian	: ascuţit 741
Slovak	: končitý 741
Spanish	: agudo 741
Swedish	: spetsig 741
Turkish	: sivri 741
Russian	: острый 741
Serbian	: шильаст 741
Ukrainian	: гострий 741

739 PLUMBER s.

Czech	: klempíř, m. 739	
Danish	: Blikkenslager, m./c.	739
Dutch	: de 'oodgieter 739	
Finnish	: peltiseppä 739	
French	: plombier, m. 739	
German	: der Klempner 739	
Hungarian	: bádogos 739	
Italian	: lattaio; piombaio, m.	739
Croatian	: limar, m. 739	
Norwegian	: blikkenslager, m.	739
Polish	: blacharz, m. 739	
Portuguese	: encanador, o 739	
Rumanian	: tinichigiul 739	
Slovak	: klampiar, m. 739	
Spanish	: hojalatero, m. 739	
Swedish	: bleckslagare-n 739	
Turkish	: tenekeci 739	
Russian	: жестянщик, m.	739
Serbian	: лимар, m. 739	
Ukrainian	: бляхар, m. 739	

742 POLICE STATION s.

Czech	: policejní stanice, f.	742
Danish	: Politistation, c.	742
Dutch	: het politiebureau 742	
Finnish	: poliisikonttori 742	
French	: poste de police, m.	742
German	: das Polizeiamt 742	
Hungarian	: a rendőrség 742	
Italian	: ufficio di polizia, m.	742
Croatian	: redarstvo, n. 742	
Norwegian	: politistasjon, m.	742
Polish	: urzad policyjny, m.	742
Portuguese	: pôsto de polícia, o	742
Rumanian	: poliţia, f. 742	
Slovak	: policaný urad, m.	742
Spanish	: Prefectura de Policía	742
Swedish	: polisstation-en 742	
Turkish	: polis dairesi 742	
Russian	: полиция, f. 742	
Serbian	: полиција, f. 742	
Ukrainian	: поліція, f. 742	

743 POMPOUS
see 518 LARGE

744 PORK s.
Czech : vepřové maso, n. 744
Danish : Svineköd, n. 744
Dutch : het varkensvleech 744
Finnish : sianliha 744
French : porc, m. 744
German : das Schweinefleisch 744
Hungarian : sertéshús 744
Italian · : carne di maiale, f. 744
Croatian : svinjetina, f. 744
Norwegian : svinekjött, n. 744
Polish : wieprzowina, f. 744
Portuguese : carne de porco, a 744
Rumanian : carnea de porc, f. 744
Slovak : bravčové mäso, n. 744
Spanish : carne de cerdo 744
Swedish : fläsk-et 744
Turkish : domuzeti 744
Russian : свинина, f. 744
Serbian : свињско месо, n. 744
Ukrainian : свиняче м'ясо, n. 744

745 PORT s. (for ships)
Czech : přístav, m.; přístaviště, n. 745
Danish : Havn, m./c. 745
Dutch : de haven 745
Finnish : satama 745
French : port, m. 745
German : der Hafen 745
Hungarian : kikötö 745
Italian : porto, m. 745
Croatian : pristanište, n. 745
Norwegian : havn, f. 745
Polish : port, m. 745
Portuguese : pôrto, o 745
Rumanian : portul 745
Slovak : prístav, m. 745
Spanish : puerto, m. 745
Swedish : hamm-en 745
Turkish : liman 745
Russian : гавань, m. 745
Serbian : пристаниште, n. 745
Ukrainian : пристань, f. 745

746 PORTER s. (a doorkeeper)
Czech : vrátný, m. 746
Danish : Portner, m. 746
Dutch : de portier 746
Finnish : porttivahti 746
French : concierge, m. 746
German : der Pförtner 746
Hungarian : kapus 746
Italian : portiere, m. 746
Croatian : vratar, m. 746
Norwegian : portner, m. 746
Polish : odźwierny, m. 746
Portuguese : porteiro, o 746
Rumanian : portarul 746
Slovak : vrátník, m. 746
Spanish : portero, m. 746
Swedish : portvakt-en 746
Turkish : kapici 746
Russian : привратник, m. 746
Serbian : вратар m. 746
Ukrainian : вовотар, m. 746

747 PORTER s. (for baggages)
Czech : nosič, m. 747
Danish : Drager, m./c. 747
Dutch : de kruier 747
Finnish : kantaja 747
French : porteur, m. 747
German : der Gepäckträger 747
Hungarian : hordár 747
Italian : facchino, m. 747
Croatian : nosač, m. 747
Norwegian : bybud, n.;barer, m. 747
Polish : numerowy, m. 747
Portuguese : carregador, o 747
Rumanian : hamalul 747
Slovak : nosič, m. 747
Spanish : mozo de cuerda, m. 747
Swedish : bärare-n 747
Turkish : hammal 747
Russian : носильщик, m. 747
Serbian : носач, m. 747
Ukrainian : носильник, m. 747

748 POSSESS v.
see 447 HAVE

749 POSTCARD s.
Czech : korespondenční lístek, m. 749
Danish : Brevkort, n. 749
Dutch : de briefkaart 749
Finnish : kortti 749
French : carte postale, f. 749
German : die Postkarte 749
Hungarian : levelezölap 749
Italian : cartolina postale, f. 749
Croatian : dopisnica, f. 749
Norwegian : brevkort, n. 749
Polish : kartka pocztowa, f. 749
Portuguese : bilhete postal, o 749
Rumanian : cartea postală, f. 749
Slovak : korešpondenčný lístok, m. 749
Spanish : tarjeta postal 749
Swedish : brevkort-et 749
Turkish : kartpostal 749
Russian : почтовая карточка, f. 749
Serbian : дописница, f. 749
Ukrainian : поштова карта, f. 749

750 POST-OFFICE s.
Czech : poštovní úřad, m. 750
Danish : Posthus, n. 750
Dutch : het postkantoor 750
Finnish : posti 750
French : bureau de poste, m. 750
German : das Postamt 750
Hungarian : postahivatal 750
Italian : ufficio postale, m. 750
Croatian : pošta, f. 750
Norwegian : posthus, n. 750
Polish : poczta, f. 750
Portuguese : agência de correio, a 750
Rumanian : oficiul postal 750
Slovak : pošta, f. 750
Spanish : correos, pl. 750
Swedish : postkontor-et 750
Turkish : postahane 750
Russian : почтовое отделение, n. 750
Serbian : пошта, f. 750
Ukrainian : пошта, f. 750

110

758 PROHIBITED

Czech	: zakázáno	758
Danish	: forbudt	758
Dutch	: verboden	758
Finnish	: kielletty	758
French	: interdit	758
German	: verboten	758
Hungarian	: tilos	758
Italian	: proibito	758
Croatian	: zabranjeno	758
Norwegian	: forbudt	758
Polish	: zabroniony, -o	758
Portuguese	: proïdo	758
Rumanian	: interzis	758
Slovak	: zakázané	758
Spanish	: prohibido	758
Swedish	: förbjudet	758
Turkish	: yasak	758
Russian	: запрещено	758
Serbian	: забрањено	758
Ukrainian	: заборонено	758

759 PROJECTILE s.

Czech	: náboj, m.	759
Danish	: Projektil, n.	759
Dutch	: het projectiel	759
Finnish	: ammus	759
French	: projectile, m.	759
German	: das Geschoss	759
Hungarian	: lövedék	759
Italian	: colpo, m.	759
Croatian	: metak, m.	759
Norwegian	: projektil, n.	759
Polish	: pocisk, m.	759
Portuguese	: projéctil, o	759
Rumanian	: projectilul	759
Slovak	: strela, f.	759
Spanish	: proyectil, m.	759
Swedish	: skott-et	759
Turkish	: mermi	759
Russian	: патрона, f.	759
Serbian	: метак, m.	759
Ukrainian	: стрільно, n.	759

760 PROMPT   see 765 PUNCTUALLY

761 PUDDING s.

Czech	: puding, m.	761
Danish	: Pudding, m./c.	761
Dutch	: de pudding	761
Finnish	: pudinki	761
French	: pudding, m.	761
German	: der Pudding	761
Hungarian	: pudding	761
Italian	: pudino, m.	761
Croatian	: puding, m.	761
Norwegian	: pudding, m.	761
Polish	: budyń, m.	761
Portuguese	: pudim, o	761
Rumanian	: pudingă, f.	761
Slovak	: puding, m.	761
Spanish	: pudín, m.	761
Swedish	: pudding-en	761
Turkish	: puding	761
Russian	: пудинг, m.	761
Serbian	: пудинг, m.	761
Ukrainian	: пудінг, m.	761

762 PULLOVER s.

Czech	: pulover, svetr, m.	762
Danish	: Pullover, m./c.	762
Dutch	: de trui	762
Finnish	: pulover	762
French	: pullover, m.	762
German	: der Pullover	762
Hungarian	: pullover	762
Italian	: pullover, m.	762
Croatian	: pulover, m.	762
Norwegian	: pullover, m.	762
Polish	: swetr, m.	762
Portuguese	: pullover, o	762
Rumanian	: puloverul	762
Slovak	: pulóver, m.	762
Spanish	: pullover, m.	762
Swedish	: pullover-n	762
Turkish	: pullover	762
Russian	: пуловер, m.	762
Serbian	: пуловер, m.	762
Ukrainian	: светер, m.	762

763 PUMP s.

Czech	: pumpa, f.	763
Danish	: Pumpe, m./c.	763
Dutch	: de pomp	763
Finnish	: pumppu	763
French	: pompe, f.	763
German	: die Pumpe	763
Hungarian	: szivattyú	763
Italian	: pompa, f.	763
Croatian	: šmrk, m.	763
Norwegian	: pumpe, f.	763
Polish	: pompa, f.	763
Portuguese	: bomba de água, a	763
Rumanian	: pompă, f.	763
Slovak	: pumpa, f.	763
Spanish	: bomba, f.	763
Swedish	: pump-en	763
Turkish	: tulumba	763
Russian	: водокачка, f.	763
Serbian	: пумпа, f.	763
Ukrainian	: смок, m.; помпа, f.	763

764 PUMPKIN s.

Czech	: tykev, f.	764
Danish	: Gräskav, n.	764
Dutch	: de pompoen	764
Finnish	: kurpitsa	764
French	: citrouille, f.	764
German	: der Kürbis	764
Hungarian	: tök	764
Italian	: zucca, f.	764
Croatian	: buča, f.	764
Norwegian	: gresskar, n.	764
Polish	: dynia, f.	764
Portuguese	: abóbora, a	764
Rumanian	: bostanul, m.	764
Slovak	: tekvica, f.	764
Spanish	: calabaza, f.	764
Swedish	: pumpa-n	764
Turkish	: kabak	764
Russian	: тыква, f.	764
Serbian	: буча; тиква, f.	764
Ukrainian	: гарбуз, m.; диня, f	764

111

751 POSTE RESTANTE

Czech : poste restante 751
Danish : poste restante 751
Dutch : poste restante 751
Finnish : noudettava 751
French : poste restante 751
German : postlagernd 751
Hungarian : postánmaradó 751
Italian : fermo posta 751
Croatian : poste restante 751
Norwegian : poste restante 751
Polish : za zgłoszeniem 751
Portuguese : posta restante, a 751
Rumanian : poste-restante 751
Slovak : poste restante 751
Spanish : poste restante 71
Swedish : postlagrande 751
Turkish : postada kalarak 751
Russian : довостребования 751
Serbian : пострестанте 751
Ukrainian : за зголошенням 751

752 POT s.

Czech : hrnec (na vaření), m. 752
Danish : Gryde, m./c. 752
Dutch : de kookpan 752
Finnish : kattila 752
French : marmite, f. 752
German : der Kochtopf 752
Hungarian : fazék 752
Italian : pentola, f. 752
Croatian : lonac za kuhanje, m. 752
Norwegian : gryte, f. 752
Polish : garnek, m. 752
Portuguese : panela, a 752
Rumanian : oală de gătit 752
Slovak : hrniec na varenie, m. 752
Spanish : olla, f. 752
Swedish : gryta-n 752
Turkish : çomlek 752
Russian : кастрюля, f. 752
Serbian : лонац, m. 752
Ukrainian : горнець, m. 752

753 POTATO s.

Czech : brambor, m.; brambory, pl. 753
Danish : Kartoffel, m. 753
Dutch : de aardappel 753
Finnish : peruna 753
French : pomme de terre, f. 753
German : die Kartoffel 753
Hungarian : burgonya 753
Italian : patata, f. 753
Croatian : krumpir, m. 753
Norwegian : potet, f. 753
Polish : kartofle, pl. 753
Portuguese : batata, a 753
Rumanian : cartoful 753
Slovak : zemiak, m. 753
Spanish : patata, f. 753
Swedish : potatis-en 753
Turkish : patates 753
Russian : картофель, f. 753
Serbian : кромпир, m. 753
Ukrainian : картопля; бараболя, f. 753

754 POULTRY s.

Czech : drůbež, f. 754
Danish : Fjekrä, n. 754
Dutch : het gevogelte 754
Finnish : siipikarja 754
French : volaille, f. 754
German : das Geflügel 754
Hungarian : szárnyas 754
Italian : volatili, pl. m. 754
Croatian : perad, f. 754
Norwegian : fugler, pl. 754
Polish : drób, m. 754
Portuguese : aves domésticas, as 754
Rumanian : păsările de curte 754
Slovak : hydina, f. 754
Spanish : aves de corral, pl. 754
Swedish : fjäderfä 754
Turkish : tavuk eti 754
Russian : птица, f. 754
Serbian : перад, f. 754
Ukrainian : дріб, f. 754

755 POWDER-BOX s.

Czech : pudřenka, f. 755
Danish : Pudderdaase, c. 755
Dutch : de poederdoos 755
Finnish : puuteri-rasia 755
French : poudrier, m. 755
German : die Puderdose 755
Hungarian : puderdoboz 755
Italian : polverino, m. 755
Croatian : doza za puder, f. 755
Norwegian : pudderdåse, m. 755
Polish : puderniczka, f. 755
Portuguese : caixinha para pó de arroz, a 755
Rumanian : pudriera, f. 755
Slovak : pudrenka, f. 755
Spanish : polvera f. 755
Swedish : puderdosa-n 755
Turkish : pudra kutusu 755
Russian : пудренница, f. 755
Serbian : кутија за пудер, f. 755
Ukrainian : пудренчка, f. 755

756 PRAISE v.

Czech : chváliti 756
Danish : rose 756
Dutch : prijzen 756
Finnish : ylistää 756
French : louer 756
German : loben 756
Hungarian : dicsérni 756
Italian : lodare 756
Croatian : hvaliti 756
Norwegian : rose 756
Polish : chwalić 756
Portuguese : elogiar 756
Rumanian : a lăuda 756
Slovak : chválit' 756
Spanish : alabar 756
Swedish : berömma 756
Turkish : medhetmek 756
Russian : хвалить 756
Serbian : хвалити 756
Ukrainian : хвалити 756

757 PRESENT see 403 GIFT

765 PUNCTUALLY *adv.*

Czech	:	přesně 765
Danish	:	präcis 765
Dutch	:	punctueel 765
Finnish	:	täsmällisesti 765
French	:	pontuellement 765
German	:	pünktlich 765
Hungarian	:	pontos 765
Italian	:	puntuale 765
Croatian	:	točno, točan 765
Norwegian	:	punktlig 765
Polish	:	puntualnie 765
Portuguese	:	pontual 765
Rumanian	:	punctual 765
Slovak	:	presne 765
Spanish	:	puntual 765
Swedish	:	icke punktlig 765
Turkish	:	vaktile 765
Russian	:	пунктуально 765
Serbian	:	тачно 765
Ukrainian	:	точно 765

766 PURE
   see 209 CLEAN

767 PURSE *s.*

Czech	:	peněženka, *f.* 767
Danish	:	Pengepung, *m./c.* 767
Dutch	:	de portemonnaie 767
Finnish	:	lompakko 767
French	:	portemonnaie, *m.* 767
German	:	die Geldtasche 767
Hungarian	:	pénztárca 767
Italian	:	portamonete, *m.* 767
Croatian	:	novčanik, m. 767
Norwegian	:	(penge) pung, *m.* 767
Polish	:	portmonetka, *f.* 767
Portuguese	:	bôlsa para dinheiro, *a* 767
Rumanian	:	punga de bani 767
Slovak	:	peňaženka *f.* 767
Spanish	:	bolsa, *f.* 757
Swedish	:	portmonnä 767
Turkish	:	ufaklik çantasi 767
Russian	:	кошелек, *m.* 767
Serbian	:	новчаник, *m.* 767
Ukrainian	:	гаманець, *m.* 767

768 PYJAMAS *s.*

Czech	:	pyžama, *n.*; noční oblek, *m.* 768
Danish	:	Pyjamas, *m./c.* 768
Dutch	:	de pyjama 768
Finnish	:	pyjama 768
French	:	pyjama, *m.* 768
German	:	der Schlafanzug 768
Hungarian	:	hálóruha 768
Italian	:	camicia da notte, *f.* 768
Croatian	:	pyjama, *f.* 768
Norwegian	:	pyjamas, *m.* 768
Polish	:	piżama, *n.* 768
Portuguese	:	pijama, *o* 768
Rumanian	:	pijamaua, *f.* 768
Slovak	:	pyžama, *n.* 768
Spanish	:	pijama, *f.* 768
Swedish	:	pyjamas 768
Turkish	:	pijama 768
Russian	:	пижама, *f.* 768
Serbian	:	спаваħе одело, *n.* 768
Ukrainian	:	спальний одяг, *m.* 768

769 QUARTER *s.*

Czech	:	čtvrt, *f.* 769
Danish	:	en Fjerdedel 769
Dutch	:	een kwart 769
Finnish	:	yksi neljäsosa 769
French	:	un quart 769
German	:	ein Viertel 769
Hungarian	:	negyed 769
Italian	:	un quarto 769
Croatian	:	četvrtina 769
Norwegian	:	en fjerdedel, en kvart 769
Polish	:	jedna czwarta 769
Portuguese	:	um quarto 769
Rumanian	:	un sfert 769
Slovak	:	jedna štvrtina 769
Spanish	:	un cuarto 769
Swedish	:	en fjärdedel 769
Turkish	:	dörtte bir 769
Russian	:	четверть 769
Serbian	:	једна четвртина 769
Ukrainian	:	одна четверта 769

770 QUESTION *v.*
   see 36 ASK or INQUIRE

771 QUICKLY *adv.*

Czech	:	rychle; spešně 771
Danish	:	hurstigt 771
Dutch	:	vlug 771
Finnish	:	nopea 771
French	:	vite 771
German	:	schnell 771
Hungarian	:	gyorsan 771
Italian	:	prestamente 771
Croatian	:	brz 771
Norwegian	:	hurtig; rask 771
Polish	:	prętko 771
Portuguese	:	depressa 771
Rumanian	:	repede; iute 771
Slovak	:	rýchlo; chytro 771
Spanish	:	pronto 771
Swedish	:	fort; rask 771
Turkish	:	çabuk 771
Russian	:	скоро 771
Serbian	:	брз 771
Ukrainian	:	швидко 771

772 RABBIT *s.*

Czech	:	králík, *m.* 772
Danish	:	Kanin, *m./c.* 772
Dutch	:	het konijn 772
Finnish	:	kaniini 772
French	:	lapin, *m.* 772
German	:	das Kaninchen 772
Hungarian	:	hazinyúl 772
Italian	:	coniglio, *m.* 772
Croatian	:	kunić, *m.* 772
Norwegian	:	kanin, *m.* 772
Polish	:	królik, *m.* 772
Portuguese	:	coelho, *o* 772
Rumanian	:	iepurele de casă 772
Slovak	:	králik, *m.* 772
Spanish	:	conejo, *m.* 722
Swedish	:	hvar-en; kanin-en 772
Turkish	:	oda tavşani 772
Russian	:	кролик, *m.* 772
Serbian	:	куниħ, *m.* 772
Ukrainian	:	кріль, *m.* 772

773 RADIO (Brit.)
see 1103 WIRELESS

777 RAILWAY STATION
see 938 STATION

774 RADISH   (red) s.

Czech	:	řetkvička, f. 774
Danish	:	Radiser, pl. 774
Dutch	:	het radijsje 774
Finnish	:	retiisi 774
French	:	radis, m. 774
German	:	das Radieschen 774
Hungarian	:	hónapos retek 774
Italian	:	ravanello, m. 774
Croatian	:	rotkvica, m. 774
Norwegian	:	reddik, m. 774
Polish	:	rzodkiewka, f. 774
Portuguese	:	rabanete, o 774
Rumanian	:	ridichea de lună, f. 774
Slovak	:	retkevka, f. 774
Spanish	:	rabanito, m. 774
Swedish	:	rädisa-n 774
Turkish	:	turp 774
Russian	:	редиска, f. 774
Serbian	:	ротквица, f. 774
Ukrainian	:	редьквиця, f. 774

775 RADISH   s. (white)

Czech	:	řetkev, r. 775
Danish	:	Raeddike, c. 775
Dutch	:	de rammenas 775
Finnish	:	retikka 775
French	:	le radis 775
German	:	der Rettich 775
Hungarian	:	retek 775
Italian	:	rafano, m. 775
Croatian	:	rotkva, f. 775
Norwegian	:	nepe, f. 775
Polish	:	rzotkiew, f. 775
Portuguese	:	rábano, o 775
Rumanian	:	ridichea, f. 775
Slovak	:	retkev, f. 775
Spanish	:	rábano, m. 775
Swedish	:	rättika-n 775
Turkish	:	karaturp 775
Russian	:	редька, f. 775
Serbian	:	ротквица, f. 775
Ukrainian	:	редька, f. 775

776 RAILWAY   s. (railroad)

Czech	:	železnice, f. 776
Danish	:	Jernbane, m./c. 776
Dutch	:	de spoorweg 776
Finnish	:	rautatie 776
French	:	chemin de fer, m. 776
German	:	die Eisenbahn 776
Hungarian	:	vasút 776
Italian	:	ferrovia, f. 776
Croatian	:	željeznica. f. 776
Norwegian	:	jernbane, m. 776
Polish	:	pociag, m. 776
Portuguese	:	caminho de ferro, o 776
Rumanian	:	calea ferată, o 776
Slovak	:	železnica, f. 776
Spanish	:	ferrocarril, m. 776
Swedish	:	järnvägståg-et 776
Turkish	:	demiryol (u) 776
Russian	:	железная дорога, f. 776
Serbian	:	железница, f. 776
Ukrainian	:	залізниця, f. 776

778 RAIN   s.

Czech	:	dešt', m. 778
Danish	:	Regn, n. 778
Dutch	:	de regen 778
Finnish	:	sade 778
French	:	pluie, f. 778
German	:	der Regen 778
Hungarian	:	esö 778
Italian	:	pioggia, f. 778
Croatian	:	kiša, f. 778
Norwegian	:	regn, n. 778
Polish	:	deszcz, m. 778
Portuguese	:	chuva, a 778
Rumanian	:	ploaiä, f. 778
Slovak	:	dážd', m. 778
Spanish	:	lluvia 778
Swedish	:	regn-et 778
Turkish	:	yağmur 778
Russian	:	дождь, m. 778
Serbian	:	киша, f. 778
Ukrainian	:	дощ, m. 778

779 RAINCOAT   s.

Czech	:	plášt' do deště, m. 779
Danish	:	Regnfrakke, m. 779
Dutch	:	de regenjas 779
Finnish	:	sadetakki 779
French	:	imperméable, m. 779
German	:	der Regenmantel 779
Hungarian	:	esököpeny 779
Italian	:	impermeabile, m. 779
Croatian	:	kišni kaput, m. 779
Norwegian	:	regnfrakk, m. 779
Polish	:	deszczownik, m. 779
Portuguese	:	impermeável, o 779
Rumanian	:	manta de ploaie, f. 779
Slovak	:	plášt' do dažd'a, m. 779
Spanish	:	impermeable, m. 779
Swedish	:	regnkappa-n 779
Turkish	:	yagmurluk 779
Russian	:	дождевик, m. 779
Serbian	:	кишни капут, m. 779
Ukrainian	:	дощівник, m. 779

780 RAKE   s.

Czech	:	hrábě, pl. 780
Danish	:	Rive, m./c. 780
Dutch	:	de hark 780
Finnish	:	harava 780
French	:	rateau, m. 780
German	:	der Rechen 780
Hungarian	:	gereblye 780
Italian	:	rastrello, m. 780
Croatian	:	grablje, pl. 780
Norwegian	:	rive, f. 780
Polish	:	grabie, pl. 780
Portuguese	:	ancinho, o 780
Rumanian	:	greblă, f. 780
Slovak	:	hrable, pl. 780
Spanish	:	rastro, m. 780
Swedish	:	räfsa-n 780
Turkish	:	tarak 780
Russian	:	грабли 780
Serbian	:	гребуља 780
Ukrainian	:	граблі 780

781 RAPE *s.* (a plant)

Czech	:	řepka, *f.* 781
Danish	:	Raps, *m./c.* 781
Dutch	:	de raps 781
Finnish	:	rapsi 781
French	:	colza, *m.* 781
German	:	der Raps 781
Hungarian	:	a repce 781
Italian	:	colza, *f.* 781
Croatian	:	uljana repica, *f.* 781
Norwegian	:	raps, *n.* 781
Polish	:	rzep, *m.* 781
Portuguese	:	colza, *a* 781
Rumanian	:	rapiţă, *f.* 781
Slovak	:	repka, *f.* 781
Spanish	:	colza, *f.* 781
Swedish	:	raps-en 781
Turkish	:	silcim 781
Russian	:	рапс, *m.* 781
Serbian	:	угьана репица, *f.* 781
Ukrainian	:	piпa, *f.* 781

782 RAPIDLY
see **771 QUICKLY**

783 RASPBERRY *s.*

Czech	:	malina, *f.* 783
Danish	:	Hindbär, *m./c.* 783
Dutch	:	de framboos 783
Finnish	:	vattu 783
French	:	framboise, *f.* 783
German	:	die Himbeere 783
Hungarian	:	málna 783
Italian	:	lampone, *m.* 783
Croatian	:	malina, *f.* 783
Norwegian	:	bringebär, *n.* 783
Polish	:	malina, *f.* 783
Portuguese	:	framboesa, *a* 783
Rumanian	:	smeura, *f.* 783
Slovak	:	malina, *f.* 783
Spanish	:	frambuesa, *f.* 783
Swedish	:	hallon-et 783
Turkish	:	agaç çileği 783
Russian	:	малина, *f.* 783
Serbian	:	малина, *f.* 783
Ukrainian	:	малина, *f.* 783

784 RAT *s.*

Czech	:	krysa, *f.* 784
Danish	:	Rotte, *m./c.* 784
Dutch	:	de rat 784
Finnish	:	rotta 784
French	:	rat, *m.* 784
German	:	die Ratte 784
Hungarian	:	patkány 784
Italian	:	ratto, *m.* 784
Croatian	:	štakor, *m.* 784
Norwegian	:	rotte, *f.* 784
Polish	:	szczur, *m.* 784
Portuguese	:	rato, *o* 784
Rumanian	:	şobolanul 784
Slovak	:	potkan, *m.* 784
Spanish	:	rata, *f.* 784
Swedish	:	råtta-n 784
Turkish	:	siçan 784
Russian	:	крыса, *f.* 784
Serbian	:	штакор, *m.* 784
Ukrainian	:	щур; пацюк, *m.* 784

785 RAZOR *s.*

Czech	:	břitva, *f.* 785
Danish	:	Barberknir, *m./c.* 785
Dutch	:	het scheermes 785
Finnish	:	partaveitsi 785
French	:	rasoir, *m.* 785
German	:	das Rasiermesser 785
Hungarian	:	borotva 785
Italian	:	rasoio, *m.* 785
Croatian	:	nož za brijanje, *m.* 785
Norwegian	:	barberkniv, *m.* 785
Polish	:	brzytwa, *f.* 785
Portuguese	:	navalha, *a* 785
Rumanian	:	briciul de ras 785
Slovak	:	britva, *f.* 785
Spanish	:	navaja, *f.* 785
Swedish	:	rakkniv-en 785
Turkish	:	ustura 785
Russian	:	бритва, *f.* 785
Serbian	:	нож за бријанье *m.* 785
Ukrainian	:	бритва, *f:* 785

786 READ *v.*

Czech	:	čísti 786
Danish	:	läse 786
Dutch	:	lezen 786
Finnish	:	lukea 786
French	:	lire 786
German	:	lesen 786
Hungarian	:	olvas 786
Italian	:	leggere 786
Croatian	:	čitati 786
Norwegian	:	lese 786
Polish	:	çzytać 786
Portuguese	:	ler 786
Rumanian	:	citi 786
Slovak	:	čítat' 786
Spanish	:	leer; indicar 786
Swedish	:	läsa 786
Turkish	:	okumak 786
Russian	:	читать 786
Serbian	:	читати 786
Ukrainian	:	читати 786

787 RECEIPT *s.*

Czech	:	potvrzenka, *f.* 787
Danish	:	Kvittering, *f.* 787
Dutch	:	de kwitantie 787
Finnish	:	kuitti 787
French	:	quittance, *f.* 787
German	:	die Quittung 787
Hungarian	:	nyugta 787
Italian	:	ricevuta, *f.* 787
Croatian	:	potvrda, *f.* 787
Norwegian	:	kvittering, *f.* 787
Polish	:	pokwitowanie, *n.* 787
Portuguese	:	recibo, *m.* 787
Rumanian	:	chitanţă, *f.* 787
Slovak	:	potvrdenka, *f.* 787
Spanish	:	la cuenta; factura 787
Swedish	:	kvitto-n 787
Turkish	:	makbuz 787
Russian	:	квитанция, *f.* 788
Serbian	:	потврда, *f.* 787
Ukrainian	:	поквитування, *f.* 787

788 RECEIVE *v.*
see **973 TAKE**

789 RED *adv.*

Czech	:	červený 789
Danish	:	röd 789
Dutch	:	rood 789
Finnish	:	punainen 789
French	:	rouge 789
German	:	rot 789
Hungarian	:	piros 789
Italian	:	rosso 789
Croatian	:	crven 789
Norwegian	:	röd 789
Polish	:	czerwony 789
Portuguese	:	vermelho 789
Rumanian	:	roşu 789
Slovak	:	červený 789
Spanish	:	rojo 789
Swedish	:	röd 789
Turkish	:	kirmizi 789
Russian	:	красный 789
Serbian	:	црвен 789
Ukrainian	:	червоний 789

790 RED CABBAGE *s.*

Czech	:	červené, zelí, n. 790
Danish	:	Rödkaal, c. 790
Dutch	:	de roode kool 790
Finnish	:	punakaali 790
French	:	chou rouge, m. 790
German	:	der Rotkohl 790
Hungarian	:	vörös káposzta 790
Italian	:	cavolo rosso, m. 790
Croatian	:	crveni kupus, m. 790
Norwegian	:	rödkål, m. 790
Polish	:	czerwona kapusta, f. 790
Portuguese	:	couve roxa, a 790
Rumanian	:	varsa rosie 790
Slovak	:	červená kapusta, f. 790
Spanish	:	berza roja 790
Swedish	:	rödkål-en 790
Turkish	:	kirmizi lahana 790
Russian	:	синяя капуста, f. 790
Serbian	:	црвени купус, m. 790
Ukrainian	:	червона капуста, f. 790

791 RED CURRANT *s.*

Czech	:	rybíz, m. 791
Danish	:	Ribs, m./c. 791
Dutch	:	de roode bes 791
Finnish	:	viinimarjat 791
French	:	groseille rouge, f. 791
German	:	die Johannisbeere 791
Hungarian	:	ribizli 791
Italian	:	ribes, m. 791
Croatian	:	ribiz, m. 791
Norwegian	:	rips, m. 791
Polish	:	porzeczka, f. 791
Portuguese	:	groselha, a 791
Rumanian	:	coacăza, f. 791
Slovak	:	ribezle, pl. 791
Spanish	:	grosella, f. 791
Swedish	:	vinbär-et 791
Turkish	:	frenk üzümü 791
Russian	:	смородина, f. 791
Serbian	:	рибизла, f. 791
Ukrainian	:	порічки, pl. 791

792 RED WINE *s.*

Czech	:	červené víno, n. 792
Danish	:	Röd Vin, m./c. 792
Dutch	:	de roode wijn 792
Finnish	:	punaviini 792
French	:	vin rouge, m. 792
German	:	der Rotwein 792
Hungarian	:	vörösbor 792
Italian	:	vino rosso, m. 792
Croatian	:	crveno vino, n. 792
Norwegian	:	röd vin, m. 792
Polish	:	czerwone wino, n. 792
Portuguese	:	vinho tinto, o 792
Rumanian	:	vinul roşu 792
Slovak	:	červené víno, n. 792
Spanish	:	vino tinto 792
Swedish	:	rödvinet 792
Turkish	:	kirmizi şarap 792
Russian	:	красное вино, n. 792
Serbian	:	чрно вино, n. 792
Ukrainian	:	червоне вино, n. 792

793 REGISTER *v.*

Czech	:	přihlásiti (se) 793
Danish	:	anmelde 793
Dutch	:	aanmelden 793
Finnish	:	ilmoittaa 793
French	:	déclarer l'arrivée 793
German	:	anmelden 793
Hungarian	:	bejelenteni 793
Italian	:	notificare 793
Croatian	:	prijaviti 793
Norwegian	:	anmelde 793
Polish	:	zameldować 793
Portuguese	:	anunciar 793
Rumanian	:	a anunţa sosirea 793
Slovak	:	prihlásiť 793
Spanish	:	declarar la llegada a la policía 793
Swedish	:	anmäla 793
Turkish	:	resmen bildirmek 793
Russian	:	прописаться 793
Serbian	:	пријавити 793
Ukrainian	:	замельдувати 793

794 REINS *s.*

Czech	:	uzda, f. 794
Danish	:	Tömme, c. 794
Dutch	:	de teugel 794
Finnish	:	ohja 794
French	:	rênes, f. pl. 794
German	:	die Zügel 794
Hungarian	:	gyeplö 794
Italian	:	redini, f. pl. 794
Croatian	:	uzda, f. 794
Norwegian	:	hestetömmer, pl. 794
Polish	:	cugle, pl. 794
Portuguese	:	rédeas, as 794
Rumanian	:	hătul 794
Slovak	:	uzda, f. 794
Spanish	:	rienda 794
Swedish	:	tygel-n 794
Turkish	:	dizgin 794
Russian	:	вожжи, pl. 794
Serbian	:	узда, f. 794
Ukrainian	:	поводи, pl. 794

795 RELIEVE
see **455 HELP**

116

796 REMAIN   v.

Czech	:	zůstati 796
Danish	:	blive 796
Dutch	:	blijven 796
Finnish	:	pysyä 796
French	:	rester; demeurer 796
German	:	bleiben 796
Hungarian	:	marad 796
Italian	:	restare 796
Croatian	:	ostati 796
Norwegian	:	bli 796
Polish	:	ostać 796
Portuguese	:	ficar 796
Rumanian	:	a sta; a rămîne 796
Slovak	:	zostat' 796
Spanish	:	restar; quedar(se) 796
Swedish	:	stanna; blive 796
Turkish	:	kalmak 796
Russian	:	оставатся 796
Serbian	:	остати 796
Ukrainian	:	залишатися 796

797 REPAIR   v.   see 586 MEND

798 REPEAT   v.

Czech	:	opakovati 798
Danish	:	gentage 798
Dutch	:	herhalen 798
Finnish	:	toistaa 798
French	:	répéter 798
German	:	wiederholen 798
Hungarian	:	(meg) ismétel 798
Italian	:	ripetere 798
Croatian	:	ponavljati 798
Norwegian	:	gjenta 798
Polish	:	powtarzać 798
Portuguese	:	repetir 798
Rumanian	:	a repeta 798
Slovak	:	opakovat' 798
Spanish	:	repetir 798
Swedish	:	upprepa; repetera 798
Turkish	:	tekrar 798
Russian	:	повторять 798
Serbian	:	понављати 798
Ukrainian	:	повторювати 798

799 REPLY   v.   see 21 ANSWER

800 REPRODUCE   v.   see 798 REPEAT

801 REQUEST   v.   see 36 ASK

802 REQUIRE   v.   see 36 ASK

803 RESIDENCE   s.   see 356 FLAT

804 RESPOND   v.   see 21 ANSWER

805 REST   s.

Czech	:	odpočinek, m.; přestávka, f. 805
Danish	:	hvile, c. 805
Dutch	:	rest 805
Finnish	:	loma 805
French	:	repos, m. 805
German	:	die Pause 805
Hungarian	:	szünet 805
Italian	:	riposo, m. 805
Croatian	:	stanka, f. 805
Norwegian	:	pause, c. 805
Polish	:	vypoczać. 805
Portuguese	:	descauso, m. 805
Rumanian	:	pauză, f. 805
Slovak	:	pauza, f. 805
Spanish	:	pausa, f. 805
Swedish	:	rest-en 805
Turkish	:	paydos; fasila 805
Russian	:	пауза, f. 805
Serbian	:	станка, f. 805
Ukrainian	:	пауза, f. 805

806 RESTAURANT   see 485 INN

807 RICH   adj.

Czech	:	bohatý 807
Danish	:	rig 807
Dutch	:	rijk 807
Finnish	:	rikas 807
French	:	riche 807
German	:	reich 807
Hungarian	:	gazdag 807
Italian	:	ricco 807
Croatian	:	bogat 807
Norwegian	:	rik 807
Polish	:	bogaty 807
Portuguese	:	rico 807
Rumanian	:	bogat 807
Slovak	:	bohatý 807
Spanish	:	rico 807
Swedish	:	rik 807
Turkish	:	zengin 807
Russian	:	богатый 807
Serbian	:	богат 807
Ukrainian	:	багатий 807

808 RICE   s.

Czech	:	rýže, f. 808
Danish	:	Ris, m./c. 808
Dutch	:	de rijst 808
Finnish	:	riisi 808
French	:	riz, m. 808
German	:	der Reis 808
Hungarian	:	rizs 808
Italian	:	riso, m. 808
Croatian	:	riža, m. 808
Norwegian	:	ris, m. 808
Polish	:	ryż, m. 808
Portuguese	:	arroz, o 808
Rumanian	:	orezul 808
Slovak	:	ryža, f. 808
Spanish	:	arroz, m. 808
Swedish	:	ris-et 808
Turkish	:	pirinc 808
Russian	:	рис, m. 808
Serbian	:	пиринач, m. 808
Ukrainian	:	риж, m. 808

117

809 RIDE v.

Czech	: jezditi (na koni) 809
Danish	: ride 809
Dutch	: rijden 809
Finnish	: ratsastaa 809
French	: aller à cheval 809
German	: reiten 809
Hungarian	: lovagolni 809
Italian	: cavalcare 809
Croatian	: jašiti 809
Norwegian	: ride 809
Polish	: jeździć na koniu 809
Portuguese	: montar 809
Rumanian	: a călări 809
Slovak	: jazdit' 809
Spanish	: cabalgar 809
Swedish	: rida 809
Turkish	: biumek 809
Russian	: ехать верхом 809
Serbian	: јахати 809
Ukrainian	: їхати верхи 809

810 RIFLE s. (a firearm)

Czech	: puška, f. 810
Danish	: Gevär, n. 810
Dutch	: het geweer 810
Finnish	: kivääri 810
French	: fusil 810
German	: das Gewehr 810
Hungarian	: fegyver 810
Italian	: fucile, m. 810
Croatian	: puška, f. 810
Norwegian	: gewär, n. 810
Polish	: karabin, m. 810
Portuguese	: espingarda, a 810
Rumanian	: puşcă, f. 810
Slovak	: puška, f. 810
Spanish	: fusil, m. 810
Swedish	: gewär-et 810
Turkish	: tüfek 810
Russian	: винтовка, f. 810
Serbian	: пушка, f. 810
Ukrainian	: кріс, m.; рушниця, f. 810

811 RIGHT see 415 GOOD

812 RING s.

Czech	: prsten, m. 812
Danish	: Ring, m./c. 812
Dutch	: de ring 812
Finnish	: sormus 812
French	: anneau, m. 812
German	: der Ring 812
Hungarian	: gyürü 812
Italian	: anello, m. 812
Croatian	: prsten, m. 812
Norwegian	: ring, m. 812
Polish	: pierścień, m. 812
Portuguese	: anel, o 812
Rumanian	: inelul, c. 812
Slovak	: prsteň, m. 812
Spanish	: sortija, f. 812
Swedish	: ring-en 812
Turkish	: yüzük 812
Russian	: кольцо. n. 812
Serbian	: прстен, m. 812
Ukrainian	: перстень, m. 812

813 RIVER s.

Czech	: řeka, f. 813
Danish	: Flod, c. 813
Dutch	: de rivier 813
Finnish	: joki 813
French	: fleuve, m. 813
German	: der Fluss 813
Hungarian	: folyó 813
Italian	: fiume, m. 813
Croatian	: rijeka, f. 813
Norwegian	: elv, f. 813
Polish	: rzeka, f. 813
Portuguese	: rio, o 813
Rumanian	: râul 813
Slovak	: rieka, f. 813
Spanish	: río, m. 813
Swedish	: flod-en 813
Turkish	: irmak 813
Russian	: река, f. 813
Serbian	: река, f. 813
Ukrainian	: ріка, f. 813

814 ROAD s.

Czech	: ulice, f. 814
Danish	: Gade, c. 814
Dutch	: de straat 814
Finnish	: katu 814
French	: route, f. 814
German	: die Strasse 814
Hungarian	: utca 814
Italian	: strada, f. 814
Croatian	: ulica; cesta, f. 814
Norwegian	: gate, f. 814
Polish	: ulica, f. 814
Portuguese	: estrada, a 814
Rumanian	: stradă, f. 814
Slovak	: cesta, f. 814
Spanish	: calle, f. 814
Swedish	: gata-n 814
Turkish	: cadde 814
Russian	: улица, f. 814
Serbian	: улица, f. 814
Ukrainian	: вулиця, f. 814

815 ROAST v.

Czech	: smažiti; péci 815
Danish	: stege 815
Dutch	: braden 815
Finnish	: paistaa 815
French	: rôtir 815
German	: braten 815
Hungarian	: sütni 815
Italian	: fare l'arrosto 815
Croatian	: peći; pržiti 815
Norwegian	: steke 815
Polish	: piec 815
Portuguese	: assar 815
Rumanian	: a präji 815
Slovak	: piect'; smažit' 815
Spanish	: asar 815
Swedish	: steka 815
Turkish	: kizarmak 815
Russian	: печь 815
Serbian	: пеħи 815
Ukrainian	: пекти 815

118

816 ROASTED-CHICKEN s.

Czech	: pečené kuře, n. 816
Danish	: stegt Höne 816
Dutch	: de gebakken kip 816
Finnish	: paistettu kana 816
French	: poulet rôti, m. 816
German	: das Brathuhn 816
Hungarian	: sült csirke 816
Italian	: pollo arrosto, m. 816
Croatian	: pečena kokoš, f. 816
Norwegian	: stekt höns 816
Polish	: pieczona kura, f. 816
Portuguese	: frango assado, o 816
Rumanian	: friptura de pasere 816
Slovak	: pečená kura, f. 816
Spanish	: pollo asado 816
Swedish	: stekt höns 816
Turkish	: tavuk kizartmasi 816
Russian	: жареная курица, f. 816
Serbian	: печена кокош, f. 816
Ukrainian	: печена курка, f. 816

817 ROASTED-GOOSE s.

Czech	: pečená husa, f. 817
Danish	: Gaasesteg, m. 817
Dutch	: de gebraden gans 817
Finnish	: paistettu hanhi 817
French	: rôti d'oie, m. 817
German	: der Gänsebraten 817
Hungarian	: libasült 817
Italian	: arrosto di oca, m. 817
Croatian	: pečena guska, f. 817
Norwegian	: gåsestek, f. 817
Polish	: pieczeń gęsia, f. 817
Portuguese	: assado de ganso, o 817
Rumanian	: friptura de gäsca 817
Slovak	: pečená hus, f. 817
Spanish	: ganso asado 817
Swedish	: gåsstek-en 817
Turkish	: kaz kizartmasi 817
Russian	: жареный гусь, m. 817
Serbian	: печена гуска, f. 817
Ukrainian	: гусяча печеня, f. 817

818 ROAST (MEAT) s.

Czech	: pečeně, f.; pečené maso, n. 818
Danish	: Steg, m./c. 818
Dutch	: het gebraden vlees 818
Finnish	: paisti 818
French	: rôti, m. 818
German	: der Braten 818
Hungarian	: sült 818
Italian	: arrosto, m. 818
Croatian	: pečenka, f. 818
Norwegian	: stek, m. 818
Polish	: pieczeń, f. 818
Portuguese	: assado, o 818
Rumanian	: friptura, f. 818
Slovak	: pečienka, f. 818
Spanish	: asado, m. 818
Swedish	: stek-en 818
Turkish	: kebab 818
Russian	: жаркое, n. 818
Serbian	: печенье, n. 818
Ukrainian	: печеня, f. 818

819 ROBE

see 290 DRESSING ROBE

820 ROLL s. (a cake, bun)

Czech	: rohlík, m.; žemle, f. 820
Danish	: Rundstykke, n. 820
Dutch	: het cadetje 820
Finnish	: sämpylä 820
French	: le petit pain 820
German	: die Semmel 820
Hungarian	: zsemle 820
Italian	: panicciuolo, m. 820
Croatian	: žemlička, f. 820
Norwegian	: rundstykke, n.; bolle, m. 820
Polish	: bułka, f. 820
Portuguese	: paôzinho, o 820
Rumanian	: frauzela, f. 820
Slovak	: žeml'a, f. 820
Spanish	: panecillo, m. 820
Swedish	: bulle-n 820
Turkish	: ufak beyaz ekmek; francala, f. 820
Russian	: булочка, f. 820
Serbian	: земльичка, f. 820
Ukrainian	: булка, f. 820

821 ROSE s.

Czech	: růže, f. 821
Danish	: Rose, f./c. 821
Dutch	: de roos 821
Finnish	: ruusu 821
French	: rose, f. 821
German	: die Rose 821
Hungarian	: rózsa 821
Italian	: rosa,f. 821
Croatian	: ruža, f. 821
Norwegian	: rose, f. 821
Polish	: róża, f. 821
Portuguese	: rosa, a 821
Rumanian	: trandafirul 821
Slovak	: ruža, f. 821
Spanish	: rosa, f. 821
Swedish	: ros-en 821
Turkish	: gül 821
Russian	: роза, f. 821
Serbian	: ружа, f. 821
Ukrainian	: рожа, f. 821

822 ROOF s.

Czech	: střecha, f. 822
Danish	: Tag, n. 822
Dutch	: het dak 822
Finnish	: katto, m. 822
French	: toît, m. 822
German	: das Dach 822
Hungarian	: tetö 822
Italian	: tetto, m. 822
Croatian	: krov, m. 822
Norwegian	: tak, n. 822
Polish	: dach, m. 822
Portuguese	: telhado, o 822
Rumanian	: acoperişul 822
Slovak	: strecha, f. 822
Spanish	: tejado, m. 822
Swedish	: tak-et 822
Turkish	: dam 822
Russian	: крыша, f. 822
Serbian	: кров, m. 822
Ukrainian	: дах, m. 822

823 ROPE *s.*

Czech	: provaz, *m.*; lano, *n.*	**823**
Danish	: Reb, *n.* 823	
Dutch	: het touw 823	
Finnish	: köysi 823	
French	: corde, *f.* 823	
German	: das Seil 823	
Hungarian	: kötel 823	
Italian	: corda, *f.* 823	
Croatian	: uže, *n.* 823	
Norwegian	: tau, *n.*; line, *f.*	**823**
Polish	: sznur, *m.* 823	
Portuguese	: corda, *a* 823	
Rumanian	: frânghiă, *f.* 823	
Slovak	: lano, *n.* 823	
Spanish	: soga, *f.* 823	
Swedish	: rep-et 823	
Turkish	: ip 823	
Russian	: канат, *m.* 823	
Serbian	: уже, *n.* 823	
Ukrainian	: мотуз, *m.* 823	

824 RUCKSACK *s.*

Czech	: bat'oh, *m.* 824
Danish	: Rygsäk 824
Dutch	: de rantsel 824
Finnish	: (selkä) reppu 824
French	: havresac, *m.* 824
German	: der Rucksack 824
Hungarian	: hátizsák 824
Italian	: zaino, *m.* 824
Croatian	: ranac, *m.* 824
Norwegian	: ryggsekk, *m.* 824
Polish	: rukzak, *m.* 824
Portuguese	: mochila, *a* 824
Rumanian	: raniță, *f.* 824
Slovak	: plecák, *m.* 824
Spanish	: saco de provisiones 824
Swedish	: ryggsäck-en 824
Turkish	: arka turbasi 824
Russian	: ранац, *m.* 824
Serbian	: ранац, *m.* 824
Ukrainian	: наплечник, *m.* 824

825 RULER *s.*

Czech	: pravítko *n.* 825
Danish	: Lineal, *m./c.* 825
Dutch	: de lineaal 825
Finnish	: viivotin 825
French	: règle, *f.* 825
German	: das Lineal 825
Hungarian	: vonalzó 825
Italian	: riga, *f.* 825
Croatian	: ravnalo, *n.* 825
Norwegian	: linjal, *m.* 825
Polish	: linjal, *m.* 825
Portuguese	: régua, *a* 825
Rumanian	: linialul, *n.* 825
Slovak	: lineár, *m.* 825
Spanish	: regla, *f.* 825
Swedish	: linjal-en 825
Turkish	: cetvel 825
Russian	: линейка, *f.* 825
Serbian	: равнало, *n.* 825
Ukrainian	: лінійка, *f.* 825

826 RUN *v.*

Czech	: běhati 826
Danish	: löbe 826
Dutch	: loopen 826
Finnish	: juosta 826
French	: courrir 826
German	: laufen 826
Hungarian	: futni 826
Italian	: correre 826
Croatian	: trčati 826
Norwegian	: löpe 826
Polish	: biegać 826
Portuguese	: correr 826
Rumanian	: a fugi 826
Slovak	: bežat' 826
Spanish	: correr 826
Swedish	: springa 826
Turkish	: koşmak 826
Russian	: бежать 826
Serbian	: трчати 826
Ukrainian	: бігати 826

827 RYE *s.*

Czech	: žito, *n.* 827
Danish	: Rug, *m./c.* 827
Dutch	: de rogge 827
Finnish	: ruis 827
French	: seigle, *m.* 827
German	: der Roggen 827
Hungarian	: rozs 827
Italian	: segale, *f.* 827
Croatian	: raž, *f.* 827
Norwegian	: rug, *m.* 827
Polish	: żyto, *n.* 827
Portuguese	: centeio, *o* 827
Rumanian	: secară, *f.* 827
Slovak	: raž, *f.* 827
Spanish	: centeno, *m.* 827
Swedish	: råg-en 827
Turkish	: çavdar 827
Russian	: рожь, *f.* 827
Serbian	: раж, *f.* 827
Ukrainian	: жіто, *n.* 827

828 SACK *s.*

Czech	: pytel, *m.* 828
Danish	: Säk, *m./c.* 828
Dutch	: de zak 828
Finnish	: säkki 828
French	: sac, *m.* 828
German	: der Sack 828
Hungarian	: zsák 828
Italian	: sacco, *m.* 828
Croatian	: vreća, *f.* 828
Norwegian	: sekk, *m.* 828
Polish	: worek, *m.* 828
Portuguese	: saco, *o* 828
Rumanian	: sacul 828
Slovak	: vrece, *m.* 828
Spanish	: saco, *m.* 828
Swedish	: säck-en 828
Turkish	: çuval 828
Russian	: мешок, *m.* 828
Serbian	: врећа, *f.* 828
Ukrainian	: мішок, *m.* 828

120

829 SAD adj.

Czech	: smutný, smutná, **smutné**	829
Danish	: bedrövet	829
Dutch	: dróvig	829
Finnish	: surullinen	829
French	: triste	829
German	: traurig	829
Hungarian	: szomorú	829
Italian	: triste	829
Croatian	: žalostan	829
Norwegian	: sörgelig	829
Polish	: smutny	829
Portuguese	: triste	829
Rumanian	: trist	829
Slovak	: smutný	829
Spanish	: triste	829
Swedish	: bedrövad	829
Turkish	: hazin; meyus	829
Russian	: печальный	829
Serbian	: жалостан	829
Ukrainian	: сумний	829

832 SAILOR s.

Czech	: námořník, m.	832
Danish	: Matros, m.	832
Dutch	: de matroos	832
Finnish	: matruusi	832
French	: matelot, m.	832
German	: der Matrose	832
Hungarian	: matróz	832
Italian	: marinaio, m.	832
Croatian	: mornar, m.	832
Norwegian	: matros, m.	832
Polish	: marynarz, m.	832
Portuguese	: marinheiro, o	832
Rumanian	: marinarul	832
Slovak	: námornik, m.	832
Spanish	: marinero, m.	832
Swedish	: matros-en	832
Turkish	: behriye neferi	832
Russian	: матрос, m.	832
Serbian	: морнар, m.	832
Ukrainian	: матрос, m.	832

830 SADDLE s.

Czech	: sedlo, n.	830
Danish	: Saddel, m.	830
Dutch	: het zadel	830
Finnish	: satula	830
French	: selle, f.	830
German	: der Sattel	830
Hungarian	: nyereg	830
Italian	: sella, f.	830
Croatian	: sedlo, n.	830
Norwegian	: sal, m.	830
Polish	: siodło, n.	830
Portuguese	: sela,a	830
Rumanian	: şeaua, f.	830
Slovak	: sedlo, n.	830
Spanish	: silla, f.	830
Swedish	: sadel-n	830
Turkish	: eğer	830
Russian	: седло, n.	830
Serbian	: седло, n.	830
Ukrainian	: сідло, n.	830

833 SALAD s.

Czech	: salát, m.	833
Danish	: Salat, m./c.	833
Dutch	: de sla	833
Finnish	: salaatti	833
French	: salade, f.	833
German	: der Salat	833
Hungarian	: saláta	833
Italian	: insalata, f.	833
Croatian	: salata, f.	833
Norwegian	: salat, m.	833
Polish	: sałata, f.	833
Portuguese	: salada, a	833
Rumanian	: salata, f.	833
Slovak	: šalát, m.	833
Spanish	: ensalada, f.	833
Swedish	: sallad-en	833
Turkish	: salata	833
Russian	: салат, m.	833
Serbian	: салата, f.	833
Ukrainian	: салата, f.	833

831 SAFETY-PIN s.

Czech	: zavírací špendlík, m.	831
Danish	: Sikkerhedsnaal, m./c.	831
Dutch	: de veiligheidsspeid	831
Finnish	: varmuusneula	831
French	: épingle de sûreté, f.	831
German	: die Sicherheitsnadel	831
Hungarian	: biztositótü	831
Italian	: spilla di sicurezza, f.	831
Croatian	: zaponka, f.	831
Norwegian	: sikkerhetsnål, f.	831
Polish	: agrafka, f.	831
Portuguese	: alfinete de segurança, o	831
Rumanian	: acul de sigurantă, f.	831
Slovak	: spínadlo, n.	831
Spanish	: imperdible, m.	831
Swedish	: säkerhetsnål-en	831
Turkish	: cengelli iğne	831
Russian	: булавка английская, f.	831
Serbian	: иглица, f.	831
Ukrainian	: аграфка, f.	831

834 SALT s.

Czech	: sůl, f.	834
Danish	: Salt. n.	834
Dutch	: het zout	834
Finnish	: suola	834
French	: sel, m.	834
German	: das Salz	834
Hungarian	: só	834
Italian	: sale, m.	834
Croatian	: so, f.	834
Norwegian	: salt, n.	834
Polish	: sól, m.	834
Portuguese	: sal, o	834
Rumanian	: sareă, f.	834
Slovak	: sol', f.	834
Spanish	: sal f.	834
Swedish	: salt-et	834
Turkish	: tuz	834
Russian	: соль, f.	834
Serbian	: со, f.	834
Ukrainian	: сіль, f.	834

835 SALT adj.

Czech	:	salt 835
Danish	:	slaný 835
Dutch	:	zout 835
Finnish	:	suolainen 835
French	:	salé 835
German	:	salzig 835
Hungarian	:	sós 835
Italian	:	salato 835
Croatian	:	slan 835
Norwegian	:	salt 835
Polish	:	słony 835
Portuguese	:	salgado 835
Rumanian	:	sărat 835
Slovak	:	slaný 835
Spanish	:	salado 835
Swedish	:	salt 835
Turkish	:	tuzlu 835
Russian	:	соленый 835
Serbian	:	слан 835
Ukrainian	:	солоний 835

836 SAND s.

Czech	:	písek, m. 836
Danish	:	Sand, m./c. 836
Dutch	:	het zand 836
Finnish	:	hiekka 836
French	:	sable, m. 836
German	:	der Sand 836
Hungarian	:	homok 836
Italian	:	rena, f. 836
Croatian	:	pijesak, m. 836
Norwegian	:	sand, m. 836
Polish	:	piasek, m. 836
Portuguese	:	areia, a 836
Rumanian	:	nisip, c. 836
Slovak	:	piesok, m. 836
Spanish	:	arena, f. 836
Swedish	:	sand-en 836
Turkish	:	kum 836
Russian	:	песок, m. 836
Serbian	:	песак, m. 836
Ukrainian	:	пісок, m. 836

837 SAPPER s. (soldier)

Czech	:	zákopník, m. 837
Danish	:	Pioner, m./c. 837
Dutch	:	de pionier 837
Finnish	:	pioneeri 837
French	:	sapeur, m. 837
German	:	der Pionier 837
Hungarian	:	utász 837
Italian	:	esploratore, m. 837
Croatian	:	pionir, m. 837
Norwegian	:	pioner, m. 837
Polish	:	pionier, m. 837
Portuguese	:	sapador, o 837
Rumanian	:	pionerul 837
Slovak	:	zákopnik, m. 837
Spanish	:	zapador, m. 837
Swedish	:	pionjär-en 837
Turkish	:	istihkâm askeri 837
Russian	:	сапяр, m. 837
Serbian	:	пионир, m. 837
Ukrainian	:	піонер, m. 837

838 SATURDAY s.

Czech	:	sobota, f. 838
Danish	:	Lördag, m. 838
Dutch	:	de zaterdag 838
Finnish	:	lauantai 838
French	:	samedi, m. 838
German	:	der Samstag 838
Hungarian	:	szombat 838
Italian	:	sabato, m. 838
Croatian	:	subota, f. 838
Norwegian	:	lördag, m. 838
Polish	:	sobota, f. 838
Portuguese	:	sábado, o 838
Rumanian	:	Sâmbătă, f. 838
Slovak	:	sobota, f. 838
Spanish	:	sábado, m. 838
Swedish	:	lördag-en 838
Turkish	:	cumaertersi 838
Russian	:	суббота, f. 838
Serbian	:	субота, f. 838
Ukrainian	:	субота, f. 838

839 SAUSAGE s.

Czech	:	salám, m. 839
Danish	:	Pölse, m./c. 839
Dutch	:	de worst 839
Finnish	:	makkara 839
French	:	sacisson, m. 839
German	:	die Wurst 839
Hungarian	:	kolbász 839
Italian	:	salame, m. 839
Croatian	:	kobasica, f. 839
Norwegian	:	pölse, f. 839
Polish	:	kiełbasa, f. 839
Portuguese	:	chouriço, o 839
Rumanian	:	cârnatul 839
Slovak	:	klobása, f. 839
Spanish	:	salchichón, m. 839
Swedish	:	korv-en 839
Turkish	:	sucuk 839
Russian	:	колбаса, f. 839
Serbian	:	кобасица, f. 839
Ukrainian	:	ковбаса, f. 839

840 SAW s. (a tool)

Czech	:	pila, f. 840
Danish	:	Sav, f./c. 840
Dutch	:	de zaag 840
Finnish	:	saha 840
French	:	scie, f. 840
German	:	die Säge 840
Hungarian	:	fürész 840
Italian	:	sega, f. 840
Croatian	:	pila, f. 840
Norwegian	:	sag, f. 840
Polish	:	piła, f. 840
Portuguese	:	serra, a 840
Rumanian	:	ferăsträul 840
Slovak	:	pilka, f. 840
Spanish	:	sierra, f. 840
Swedish	:	såg-en 840
Turkish	:	destere 840
Russian	:	пила, f. 840
Serbian	:	тестера, f. 840
Ukrainian	:	пила, f. 840

841 SAY AGAIN
    see **798 REPEAT**

842 SCAFFOLDING *s.*

Czech	: lešení, *n.* 842
Danish	: Tömrer; Stillads, *n.* 842
Dutch	: de stellage 842
Finnish	: telineet 842
French	: échafaudage, *m.* 842
German	: das Gerüst 842
Hungarian	: állvány 842
Italian	: armatura, *f.* 842
Croatian	: skela, *f.* 842
Norwegian	: stillas, *n.* 842
Polish	: rusztowanie, *n.* 842
Portuguese	: andaime, *o* 842
Rumanian	: schelă, *f.* 842
Slovak	: lešenie, *n.* 842
Spanish	: andamio, *m.* 842
Swedish	: byggnads-ställning-en 842
Turkish	: allvany 842
Russian	: леса, *pl.* 842
Serbian	: скела, *f.* 842
Ukrainian	: риштовання, *f.* 842

843 SCARF *s.*

Czech	: šátek (na krk) *m.* 843
Danish	: Halstórkläde, *n.* 843
Dutch	: de halsdoek 843
Finnish	: kaulaliina 843
French	: le cache-nez 843
German	: das Halstuch 843
Hungarian	: sál 843
Italian	: sciarpa, *f.* 843
Croatian	: rubac za vrat, *m.* 843
Norwegian	: halstörklä, *n.* 843
Polish	: szalik, *m.* 843
Portuguese	: chale, *o* 843
Rumanian	: fularul 843
Slovak	: šatka na hrdlo, *f.* 843
Spanish	: pañuelo de cuello, *m.* 843
Swedish	: halsduk-en 843
Turkish	: atki 843
Russian	: шейный платок, *m.* 843
Serbian	: поша, *f.* 843
Ukrainian	: хустника на шию, *f.* 843

844 SCHOOL *s.*

Czech	: škola, *f.* 844
Danish	: skole, *c.* 844
Dutch	: school 844
Finnish	: koulu 844
French	: école, *f.* 844
German	: die Schule 844
Hungarian	: iskola 844
Italian	: scuola, *f.* 844
Croatian	: škola, *f.* 844
Norwegian	: skole, *c.* 844
Polish	: szkola, *f.* 844
Portuguese	: escola, *f.* 844
Rumanian	: scoală, *f.* 844
Slovak	: škola, *f.* 844
Spanish	: escuela, *f.* 844
Swedish	: skola, *f.* 844
Turkish	: mektep 844
Russian	: школа, *f.* 844
Serbian	: школа, *f.* 844
Ukrainian	: школа, *f.* 844

845 SCISSORS *s.*

Czech	: nůžky, *pl.* 845
Danish	: Saks, *m./c.* 845
Dutch	: de schaar 845
Finnish	: sakset 845
French	: ciseaux, *m. pl.* 845
German	: die Schere 845
Hungarian	: olló 845
Italian	: forbici, *f. pl.* 845
Croatian	: nožice. *pl.* 845
Norwegian	: saks, *f.* 845
Polish	: nożyce, *pl.* 845
Portuguese	: tesoura, *a* 845
Rumanian	: foarfecele, *f.* 845
Slovak	: nožnice, *pl.* 845
Spanish	: tijeras, *pl.* 845
Swedish	: sax-en 845
Turkish	: makas 845
Russian	: ножницы, *pl.* 845
Serbian	: маказе, *pl.* 845
Ukrainian	: ножиці, *pl.* 845

846 SCRAMBLED EGG *s.*

Czech	: míchané vejce, *n.* 846
Danish	: Röräg, *c.* 846
Dutch	: het roerei 846
Finnish	: munakokkeli(a) 846
French	: oeuf brouillé, *m.* 846
German	: das Rührei 846
Hungarian	: rántotta 846
Italian	: uovo al tegame, *m.* 846
Croatian	: kajgana, *f.* 846
Norwegian	: eggeröre, *f.* 846
Polish	: jajecznica, *f.* 846
Portuguese	: ovos mexidos, *os* 846
Rumanian	: jumările, *f.* 846
Slovak	: praženica, *f.* 846
Spanish	: huevos revueltos *pl.* 846
Swedish	: äggröra-n 846
Turkish	: omlet 846
Russian	: яичница *f.* 846
Serbian	: кајгана, *f.* 846
Ukrainian	: яэшниця, *f.* 846

847 SCREW *s.*

Czech	: šroub *m.* 847
Danish	: Skrue, *m./c.* 847
Dutch	: de schroef 847
Finnish	: ruuvi 847
French	: vis, *f.* 847
German	: die Schraube 847
Hungarian	: csavar 847
Italian	: vite, *f.* 847
Croatian	: vijak, *m.* 847
Norwegian	: skrue, *m.* 847
Polish	: śruba, *f.* 847
Portuguese	: parafuso, *o* 847
Rumanian	: şurubul 847
Slovak	: skrutka, *f.* 847
Spanish	: tornillo, *m.* 847
Swedish	: skruv-en 847
Turkish	: vida 847
Russian	: винт; шуруп, *m.* 847
Serbian	: шараф, *m.* 847
Ukrainian	: шруба, *f.* 847

848 SCREW-DRIVER s.

Czech : šroubovák, *m.* 848
Danish : Skrueträkker, *m./c.* 848
Dutch : de schroevendraaier 848
Finnish : ruuvitaltta 848
French : tourne-vis, *m.* 848
German : der Schraubenzieher 848
Hungarian : csavarhúzó 848
Italian : cacciavite, *m.* 848
Croatian : vadi-šaraf, *m.* 848
Norwegian : skrujern, *n.* 848
Polish : wkrętak, *m.* 848
Pórtuguese : escariador, *o* 848
Rumanian : şurupelniţă, *f.* 848
Slovak : vývrtka, *f.* 848
Spanish : destornillador, *m.* 848
Swedish : skruvmejsel-en 848
Turkish : tornavida 848
Russian : отвертка, *f.* 848
Serbian : вади-шараф, *m.* 848
Ukrainian : орзшрубник, *m.* 848

849 SEA v.

Czech : moře, *n.* 849
Danish : Hav, *n.* 849
Dutch : de zee 849
Finnish : meri 849
French : mer, *f.* 849
German : das Meer 849
Hungarian : a tenger 849
Italian : mare, *m.* 849
Croatian : more, *n.* 849
Norwegian : hav, *n.* 849
Polish : morze, *n.* 849
Portuguese : mar, *o* 849
Rumanian : mareă, *f.* 849
Slovak : more, *m.* 849
Spanish : mar, *m.* 849
Swedish : sjö-n 849
Turkish : deniz 849
Russian : море, *n.* 849
Serbian : море, *n.* 849
Ukrainian : море, *n.* 849

850 SEAL see 932 STAMP

851 SEAT see 87 BENCH

852 SECOND s.

Czech : vteřina, *f.* 852
Danish : Sekund, *f.* 852
Dutch : de seconde 852
Finnish : secunti 852
French : seconde, *f.* 852
German : die Sekunde 852
Hungarian : másodperec 852
Italian : secondo, *m.* 852
Croatian : sekunda, *f.* 852
Norwegian : sekund, *n.* 852
Polish : sekunda, *f.* 852
Portuguese : segundo, *o* 852
Rumanian : secunda, *f.* 852
Slovak : sekunda, *f.* 852
Spanish : segundo, *m.* 852
Swedish : sekund-en 852
Turkish : saniye 852
Russian : секунда, *f.* 852
Serbian : секунда, *f.* 852
Ukrainian : секунда, *f.* 852

853 SECRETARY s. f.

Czech : sekretářka, f.; sekretář, *m.* 853
Danish : Sekretär, *m./c.* 853
Dutch : de secretaresse 853
Finnish : sihteeri 853
French : secrétaire, *f.* 853
German : die Sekretärin, *f.*; der Sekretär, *m.* 853
Hungarian : titkárnö 853
Italian : segretaria, *f.* 853
Croatian : sekretarica, *f.* 853
Norwegian : sekretär, *m.* 853
Polish : sekretarka, *f.*; sekretar, *m.* 853
Portuguese : secretária, *a* 853
Rumanian : secretară, *f.* 853
Slovak : tajomníčka, *f.*; tajomník, *m.* 853
Spanish : secretaria, *f.* 853
Swedish : sekretarare-n 853
Turkish : yazici kız 853
Russian : секретарша, *f.* 853
Serbian : секретарица, *f.* 853
Ukrainian : секретарка, *f.* 853

854 SEE v.

Czech : viděti; dívati se 854
Danish : se 854
Dutch : zien 854
Finnish : nähdä 854
French : voir 854
German : sehen 854
Hungarian : lát; néz 854
Italian : vedere 854
Croatian : vidjeti 854
Norwegian : se 854
Polish : widzieć 854
Portuguese : ver 854
Rumanian : a vedea 854
Slovak : vidiet'; pozerat' 854
Spanish : ver 854
Swedish : se 854
Turkish : görmek; bakmak 854
Russian : видеть 854
Serbian : видјети 854
Ukrainian : бачити 854

855 SELL v.

Czech : prodati; prodávati 855
Danish : sälge 855
Dutch : verkopen 855
Finnish : myydä 855
French : vendre 855
German : verkaufen 855
Hungarian : elad 855
Italian : vendere 855
Croatian : prodati 855
Norwegian : selge 855
Polish : sprzedawać 855
Portuguese : vender 855
Rumanian : a vinde 855
Slovak : predat' 855
Spanish : vender 855
Swedish : sälja 855
Turkish : satmak 855
Russian : прода(ва)ть 855
Serbian : продати 855
Ukrainian : продавати 855

856 SEPTEMBER s.

Czech	:	září, n. 856
Danish	:	September 856
Dutch	:	September 856
Finnish	:	syyskuu 856
French	:	septembre, m. 856
German	:	der September 856
Hungarian	:	szeptember 856
Italian	:	settembre 856
Croatian	:	rujan, m. 856
Norwegian	:	september 856
Polish	:	wrzesień 856
Portuguese	:	setembro 856
Rumanian	:	Septembrie 856
Slovak	:	september 856
Spanish	:	setiembre 856
Swedish	:	september 856
Turkish	:	eylul 856
Russian	:	сентябрь 856
Serbian	:	Септембар 856
Ukrainian	:	Вересень 856

857 SEVEN

Czech	:	sedm 857
Danish	:	syv 857
Dutch	:	zeven 857
Finnish	:	seitsemän 857
French	:	sept 857
German	:	sieben 857
Hungarian	:	hét 857
Italian	:	sette 857
Croatian	:	sedam 857
Norwegian	:	syv 857
Polish	:	siedem 857
Portuguese	:	sete 857
Rumanian	:	şapte 857
Slovak	:	sedem 857
Spanish	:	siete 857
Swedish	:	sju 857
Turkish	:	yedi 857
Russian	:	семь 857
Serbian	:	седам 857
Ukrainian	:	сім 857

858 SEVENTEEN

Czech	:	sedmnáct 858
Danish	:	sytten 858
Dutch	:	zeventien 858
Finnish	:	seitsemäntoista 858
French	:	dix-sept 858
German	:	siebzehn 858
Hungarian	:	tizenhét 858
Italian	:	diciasétte 858
Croatian	:	sedamnaest 858
Norwegian	:	sytten 858
Polish	:	siedemnaście 858
Portuguese	:	dezassete 858
Rumanian	:	şaptesprezece 858
Slovak	:	sedemnást' 858
Spanish	:	diez y siete 858
Swedish	:	sjuton 858
Turkish	:	on yedi 858
Russian	:	семнадцать 858
Serbian	:	седамнаест 858
Ukrainian	:	сімнадцять 858

859 SEVENTY

Czech	:	sedmdesát 859
Danish	:	halvfjerds 859
Dutch	:	zeventig 859
Finnish	:	seitsemänkymmentä 859
French	:	soixante-dix 859
German	:	siebzig 859
Hungarian	:	hetven 859
Italian	:	settanta 859
Croatian	:	sedamdeset 859
Norwegian	:	sytti 859
Polish	:	siedemdziesiąt 859
Portuguese	:	setenta 859
Rumanian	:	şaptezeci 859
Slovak	:	sedemdesiat 859
Spanish	:	setenta 859
Swedish	:	sjuttio 859
Turkish	:	yetmiş 859
Russian	:	семьдесят 859
Serbian	:	седамдесет 859
Ukrainian	:	сімдесять 859

860 SEWING-MACHINE s.

Czech	:	šicí stroj, m. 860
Danish	:	Symaskine, c. 860
Dutch	:	de naaimachine 860
Finnish	:	ompelukone 860
French	:	machine à coudre, f. 860
German	:	die Nähmaschine 860
Hungarian	:	a varrógép 860
Italian	:	macchina da cucire, f. 860
Croatian	:	šivaća mašina, f. 860
Norwegian	:	symaskin, m. 860
Polish	:	maszyna do szycia, f. 860
Portuguese	:	máquina de costura, a 860
Rumanian	:	maşina de cusut, f. 860
Slovak	:	šijací stroj, m. 860
Spanish	:	la máquina de coser 860
Swedish	:	symaskin-en 860
Turkish	:	dikiş makinasi 860
Russian	:	швейная машина, f. 860
Serbian	:	шиваћа машина, f. 860
Ukrainian	:	машина до шиття, f. 860

861 SEWING THREAD s.

Czech	:	nit, f. 861
Danish	:	Sygarn, m./c. 861
Dutch	:	het naaigaren 861
Finnish	:	ompelulanka 861
French	:	fil à coudre, m. 861
German	:	das Nähgarn 861
Hungarian	:	varró cérna 861
Italian	:	filo da cucire, m. 861
Croatian	:	konac za šivanje, m. 861
Norwegian	:	sytråd, m. 861
Polish	:	nici do szycia, pl. 861
Portuguese	:	linha para costura, a 861
Rumanian	:	aţa de cusut 861
Slovak	:	nit', f. 861
Spanish	:	hilo de coser, m. 861
Swedish	:	stoppgarn-et 861
Turkish	:	dikis ipliği 861
Russian	:	нитки, pl. 861
Serbian	:	конац за шивање, f. 861
Ukrainian	:	нитки, pl. 861

862 SEW ON v.

Czech	:	přišíti 862
Danish	:	sy i 862
Dutch	:	aannaaien 862
Finnish	:	ommella 862
French	:	coudre 862
German	:	annähen 862
Hungarian	:	rávarrni 862
Italian	:	cucire 862
Croatian	:	prišiti 862
Norwegian	:	sy på 862
Polish	:	przyszyć 862
Portuguese	:	coser 862
Rumanian	:	a coase 862
Slovak	:	prišit' 862
Spanish	:	coser 862
Swedish	:	sy fast 862
Turkish	:	dikmek 862
Russian	:	пришивать 862
Serbian	:	сашити 862
Ukrainian	:	пришити 862

865 SHAVING-BRUSH s.

Czech	:	štětka na holení, f. 865
Danish	:	Barberkost, m. 865
Dutch	:	de scheerkwast 865
Finnish	:	partasuti 865
French	:	blaireau, m. 865
German	:	der Rasierpinsel 865
Hungarian	:	borotvaecset 865
Italian	:	pennello per la barba, m. 865
Croatian	:	četka za brijanje, f. 865
Norwegian	:	barberkost, m. 865
Polish	:	pędzel do golenia, m. 865
Portuguese	:	pincel para barba, o 865
Rumanian	:	pensula de ras 865
Slovak	:	štetka na holenie, f. 865
Spanish	:	brocha de afeitar, f. 865
Swedish	:	rakborste-n 865
Turkish	:	tiraş fırçası 865
Russian	:	кисть для бритья, f. 865
Serbian	:	четка за бријање, f. 865
Ukrainian	:	пендзель до голення, m. 865

863 SHANK s.

Czech	:	holeň. f. 863
Danish	:	Underben 863
Dutch	:	de onderdij 863
Finnish	:	sääri 863
French	:	jambe, f. (partie inferieure) 863
German	:	der Unterschenkel 863
Hungarian	:	alsólábszár 863
Italian	:	avangamba, f. 863
Croatian	:	golen, f. 863
Norwegian	:	skank, m. 863
Polish	:	goleń, f. 863
Portuguese	:	perna, a 863
Rumanian	:	pulpa, f. 863
Slovak	:	stehno, n. 863
Spanish	:	pierna, f. 863
Swedish	:	ben-et 863
Turkish	:	baldir 863
Russian	:	голень, f. 863
Serbian	:	голен, m. 863
Ukrainian	:	підстегня, f. 863

866 SHAWL s.

Czech	:	šál, m. 866
Danish	:	Halstørkläde, m. 866
Dutch	:	de sjaal 866
Finnish	:	shaali 866
French	:	le châle 866
German	:	der Schal 866
Hungarian	:	sál 866
Italian	:	scialle, m. 866
Croatian	:	šal, m. 866
Norwegian	:	halstörklä, n. 866
Polish	:	szal, m. 866
Portuguese	:	chale, o 866
Rumanian	:	fularul 866
Slovak	:	šál, m. 866
Spanish	:	chal, m. 866
Swedish	:	halsduk-en 866
Turkish	:	şäl 866
Russian	:	кашнэ n. 866
Serbian	:	шал, m. 866
Ukrainian	:	щаль, m. 866

864 SHAVE v.

Czech	:	holiti 864
Danish	:	barbere 864
Dutch	:	scheren 864
Finnish	:	parta 864
French	:	raser 864
German	:	rasieren 864
Hungarian	:	borotválni 864
Italian	:	farsi la barba 864
Croatian	:	brijati 864
Norwegian	:	barbere 864
Polish	:	golić 864
Portuguese	:	fazer a barba 864
Rumanian	:	a bărbieri 864
Slovak	:	holit' 864
Spanish	:	afeitar 864
Swedish	:	raka sig 864
Turkish	:	traş etmek 864
Russian	:	брить 864
Serbian	:	бријати 864
Ukrainian	:	голити 864

867 SHELL s.

Czech	:	mušle, f. 867
Danish	:	Musling, m./c. 867
Dutch	:	de mossel 867
Finnish	:	simpukka 867
French	:	moule, f. 867
German	:	die Muschel 867
Hungarian	:	kagyló 867
Italian	:	conchiglia, f. 867
Croatian	:	školjka, f. 867
Norwegian	:	musling, m. 867
Polish	:	muszla, f. 867
Portuguese	:	marisco, o 867
Rumanian	:	scoica, f. 867
Slovak	:	mušľa, f. 867
Spanish	:	marisco, m. 867
Swedish	:	mussla-n 867
Turkish	:	midiya 867
Russian	:	ракушка, f. 867
Serbian	:	школька, f. 867
Ukrainian	:	мушля, f. 867

868 SHEEP *s.*

Czech	:	ovce, *f.* 868
Danish	:	For, *c.* 868
Dutch	:	het schaap 868
Finnish	:	lammas 868
French	:	brebis, *f.* 868
German	:	das Schaf 868
Hungarian	:	juh 868
Italian	:	pecora, *f.* 868
Croatian	:	ovca, *f.* 868
Norwegian	:	sau, *m.* 868
Polish	:	owca, *f.* 868
Portuguese	:	ovelha, *a* 868
Rumanian	:	oaiä, *f.* 868
Slovak	:	ovca, *f.* 868
Spanish	:	oveja, *f.* 868
Swedish	:	får-et 868
Turkish	:	dişi koyun 868
Russian	:	овца, *f.* 868
Serbian	:	овца, *f.* 868
Ukrainian	:	вівця, *f.* 868

869 SHELVES *s.*

Czech	:	regál, *m.*; regály, *pl.* 869
Danish	:	Dokument-skab, *n.* 869
Dutch	:	de actenkast 869
Finnish	:	asiakirjakaappi 869
French	:	armoire à dossiers, *f.* 869
German	:	der Aktenschrank 869
Hungarian	:	iratszekrény 869
Italian	:	armadio (per ufficio), *m.* 869
Croatian	:	ormar za akta, *m.* 869
Norwegian	:	dokumentskap, *n.* 869
Polish	:	szafka na akty, *f.* 869
Portuguese	:	arquivo, *o* 869
Rumanian	:	dulapul pentru acte 869
Slovak	:	skriňa na spisy, *f.* 869
Spanish	:	archivo, *m.* 869
Swedish	:	dokuments-kåp-et 869
Turkish	:	dosya dolabi 869
Russian	:	шкаф с делами, *m.* 869
Serbian	:	ормар за акта, *m.* 869
Ukrainian	:	шафа на акта, *f.* 869

870 SHIN (SHINBONE) *s.*

Czech	:	holeň, *f.* 870
Danish	:	Skinneben, *n.* 870
Dutch	:	scheenbeen, n. 870
Finnish	:	sääriluu 870
French	:	le tibia 870
German	:	das Schienbein 870
Hungarian	:	sincsont 870
Italian	:	stinco, *m.* 870
Croatian	:	cjevanica, *f.* 870
Norwegian	:	skinneben, *n.* 870
Polish	:	podkolenie, *n.* 870
Portuguese	:	canela, *a* 870
Rumanian	:	tibie. *f.* 870
Slovak	:	holenná kosť, *f.* 870
Spanish	:	canilla, *f.* 870
Swedish	:	skenben-et 870
Turkish	:	bacak gemiği 870
Russian	:	берцо, *n.*; голень, *f.* 870
Serbian	:	цеваница, *f.* 870
Ukrainian	:	підкоління, *n.* 870

871 SHIRT *s.*

Czech	:	košile, *f.* 871
Danish	:	Skjorte, *m./c.* 871
Dutch	:	het hemd 871
Finnish	:	paita 871
French	:	chemise, *f.* 871
German	:	das Hemd 871
Hungarian	:	ing 871
Italian	:	camicia, *f.* 871
Croatian	:	košulja, *f.* 871
Norwegian	:	skjorte, *f.* 871
Polish	:	koszula, *f.* 871
Portuguese	:	camisa, *a* 871
Rumanian	:	cămaşa, *f.* 871
Slovak	:	košeľa,, *f.* 871
Spanish	:	camisa, *f.* 871
Swedish	:	skjortan 871
Turkish	:	gömlek 871
Russian	:	сорочка, *f.* 871
Serbian	:	кошуља, *f.* 871
Ukrainian	:	сорочка, *f.* 871

872 SHOE *s.*

Czech	:	bota, *f.*; 872
Danish	:	Stövle, *pl.* 872
Dutch	:	de schoen 872
Finnish	:	kengät 872
French	:	chaussures, *f.* 872
German	:	der Schuh 872
Hungarian	:	cipö 872
Italian	:	scarpe, *f. pl.* 872
Croatian	:	cipela, *f.* 872
Norwegian	:	sko, *c./pl.* 872
Polish	:	buciki, *pl.* 872
Portuguese	:	bota, *a* 872
Rumanian	:	gheata, *f.* 872
Slovak	:	topánka, *pl.* 872
Spanish	:	zapatos, *pl.* 872
Swedish	:	känga-n, *pl.* 872
Turkish	:	ayak kaplari 872
Russian	:	ботинки, *pl.* 872
Serbian	:	ципела, *f.* 872
Ukrainian	:	черевики високі, *pl.* 872

873 SHOE-BRUSH *s.*

Czech	:	kartáč na boty, *m.* 873
Danish	:	Skobörste, *m./c.* 873
Dutch	:	de schoenenborstel 873
Finnish	:	kengänharja 873
French	:	brosse à chaussures, *f.* 873
German	:	die Schuhbürste 873
Hungarian	:	cipökefe 873
Italian	:	spazzola per le scarpe, *f.* 873
Croatian	:	četka za cipele, *f.* 873
Norwegian	:	skobörste, *m.* 873
Polish	:	szczotka do butów, *f.* 873
Portuguese	:	escôva para sapatos, *a* 873
Rumanian	:	peria de ghete, *f.* 873
Slovak	:	kefa na topánky, *f.* 873
Spanish	:	cepillo para el calzado *m.* 873
Swedish	:	skoborste-n 873
Turkish	:	ayakkabi firçasi 873
Russian	:	щетка сапожная, *f.* 873
Serbian	:	четка за ципеле, *f.* 873
Ukrainian	:	щітка до черевик, *f.* 873

874 SHOE-LACE s.

Czech	: tkanička, *f.* 874
Danish	: Snórebaand, *n.* 874
Dutch	: de veter 874
Finnish	: kenkänauha 874
French	: lacet, *m.* 874
German	: das Schuhband 874
Hungarian	: cipözsinór 874
Italian	: laccio per le scarpe,*m.* 874
Croatian	: vrpca za cipele, *f.* 874
Norwegian	: skolisse, *m.* 874
Polish	: sznorówka, *f.* 874
Portuguese	: atacador, *o* 874
Rumanian	: siretul de ghete 874
Slovak	: šnúrky do topanky, *pl.* 874
Spanish	: cordón de zapato 874
Swedish	: skosnöre-t 874
Turkish	: ayak kabi bağisi 874
Russian	: шнурок, *m.* 874
Serbian	: врпца за ципеле, *f.* 874
Ukrainian	: шнурівка, *f.* 874

877 SHORT adj.

Czech	: krátký 877
Danish	: kort 877
Dutch	: kort 877
Finnish	: lyhyt 877
French	: court 877
German	: kurz 877
Hungarian	: rövid 877
Italian	: corto 877
Croatian	: kratak 877
Norwegian	: kort 877
Polish	: krótki 877
Portuguese	: curto 877
Rumanian	: scurt 877
Slovak	: krátký 877
Spanish	: corto 877
Swedish	: kort 877
Turkish	: kisa 877
Russian	: короткий 877
Serbian	: кратак 877
Ukrainian	: короткий 877

875 SHOEMAKER s.

Czech	: obuvník, *m.* 875
Danish	: Skomager, *m.* 875
Dutch	: de schoenmaker 875
Finnish	: suutari 875
French	: cordonnier, *m.*
German	: der Schuhmacher 875
Hungarian	: cipész 875
Italian	: calzolaio, *m.* 875
Croatian	: obućar, *m.* 875
Norwegian	: skomaker, *m.* 875
Polish	: szewe, *m.* 875
Portuguese	: sapateiro, *o* 875
Rumanian	: cizmarul 875
Slovak	: obuvník, *m.*; čizmar, *m.* 875
Spanish	: zapatero, *m.* 875
Swedish	: skomakare-n 875
Turkish	: kuntraci 875
Russian	: сапожник, *m.* 875
Serbian	: обуħар, *m.* 875
Ukrainian	: швець, *m.* 875

878 SHOULDER s.

Czech	: rameno, *n.* 878
Danish	: Skulder, *m./c.* 878
Dutch	: de schouder 878
Finnish	: oikapää 878
French	: épaule, *f.* 878
German	: die Schulter 878
Hungarian	: váll 878
Italian	: spalla, *f.* 878
Croatian	: rame, *n.* 878
Norwegian	: skulder, *m.* 878
Polish	: ramię, *n.* 878
Portuguese	: ombro, *o* 878
Rumanian	: umärul 878
Slovak	: plece, *n.* 878
Spanish	: hombro, *m.* 878
Swedish	: skuldra-n 878
Turkish	: omuz 878
Russian	: плечо, *n.* 878
Serbian	: раме, *n.* 878
Ukrainian	: рамя, *f.* 878

876 SHOP s.

Czech	: obchod, *m.* 876
Danish	: Butik, *m./c.* 876
Dutch	: de winkel 876
Finnish	: myymäla 876
French	: boutique, *f.* 876
German	: der Laden 876
Hungarian	: üzlet 876
Italian	: bottega, *f.* 876
Croatian	: dućan, *m.* 876
Norwegian	: butikk, *m.*; forretning, *m.* 876
Polish	: sklep, *m.* 876
Portuguese	: loja, *a* 876
Rumanian	: prävälia, *f.* 876
Slovak	: obchod, *m.* 876
Spanish	: tienda, *f.* 876
Swedish	: butik-en 876
Turkish	: dukân 876
Russian	: магазин, *m.*; лавка, *f.* 876
Serbian	: дуħан, *m.* 876
Ukrainian	: крамниця, *f.* 876

879 SHOVEL s.

Czech	: lopata, *f.* 879
Danish	: Skovl; Skuffe 879
Dutch	: de schop; schep 879
Finnish	: lapio 879
French	: pèle, *f.* 879
German	: die Schaufel 879
Hungarian	: lapát 879
Italian	: Pala, *f.* 879
Croatian	: lopata, *f.* 879
Norwegian	: skuffe, *c.* 879
Polish	: szufla, *f.* 879
Portuguese	: pá, *a* 879
Rumanian	: lopată, *f.* 879
Slovak	: lopata, *f.* 879
Spanish	: pala, *f.* 879
Swedish	: spade-n 879
Turkish	: kürek 879
Russian	: лопата, *f.* 879
Serbian	: лопата, *f.* 879
Ukrainian	: лопата, *f.* 879

880 SICK *see* 475 ILL

881 SIEVE *s.*

Czech	:	síto, *n.* 881
Danish	:	sikt, *c.* 881
Dutch	:	de zeef 881
Finnish	:	seula 881
French	:	tamis, *m.* 881
German	:	das Sieb 881
Hungarian	:	szita 881
Italian	:	staccio, *m.* 881
Croatian	:	sito, *n.* 881
Norwegian	:	sil, *m.* 881
Polish	:	sito, *n.* 881
Portuguese	:	peneira, *a* 881
Rumanian	:	sită, *f.* 881
Slovak	:	sito, *n.* 881
Spanish	:	tamiz 881
Swedish	:	såll-et 881
Turkish	:	süzgeç 881
Russian	:	решето, *n.* 881
Serbian	:	сито, *n.* 881
Ukrainian	:	сито, *n.* 881

882 SIGNATURE *s.*

Czech	:	podpis, *m.* 882
Danish	:	Underskrift, *m./c.* 882
Dutch	:	de handteekening 882
Finnish	:	allekirjoitus 882
French	:	signature, *f.* 882
German	:	die Unterschrift 882
Hungarian	:	aláirás 882
Italian	:	firma, *f.* 882
Croatian	:	potpis, *m.* 882
Norwegian	:	underskrift, *f.* 882
Polish	:	podpis, *m.* 882
Portuguese	:	assinatura, *a* 882
Rumanian	:	iscălitura, *f.* 882
Slovak	:	podpis, *m.* 882
Spanish	:	firma, *f.* 882
Swedish	:	underskrift-en 882
Turkish	:	imza 882
Russian	:	подпись 882
Serbian	:	потпис, *m.* 882
Ukrainian	:	підпись, *m̦.* 882

883 SILK *s.*

Czech	:	hedvábí, *n.* 883
Danish	:	Silke, *m./c.* 883
Dutch	:	de zijde 883
Finnish	:	silkki 883
French	:	soie, *f.* 883
German	:	die Seide 883
Hungarian	:	selyem 883
Italian	:	seta, *f.* 883
Croatian	:	svila, *f.* 883
Norwegian	:	silke, *m.* 883
Polish	:	jedwab, *m.* 883
Portuguese	:	sêda, *a* 883
Rumanian	:	mătasă, *f.* 883
Slovak	:	hodváb, *m.* 883
Spanish	:	seda, *f.* 883
Swedish	:	siden 883
Turkish	:	ipek 883
Russian	:	шелк, *m.* 8883
Serbian	:	свила, *f.* 883
Ukrainian	:	шовк, *m.* 883

884 SING *v.*

Czech	:	zpívati 884
Danish	:	synge 884
Dutch	:	zingen 884
Finnish	:	laulaa 884
French	:	chanter 884
German	:	singen 884
Hungarian	:	énekelni 884
Italian	:	cantare 884
Croatian	:	pjevati 884
Norwegian	:	synge 884
Polish	:	śpiewać 884
Portuguese	:	cantar 884
Rumanian	:	a cînta 884
Slovak	:	spievat' 884
Spanish	:	cantar 884
Swedish	:	sjunga 884
Turkish	:	sarki söylemek 884
Russian	:	петь 884
Serbian	:	пјевати 884
Ukrainian	:	співати 884

885 SINGLE *adj.*

Czech	:	sám; jediný; svobodný 885
Danish	:	enkelt 885
Dutch	:	enkel 885
Finnish	:	vapaa; yksityinen 885
French	:	seul; célebataire 885
German	:	ledig; einzeln 885
Hungarian	:	egyes 885
Italian	:	solo; celibe 885
Croatian	:	jedini; slobodan 885
Norwegian	:	enkelt; ledig 885
Polish	:	swobodny 885
Portuguese	:	só; singelo 885
Rumanian	:	neinsurat; singur 885
Slovak	:	jediný; slobodný 885
Spanish	:	solo; soltero 885
Swedish	:	enda; enkel 885
Turkish	:	tek; bekâr 885
Russian	:	единый; свободный 885
Serbian	:	јединн; слободан 885
Ukrainian	:	один; неодружений 885

886 SIR *s.*

Czech	:	pán; Pane! *m.* 886
Danish	:	herre; Hr., *m.* 886
Dutch	:	Mijnheer, *m.* 886
Finnish	:	herra 886
French	:	Monsieur, *m.* 886
German	:	der Herr 886
Hungarian	:	úr 886
Italian	:	Signore, *m.* 886
Croatian	:	gospodin, *m.* 886
Norwegian	:	herre, *c.*; *herr* ... 886
Polish	:	pan; Pane! 886
Portuguese	:	senhor, *m.* 886
Rumanian	:	domn; Domnule! 886
Slovak	:	pán, *m.*; pane! 886
Spanish	:	señor, *m.* 886
Swedish	:	herre (hr.); Min herre! 886
Turkish	:	bay; sahib; efendi 886
Russian	:	господин, *m.* 886
Serbian	:	господин, *m.* 886
Ukrainian	:	пан, *m.* 886

887 SIREN s.

Czech	: siréna, f.	887
Danish	: Sirene, m./c.	887
Dutch	: de sirene	887
Finnish	: sireeni	887
French	: sirène, f.	887
German	: die Sirene	887
Hungarian	: a sziréna	887
Italian	: sirena, f.	887
Croatian	: sirena, f.	887
Norwegian	: sirene, f.	887
Polish	: syrena, f.	887
Portuguese	: sereia, a	887
Rumanian	: sirena	887
Slovak	: siréna, f.	887
Spanish	: sirena, f.	887
Swedish	: siren-en	887
Turkish	: canavar düdügü	887
Russian	: сирена, f.	887
Serbian	: сирена, f.	887
Ukrainian	: сирена, f.	887

890 SIX

Czech	: šest	890
Danish	: seks	890
Dutch	: zes	890
Finnish	: kuusi	890
French	: six	890
German	: sechs	890
Hungarian	: hat	890
Italian	: sei	890
Croatian	: šest	890
Norwegian	: seks	890
Polish	: sześć	890
Portuguese	: seis	890
Rumanian	: şase	890
Slovak	: šest	890
Spanish	: seis	890
Swedish	: sex	890
Turkish	: alti	890
Russian	: шесть	890
Serbian	: шест	890
Ukrainian	: шість	890

888 SIT v.

Czech	: seděti	888
Danish	: sidde	888
Dutch	: zitten	888
Finnish	: istua	888
French	: être assis	888
German	: sitzen	888
Hungarian	: ülni	888
Italian	: essere seduto	888
Croatian	: sjediti	888
Norwegian	: sitte	888
Polish	: siedzieć	888
Portuguese	: estar sentado	888
Rumanian	: a sedea	888
Slovak	: sediet'	888
Spanish	: estar sentado	888
Swedish	: sitta	888
Turkish	: oturmak	888
Russian	: сидеть	888
Serbian	: седети	888
Ukrainian	: сидіти	888

891 SIXTEEN

Czech	: šestnáct	891
Danish	: seksten	891
Dutch	: zestien	891
Finnish	: kuusitoista	891
French	: seize	891
German	: sechzehn	891
Hungarian	: tizenhat	891
Italian	: sédici	891
Croatian	: šestnaest	891
Norwegian	: seksten	891
Polish	: szesnacie	891
Portuguese	: dezasseis	891
Rumanian	: şaisprezece	891
Slovak	: šestnást'	891
Spanish	: diez y seis	891
Swedish	: sexton	891
Turkish	: on alti	891
Russian	: шестнадцать	891
Serbian	: шестнаест	891
Ukrainian	: шістнадцять	891

889 SIT DOWN v.

Czech	: sednouti si; posaditi se	889
Danish	: saette sig	889
Dutch	: ga zitten!	889
Finnish	: asettua	889
French	: s'asseoir	889
German	: sich setzen	889
Hungarian	: tesz; helyez	889
Italian	: sedere	889
Croatian	: sjesti	889
Norwegian	: sette	889
Polish	: siadać	889
Portuguese	: assentar-se	889
Rumanian	: a se ascza; a lua loc	889
Slovak	: sadnút' si	889
Spanish	: sentar(se)	889
Swedish	: sitta ned	889
Turkish	: oturmak	889
Russian	: садиться	889
Serbian	: cjести	889
Ukrainian	: сідати	889

892 SIXTY

Czech	: šedesát	892
Danish	: tres	892
Dutch	: zestig	892
Finnish	: kuusikymmentä	892
French	: soixante	892
German	: sechzig	892
Hungarian	: hatvan	892
Italian	: sessanta	892
Croatian	: šesdeset	892
Norwegian	: seksti	892
Polish	: sześdziesiąt	892
Portuguese	: sessenta	892
Rumanian	: sasezeci	892
Slovak	: šest'desiat	892
Spanish	: sesenta	892
Swedish	: sextio	892
Turkish	: altmiş	892
Russian	: шестьдесят	892
Serbian	: шездесет	892
Ukrainian	: шістьдесять	892

893 SKIS	s. pl.
Czech	: lyže, pl. 893
Danish	: Ski, f./c. 893
Dutch	: de ski 893
Finnish	: suksi 893
French	: skis, m. pl. 893
German	: der Ski 893
Hungarian	: sí 893
Italian	: sci, m. pl. 893
Croatian	: smučke, pl. 893
Norwegian	: ski, f. 893
Polish	: narty, pl. 893
Portuguese	: ski, o 893
Rumanian	: schiurile, pl. 893
Slovak	: lyža, f. lyže, pl. 893
Spanish	: esquies, pl. 893
Swedish	: skidor-na 893
Turkish	: ski 893
Russian	: лыжи, pl. 893
Serbian	: смучка, f. 893
Ukrainian	: соъги; лещети, pl. 893

896 SLEEPING-CAR	s.
Czech	: spací vůz, m. 896
Danish	: Sovevogn, m./c. 896
Dutch	: de slaap-wagen 896
Finnish	: makuuvaunu 896
French	: wagon-lit, m. 896
German	: der Schlafwagen 896
Hungarian	: hálókocsi 896
Italian	: carrozza letti, f. 896
Croatian	: spavaća kola, pl. 896
Norwegian	: sovevogn, m. 896
Polish	: wóz sypialny, m. 896
Portuguese	: vagão-leito, o 896
Rumanian	: vagonul de dormit 896
Slovak	: spací vozeň, m. 896
Spanish	: coche-cama 896
Swedish	: sovvagn-en 896
Turkish	: yatak arabasi 896
Russian	: спальный вагон, m. 896
Serbian	: спаваћа кола, f. 896
Ukrainian	: спальний вагон, m. 896

894 SLEDGE	s.
Czech	: sáně, (pl.) 894
Danish	: Släde, m./c. 894
Dutch	: de slee 894
Finnish	: reki; kelkka 894
French	: traîneau, m. 894
German	: der Schlitten 894
Hungarian	: szánkó 894
Italian	: slitta, f. 894
Croatian	: saonice, pl. 894
Norwegian	: slede, m.; kjelke, m. 894
Polish	: sanie, pl. 894
Portuguese	: trenó, o 894
Rumanian	: saniă, pl. 894
Slovak	: sane, pl. 894
Spanish	: trineo, m. 894
Swedish	: släde-n 894
Turkish	: kizak 894
Russian	: сани, pl. 894
Serbian	: саонице, pl. 894
Ukrainian	: сани, pl. 894

897 SISTER	s.
Czech	: sestra, f. 897
Danish	: söster, f. 897
Dutch	: zuster, f. 897
Finnish	: sisar 897
French	: soeur, f. 897
German	: die Schwester 897
Hungarian	: nővér 897
Italian	: sorella, f. 897
Croatian	: sestra, f. 897
Norwegian	: söster, c./f. 897
Polish	: siostra, f. 897
Portuguese	: irmã, f. 897
Rumanian	: soră, f. 897
Slovak	: sestra, f. 897
Spanish	: hermana, f. 897
Swedish	: syster, f. 897
Turkish	: hemşire 897
Russian	: сестра, f. 897
Serbian	: сестра, f 897
Ukrainian	: сестра, f. 897

895 SLEEP	v.
Czech	: spáti 895
Danish	: sove 895
Dutch	: slapen 895
Finnish	: nukkua 895
French	: dormir 895
German	: schlafen 895
Hungarian	: aludni 895
Italian	: dormire 895
Croatian	: spavati 895
Norwegian	: sove 895
Polish	: spać 895
Portuguese	: dormir. 895
Rumanian	: a dormi 895
Slovak	: spat' 895
Spanish	: dormir 895
Swedish	: sova 895
Turkish	: uyumak 895
Russian	: спать 895
Serbian	: спавати 895
Ukrainian	: спати 895

898 SLIPPERS	s.
Czech	: trepky, f., pl.; domácí střevíce, pl. 898
Danish	: Tófler, m./c. 898
Dutch	: de pantoffel 898
Finnish	: tohvelit 898
French	: pantoufle, m. 898
German	: der Pantoffel 898
Hungarian	: papucs 898
Italian	: le pantofole 898
Croatian	: papuča, f. 898
Norwegian	: töffel, m. 898
Polish	: pantofle, pl. 898
Portuguese	: chinela, a 898
Rumanian	: pantofii de casă, pl. 898
Slovak	: domáca obuv, f. 898
Spanish	: zapatillas, pl. 898
Swedish	: tofflor-na 898
Turkish	: terlik 898
Russian	: туфли, pl. 898
Serbian	: папуча, f. 898
Ukrainian	: туфлі, pl. 898

899 SLIPS   see 119 BOW

900 SLOWLY   adv.

Czech	:	pomalu; zvolna 900
Danish	:	langsom 900
Dutch	:	langzaam 900
Finnish	:	hidas 900
French	:	lentement 900
German	:	langsam 900
Hungarian	:	lassú; lassan 900
Italian	:	lentamente 900
Croatian	:	polagano 900
Norwegian	:	langsom 900
Polish	:	powolniej 900
Portuguese	:	dewagar 900
Rumanian	:	încet 900
Slovak	:	pomlý; zvolna 900
Spanish	:	lentamente 900
Swedish	:	långsam 900
Turkish	:	yavas; ağir 900
Russian	:	медленный; -o 900
Serbian	:	полагано 900
Ukrainian	:	повільно; тихо 900

901 SMALL   adj.

Czech	:	malý 901
Danish	:	liden 901
Dutch	:	klein 901
Finnish	:	pieni 901
French	:	petit 901
German	:	klein 901
Hungarian	:	kicsiny 901
Italian	:	piccolo 901
Croatian	:	mali 901
Norwegian	:	liten 901
Polish	:	mały 901
Portuguese	:	pequeno 901
Rumanian	:	mic 901
Slovak	:	malý 901
Spanish	:	pequeño 901
Swedish	:	liten 901
Turkish	:	küçük 901
Russian	:	маленький 901
Serbian	:	мал 901
Ukrainian	:	малий 901

902 SMITH   s.

Czech	:	kovář, m. 902
Danish	:	Smed, m. 902
Dutch	:	de smid 902
Finnish	:	seppä 902
French	:	forgeron, m. 902
German	:	der Schmied 902
Hungarian	:	kovács 902
Italian	:	fabbro, m. 902
Croatian	:	kovač, m. 902
Norwegian	:	smed, m. 902
Polish	:	kowal, m. 902
Portuguese	:	ferreiro, o 902
Rumanian	:	ferarul 902
Slovak	:	kováč, m. 902
Spanish	:	herrero, m. 902
Swedish	:	smed-en 902
Turkish	:	demirci 902
Russian	:	кузнец, m. 902
Serbian	:	ковач, m. 902
Ukrainian	:	коваль, m. 902

903 SNAKE   s.

Czech	:	had, m. 903
Danish	:	Slange, m./c. 903
Dutch	:	de slang 903
Finnish	:	käärme 903
French	:	serpent, m. 903
German	:	die Schlange 903
Hungarian	:	kígyó 903
Italian	:	serpente, m. 903
Croatian	:	zmija, f. 903
Norwegian	:	slange, m. 903
Polish	:	wąż; zmija, f. 903
Portuguese	:	cobra, a 903
Rumanian	:	şarpele, m. 903
Slovak	:	had, m. 903
Spanish	:	culebra, f. 903
Swedish	:	orm-en 903
Turkish	:	yilan 903
Russian	:	змея, f. 903
Serbian	:	змија, f. 903
Ukrainian	:	змія, f. 903

904 SNOW   s.

Czech	:	sníh, m. 904
Danish	:	Sne, m./c. 904
Dutch	:	de sneeuw 904
Finnish	:	lumi 904
French	:	neige, f. 904
German	:	der Schnee 904
Hungarian	:	hó 904
Italian	:	neve, f. 904
Croatian	:	snijeg, m. 904
Norwegian	:	sne, m. 904
Polish	:	śnieg, m. 904
Portuguese	:	neve, a 904
Rumanian	:	zapadă, f. 904
Slovak	:	sneh, m. 904
Spanish	:	nieve, f. 904
Swedish	:	snö-n 904
Turkish	:	kar 904
Russian	:	снег, m. 904
Serbian	:	снег, m. 904
Ukrainian	:	сніг, m. 904

905 SOAP   s.

Czech	:	mýdlo, n. 905
Danish	:	Säbe, m. 905
Dutch	:	de zeep 905
Finnish	:	saippua 905
French	:	savon, m. 905
German	:	die Seife 905
Hungarian	:	szappan 905
Italian	:	sapone, m. 905
Croatian	:	sapun, m. 905
Norwegian	:	såpe, f. 905
Polish	:	mydło, n. 905
Portuguese	:	sabão, o 905
Rumanian	:	săpunul 905
Slovak	:	mydlo, n. 905
Spanish	:	jabón, m. 905
Swedish	:	tvål-en 905
Turkish	:	sabun 905
Russian	:	мыло, n. 905
Serbian	:	сапун, m. 905
Ukrainian	:	мило, n. 905

906 SOCKS *s. pl.*

Czech : ponožky, *f. pl.* 906
Danish : Herresokker, *pl.* 906
Dutch : de socken 906
Finnish : puolisukka 906
French : chaussettes *f. pl.* 906
German : die Socken, *pl.* 906
Hungarian : rövid harisnya 906
Italian : calzetti, *m. pl.* 906
Croatian : čarapa, *f.* 906
Norwegian : sokker; herreströmper, *pl.* 906
Polish : skarpetki, *pl.* 906
Portuguese : peúga, *a* 906
Rumanian : ciorapul scurt 906
Slovak : ponožky, *f. pl.* 906
Spanish : calcetines, *pl.* 906
Swedish : herrstrumpor-na 906
Turkish : çoraplar 906
Russian : носки, *pl.* 906
Serbian : чарапа, *f.* 906
Ukrainian : шкарпетки, *pl.* 906

907 SOFA *s.*

Czech : pohovka, *f.* 907
Danish : sofa, *m./c.* 907
Dutch : de canapee 907
Finnish : sohva 907
French : canapé, *m.* 907
German : das Sofa 907
Hungarian : diván 907
Italian : sofa, *m.* 907
Croatian : sofa, *f.* 907
Norwegian : sofa, *m.* 907
Polish : kanapa, *f.* 907
Portuguese : sofá, *o* 907
Rumanian : sofană, *f.* 907
Slovak : pohovka, *f.* 907
Spanish : sofá, *m.* 907
Swedish : soffa-n 907
Turkish : minder 907
Russian : диван, *m.* 907
Serbian : зофа, *f.* 907
Ukrainian : канапа, *f.* 907

908 SOLDIER *s.*

Czech : voják, *m.* 908
Danish : soldat, *m.* 908
Dutch : soldaat, *m.* 908
Finnish : sotilas 908
French : soldat, *m.* 908
German : der Soldat 908
Hungarian : katona 908
Italian : soldato, *m.* 908
Croatian : vojnik, *m.* 908
Norwegian : soldat, *m.* 908
Polish : zotniesz, *m.* 908
Portuguese : soldato, *m.* 908
Rumanian : soldat-ul 908
Slovak : vojak, *m.* 908
Spanish : soldado *m.* 908
Swedish : soldat-en 908
Turkish : asker 908
Russian : солдат, *m.* 908
Serbian : војник, *m.* 908
Ukrainian : солдат; вояк, *m.* 908

909 SOLE *s.*

Czech : podrážka, *f.*; podešev, *f.* 909
Danish : Saal, *m./c.* 909
Dutch : de zool 909
Finnish : puolipohja 909
French : semelle, *f.* 909
German : die Sohle 909
Hungarian : talp 909
Italian : suola, *f.* 909
Croatian : taban, *m.*; djon, *m.* 909
Norwegian : såle, *c.* 909
Polish : podeszwa, *f.* 909
Portuguese : sola, *a* 909
Rumanian : talpa, *f.* 909
Slovak : podošva, *f.* 909
Spanish : suela, *f.* 909
Swedish : skosula-n 909
Turkish : taban 909
Russian : подметка, *f.* 909
Serbian : табан, *m.* 909
Ukrainian : підошва, *f.* 909

910 SON *s.*

Czech : syn, *m.* 910
Danish : son, *m.* 910
Dutch : zoon, *m.* 910
Finnish : poika 910
French : fils, *m.* 910
German : der Sohn 910
Hungarian : fiú, *m.* 910
Italian : figlio, *m.* 910
Croatian : sin, *m.* 910
Norwegian : sönn, *m.* 910
Polish : syn, *m.* 910
Portuguese : filho, *m.* 910
Rumanian : flăcău, *m.* 910
Slovak : syn, *m.* 910
Spanish : hijo, *m.* 910
Swedish : son, *m.* 910
Turkish : oğul 910
Russian : сын, *m.* 910
Serbian : син, *m.* 910
Ukrainian : син, *m.* 910

911 SORROWFUL
see 829 SAD

912 SORRY *adv.*

Czech : litující; smutný; je mi líto; bohužel 912
Danish : bedrövet 912
Dutch : bedroefd 912
Finnish : valitettavasti 912
French : fâché; je regrette 912
German : leider; es tut mir leid 912
Hungarian : sajnos 912
Italian : tristo; affannato 912
Croatian : nažalost; žao mi je 912
Norwegian : dessverre 912
Polish : smutny; ja jestem smutny 912
Portuguese : triste 912
Rumanian : din păcate; de 912
Slovak : žiaľbohu 912
Spanish : triste; lo siento; me pesa 912
Swedish : sorgsen; ledsen 912
Turkish : heyhat; müteesirin 912
Russian : мне жаль; к сожалению 912
Serbian : нажалост; жао ми је 912
Ukrainian : засмучений; вибачте! 912

913 SOUTH s.

Czech	:	jih, m. 913
Danish	:	syd, c. 913
Dutch	:	zuiden 913
Finnish	:	etelä 913
French	:	sud, m. 913
German	:	der Süden 913
Hungarian	:	dél 913
Italian	:	mezzodi; meriggio, m. 913
Croatian	:	jug, m. 913
Norwegian	:	sör, c. 913
Polish	:	jug, m. 913
Portuguese	:	sul, m. 913
Rumanian	:	sud, c. 913
Slovak	:	juh, m. 913
Spanish	:	sur; sud, m. 913
Swedish	:	syd 913
Turkish	:	cenub 913
Russian	:	юг, m. 913
Serbian	:	jyr, m. 913
Ukrainian	:	південь 913

916 SOUR adj.

Czech	:	kyselý 916
Danish	:	sur 916
Dutch	:	zuur 916
Finnish	:	hapan 916
French	:	aigre 916
German	:	sauer 916
Hungarian	:	savanyú 916
Italian	:	acido 916
Croatian	:	kiselo 916
Norwegian	:	sur 916
Polish	:	kwaśny 916
Portuguese	:	azêdo 916
Rumanian	:	acru 916
Slovak	:	kyslý 916
Spanish	:	agrio 916
Swedish	:	sur 916
Turkish	:	ekşi 916
Russian	:	кислый 916
Serbian	:	кисео 916
Ukrainian	:	квасний 916

914 SOUND adj.

Czech	:	zdravý 914
Danish	:	sund 914
Dutch	:	gezond 914
Finnish	:	terve 914
French	:	sain 914
German	:	gesund 914
Hungarian	:	egészséges 914
Italian	:	sano 914
Croatian	:	zdrav 914
Norwegian	:	frisk 914
Polish	:	zdrowy 914
Portuguese	:	são 914
Rumanian	:	sănătos 914
Slovak	:	zdravý 914
Spanish	:	sano 914
Swedish	:	frisk 914
Turkish	:	saglam 914
Russian	:	здоровый 914
Serbian	:	здрав 914
Ukrainian	:	здоровий 914

917 SOW v.

Czech	:	síti 917
Danish	:	saa 917
Dutch	:	zaaien 917
Finnish	:	kylvää 917
French	:	semer 917
German	:	säen 917
Hungarian	:	vetni 917
Italian	:	seminare 917
Croatian	:	sijati 917
Norwegian	:	så 917
Polish	:	siać 917
Portuguese	:	semear 917
Rumanian	:	a sămăna 917
Slovak	:	siat' 917
Spanish	:	sembrar 917
Swedish	:	så 917
Turkish	:	ekmek 917
Russian	:	сеять 917
Serbian	:	сејати 917
Ukrainian	:	сіяти 917

915 SOUP s.

Czech	:	polévka, f. 915
Danish	:	suppe, m./c. 915
Dutch	:	de soep 915
Finnish	:	keitto 915
French	:	potage, m. 915
German	:	die Suppe 915
Hungarian	:	leves 915
Italian	:	minestra, f. 915
Croatian	:	juha, f. 915
Norwegian	:	suppe, f. 915
Polish	:	zupa, f. 915
Portuguese	:	sopa, a 915
Rumanian	:	supă, f. 915
Slovak	:	polievka, f. 915
Spanish	:	sopa f. 915
Swedish	:	soppa-n 915
Turkish	:	çorba 915
Russian	:	суп, m. 915
Serbian	:	jyxa, f. 915
Ukrainian	:	юшка; зупа, f. 915

918 SPADE s.

Czech	:	rýč, m. 918
Danish	:	Spade, m./c. 918
Dutch	:	de schop 918
Finnish	:	lapio 918
French	:	bêche, f. 918
German	:	der Spaten 918
Hungarian	:	ásó 918
Italian	:	accetta, f. 918
Croatian	:	lopata, f. 918
Norwegian	:	spade, m. 918
Polish	:	rydel, m. 918
Portuguese	:	pá, a 918
Rumanian	:	hîrleţul 918
Slovak	:	rýl', m. 918
Spanish	:	pala, f. 918
Swedish	:	spad-en 918
Turkish	:	kürek 918
Russian	:	лопата, f. 918
Serbian	:	ашов, m. 918
Ukrainian	:	лопата, f. 918

919 SPEAK v.

Czech	:	mluviti 919
Danish	:	tale 919
Dutch	:	spreken 919
Finnish	:	puhua 919
French	:	parler 919
German	:	sprechen 919
Hungarian	:	beszélni 919
Italian	:	parlare 919
Croatian	:	govoriti 919
Norwegian	:	tale, snakke 919
Polish	:	mówić 919
Portuguese	:	falar 919
Rumanian	:	a vorbi 919
Slovak	:	hovorit' 919
Spanish	:	hablar 919
Swedish	:	tala 919
Turkish	:	söylemek 919
Russian	:	говорить 919
Serbian	:	говорити 919
Ukrainian	:	говорити 919

920 SPECTACLES see 327 EYE GLASSES

921 SPINACH s.

Czech	:	špenát, m. 921
Danish	:	Spinat, m./c. 921
Dutch	:	de spinazie 921
Finnish	:	pinaatti 921
French	:	épinards, m. pl. 921
German	:	der Spinat 921
Hungarian	:	spenót 921
Italian	:	spinacci, m. pl. 921
Croatian	:	spinača, f. 921
Norwegian	:	spinat, m. 921
Polish	:	szpinak, m. 921
Portuguese	:	espinafre, o 921
Rumanian	:	spanacul, m. 921
Slovak	:	špenát, m. 921
Spanish	:	espinaca, f. 921
Swedish	:	spenat-en 921
Turkish	:	ispanak 921
Russian	:	шпинат, m. 921
Serbian	:	спинача, f. 921
Ukrainian	:	шпінат, m. 921

922 SPIRIT-LEVEL s. (water level)

Czech	:	vodováha, f.; libela, f. 922
Danish	:	Vaterpass, n. 922
Dutch	:	de waterpas 922
Finnish	:	vesivaaka 922
French	:	niveau, m. 922
German	:	die Wasserwaage 922
Hungarian	:	vizmértek 922
Italian	:	livellatore, m. 922
Croatian	:	razulja, f. 922
Norwegian	:	vaterpass, n. 922
Polish	:	poziomnica, f. 922
Portuguese	:	nivel de água, o 922
Rumanian	:	nivelul, c. 922
Slovak	:	vodná váha, f. 922
Spanish	:	nivel de agua, m. 922
Swedish	:	vattenpass-et 922
Turkish	:	suterazisi 922
Russian	:	ватерпас, m. 922
Serbian	:	нивела, f. 922
Ukrainian	:	водоважок, m. 922

923 SPOON s.

Czech	:	lžíce, f. 923
Danish	:	Ske, m.c. 923
Dutch	:	de lepel 923
Finnish	:	lusikka 923
French	:	cuiller, f. 923
German	:	der Löffel 923
Hungarian	:	kanál 923
Italian	:	cucchiaio, m. 923
Croatian	:	kašika, f. 923
Norwegian	:	skje, m. 923
Polish	:	lyžka, f. 923
Portuguese	:	colhér, a 923
Rumanian	:	lingură, f. 923
Slovak	:	lyžica, f. 923
Spanish	:	cuchara, f. 923
Swedish	:	sked-en 923
Turkish	:	yemek kaşigi 923
Russian	:	ложка, f. 923
Serbian	:	кашика, f. 923
Ukrainian	:	ложка, f. 923

924 SPORTING SHIRT s.

Czech	:	sportovní košile, f. 924
Danish	:	Sportsskjorte, m./c. 924
Dutch	:	hed sporthemd 924
Finnish	:	urheilupaita 924
French	:	la chemise de sport, f. 924
German	:	das Sporthemd 924
Hungarian	:	sporting 924
Italian	:	camicia, f. 924
Croatian	:	sportska košulja, f. 924
Norwegian	:	sportsskjorte, m. 924
Polish	:	sportowa koszula, f. 924
Portuguese	:	camisa de esporte, a 924
Rumanian	:	cămaşa de sport, f. 924
Slovak	:	športová košel'a 924
Spanish	:	camisa de deporte, f. 924
Swedish	:	sportskjorta-n 924
Turkish	:	spor gómleği 924
Russian	:	спортивная рубашка, f. 924
Serbian	:	спортска кошуља, f. 924
Ukrainian	:	спортова сорочка, f. 924

925 SPORTING-SHOE s.

Czech	:	sportovní bota, f. 925
Danish	:	Sportssko, m./c. 925
Dutch	:	de sportschoen 925
Finnish	:	urheilukenkä 925
French	:	chaussure de sport, f. 925
German	:	der Sportschuh 925
Hungarian	:	sportcipő 925
Italian	:	scarpa da passeggio, f. 925
Croatian	:	sportska cipela, f. 925
Norwegian	:	sportssko, m. 925
Polish	:	bucik sportowy m. 925
Portuguese	:	sapato de esporte, o 925
Rumanian	:	pantoful de sport 925
Slovak	:	športová topánka, f. 925
Spanish	:	bota deportiva, f. 925
Swedish	:	sportskor-na, pl. 925
Turkish	:	spor ayak kabi 925
Russian	:	спортивные ботинки, pl. 925
Serbian	:	спортска обуђа, f. 925
Ukrainian	:	спортовий черевик, m. 925

926 SPRING s. (a season)

Czech	:	jaro, *n.* 926
Danish	:	foraar, *m.* 926
Dutch	:	de lente 926
Finnish	:	kevät 926
French	:	printemps, *m.* 926
German	:	der Frühling 926
Hungarian	:	tavasz 926
Italian	:	primavera, *f.* 926
Croatian	:	proljeće, *n.* 926
Norwegian	:	vår, *m.* 926
Polish	:	wiosna, *f.* 926
Portuguese	:	primavera, *a* 926
Rumanian	:	primăvara, *f.* 926
Slovak	:	jar, *f.* 926
Spanish	:	primavera, *f.* 926
Swedish	:	vår-en 926
Turkish	:	bahar 926
Russian	:	весна, *f.* 926
Serbian	:	пролеће, *n.* 926
Ukrainian	:	весна, *f.* 926

929 STAG s. (an adult male deer)

Czech	:	jelen, *m.* 929
Danish	:	Hjort, *m.* 929
Dutch	:	het hert 929
Finnish	:	saksanhirvi 929
French	:	cerf, *m.* 929
German	:	der Hirsch 929
Hungarian	:	szarvas 929
Italian	:	cervo, *m.* 929
Croatian	:	jelen, *m.* 929
Norwegian	:	hjort, *m.* 929
Polish	:	jeleń, *m.* 929
Portuguese	:	veado, *o* 929
Rumanian	:	cerbul 929
Slovak	:	jeleň, *m.* 929
Spanish	:	ciervo, *m.* 929
Swedish	:	hjort-en 929
Turkish	:	geyik 929
Russian	:	олень, *m.* 929
Serbian	:	јелен, *m.* 929
Ukrainian	:	олень, *m.* 929

927 SQUARE s. (an area in a city)

Czech	:	náměstí, *n.* 927
Danish	:	plads, *m./c.* 927
Dutch	:	het plein 927
Finnish	:	tori 927
French	:	place, *f.* 927
German	:	der Platz 927
Hungarian	:	tér 927
Italian	:	piazza, *f.* 927
Croatian	:	trg, *m.* 927
Norwegian	:	plass, *m.* 927
Polish	:	plac, *m.* 927
Portuguese	:	praça, *a* 927
Rumanian	:	piaţă, *f.* 927
Slovak	:	námestie, *n.* 927
Spanish	:	plaza, *f.* 927
Swedish	:	torg-et 927
Turkish	:	meidan 927
Russian	:	площадь, *f.* 927
Serbian	:	тгр, *m.* 927
Ukrainian	:	площа, *f.* 927

930 STAIR-CASE s.

Czech	:	schody, *pl.* 930
Danish	:	Trappe, *c.* 930
Dutch	:	de trap 930
Finnish	:	portaat 930
French	:	escalier, *m.* 930
German	:	die Treppe 930
Hungarian	:	lépcsö 930
Italian	:	scala, *f.* 930
Croatian	:	stepenice, *f., pl.* 930
Norwegian	:	trapp, *f.* 930
Polish	:	schody, *pl.* 930
Portuguese	:	escada, *a* 930
Rumanian	:	scară, *f.* 930
Slovak	:	schody, *pl.* 930
Spanish	:	escalera, *f.* 930
Swedish	:	trappa-n 930
Turkish	:	merdiven 930
Russian	:	лестница, *f.* 930
Serbian	:	степенице, *pl.* 930
Ukrainian	:	сходи, *pl.* 930

928 STABLE s.

Czech	:	chlév, *m.*; stáj, *f.* **928**
Danish	:	Stald, *c.* 928
Dutch	:	de stal 928
Finnish	:	talli 928
French	:	étable, *f.* 928
German	:	der Stall 928
Hungarian	:	istálló 928
Italian	:	stalla, *f.* 928
Croatian	:	staja, *f.* 928
Norwegian	:	stall, *m.*; fjös, *n.* **928**
Polish	:	stajnia, *f.* 928
Portuguese	:	cocheira, *a* 928
Rumanian	:	grajdul 928
Slovak	:	stajňa, *f.* 928
Spanish	:	cuadra, *f.* 928
Swedish	:	stall-et 928
Turkish	:	ahur 928
Russian	:	хлев, *m.* 928
Serbian	:	стаја, *f.* 928
Ukrainian	:	стайня, *f.* **928**

931 STAMP s. (for letters)

Czech	:	(poštovní) známka, *f.* **931**
Danish	:	Frimärke, *n.* 931
Dutch	:	de postzegel 931
Finnish	:	postimerkki 931
French	:	timbre, *m.* 931
German	:	die Briefmarke 931
Hungarian	:	bélyeg 931
Italian	:	francobollo, *m.* 931
Croatian	:	poštanska marka, *f.* **931**
Norwegian	:	frimerke, *n.* 931
Polish	:	znaczek pocztowy, *m.* **931**
Portuguese	:	sêlo, *o* 931
Rumanian	:	timbrul postal, *n.* 931
Slovak	:	poštová známka, *f.* 931
Spanish	:	sello, *m.* 931
Swedish	:	frimärke-t 931
Turkish	:	pul 931
Russian	:	почтовая марка, *f.* **931**
Serbian	:	поштанска марка, *f.* **931**
Ukrainian	:	значок на ліст, *m.* 931

932 STAMP	s. (seal)
Czech	: razítko, n. 932
Danish	: stempel, n. 932
Dutch	: de stempel 932
Finnish	: leima 932
French	: cachet, m. 932
German	: der Stempel 932
Hungarian	: pecsét 932
Italian	: timbro, m. 932
Croatian	: pečat, m. 932
Norwegian	: stempel, n. 932
Polish	: pieczątka, f. 932
Portuguese	: carimbo, o 932
Rumanian	: stampilă, f. 932
Slovak	: pečiatka, f. 932
Spanish	: sello, m. 932
Swedish	: stämpel-n 932
Turkish	: mühür 932
Russian	: штемпель, m. 932
Serbian	: печат 932
Ukrainian	: печатка, f. 932

933 STAND	v.
Czech	: státi 933
Danish	: staa 933
Dutch	: staan 933
Finnish	: seisoa 933
French	: être debout 933
German	: stehen 933
Hungarian	: áll 933
Italian	: stare in piedi 933
Croatian	: stajati 933
Norwegian	: stå 933
Polish	: stać 933
Portuguese	: estar em pé 933
Rumanian	: a sta 933
Slovak	: stát' 933
Spanish	: estar de pie 933
Swedish	: stå 933
Turkish	: durmak 933
Russian	: стоять 933
Serbian	: стајати 933
Ukrainian	: стояти 933

934 STANDING-LAMP	s.
Czech	: stolní lampa, f. 934
Danish	: staalampe, m. 934
Dutch	: de staande lamp 934
Finnish	: jalkalamppu 934
French	: lampe transportable, f. 934
German	: die Stehlampe 934
Hungarian	: állólámpa 934
Italian	: lampada transportabile, f. 934
Croatian	: svjetiljka na stolu, f. 934
Norwegian	: stålampe, f. 934
Polish	: latarka ręczna, f. 934
Portuguese	: lâmpada de pé alto, a 934
Rumanian	: lampa de masă, f. 934
Slovak	: stolná lampa, f. 934
Spanish	: lámpara de pie 934
Swedish	: bordslampan 934
Turkish	: masa lambasi 934
Russian	: стоячая лампа, f. 934
Serbian	: стојећа лампа, f. 934
Ukrainian	: стаяча ляма, f. 934

935 STAR	s.
Czech	: hvězda, f. 935
Danish	: stjerner, pl. 935
Dutch	: de ster 935
Finnish	: tahti 935
French	: étoile, f. 935
German	: der Stern 935
Hungarian	: csillag 935
Italian	: stelle, f. pl. 935
Croatian	: zvijezda, f. 935
Norwegian	: stjerne, f. 935
Polish	: gwiazdy, f. pl. 935
Portuguese	: estrêla, a 935
Rumanian	: steaua, f. 935
Slovak	: hviezda, f. 935
Spanish	: estrella f. 935
Swedish	: stjärnor-na, pl. 935
Turkish	: yildizler 935
Russian	: звезда, f. 935
Serbian	: звезда, f. 935
Ukrainian	: зоря; звізда, f. 935

936 START	s.
Czech	: odjezd; začátek, m. 936
Danish	: udrejse 936
Dutch	: de uitreis 936
Finnish	: maastalähtö 936
French	: départ, f. 936
German	: die Ausreise, Start 936
Hungarian	: kiutazás 936
Italian	: l'uscita, f. 936
Croatian	: izlaz (iz države), m. 936
Norwegian	: utreise, f. 936
Polish	: wyjazd, m. 936
Portuguese	: viagem (de saída), f. 936
Rumanian	: iesire (din tară), f. 936
Slovak	: vycestovanie, n. 936
Spanish	: salida, f. 936
Swedish	: utresa-n 936
Turkish	: Azimet 936
Russian	: выезд, m. 936
Serbian	: излаз; путованье из ... m. 936
Ukrainian	: виізд. 936

937 START v. see 83 BEGIN

938 STATION	s.
Czech	: nádraží, n. 938
Danish	: jernbanestation, m./c. 938
Dutch	: het station 938
Finnish	: asema 938
French	: gare, f. 938
German	: der Bahnhof 938
Hungarian	: pályaudvar 938
Italian	: stazione, f. 938
Croatian	: stanica, f. 938
Norwegian	: jernbane-stasjon, m. 938
Polish	: dworzec kolejowy, m. 938
Portuguese	: estação, a 938
Rumanian	: gară, f. 938
Slovak	: stanica, f. 938
Spanish	: estación, f. 938
Swedish	: station-en 938
Turkish	: istasion 938
Russian	: вокзал, m. 938
Serbian	: станица, f. 938
Ukrainian	: двірець, m. 938

939 STATION-MASTER *s.*

Czech	: přednosta stanice, *m.*	939
Danish	: stationsforstander, *m./c.*	939
Dutch	: de stationschef	939
Finnish	: asemapäällikkö	939
French	: chef de gare, *m.*	939
German	: der Stationsvorsteher	939
Hungarian	: állomásfönök	939
Italian	: capostazione, *m.*	939
Croatian	: šef stanice, *m.*	939
Norwegian	: stasjonsmester, *m.*	939
Polish	: naczelnik stacji, *m.*	939
Portuguese	: chefe de estação, *o*	939
Rumanian	: şeful de garä	939
Slovak	: prednosta stanice, *m.*	939
Spanish	: jefe de estación, *m.*	939
Swedish	: stations-inspektor, *m.*	939
Turkish	: istasyon şefi	939
Russian	: начальник станции, *m.*	939
Serbian	: шеф станице, *m.*	939
Ukrainian	: начальник станції, *m.*	939

943 STICK *s.* (of wood)

Czech	: hůl, *f.*	943
Danish	: spadserestok, *m./c.*	943
Dutch	: de wandelstock	943
Finnish	: hävelykeppi	943
French	: la canne	943
German	: der Spazierstock	943
Hungarian	: sétapálca	943
Italian	: Bastone da passeggio, *m.*	943
Croatian	: palica za šetnju, *f.*	943
Norwegian	: spaserstokk, *c.*	943
Polish	: spacerowa laska, *f.*	943
Portuguese	: bengala, *a*	943
Rumanian	: bastonul	943
Slovak	: palica, *f.*	943
Spanish	: bastón, *m.*	943
Swedish	: spatserkäpp-en	943
Turkish	: baston	943
Russian	: трость, *f.*	943
Serbian	: палица за шетњу, *f.*	943
Ukrainian	: палиця, *f.*	943

940 STAY see **796 REMAIN**

941 STEEL *s.*

Czech	: ocel, *f.*	941
Danish	: staal, *n.*	941
Dutch	: het staal	941
Finnish	: teräs	941
French	: acier, *m.*	941
German	: der Stahl	941
Hungarian	: acél	941
Italian	: acciaio, *m.*	941
Croatian	: čelik, *m.*	941
Norwegian	: stål, *n.*	941
Polish	: stal, *f.*	941
Portuguese	: aço, *o*	941
Rumanian	: oţelul	941
Slovak	: ocel', *f.*	941
Spanish	: acero, *m.*	941
Swedish	: stål-et	941
Turkish	: çelik	941
Russian	: сталь, *f.*	941
Serbian	: челик, *m.*	941
Ukrainian	: сталь, *f.*	941

944 STING *v.*

Czech	: píchati	944
Danish	: stikke	944
Dutch	: steken	944
Finnish	: pistää	944
French	: piquer	944
German	: stechen	944
Hungarian	: szúrni	944
Italian	: pungere	944
Croatian	: bosti	944
Norwegian	: stikke	944
Polish	: kłóć	944
Portuguese	: picar	944
Rumanian	: a inţepa	944
Slovak	: pichat'	944
Spanish	: pinchar	944
Swedish	: sticka	944
Turkish	: saplamak	944
Russian	: колоть; кусать	944
Serbian	: бости	944
Ukrainian	: кусати	944

942 STEEL-HELMET *s.*

Czech	: přilba, *f.*	942
Danish	: staalhjelm, *m./c.*	942
Dutch	: de staalhelm	942
Finnish	: teräskypärä	942
French	: casque d'acier, *m.*	942
German	: der Stahlhelm	942
Hungarian	: rohamsisak	942
Italian	: elmo, *m.*	942
Croatian	: šljem, *m.*	942
Norwegian	: stålhjelm, *m.*	942
Polish	: hełm, *m.*	942
Portuguese	: capacete de aço, *o*	942
Rumanian	: cască de otel, *f.*	942
Slovak	: prilba, *f.*	942
Spanish	: casco de acero, *m.*	942
Swedish	: stalhjälm-en	942
Turkish	: mihver	942
Russian	: стальной шлем, *m.*	942
Serbian	: шлем, *m.*	942
Ukrainian	: шолом, *m.*	942

945 STOCKINGS *s. pl.*

Czech	: punčochy, *f. pl.*	945
Danish	: strömpe, *pl.*	945
Dutch	: de kous	945
Finnish	: sukat	945
French	: bas, *m.*	945
German	: der Strumpf; die Strümpfe *pl.*	945
Hungarian	: harisnya	945
Italian	: calze, *f. pl.*	945
Croatian	: čarapa, *f.*	945
Norwegian	: strömpe, *m.*	945
Polish	: pończochy, *pl.*	945
Portuguese	: meia, *a*	945
Rumanian	: ciorapii, *pl.*	945
Slovak	: pančuchy, *f. pl.*	945
Spanish	: medias *f.*	945
Swedish	: strumpor-na, *pl.*	945
Turkish	: çoraplar, *pl.*	945
Russian	: чулок, *m.*	945
Serbian	: чарапа, *f.*	945
Ukrainian	: чулок. *m.* панчохи, *pl.*	945

138

848

946 STONE s.

Czech	: kámen, *m.* 946
Danish	: sten, *m./c.* 946
Dutch	: de steen 946
Finnish	: kivi 946
French	: pierre, *f.* 946
German	: der Stein 946
Hungarian	: kö 946
Italian	: pietra, *f.* 946
Croatian	: kamen, *m.* 946
Norwegian	: sten, *m.* 946
Polish	: kamień, *m.* 946
Portuguese	: pedra, *a* 946
Rumanian	: piatră, *f.* 946
Slovak	: kameň, *m.* 946
Spanish	: piedra, *f.* 946
Swedish	: sten-en 946
Turkish	: taş 946
Russian	: камень, *m.* 946
Serbian	: камен, *m.* 946
Ukrainian	: камінь, *m.* 946

947 STONE-PINE s.

Czech	: pinie, *f.* 947
Danish	: pinie, *f./c.* 947
Dutch	: de pijnboom 947
Finnish	: pinus 947
French	: pin cultivé, *m.* 947
German	: die Pinie 947
Hungarian	: mandolufenyö 497
Italian	: pigna, *f.* 947
Croatian	: pinija, *f.* 947
Norwegian	: pinje, *f.* 947
Polish	: pińja, *f.* 947
Portuguese	: pinheiro manso, *o* 947
Rumanian	: pinul 947
Slovak	: pínia, *f.* 947
Spanish	: pino negro, *m.* 947
Swedish	: pinje-n 947
Turkish	: çam fistiği 947
Russian	: пиния, *f.* 947
Serbian	: пинија, *f.* 947
Ukrainian	: піннія, *f.* 947

948 STOP s.

Czech	: zastávka, *f.* 948
Danish	: stoppested, *c.* 948
Dutch	: de halte 948
Finnish	: seisake 948
French	: arrêt, *m.* 948
German	: die Haltestelle 948
Hungarian	: megállóhely 948
Italian	: fermata, *f.* 948
Croatian	: stanica, *f.* 948
Norwegian	: stoppested, *n.* 948
Polish	: przestanek, *m.* 948
Portuguese	: paragem, *a* 948
Rumanian	: staţiă, *f.* 948
Slovak	: zastávka, *f.* 948
Spanish	: parada, *f.* 948
Swedish	: hållplats-en 948
Turkish	: durak yeri 948
Russian	: остановка, *f.* 948
Serbian	: станица, *f.* 948
Ukrainian	: перестанок, *m.* 948

949 STORM s.

Czech	: bouřka, *f.* 949
Danish	: storm, *m./c.* 949
Dutch	: de storm 949
Finnish	: myrsky 949
French	: tempête, *f.* 949
German	: der Sturm 949
Hungarian	: a vihar 949
Italian	: tempesta, *f.* 949
Croatian	: bura, *f.* 949
Norwegian	: storm, *m.* 949
Polish	: burza, *f.* 949
Portuguese	: tempestade, *a* 949
Rumanian	: furtuna, *f.* 949
Slovak	: víchor, *m.* 949
Spanish	: tempestad, *f.* 949
Swedish	: storm-en 949
Turkish	: bora 949
Russian	: буря, *f.* 949
Serbian	: непогода, *f.* 949
Ukrainian	: буря, *f.* 949

950 STOVE s.

Czech	: kamna, *pl.* 950
Danish	: ovn, *m./c.* 950
Dutch	: de kachel 950
Finnish	: uuni 950
French	: poêle, *m.* 950
German	: der Ofen 950
Hungarian	: kályha 950
Italian	: stufa, *f.* 950
Croatian	: peč, *f.* 950
Norwegian	: ovn, *m.* 950
Polish	: piec, *m.* 950
Portuguese	: fogão, *o* 950
Rumanian	: sobă, *f.* 950
Slovak	: kachle, *pl.* 950
Spanish	: estufa, *f.* 950
Swedish	: ugn-en 950
Turkish	: ocak; soba 950
Russian	: печка, *f.* 950
Serbian	: пећ, *f.* 950
Ukrainian	: піч, *f.* 950

951 STRAIGHT AHEAD adv.

Czech	: přímo; rovně 951
Danish	: redelig; ligend 951
Dutch	: rechtuit 951
Finnish	: suoraan eteenpäin 951
French	: directement 951
German	: geradeaus 951
Hungarian	: egyenes 951
Italian	: direttamente 951
Croatian	: ravno 951
Norwegian	: like ut 951
Polish	: ravno 951
Portuguese	: direito 951
Rumanian	: de-a dreptul 951
Slovak	: priamo; rovno 951
Spanish	: directamente 951
Swedish	: rakt 951
Turkish	: ileriye doğru 951
Russian	: пряжо 951
Serbian	: равно 951
Ukrainian	: прямо 951

952 STRAW *s.*

Czech	:	sláma, *f.* 952
Danish	:	Halm, *m./c.* 952
Dutch	:	het stroo 952
Finnish	:	oljet 952
French	:	paille, *f.* 952
German	:	das Stroh 952
Hungarian	:	szalma 952
Italian	:	paglia, *f.* 952
Croatian	:	slama, *f.* 952
Norwegian	:	halm, *m.* 952
Polish	:	słoma, *f.* 952
Portuguese	:	palha, *a* 952
Rumanian	:	paiele 952
Slovak	:	slama, *f.* 952
Spanish	:	paja, *f.* 952
Swedish	:	halm-en 952
Turkish	:	saman 952
Russian	:	солома, *f.* 952
Serbian	:	слама, *f.* 952
Ukrainian	:	солома, *f.* 952

953 STRAWBERRY *s.*

Czech	:	jahoda, *f.* 953
Danish	:	jordbär, *m./c.* 953
Dutch	:	de aardbei 953
Finnish	:	mansikka 953
French	:	fraise, *f.* 953
German	:	die Erdbeere 953
Hungarian	:	földieper 953
Italian	:	fragola, *f.* 953
Croatian	:	jagoda, *f.* 953
Norwegian	:	jordbär, *m.* 953
Polish	:	poziomka, *f.* 953
Portuguese	:	morango, *o* 953
Rumanian	:	fraga, *f.* 953
Slovak	:	jahoda, *f.* 953
Spanish	:	fresa *f.* 953
Swedish	:	smultron-et 953
Turkish	:	çilek 953
Russian	:	клубника, *f.* 953
Serbian	:	jагода, *f.* 953
Ukrainian	:	суниця; полуница, *f.* 953

954 STUD *s.* (a button)

Czech	:	knoflík, *m.* (do límečku) 954
Danish	:	Kraveknap, *m./c.* 954
Dutch	:	het boordenknoopje 954
Finnish	:	kauluksennappi 954
French	:	bouton de faux col, *m.* 954
German	:	der Kragenknopf 954
Hungarian	:	gallérgomb 954
Italian	:	gemello, *m.* 954
Croatian	:	dugme za ovratnik, *m.* 954
Norwegian	:	kraveknapp, *m.* 954
Polish	:	spinka, *f.* 954
Portuguese	:	botão para colarinho, *o* 954
Rumanian	:	butonul 954
Slovak	:	gombička do goliera, *f.* 954
Spanish	:	botón de cuello, *m.* 954
Swedish	:	kragknapp-en 954
Turkish	:	yaka düğmesi 954
Russian	:	запонка, *f.* 954
Serbian	:	дугме за jаку, *n.* 954
Ukrainian	:	спинка, *f.* 954

955 STUFF *s.*

Czech	:	látka, *f.* 955
Danish	:	stof, *n.* 955
Dutch	:	de stof 955
Finnish	:	kankaat 955
French	:	les étoffes, *pl.* 955
German	:	der Stoff 955
Hungarian	:	anyag 955
Italian	:	stoffe, *f. pl.* 955
Croatian	:	tkanina, *f.* 955
Norwegian	:	stoff, *n.* 955
Polish	:	material', *f.* 955
Portuguese	:	tecido, *o* 955
Rumanian	:	stofele 955
Slovak	:	látka, *f.* 955
Spanish	:	telas, *pl.* 955
Swedish	:	tyg-et 955
Turkish	:	kumaş 955
Russian	:	материя; ткань, *f.* 955
Serbian	:	тканина, *f.* 955
Ukrainian	:	матерії, *pl.* 955

956 SUFFERING *s.*
see 688 PAIN

957 SUGAR *s.*

Czech	:	cukr, *m.* 957
Danish	:	sukker, *n.* 957
Dutch	:	de suiker 957
Finnish	:	sokeri 957
French	:	sucre, *m.* 957
German	:	der Zucker 957
Hungarian	:	cukor 957
Italian	:	zucchero, *m.* 957
Croatian	:	šećer, *m.* 957
Norwegian	:	sukker, *n.* 957
Polish	:	cukier, *m.* 957
Portuguese	:	açúcar, *o* 957
Rumanian	:	zahărul 957
Slovak	:	cukor, *m.* 957
Spanish	:	azúcar, *m.* 957
Swedish	:	socker 957
Turkish	:	şeker 957
Russian	:	сахар, *m.* 957
Serbian	:	шечер, *m.* 957
Ukrainian	:	цукор, *m.* 957

958 SUITCASE
see 54 A TRAVELING BAG

959 SUM *s.*
see 661 NUMBER

960 SUMMER *s.*

Czech	:	léto, *n.* 960
Danish	:	sommer, *m.* 960
Dutch	:	de zomer 960
Finnish	:	kesä 960
French	:	été, *m.* 960
German	:	der Sommer 960
Hungarian	:	nyár 960
Italian	:	estate, *f.* 960
Croatian	:	ljeto, *n.* 960
Norwegian	:	sommer, *m.* 960
Polish	:	lato, *n.* 960
Portuguese	:	verão, *o* 960
Rumanian	:	vară, *f.* 960
Slovak	:	leto, *n.* 960
Spanish	:	verano, *m.* 960
Swedish	:	sommar-en 960
Turkish	:	yaz 960
Russian	:	лето, *n.* 960
Serbian	:	лето, *n.* 960
Ukrainian	:	літо, *n.* 960

961 SUN *s.*

Czech	:	slunce, *n.* 961
Danish	:	sol, *m./c.* 961
Dutch	:	de zon 961
Finnish	:	aurinko 961
French	:	soleil, *m.* 961
German	:	die Sonne 961
Hungarian	:	nap 961
Italian	:	sole, *m.* 961
Croatian	:	sunce, *n.* 961
Norwegian	:	sol, *f.* 961
Polish	:	słońce, *n.* 961
Portuguese	:	sol, *o* 961
Rumanian	:	soarele 961
Slovak	:	slnko, *n.* 961
Spanish	:	sol, *m.* 961
Swedish	:	sol-en 961
Turkish	:	günes 961
Russian	:	солнце, *n.* 961
Serbian	:	сунце, *n.* 961
Ukrainian	:	сонце, *n.* 961

962 SUNDAY *s.*

Czech	:	neděle, *f.* 962
Danish	:	söndag, *m./c.* 962
Dutch	:	de zondag 962
Finnish	:	sunnuntai 962
French	:	dimanche, *m.* 962
German	:	der Sonntag 962
Hungarian	:	vasárnap 962
Italian	:	domenica, *f.* 962
Croatian	:	nedelja, *f.* 962
Norwegian	:	söndag, *m.* 962
Polish	:	niedziela, *f.* 962
Portuguese	:	domingo, *o* 962
Rumanian	:	duminică, *f.* 962
Slovak	:	nedel'a, *f.* 962
Spanish	:	domingo, *m.* 962
Swedish	:	söndagen 962
Turkish	:	pazar 962
Russian	:	воскресенье, *n.* 962
Serbian	:	недеља, *f.* 962
Ukrainian	:	неділя, *f.* 962

963 SUPPER *s.*

Czech	:	večeře, *f.* 963
Danish	:	aftensmad, *m./c.* 963
Dutch	:	het avondeten 963
Finnish	:	iilallinen 963
French	:	dîner; souper, *m.* 963
German	:	das Abendessen 963
Hungarian	:	vacsora 963
Italian	:	cena, *f.* 963
Croatian	:	večera, *f.* 963
Norwegian	:	aftensmat, *m.* 963
Polish	:	kolacja, *f.* 963
Portuguese	:	jantar, *a* 963
Rumanian	:	cină, *f.* 963
Slovak	:	večera, *f.* 963
Spanish	:	cena, *f.* 963
Swedish	:	kvällsmat-en 963
Turkish	:	akşam yemeği 963
Russian	:	ужин, *m.* 963
Serbian	:	вечера, *f.* 963
Ukrainian	:	вечеря, *f.* 963

964 SUSPENDERS *pl.*

Czech	:	podvazky, *pl. m.* 964
Danish	:	sokkeholder, *m.* 964
Dutch	:	de sokkendragers 964
Finnish	:	sukanpidin 964
French	:	support-chaussettes, *pl.* 964
German	:	der Sockenhalter 964
Hungarian	:	harisnyatartó 964
Italian	:	reggicalze, *m. pl.* 964
Croatian	:	podvezica, *f.* 964
Norwegian	:	sokkeholder, *m.* 964
Polish	:	podwiązki, *pl.* 964
Portuguese	:	liga, *a* 964
Rumanian	:	jartierele, *pl.* 964
Slovak	:	podväzok, *m.* 964
Spanish	:	liga, *f.* 964
Swedish	:	herrstrumpeband-en 964
Turkish	:	corap bağleri 964
Russian	:	подвязки, *pl.* 964
Serbian	:	подвезице, *f.* 964
Ukrainian	:	підвязки, *pl.* 964

965 SWEEP *v.*

Czech	:	mésti 965
Danish	:	jefe 965
Dutch	:	vegen 965
Finnish	:	lakaista 965
French	:	balayer 965
German	:	fegen 965
Hungarian	:	söpörni 965
Italian	:	scopare 965
Croatian	:	mesti 965
Norwegian	:	feie 965
Polish	:	wymiatać 965
Portuguese	:	varrer 965
Rumanian	:	a mătura 965
Slovak	:	zametat' 965
Spanish	:	barrer 965
Swedish	:	sopa 965
Turkish	:	süpürmek 965
Russian	:	мести 965
Serbian	:	чистити метлом 965
Ukrainian	:	вимітати 965

966 SWEET *adj.*

Czech	:	sladký 966
Danish	:	söd 966
Dutch	:	zoet 966
Finnish	:	makea 966
French	:	doux 966
German	:	süss 966
Hungarian	:	édes 966
Italian	:	dolce 966
Croatian	:	sladak 966
Norwegian	:	söt 966
Polish	:	słodki 966
Portuguese	:	doce 966
Rumanian	:	dulce 966
Slovak	:	sladký 966
Spanish	:	dulce 966
Swedish	:	söt 966
Turkish	:	tatli 966
Russian	:	сладкий 966
Serbian	:	сладак 966
Ukrainian	:	солодкий 966

967 SWIM *v.* see 67 BATHE

968 SWIMMING *s.*

Czech	:	plavání, *n.* 968
Danish	:	svömning, *c.* 968
Dutch	:	het zwemmen 968
Finnish	:	uida 968
French	:	nage, *f.* 968
German	:	das Schwimmen 968
Hungarian	:	úszás 968
Italian	:	nuotare; nuoto, *m.* 968
Croatian	:	plivanje, *n.* 968
Norwegian	:	svömming, *m.* 968
Polish	:	pływanie, *n.* 968
Portuguese	:	nadar, *o* 968
Rumanian	:	inotul 968
Slovak	:	plávanie, *n.* 968
Spanish	:	nadar 968
Swedish	:	simma 968
Turkish	:	yüsmek 968
Russian	:	плавание, *n.* 968
Serbian	:	пливанье, *n.* 968
Ukrainian	:	плавання, *f.* 968

969 SWITSCH *s.*

Czech	:	vypinač, *m.* 969
Danish	:	kontakt, *m./c.* 969
Dutch	:	de schakelaar 969
Finnish	:	kytkin 969
French	:	commutateur, *m.* 969
German	:	der Schalter 969
Hungarian	:	kapcsoló 969
Italian	:	interruttore, *m.* 969
Croatian	:	šalter, *m.* 969
Norwegian	:	bryter, *m.* 969
Polish	:	wyłącznik, *m.* 969
Portuguese	:	interruptor, *o* 969
Rumanian	:	comutatorul 969
Slovak	:	vypínač, *m.* 969
Spanish	:	interruptor, *m.* 969
Swedish	:	elektriska knappen 969
Turkish	:	dügmesi 969
Russian	:	выключатель, *m.* 969
Serbian	:	шалтер, *m.* 969
Ukrainian	:	лучник, *m.* 969

970 TABLE *s.*

Czech	:	stůl, *m.* 970
Danish	:	Bord, *n.* 970
Dutch	:	de tafel 970
Finnish	:	pöytä 970
French	:	table, *f.* 970
German	:	der Tisch 970
Hungarian	:	asztal 970
Italian	:	tavola, *f.* 970
Croatian	:	sto, *m.* 970
Norwegian	:	bord, *n.* 970
Polish	:	stól, *m.* 970
Portuguese	:	mesa, *a* 970
Rumanian	:	masă, *f.* 970
Slovak	:	stôl, *m.* 970
Spanish	:	mesa *f.* 970
Swedish	:	bord-et 970
Turkish	:	masa 970
Russian	:	стол, *m.* 970
Serbian	:	сто, *m.* 970
Ukrainian	:	стіл, *m.* 970

971 TABLET *s.* (medicine)

Czech	:	tabletka, *f.* 971
Danish	:	Tablet, *m./c.* 971
Dutch	:	de pil 971
Finnish	:	tabletti 971
French	:	comprimé, *m.* 971
German	:	die Tablette 971
Hungarian	:	tabletta 971
Italian	:	tavoletta, *f.* 971
Croatian	:	tableta, *m.* 971
Norwegian	:	tablett, *m.* 971
Polish	:	pigulka, *f.* 971
Portuguese	:	comprimido, *o* 971
Rumanian	:	tabletă, *f.* 971
Slovak	:	tabletka, *f.* 971
Spanish	:	tableta, *f.* 971
Swedish	:	tablett-en 971
Turkish	:	tablet 971
Russian	:	пилюля; таблетка, *f.* 971
Serbian	:	таблета, *f.* 971
Ukrainian	:	пілюля, *f.* 971

972 TAILOR *s.*

Czech	:	krejčí, *m.* 972
Danish	:	Skrädder, *m./c.* 972
Dutch	:	de kleermaker 972
Finnish	:	räätäli 972
French	:	tailleur, *m.* 972
German	:	der Schneider 972
Hungarian	:	szabó 972
Italian	:	sarto, *m.* 972
Croatian	:	krojač, *m.* 972
Norwegian	:	skredder, *m.* 972
Polish	:	krawiec, *m.* 972
Portuguese	:	alfaiate, *o* 972
Rumanian	:	croitorul 972
Slovak	:	krajčír, *m.* 972
Spanish	:	sastre, *m.* 972
Swedish	:	skräddare-n 972
Turkish	:	terzi 972
Russian	:	портной, *m.* 972
Serbian	:	кројач, *m.* 972
Ukrainian	:	кравець, *m.* 972

973 TAKE v.

Czech	: vzíti; bráti 973
Danish	: tage; bringe 973
Dutch	: nemen 973
Finnish	: ottaa 973
French	: prendre 973
German	: nehmen 973
Hungarian	: vesz 973
Italian	: prendere 973
Croatian	: uzimati 973
Norwegian	: ta 973
Polish	: vzić 973
Portuguese	: tomar 973
Rumanian	: a lua 973
Slovak	: vziat'; brat' 973
Spanish	: tomar; coger 973
Swedish	: taga 973
Turkish	: almak 973
Russian	: брать 973
Serbian	: та 973
Ukrainian	: взяти; брати 973

974 TANK s. (an armored vehicle moving on a caterpillar tread)

Czech	: pancéřový vůz, m.; tank, m. 974
Danish	: tank, m./c. 974
Dutch	: de vechtwagen 974
Finnish	: tankki 974
French	: char blindé, m. 974
German	: der Panzer 974
Hungarian	: harckocsi 974
Italian	: corazza, f. 974
Croatian	: tank, m. 974
Norwegian	: panser, m. 974
Polish	: czołg, m. 974
Portuguese	: carro blindado, m.; tanque, o 974
Rumanian	: tancul 974
Slovak	: panciernik, m. 974
Spanish	: tanque, m. 974
Swedish	: stridsvagn-en 974
Turkish	: zirihli araba 974
Russian	: танк, m. 974
Serbian	: тенк, m. 974
Ukrainian	: танк, m. 974

975 TAPE-MEASURE s. (European)

Czech	: metr, m. 975
Danish	: metermaal, n. 975
Dutch	: de metermaat 975
Finnish	: metrimitta 975
French	: mètre, m. 975
German	: das Metermass 975
Hungarian	: mérce 975
Italian	: metro, m. 975
Croatian	: meter za merenje, m. 975
Norwegian	: metermål, n. 975
Polish	: metrówka, f. 975
Portuguese	: metro, o 975
Rumanian	: metrul 975
Slovak	: meter, m. 975
Spanish	: cinta métrica, f. 975
Swedish	: metermått-et 975
Turkish	: metre ölçüsü 975
Russian	: метр, m. 975
Serbian	: мерило, n. 975
Ukrainian	: метер, m. 975

976 TART s.

Czech	: dort, m. 976
Danish	: Lagkage, c. 976
Dutch	: de taart 976
Finnish	: torttu 976
French	: la tarte 976
German	: die Torte 976
Hungarian	: torta 976
Italian	: torta, f. 976
Croatian	: kolač, m. 976
Norwegian	: blötkake, m. 976
Polish	: tort, m. 976
Portuguese	: torta, a 976
Rumanian	: torta, f. 976
Slovak	: torta, f. 976
Spanish	: torta, f. 976
Swedish	: tårta-n 976
Turkish	: pasta 976
Russian	: торт, m. 976
Serbian	: торта, f. 976
Ukrainian	: торт, m. 976

977 TEA s.

Czech	: čaj, m. 977
Danish	: te, m./c. 977
Dutch	: de thee 977
Finnish	: tee 977
French	: thé, m. 977
German	: der Tee 977
Hungarian	: tea 977
Italian	: tè, m. 977
Croatian	: čaj, m. 977
Norwegian	: te, m. 977
Polish	: herbata, f. 977
Portuguese	: chá, o 977
Rumanian	: ceaiul 977
Slovak	: čaj, m. 977
Spanish	: té, m. 977
Swedish	: té-et 977
Turkish	: çay 977
Russian	: чай, m. 977
Serbian	: чај, m. 977
Ukrainian	: чай, m. 977

978 TELEGRAM s.

Czech	: telegram, m. 978
Danish	: telegram, n. 978
Dutch	: het telegram 978
Finnish	: sähke 978
French	: télégramme, m. 978
German	: das Telegramm 978
Hungarian	: távirat 978
Italian	: telegramma, m. 978
Croatian	: telegram, m. 978
Norwegian	: telegram, m. 978
Polish	: telegram, m. 978
Portuguese	: telegrama, o 978
Rumanian	: telegramă, f. 978
Slovak	: telegram, m. 978
Spanish	: telegrama, m. 978
Swedish	: telegramm-et 978
Turkish	: telegram 978
Russian	: телеграма, f. 978
Serbian	: телеграм, m. 978
Ukrainian	: телеграма, f. 978

979 TELEPHONE s.

Czech	: telefon, *m.*	979
Danish	: telefon, *m./c.*	979
Dutch	: de telefon	979
Finnish	: puhelin	979
French	: téléphone, *m.*	979
German	: das Telefon	979
Hungarian	: távbeszélö	979
Italian	: telefono, *m.*	979
Croatian	: telefon, *m.*	979
Norwegian	: telefon, *m.*	979
Polish	: telefon, *m.*	979
Portuguese	: telefone, *o*	979
Rumanian	: telefonul	979
Slovak	: telefón, *m.*	979
Spanish	: teléfono, *m.*	979
Swedish	: telefon-en	979
Turkish	: telefon	979
Russian	: телефон, *m.*	979
Serbian	: телефон, *m.*	979
Ukrainian	: телефон, *m.*	979

980 TELEPHONE v. see CALL

981 TELL v.

Czech	: říci; vyprávěti; sděliti	981
Danish	: sige; fortälle	981
Dutch	: tellen	981
Finnish	: sanoa	981
French	: dire; raconter	981
German	: sagen	981
Hungarian	: mond	981
Italian	: dire	981
Croatian	: kazati	981
Norwegian	: si	981
Polish	: mówić; powiedzieć	981
Portuguese	: dizer	981
Rumanian	: a spune; a zice	981
Slovak	: hovorit'; povedat'	981
Spanish	: decir; contar	981
Swedish	: tala; urskilja	981
Turkish	: demek	981
Russian	: говорить	981
Serbian	: казати	981
Ukrainian	: говорити; сказати	981

982 TEN

Czech	: deset	982
Danish	: ti	982
Dutch	: tien	982
Finnish	: kymmenen	982
French	: dix	982
German	: zehn	982
Hungarian	: tíz	982
Italian	: dieci	982
Croatian	: deset	982
Norwegian	: ti	982
Polish	: dziesięc	982
Portuguese	: dez	982
Rumanian	: zece	982
Slovak	: desat'	982
Spanish	: diez	982
Swedish	: tio	982
Turkish	: on	982
Russian	: десять	982
Serbian	: десет	982
Ukrainian	: десять	982

983 THANKS

Czech	: děkuji; díky	983
Danish	: tak	983
Dutch	: dank U; dank je	**983**
Finnish	: kiitos	983
French	: merci	983
German	: danke	983
Hungarian	: köszönöm	983
Italian	: grazie	983
Croatian	: hvala	983
Norwegian	: takk	983
Polish	: dziękuję	983
Portuguese	: obrigado	983
Rumanian	: multumesc	983
Slovak	: d'akujem	983
Spanish	: gracias	983
Swedish	: tack	983
Turkish	: tesekkür; ederim	**983**
Russian	: благодарю; спасибо	**983**
Serbian	: хвала	983
Ukrainian	: дякую	983

984 THEATRE s.

Czech	: divadlo, *n.*	984
Danish	: teater, *n.*	984
Dutch	: het theater	984
Finnish	: teatteri	984
French	: théâtre, *m.*	984
German	: das Theater	984
Hungarian	: szinház	984
Italian	: teatro, *m.*	984
Croatian	: kazalište, *n.*	984
Norwegian	: teater, *n.*	984
Polish	: teater, *m.*	984
Portuguese	: teatro, *o*	984
Rumanian	: teatrul	984
Slovak	: divadlo, *n.*	984
Spanish	: teatro, *m.*	984
Swedish	: teater-n	984
Turkish	: tiyatro	984
Russian	: театр *m.*	984
Serbian	: позориште, *n.*	**984**
Ukrainian	: театер, *m.*	984

985 THERE adv.

Czech	: tam	985
Danish	: der	985
Dutch	: daar	985
Finnish	: tuolla, (tuossa)	985
French	: là	985
German	: dort	985
Hungarian	: ott	985
Italian	: là	985
Croatian	: ondje	985
Norwegian	: der	985
Polish	: tam	985
Portuguese	: ali; aí; acolá	985
Rumanian	: acolo	985
Slovak	: tam	985
Spanish	: ahí, allí	985
Swedish	: där	985
Turkish	: orada	985
Russian	: там	985
Serbian	: Tамо	985
Ukrainian	: Там	985

986 THERMOMETER
see 210 CLINICAL THERMOMETER

987 THICK adj.

Czech	: tlustý 987
Danish	: tyk 987
Dutch	: dik 987
Finnish	: paksu 987
French	: épais 987
German	: dick 987
Hungarian	: vastag 987
Italian	: grosso 987
Croatian	: debeo 987
Norwegian	: tykk 987
Polish	: gruby 987
Portuguese	: gordo 987
Rumanian	: gros 987
Slovak	: tlstý 987
Spanish	: grueso 987
Swedish	: tjock 987
Turkish	: kalin 987
Russian	: толстый 987
Serbian	: дебео 987
Ukrainian	: грубий 987

990 THIN adj.

Czech	: tenký 990
Danish	: tynd 990
Dutch	: dun 990
Finnish	: ohut 990
French	: mince 990
German	: dünn 990
Hungarian	: vékony 990
Italian	: sottile 990
Croatian	: tanak 990
Norwegian	: tynn 990
Polish	: cienki 990
Portuguese	: magro 990
Rumanian	: subtire 990
Slovak	: tenký 990
Spanish	: delgado 990
Swedish	: tunn 990
Turkish	: ince 990
Russian	: тонкий 990
Serbian	: танак 990
Ukrainian	: тонкий 990

988 THIGH s.

Czech	: stehno, n. 988
Danish	: laar 988
Dutch	: de dij 988
Finnish	: reisi 988
French	: cuisse, f. 988
German	: der Oberschenkel 988
Hungarian	: felsölábszár 988
Italian	: coscia, f. 988
Croatian	: stegno, n. 988
Norwegian	: lår, n. 988
Polish	: udo, n. 988
Portuguese	: coxa, a 988
Rumanian	: coapsa 988
Slovak	: stehno, n. 988
Spanish	: muslo, m. 988
Swedish	: lår-et 988
Turkish	: uyluk 988
Russian	: ляшка, f. 988
Serbian	: бутина, f. 988
Ukrainian	: стегно, n. 988

991 THING s.

Czech	: věc; předmět 991
Danish	: ting; sag, c. 991
Dutch	: ding; zaak 991
Finnish	: asia; esine 991
French	: chose, f.; objet 991
German	: die Sache 991
Hungarian	: dolog 991
Italian	: cosa, f. 991
Croatian	: stvar, m.; posao, n. 991
Norwegian	: sak,c. 991
Polish	: przedmiot, m. 991
Portuguese	: coisa, f. 991
Rumanian	: lucru, c.; obiet, c. 991
Slovak	: vec, f. 991
Spanish	: cosa, f. 991
Swedish	: ting; sak 991
Turkish	: şey; iş 991
Russian	: вещь, f. 991
Serbian	: ствар; посао 991
Ukrainian	: предмет, m. 991

989 THIMBLE s.

Czech	: náprstek, m. 989
Danish	: fingerböl, n. 989
Dutch	: de vingerhoed 989
Finnish	: sormustin 989
French	: dé à coudre, m. 989
German	: der Fingerhut 989
Hungarian	: gyüszü 989
Italian	: ditale, m. 989
Croatian	: naprstak, m. 989
Norwegian	: fingerböl, n. 989
Polish	: naparstek, m. 989
Portuguese	: dedal, o 989
Rumanian	: degetarul 989
Slovak	: náprstok, m. 989
Spanish	: dedal, m. 989
Swedish	: fingerborg-en 989
Turkish	: yüksük 989
Russian	: наперсток, m. 989
Serbian	: напрстак, m. 989
Ukrainian	: наперсток, m. 989

992 THIRD s.

Czech	: třetina, f. 992
Danish	: en trediedel 992
Dutch	: een derde 992
Finnish	: kolmasosa 992
French	: un tiers 992
German	: ein Drittel 992
Hungarian	: egy harmad 992
Italian	: un terzo 992
Croatian	: trećina 992
Norwegian	: en tredjedel 992
Polish	: jedna trzecia 992
Portuguese	: um terço 992
Rumanian	: o treime 992
Slovak	: jedna tretina 992
Spanish	: un tercio 992
Swedish	: en tredjedel 992
Turkish	: üçte biri 992
Russian	: треть 992
Serbian	: трећина 992
Ukrainian	: одна третя 992

993 THIRSTY *adj.*

Czech	:	žíznivý	993
Danish	:	törstig	993
Dutch	:	dorst	993
Finnish	:	janoinen	993
French	:	avoir soif	993
German	:	durstig	993
Hungarian	:	szomjas(an)	993
Italian	:	sitıbondo; bramoso	993
Croatian	:	žeden	993
Norwegian	:	törstig	993
Polish	:	pragnacy	993
Portuguese	:	sedento	993
Rumanian	:	insetat; setos	993
Slovak	:	smädny	993
Spanish	:	sediento	993
Swedish	:	törstig	993
Turkish	:	susamiş	993
Russian	:	хочется пить	993
Serbian	:	жедан	993
Ukrainian	:	хочется пити	993

994 THIRTEEN

Czech	:	třináct	994
Danish	:	tretten	994
Dutch	:	dertien	994
Finnish	:	kolmetoista	994
French	:	treize	994
German	:	dreizehn	994
Hungarian	:	tizenhárom	994
Italian	:	trédici	994
Croatian	:	trinaest	994
Norwegian	:	tretten	994
Polish	:	trzynaśćie	994
Portuguese	:	treze	994
Rumanian	:	treisprezece	994
Slovak	:	trinást'	994
Spanish	:	trece	994
Swedish	:	tretton	994
Turkish	:	on üç	994
Russian	:	тринадцать	994
Serbian	:	тринаест	994
Ukrainian	:	тринадцять	994

995 THIRTY

Czech	:	třicet	995
Danish	:	tredive	995
Dutch	:	dertig	995
Finnish	:	kolmekymmentä	995
French	:	trente	995
German	:	dreissig	995
Hungarian	:	harminc	995
Italian	:	trenta	995
Croatian	:	trideset	995
Norwegian	:	tredve	995
Polish	:	trzydzieśći	995
Portuguese	:	trinta	995
Rumanian	:	treizeci	995
Slovak	:	tridsat'	995
Spanish	:	treinta	995
Swedish	:	trettio	995
Turkish	:	otuz	995
Russian	:	тридцать	995
Serbian	:	тридесет	995
Ukrainian	:	трийцять	995

996 THOUSAND

Czech	:	tisíc	996
Danish	:	tusind	996
Dutch	:	duizend	996
Finnish	:	tuhat	996
French	:	mille	996
German	:	tausend	996
Hungarian	:	ezer	996
Italian	:	mille	996
Croatian	:	hiljada	996
Norwegian	:	tusen	996
Polish	:	tysiąc	996
Portuguese	:	mil	996
Rumanian	:	una mie	996
Slovak	:	tisíc	996
Spanish	:	mil	996
Swedish	:	tusen	996
Turkish	:	bin	996
Russian	:	тысяча	996
Serbian	:	хилада	996
Ukrainian	:	тисяча	996

997 THREE

Czech	:	tři	997
Danish	:	tre	997
Dutch	:	drie	997
Finnish	:	kolme	997
French	:	trois	997
German	:	drei	997
Hungarian	:	három	997
Italian	:	tre	997
Croatian	:	tri	997
Norwegian	:	tre	997
Polish	:	trzy	997
Portuguese	:	três	997
Rumanian	:	trei	997
Slovak	:	tri	997
Spanish	:	tres	997
Swedish	:	tre	997
Turkish	:	üç	997
Russian	:	три	997
Serbian	:	три	997
Ukrainian	:	три	997

998 THROAT *s.*

Czech	:	hrdlo, *n.*	998
Danish	:	strube, *m./c.*	998
Dutch	:	de keel	998
Finnish	:	kurkku	998
French	:	gorge, *f.*	998
German	:	die Kehle	998
Hungarian	:	gége	998
Italian	:	gola, *f.*	998
Croatian	:	grkljan, *m.*	998
Norwegian	:	strupe, *m.*	998
Polish	:	gardło, *m.*	998
Portuguese	:	garganta, *a*	998
Rumanian	:	gîtlej, *m/f.*	998
Slovak	:	hrdlo, *n.*	998
Spanish	:	garganta, *f.*	998
Swedish	:	strupe-n	998
Turkish	:	boğaz	998
Russian	:	горло, *n.*	998
Serbian	:	гркльан, *m.*	998
Ukrainian	:	горло, *n.*	998

146

999 THUMB s.

Czech	: palec, m. 999
Danish	: tommelfinger, m./c. 999
Dutch	: de duim 999
Finnish	: peukalo 999
French	: pouce, m. 999
German	: der Daumen 999
Hungarian	: hüvelykujj 999
Italian	: pollice, m. 999
Croatian	: palac, m. 999
Norwegian	: tommel-finger, m. 999
Polish	: kciuk, m. 999
Portuguese	: polegar, o 999
Rumanian	: degetul cel mare 999
Slovak	: palec, m. 999
Spanish	: pulgar, m. 999
Swedish	: tumme-n 999
Turkish	: baş parmak 999
Russian	: большой палец, m. 999
Serbian	: палац 999
Ukrainian	: палюх 999

1002 TICKET s.

Czech	: jízdenka, f. 1002
Danish	: billet, m./c. 1002
Dutch	: het treinkaartje 1002
Finnish	: matkalippu 1002
French	: billet, m. 1002
German	: die Fahrkarte 1002
Hungarian	: menetjegy 1002
Italian	: biglietto, m. 1002
Croatian	: vozna karta, f. 1002
Norwegian	: billett, m. 1002
Polish	: bilet, m. 1002
Portuguese	: bilhete, o 1002
Rumanian	: biletul 1002
Slovak	: cestovný lístok, m. 1002
Spanish	: billete, m. 1002
Swedish	: biljett-en 1002
Turkish	: seyahat billeti 1002
Russian	: билет, m. 1002
Serbian	: возна карта, f. 1002
Ukrainian	: білет, m. 1002

1000 THUNDER s.

Czech	: hrom, m. 1000
Danish	: torden, n. 1000
Dutch	: de donder 1000
Finnish	: ukkonen 1000
French	: tonnerre, m. 1000
German	: der Donner 1000
Hungarian	: a dörgés 1000
Italian	: tuono, m. 1000
Croatian	: grom, m. 1000
Norwegian	: torden, n. 1000
Polish	: piorun, m.; grzmot, m. 1000
Portuguese	: trovão, o 1000
Rumanian	: tunetul 1000
Slovak	: hrom, m. 1000
Spanish	: trueno, m. 1000
Swedish	: åska-n 1000
Turkish	: gökgürlemsi 1000
Russian	: гром m. 1000
Serbian	: гром, m. 1000
Ukrainian	: грім; перун, m. 1000

1003 TIE s.

Czech	: vázanka, f. 1003
Danish	: slips, n. 1003
Dutch	: de das 1003
Finnish	: kravatti 1003
French	: cravatte, f. 1003
German	: die Krawatte 1003
Hungarian	: nyakkendö 1003
Italian	: cravatta, f. 1003
Croatian	: kravata, f. 1003
Norwegian	: slips, n. 1003
Polish	: krawat, f. 1003
Portuguese	: gravata, a 1003
Rumanian	: cravata, f. 1003
Slovak	: viazanka, f. 1003
Spanish	: corbata f. 1003
Swedish	: slips-en 1003
Turkish	: boyunbaği 1003
Russian	: галстук, m. 1003
Serbian	: кравата, f. 1003
Ukrainian	: краватка, f. 1003

1001 THURSDAY s.

Czech	: čtvrtek, m. 1001
Danish	: tordsdag, m. 1001
Dutch	: de donderdag 1001
Finnish	: torstai 1001
French	: jeudi, m. 1001
German	: der Donnerstag 1001
Hungarian	: csütörtök 1001
Italian	: giovedi, m. 1001
Croatian	: četvrtak, m. 1001
Norwegian	: torsdag, m. 1001
Polish	: czwartek, m. 1001
Portuguese	: quinta-feira, a 1001
Rumanian	: perşembe 1001
Slovak	: štvrtok, m. 1001
Spanish	: jueves, m. 1001
Swedish	: torsdag-en 1001
Turkish	: perşenbe 1001
Russian	: четверг, m. 1001
Serbian	: четвртак, m. 1001
Ukrainian	: четвер, m. 1001

1004 TIME s.

Czech	: čas, m. 1004
Danish	: tiden 1004
Dutch	: de tijd 1004
Finnish	: aika 1004
French	: le temps 1004
German	: die Zeit 1004
Hungarian	: idö 1004
Italian	: tempo, m. 1004
Croatian	: vrijeme 1004
Norwegian	: tiden 1004
Polish	: czas 1004
Portuguese	: tempo, o 1004
Rumanian	: timpul 1004
Slovak	: čas, m. 1004
Spanish	: tiempo 1004
Swedish	: tid-en 1004
Turkish	: zamau 1004
Russian	: время, n. 1004
Serbian	: време, n. 1004
Ukrainian	: час, m. 1004

1005 TIN *s.* (a metallic element)

Czech	: cín, *m.* 1005	
Danish	: tin, *n.* 1005	
Dutch	: het tin 1005	
Finnish	: tina 1005	
French	: étain, *m.* 1005	
German	: das Zinn 1005	
Hungarian	: as ón 1005	
Italian	: stagno, *m.* 1005	
Croatian	: kositar; kalaj, *m.* 1005	
Norwegian	: tinn, *n.* 1005	
Polish	: cyna, *f.* 1005	
Portuguese	: estanho, *o* 1005	
Rumanian	: cositorul 1005	
Slovak	: cín, *m.* 1005	
Spanish	: estaño, *m.* 1005	
Swedish	: tenn-et 1005	
Turkish	: kalay 1005	
Russian	: олово, *n.* 1005	
Serbian	: цин, *m.* 1005	
Ukrainian	: цина, *f.* 1005	

1008 TOBACCO *s.*

Czech	: tabák, *m.* 1008
Danish	: tobak, *m./c.* 1008
Dutch	: de tabak 1008
Finnish	: tupakka 1008
French	: tabac, *m.* 1008
German	: der Tabak 1008
Hungarian	: dohány 1008
Italian	: tabacco, *m.* 1008
Croatian	: duhan, m. 1008
Norwegian	: tobakk, *m.* 1008
Polish	: tytoń, *m.* 1008
Portuguese	: tabaco, *o* 1008
Rumanian	: tutunul 1008
Slovak	: tabak, *m.* 1008
Spanish	: tabaco 1008
Swedish	: tobak-en 1008
Turkish	: tütün 1008
Russian	: табак, *m.* 1008
Serbian	: дубан, *m.* 1008
Ukrainian	: тютюн, *m.* 1008

1006 TIN-OPENER *s.*

Czech	: otevírač konserv, *m.* 1006
Danish	: daaseaabner, *m./c.* 1006
Dutch	: de busopenaar 1006
Finnish	: tölkinavaaja 1006
French	: ouvre-boîte, *m.* 1006
German	: der Büchsenöffner 1006
Hungarian	: konzervnyitó 1006
Italian	: chiavetta per scatole, *f.* 1006
Croatian	: ključ za otvaranje konzervi 1006
Norwegian	: hermetikåpner, *m.* 1006
Polish	: otwieracz do puszek, *m.* 1006
Portuguese	: abridor de latas, *o* 1006
Rumanian	: deschizatorul pentra conserve 1006
Slovak	: otvarač na konzervy, *m.* 1006
Spanish	: abrelatas, *m.* 1006
Swedish	: konservöppnare-n 1006
Turkish	: kutu-açmakul 1006
Russian	: консервный ключ *m.* 1006
Serbian	: кльуч за отваранье конзерви, *m.* 1006
Ukrainian	: ключ до консерв, *m.* 1006

1009 TOBACCONIST *s.*

Czech	: trafika, *f.* 1009
Danish	: cigarbutik, *m./c.* 1009
Dutch	: de sigarenwinkel 1009
Finnish	: tupakkakauppa 1009
French	: bureau de tabac, *m.* 1009
German	: der Zigarrenladen 1009
Hungarian	: trafik 1009
Italian	: tabacchino, *m.* 1009
Croatian	: trafika, *f.* 1009
Norwegian	: sigarforretning, *m.* 1009
Polish	: trafika, *f.* 1009
Portuguese	: tabacaria, *a* 1009
Rumanian	: tutungeriă, *f.* 1009
Slovak	: trafika, *f.* 1009
Spanish	: estanco, *m.* 1009
Swedish	: sigarrbutik-en 1009
Turkish	: cigara dukâni 1009
Russian	: табачный магазин, *m.* 1009
Serbian	: трафика, *f.* 1009
Ukrainian	: склеп з цигарками, *m.* 1009

1007 TIRED *adj.*

Czech	: unaven; unavený 1007
Danish	: trät 1007
Dutch	: moe 1007
Finnish	: väsynyt 1007
French	: fatigué 1007
German	: müde 1007
Hungarian	: fáradt 1007
Italian	: stanco 1007
Croatian	: umoran 1007
Norwegian	: trett 1007
Polish	: smęczeny 1007
Portuguese	: trät 1007
Rumanian	: obosit 1007
Slovak	: unavený 1007
Spanish	: fatigado 1007
Swedish	: trött 1007
Turkish	: yorgun 1007
Russian	: усталый 1007
Serbian	: уморан 1007
Ukrainian	: зморений 1007

1010 TODAY *adv.*

Czech	: dnes 1010
Danish	: i dag 1010
Dutch	: vandaag, heden 1010
Finnish	: tänään 1010
French	: aujourd'hui 1010
German	: heute 1010
Hungarian	: ma 1010
Italian	: oggi 1010
Croatian	: danas 1010
Norwegian	: idag 1010
Polish	: dzisiaj 1010
Portuguese	: hoje 1010
Rumanian	: azi 1010
Slovak	: dnes 1010
Spanish	: hoy 1010
Swedish	: i dag 1010
Turkish	: bugün 1010
Russian	: сегодня 1010
Serbian	: данас 1010
Ukrainian	: сьогодні; нині 1010

148

1011 TOE s.

Czech	:	prst (u nohy), *m.* 1011
Danish	:	täer, *m./c.* 1011
Dutch	:	de teen 1011
Finnish	:	varpaat, *pl.* 1011
French	:	orteil, *m.* 1011
German	:	die Zehe 1011
Hungarian	:	lábujj 1011
Italian	:	dita dei piedi, *m. pl.* 1011
Croatian	:	prst na nozi, *m.* 1011
Norwegian	:	tå, *m.* 1011
Polish	:	palce u nogi, *pl.* 1011
Portuguese	:	dedo do pé, *o* 1011
Rumanian	:	degetul dela picior 1011
Slovak	:	'palce (na nohe), *m. pl.* 1011
Spanish	:	dedos *pl.* 1011
Swedish	:	tå-n, tår-na, *pl.* 1011
Turkish	:	ayak parmaklari 1011
Russian	:	палец ноги, *m.* 1011
Serbian	:	прст на нози, *m.* 1011
Ukrainian	:	пальці в нозі, *pl.* 1011

1014 TOMORROW adv.

Czech	:	zítra 1014
Danish	:	i morgen 1014
Dutch	:	morgen 1014
Finnish	:	huomenna 1014
French	:	demain 1014
German	:	morgen 1014
Hungarian	:	holnap 1014
Italian	:	domani 1014
Croatian	:	sutra 1014
Norwegian	:	imorgen 1014
Polish	:	jutro 1014
Portuguese	:	amanhã 1014
Rumanian	:	mäine 1014
Slovak	:	zajtra 1014
Spanish	:	mañana 1014
Swedish	:	i morgon 1014
Turkish	:	yarin 1014
Russian	:	завтра 1014
Serbian	:	сутра 1014
Ukrainian	:	завтра 1014

1012 TOILET, W. C. (Lavatory) s.

Czech	:	toaleta, *f.* 1012
Danish	:	W. C. 1012
Dutch	:	de W. C. 1012
Finnish	:	käymälä 1012
French	:	cabinet, *m.* 1012
German	:	der Abort 1012
Hungarian	:	arnyékszék 1012
Italian	:	gabinetto, *m.* 1012
Croatian	:	nužnik, *m.* 1012
Norwegian	:	W. C. 1012
Polish	:	wychodek, *m.* 1012
Portuguese	:	retrete, *a* 1012
Rumanian	:	closetul 1012
Slovak	:	záchod, *m.* 1012
Spanish	:	excusado, *m.* 1012
Swedish	:	toalett-en 1012
Turkish	:	halâ 1012
Russian	:	уборная, *f.* 1012
Serbian	:	нужник, *m.* 1012
Ukrainian	:	виходок, *m.* 1012

1015 TONGS s.

Czech	:	kleště, *pl.* 1015
Danish	:	tang, *m./c.* 1015
Dutch	:	de tang 1015
Finnish	:	pihdit 1015
French	:	tenaille, *f.* 1015
German	:	die Zange 1015
Hungarian	:	fogó 1015
Italian	:	tenaglie, *f. pl.* 1015
Croatian	:	kliješta, *pl.* 1015
Norwegian	:	tang, *f.* 1015
Polish	:	obcegi, *pl.* 1015
Portuguese	:	turquês, *a* 1015
Rumanian	:	cleștele 1015
Slovak	:	kliešte, *pl.* 1015
Spanish	:	tenazas, *pl.* 1015
Swedish	:	tång-en 1015
Turkish	:	kerpeten 1015
Russian	:	клещи, *pl.* 1015
Serbian	:	клешта, *pl.* 1015
Ukrainian	:	кліщі, *pl.* 1015

1013 TOMATO s.

Czech	:	rajské jablíčko, *n.* 1013
Danish	:	tomat, *m./c.* 1013
Dutch	:	de tomaat 1013
Finnish	:	tomaatti 1013
French	:	tomate, *f.* 1013
German	:	die Tomate 1013
Hungarian	:	paradicsom 1013
Italian	:	pomodoro, *m.* 1013
Croatian	:	paradajz, *m.* 1013
Norwegian	:	tomat, *m.* 1013
Polish	:	pomidor, *m.* 1013
Portuguese	:	tomate, *o* 1013
Rumanian	:	patlajeaua roșie, *f.* 1013
Slovak	:	rajčina, *f.* 1013
Spanish	:	tomate, *m.* 1013
Swedish	:	tomat-en 1013
Turkish	:	tomates 1013
Russian	:	томат.; помидор, *m.* 1013
Serbian	:	парадајз, *m.* 1013
Ukrainian	:	помідор, *m.* 1013

1016 TONGUE s.

Czech	:	jazyk, *m.* 1016
Danish	:	tunge, *m./c.* 1016
Dutch	:	de tong 1016
Finnish	:	kieli 1016
French	:	langue, *f.* 1016
German	:	die Zunge 1016
Hungarian	:	nyelv 1016
Italian	:	lingua, *f.* 1016
Croatian	:	jezik, *m.* 1016
Norwegian	:	tunge, *f.* 1016
Polish	:	język, *m:* 1016
Portuguese	:	língua, *a* 1016
Rumanian	:	limba, *f.* 1016
Slovak	:	jazyk *m.* 1016
Spanish	:	lengua *f.* 1016
Swedish	:	tunga-n 1016
Turkish	:	dil 1016
Russian	:	язык *m.* 1016
Serbian	:	језик, *m.* 1016
Ukrainian	:	язик 1016

1017 TOOTH *(teeth pl.)* s.

Czech	:	zub, *m.*; zuby, *pl.* 1017
Danish	:	tänder, *pl.* 1017
Dutch	:	de tand 1017
Finnish	:	hammas 1017
French	:	dent, *f.* 1017
German	:	der Zahn, die Zähne, *pl.* 1017
Hungarian	:	fog 1017
Italian	:	dent, denti, *m. pl.* 1017
Croatian	:	zub, zubi, *m. pl.* 1017
Norwegian	:	tann, *f.* 1017
Polish	:	zab, *m.*; zęby, *pl.* 1017
Portuguese	:	dente, *o* 1017
Rumanian	:	dintele, *pl.* 1017
Slovak	:	zub, zuby, *m. pl.* 1017
Spanish	:	dientes, *pl.* 1017
Swedish	:	tand-en, tänder-na, *pl.* 1017
Turkish	:	dişler 1017
Russian	:	зубы, *pl.* 1017
Serbian	:	зуби, *pl.* 1017
Ukrainian	:	зуби, *pl.* 1017

1018 TOOTH-BRUSH s.

Czech	:	kartáček na zuby, *m.* 1018
Danish	:	tandbörste, *c.* 1018
Dutch	:	de tandeborstel 1018
Finnish	:	hammasharja 1018
French	:	brosse à dents, *f.* 1018
German	:	die Zahnbürste 1018
Hungarian	:	fogkefe 1018
Italian	:	spazzolino per i denti, *m.* 1018
Croatian	:	četka za zube, *f.* 1018
Norwegian	:	tannbörste, *m.* 1018
Polish	:	szczotka do zębów, *f.* 1018
Portuguese	:	escova de dentes, *a* 1018
Rumanian	:	periä de dinti, *f.* 1018
Slovak	:	kefka na zuby 1018
Spanish	:	cepillo para los dientes 1018
Swedish	:	tandborste-n 1018
Turkish	:	diş fırçasi 1018
Russian	:	зубная щетка, *f.* 1018
Serbian	:	четка за зубе 1018
Ukrainian	:	щітка до зубів 1018

1019 TOOTH-PASTE s.

Czech	:	zubní pasta, *f.* 1019
Danish	:	tandpaste, *c.* 1019
Dutch	:	de tandpasta 1019
Finnish	:	hammastahna 1019
French	:	pâte dentifrice, *f.* 1019
German	:	die Zahnpaste 1019
Hungarian	:	fogkrém 1019
Italian	:	pasta dentifricia, *f.* 1019
Croatian	:	pasta za zube, *f.* 1019
Norwegian	:	tannpasta, *m.* 1019
Polish	:	pasta do zębow 1019
Portuguese	:	pasta dentífrica, *a* 1019
Rumanian	:	pasta de dinţi 1019
Slovak	:	zubná pasta, *f.* 1019
Spanish	:	pasta dentífrica, *f.* 1019
Swedish	:	tandkräm-en 1019
Turkish	:	diş pati 1019
Russian	:	зубная паста, *f.* 1019
Serbian	:	паста за зубе, *f.* 1019
Ukrainian	:	паста до зубів, *f.* 1019

1020 TORTOISE s.

Czech	:	želva, *f.* 1020
Danish	:	skildpadde, *m.* 1020
Dutch	:	de schildpad 1020
Finnish	:	kilpikonna 1020
French	:	tortue 1020
German	:	die Schildkröte 1020
Hungarian	:	teknösbéka 1020
Italian	:	tartaruga, *f.* 1020
Croatian	:	kornjača, *f.* 1020
Norwegian	:	skildpadde, *f.* 1020
Polish	:	żołw, *m.* 1020
Portuguese	:	tartaruga, *a* 1020
Rumanian	:	broasca ţestoasä, *f.* 1020
Slovak	:	korytnačka, *f.* 1020
Spanish	:	tortuga, *f.* 1020
Swedish	:	sköldpadda-n 1020
Turkish	:	kaplumbağa 1020
Russian	:	черепаха, *f.* 1020
Serbian	:	корњаѕа, *f.* 1020
Ukrainian	:	черепаха, *f.* 1020

1021 TOWEL s.

Czech	:	ručník, *m.* 1021
Danish	:	haandkläde, *n.* 1021
Dutch	:	de handdoek 1021
Finnish	:	pyyheliina 1021
French	:	essuie-main, *m.* 1021
German	:	das Handtuch 1021
Hungarian	:	torülközö 1021
Italian	:	asciugamano, *m.* 1021
Croatian	:	ručnik, *m.* 1021
Norwegian	:	håndklä, *n.* 1021
Polish	:	ręcznik, *m.* 1021
Portuguese	:	toalha, *a* 1021
Rumanian	:	prosapul 1021
Slovak	:	uterák, *m.* 1021
Spanish	:	toalla, *f.* 1021
Swedish	:	handduk-en 1021
Turkish	:	havlu 1021
Russian	:	полотенце, *n.* 1021
Serbian	:	убрус, *m.* 1021
Ukrainian	:	рушник, *m.* 1021

1022 TOWN s.

Czech	:	město, *n.* 1022
Danish	:	by, *m./c.* 1022
Dutch	:	de stad 1022
Finnish	:	kaupunki 1022
French	:	ville, *f.* 1022
German	:	die Stadt 1022
Hungarian	:	város 1022
Italian	:	città, *f.* 1022
Croatian	:	grad, *m.* 1022
Norwegian	:	by, *m.* 1022
Polish	:	miasto, *n.* 1022
Portuguese	:	a cidade 1022
Rumanian	:	oraşul 1022
Slovak	:	mesto, *n.* 1022
Spanish	:	ciudad, *m.* 1022
Swedish	:	stad-en 1022
Turkish	:	şehir 1022
Russian	:	город, *m.* 1022
Serbian	:	варош, *f.* 1022
Ukrainian	:	місто, *n.* 1022

1023 TOWN-HALL s.

Czech	:	radnice, f. 1023
Danish	:	raadhus, n. 1023
Dutch	:	het stadhuis 1023
Finnish	:	kaupungintalo 1023
French	:	hôtel de ville, m. 1023
German	:	das Rathaus 1023
Hungarian	:	városháza 1023
Italian	:	casa della città, f. 1023
Croatian	:	vijećnica, f. 1023
Norwegian	:	rådhus, n. 1023
Polish	:	ratusz, m. 1023
Portuguese	:	cámara municipal, a 1023
Rumanian	:	primäria, f. 1023
Slovak	:	radnica, f. 1023
Spanish	:	ayuntamiento, m. 1023
Swedish	:	rådhus-et 1023
Turkish	:	belediye daygresi 1023
Russian	:	ратуша, f. 1023
Serbian	:	већница, f. 1023
Ukrainian	:	ратуш, m. 1023

1024 TRACTOR s.

Czech	:	traktor, m. 1024
Danish	:	traktor, m./c. 1024
Dutch	:	de tractor 1024
Finnish	:	traktori 1024
French	:	tracteur, m. 1024
German	:	der Traktor 1024
Hungarian	:	traktor 1024
Italian	:	tractore, m. 1024
Croatian	:	traktor, m. 1024
Norwegian	:	traktor, m. 1024
Polish	:	traktor, m. 1024
Portuguese	:	tractor, o 1024
Rumanian	:	tractorul 1024
Slovak	:	traktor, m. 1024
Spanish	:	tractor, m. 1024
Swedish	:	traktor-n 1024
Turkish	:	tratör 1024
Russian	:	трактор, m. 1024
Serbian	:	трактор, m. 1024
Ukrainian	:	трактор, m. 1024

1025 TRADE   see 143 BUSINESS

1026 TRAMWAY s.

Czech	:	elektrická dráha, f. 1026
Danish	:	sporvogn, c. 1026
Dutch	:	de tram 1026
Finnish	:	raitiotie 1026
French	:	tramway, m. 1026
German	:	die Strassenbahn 1026
Hungarian	:	villamos 1026
Italian	:	tranvai, m. 1026
Croatian	:	tramvaj. m. 1026
Norwegian	:	trikk, m. 1026
Polish	:	tramwaj, m. 1026
Portuguese	:	eléctrico, o 1026
Rumanian	:	tramvaiul 1026
Slovak	:	električka, f. 1026
Spanish	:	tranvía, f. 1026
Swedish	:	spårvagn-en 1026
Turkish	:	tramway 1026
Russian	:	трамвай, m. 1026
Serbian	:	трамвај, m. 1026
Ukrainian	:	трамвай, m. 1026

1027 TRANSLATE v.

Czech	:	přeložiti; překládati 1027
Danish	:	oversätte 1027
Dutch	:	verplaatsen 1027
Finnish	:	kääntää 1027
French	:	traduire 1027
German	:	übersetzen 1027
Hungarian	:	lefordét 1027
Italian	:	translare 1027
Croatian	:	prelaziti 1027
Norwegian	:	oversette 1027
Polish	:	przetlumatrć 1027
Portuguese	:	traduzir 1027
Rumanian	:	a traduce 1027
Slovak	:	preložit' 1027
Spanish	:	traducir; trasladar 1027
Swedish	:	översätta 1027
Turkish	:	çevirmak 1027
Russian	:	переводить 1027
Serbian	:	прелазити 1027
Ukrainian	:	перекладати 1027

1028 TRAVEL v.

Czech	:	cestovati 1028
Danish	:	rejse 1028
Dutch	:	reizen 1028
Finnish	:	matkustaa 1028
French	:	voyager 1028
German	:	reisen 1028
Hungarian	:	utazik 1028
Italian	:	viaggio 1028
Croatian	:	putovati 1028
Norwegian	:	reise 1028
Polish	:	podroźować 1028
Portuguese	:	viagar 1028
Rumanian	:	a calatore 1028
Slovak	:	cestovat' 1028
Spanish	:	viajar 1028
Swedish	:	resa 1028
Turkish	:	seyahat 1028
Russian	:	ехать; поехать; ездить 1028
Serbian	:	путовати 1028
Ukrainian	:	подорожувати 1028

1029 THREAD s.   see 861 sewing thread

1030 TREE s.

Czech	:	strom, m. 1030
Danish	:	träd, n. 1030
Dutch	:	de boom 1030
Finnish	:	puu 1030
French	:	arbre, m. 1030
German	:	der Baum 1030
Hungarian	:	fa 1030
Italian	:	albero, m. 1030
Croatian	:	stablo, n. 1030
Norwegian	:	tre, n. 1030
Polish	:	drzewo, n. 1030
Portuguese	:	árvore, a 1030
Rumanian	:	copacul 1030
Slovak	:	strom, m. 1030
Spanish	:	árbol, m. 1030
Swedish	:	träd-et 1030
Turkish	:	ağaç 1030
Russian	:	дерево, n. 1030
Serbian	:	дрво, n. 1030
Ukrainian	:	дерево, n. 1030

1031 TROUBLE s.

Czech	:	nesnáz; starost; mrzutost, f. 1031
Danish	:	bekymring, c. 1031
Dutch	:	onrust; storen 1031
Finnish	:	vaikeus; suru 1031
French	:	trouble, m. 1031
German	:	die Sorge; der Kummer 1031
Hungarian	:	gond 1031
Italian	:	disturbamento, m. 1031
Croatian	:	tuga, f. 1031
Norwegian	:	sorg, c. 1031
Polish	:	opieka, f. 1031
Portuguese	:	pena, f.; molestia, f. 1031
Rumanian	:	grijă, f. 1031
Slovak	:	starost', f. 1031
Spanish	:	perturbación, f.; pena, f. 1031
Swedish	:	oreda; oro; plaga 1031
Turkish	:	keder; dert 1031
Russian	:	горе, n.; забота, f. 1031
Serbian	:	туга, f. 1031
Ukrainian	:	горе; біда, f. 1031

1032 TROUSERS s.

Czech	:	kalhoty, pl. 1032
Danish	:	bukser; benkläder, pl. 1032
Dutch	:	de broek 1032
Finnish	:	housut 1032
French	:	pantalon, m. 1032
German	:	die Hose 1032
Hungarian	:	nadrág 1032
Italian	:	calzoni, pl. m. 1032
Croatian	:	hlače, pl. 1032
Norwegian	:	bukser, pl. 1032
Polish	:	spodnie, pl. 1032
Portuguese	:	calças, as 1032
Rumanian	:	pantalonii, pl. 1032
Slovak	:	nohavice, f. pl. 1032
Spanish	:	pantalones, pl. 1032
Swedish	:	hyxor-na 1032
Turkish	:	pantalon 1032
Russian	:	штаны; брюки, pl. 1032
Serbian	:	панталоне, pl. 1032
Ukrainian	:	штани, pl. 1032

1033 TRUCK see **614 MOTOR TRUCK**

1034 TRUMPET s.

Czech	:	trumpeta, f. 1034
Danish	:	trompet, m./c. 1034
Dutch	:	de trompet 1034
Finnish	:	torvi; vaskitorvi 1034
French	:	trompette, f. 1034
German	:	die Trompete
Hungarian	:	kürt 1034
Italian	:	cornetta, f. 1034
Croatian	:	truba, f. 1034
Norwegian	:	trompet, m. 1034
Polish	:	trąba, f. 1034
Portuguese	:	clarim, a 1034
Rumanian	:	trompetă, f. 1034
Slovak	:	trúba, f. 1034
Spanish	:	trompeta f. 1034
Swedish	:	trumpet-en 1034
Turkish	:	trampet 1034
Russian	:	корнет, m. 1034
Serbian	:	труба, f. 1034
Ukrainian	:	труба, f. 1034

1035 TRY v.

Czech	:	zkoušeti; pokusiti se 1035
Danish	:	pröve 1035
Dutch	:	proef 1035
Finnish	:	koettaa 1035
French	:	essayer 1035
German	:	versuchen 1035
Hungarian	:	kisérletezik 1035
Italian	:	provare 1035
Croatian	:	kušati 1035
Norwegian	:	forsöke 1035
Polish	:	kuszać 1035
Portuguese	:	provar 1035
Rumanian	:	a încerca 1035
Slovak	:	skúsit' 1035
Spanish	:	probar; ensayar 1035
Swedish	:	pröva; försöka 1035
Turkish	:	tecrübe 1035
Russian	:	пробовать 1035
Serbian	:	кушати 1035
Ukrainian	:	пробувати 1035

1036 TUESDAY s.

Czech	:	úterý, n. 1036
Danish	:	tirsdag, m. 1036
Dutch	:	de dinsdag 1036
Finnish	:	tiistai 1036
French	:	mardi, m. 1036
German	:	der Dienstag 1036
Hungarian	:	kedd 1036
Italian	:	martedi, m. 1036
Croatian	:	utorak, m. 1036
Norwegian	:	tirsdag, m. 1036
Polish	:	wtorek, m. 1036
Portuguese	:	têrça-feira, a 1036
Rumanian	:	Marti, f. 1036
Slovak	:	utorok, m. 1036
Spanish	:	martes, m. 1036
Swedish	:	tisdagen 1036
Turkish	:	sali 1036
Russian	:	вторник, m. 1036
Serbian	:	уторак, m. 1036
Ukrainian	:	вівторок, m. 1036

1037 TULIP s.

Czech	:	tulipán, m. 1037
Danish	:	tulipan, m./c. 1037
Dutch	:	de tulp 1037
Finnish	:	tulppaani 1037
French	:	tulipe, f. 1037
German	:	die Tulpe 1037
Hungarian	:	tulipán 1037
Italian	:	tulipano, m. 1037
Croatian	:	lala, f. 1037
Norwegian	:	tulipan, m. 1037
Polish	:	tulipan, m. 1037
Portuguese	:	tulipa, a 1037
Rumanian	:	garoafă, f. 1037
Slovak	:	tulipán, m. 1037
Spanish	:	tulipán, m. 1037
Swedish	:	tulpan-en 1037
Turkish	:	lâle 1037
Russian	:	тюльпан, m. 1037
Serbian	:	лала, f. 1037
Ukrainian	:	тульпан, m. 1037

1038 TWELVE

Czech	:	dvanáct 1038
Danish	:	tolv 1038
Dutch	:	twaalf 1038
Finnish	:	kaksitoista 1038
French	:	douze 1038
German	:	zwölf 1038
Hungarian	:	tizenkettö 1038
Italian	:	dódici 1038
Croatian	:	dvanaest 1038
Norwegian	:	tolv 1038
Polish	:	dwanaście 1038
Portuguese	:	doze 1038
Rumanian	:	doisprezece 1038
Slovak	:	dvanást' 1038
Spanish	:	doce 1038
Swedish	:	tolf 1038
Turkish	:	on iki 1038
Russian	:	двенадцат 1038
Serbian	:	дванаест 1038
Ukrainian	:	дванадцять 1038

1039 TWENTY

Czech	:	dvacet 1039
Danish	:	tyve 1039
Dutch	:	twintig 1039
Finnish	:	kaksikymmentä 1039
French	:	vingt 1039
German	:	zwanzig 1039
Hungarian	:	húsz 1039
Italian	:	venti 1039
Croatian	:	dvadeset 1039
Norwegian	:	tyve 1039
Polish	:	dwadzieścia 1039
Portuguese	:	vinte 1039
Rumanian	:	douăzeci 1039
Slovak	:	dvadsat' 1039
Spanish	:	veinte 1039
Swedish	:	tjugo 1039
Turkish	:	yirmi 1039
Russian	:	двадцать 1039
Serbian	:	двадесет 1039
Ukrainian	:	двайцять 1039

1040 TWICE adv.

Czech	:	dvakrát 1040
Danish	:	to gange 1040
Dutch	:	tweemaal 1040
Finnish	:	kaksikertaa 1040
French	:	deux fois 1040
German	:	zweimal 1040
Hungarian	:	kétszer 1040
Italian	:	due per 1040
Croatian	:	dva puta 1040
Norwegian	:	to ganger 1040
Polish	:	dwa razy 1040
Portuguese	:	duas vezes 1040
Rumanian	:	de două ori 1040
Slovak	:	dvakrát 1040
Spanish	:	dos veces 1040
Swedish	:	två gånger 1040
Turkish	:	iki kere 1040
Russian	:	два раза 1040
Serbian	:	два пут 1040
Ukrainian	:	два рази 1040

1041 TWO

Czech	:	dvě 1041
Danish	:	to 1041
Dutch	:	twee 1041
Finnish	:	kaksi 1041
French	:	deux 1041
German	:	zwei 1041
Hungarian	:	kettö 1041
Italian	:	due 1041
Croatian	:	dva 1041
Norwegian	:	to 1041
Polish	:	dwa 1041
Portuguese	:	dois 1041
Rumanian	:	doi 1041
Slovak	:	dve 1041
Spanish	:	dos 1041
Swedish	:	två 1041
Turkish	:	iki 1041
Russian	:	два 1041
Serbian	:	два 1041
Ukrainian	:	два 1041

1042 TYPEWRITER s.

Czech	:	psací stroj, m. 1042
Danish	:	skrivemaskine, m./c. 1042
Dutch	:	de schrijfmachine 1042
Finnish	:	kirjoituskone 1042
French	:	machine à écrire, f. 1042
German	:	die Schreibmaschine 1042
Hungarian	:	irógép 1042
Italian	:	macchina da scrivere, f. 1042
Croatian	:	pisaća mašina, f. 1042
Norwegian	:	skrivemaskin, m. 1042
Polish	:	maszyna do pisania, f. 1042
Portuguese	:	máquina para escrever, a 1042
Rumanian	:	masină de scris, f. 1042
Slovak	:	písací stroj, m. 1042
Spanish	:	máquina de escribir, f. 1042
Swedish	:	skrivmaskin-en 1042
Turkish	:	yazi makinasi 1042
Russian	:	пишущяя машина, f. 1042
Serbian	:	писаћа машина, f. 1042
Ukrainian	:	машина до писання, f. 1042

1043 TIRE s.

Czech	:	pneumatika, f. 1043
Danish	:	gummiring, m./c. 1043
Dutch	:	de band 1043
Finnish	:	rengas 1043
French	:	pneu, m. 1043
German	:	der Reifen 1043
Hungarian	:	abrones 1043
Italian	:	copertone, m. 1043
Croatian	:	obruč, m. 1043
Norwegian	:	gummiring, m. 1043
Polish	:	obręcz, m. 1403
Portuguese	:	pneumático, o 1043
Rumanian	:	cauciucul 1043
Slovak	:	pneumatika, f. 1043
Spanish	:	neumático, m. 1043
Swedish	:	ring-en; däck-et 1043
Turkish	:	otomobil lastiği 1043
Russian	:	шина, f. 1043
Serbian	:	обруч, m. 1043
Ukrainian	:	обруч, m. 1043

1044 UGLY	adj.		
Czech	:	ošklivý	1044
Danish	:	grim	1044
Dutch	:	leelijk	1044
Finnish	:	ruma	1044
French	:	laid	1044
German	:	hässlich	1044
Hungarian	:	csúnya	1044
Italian	:	brutto	1044
Croatian	:	ružan	1044
Norwegian	:	stygg	1044
Polish	:	brzydki	1044
Portuguese	:	feio	1044
Rumanian	:	urât	1044
Slovak	:	škaredý	1044
Spanish	:	feo	1044
Swedish	:	ful	1044
Turkish	:	çirkin	1044
Russian	:	уродливо; -ый	1044
Serbian	:	ружно	1044
Ukrainian	:	поганий	1044

1045 UMBRELLA	s.		
Czech	:	deštník, m.	1045
Danish	:	Paraply, c.	1045
Dutch	:	de paraplu	1045
Finnish	:	sateenvarjo	1045
French	:	le parapluie	1045
German	:	der (Regen) schirm	1045
Hungarian	:	esernyö	1045
Italian	:	Ombrello, m.	1045
Croatian	:	kišobran, m.	1045
Norwegian	:	paraply, c.	1045
Polish	:	parasol, m.	1045
Portuguese	:	guarda-chuva, o	1045
Rumanian	:	umbrela, f.	1045
Slovak	:	dáždnik, m.	1045
Spanish	:	paraguas, m.	1045
Swedish	:	paraply-et	1045
Turkish	:	şemsiye	1045
Russian	:	зонтік, m.	1045
Serbian	:	кишобран, m.	1045
Ukrainian	:	паросоля, f.	1045

1046 UNCLE	s.		
Czech	:	strýc, m.	1046
Danish	:	onkel, c.	1046
Dutch	:	oom, m.	1046
Finnish	:	setä; eno	1046
French	:	oncle, m.	1046
German	:	der Onkel	1046
Hungarian	:	nagybátya	1046
Italian	:	zio, m.	1046
Croatian	:	stric; ujak	1046
Norwegian	:	onkel, c.	1046
Polish	:	stryj, m.	1046
Portuguese	:	tio, m.	1046
Rumanian	:	unchi, m.	1046
Slovak	:	strýc; ujec	1046
Spanish	:	tío, m.	1046
Swedish	:	farbror, m.	1046
Turkish	:	amca; dayi	1046
Russian	:	дядя, m.	1046
Serbian	:	стриц, m.	1046
Ukrainian	:	дядько, m.	1046

1047 UNCLEAN see 279 DIRTY

1048 UNDERSTAND	v.		
Czech	:	rozuměti	1048
Danish	:	forstaa	1048
Dutch	:	verstaan; begrijpen	1048
Finnish	:	ymmärtää	1048
French	:	comprendre	1048
German	:	verstehen	1048
Hungarian	:	megérteni	1048
Italian	:	capire	1048
Croatian	:	razumjeti	1048
Norwegian	:	forstå	1048
Polish	:	rozumieć	1048
Portuguese	:	compreender	1048
Rumanian	:	a întelege	1048
Slovak	:	rozumiet'	1048
Spanish	:	entender	1048
Swedish	:	förstå	1048
Turkish	:	anlamak	1048
Russian	:	понимать	1048
Serbian	:	разумети	1048
Ukrainian	:	розуміти,	1048

1049 UNIFORM	s.		
Czech	:	stejnokroj, m.	1049
Danish	:	uniform, m./c.	1049
Dutch	:	het uniform	1049
Finnish	:	univormu; virkapuku	1049
French	:	uniforme, m.	1049
German	:	die Uniform	1049
Hungarian	:	egyenruha	1049
Italian	:	divisa, f.	1049
Croatian	:	uniforma, f.	1049
Norwegian	:	uniform, m.	1049
Polish	:	mundur, m.	1049
Portuguese	:	farda, a	1049
Rumanian	:	uniforma, f.	1049
Slovak	:	rovnošata, f.; uniforma	1049
Spanish	:	uniforme, m.	1049
Swedish	:	uniform-en	1049
Turkish	:	uniforma	1049
Russian	:	форма, f.	1049
Serbian	:	униформа, f.	1049
Ukrainian	:	однострій, m.	1049

1050 UNMARRIED see 885 SINGLE

1051 UNPUNCTUALLY	adv.		
Czech	:	nepřesně	1051
Danish	:	upräcis	1051
Dutch	:	niet op tijd	1051
Finnish	:	epätäsmällisesti	1051
French	:	non ponctuellement	1051
German	:	unpünktlich	1051
Hungarian	:	pontatlan	1051
Italian	:	non punctuale	1051
Croatian	:	netočno, netočan	1051
Norwegian	:	upresis, upunktlig	1051
Polish	:	niepunktualnie	1051
Portuguese	:	não pontual	1051
Rumanian	:	nepunctual	1051
Slovak	:	nepresne	1051
Spanish	:	poco puntual	1051
Swedish	:	icke punktlig	1051
Turkish	:	vaktisiz	1051
Russian	:	непунктуально	1051
Serbian	:	нетачно	1051
Ukrainian	:	не точно	1051

1052 UPPER-ARM s.

Czech	:	nadloktí, n. 1052
Danish	:	Overarm, m./c. 1052
Dutch	:	de bovenarm 1052
Finnish	:	olkavarsi 1052
French	:	bras supérieur, m. 1052
German	:	der Oberarm 1052
Hungarian	:	felsökar 1052
Italian	:	omero, m. 1052
Croatian	:	nadlaktica, f. 1052
Norwegian	:	overarm, m. 1052
Polish	:	nadramię, n. 1052
Portuguese	:	braço, o 1052
Rumanian	:	braţul 1052
Slovak	:	nadlaktie, n. 1052
Spanish	:	brazo, m. 1052
Swedish	:	överarm-en 1052
Turkish	:	kol 1052
Russian	:	верхняя часть руки, f. 1052
Serbian	:	надлактица, f. 1052
Ukrainian	:	горішне рамя, n. 1052

1055 VEGETABLE s.

Czech	:	zelenina, f. 1055
Danish	:	Grönnsager, pl. 1055
Dutch	:	de groente 1055
Finnish	:	vihanneksia 1055
French	:	légume, m. 1055
German	:	das Gemüse 1055
Hungarian	:	fözelék 1055
Italian	:	verdura, f. 1055
Croatian	:	povrće, n. 1055
Norwegian	:	grönnsaker, pl. 1055
Polish	:	jarzyna, f. 1055
Portuguese	:	legumes, os 1055
Rumanian	:	zarzavatul 1055
Slovak	:	zelenina, f. 1055
Spanish	:	legumbres, pl. 1055
Swedish	:	grönsaker-na, pl. 1055
Turkish	:	sebzevat 1055
Russian	:	овощи, pl. 1055
Serbian	:	поврђе, n. 1055
Ukrainian	:	ярина; городина, f. 1055

1053 VALLEY s.

Czech	:	údolí, n. 1053
Danish	:	Dal, m./c. 1053
Dutch	:	het dal 1053
Finnish	:	laakso 1053
French	:	vallée, f. 1053
German	:	das Tal 1053
Hungarian	:	völgy 1053
Italian	:	valle, f. 1053
Croatian	:	dolina, f. 1053
Norwegian	:	dal, m. 1053
Polish	:	dolina, f. 1053
Portuguese	:	vale, o 1053
Rumanian	:	valeă, f. 1053
Slovak	:	údolie, n. 1053
Spanish	:	valle, f. 1053
Swedish	:	dal-en 1053
Turkish	:	vadi 1053
Russian	:	долина, f. 1053
Serbian	:	долина, f. 1053
Ukrainian	:	долина, f. 1053

1056 VELVET s.

Czech	:	samet, m. 1056
Danish	:	Flöjl, m./c. 1056
Dutch	:	het fluweel 1056
Finnish	:	sametti 1056
French	:	velours, m. 1056
German	:	der Samt 1056
Hungarian	:	bársony 1056
Italian	:	velluto, m. 1056
Croatian	:	kadifa, f. 1056
Norwegian	:	flöyl, m. 1056
Polish	:	aksamit, m. 1056
Portuguese	:	veludo, o 1056
Rumanian	:	catifeă, f. 1056
Slovak	:	zamat, m. 1056
Spanish	:	terciopelo, m. 1056
Swedish	:	sammet-en 1056
Turkish	:	kadife 1056
Russian	:	бархат m. 1056
Serbian	:	кадифа, f. 1056
Ukrainian	:	оксамит, m. 1056

1054 VEAL s.

Czech	:	telecí maso, n. 1054
Danish	:	Kalveköd, n. 1054
Dutch	:	het kalfsvlees 1054
Finnish	:	vasikanliha 1054
French	:	veau, m. 1054
German	:	das Kalbfleisch 1054
Hungarian	:	borjúhús 1054
Italian	:	carne di vitello, f. 1054
Croatian	:	teletina, f. 1054
Norwegian	:	kalvekjött, n. 1054
Polish	:	mięso cielęce, n. 1054
Portuguese	:	carne de vitela, a 1054
Rumanian	:	carnea de viţel 1054
Slovak	:	telacie mäso, n. 1054
Spanish	:	ternera, f. 1054
Swedish	:	kalvkött-et 1054
Turkish	:	dana eti 1054
Russian	:	телятина, f. 1054
Serbian	:	мелетина, f. 1054
Ukrainian	:	теляче мясо, n. 1054

1057 VERY adv.

Czech	:	velmi 1057
Danish	:	meget 1057
Dutch	:	waar; zeer 1057
Finnish	:	hyvin 1057
French	:	très 1057
German	:	sehr 1057
Hungarian	:	nagyon 1057
Italian	:	vero; molto 1057
Croatian	:	veoma; vrlo 1057
Norwegian	:	meget 1057
Polish	:	bardzo 1057
Portuguese	:	muito 1057
Rumanian	:	foarte; mult 1057
Slovak	:	veľmi; veľa 1057
Spanish	:	muy 1057
Swedish	:	mycket 1057
Turkish	:	çok; pek 1057
Russian	:	очень 1057
Serbian	:	веома 1057
Ukrainian	:	дуже; сильно 1057

1058 VESSEL s. see 105 BOAT

1059 VEST s. see 1067 (Brit.) waist-coat

1060 VILLAGE s.

Czech : vesnice, f. 1060
Danish : Landsby, m./c. 1060
Dutch : het dorp 1060
Finnish : kylä 1060
French : village, m. 1060
German : das Dorf 1060
Hungarian : falu 1060
Italian : villaggio, m. 1060
Croatian : selo, n. 1060
Norwegian : landsby, m. 1060
Polish : wieś, f. 1060
Portuguese : aldeia, a 1060
Rumanian : satul 1060
Slovak : dedina, f. 1060
Spanish : aldea, f. 1060
Swedish : by-n 1060
Turkish : köy 1060
Russian : деревня, f. 1060
Serbian : село, n. 1060
Ukrainian : село, n. 1060

1061 VINEGAR s.

Czech : ocet, m. 1061
Danish : Eddike, c. 1061
Dutch : de azijn 1061
Finnish : etikka 1061
French : vinaigre, m. 1061
German : der Essig 1061
Hungarian : ecet 1061
Italian : aceto, m. 1061
Croatian : ocat, m. 1061
Norwegian : eddik, m. 1061
Polish : ocet, m. 1061
Portuguese : vinagre, o 1061
Rumanian : oţet, n. 1061
Slovak : ocot, m. 1061
Spanish : vinagre, m. 1061
Swedish : ättika-n 1061
Turkish : sirke 1061
Russian : уксус, m. 1061
Serbian : сирће, n. 1061
Ukrainian : оцет, m. 1061

1062 VIOLET s.

Czech : fialka, f. 1062
Danish : Viol, m./c. 1062
Dutch : het viooltje 1062
Finnish : orvokki 1062
French : violette, f. 1062
German : das Veilchen 1062
Hungarian : ibolya 1062
Italian : violetta, f. 1062
Croatian : ljubičica, f. 1062
Norwegian : fiol, m. 1062
Polish : fiołek, m. 1062
Portuguese : violeta, a 1062
Rumanian : vioreă, f. 1062
Slovak : fialka, f. 1062
Spanish : violeta, f. 1062
Swedish : viol-en 1062
Turkish : menekşe 1062
Russian : фиалка, f. 1062
Serbian : љубичица, f. 1062
Ukrainian : фіялка, f. 1062

1063 VIOLET-PURPLE adj.

Czech : fialový 1063
Danish : violet 1063
Dutch : lila 1063
Finnish : sinipunainen 1063
French : violet 1063
German : violett 1063
Hungarian : ibolya színü 1063
Italian : violetto 1063
Croatian : ljubičast 1063
Norwegian : fiolett 1063
Polish : fijoletowy 1063
Portuguese : côr violete 1063
Rumanian : violet 1063
Slovak : fialový 1063
Spanish : color violeta 1063
Swedish : violett 1063
Turkish : menekşe 1063
Russian : фиолетовый 1063
Serbian : љубичаст 1063
Ukrainian : фіолетний 1063

1064 VIOLIN s.

Czech : housle, pl. 1064
Danish : Violin, m./c. 1064
Dutch : de viool 1064
Finnish : viulu 1064
French : violon, m. 1064
German : die Geige 1064
Hungarian : hegedü 1064
Italian : violino, m. 1064
Croatian : gulse, pl. 1064
Norwegian : fiolin, m. 1064
Polish : skrzypce, pl. 1064
Portuguese : violino, o 1064
Rumanian : vioară, f. 1064
Slovak : husle, pl. 1064
Spanish : violín, m. 1064
Swedish : fiol-en 1064
Turkish : keman 1064
Russian : скрипка, f. 1064
Serbian : гусле, pl. 1064
Ukrainian : скрипка, f. 1064

1065 VIOLONCELLO s.

Czech : čelo, n. 1065
Danish : Cello, c. 1065
Dutch : de cello 1065
Finnish : cello 1065
French : violoncelle, m. 1065
German : das Cello 1065
Hungarian : cselló 1065
Italian : violoncello, m. 1065
Croatian : čelo, n. 1065
Norwegian : cello, m. 1065
Polish : czelo, n. 1065
Portuguese : violoncelo, o 1065
Rumanian : violoncelul 1065
Slovak : čelo, n. 1065
Spanish : violoncelo, m. 1065
Swedish : cello-n 1065
Turkish : cello 1065
Russian : виолончель, f. 1065
Serbian : чело, n. 1065
Ukrainian : віольончеля, f. 1065

1066 W. C. see 1012 TOILET

1067 WAISTCOAT s.

Czech	: vesta, *f.* 1067
Danish	: Vest, *m./c.* 1067
Dutch	: het vest 1067
Finnish	: liivit 1067
French	: gilet, *m.* 1067
German	: die Weste 1067
Hungarian	: mellény 1067
Italian	: panciotto, *m.* 1067
Croatian	: prsluk, *m.* 1067
Norwegian	: vest, *m.* 1067
Polish	: kamizelka, *f.* 1067
Portuguese	: colete, *o* 1067
Rumanian	: vesta, *f.* 1067
Slovak	: vesta, *f.* 1067
Spanish	: chaleco, *m.* 1067
Swedish	: väst-en 1067
Turkish	: yelek 1067
Russian	: жилетка, *f.* 1067
Serbian	: прслук, *m.* 1067
Ukrainian	: камізелька, *f.* 1067

1068 WAIT v.

Czech	: čekati 1068
Danish	: vente 1068
Dutch	: wachten 1068
Finnish	: odottaa 1068
French	: attendre 1068
German	: warten 1068
Hungarian	: várni 1068
Italian	: aspettare 1068
Croatian	: čekati 1068
Norwegian	: vente 1068
Polish	: czekać 1068
Portuguese	: esperar 1068
Rumanian	: a aştepta 1068
Slovak	: čakat' 1068
Spanish	: esperar 1068
Swedish	: vänta 1068
Turkish	: beklemek 1068
Russian	: ждать 1068
Serbian	: чекати 1068
Ukrainian	: чекати 1068

1069 WAITER s.

Czech	: číšník, *m.* 1069
Danish	: Tjener, *m./c.* 1069
Dutch	: de kellner 1069
Finnish	: tarjoilija 1069
French	: garçon de café, *m.* 1069
German	: der Kellner 1069
Hungarian	: pincér 1069
Italian	: cameriere, *m.* 1069
Croatian	: konobar, *m.* 1069
Norwegian	: kelner, *m.* 1069
Polish	: kelner, *m.* 1069
Portuguese	: criado, *o* 1069
Rumanian	: chelnerul 1069
Slovak	: čašník, *m.* 1069
Spanish	: mozo, *m.* 1069
Swedish	: kyparen 1069
Turkish	: garson 1069
Russian	: кельнер, *m.* 1069
Serbian	: конобар, *m.* 1069
Ukrainian	: кельнер, *m.* 1069

1070 WALK v.

Czech	: choditi 1070
Danish	: gaa 1070
Dutch	: gaan 1070
Finnish	: käydä, mennä 1070
French	: marcher 1070
German	: gehen 1070
Hungarian	: menni 1070
Italian	: andare 1070
Croatian	: ići 1070
Norwegian	: gå 1070
Polish	: iść 1070
Portuguese	: andar, ir 1070
Rumanian	: a merge 1070
Slovak	: íst' 1070
Spanish	: andar 1070
Swedish	: gå 1070
Turkish	: gitmek 1070
Russian	: итти 1070
Serbian	: иħи 1070
Ukrainian	: іти 1070

1071 WALLET s.

Czech	: náprsní taška, *f.* 1071
Danish	: Tegnebog, *f.* 1071
Dutch	: de portefeuille 1071
Finnish	: lompakko 1071
French	: porte-feuille, *m.* 1071
German	: die Brieftasche 1071
Hungarian	: pénztárca 1071
Italian	: portafogli, *m.* 1071
Croatian	: budjelar, *f.* 1071
Norwegian	: lommebok, *f.* 1071
Polish	: portfel, *m.* 1071
Portuguese	: carteira, *a* 1071
Rumanian	: portofoliul 1071
Slovak	: náprsná taška, *f.* 1071
Spanish	: cartera, *f.* 1071
Swedish	: plånbok-en 1071
Turkish	: cüzdan 1071
Russian	: бумажник, *m.* 1071
Serbian	: буħелар, *m.* 1071
Ukrainian	: портфель, *m.* 1071

1072 WALNUT s.

Czech	: vlašský ořech, *m.* 1072
Danish	: Valnöd, *m./c.* 1072
Dutch	: de walnoot 1072
Finnish	: saksanpähkinä 1072
French	: noix, *f.* 1072
German	: die Walnuss 1072
Hungarian	: dió 1072
Italian	: noce, *f.* 1072
Croatian	: orah, *m.* 1072
Norwegian	: valnött, *f.* 1072
Polish	: orzech włoski, *m.* 1072
Portuguese	: noz, *a* 1072
Rumanian	: nuca, *f.* 1072
Slovak	: orech, *m.* 1072
Spanish	: nuez, *m.* 1072
Swedish	: valnöt-en 1072
Turkish	: ceviz 1072
Russian	: грецкии орех, *m.* 1072
Serbian	: орах, *m.* 1072
Ukrainian	: волоський горіх, *m.* 1072

1073 WARDROBE s.

Czech	:	skříň, f. 1073
Danish	:	Skab, n. 1073
Dutch	:	de kast 1073
Finnish	:	kaappi 1073
French	:	armoire, f. 1073
German	:	der Schrank 1073
Hungarian	:	szekrény 1073
Italian	:	armadio, m. 1073
Croatian	:	ormar, m. 1073
Norwegian	:	skap, n. 1073
Polish	:	szafa, f. 1073
Portuguese	:	guarda-fato, o 1073
Rumanian	:	dulapul 1073
Slovak	:	skriňa, f. 1073
Spanish	:	armario, m. 1073
Swedish	:	skåp-et 1073
Turkish	:	dolap 1073
Russian	:	шкаф, m. 1073
Serbian	:	ормар, m. 1073
Ukrainian	:	шафа, f. 1073

1074 WAREHOUSE s.

Czech	:	obchodní dům, m. 1074
Danish	:	Varehus, n. 1074
Dutch	:	het magazijn 1074
Finnish	:	kauppaliike 1074
French	:	bazar, m. 1074
German	:	das Kaufhaus 1074
Hungarian	:	áruház 1074
Italian	:	negozio, m. 1074
Croatian	:	trgovačka kuća, f. 1074
Norwegian	:	handelshus, n. 1074
Polish	:	dom handlowy, m. 1074
Portuguese	:	casa comercial, a 1074
Rumanian	:	magazinul universal 1074
Slovak	:	obchodný dom, m. 1074
Spanish	:	almacén; depósito, m. 1074
Swedish	:	varuhus-et 1074
Turkish	:	ticarethane 1074
Russian	:	универмаг, m.1074
Serbian	:	продаваоница, f. 1074
Ukrainian	:	торговельний дім, m. 1074

1075 WARM adj.

Czech	:	teplý 1075
Danish	:	varm 1075
Dutch	:	warm 1075
Finnish	:	lämmin 1075
French	:	chaud 1075
German	:	warm 1075
Hungarian	:	meleg 1075
Italian	:	caldo 1075
Croatian	:	topao 1075
Norwegian	:	varm 1075
Polish	:	ciepły 1075
Portuguese	:	quente 1075
Rumanian	:	cald 1075
Slovak	:	teplý 1075
Spanish	:	cálido 1075
Swedish	:	varm 1075
Turkish	:	siçak 1075
Russian	:	тепло; -ый 1075
Serbian	:	топао 1075
Ukrainian	:	теплий 1075

1076 WASH v.

Czech	:	mýti (se) 1076
Danish	:	vaske 1076
Dutch	:	wasschen 1076
Finnish	:	pestä 1076
French	:	laver 1076
German	:	waschen 1076
Hungarian	:	mosni 1076
Italian	:	lavare 1076
Croatian	:	prati 1076
Norwegian	:	vaske 1076
Polish	:	prać 1076
Portuguese	:	lavar 1076
Rumanian	:	a späla 1076
Slovak	:	umývat' 1076
Spanish	:	lavar 1076
Swedish	:	tvätta 1076
Turkish	:	yikamak 1076
Russian	:	мыть 1076
Serbian	:	прати 1076
Ukrainian	:	прати 1076

1077 WASH-ROOM s.

Czech	:	umývárna, f. 1077
Danish	:	Vaskerum, n. 1077
Dutch	:	de waschruimte 1077
Finnish	:	pesuhuone 1077
French	:	lavabos, m. pl. 1077
German	:	der Waschraum 1077
Hungarian	:	mosdóhelyiség 1077
Italian	:	lavatoio, m. 1077
Croatian	:	umivaonica, f. 1077
Norwegian	:	vaskerum, n. 1077
Polish	:	umywalnia, f. 1077
Portuguese	:	lavatório, o 1077
Rumanian	:	spälatorul 1077
Slovak	:	umyváreň, f. 1077
Spanish	:	lavabo, m. 1077
Swedish	:	tvättrumm-et 1077
Turkish	:	yikama odasi 1077
Russian	:	умывальная, f. 1077
Serbian	:	умиваоница, f. 1077
Ukrainian	:	умивальня, f. 1077

1078 WASP s.

Czech	:	vosa, f. 1078
Danish	:	Hveps, m./c. 1078
Dutch	:	de wesp 1078
Finnish	:	ampiainen 1078
French	:	guêpe, f. 1078
German	:	die Wespe 1078
Hungarian	:	darázs 1078
Italian	:	vespa, f. 1078
Croatian	:	osa, f. 1078
Norwegian	:	hveps, m. 1078
Polish	:	osa, f. 1078
Portuguese	:	vespa, a 1078
Rumanian	:	viespea 1078
Slovak	:	osa, f. 1078
Spanish	:	avispa, f. 1078
Swedish	:	getin-en 1078
Turkish	:	eşek arisi 1078
Russian	:	oca, f. 1078
Serbian	:	oca, f. 1078
Ukrainian	:	oca, f. 1078

1079 WATCH s.

Czech	: hodinky, *pl.*	1079
Danish	: Lommeur, *n.*	1079
Dutch	: het horloge	1079
Finnish	: taskukello	1079
French	: montre de poche	1079
German	: die Taschenuhr	1079
Hungarian	: zsebóra	1079
Italian	: orologio da tasca, *m.*	1079
Croatian	: džepni sat, *m.*	1079
Norwegian	: lommeur, *n.*	1079
Polish	: zegarek kieszonkowy, *m.*	1079
Portuguese	: relógio de algibeira, *o*	1079
Rumanian	: ceasul de buzunar	1079
Slovak	: vreckové hodinky	1079
Spanish	: reloj de bolsillo	1079
Swedish	: fickur-et	1079
Turkish	: cep saati	1079
Russian	: часы карманные, *pl.*	1079
Serbian	: џепни сат, *m.*	1079
Ukrainian	: кишеньковий годинник, *m.*	1079

1080 WATER s.

Czech	: voda, *f.*	1080
Danish	: Vand, *c.*	1080
Dutch	: het water	1080
Finnish	: vesi	1080
French	: eau, *f.*	1080
German	: das Wasser	1080
Hungarian	: viz	1080
Italian	: acqua, *f.*	1080
Croatian	: voda, *f.*	1080
Norwegian	: vann	1080
Polish	: woda, *f.*	1080
Portuguese	: água, *a*	1080
Rumanian	: apă, *f.*	1080
Slovak	: voda, *f.*	1080
Spanish	: agua, *f.*	1080
Swedish	: vatten; vattnet	1080
Turkish	: su	1080
Russian	: вода, *f.*	1080
Serbian	: вода, *f.*	1080
Ukrainian	: вода, *f.*	1080

1081 WATER LEVEL see 922 SPIRIT LEVEL

1082 WAY s.

Czech	: cesta, *f.*	1082
Danish	: Vej, *m./c.*	1082
Dutch	: de weg	1082
Finnish	: tie	1082
French	: chemin, *m.*	1082
German	: der Weg	1082
Hungarian	: az út	1082
Italian	: pia, *f.*	1082
Croatian	: put	1082
Norwegian	: vei, *m.*	1082
Polish	: droga, *f.*	1082
Portuguese	: caminho, *o*	1082
Rumanian	: drumul	1082
Slovak	: cesta, *f.*	1082
Spanish	: camino, *m.*	1082
Swedish	: väg-en	1082
Turkish	: yol	1082
Russian	: дорога, *f.*	1082
Serbian	: пут, *m.*	1082
Ukrainian	: дорога, *f.*	1082

1083 WEDDING s.

Czech	: svatba, *f.*	1083
Danish	: Bryllup, *n.*	1083
Dutch	: de bruiloft	1083
Finnish	: häät	1083
French	: noce	1083
German	: die Hochzeit	1083
Hungarian	: esküvö	1083
Italian	: nozze, *f. pl.*	1083
Croatian	: svadba, *f.*	1083
Norwegian	: bryllup, *n.*	1083
Polish	: wesele, *n.*	1083
Portuguese	: casamento, *o*	1083
Rumanian	: nunta, *f.*	1083
Slovak	: svatba, *f.*	1083
Spanish	: boda, *f.*	1083
Swedish	: bröllop-et	1083
Turkish	: dügün	1083
Russian	: свадба, *f.*	1083
Serbian	: свадба, *f.*	1083
Ukrainian	: весілля, *f.*	1083

1084 WEDDING-RING s.

Czech	: snubní prsten, *m.*	1084
Danish	: Vielsesring, *m./c.*	1084
Dutch	: de trouwring	1084
Finnish	: vihkisormus	1084
French	: alliance, *m.*	1084
German	: der Trauring	1084
Hungarian	: jegygyürü	1084
Italian	: fede, *f.*	1084
Croatian	: vjerenički prsten, *m.*	1084
Norwegian	: vielsesring, *m.*	1084
Polish	: pierścień ślubny, *m.*	1084
Portuguese	: anel de casamento, *o*	1084
Rumanian	: verigeta, *f.*	1084
Slovak	: snubný prsteň, *m.*	1084
Spanish	: anillo nupcial, *m.*	1084
Swedish	: vigselring-en	1084
Turkish	: nikâh yüzüğü	1084
Russian	: обручальное кольцо, *n.*	1084
Serbian	: веренички прстен, *m.*	1084
Ukrainian	: шлюбний перстень, *m.*	1084

1085 WEDNESDAY s.

Czech	: středa, *f.*	1085
Danish	: Onsdag, *m.*	1085
Dutch	: de woensdag	1085
Finnish	: keskiviikkoo	1085
French	: mercredi, *m.*	1085
German	: der Mittwoch	1085
Hungarian	: szerdda	1085
Italian	: mercoledi, *m.*	1085
Croatian	: srieda, *f.*	1085
Norwegian	: onsdag, *m.*	1085
Polish	: środa, *f.*	1085
Portuguese	: quarta-feira, *a*	1085
Rumanian	: Miercuri, *f.*	1085
Slovak	: streda, *f.*	1085
Spanish	: miércoles, *m.*	1085
Swedish	: onsdagen	1085
Turkish	: çarşenbe	1085
Russian	: среда, *f.*	1085
Serbian	: среда, *f.*	1085
Ukrainian	: середа, *f.*	1085

1086 WEEK s.

Czech	:	týden, m.	1086
Danish	:	Uge, m.	1086
Dutch	:	de week	1086
Finnish	:	viikko	1086
French	:	semaine, f.	1086
German	:	die Woche	1086
Hungarian	:	hét	1086
Italian	:	settimana, f.	1086
Croatian	:	sedmica, f.	1086
Norwegian	:	uke, f.	1086
Polish	:	tydzień, m.	1086
Portuguese	:	semana, a	1086
Rumanian	:	săptămîna, f.	1086
Slovak	:	týždeň, m.	1086
Spanish	:	semana, f.	1086
Swedish	:	veckan	1086
Turkish	:	hafta	1086
Russian	:	неделя, f.	1086
Serbian	:	седмица, f.	1086
Ukrainian	:	тiждень, m.	1086

1089 WHAT pron.

Czech	:	co; což; jaký	1089	
Danish	:	hvilken; hvad for en	1089	1089
Dutch	:	wat; welk	1089	
Finnish	:	mikä; mitä	1089	
French	:	quoi; que; quel ...	1089	1089
German	:	was; was für ein ...	1089	1089
Hungarian	:	mi? micsoda	1089	
Italian	:	che; che cosa	1089	
Croatian	:	što	1089	
Norwegian	:	hva	1089	
Polish	:	co	1089	
Portuguese	:	que; qual	1089	
Rumanian	:	ce; ceea ce	1089	
Slovak	:	čo; aký	1089	
Spanish	:	que; que cosa	1089	
Swedish	:	vad; vilken	1089	
Turkish	:	ne; nedir	1089	
Russian	:	что	1089	
Serbian	:	што	1089	
Ukrainian	:	що	1089	

1087 WELL s. (in the earth)

Czech	:	studna, f.	1087
Danish	:	Brönd, m./c.	1087
Dutch	:	de put	1087
Finnish	:	kaivo	1087
French	:	puits, m.	1087
German	:	der Brunnen	1087
Hungarian	:	kút	1087
Italian	:	fontana, f.	1087
Croatian	:	bunar, m.	1087
Norwegian	:	brönn, m.	1087
Polish	:	studnia, f.	1087
Portuguese	:	poço, o	1087
Rumanian	:	fîntâna, f.	1087
Slovak	:	studňa, f.	1087
Spanish	:	pozo, m.	1087
Swedish	:	brunn-en	1087
Turkish	:	çeşme	1087
Russian	:	колодезь, ·m.	1087
Serbian	:	бунар, m.	1087
Ukrainian	:	студня; .криниця, f.	1087

1090 WHEAT s.

Czech	:	pšenice, f.	1090
Danish	:	hvede. m./c.	1090
Dutch	:	de tarwe	1090
Finnish	:	vehnä	1090
French	:	blé, m.	1090
German	:	der Weizen	1090
Hungarian	:	búza	1090
Italian	:	frumento, m.	1090
Croatian	:	pšenica, f.	1090
Norwegian	:	hvete, m.	1090
Polish	:	pszenica, f.	1090
Portuguese	:	trigo, o	1090
Rumanian	:	grâul	1090
Slovak	:	pšenica, f.	1090
Spanish	:	trigo, m.	1090
Swedish	:	vete-t	1090
Turkish	:	buğday	1090
Russian	:	пшеница, f.	1090
Serbian	:	пшеница, f.	1090
Ukrainian	:	пшениця, f.	1090

1088 WEST s.

Czech	:	západ, m.	1088	
Danish	:	Vest, n.	1088	
Dutch	:	Westen	1088	
Finnish	:	länsi	1088	
French	:	ouest; occident, m.	1088	
German	:	der West (en)	1088	
Hungarian	:	nyugat	1088	
Italian	:	occidente; occaso, m.	1088	
Croatian	:	zapad, m.	1088	
Norwegian	:	vest, c.	1088	
Polish	:	zapad, m.	1088	
Portuguese	:	oeste, m.	1088	
Rumanian	:	vest, c.	1088	
Slovak	:	západ, m.	1088	
Spanish	:	oeste; occidente, m.	1088	
Swedish	:	väst (an)	1088	
Turkish	:	garp	1088	
Russian	:	запад, m.	1088	
Serbian	:	запад, m.	1088	
Ukrainian	:	захiд, m.	1088	

1091 WHERE?

Czech	:	kde	1091
Danish	:	hvor	1091
Dutch	:	waar	1091
Finnish	:	missä	1091
French	:	où	1091
German	:	wo	1091
Hungarian	:	hol	1091
Italian	:	dove	1091
Croatian	:	gdje	1091
Norwegian	:	hvor	1091
Polish	:	gdzie	1091
Portuguese	:	onde	1091
Rumanian	:	unde	1091
Slovak	:	kde	1091
Spanish	:	dónde	1091
Swedish	:	var	1091
Turkish	:	nerde	1091
Russian	:	Где?	1091
Serbian	:	Где?	1091
Ukrainian	:	Де?	1091

1092 WHERE FROM?

Czech	:	odkud 1092
Danish	:	hvorfra 1092
Dutch	:	vanwaar 1092
Finnish	:	mistä 1092
French	:	d'où 1092
German	:	woher 1092
Hungarian	:	honnan 1092
Italian	:	da dove 1092
Croatian	:	otkuda 1092
Norwegian	:	hvorfra 1092
Polish	:	skad 1092
Portuguese	:	donde 1092
Rumanian	:	de unde 1092
Slovak	:	odkial' 1092
Spanish	:	de dónde 1092
Swedish	:	varifrån 1092
Turkish	:	nereden 1092
Russian	:	Откуда? 1092
Serbian	:	Откуда? 1092
Ukrainian	:	Звідки? 1092

1093 WHERE TO?

Czech	:	kam 1093
Danish	:	hvorhen 1093
Dutch	:	waarheen 1093
Finnish	:	minne 1093
French	:	où 1093
German	:	wohin 1093
Hungarian	:	hová 1093
Italian	:	dove; per dove 1093
Croatian	:	kamo 1093
Norwegian	:	hvorhen 1093
Polish	:	którędy 1093
Portuguese	:	para onde 1093
Rumanian	:	încotro 1093
Slovak	:	kam 1093
Spanish	:	adónde? 1093
Swedish	:	varthän 1093
Turkish	:	nereye 1093
Russian	:	куда? 1093
Serbian	:	Камо? 1093
Ukrainian	:	Куди? 1093

1094 WHITE adj.

Czech	:	bílý 1094
Danish	:	hvid 1094
Dutch	:	wit 1094
Finnish	:	valkea 1094
French	:	blanc 1094
German	:	weiss 1094
Hungarian	:	fehér 1094
Italian	:	bianco 1094
Croatian	:	bijel 1094
Norwegian	:	hvit 1094
Polish	:	biały 1094
Portuguese	:	branco 1094
Rumanian	:	alb 1094
Slovak	:	biely 1094
Spanish	:	blanco 1094
Swedish	:	vit 1094
Turkish	:	beyaz, ak 1094
Russian	:	белый 1094
Serbian	:	бео 1094
Ukrainian	:	білий 1094

1095 WHITE WINE s.

Czech	:	bílé víno, n. 1095
Danish	:	Hvid Vin, m./c. 1095
Dutch	:	de witte wijn 1095
Finnish	:	valkoviini 1095
French	:	vin blanc, m. 1095
German	:	der Weisswein 1095
Hungarian	:	fehérbor 1095
Italian	:	vino bianco, m. 1095
Croatian	:	bijelo vino, n. 1095
Norwegian	:	hvit vin, m. 1095
Polish	:	białe wino, n. 1095
Portuguese	:	vinho branco, o 1095
Rumanian	:	vinul alb 1095
Slovak	:	biele víno, n. 1095
Spanish	:	vino blanco, m. 1095
Swedish	:	vitt-vinet 1095
Turkish	:	beyaz şarap 1095
Russian	:	белое вино, n. 1095
Serbian	:	бело вино, n. 1095
Ukrainian	:	біле вино, n. 1095

1096 WHY?

Czech	:	proč 1096
Danish	:	hvorfor 1096
Dutch	:	waarom 1096
Finnish	:	miksi 1096
French	:	pourquoi 1096
German	:	warum 1096
Hungarian	:	miért 1096
Italian	:	perché 1096
Croatian	:	zašto 1096
Norwegian	:	hvorfor 1096
Polish	:	czemu 1096
Portuguese	:	porque 1096
Rumanian	:	dece 1096
Slovak	:	prečo 1096
Spanish	:	por qué 1096
Swedish	:	varför 1096
Turkish	:	niçin 1096
Russian	:	Почему? 1096
Serbian	:	Зашто? 1096
Ukrainian	:	Чому? 1096

1097 WIFE   see 1105 WOMAN

1098 WILD PIG s. (boar)

Czech	:	divoké prase, n. 1098
Danish	:	Vildsvin, n. 1098
Dutch	:	het wilde zwijn 1098
Finnish	:	metsäkarju 1098
French	:	sanglier, m. 1098
German	:	das Wildschwein 1098
Hungarian	:	vaddisznó 1098
Italian	:	cinghiale, m. 1098
Croatian	:	divlja svinja, f. 1098
Norwegian	:	villsvin, n. 1098
Polish	:	dzik, m. 1098
Portuguese	:	javali, o 1098
Rumanian	:	porcul mistret 1098
Slovak	:	diviak, m. 1098
Spanish	:	jabalí, m. 1098
Swedish	:	vild svin-et 1098
Turkish	:	yabani domuz 1098
Russian	:	дикая свинья, f. 1098
Serbian	:	дивльа свиньа, f. 1098
Ukrainian	:	дика свиня, f. 1098

1099 WILLOW s.

Czech	:	vrba, f. 1099
Danish	:	Pil; Piletrae, n.; Vidie 1099
Dutch	:	de wilg 1099
Finnish	:	paju 1099
French	:	saule, m. 1099
German	:	die Weide 1099
Hungarian	:	füzfa 1099
Italian	:	salice, m. 1099
Croatian	:	vrba, f. 1099
Norwegian	:	pil; vidje, f. 1099
Polish	:	wierzba, b. 1099
Portuguese	:	vimeiro, o 1099
Rumanian	:	salciä, f. 1099
Slovak	:	vrba, f. 1099
Spanish	:	mimbrera, f. 1099
Swedish	:	videträd-et 1099
Turkish	:	suyut ağaci 1099
Russian	:	ива, f. 1099
Serbian	:	врба, f. 1099
Ukrainian	:	верба, f. 1099

1102 WINTER s.

Czech	:	zima, f. 1102
Danish	:	Vinter, m. 1102
Dutch	:	de winter 1102
Finnish	:	talvi 1102
French	:	hiver, m. 1102
German	:	der Winter 1102
Hungarian	:	tél 1102
Italian	:	inverno, m. 1102
Croatian	:	zima, f. 1102
Norwegian	:	vinter, m. 1102
Polish	:	zima, f. 1102
Portuguese	:	inverno, o 1102
Rumanian	:	iarnä, f. 1102
Slovak	:	zima, f. 1102
Spanish	:	invierno, m. 1102
Swedish	:	vinter-n 1102
Turkish	:	kiş 1102
Russian	:	зима, f. 1102
Serbian	:	зима, f. 1102
Ukrainian	:	зима, f. 1102

1100 WIND s.

Czech	:	vítr, m. 1100
Danish	:	Vind, m. 1100
Dutch	:	de wind 1100
Finnish	:	tuuli 1100
French	:	vent, m. 1100
German	:	der Wind 1100
Hungarian	:	szél 1100
Italian	:	vento, m. 1100
Croatian	:	vjetar, m. 1100
Norwegian	:	vind, m. 1100
Polish	:	wiatr, m. 1100
Portuguese	:	vento, o 1100
Rumanian	:	văntul 1100
Slovak	:	vietor, m. 1100
Spanish	:	viento, m. 1100
Swedish	:	vind-en 1100
Turkish	:	rüzğâr 1100
Russian	:	ветер, m. 1100
Serbian	:	ветар, m. 1100
Ukrainian	:	вітер, m. 1100

1103 WIRELESS s. (Radio)

Czech	:	radio, n. 1103
Danish	:	Radio, m. 1103
Dutch	:	het radio 1103
Finnish	:	radio 1103
French	:	radio, f. 1103
German	:	das Radio 1103
Hungarian	:	a rádió 1103
Italian	:	radio, f. 1103
Croatian	:	radio, n. 1103
Norwegian	:	radio, n. 1103
Polish	:	rádio, n. 1103
Portuguese	:	rádio, o 1103
Rumanian	:	aparatul de radio 1103
Slovak	:	rádio, n. 1103
Spanish	:	el aparato de radio 1103
Swedish	:	radio-n 1103
Turkish	:	radio 1103
Russian	:	радиоапарат, m. 1103
Serbian	:	радио, n. 1103
Ukrainian	:	радійо, n. 1103

1101 WINDOW s.

Czech	:	okno, n. 1101
Danish	:	Vindu, c. 1101
Dutch	:	het raam 1101
Finnish	:	ikkuna 1101
French	:	fenêtre, f. 1101
German	:	das Fenster 1101
Hungarian	:	ablak 1101
Italian	:	finestra, f. 1101
Croatian	:	prozor, m. 1101
Norwegian	:	vindu, n. 1101
Polish	:	okno, n. 1101
Portuguese	:	janela, a 1101
Rumanian	:	fereastră, f. 1101
Slovak	:	oblok, m. 1101
Spanish	:	ventana, f. 1101
Swedish	:	fönster-et 1101
Turkish	:	pencere 1101
Russian	:	окно, n. 1101
Serbian	:	прозор, m. 1101
Ukrainian	:	вікно, n. 1101

1104 WIRE-SHEARS s.

Czech	:	nůžky na drát, pl. 1104
Danish	:	Traadsaks, m./c. 1104
Dutch	:	de draadschaar 1104
Finnish	:	rautalankasakset 1104
French	:	cisailles, f. pl. 1104
German	:	die Drahtschere 1104
Hungarian	:	drótvagóolló 1104
Italian	:	pinzetta, f. 1104
Croatian	:	skare za žicu, pl. 1104
Norwegian	:	trådsaks, f. 1104
Polish	:	nożyce blacharskie, n. pl. 1104
Portuguese	:	tesoura para arame, a 1104
Rumanian	:	foarfecele de täiat sârma 1104
Slovak	:	nožnice na drót, pl. 1104
Spanish	:	pinzas para alambre 1104
Swedish	:	trådsax-en 1104
Turkish	:	tel makasi 1104
Russian	:	ножницы для проволоки, pl. 1104
Serbian	:	маказе за жицу, pl. 1104
Ukrainian	:	ножиці блягарські, pl. 1104

162

1105 WOMAN s.

Czech	:	žena, f. 1105
Danish	:	Kvinde, f. 1105
Dutch	:	de vrouw 1105
Finnish	:	rouva 1105
French	:	femme, f. 1105
German	:	die Frau; das Weib 1105
Hungarian	:	nö 1105
Italian	:	donna, f. 1105
Croatian	:	žena, f. 1105
Norwegian	:	kvinne, f. 1105
Polish	:	kobieta, f. 1105
Portuguese	:	mulher, a 1105
Rumanian	:	femea 1105
Slovak	:	žena, f. 1105
Spanish	:	mujer, f. 1105
Swedish	:	kvinna-n 1105
Turkish	:	kadin 1105
Russian	:	женщина, f. 1105
Serbian	:	жена, f. 1105
Ukrainian	:	жінка, f. 1105

1106 WOOD s. (forest)

Czech	:	les, m. 1106
Danish	:	Skov, m./c. 1106
Dutch	:	het bosch 1106
Finnish	:	metsä 1106
French	:	forêt, f. 1106
German	:	der Wald 1106
Hungarian	:	erdö 1106
Italian	:	bosco, m. 1106
Croatian	:	šuma, f. 1106
Norwegian	:	skog, m. 1106
Polish	:	las, m. 1106
Portuguese	:	floresta, a 1106
Rumanian	:	pädurea, f. 1106
Slovak	:	les, m. 1106
Spanish	:	bosque, m. 1106
Swedish	:	skog-en 1106
Turkish	:	orman 1106
Russian	:	лес,1106
Serbian	:	шума, f. 1106
Ukrainian	:	ліс, m. 1106

1107 WOOL s.

Czech	:	vlna, f. 1107
Danish	:	Uld, m./c. 1107
Dutch	:	de wol 1107
Finnish	:	villa 1107
French	:	laine, f. 1107
German	:	die Wolle 1107
Hungarian	:	gyapjú 1107
Italian	:	lana, f. 1107
Croatian	:	vuna, f. 1107
Norwegian	:	ull, f. 1107
Polish	:	wełna, f. 1107
Portuguese	:	lã, a 1107
Rumanian	:	lâna, f. 1107
Slovak	:	vlna, f. 1107
Spanish	:	lana, f. 1107
Swedish	:	ylle-t 1107
Turkish	:	yun 1107
Russian	:	шерсть, m. 1107
Serbian	:	вуна, f. 1107
Ukrainian	:	вовна, f. 1107

1108 WORK v.

Czech	:	pracovati 1108
Danish	:	Arbejde 1108
Dutch	:	werken 1108
Finnish	:	tehdä työtä 1108
French	:	travailler 1108
German	:	arbeiten 1108
Hungarian	:	dolgozni 1108
Italian	:	lavorare 1108
Croatian	:	raditi 1108
Norwegian	:	arbeide 1108
Polish	:	pracować 1108
Portuguese	:	trabalhar 1108
Rumanian	:	a lucra 1108
Slovak	:	pracovat' 1108
Spanish	:	trabajar 1108
Swedish	:	arbeta 1108
Turkish	:	çalişmak 1108
Russian	:	работать 1108
Serbian	:	радити 1108
Ukrainian	:	працювати 1108

1109 WORKMAN s.

Czech	:	dělník, m. 1109
Danish	:	Arbeider, c. 1109
Dutch	:	de arbeider 1109
Finnish	:	työläinen 1109
French	:	ouvrier, m. 1109
German	:	der Arbeiter 1109
Hungarian	:	a munkás 1109
Italian	:	operaio, m. 1109
Croatian	:	radnik, m. 1109
Norwegian	:	arbeider, m. 1109
Polish	:	robotnik, m. 1109
Portuguese	:	operário, o 1109
Rumanian	:	lucrätorul 1109
Slovak	:	robotník, m. 1109
Spanish	:	obrero, m. 1109
Swedish	:	arbetare-n 1109
Turkish	:	isçi 1109
Russian	:	работник, m. 1109
Serbian	:	радник, 1109
Ukrainian	:	робітник, m. 1109

1110 WORKWOMAN s.

Czech	:	dělnice, f. 1110
Danish	:	Arbeider, c. 1110
Dutch	:	de arbeidster 1110
Finnish	:	työläisnaien 1110
French	:	l'ouvrière, f. 1110
German	:	die Arbeiterin 1110
Hungarian	:	a munkásnő 1110
Italian	:	operaia, f. 1110
Croatian	:	radnica, f. 1110
Norwegian	:	kvinnelig; arbeider, m. 1110
Polish	:	robotnica, f. 1110
Portuguese	:	operária, a 1110
Rumanian	:	lucrätoareă, f. 1110
Slovak	:	robotníčka, f. 1110
Spanish	:	obrera, f. 1110
Swedish	:	arbeterska-n 1110
Turkish	:	işci kadin 1110
Russian	:	работница, f. 1110
Serbian	:	радница, f. 1110
Ukrainian	:	робітниця, f. 1110

1111 WORRY *s.*   see **1031 TROUBLE**

1112 WREATH *s.*

Czech	: věnec, *m.* 1112
Danish	: Krans, *m./c.* 1112
Dutch	: de krans 1112
Finnish	: seppele 1112
French	: couronne, *f.* 1112
German	: der Kranz 1112
Hungarian	: koszorú 1112
Italian	: corona, *f.*; ghirlanda, *f.* 1112
Croatian	: vijenac, *m.* 1112
Norwegian	: krans, *m.* 1112
Polish	: wianek, *m.* 1112
Portuguese	: corôa (de flores), *f.* 1112
Rumanian	: coroană, *f.* 1112
Slovak	: veniec, *m.* 1112
Spanish	: corona, *f.* 1112
Swedish	: krans-en 1112
Turkish	: çelenk 1112
Russian	: венок, *f.* 1112
Serbian	: венац, *m.* 1112
Ukrainian	: вінок, *m.* 1112

1113 WRENCH *s.*

Czech	: šroubový (francouzský) klíč, *m.* 1113
Danish	: Skruenökkel, *m./c.* 1113
Dutch	: de schroefsleutel 1113
Finnish	: ruuviavain 1113
French	: clef à écrous, *f.* 1113
German	: der Schraubenschlüssel 1113
Hungarian	: csavarkulcs 1113
Italian	: chiave per viti, *f.* 1113
Croatian	: franzuz, *m.* 1113
Norwegian	: skrunökkel, *m.* 1113
Polish	: odkrętka, *f.* 1113
Portuguese	: chave de parafusos, *a* 1113
Rumanian	: cheia franceza, *f.* 1113
Slovak	: skrutkový kľúč, *m.* 1113
Spanish	: llave para tuerca 1113
Swedish	: skruvnyckel-n 1113
Turkish	: vida anahtori 1113
Russian	: гачный ключ, *m* 1113
Serbian	: франзуз, *m.* 1113
Ukrainian	: шрубоключ, *m.* 1113

1114 WRIST WATCH *s.*

Czech	: náramkové hodinky 1114
Danish	: Armbaandsur, *n.* 1114
Dutch	: het polshorloge 1114
Finnish	: rannekello 1114
French	: montre-bracelet, *f.* 1114
German	: die Armbanduhr 1114
Hungarian	: karóra 1114
Italian	: orologio da polso, *m.* 1114
Croatian	: ručni sat, *m.* 1114
Norwegian	: armbåndsur, *n.* 1114
Polish	: zegarek na rękę, *m.* 1114
Portuguese	: relógio de pulso, *o* 1114
Rumanian	: ceasul de mâna 1114
Slovak	: naramkove hodinky, *pl.* 1114
Spanish	: reloj de pulsera, *m.* 1114
Swedish	: armbandsur-et 1114
Turkish	: kol saati 1114
Russian	: часы наручные, *pl.* 1114
Serbian	: ручни сат, *m.* 1114
Ukrainian	: наручний годинник, *m.* 1114

1115 YEAR *s.*

Czech	: rok, *m.* 1115
Danish	: Aar, *n.* 1115
Dutch	: het jaar 1115
Finnish	: vuosi 1115
French	: année, *f.* 1115
German	: das Jahr 1115
Hungarian	: év 1115
Italian	: anno, *m.* 1115
Croatian	: godina, *f.* 1115
Norwegian	: år, *n.* 1115
Polish	: rok, *m.* 1115
Portuguese	: ano, *o* 1115
Rumanian	: an, *m.* 1115
Slovak	: rok, *m.* 1115
Spanish	: año, *m.* 1115
Swedish	: år-et 1115
Turkish	: sene 1115
Russian	: год, *m.* 1115
Serbian	: година, *f.* 1115
Ukrainian	: рік, *m.* 1115

1116 YELLOW *adj.*

Czech	: žlutý 1116
Danish	: gul 1116
Dutch	: geel 1116
Finnish	: keltainen 1116
French	: jaune 1116
German	: gelb 1116
Hungarian	: sárga 1116
Italian	: giallo 1116
Croatian	: žut 1116
Norwegian	: gul 1116
Polish	: żółty 1116
Portuguese	: amarelo 1116
Rumanian	: galben 1116
Slovak	: žltý 1116
Spanish	: amarillo 1116
Swedish	: gul 1116
Turkish	: sarga 1116
Russian	: желтый 1116
Serbian	: жут 1116
Ukrainian	: жовтий 1116

1117 YES

Czech	: ano 1117
Danish	: ja 1117
Dutch	: ja 1117
Finnish	: niin, kyllä 1117
French	: oui 1117
German	: ja 1117
Hungarian	: igen 1117
Italian	: si 1117
Croatian	: da 1117
Norwegian	: ja 1117
Polish	: tak 1117
Portuguese	: sim 1117
Rumanian	: da 1117
Slovak	: áno 1117
Spanish	: sí 1117
Swedish	: ja 1117
Turkish	: evet 1117
Russian	: дн 1117
Serbian	: да 1117
Ukrainian	: так 1117

1118 YESTERDAY *adv.*

Czech	: včera 1118
Danish	: i Gaar 1118
Dutch	: gisteren 1118
Finnish	: eilen 1118
French	: hier 1118
German	: gestern 1118
Hungarian	: tegnap 1118
Italian	: ieri 1118
Croatian	: jučer 1118
Norwegian	: igår 1118
Polish	: wczoraj 1118
Portuguese	: óntem 1118
Rumanian	: ieri 1118
Slovak	: včera 1118
Spanish	: ayer 1118
Swedish	: i går 1118
Turkish	: dun 1118
Russian	: вчера 1118
Serbian	: јуче 1118
Ukrainian	: вчора 1118

1119 YOUNG WOMAN see **597 MISS or LADY**

1120 ZERO *s.*

Czech	: nula, *f.* 1120
Danish	: Nul, *n.* 1120
Dutch	: nul 1120
Finnish	: nolla 1120
French	: zéro,*m.* 1120
German	: die Null 1120
Hungarian	: nulla 1120
Italian	: zero, *m.* 1120
Croatian	: nula, *f.* 1120
Norwegian	: null, *n.* 1120
Polish	: zero, 1120
Portuguese	: zéro, *o* 1120
Rumanian	: zero, *m.* 1120
Slovak	: nula, *f.* 1120
Spanish	: cero, *m.* 1120
Swedish	: noll 1120
Turkish	: sifir 1120
Russian	: нуль, *m.* 1120
Serbian	: нула, *f.* 1120
Ukrainian	: зеро, *n.* 1120

1121 ZINC *s.*

Czech	: zinek, *m.* 1121
Danish	: Zink, *n.* 1121
Dutch	: het zink 1121
Finnish	: sinkii 1121
French	: zink, *m.* 1121
German	: das Zink 1121
Hungarian	: a horgany 1121
Italian	: zingo, *m.* 1121
Croatian	: cink, *m.* 1121
Norwegian	: sink, *n.* 1121
Polish	: cynk, *m.* 1121
Portuguese	: zinco, *o* 1121
Rumanian	: zincul 1121
Slovak	: cink, *m.* 1121
Spanish	: zinc, *m.* 1121
Swedish	: zink-et 1121
Turkish	: çinko 1121
Russian	: цинк, *m.* 1121
Serbian	: цинк, *m.* 1121
Ukrainian	: цинк, *m.* 1121

1122 ZITHER *s.*

Czech	: citera, *f.* 1122
Danish	: Citer, *c.* 1122
Dutch	: de cither 1122
Finnish	: kantele 1122
French	: zither, *f.* 1122
German	: die Zither 1122
Hungarian	: citera 1122
Italian	: cetra, *f.* 1122
Croatian	: citra, *f.* 1122
Norwegian	: citar, *m.* 1122
Polish	: cytra, *f.* 1122
Portuguese	: cítara, *a* 1122
Rumanian	: citeră, *f.* 1122
Slovak	: citara, *f.* 1122
Spanish	: cítara, *f.* 1122
Swedish	: cittra-n 1122
Turkish	: kitara 1122
Russian	: цитра, *f.* 1122
Serbian	: цитра, *f.* 1122
Ukrainian	: цитра, *f.* 1122

1123 ZITHERN see **1122 ZITHER**

1124 Zn. see **1121 CHEM. ZINC**

EXPRESSIONS

1125 SUNDRIES

Czech	:	všeobecné 1125
Danish	:	Forskelligt 1125
Dutch	:	diverse 1125
Finnish	:	yleistä 1125
French	:	généralités 1125
German	:	allgemeines 1125
Hungarian	:	általános 1125
Italian	:	diverse cose 1125
Croatian	:	općenito 1125
Norwegian	:	forskjellig 1125
Polish	:	ogólne 1125
Portuguese	:	diversos 1125
Rumanian	:	diverse 1125
Slovak	:	všeobecné 1125
Spanish	:	generalidades 1125
Swedish	:	allmänt 1125
Turkish	:	umumi şeylar 1125
Russian	:	общее 1125
Serbian	:	обште 1125
Ukrainian	:	загальне 1125

1126 GOOD MORNING

Czech	:	Dobré jitro 1126
Danish	:	God Morgen 1126
Dutch	:	Goeden morgen 1126
Finnish	:	hyvää huomenta 1126
French	:	Bon jour 1126
German	:	Guten Morgen 1126
Hungarian	:	Jo reggelt 1126
Italian	:	Buon giorno 1126
Croatian	:	Dobro jutro 1126
Norwegian	:	God morgen 1126
Polish	:	Dobry ranek 1126
Portuguese	:	Bom dia 1126
Rumanian	:	Bună dimineata 1126
Slovak	:	Dobré ráno 1126
Spanish	:	Buenos días 1126
Swedish	:	God morgon 1126
Turkish	:	Gün aydin 1126
Russian	:	Доброе утро! 1126
Serbian	:	Добро јутро! 1126
Ukrainian	:	Доброго ранку! 1126

1127 GOOD DAY

Czech	:	Dobrý den 1127
Danish	:	God Dag 1127
Dutch	:	Goeden dag 1127
Finnish	:	Hyvää päivää 1127
French	:	Bonjour 1127
German	:	Guten Tag 1127
Hungarian	:	Jó napot 1127
Italian	:	Buona giornata 1127
Croatian	:	Dobar dan 1127
Norwegian	:	God dag 1127
Polish	:	Dzień dobry 1127
Portuguese	:	Bom dia 1127
Rumanian	:	Bună ziua 1127
Slovak	:	Dobrý deň 1127
Spanish	:	Buen día 1127
Swedish	:	God dag 1127
Turkish	:	Gün aydin 1127
Russian	:	Добрый день! 1127
Serbian	:	Добар дан! 1127
Ukrainian	:	Добрий день! 1127

1128 GOOD EVENING

Czech	:	Dobrý večer 1128
Danish	:	God Aften 1128
Dutch	:	Goeden avond 1128
Finnish	:	Hyvää iltaa 1128
French	:	Bon soir 1128
German	:	Guten Abend 1128
Hungarian	:	Jó estét 1128
Italian	:	Buona sera 1128
Croatian	:	Dobro veče 1128
Norwegian	:	God aften 1128
Polish	:	Dobry wieczór 1128
Portuguese	:	Boa noite 1128
Rumanian	:	Bună seara 1128
Slovak	:	Dobrý večer 1128
Spanish	:	Buenas tardes 1128
Swedish	:	God kväll; God afton 1128
Turkish	:	Aksaminiz hayir olsun 1128
Russian	:	Добрый вечер! 1128
Serbian	:	Добро вече! 1128
Ukrainian	:	Добрий вечір! 1128

1129 GOOD NIGHT

Czech	:	Dobrou noc 1129
Danish	:	God Nat 1129
Dutch	:	Goede Nacht 1129
Finnish	:	Hyvää yötä 1129
French	:	Bonne nuit 1129
German	:	Gute Nacht 1129
Hungarian	:	Jó éjszakát 1129
Italian	:	Buona notte 1129
Croatian	:	Laků noć 1129
Norwegian	:	God natt 1129
Polish	:	Dobra noc 1129
Portuguese	:	Boa noite 1128
Rumanian	:	Noapte bună 1129
Slovak	:	Dobrú noc 1129
Spanish	:	Buenas noches 1129
Swedish	:	God natt 1129
Turkish	:	Geceniz hayir olsun 1129
Russian	:	Спокойной ночи! 1129
Serbian	:	Лаку ноћ! 1129
Ukrainian	:	Добраніч! 1129

1130 SO LONG

Czech	:	Na shledanou 1130
Danish	:	Paa Gensyn 1130
Dutch	:	Tot ziens 1130
Finnish	:	Näkemiin 1130
French	:	Au revoir 1130
German	:	Auf Wiedersehen 1130
Hungarian	:	Viszontlátásra 1130
Italian	:	A rivederci 1130
Croatian	:	Do vidjenja 1130
Norwegian	:	På giensyn 1130
Polish	:	Do widzenia 1130
Portuguese	:	Até logo 1130
Rumanian	:	La revedere 1130
Slovak	:	Do videnia 1130
Spanish	:	Hasta la vista 1130
Swedish	:	På återseende 1130
Turkish	:	Yine görüşelim 1130
Russian	:	Досвидание! 1130
Serbian	:	До виђења! 1130
Ukrainian	:	До побачення! 1130

1131 HOW ARE YOU?

Czech	:	Jak se máte? Jak se máš? 1131
Danish	:	Hvordan har De det? 1131
Dutch	:	Hoe gaat het met U? 1131
Finnish	:	Kuinka voitte? 1131
French	:	Comment allez-vous? 1131
German	:	Wie geht es Ihnen?
Hungarian	:	Hogy van? 1131
Italian	:	Come sta? 1131
Croatian	:	Kako ste? 1131
Norwegian	:	Hvordan har De det? 1131
Polish	:	Jak się czujesz? 1131
Portuguese	:	Como passa?
Rumanian	:	Ce mal faceţi? 1131
Slovak	:	Ako sa mate? 1131
Spanish	:	¿Cómo está? 1131
Swedish	:	Huru mår ni? 1131
Turkish	:	Nasilsiniz? 1131
Russian	:	Как Вы поживаете! 1131
Serbian	:	Како сте? 1131
Ukrainian	:	Як ся маете? 1131

1132 I LOOK FOR A ROOM

Czech	:	Hledám byt 1132
Danish	:	Jeg söger Kvarter 1132
Dutch	:	Ik zoek onderdak 1132
Finnish	:	Etsin yösijaa 1132
French	:	Je cherche une chambre 1132
German	:	Ich suche Quartier 1132
Hungarian	:	szállást keresek 1132
Italian	:	Cerco un alloggio 1132
Croatian	:	Tražim stan 1132
Norwegian	:	Jeg söker et sted å bo 1132
Polish	:	Szukam pomieszkania 1132
Portuguese	:	Procurar a habitação 1132
Rumanian	:	Eu căut locuintă 1132
Slovak	:	hl'adám byt 1132
Spanish	:	Busco alojamiento 1132
Swedish	:	Jag söker rum 1132
Turkish	:	Ikamet ariyorum 1132
Russian	:	ищу квартиру 1132
Serbian	:	тражим стан 1132
Ukrainian	:	шукаю помешкання 1132

1133 I WANT TO EAT

Czech	:	chci jísti 1133
Danish	:	Jeg vil spise 1133
Dutch	:	Ik wil eten 1133
Finnish	:	haluaisin syödä 1133
French	:	Je veux manger 1133
German	:	Ich will essen 1133
Hungarian	:	Enni akarok 1133
Italian	:	Io voglio mangiare 1133
Croatian	:	hoću jesti 1133
Norwegian	:	Jeg vil pise 1133
Polish	:	Chcę jeść 1133
Portuguese	:	Quero comer 1133
Rumanian	:	Vreau să 1133
Slovak	:	(ja) chcem jest' 1133
Spanish	:	deseo comer 1133
Swedish	:	ag will äta 1133
Turkish	:	Yemek isteyorum 1133
Russian	:	я хочу есть 1133
Serbian	:	хоћу ести 1133
Ukrainian	:	я хочу їсти 1133

1134 I WANT TO DRINK

Czech	:	Chci píti 1134
Danish	:	Jeg vil drikke 1134
Dutch	:	Ik wil drinken 1134
Finnish	:	Haluaisin juoda 1134
French	:	Je veux boire 1134
German	:	Ich will trinken 1134
Hungarian	:	Inni akarok 1134
Italian	:	Io voglio bere 1134
Croatian	:	Hoću piti 1134
Norwegian	:	Jeg vil drikke 1134
Polish	:	Chcę pić 1134
Portuguese	:	Quero beber 1134
Rumanian	:	Vreau să beau 1134
Slovak	:	(Ja) chcem pit' 1134
Spanish	:	Deseo beber 1134
Swedish	:	Jag will dricka 1134
Turkish	:	Içmek isteyorum 1134
Russian	:	я хочу пить 1134
Serbian	:	хоћу пити 1134
Ukrainian	:	я хочу пити 1134

1135 WHAT IS YOUR NAME?

Czech	:	Jak se jmenujete? 1135
Danish	:	Hvad er Deres Navn? 1135
Dutch	:	Hoe heet U? 1135
Finnish	:	Mikkä on heidän nimi? 1135
French	:	Comment vous appelez-vous? 1135
German	:	Wie heissen Sie? 1135
Hungarian	:	Hogy hívnak? 1135
Italian	:	Come si chiama lei? 1135
Croatian	:	Kako vi zvate se? 1135
Norwegian	:	Hva er Deres navn? 1135
Polish	:	Nazwisko poprosze ... 1135
Portuguese	:	Como se chama? 1135
Rumanian	:	Care tău nume? 1135
Slovak	:	Ako sa volate? 1135
Spanish	:	¿Cómo se llama? 1135
Swedish	:	Hvad är din namn? 1135
Turkish	:	Isminiz ne? 1135
Russian	:	Как Вас зовут? 1135
Serbian	:	Како ви звате се? 1135
Ukrainian	:	Як ви називатеся? 1135

1138 WHERE IS THAT?

Czech	:	Kde je to? 1138
Danish	:	Hvor er det? 1138
Dutch	:	Waar is dat? 1138
Finnish	:	Missä on tämä? 1138
French	:	Où est cela? 1138
German	:	Wo ist das? 1138
Hungarian	:	Ho van az? 1138
Italian	:	Dove è? 1138
Croatian	:	Gdje je to? 1138
Norwegian	:	Hvor er det? 1138
Polish	:	Gdzie to jest? 1138
Portuguese	:	Onde está isso? 1138
Rumanian	:	Unde este aceasta? 1138
Slovak	:	Kde je to? 1138
Spanish	:	¿Dónde está esto? 1138
Swedish	:	Var är det? 1138
Turkish	:	Bu nerede? 1138
Russian	:	Где это? 1138
Serbian	:	Где је то? 1138
Ukrainian	:	Де це е? 1138

1136 DID YOU UNDERSTAND?

Czech	:	Rozuměl jste? 1136
Danish	:	Har De forstaaet? 1136
Dutch	:	Hebt U begrepen? 1136
Finnish	:	Oletteko ymmärtänyt? 1136
French	:	Avez-vous compris? 1136
German	:	Haben Sie verstanden? 1136
Hungarian	:	Megértette? 1136
Italian	:	Avete capito? 1136
Croatian	:	Jeste li razumjeli? 1136
Norwegian	:	Har De forstått? 1136
Polish	:	Czy zrozumieliście? 1136
Portuguese	:	O senhor compreenden? 1136
Rumanian	:	Ați înteles? 1136
Slovak	:	Rozumeli ste? 1136
Spanish	:	¿Ha entendido? 1136
Swedish	:	Har Ni förstått? 1136
Turkish	:	Anladiniz mi? 1136
Russian	:	Поняли? 1136
Serbian	:	јесте ли разумели? 1136
Ukrainian	:	Чи ви зрозуміли? 1136

1139 SHOW ME ...

Czech	:	Ukažte mi ... 1139
Danish	:	Vil De vise mig ... 1139
Dutch	:	Laat U me ... zien 1139
Finnish	:	Olkaa hyvä ja näyttäkää minulle 1139
French	:	Montrez-moi ... 1139
German	:	Zeigen Sie mir ... 1139
Hungarian	:	Mutassa meg nekem ... 1139
Italian	:	Indicate mi ... 1139
Croatian	:	Pokažite mi ... 1139
Norwegian	:	Vil De väre så snild å vise meg ... 1139
Polish	:	Pokaźcie mnie ... 1139
Portuguese	:	mostre-me ... 1139
Rumanian	:	Aratati-mi ... 1139
Slovak	:	Ukážte mi ... 1139
Spanish	:	Muéstreme usted ... 1139
Swedish	:	Visa mig ... 1139
Turkish	:	Bana gösteriniz 1139
Russian	:	покажите мне ... 1139
Serbian	:	покажите ми ... 1139
Ukrainian	:	покажіть мені ... 1139

1137 WHAT IS THIS?

Czech	:	Co je to? 1137
Danish	:	Hvad er det? 1137
Dutch	:	Wat is dat? 1137
Finnish	:	Mikä on tämä? 1137
French	:	Qu'est-ce que c'est? 1137
German	:	Was ist das? 1137
Hungarian	:	Mi az? 1137
Italian	:	Che cosa è (questo)? 1137
Croatian	:	Šta je to? 1137
Norwegian	:	Hvad er det? 1137
Polish	:	Co to jest? 1137
Portuguese	:	O que é isso (... isto?) 1137
Rumanian	:	Ce-i aceasta? 1137
Slovak	:	Čo je to? 1137
Spanish	:	¿Qué es esto? 1137
Swedish	:	Vad är det? 1137
Turkish	:	Bu nedir? 1137
Russian	:	Что это такое? 1137
Serbian	:	Шта је то? 1137
Ukrainian	:	Що це е? 1137

1140 GIVE ME ...

Czech	:	Dejte mi ... 1140
Danish	:	Vil De give mig ... 1140
Dutch	:	Geeft U mij ... 1140
Finnish	:	Olkaa hyvä ja antakaa minulle 1140
French	:	Donnez-moi ... 1140
German	:	Geben Sie mir ... 1140
Hungarian	:	Adja Ön ide ... 1140
Italian	:	Datemi ... 1140
Croatian	:	Dajte mi 1140
Norwegian	:	Vil De väre så snild å gi meg ... 1140
Polish	:	Dajcie mnie ... 1140
Portuguese	:	Dê-me ... 1140
Rumanian	:	Dați-mi ... 1140
Slovak	:	Dajte mi ... 1140
Spanish	:	Deme usted ... 1140
Swedish	:	giv mig ... 1140
Turkish	:	Bana veriniz ... 1140
Russian	:	дайте мне ... 1140
Serbian	:	дајте ми ... 1140
Ukrainian	:	дайте мені ... 1140

1141 HOW MUCH IS THIS ... ?

Czech	:	Kolik to stojí? 1141
Danish	:	Hvad koster det? 1141
Dutch	:	Wat kost dat? 1141
Finnish	:	Mitä tämä maksaa? 1141
French	:	Combien cela coûte-t-il? 1141
German	:	Was kostet das? 1141
Hungarian	:	Mennyibe kerül az? 1141
Italian	:	Quanto costa? 1141
Croatian	:	Što to stoji? 1141
Norwegian	:	Hvad koster det? 1141
Polish	:	Co to kosztuje? 1141
Portuguese	:	Quanto custa? 1141
Rumanian	:	Cât costă? 1141
Slovak	:	Čo to stojí? 1141
Spanish	:	¿Cuánto vale esto? 1141
Swedish	:	Vad kostar det? 1141
Turkish	:	Bu kaçadir? 1141
Russian	:	Сколько это стоит? 1141
Serbian	:	шта стаје то? 1141
Ukrainian	:	Що це коштує? 1141

1144 ON THE RIGHT

Czech	:	Vpravo 1144
Danish	:	Til hójre 1144
Dutch	:	Rechts 1144
Finnish	:	Oikealla 1144
French	:	À droite 1144
German	:	Rechts 1144
Hungarian	:	Jobbra 1144
Italian	:	A destra 1144
Croatian	:	Desno 1144
Norwegian	:	Til hörye 1144
Polish	:	Na prawo 1144
Portuguese	:	À direita 1144
Rumanian	:	La dreapta 1144
Slovak	:	Vpravo 1144
Spanish	:	A la derecha 1144
Swedish	:	Till höger 1144
Turkish	:	Sağda 1144
Russian	:	Направо 1144
Serbian	:	Десно 1144
Ukrainian	:	Нн право 1144

1142 KNITTED JACKET s.

Czech	:	pletená kazajka, f. 1142
Danish	:	Jumper, m. 1142
Dutch	:	het gebreide vest 1142
Finnish	:	neulenuttu 1142
French	:	jaçuette de lainage, f. 1142
German	:	die Strickjacke 1142
Hungarian	:	kötöttkabát 1142
Italian	:	maglia, f. 1142
Croatian	:	pletena bluza, f. 1142
Norwegian	:	jumper, m.; strikkyakke, f. 1142
Polish	:	żakiet trykotowy, m. 1142
Portuguese	:	casaco de malha, o 1142
Rumanian	:	jerseul 1142
Slovak	:	pletená vesta, f. 1142
Spanish	:	jubón de punto, m. 1142
Swedish	:	tröja-n 1142
Turkish	:	örgü çaketti 1142
Russian	:	кофта вязанная, f. 1142
Serbian	:	плетена блуза, f. 1142
Ukrainian	:	плетенний каптаник, m. 1142

1145 ON THE LEFT

Czech	:	Vlevo 1145
Danish	:	Til venstre 1145
Dutch	:	Links 1145
Finnish	:	Vasemmalla 1145
French	:	À gauche 1145
German	:	Links 1145
Hungarian	:	Balra 1145
Italian	:	A sinistra 1145
Croatian	:	Lijevo 1145
Norwegian	:	Til venstre 1145
Polish	:	Na levo 1145
Portuguese	:	À esquerda 1145
Rumanian	:	La stinga 1145
Slovak	:	vľavo 1145
Spanish	:	A la izquierda 1145
Swedish	:	Till vänster 1145
Turkish	:	Sola 1145
Russian	:	Налево 1145
Serbian	:	Лево 1145
Ukrainian	:	На ліво 1145

1143 WHERE ARE THERE ... ?

Czech	:	Kde se dostane ... ? 1143
Danish	:	Hvor kan man faa ...? 1143
Dutch	:	Waar is er ... te krijgen? 1143
Finnish	:	Missä saan ... 1143
French	:	Où y a-t-il? 1143
German	:	Wo gibt es? 1143
Hungarian	:	Hol van ... ? 1143
Italian	:	Dove si può trovare? 1143
Croatian	:	Gdje je to? 1143
Norwegian	:	Hvor får man? 1143
Polish	:	Gdzie to się znajduje? 1143
Portuguese	:	Onde há isso ... ? 1143
Rumanian	:	Unde se găseşte? 1143
Slovak	:	Kde je to ... ? 1143
Spanish	:	¿Dónde hay ... ? 1143
Swedish	:	Var finns det? 1143
Turkish	:	Nerde var ... ? 1143
Russian	:	Где это можно найти? 1143
Serbian	:	Где је то? 1143
Ukrainian	:	Де це находитьтя? 1143

1146 TO WASH THE HAIR

Czech	:	mýti vlasy 1146
Danish	:	vaske Haaret 1146
Dutch	:	haarwasschen 1146
Finnish	:	hiuspesu 1146
French	:	laver les cheveux 1146
German	:	Haar waschen 1146
Hungarian	:	hajat mosni 1146
Italian	:	lavare i capelli 1146
Croatian	:	prati kosu 1146
Norwegian	:	vaske håret 1146
Polish	:	myć włosy 1146
Portuguese	:	lavar o cabelo 1146
Rumanian	:	a-şi spala părul 1146
Slovak	:	umývat' vlasy 1146
Spanish	:	lavar el cabello 1146
Swedish	:	tvätta håret 1146
Turkish	:	sac yikamak 1146
Russian	:	мыть голову 1146
Serbian	:	прати косу 1146
Ukrainian	:	мити волосся 1146

1147 TO CUT THE HAIR

Czech	:	stříhati vlasy 1147
Danish	:	klippe Haaret 1147
Dutch	:	haar knippen 1147
Finnish	:	leikkuuttaa tukkansa 1147
French	:	couper les cheveux 1147
German	:	Haare schneiden 1147
Hungarian	:	nyírni hajat 1147
Italian	:	tagliare i capelli 1147
Croatian	:	šišati kosu 1147
Norwegian	:	klippe håret 1147
Polish	:	strzyc wlosy 1147
Portuguese	:	cortar o cabelo 1147
Rumanian	:	a tunde părul 1147
Slovak	:	strihat' vlasy 1147
Spanish	:	cortar el pelo 1147
Swedish	:	klippa hår-et 1147
Turkish	:	saç kesmek 1147
Russian	:	стричь волосы 1147
Serbian	:	шишати косу 1147
Ukrainian	:	стригти волосся 1147

1150 FIVE O'CLOCK

Czech	:	pět hodin 1150
Danish	:	Klokken fem 1150
Dutch	:	vijf uur 1150
Finnish	:	kello viisi 1150
French	:	cinq heures, f. pl. 1150
German	:	fünf Uhr 1150
Hungarian	:	öt ora 1150
Italian	:	le cinque 1150
Croatian	:	pet sati 1150
Norwegian	:	klokken fem 1150
Polish	:	piąta godzina 1150
Portuguese	:	cinco horas 1150
Rumanian	:	orele cinci 1150
Slovak	:	pät' hodín 1150
Spanish	:	las cinco 1150
Swedish	:	klockan fem 1150
Turkish	:	saat beş 1150
Russian	:	пять часов 1150
Serbian	:	пет сати 1150
Ukrainian	:	пята година 1150

1148 TO SEE THE DOCTOR

Czech	:	jíti k lékaři 1148
Danish	:	gaa til Läge 1148
Dutch	:	naar den dokter 1148
Finnish	:	mennä lääkärille 1148
French	:	aller chez le médecin 1148
German	:	zum Arzt gehen 1148
Hungarian	:	orvoshoz menni 1148
Italian	:	andare del medico 1148
Croatian	:	ići liječniku 1148
Norwegian	:	gå til lege 1148
Polish	:	iść do lekarza 1148
Portuguese	:	ir ao médico 1148
Rumanian	:	a merge la doctor 1148
Slovak	:	íst'k lekárovi 1148
Spanish	:	ir al médico 1148
Swedish	:	gå till läkaren 1148
Turkish	:	doktora gitmek 1148
Russian	:	итти к врачу 1148
Serbian	:	ићи лекару 1148
Ukrainian	:	іти до лікаря 1148

1151 A QUARTER PAST FIVE

Czech	:	čtvrt na šest 1151
Danish	:	et Kvarter over fem 1151
Dutch	:	kwart over vijf 1151
Finnish	:	neljännes yli viisi 1151
French	:	cinq heures quinze 1151
German	:	ein Viertel nach fünf 1151
Hungarian	:	öt ora fizenöt 1151
Italian	:	le cinque ed un quarto 1151
Croatian	:	pet i petnaest 1151
Norwegian	:	klokke fem en kvart 1151
Polish	:	kwadrans na szósta 1151
Portuguese	:	cinco (horas) e um quarto 1151
Rumanian	:	orele cinci și un sfert 1151
Slovak	:	pät hodín patnáct 1151
Spanish	:	las cinco y cuarto 1151
Swedish	:	en kvart över fem 1151
Turkish	:	bes i on beş 1151
Russian	:	пять часов пятнадцать минут 1151
Serbian	:	пет и четверт 1151
Ukrainian	:	чверть на шосту 1151

1149 WHAT TIME IS IT?

Czech	:	Kolik je hodin? 1149
Danish	:	Hvad er Klokken? 1149
Dutch	:	Hoe laat is het? 1149
Finnish	:	Paljonko kello on? 1149
French	:	Quelle heure est-il? 1149
German	:	Wie spät ist es? 1149
Hungarian	:	Hány óra van? 1149
Italian	:	Che ora è? 1149
Croatian	:	Koliko je sati? 1149
Norwegian	:	Hvor meget er klokken? 1149
Polish	:	Która godzina? 1149
Portuguese	:	Que horas são? 1149
Rumanian	:	Ce orä e? 1149
Slovak	:	Kol'ko je hodin? 1149
Spanish	:	¿Qué hora es? 1149
Swedish	:	Hur myket är klockan? 1149
Turkish	:	Saat kaçtir? 1149
Russian	:	Который час? 1149
Serbian	:	Колика је сати? 1149
Ukrainian	:	Ктора година? 1149

1152 HALF PAST FIVE

Czech	:	půl šesté 1152
Danish	:	halv seks 1152
Dutch	:	half zes 1152
Finnish	:	puoli kuusi 1152
French	:	cinq heures et demie 1152
German	:	Halb sechs 1152
Hungarian	:	fél hat 1152
Italian	:	le cinque e mezzo 1152
Croatian	:	pola šest 1152
Norwegian	:	klokke half seks 1152
Polish	:	pół do szóstej 1152
Portuguese	:	cinco e trínta 1152
Rumanian	:	orele cinci și jumătate 1152
Slovak	:	pol šiestej 1152
Spanish	:	las cinco y media 1152
Swedish	:	halv sex 1152
Turkish	:	beş buçuk 1152
Russian	:	пол шестого 1152
Serbian	:	пет и то 1152
Ukrainian	:	пів до шостої 1152

1153 A QUARTER TO SEVEN

Czech	: tři čtvrti na sedm 1153
Danish	: et kvarter is syv 1153
Dutch	: kwart voor zeven 1153
Finnish	: neljännestä vaille seitsemän 1153
French	: sept heures moins le quart 1153
German	: drei Viertel auf sieben 1153
Hungarian	: háromnegyed het 1153
Italian	: le sette meno un quarto 1153
Croatian	: sedam manje četvrt 1153
Norwegian	: klokke kvart i syv 1153
Polish	: trzy na siódma 1153
Portuguese	: seis (horas) o três quartos 1153
Rumanian	: orele şapte fără un sfert 1153
Slovak	: tri štvrte na sedem 1153
Spanish	: las siete menos cuarto 1153
Swedish	: en kvart i sju 1153
Turkish	: yediye çeyrek var 1153
Russian	: три четверти седьмого 1153
Serbian	: шест и тричетврт 1153
Ukrainian	: три чверти на сему 1153

1156 I AM

Czech	: jsem 1156
Danish	: jeg er 1156
Dutch	: ik ben 1156
Finnish	: olen 1156
French	: je suis 1156
German	: ich bin 1156
Hungarian	: én vagyok 1156
Italian	: io sono 1156
Croatian	: ja sam 156
Norwegian	: jeg er 1156
Polish	: ja jestem 1156
Portuguese	: eu sou; estou 1156
Rumanian	: eu sunt 1156
Slovak	: ja som 1156
Spanish	: soy; estoy 1156
Swedish	: jag är 1156
Turkish	: benim 1156
Russian	: я (есьм) 1156
Serbian	: ja сам 1156
Ukrainian	: я е 1156

1154 TOO EARLY

Czech	: příliš brzy 1154
Danish	: for tidlight 1154
Dutch	: te vroeg 1154
Finnish	: aikaisin 1154
French	: trop tôt 1154
German	: zu früh 1154
Hungarian	: túl korán 1154
Italian	: troppo presto 1154
Croatian	: prerano 1154
Norwegian	: for tidlig 1154
Polish	: zawcześnie 1154
Portuguese	: muito cedo 1154
Rumanian	: prea devreme 1154
Slovak	: vel'mi zavčasu 1154
Spanish	: demasiado temprano 1154
Swedish	: för tidigt 1154
Turkish	: çok erken 1154
Russian	: слишком рано 1154
Serbian	: прерано 1154
Ukrainian	: за скояо 1154

1157 YOU ARE (thou art)

Czech	: jste; jsi 1157
Danish	: De er; du er 1157
Dutch	: je bent; U bent 1157
Finnish	: Te olette; sinä olet 1157
French	: vous êtes; tu es 1157
German	: Sie sind; du bist 1157
Hungarian	: ön van; te vagy 1157
Italian	: egli è; lei è; tu sei 1157
Croatian	: Vi ste; ti si 1157
Norwegian	: De er; Du er 1157
Polish	: oni as; ty jestés 1157
Portuguese	: êles (elas) são; tu és 1157
Rumanian	: Dumnea voastră sunteti; tu esti 1157
Slovak	: Vy ste; Ty si 1157
Spanish	: Vd. es, está; eres, estás 1157
Swedish	: Ni är; du är 1157
Turkish	: onlar dir; sen sin 1157
Russian	: ты (есьм) 1157
Serbian	: ти си 1157
Ukrainian	: ти е 1157

1155 TOO LATE

Czech	: příliš pozdě 1155
Danish	: for sent 1155
Dutch	: te laat 1155
Finnish	: liian myöhään 1155
French	: trop tard 1155
German	: zu spät 1155
Hungarian	: túl késö 1155
Italian	: troppo tardi 1155
Croatian	: prekasno 1155
Norwegian	: for sent 1155
Polish	: zapóźno 1155
Portuguese	: muito tarde 1155
Rumanian	: prea tirziu 1155
Slovak	: vel'mi neskoro 1155
Spanish	: demasiado tarde 1155
Swedish	: för sent 1155
Turkish	: çok gec 1155
Russian	: слишком поздно 1155
Serbian	: прекасно 1155
Ukrainian	: за пізно 1155

1158 HE, SHE, IT IS

Czech	: on, ona, ono jest 1158
Danish	: han, hun, den, det er 1158
Dutch	: hij, zij, het is 1158
Finnish	: hän von 1158
French	: il, elle est 1158
German	: er, sie, es ist 1158
Hungarian	: ö van 1158
Italian	: egli, lei è 1158
Croatian	: on, ona, ono je 1158
Norwegian	: han, hun, den det er 1158
Polish	: on, ona, ono jest 1158
Portuguese	: êle, ela é 1158
Rumanian	: el, ea e 1158
Slovak	: on, ona, on je 1158
Spanish	: él, ella es, está 1158
Swedish	: han, hon, det är 1158
Turkish	: o (iste) 1158
Russian	: он, она, оно (есьм) 1158
Serbian	: оа, она, оно je 1158
Ukrainian	: він, вона, воно е 1158

1159 WE ARE

Czech	:	jsme 1159
Danish	:	vi er 1159
Dutch	:	wij zijn 1159
Finnish	:	olemme 1159
French	:	nous sommes 1159
German	:	wir sind 1159
Hungarian	:	mi vagyunk 1159
Italian	:	noi siamo 1159
Croatian	:	mi smo 1159
Norwegian	:	vi er 1159
Polish	:	my jesteśmy 1159
Portuguese	:	nós somos 1159
Rumanian	:	noi suntem 1159
Slovak	:	my sme 1159
Spanish	:	somos; estamos 1159
Swedish	:	vi äro 1159
Turkish	:	biz iz 1159
Russian	:	мы (есьм) 1159
Serbian	:	ми смо 1159
Ukrainian	:	ми е 1159

1160 YOU ARE (pl.)

Czech	:	jste 1160
Danish	:	I er 1160
Dutch	:	gij zijt 1160
Finnish	:	olette 1160
French	:	vous êtes 1160
German	:	ihr seid 1160
Hungarian	:	ti vagytok 1160
Italian	:	voi siete 1160
Croatian	:	vi ste 1160
Norwegian	:	dere er 1160
Polish	:	wy jesteście 1160
Portuguese	:	vós sois 1160
Rumanian	:	voi sunteti 1160
Slovak	:	vy ste 1160
Spanish	:	sois estáis 1160
Swedish	:	ni är 1160
Turkish	:	siz siniz 1160
Russian	:	вы (есьм) 1160
Serbian	:	ви сте 1160
Ukrainian	:	ви е 1160

1161 THEY ARE

Czech	:	jsou 1161
Danish	:	de er 1161
Dutch	:	zij zijn 1161
Finnish	:	he ovat 1161
French	:	ils sont 1161
German	:	sie sind 1161
Hungarian	:	ök vannak 1161
Italian	:	loro sono 1161
Croatian	:	oni su 1161
Norwegian	:	de er 1161
Polish	:	oni sa 1161 1161
Portuguese	:	êles são; estão 1161
Rumanian	:	ei sunt 1161
Slovak	:	oni sú 1161
Spanish	:	son; están 1161
Swedish	:	de äro 1161
Turkish	:	onlar dirler 1161
Russian	:	они (есьм) 1161
Serbian	:	ани су 1161
Ukrainian	:	вони е 1161

1162 I HAVE

Czech	:	(ja) mám 1162
Danish	:	Jeg har 1162
Dutch	:	ik heb 1162
Finnish	:	minulla on 1162
French	:	j'ai 1162
German	:	ich habe 1162
Hungarian	:	nekem van 1162
Italian	:	io ho 1162
Croatian	:	ja imam 1162
Norwegian	:	jeg har 1162
Polish	:	ja mam 1162
Portuguese	:	eu tenho 1162
Rumanian	:	eu am 1162
Slovak	:	(ja) mám 1162
Spanish	:	tengo, he 1162
Swedish	:	jag har 1162
Turkish	:	benim var 1162
Russian	:	я имею 1162
Serbian	:	ja имам 1162
Ukrainian	:	я маю 1162

1163 YOU HAVE

Czech	:	(vy) máte; (ty) máš 1163
Danish	:	De har; du her 1163
Dutch	:	U hebt; je hebt 1163
Finnish	:	Teillä on; sinulla on 1163
French	:	Vous avez; tu as 1163
German	:	Sie haben; du hast 1163
Hungarian	:	Önnek van; neked van 1163
Italian	:	voi avete; tu hai 1163
Croatian	:	Vi imate; ti imaš 1163
Norwegian	:	De har; du har 1163
Polish	:	Oni maja; tymasz 1163
Portuguese	:	o senhor (a senhora) tem; tu tens 1163
Rumanian	:	ei au; tu ai 1163
Slovak	:	(vy) máte; (ty) máš 1163
Spanish	:	Vd. tiene, ha; tienes, has 1163
Swedish	:	Ni har; du har 1163
Turkish	:	Sizin var; senin var 1163
Russian	:	ты имееш 1163
Serbian	:	ти имаш 1163
Ukrainian	:	ти маеш 1163

1164 HE, SHE, IT HAS

Czech	:	on, ona, ono má 1164
Danish	:	han, hun, den, det har 1164
Dutch	:	hij, zij, het heeft 1164
Finnish	:	hänellä on, sillä on 1164
French	:	il, elle, il a 1164
German	:	er, sie, es hat 1164
Hungarian	:	neki van 1164
Italian	:	egli, lei ha 1164
Croatian	:	on, ona ono ima 1164
Norwegian	:	han, hun, den, det har 1164
Polish	:	on, ona, ono ma 1164
Portuguese	:	êle, ela tem 1164
Rumanian	:	el, ea, are 1164
Slovak	:	on, ona, ono má 1164
Spanish	:	él, ella ha 1164
Swedish	:	han, hon, det ar 1164
Turkish	:	onun var 1164
Russian	:	он, она, оно имеет 1164
Serbian	:	он, она, оно има 1164
Ukrainian	:	він, вона, воно мае 1164

1165 WE HAVE

Czech	:	(my) máme 1165
Danish	:	vi har 1165
Dutch	:	wij hebben 1165
Finnish	:	meillä on 1165
French	:	nous avons 1165
German	:	wir haben 1165
Hungarian	:	nekünk van 1165
Italian	:	noi abbiamo 1165
Croatian	:	mi imamo 1165
Norwegian	:	vi har 1165
Polish	:	my mamy 1165
Portuguese	:	nós temos 1165
Rumanian	:	noi avem 1165
Slovak	:	my máme 1165
Spanish	:	tenemos, hemos 1165
Swedish	:	vi ha (-va) 1165
Turkish	:	bizim var 1165
Russian	:	мы имеем 1165
Serbian	:	ми имамо 1165
Ukrainian	:	ми маемо 1165

1166 YOU HAVE (pl.)

Czech	:	(vy) máte 1166
Danish	:	I har 1166
Dutch	:	jullie hebt 1166
Finnish	:	teillä on 1166
French	:	vous avez 1166
German	:	ihr habt 1166
Hungarian	:	neektek van 116
Italian	:	voi avete 1166
Croatian	:	vi imate 1166
Norwegian	:	dere har 1166
Polish	:	wy macie 1166
Portuguese	:	vós tendes 1166
Rumanian	:	voi aveti 1166
Slovak	:	vy máte 1166
Spanish	:	tenéis, habéis 1166
Swedish	:	Ni ha 1166
Turkish	:	sizin var 1166
Russian	:	вы имеете 1166
Serbian	:	ви имате 1166
Ukrainian	:	ви маете 1166

1167 THEY HAVE

Czech	:	oni mají 1167
Danish	:	de har 1167
Dutch	:	zij hebben 1167
Finnish	:	heillä on 1167
French	:	ils ont 1167
German	:	sie haben 1167
Hungarian	:	nekik van 1167
Italian	:	loro hanno 1167
Croatian	:	oni imaju 167
Norwegian	:	de har 1167
Polish	:	oni mają 1167
Portuguese	:	êles têm 1167
Rumanian	:	ei au 1167
Slovak	:	ei au 1167
Spanish	:	ellos (ellas) tienen, han 1167
Swedish	:	de ha 1167
Turkish	:	onlarin var 1167
Russian	:	они имеют 1167
Serbian	:	они имају 1167
Ukrainian	:	вони мають 1167

1168 HAVE YOU ... ?

Czech	:	Máte ... ? 1168
Danish	:	Har De ... ? 1168
Dutch	:	Hebt U ... ? 1168
Finnish	:	Onko Teillä ... ? 1168
French	:	Avez-vous ...? 1168
German	:	Haben Sie ... ? 1168
Hungarian	:	Van önnek ... ? 1168
Italian	:	Avete ... ? 1168
Croatian	:	Imate li ... ? 1168
Norwegian	:	Har De ... ? 1168
Polish	:	Czy macie ... ? 1168
Portuguese	:	O senhor tem ... ? 1168
Rumanian	:	Aveţi ... ? 1168
Slovak	:	Máte ... ? 1168
Spanish	:	¿ Ha ... Vd.? (¿ Tiene Vd.?) 1168
Swedish	:	Har Ni ... ? 1168
Turkish	:	Sizde var mi? 1168
Russian	:	Имеете ли? 1168
Serbian	:	имате ли? 1168
Ukrainian	:	Чи ви маете? 1168

1169 I KNOW

Czech	:	Vím 1169
Danish	:	Jeg ved 1169
Dutch	:	Ik weet 1169
Finnish	:	Tiedän 1169
French	:	Je sais 1169
German	:	Ich weiss 1169
Hungarian	:	Tudom 1169
Italian	:	Io so 1169
Croatian	:	Znam 1169
Norwegian	:	Jeg vet 1169
Polish	:	Ja wiem 1169
Portuguese	:	Eu sei 1169
Rumanian	:	Stiu 1169
Slovak	:	Viem 1169
Spanish	:	Yo sé 1169
Swedish	:	Jag vet 1169
Turkish	:	Bilirim 1169
Russian	:	(я) знаю 1169
Serbian	:	знам 1169
Ukrainian	:	я знаю 1169

1170 I DON'T KNOW

Czech	:	Nevím 1170
Danish	:	Jeg ved ikke 1170
Dutch	:	Ik weet niet 1170
Finnish	:	En tiedä 1170
French	:	Je ne sais pas 1170
German	:	Ich weiss nicht 1170
Hungarian	:	Nem tudom 1170
Italian	:	Io non so 1170
Croatian	:	Ne znam 1170
Norwegian	:	Jeg vet ikke 1170
Polish	:	Ja niewiem 1170
Portuguese	:	Eu não sei 1170
Rumanian	:	Nu stiu 1170
Slovak	:	Neviem 1170
Spanish	:	No sé 1170
Swedish	:	Jag vet inte 1170
Turkish	:	Bilmem 1170
Russian	:	я не знаю 1170
Serbian	:	не знам 1170
Ukrainian	:	я не знаю 1170

INDEX

All the entries (words and phrases) in *the main vocabulary* are numbered consecutively from 1-1170. The entries in this Index—where you find alphabetical word lists in all twenty languages—refer to these numbers.

CZECH

matka, *f.* 608
matrace, *f.* 577
med, *m.* 461
měd', *f.* 236
meloun, *m.* 585
merunka, *f.* 28
měsíc, *m.* 602
měsíc, *m.* 604
město, *n.* 1022
metr, *m.* 975
mésti 965
mezek, *m.*; soumar, *m.* 627
míchané vejce, *n.* 846
milovati 550
milý 499
minerální voda, *f.* 594
minuta, *f.* 595
mirabelka, *f.* 596
mísa, *f.* 120
mistr, *m.* 575
míti; vlastniti 447
mléko, *n.* 592
mluviti 919
mnoho 626
modrý 102
moře, *n.* 849
mosaz, *f.* 125
most, *m.* 130
motocykl, *m.* 613
motor, *m.* 610
motyka, *f.* 460
motýl, *m.* 146
motýlek, *m.* 119
moucha, *f.* 362
mouka, *f.* 359
možná 579
mrak, *m.* 215
mrkev, *f.* 173
mrzutost, *f.* 1031
můj, má, mé 633
muškát, *m.* 663
mušle, *f.* 867
muž; manžel, *m.* 566
mýdlo, *n.* 905
myš, *f.* 617
mýti (se) 1076
náboj, *m.* 759
nadloktí, *n.* 1052
nádraží, *n.* 938
náhrdelník, *m.* 641
nákladní auto, *n.* 614
nákladný 323
nálevka, *f.* 388
nalézti; nalézati 347
náměstí, *n.* 927
námořník, *m.* 832
náprsní taška, *f.* 1071
náprstek, *m.* 989
náramek, *m.* 123
náramkové hodinky 1114
narození, *n.* 93
narozeniny, *pl.* 94
nástupiště, *n.* 730
naušnice, *f.* 299
název 636
ne 654
nebezpečí, *n.* 258
neděle, *f.* 962
nehet, *m.* 349
nemluvně 49

nemocnice, *f.* 466
nemocný 475
nepřesně 1051
nesnáz 1031
nésti; přinésti 132
nikl, *m.* 647
nit, *f.* 861
noc, *f.* 648
noční košile, *f.* 649
noční oblek, *m.* 768
noční stolek, *m.* 650
noha, *f.* 363
noha, *f.* 524
nos, *m.* 658
nosič, *m.* 747
noty, *pl. f.* 630
noviny, *pl.* 645
nový, nová, nové 644
nudle, *f. pl.* 655
nula, *f.* 1120
nůž, *m.* 504
nůžky, *pl.* 845
nůžky na drát, *pl.* 1104
oběd, *m.* 278
obchod, *m.* 876
obchod; obchodní záležitost 143
obchodní dům, *m.* 1074
obchodní loď, *f.* 588
obličej, *m.* 328
obraz 689
obuvník, *m.* 875
obvaz, *m.* 289
obvaz, *m.* 60
obývací pokoj, *m.* 545
ocel, *f.* 941
ocet, *m.* 1061
oddělení, *n.* 230
oděv, *m.* (mužský) 214
odhlásiti (se) 659
odjeti; opustiti 522
odjezd; začátek, *m.* 936
odkud 1092
odpočinek, *m.*; přestávka, *f.* 805
odpoledne, *n.* 6
odpověděti 21
odpustiti 318
oheň, *m.* 350
oko, *n.*; oči, *pl.* 326
okno, *n.* 1101
okurka, *f.* 251
olej, *m.* 672
olejové sardinky, *pl.* 673
oliva, *f.* 676
olovo *n.* 520
omáčka, *f.* 424
opakovati 798
opasek, *m.* 86
opustiti 522
orati 736
ordinační hodina, *f.* 233
osel, *m.* 285
osm 304
osobní auto, *n.* 612
osmdesát 306
osmnáct 305
ošetřovatelka 622
ošklivý 1044
otec, *m.* 334
otevírač konserv, *m.* 1006
otevřený 680

psací stůl, *m.* 274
psaní 526
pšenice, *f.* 1090
pták, *m.* 92
půda, *f.* 42
puding, *m.* 761
pudřenka, *f.* 755
půl; polovina, *f.* 435
pumpa, *f.* 763
punčochy, *f. pl.* 945
puška, *f.* 810
pytel, *m.* 828
pyžama 768
rád 406
radio, *n.* 1103
radnice, *f.* 1023
radostný 589
rak (mořský), *m.* 546
rajské jablíčko, *n.* 1013
rameno, *n.* 878
razítko, *n.* 932
regál, *m.*; regály, *pl.* 869
ret, *m.*; rty, *pl.* 539
rodiče, *m. pl.* 698
rohlík, *m.*; žemle, *f.* 820
rok, *m.* 1115
rolník, *m.* 707
rovně 951
rozuměti 1048
ruční granát, *m.* 440
ručník, *m.* 1021
ruda, *f.* 682
ruka, *f.*; ruce, *pl.* 439
rukavice, *f.* 409
růže, *f.* 821
ryba, *f.* 353
rýč, *m.* 918
rybíz, *m.* 791
rychle; spěšně 771
rýže, *f.* 808
řeka, *f.* 813
řemen 86
řepka, *f.* 781
řetkev, *r.* 775
řetkvička, *f.* 774
řezati; stříhati 254
řezník, *m.* 144
říci; vyprávěti; sděliti 981
říjen, *m.* 669
sad, *m.*; sady, *pl.* 699
sádlo, *n.* 517
sako 491
salám, *m.* 839
salát, *m.* 833
sám 885
samet, *m.* 1056
sáně, (*pl.*) 894
Sbohem; žijte blaze 416
sděliti 981
seděti 888
sedlák 707
sedlo, *n.* 830
sedm 857
sedmdesát 859
sedmnáct 858
sednouti si; posaditi se 889
sejíti se; shromážditi 584
sekera, *f.* 48
sekretářka, f.; sekretář, *m.* 853
selka 708

selské stavení, *n.* 333
selský dvůr 332
seno, *n.* 458
sestra, *f.* 662
sestra, *f.* 897
setkati se 584
sever, *m.* 657
shromážditi 584
schody, *pl.* 930
schopný; schopen 1
silnice, *f.* 459
siréna, *f.* 887
síť', *f.* 643
síti 917
síto, *n.* 881
sklenice, *f.* 407
sklep, *m.* 64
sklízeti 444
skopové maso, *n.* 632
skříň, *f.* 1073
sladký 966
sláma, *f.* 952
slaneček, *m.* 457
slanina, *f.* 52
slaný 834
slunce, *n.* 961
slečna, *f.* 597
služebná, *f.* 562
smažiti 815
směnárna, *f.* 317
smeták, *m.* 135
smetana, *f.* 249
smrk, *m.* 725
smrt, *f.* 266
smutný 912
smutný, smutná, **smutné** 829
smyčec houslový 118
snad 579
snídaně, *f.* 127
sníh, *m.* 904
snubní prsten, *m.* 1084
sobota, *f.* 838
soumar 627
spací vůz, *m.* 896
spáti 895
spěchati 445
spěšně 771
spis 283
spodní kalhoty, *pl.* 287
sponka, *f.*; svorka, *f.* 211
sportovní bota, *f.* 925
sportovní košile, *f.* 924
srdce, *n.* 452
srnec, *m.*; srnka, *f.* 268
srpen, *m.* 43
ssací papír, *m.* 100
stáj 928
starost 1031
starý 675
statek 333
státi 933
stehno, *n.* 988
stejnokroj, *m.* 1049
sto 470
stodola, *f.* 62
stolní lampa, *f.* 934
stroj 560
strojní puška 561
strom, *m.* 1030
strýc, *m.* 1046

voda, *f.* 1080
vodotrysk 375
vodováha 922
voják, *m.* 908
vojenská nemocnice, *f.* 591
vojsko 32
volati; zavolati 153
volný (-o) 379
vosa, *f.* 1078
vrata, *pl.* 400
vrátný, *m.* 746
vrátný, *m.* 436
vrba, *f.* 1099
vrták, *m.* 117
vteřina, *f.* 852
vůl, *m.* 686
vůz, *m.* 174
výdejna jízdenek, *f.* 113
východ, *m.* 300
východ, *m.* 322
vypinač, *m.* 969
vyprávěti 981
výtah 309
vývrtka, *f.* 237
vzíti 973
začátek 936
záclona, *f.* 253
začíti; začínati 83
záda, *pl.* 50
zadní strana; záda 51
zahrada, *f.* 395
záchranný pás, *m.* 528
zajíc, *m.* 442
zakázáno 758
zákopník, *m.* 837
zámek, *m.* 547
zámek, *m.* 176
západ, *m.* 1088
zápalka, *f.* 576
zápalná bomba, *f.* 477

zaplatiti 704
zapomenouti; zapomněti 369
září, *n.* 856
zastávka, *f.* 948
zástěra, *f.* 30
zavazadlo, *n.* 555
zavírací špendlík, *m.* 831
zavolati 153
zavřený 213
zde 456
zdravý 914
zdviž, *f.*; výtah, *m.* 309
zedník, *m.* 129
zelenina, *f.* 1055
zelený 426
zelí, *n.* 150
zima, *f.* 1102
zinek, *m.* 1121
zítra 1014
zkoušeti 1035
zmrzlina, *f.* 474
zpívati 884
zub, *m.*; zuby, *pl.* 1017
zubní pasta, *f.* 1019
zůstati 796
zvěřina, *f.* 393
zvíře 19
zvolna 900
žebřík, *m.* 507
žehlička, *f.* 489
železnice, *f.* 776
železo, *n.* 488
želva, *f.* 1020
žena, *f.* 1105
židle, *f.* 184
žijte blaze 416
žito, *n.* 827
žíznivý 993
žlutý 1116
župan, *m.* 290

VŠEOBECNÉ 1125
Dobré jitro 1126
Dobrý den 1127
Dobrý večer 1128
Dobrou noc 1129
Na shledanou 1130
Jak se máte? 1131
Hledám byt 1132
Chci jísti 1133
Chci píti 1134
Jak se jmenujete? 1135
Rozuměl jste? 1136
Co je to? 1137
Kde je to? 1138
Ukažte mi ... 1139
Dejte mi ... 1140
Kolik to stojí? 1141
pletená kazajka, *f.* 1142
Kde se dostane ...? 1143
Vpravo 1144
Vlevo 1145
mýti vlasy 1146
stříhati vlasy 1147

jíti k lékaři 1148
Kolik je hodin? 1149
pět hodin 1150
čtvrt na šest 1151
půl šesté 1152
tři čtvrti na sedm 1153
příliš brzy 1154
příliš pozdě 1155
jsem 1156
jste; jsi 1157
on, ona, ono jest 1158
jsme 1159
jste 1160
jsou 1161
(já) mám 1162
(vy) máte; (ty) máš 1163
on, ona, ono má 1164
(my) máme 1165
(vy) máte 1166
oni mají 1167
Máte ...? 1168
Vím 1169
Nevím 1170

DANISH

Abrikos, *c.* 28
adresse, *c.* 4
afmelde 659
Aften, *m.* 316
aftensmad, *m./c.* 963
Agerhöne, *f./c.* 701
Albue, *m./c.* 307
Aluminium, *n.* 15
Ambolt, *m.* 22
Ananas, *m./c.* 16
Ager, *m./c.* 3
Agurk, *m./c.* 251
And, *m./c.* 296
Ankel, *s.* 20
Anker, *n.* 17
anmelde 793
Ansigt, *n.* 328
Appelsin, *m./c.* 681
Apotek, *n.* 716
April 29
Arbejde 1108
Arbejder, *c.* 1109
Arbejder, *c.* 1110
Armbaand, *n.* 123
Armbaandsur, *n.* 1114
Asparges, *pl.* 37
Asters, *pl.* 40
atten 305
August 43
Avis, *m./c.* 645
Baad, *m./c.* 105
bade 67
Badedragt, *c.* 66
Badehaandkläde, *n.* 69
Badekaabe, *c.* 68
Badekar, *n.* 70
Bagage, *m./c.* 555
bage 56
Bager, *m./c.* 57
Bagside, *m.* 51
Balkon, *m./c.* 58
Banan, *c.* 59
barbere 864
Barberkniv, *m./c.* 785
Barberkost, *m.* 865
bedrövet 829
bedrövet 912
begynde 83
bekymring, *c.* 1031
Ben, *n.* 524
Benzin. *m./c.* 399
Beskyttelsesrum, *n.* 10
betale 704
Bi, *f./c.* 77
Bil, *m./c.* 612
Billard, *m./c.* 91
billet, *m./c.* 1002
Billethul, *n.* 113
billigt 188
Bind, *n.*; Bandage 60
Biograf, *c.* 622
bitter 96
Bjerg, *n.* 615
Bjergkäde, *m./c.* 616
Bläkhus, *n.* 484
blaa 102
Blaabär, *m./c.* 103

Blikkenslager, *m./c.* 739
blive 796
Blomkaal, *c.* 181
Blomme, *c.* 738
Blomst, *m/c.* 360
Blonder, *pl.* 506
Bluse, *m./c.* 101
Bly, *n.* 520
Blyant, *m./c.* 710
Bog, *m./c.* 111
Boghandel, *m./c.* 115
Bogholder, *m./c.* 114
Bogskab, *n.* 112
Bolig; Lejlighed 356
Bombe, *m./c.* 110
Bomuld, *m./c.* 243
Bonde, *m.* 707
Bondegaard, *m./c.* 332
Bondehus, *n.* 333
Bondekone, *f.* 708
Bor, *m./c.* 117
Bord, *n.* 970
Brandbombe, *c.* 477
Brev, *n.* 526
Brevkort, *n.* 749
Briller, *pl.* 327
bringe 132
Bro, *m./c.* 130
Broche, *m./c.* 133
brun 136
Bryllup, *n.* 1083
Bryst, *n.* 194
Bröd, *n.* 126
Brönd, *m./c.* 1087
Buket, *m./c.* 141
bukser; benkläder, *pl.* 1032
Buntmager, *m.* 391
Butik, *m./c.* 876
by, *m./c.* 1022
Byg, *m./c.* 61
Bäk, *m./c.* 134
Bälte, *n.* 86
Bänk, *m./c.* 87
Böfsteg, *m./c.* 80
Bög, *m./c.* 78
Bönner, *pl.* 73
börste 138
Cafe, *m./c.* 152
Cello, *c.* 1065
Cigar, *m./c.* 203
cigarbutik, *m./c.* 1009
Cigaret, *m./c.* 204
Citron, *m./c.* 525
Champagne, *c.* 187
Chauffeur, *m.* 293
Chokolade, *m./c.* 201
Chokolade, *c.* 220
Citer, *c.* 1122
Clips, *c.* 211
Cykel, *m./c.* 89
Cykellygte, *c.* 531
Cypres, *m./c.* 256
daaseaabner, *m./c.* 1006
dadle 98
Dag, *m.* 262
i dag 1010
Dagligstue, *m./c.* 545

Kompas, n./c. 231
konge, m. 500
Konsulat, n. 232
Konsultationstid 233
kontakt, m./c. 969
Kontor, f./c. 670
Kontorchef, m./c. 450
kontrol, c. 234
Kop, c. 252
Korset, c. 240
kort 877
Kotelet, c. 255
Kran, m./c. 248
Krans, m./c. 1112
Kraveknap, m./c. 954
Krybbe, m./c. 250
Kulskuffe, m./c. 219
Kunstsilke, m./c. 35
Kupe, m./c. 230
Kurv, m./c. 65
Kvinde, f. 1105
Kvindelig 1109
Kvittering, f. 787
Kvistkammer, n. 397
Kväg, c.; Okse, m. 180
kys, n. 501
Kälder, m./c. 64
köbe 148
Köd, n. 582
Kökken, n. 502
köre 292
Kaabe, c. 512
Kaalrabi, m./c. 505
Lade, m./c. 62
Lagkage, c. 976
Lampe, c. 183
Landevej, m./c. 459
Landkort, n. 568
Landsby, m./c. 1060
Landskab, n. 515
lang 548
langsom 900
Lastbil, m./c. 614
lave; göre 564
Lazaret, n. 591
Legeme, n. 85
lejr, c. 159
Letmetal, n. 532
Lever, m./c. 544
liden 901
ligge 527
Ligtorn, m. 238
Likör, m./c. 541
Liljekonval, m./c. 535
Lim, c. 410
Lindeträ, n. 536
Lineal, m./c. 825
Lokomotiv, n. 311
Lommekniv, m./c. 740
Lommelygte 71
Lommetörkläde, n. 441
Lommeur, n. 1079
Loppe, m./c. 358
lukket 213
Lunge, m. 557
Lus, m./c. 549
Lygte, f./c. 516
Lyn, n. 533
lys 530
Lyspäre, m./c. 308

Läber, pl. 539
Läbestift, m./c. 540
Läg 156
Läge, m. 717
Länestol, m./c. 31
laere 521
Lärred, n. 537
läse 786
löbe 826
Lög, m./c. 679
Lördag, m. 838
laar 988
Laas, c. 547
madres, c. 577
Makaroni, pl. 559
maskine, c. 560
Maskingevär, n. 561
Maj 578
Majs, m./c. 563
Maleri, n. 689
malke 593
Malm, c. 682
Mand, m. 566
Mandag, m. 599
Mandolin, m./c. 567
Margarine, c. 570
Marketenderi, c. 163
Marmelade, m./c. 572
Marts 569
Matros, m. 832
Medicin, m./c. 583
megen; mange 626
meget 1057
Mejsel, m./c. 199
Mel, n. 359
Melon, m./c. 585
Mennesket 565
Messing, n. 125
Mester, m. 575
Metal, n. 590
metermaal, n. 975
Middag, m. 656
Middagsmad, m./c. 278
Militär, n. 32
min, mit, mine 633
Mindesmärke, n./c. 603
Mineralvand, n. 594
Minut 595
Mirabel, c. 596
moder, f./c. 608
Morgen, m. 605
i morgen 1014
Morgenkjole. c. 290
Morgenmad, c. 127
Motor, m./c. 610
Motorcykel, c. 613
Muldvarp, m./c. 598
Muldyr, n. 627
Mund, m. 618
Mundharmonika, c. 619
Mundvand, n. 620
munter; lystig 589
Murer, m. 129
Mursten, c. 128
Mus, m./c. 617
musik, c. 629
Musikinstrument, c. 631
Muskatnöd, m./c. 663
Musling, m./c. 867
Myg, m./c. 607

188   INDEX

Örebeskytter, *m./c.* 298
Örering, *m./c.* 299
öst, *c.* 300
Östers, *pl.* 687

aaben 680
Aal, *m./c.* 302
Aar, *n.* 1115
Aare, *m./c.* 665

FORSKELLIGT 1125
God Morgen 1126
God Dag 1127
God Aften 1128
God Nat 1129
Paa Gensyn 1130
Hvordan har De det? 1131
Jeg söger Kvarter 1132
Jeg vil spise 1133
Jeg vil drikke 1134
Hvad er Deres Navn? 1135
Har De forstaaet? 1136
Hvad er det? 1137
Hvor er det? 1138
Vil De vise mig . . . 1139
Vil De give mig . . . 1140
Hvad koster det? 1141
Jumper 1142
Hvor kan man faa . . .? 1143
Til hójre 1144
Til venstre 1145
vaske Haaret 1146
klippe Haaret 1147

gaa til Läge 1148
Hvad er Klokken? 1149
Klokken fem 1150
et Kvarter over fem 1151
halv seks 1152
et kvarter i syv 1153
for tidlig 1154
for sen 1155
jeg er 1156
De er; du er 1157
han, hun, den, det er 1158
vi er 1159
I er 1160
de er 1161
Jeg har 1162
De har; du her 1163
han, hun, den, det har 1164
vi har 1165
I har 1166
de har 1167
Har De . . . ? 1168
Jeg ved 1169
Jeg ved ikke 1170

DUTCH

de chocolade 201
de cigaret 204
de cither 1122
de citroen 525
de clarinet 207
de clip 211
de cognac 222
het colbert 491
de commode 196
het consulaat 232
controle 234
het corset 240
de coupé 230
de cypres 256
daar 985
de dadel 260
de dag 262
het dak 822
het dal 1053
het dameshemd 191
de dameshoed 508
de damesschoen 509
dank U; dank je 983
de dans 257
de das 119
de das 1003
December 267
deken 99
de den 352
de denneboom 265
een derde 992
dertig 995
dertien 994
de deur 286
het dier 19
de dij 988
dik 987
ding; zaak 991
de dinsdag 1036
diverse 1125
de dobbelsteen 275
dochter 261
de dokter 717
de dom 179
de donder 1000
de donderdag 1001
donker 259
de dood 266
het dorp 1060
dorst 993
de draadschaar 1104
drie 997
drinken 291
drövig 829
de druif 423
de duif 721
de duim 999
duizend 996
dun 990
duur 323
één 678
de eend 296
eenmaal 677
eergisteren 264
de eerste verdieping 351
de eetkamer 277
het ei 303
het eksteroog 238
de elboog 307
elf 310

en 14
Engels 312
de enkel 20
enkel 885
het erts 682
de erwt 706
eten 301
de ezel 285
de fabriek 329
Februari 336
de fiets 89
de film 346
de fluit 361
het fluweel 1056
het fontein 375
het formulier 372
het fototoestel 158
de framboos 783
het fruit 386
gaan 1070
de gans 417
de garage 394
gas 398
gave 403
de gebakken aardappel, pl. 382
de gebakken kip 816
de gebakken vis 381
het gebergte 616
de geboorte 93
de gebraden gans 817
het gebraden vlees 818
het gekookte ei 107
de gekookte vis 108
geel 1116
de geit 412
het geld 600
de gems 186
de gerst 61
het geschut 162
gesloten 213
het getal 661
Gevaar 258
geven 405
het gevogelte 754
het geweer 810
het gezicht 323
gezond 914
gisteren 1118
de gitaar 429
het glas 407
God, m. 414
goed 415
goedkoop 188
het gom 479
het gordijn 253
de grenadier 481
grijs 427
groen 426
de groente 1055
groot 518
de gymnastiek 430
de haan 218
de handgranaat, m. 440
het haar 432
de haarborstel 433
de haas 442
zich haasten 445
Hagel, n. 431
de hak 454
een half 435

de lage schoen 554
landkaart 568
het landschap 515
de landstraat 459
lang 548
de langouste 546
langzaam 900
de lantaarn 516
de laars 116
het lazaret 591
leelijk 1044
het lelietje-van-dalen 535
de lente 926
de lepel 923
leren 521
de leuningstoel 31
de lever 544
lezen 786
licht 530
het licht 531
het lichtmetaal 532
de lift 309
liefhebben 550
liggen 527
de lijm 410
lila 1063
de linde 536
de lineaal 825
het linnen 537
de lip 539
de lippenstift 540
de liqueur 541
de locomotief 311
het loket 113
de long 557
het lood 520
de loodgieter 739
loopen 826
de lucifer 576
de luis 549
maaien 623
de maaltijd 581
de maan 604
de maand 602
de maandag 599
Maart 569
de macaroni 559
machine, c. 560
het magazijn 1074
de mais 563
maken 564
de man 566
de mand 65
de mandoline 567
de mantel 512
het mantelpak 242
de margarine 570
de markt 571
matras 577
de matroos 832
het medicijn 583
het meel 359
het meer 514
de meester 575
Mei 578
de meid 562
het meisje 404
Mejuffrouw 597
de melk 592
melken 593

de meloen 585
de mens 565
het menu 587
het mes 504
het messing 125
het metaal 590
de metermaat 975
de metselaar 129
Mevrouw 625
de middag 656
het middageten 278
mijn 633
Mijnheer, m. 886
het militair 32
het mineraal water 594
de minuut 595
de mirabelle 596
misschien 579
de mitrailleur 561
moe 1007
moeder, f./c. 608
de mol 598
de mond 618
de mondharmonika 619
het mondwater 620
morgen 1014
de mortel 606
de mossel 867
de motor 610
de motorfiets 613
de mug 607
het muildier 627
de muis 617
muziek, c. 629
het muziekinstrument 631
de naaid 642
het naaigaren 861
de naaimachine 860
de nacht 648
het nachthemd 649
het nachtkastje 650
de nagel 349
de nagelvijl 635
de namiddag 6
neen 654
negen 651
negentien 652
negentig 653
de nek 638
nemen 973
het net 643
de neus 658
de nier 497
niet op tijd 1051
het nikkel 647
Noorden 657
de noot 630
de nootmuskaat 663
November 660
nömen 636
nul 1120
de ochtend 605
October 669
de oester 687
de officier 671
de olie 672
de olijf 676
de onderarm 553
de onderbroek 287
de onderdij 863

de schrijfmachine 1042
de schrijftafel 274
de schroef 847
de schroefsleutel 1113
de schroevendraaier 848
de schuilkelder 10
de schuur 62
de seconde 852
de secretaresse 853
September 856
de sering 534
de sigaar 203
de sigarenwinkel 1009
de sinaasappel 681
de sirene 887
de sjaal 866
de ski 893
de sla 833
de slaap-wagen 896
de slager 144
de slang 903
slapen 895
de slaapkamer 76
de slee 894
slecht 53
de sleutel 496
het slot 176
het slot 547
de smid 902
snede 254
de sneeuw 904
de soep 915
de socken 906
de sokkendragers 964
soldaat, *m.* 908
de speelkaart 731
het spek 52
de speld 724
de spijker 634
de spinazie 921
spits 741
de spoorweg 776
hed sporthemd 924
de sportschoen 925
het spreekuur 233
spreken 919
het staal 941
de staalhelm 942
staan 933
de staande lamp 934
de stad 1022
het stadhuis 1023
de stal 928
het standbeeld 603
het station 938
de stationschef 939
de steen 946
steken 944
de stellage 842
de stempel 932
de ster 935
de stoel 184
de stof 955
stomp 104
het stopkontact 737
stoppen 586
de storm 949
de straat 814
het strijkijzer 489
de strijkplank 490

strijkstok 118
het stroo 952
de suiker 957
de taart 976
de tabak 1008
tachtig 306
de tafel 970
de tamme kastanje 573
de tand 1017
de tang 1015
de tandpasta 1019
de tandeborstel 1018
tante, f. 44
het tapijt 172
de tarwe 1090
de teen 1011
tegenkomen 584
de telefoon 979
het telegram 978
tellen 981
de teugel 794
het theater 984
de thee 977
de thermometer 210
tien 982
de tijd 1004
de timmerman 493
de timmerman 171
het tin 1005
tolk, m. 487
de tomaat 1013
de ton 63
de tong 1016
het touw 823
de tractor 1024
de tram 1026
de trap 930
de trechter 388
het treinkaartje 1002
de trommel 295
de trompet 1034
het trottoir 703
de trouwring 1084
de trui 762
de tuin 395
de tulp 1037
twaalf 1038
twee 1041
tweemaal 1040
twintig 1039
de ui 679
de uitgang 322
de uitreis 936
het uniform 1049
het uur 468
vader, m. 334
vandaag, heden 1010
vangen 178
vanwaar 1092
het varken 720
het varkensvet 517
het varkensvlees 744
de vechtwagen 974
veel 626
de veer 338
veertien 373
veertig 374
vegen 965
de veiligheidsspeid 831
ver 331

zuiden 913
zuster, *f.* 897
zuster 662

zuur 916
zwart 97
het zwemmen 968

DIVERSE 1125
Goeden morgen 1126
Goeden dag 1127
Goeden avond 1128
Goede Nacht 1129
Tot ziens 1130
Hoe gaat het met U? 1131
Ik zoek onderdak 1132
Ik wil eten 1133
Ik wil drinken 1134
Hoe heet U? 1135
Hebt U begrepen? 1136
Wat is dat? 1137
Waar is dat? 1138
Laat U me ... zien 1139
Geeft U mij ... 1140
Wat kost dat? 1141
het gebreide vest 1142
Waar is er ... te krijgen? 1143
Rechts 1144
Links 1145
haar wasschen 1146
haar knippen 1147

naar den doktor 1148
Hoe laat is het? 1149
vijf uur 1150
kwart over vijf 1151
half zes 1152
kwart voor zeven 1153
Te vroeg 1154
te laat 1155
ik ben 1156
je bent; U bent 1157
hij, zij, het is 1158
wij zijn 1159
gij zijt 1160
zij zijn 1161
ik heb 1162
U hebt; je hebt 1163
hij, zij, het heeft 1164
wij hebben 1165
jullie hebt 1166
zij hebben 1167
Hebt U ...? 1168
Ik weet 1169
Ik weet niet 1170

FINNISH

kukkakaali 181
kukkavihko 141
kukko 218
kulkea 292
kumina 169
kuningas 500
kuolema 266
kuorma-auto 614
kupari 236
kuppi 252
kurkku 251
kurkku 998
kurpitsa 764
kuttu 412
kuu 604
kuukausi 602
lämpömittari 210
kuusi 725
kuusi 890
kuusikymmentä 892
kuusitoista 891
kykenevä 1
kylmä 223
kylpeä 67
kylpyamme 70
kylpyliina 69
kylpyviitta 68
kylvää 917
kylä 1060
kymmenen 982
kynsi 349
kynsiviila 635
kynttilä 161
kyntää 736
kynä 709
kysyä 36
kytkin 969
kyyhkynen 721
kyynärpää 307
kyynärvarsi 553
käymälä 1012
kärpänen 362
kärryt 174
käsi 439
käsikranaati 440
käsilaukku 54
käsineet 409
kävelykeppi 943
käydä, mennä 1070
kääntää 1027
käärme 903
köysi 823
lääkäri 717
laasti 606
lahja 403
lakaista 965
lakki 164
lammas 868
lampaanliha 632
lapio ·879
lapio 918
lapiolamppu 183
lapsi 49
laakso 1053
lasi 407
lasku 90
laskuvarjo 695
lato; riihi 62
lauantai 338
laukka 523

laulaa 884
lautanen 729
lautta 338
lehmus 536
lehmä 245
lehti 645
leikata 444
leikata 254
leima 932
leipoa 56
leipä 126
leipuri 57
lemmikki 370
leninki 288
lentokenttä 8
lentokone 5
lentäjä 47
leuka 198
liha 582
liikavarvas 238
liima 410
liivit 1067
likainen 279
likööri 541
linja-auto 611
linna 176
lintu 92
lippumyynti 113
lokakuu 669
loma 805
lompakko 767
lompakko 1071
lounas 278
lude 139
lukea 786
lukko 547
lumi 904
lusikka 923
luumu 738
luuta 135
lyhty 516
lyhyt 877
lyijy 520
lyijykynä 710
lypsää 593
lämmin 1075
Lämpömittari 210
länsi 1088
lääke 583
löytää 347
maahantulo 33
maaliskuu 569
maamyyrä 598
maanantai 599
maantie 459
maata 527
maastalähtö 936
maisema 515
maissi 563
maito 592
makarooneia 655
makarooneja 559
makea 966
makkara 839
maksa 544
maksaa 704
makuuhuone 76
makuuvaunu 896
malmi 682
mandoliini 567

mansikka 953
margariini 570
marmelaadi 572
marraskuu 660
matkalippu 1002
matkatavara 555
matkatavarain säilytys 556
matkustaa 522
matkustaa 1028
matruusi 832
matto 172
mausteneilikka 216
mehiläinen 77
meisseli 199
melooni 585
meri 849
messinki 125
mestari 575
metalli 590
metrimitta 975
metsä 1106
metsäkarju 1098
metsäkauris 268
mies 566
miksi 1096
mikä; mitä 1089
minne 1093
minun 633
minuutti 595
missä 1091
mistä 1092
moittia 98
moottori 610
moottoripyörä 613
muistomerkki 603
muna 303
munakokkeli(a) 846
munuainen 497
muuli 627
musiikki 629
muskottipähkinä 663
musta 97
mustepullo 484
mustikat, pl. 103
muurari 129
myydä 855
myymäla 876
myrsky 949
mänty 265
naistenhattu 508
naistenkengät 509
naistenpaita 191
naistenviitta 512
nappi 147
naudanliha 79
naula 634
nauta 180
neilikka 170
neiti 597
neljä 377
neljäkymmentä 374
neljätoista 373
nenä 658
nenäliina 441
neula 642
niin, kyllä 1117
niitty 580
niittää 623
nikkeli 647
nilkkanivel 20

nimi 636
niska 638
nojatuoli 31
nolla 1120
nopea 771
noppa; kuutio 275
nosturi 248
noudettava 751
nukkua 895
numero 661
nuottia 630
nuppineula 724
nurja puoli; tausta 51
nyrkki 354
nähdä 854
Näkemiin 1130
nälkäinen 471
odottaa 1068
ohja 794
ohra 61
ohut 990
oikapää 878
oljet 952
olkaa hyvä 732
(housunkannatimet); olkaimet 124
olkavarsi 1052
olla 72
olut 81
omata 447
omena 26
ommella 862
ompelukone 860
ompelulanka 861
onki 18
oppia 521
oranssi 681
orvokki 1062
osasto 230
osoite 4
ostaa 148
osteri 687
otsa 367
ottaa 178
ottaa 973
ovi 286
paistaa 815
paistettu hanhi 817
paistettuja perunoita 382
paistettu kala 381
paistettu kana 816
paistettu metsänriista 393
paisti 818
paistinpannu 387
paita 871
paju 1099
paketti 696
paksu 987
paljo; moni 626
palmu 690
palopommi 477
paperi 693
paprika 694
papuja pavut 73
parsa 37
parsia 586
parta 864
partasuti 865
partaveitsi 785
parturi 434
parveke 58

FRENCH

bureau, *m.* 274
bureau, *m.* 670
le bureau de change 317
bureau de poste, *m.* 750
bureau de renseignements, *m.* 483
bureau de tabac, *m.* 1009
buvard, *m.* 100
cabaret, *m.* 149
cabine, *f.* 151
cabinet, *m.* 1012
cacao, *m.* 220
le cache-nez 843
cachet, *m.* 932
café, *m.* 221
café, *m.* 152
caleçon, *m.* 287
camion, *m.* 614
camp, *m.* 159
canapé, *m.* 907
canard, *m.* 296
canif, *m.* 740
la canne 943
canon, *m.* 162
canot, *m.* 105
cantine, *f.* 163
capable 1
cape, *f.* 165
capitaine, *m.* 166
carottes, *pl. f.* 173
carte, *f.* 568
carte postale, *f.* 749
cartes à jouer, *f. pl.* 731
casque d'acier, *m.* 942
casquette, *f.* 164
cathédrale, *f.* 179
cave, *f.* 64
cave-abris, *f.* 10
ceinture, *f.* 86
ceinture de sauvetage, *f.* 528
cent 470
cerf, *m.* 929
cerise, *f.* 192
chaise, *f.* 184
le châle 866
chambre à coucher 76
chameau, *m.* 157
chamois, *m.* 186
champ, *m.* 3
champignon, *m.* 628
chanter 884
chapeau, *m.* 446
chapeau, *m.* 508
char blindé, *m.* 974
charpentier, *m.* 493
charrue, *f.* 735
chat, *m.* 177
château, *m.* 176
chaud 1075
chaudron, *m.* 109
chauffeur, *m.* 293
chaussettes *f. pl.* 906
chaussure de sport, *f.* 925
chaussures, *f. pl.* 509
chaussures, *f.* 872
chef de bureau, *m.* 450
chef de gare, *m.* 939
chemin, *m.* 1082
chemin de fer, *m.* 776
chemise, *f.* 191
chemise, *f.* 871

chemise de nuit, *f.* 649
la chemise de sport, *f.* 924
chêne, *m.* 664
cher; coûteux 323
cheval, *m.* 463
cheveux, *m. pl.* 432
cheville, *f.* 20
chèvre, *f.* 412
chevreuil, *m.* 268
chien, *m.* 284
chocolat, *m.* 201
chou blanc, *m.* 150
choufleur, *m.* 181
chou-rave, *m.* 505
chose, *f.*; objet 991
chou rouge, *m.* 790
la ciboulette 200
cigare, *m.* 203
cigarette, *f.* 204
cinéma, *m.* 622
cinq 355
cinquante 342
cisailles, *f. pl.* 1104
ciseau, *m.* 92
ciseau, *m.* 199
ciseaux, *m. pl.* 845
citron, *m.* 525
citrouille, *f.* 764
clair 530
clarinette, *f.* 207
clé, *f.* 496
clef à écrous, *f.* 1113
clou, *m.* 634
clous de girofle, *m. pl.* 216
coeur, *m.* 452
coiffeur, *m.* 434
cognac, *m.* 222
colza, *m.* 781
col, *m.* 224
col de fourrure 390
colle, *f.* 410
collier, *m.* 641
commencer 83
commerce, *m.* 143
commode, *f.* 196
commutateur, *m.* 969
compartiment, *m.* 230
comprendre 1048
comprimé, *m.* 971
comptable, *m.* 114
concierge, *m.* 746
concombre; cornichon, *m.* 251
confiture, *f.* 572
corset, *m.* 240
consigne, *f.* 556
consulat, *m.* 232
contrôle, *m.* 234
coq, *m.* 218
cor, *m.* 238
corbeille, *f.* 65
corde, *f.* 823
cordonnier 875
cornet, *m.* 275
côtelette, *f.* 255
coton, *m.* 243
cou, *m.* 640
coude, *m.* 307
coudre 862
couleur, *f.* 226
couper; séparer 254

garçon de café, *m.* 1069
gare, *f.* 938
gâteau, *m.* 154
gaz, *m.* 398
genou, *m.* 503
genre; bon 499
gilet, *m.* 1067
glace, *f.* 474
gomme, *f.* 479
gorge, *f.* 998
grand 518
grange, *f.* 62
grêle 431
grenade à main, *f.* 440
grenier, *m.* 42
gris 427
groseille à maquereau, *f.* 418
groseille rouge, *f.* 791
grue, *f.* 248
guêpe, *f.* 1078
guichet, *m.* 113
guitare, *f.* 429
gymnastique, *f.* 430
hache, *f.* 48
hareng, *m.* 457
haricot, *m.* 73
harmonica, *m.* 619
hâter; accélérér 445
havresac, *m.* 824
hêtre, *m.* 78
heure, *f.* 468
heure de visite 233
heureux; content 406
hier 1118
hiver, *m.* 1102
homard, *m.* 546
l'homme 565
homme, *m.* 566
hôpital, *m.* 466
hôpital militaire, *m.* 591
hôtel, *m.* 467
hôtel de ville, *m.* 1023
huile, *f.* 672
huit 304
huître, *f.* 687
ici 456
imperméable, *m.* 779
index, *m.* 366
infirmière, *f.* 662
l'instrument de musique 631
interdit 758
interprète *m.* 487
jambe, *f.* 524
jambe, *f.* (partie inferieure) 863
jambon, *m.* 437
janvier, *m.* 492
jardin, *m.* 395
jarretelle, *f.* 513
jaune 1116
jeu de football, *m.* 364
jeudi, *m.* 1001
joue, *f.* 189
jour, *m.* 262
journal, *m.* 645
juillet, *m.* 494
juin, *m.* 495
jupe, *f.* 384
un kilogramme 498
kummel, *m.* 169
là 985

labourer 736
lac, *m.* 514
lacet, *m.* 874
laid 1044
lait, *m.* 592
laine, *f.* 1107
laiton, *m.* 125
lampe de poche, *f.* 71
lampe plafond, *m.* 183
lampe transportable, *f.* 934
langue, *f.* 1016
lanterne, *f.* 516
lapin, *m.* 772
lard, *m.* 52
lavabos, *m. pl.* 1077
laver 1076
ligne de pêche, *f.* 18
légume, *m.* 1055
lettre, *f.* 526
lentement 900
lèvre, *f.* 539
librairie, *m.* 115
libre 379
lièvre, *m.* 442
lilas, *m.* 534
lime, *f.* 344
lime à angle, *f.* 635
lin, *m.* 357
lin, *m.* 537
liqueur, *f.* 541
lire 786
lit, *m.* 75
livre, *m.* 111
locomotive, *f.* 311
loin 331
long 548
louer 756
lumière, *f.* 531
lundi, *m.* 599
lune, *f.* 604
lunettes, *f. pl.* 327
macaronis, *m. pl.* 559
machine, *f.* 560
machine à coudre, *f.* 860
machine à écrire, *f.* 1042
maçon, *m.* 129
Mademoiselle, *f.* 597
mai, *m.* 578
maillot de bain, *m.* 66
main, *f.* 439
maïs, *m.* 563
la maison 469
maître, *m.* 575
malade 475
mandat-poste, *m.* 601
mandoline, *f.* 567
manger 301
mansarde, *f.* 397
manteau, *m.* 512
marché, *m.* 571
marcher 1070
mardi, *m.* 1036
margarine, *f.* 570
le mariage 574
marmite, *f.* 752
marron, *m.* 573
mars, *m.* 569
marteau, *m.* 438
le mateau de fourrure 389
matelas, *m.* 577

zéro,*m.* 1120

zither, *f.* 1122

zink, *m.* 1121

généralités 1125
Bon jour 1126
Bonjour 1127
Bon soir 1128
Bonne nuit 1129
Au revoir 1130
Comment allez-vous? 1131
Je cherche une chambre 1132
Je veux manger 1133
Je veux boire 1134
Comment vous appelez-vous? 1135
Avez-vous compris? 1136
Qu'est-ce que c'est? 1137
Où est cela? 1138
Montrez-moi . . . 1139
Donnez-moi . . . 1140
Combien cela coûte-t-il? 1141
jaquette de lainage, *f.* 1142
Où y a-t-il? 1143
À droite 1144
À gauche 1145
laver les cheveux 1146
couper les cheveux 1147

aller chez le médecin 1148
Quelle heure est-il? 1149
cinq heures, *f. pl.* 1150
cinq heures quinze 1151
cinq heures et demie 1152
sept heures moins le quart 1153
trop tôt 1154
trop tard 1155
je suis 1156
vous êtes; tu es 1157
il, elle est 1158
nous sommes 1159
vous êtes 1160
ils sont 1161
j'ai 1162
Vous avez; tu as 1163
il, elle, il a 1164
nous avons 1165
vous avez 1166
ils ont 1167
Avez-vous . . .? 1168
Je sais 1169
Je ne sais pas 1170

GERMAN

der Aal   302
der Abend   316
das Abendessen   963
abmelden   659
der Abort   1012
abreisen; hinterlassen   522
der Absatz   454
das Abteil   230
acht   304
achtzehn   305
achtzig   306
der Acker   3
die Adresse   4
der Aktenschrank   869
alt   675
das Aluminium   15
der Amboss   22
die Ananas   16
die Angel   18
der Anker   17
anmelden   793
annähen   862
antworten   21
der Apfel   26
die Apotheke   716
die Aprikose   28
der April   29
arbeiten   1108
der Arbeiter   1109
die Arbeiterin   1110
das Armband   123
die Armbanduhr   1114
der Arzt   717
die Aster   40
das Auge   326
der August   43
der Ausgang   322
die Auskunftsstelle   483
die Ausreise, Start   936
die Auster   687
der Autobus   611
der Bäcker   57
der Bach   134
backen   56
der Badeanzug   66
der Bademantel   68
baden   67
das Badetuch   69
die Badewanne   70
der Bahnhof   938
der Bahnsteig   730
der Balkon   58
die Banane   59
die Bank   87
der Bauer   707
die Bäuerin   708
der Baum   1030
das Bauernhaus   333
der Bauernhof   332
die Baumwolle   243
das Beefsteak   80
begegnen; zusammentreffen   584
beginnen   83
das Beil   48
das Bein   524
das Benzin   399
der Berg   615

der Besen   135
das Bett   75
die Biene   77
das Bier   81
das Billard   91
billig   188
die Binde   60
die Birne   705
bitte   732
bitter   96
blau   102
das Blei   520
bleiben   796
der Bleistift   710
der Blitz   533
die Blume   360
der Blumenkohl   181
der Blumenstrauss   141
die Bluse   101
der Bogen   118
die Bohne   73
der Bohrer   117
die Bombe   110
das Boot   105
die Brandbombe   477
braten   815
der Braten   818
das Brathuhn   816
die Bratkartoffel   382
die Bratpfanne   387
braun   136
der Brief   526
die Briefmarke   931
die Brieftasche   1071
die Brille   327
bringen   132
die Brosche   133
das Brot   126
der Brunnen   1087
die Brust   194
die Brücke   130
das Buch   111
die Buche   78
der Buchhalter   114
der Buchladen   115
die Butter   145
der Bücherschrank   112
der Büchsenöffner   1006
das Bügelbrett   490
das Bügeleisen   489
der Bürgersteig   703
das Büro   670
die Büroklammer   211
der Bürovorsteher   450
bürsten   138
das Caféhaus   152
das Cello   1065
der Chauffeur   293
das Dach   822
die Dachkammer   397
das Damenhemd   191
der Damenhut   508
die Damenkleidung   511
der Damenmantel   512
der Damenschuh   509
danke   983
die Dattel   260

der Daumen 999
die (wollene) Decke **99**
die Deckenlampe 183
das Denkmal 603
der Dezember 267
dick 987
der Dienstag 1036
der Dolmetscher, *m.* **487**
der Dom 179
der Donner 1000
der Donnerstag 1001
das Dorf 1060
dort 985
die Drahtschere 1104
drei 997
dreissig 995
dreizehn 994
ein Drittel 992
dunkel 259
dünn 990
durstig 993
die Ehe 574
das Ei 303
die Eiche 664
der Eingang 314
einhalb 435
eilen 445
einmal 677
die Einreise 33
eins 678
das Eis 474
das Eisen 488
die Eisenbahn 776
elf 310
der Ellbogen 307
die Eltern, *pl.* 698
englisch 312
entschuldigen 318
die Ente 296
die Erbse 706
die Erdbeere 953
das Erdgeschoss **428**
erlaubt 714
ernten 444
der erste Stock 351
das Erz 682
der Esel 285
essen 301
der Essig 1061
das Esszimmer **277**
die Fabrik 329
fähig 1
die Fähre 338
fahren 292
die Fahrkarte 1002
das Fahrrad 89
der Fahrstuhl 309
der Fallschirm 695
fangen 178
die Farbe 226
das Fass 63
die Faust 354
der Februar 336
die Feder 709
fegen 965
die Feige 343
die Feile 344
das Fenster 1101
die Ferse 453
das Feuer 350

die Fichte 725
der Film 346
finden 347
der Finger 348
der Fingerhut 989
der Fingernagel **349**
der Fisch 353
der Flachs 357
das Fleisch 582
der Fleischer 144
der Flieder 534
die Fliege 362
der Flieger 47
der Floh 358
die Flöte 361
der Flugplatz 8
das Flugzeug 5
der Fluss 813
das Formular 372
fragen 36
frei 379
der Freitag 380
der Freund; die **Freundin** **383**
der Friseur 434
die Frau 625
die Frau; das Weib **1105**
das Fräulein 597
froh; gern 406
fröhlich; lustig 589
der Frühling 926
das Frühstück 127
der Fuchs 378
der Füllhalter 376
fünf 355
fünfzehn 341
fünfzig 342
der Fuss 363
das Fussballspiel 364
das Fussgelenk 20
füttern 337
der Futterstoff 538
die Gabel 371
die Gans 417
der Gänsebraten **817**
die Garage 394
der Garten 395
das Gas 398
das Gasthaus 485
der gebackene Fisch **381**
geben 405
das Gebirge 616
die Geburt 93
der Geburtstag **94**
die Gefahr 258
das Geflügel 754
gehen 1070
die Geige 1064
das gekochte Ei 107
der gekochte Fisch **108**
gelb 1116
das Geld 600
die Geldtasche 767
das Gemälde 689
die Gemse 186
das Gemüse 1055
das Genick 638
das Gepäck 555
die Gepäckaufbewahrung **556**
der Gepäckträger 747
geradeaus 951

der König   500
die Kontrolle   234
der Kopf   449
das Kopfkissen   722
das Kopftuch   451
der Korb   65
der Korkzieher   237
das Korsett   240
das Kotelett   255
der Kragen   224
der Kragenknopf   **954**
der Kran   248
krank   475
das Krankenhaus   **466**
der Kranz   1112
die Krawatte   1003
die Krippe   250
die Küche   502
der Kuchen   154
die Kuh   245
der Kümmel   169
die Kunstseide   35
das Kupfer   236
der Kürbis   764
der Kürschner   391
kurz   877
der Kuss   501
der Laden   876
die Landkarte   568
die Landschaft   515
die Landstrasse   459
der Lager   159
lang   548
langsam   900
das Lastauto   614
die Laterne   516
der Lauch   523
laufen   326
die Laus   549
das Lazarett   591
die Leber   544
Lebewohl, *n.*   416
ledig; einzeln   885
der Lehnstuhl   31
der Leib; der Bauch   85
das Leichtmetall   532
leider; es tut mir leid   **912**
das Leinen   537
die Leiter   507
lernen   521
lesen   786
das Licht   531
lieben   550
liegen   527
der Likör   541
die Linde   536
das Lineal   825
die Lippe   539
der Lippenstift   540
loben   756
der Löffel   923
die Lokomotive   311
der Löscher   100
der Luftschutzkeller   10
die Lunge   557
machen   564
das Mädchen   404
die Magd; das Dienstmädchen   **562**
mähen   623
die Mahlzeit   581

der Mai   578
das Maiglöckchen   **535**
der Mais   563
die Makkaroni   559
die Mandoline   567
der Mann, (Ehe-**mann**)   **566**
der Mantel   683
die Margarine   570
der Markt   571
die Marmelade   572
die Marone   573
der März   569
die Maschine   560
das Maschinengewehr   **561**
die Matratze   577
der Matrose   832
das Maultier   627
der Maulwurf   598
der Maurer   129
die Maus   617
das Meer   849
die Medizin   583
das Mehl   359
mein, meine, mein; meine, *pl.*   **633**
der Meissel   199
der Meister   575
melken   593
die Melone   585
der Mensch   565
das Messer   504
das Messing   125
das Metall   590
das Metermass   975
die Milch   592
das Militär   32
das Mineralwasser   **594**
die Minute, *f.*   595
die Mirabelle   596
der Mittag   656
das Mittagessen   278
der Mittwoch   1085
die Möhre   173
der Monat   602
der Mond   604
der Montag   599
der Morgen   605
morgen   1014
der Morgenrock   290
der Mörtel   606
der Motor   610
das Motorrad   613
müde   1007
der Mund   618
die Mundharmonika   **619**
das Mundwasser   620
die Muschel   867
die Musik   629
das Musikinstrument   **631**
die Muskatnuss   663
die Mutter   608
die Mütze   164
der Nachmittag   6
die Nacht   648
das Nachthemd   649
der Nachttisch   650
die Nadel   642
der Nagel   634
die Nagelfeile   635
das Nähgarn   861
die Nähmaschine   860

die Scheune 62
das Schienbein 870
die Schildkröte 1020
der Schinken 437
der Schlafanzug 768
schlafen 895
der Schlafwagen 896
das Schlafzimmer 76
die Schlange 903
schlecht 53
die Schleife 119
der Schlitten 894
das Schloss 176
das Schloss 547
der Schlüssel 496
das Schmalz 517
der Schmerz 688
der Schmetterling 146
der Schmied 902
schmutzig 279
der Schnee 904
schneiden 254
der Schneider 972
schnell 771
der Schnittlauch 200
die Schokolade 201
schön 74
der Schrank 1073
die Schraube 847
der Schraubenschlüssel 1113
der Schraubenzieher 848
die Schreibmaschine 1042
der Schreibtisch 274
der Schreiner 171
der Schuh 872
das Schuhband 874
die Schuhbürste 873
der Schuhmacher 875
die Schule 844
die Schulter 878
die Schürze 30
die Schüssel 120
schwarz 97
das Schwein 720
das Schweinefleisch 744
die Schwester 662
die Schwester 897
das Schwimmen 968
sechs 890
sechzehn 891
sechzig 892
der See 514
sehen 854
sehr 1057
die Seide 883
die Seife 905
das Seil 823
sein 72
die Sekretärin, f.; der Sekretär, m. 853
der Sekt 187
die Sekunde 852
die Semmel 820
der September 856
sich setzen 889
die Sicherheitsnadel 831
das Sieb 881
sieben 857
siebzehn 858
siebzig 859
singen 884

die Sirene 887
sitzen 888
der Ski 893
die Socken, pl. 906
der Sockenhalter 964
das Sofa 907
die Sohle 909
der Sohn 910
der Soldat 908
der Sommer 960
die Sonne 961
der Sonntag 962
die Sorge; der Kummer 1031
der Spargel 37
der Spaten 918
der Spazierstock 943
der Speck 52
der Speicher 42
die Speisekarte 587
der Speisewagen 276
die Spielkarte 731
der Spinat 921
spitz 741
die Spitze 506
das Sporthemd 924
der Sportschuh 925
sprechen 919
die Sprechstunde 233
der Springbrunnen 375
die Stachelbeere 418
die Stadt 1022
der Stahl 941
der Stahlhelm 942
der Stall 928
der Stationsvorsteher 939
stechen 944
die Stechmücke 607
der Steckkontakt 737
die Stecknadel 724
stehen 933
die Stehlampe 934
der Stein 946
der Stempel 932
der Stern 935
der Stiefel 116
die Stirn 367
der Stuhl 184
stumpf 104
der Stoff 955
stopfen 586
die Strasse 814
die Strassenbahn 1026
das Streichholz 576
die Strickjacke 1142
das Stroh 952
der Strumpf; die Strümpfe pl. 945
der Strumpfhalter 513
die Stunde 468
der Sturm 949
der Süden 913
die Suppe 915
süss 966
der Tabak 1008
die Tablette 971
tadeln 98
der Tag 262
das Tal 1053
die Tankstelle 345
die Tanne 352
die Tante 44

HUNGARIAN

édes 966
egér 617
egészséges 914
egres 418
egy 678
egyenes 951
egyenruha 1049
egy harmad 992
egyes 885
egy kiló 498
egyszer 677
éhes (en) 471
éjjeliszekrény 650
éjszaka 648
az ejtôernyö 695
eke 735
elad 855
elfelejt 369
ellenörzés 234
elsö emelet 351
elutazik 522
elválaszt 254
ember 565
emlékmű 603
énekelni 884
enni 301
enyém 633
érc 590
érc; fém 682
erkély 58
erdeifenyö 265
erdö 1106
es; meg 14
esernyö 1045
esküvö 1083
esö 778
esököpeny 779
este 316
észak 657
etetni 337
az étkezés 581
étkezökocsi 276
étlap 587
év 1115
evezö 665
ezer 996
fa 1030
fagylalt 474
fájdalom 688
falicsatlakozó 737
falu 1060
fáradt 1007
fazék 752
február 336
fegyver 810
fehér 1094
fehérbor 1095
fej 449
fejkendö 451
fejni 593
fejsze 48
fekete 97
feküdni 527
fél 435
félcipö 554
felelni 21
felhö 215
felsökar 1052
felsölábszár 988
felvilágositó iroda 483

felvenó 309
a fény 531
fényképezögép 158
fenyö 352
féril 566
a festmény 689
fésü 228
a film 346
a fiókos szekrény 196
fiú 121
fiú, m. 910
fizet 704
fodrász 434
fog 1017
fogadóóra 233
fogkefe 1018
fogkrém 1019
fogni 178
fogó 1015
fogoly 701
fokhagyma 396
foltozni 586
folyó 813
fotel 31
földieper 953
földszint 428
fött hal 108
fött tojás 107
fözelék 1055
fözni 106
fözni 235
fúró 117
futni 826
fuvola 361
füge 343
függöny 253
fül 297
fülbevaló 299
fülvédő 298
fürdökád 70
fürdököpeny 68
fürdölepedö 69
fürdöruha 66
fürész 840
füródni 67
füzfa 1099
füzö 240
galamb 721
gallér 224
gallérgomb 954
a garázs 394
gáz 398
gazda 707
gazdag 807
gazdasszony 708
gége 998
gép 560
gépfegyver 561
gépkocsivezetö 293
gereblye 780
gesztenye 573
gitár 429
gomb 147
gomba 628
gombostü 724
gond 1031
gyalogos 481
gyalu 728
gyapjú 1107
gyapot 243

tavasz 926
távbeszélö 979
távirat 978
tea 977
tégla 128
tegnap 1118
tegnapelött 264
tehén 245
teherauto 614
tej 592
tejszin 249
teknösbéka 1020
tél 1102
tér 927
templom 202
a tenger 849
térd 503
térkép 568
tessék 732
tesz; helyez 889
tészta 154
tetö 822
tetü 549
teve 157
tilos 758
tintatartó 484
tiszt 671
titkárnö 853
tíz 982
tizenhat 891
tizenhét 858
tizenegy 310
tizenhárom 994
tizenkettö 1038
tizenkilenc 652
tizennégy 373
tizennyolc 305
tizenöt 341
tizzta 209
tó 514
tojás 303
toll 709
tolmács 487
tompa 104
a torna 430
torta 976
torülközö 1021
tök 764
tölcsér 388
tölgy 664
töltötoll 376
törzs 85
trafik 1009
traktor 1024
tulipán 1037
tü 642
tüdö 557
tüz 350
tyúk 197
tyúkszem 238
uborka 251
új 644
ujj 348
ujság 645
úr 886
úszás 968
az út 1082
utász 837
utazik 1028
utazni 292

utca 814
útlevél 702
ügy; üzlet 143
ügyirat 283
üllö 22
ülni 888
ürlap 372
ürühús 632
üst 109
üzlet 876
vacsora 963
vad 393
vaddisznó 1098
vadnyúl 442
vaj 145
vakolat 606
vakondok 598
váll 878
van; lenni 72
vánkos 722
van vmije; bir vmivel 447
város 1022
városháza 1023
várni 1068
varró cérna 861
a varrógép 860
vas 488
vasaló 489
a vasalódeszka 490
vasárnap 962
vastag 987
vasút 776
vászon 537
vékony 990
vendéglö 485
venni 148
verés áfonya 246
vese 497
vésö 199
vesz 973
veszedelem 258
vetni 917
vidám 406
vidám 589
vidék 515
a vihar 949
világos 530
villa 371
villám 533
villamos 1026
villanykörte 308
a virág 360
virágcsokor 141
viz 1080
vizmértek 922
vonalzó 825
vonó 118
völgy 1053
vörösbor 792
vörös káposzta 790
zab 666
zárva 213
zene 629
zerge 186
zongora 422
zongora; piano 718
zöld 426
zsák 828
zsebkendö 441
zsebkés 740

ITALIAN

calzetti, *m. pl.* 906
calzolaio, *m.* 875
calzoni, *pl. m.* 1032
camera, *f.* 76
cameriera, *f.* 185
cameriere, *m.* 1069
camicia, *f.* 924
camicia, *f.* 871
camicia da notte, *f.* 649
camicia da notte, *f.* 768
camicia per signora, *f.* 191
camicietta, *f.* 101
camione, *m.* 614
cammello, *m.* 157
camoscio, *m.* 186
campo, *m.* 3
campo, *m.* 159
candela, *f.* 161
cane, *m.* 284
cannone, *m.* 162
cantare 884
cantina, *f.* 163
cantina, *f.* 64
capire 1048
capitano, *m.* 166
capriolo, *m.* 268
capanna, *f.* 62
capelli, *m. pl.* 432
capo, *m.* 575
capostazione, *m.* 939
cappelino, *m.* 508
cappello, *m.* 446
capra, *f.* 412
capufficio, *m.* 450
carne, *f.* 582
carne di maiale *f.* 744
carne di manzo *f.* 79
la carne di montone 632
carne di vitello, *f.* 1054
carote, *f. pl.* 173
carpentiere, *m.* 493
carriola, *f.* 174
carrozza ristorante, *f.* 276
carrozza letti, *f.* 896
carta, *f.* 693
carta assorbente, *f.* 100
carta dei cibi, *f.* 587
carta geografica, *f.* 568
carte da giuoco, *f. pl.* 731
cartolina postale, *f.* 749
casa, *f.* 469
casa del contadino, *f.* 333
casa della città, *f.* 1023
cassetta, *f.* 175
cassettone, *m.* 196
castagna, *f.* 573
castello, *m.* 176
cattivo; male 53
cavalcare 809
cavallo, *m.* 463
cavaturaccioli, *m.* 237
cavolo bianco, *m.* 150
cavolo fiore, *m.* 181
cavolo rapa, *m.* 505
cavolo rosso, *m.* 790
cena, *f.* 963
cento 470
cervo, *m.* 929
cesta, *f.* 65
cetra, *f.* 1122

che; che cosa 1089
chiamare 153
chiaro 530
chiatta, *m.* 338
chiave, *f.* 496
chiave per viti, *f.* 1113
chiavetta per scatole, *f.* 1006
chiesa, *f.* 202
un chilogramma 498
chiodo, *m.* 634
chitarra, *f.* 429
chiuso 213
ciliege, *f.* 192
cimice, *f.* 139
cinema, *m.* 622
cinghiale, *m.* 1098
cinquanta 342
cinque 355
cintura, *f.* 86
cioccolata, *f.* 201
cipolla, *f.* 679
cipresso, *m.* 256
il citriolo 251
città, *f.* 1022
clarinetto, *m.* 207
cognac, *m.* 222
colazione, *m.* 127
colla, *f.* 410
collana, *f.* 641
colletto, m. 224
collo, *m.* 640
colore, *m.* 226
colpo, *m.* 759
coltello, *m.* 504
colza, *f.* 781
cominciare 83
comino, *m.* 169
comodino, *m.* 650
comprare 148
conchiglia, *f.* 867
coniglio, *m.* 772
consolato, *m.* 232
contabile, *m.* 114
contadina, *f.* 708
contadino, *m.* 707
contatto, *m.* 737
contento; allegro 406
Il conto 90
coperta da letto, *f.* 99
copertone, *m.* 1043
corazza, *f.* 974
corda, *f.* 823
cornetta, *f.* 1034
corona, *f.*; ghirlanda, *f.* 1112
correre 826
corsa di cavalli 464
corsetto, *m.* 240
corto 877
cosa, *f.* 991
coscia, *f.* 988
costume *m.* 242
costume da bagno, *m.* 66
cotoletta, *f.* 255
cotone, *m.* 243
cravatta, *f.* 1003
cucchiaio, *m.* 923
cucina, *f.* 502
cucire 862
cuocere 235
cuocere 106

grappette, *f. pl.* **211**
gravatta, *f.* 119
grazie 983
grembiale, *m.* 30
grigio 427
grosso 987
gru, *f.* 248
guancia, *f.* 189
guanciale, *m.* 722
guanto, *m.* 409
ieri 1118
ieri l'altro 264
l'imbuto, *m.* 388
impermeabile, *m.* **779**
incontrare 584
incudine, *f.* 22
indice, *m.* 366
indirizzo, *m.* 4
indumenti (maschili), *m. pl.* **214**
indumenti femminili, *f. pl.* **511**
inglese 312
ingresso, *m.* 314
insalata, *f.* 833
insegnare 521
interprete, *m.* 487
interruttore, *m.* 969
inverno, *m.* 1102
là 985
labbra, *f. pl.* 539
laccio per le scarpe,*m.* 874
lago, *m.* 514
lampada per il soffitto, *f.* **183**
lampada tascabile, *f.* 71
lampada transportabile, *f.* **934**
lampadina, *f.* 308
lampo, *m.*; fulmine, *m.* **533**
lampone, *m.* 783
lana, *f.* 1107
lanterna, *f.* 516
lardo, *m.* 52
lasciare; abbandonare **522**
lattaio; piombaio, *m.* **739**
latte, *m.* 592
lavatoio, *m.* 1077
lavare 1076
lavorare 1108
lazzaretto, *m.* 591
leggere 786
lentamente 900
lepre, *f.* 442
lettera, *f.* 526
letto, *m.* 75
levante; oriente; est, *m.* **300**
libero 379
libreria, *f.* 115
libro, *m.* 111
lillà, *m.* 534
lima, *f.* 344
lime a per le unghie, *f.* **635**
limone, *m.* 525
lingua, *f.* 1016
lino, *m.* 357
lino, *m.* 537
liquore, *m.* 541
livellatore, *m.* 922
locanda, *f.* 485
locomotiva, *f.* 311
lodare 756
lontano 331
luce, *f.* 531

luglio, *m.* 494
luna, *f.* 604
lunedi, *m.* 599
lungo 548
maccheroni, *m. pl.* **559**
macchina, *f.* 560
macchina da cucire, *f.* **860**
macchina da scrivere, *f.* **1042**
macellaio *m.* 144
madre, *f.* 608
maggio, *m.* 578
maiale, *m.* 720
mandolino, *m.* 567
mangiare 301
mangiatoa, *f.* 250
mano, *f.* 439
mantellina, *f.* 165
manzo, *m.* 180
marciapiede, *m.* **703**
margarina, *f.* 570
mare, *m.* 849
marinaio, *m.* 832
marmellata, *f.* 572
marrone 136
martedi, *m.* 1036
martello, *m.* 438
marzo, *m.* 569
mattina, *f.* 605
materassa, *f.* 577
matita, *f.* 710
matrimonio, *m.* 574
mattone, *m.* 128
mazzo di fiori, *m.* **141**
medicina, *f.* 583
medico, *m.* 717
mela, *f.* 26
melone, *m.* 585
mente, *m.* 198
mercato, *n.* 571
mercoledi, *m.* 1085
merletto, *m.* 506
mese, *m.* 602
una metà 435
metalli, *m. pl.* 590
metallo leggero, *m.* **532**
metro, *m.* 975
mezzodi; meriggio, *m.* **913**
mezzogiorno, *m.* **656**
miele, *m.* 461
militare, *m.* 32
mille 996
minerale, *m.* 682
minestra, *f.* 915
minuto, *m.* 595
mio, mia, mie 633
mirabella, *f.* 596
mitragliatrice, *f.* **561**
modulo, *m.* 372
molto 626
monomento, *m.* 603
montagna, *f.* 616
monte, *m.* 615
morte, *f.* 266
mosca, *f.* 362
motocicletta, *f.* **613**
motore, *m.* 610
mughetto, *m.* 535
mulo, *m.* 627
mungere 593
muratore, *m.* **129**

snotificare 659
sofa, *m.* 907
soffitta, *f.* 397
soldato, *m.* 908
soldato coloniale **225**
sole, *m.* 961
solo; celibe 885
soprabito, *m.* 683
soprabito per signora, *m.* **512**
soprascarpe, *m.* **684**
sorella, *f.* 897
sottile 990
spalla, *f.* 878
spazzola per i capelli, *f.* **433**
spazzola per le scarpe, *f.* **873**
spazzolino per i denti, *m.* **1018**
spazzolare 138
spilla, *f.* 724
spilla di sicurezza, *f.* **831**
spillo, *m.* 133
spinacci, *m. pl.* **921**
sporco 279
sportello, *m.* 113
spumante, *m.* 187
staccio, *m.* 881
stagno, *m.* 1005
stoffe, *f. pl.* 955
stalla, *f.* 928
stanco 1007
stare in piedi 933
stazione, *f.* 938
stelle, *f. pl.* 935
stinco, *m.* 870
stivale, *m.* 116
strada, *f.* 814
strada di campagna, *f.* **459**
strumenti musicali, *m. pl.* **631**
strutto, *m.* 517
stufa, *f.* 950
suola, *f.* 909
suora, *f.* 662
tabacchino, *m.* 1009
tabacco, *m.* 1008
tacco, *m.* 454
tafano, *m.* 607
tagliare; separare **254**
talpa, *f.* 598
tamburo, *m.* 295
tappeto, *m.* 172
tartaruga, *f.* 1020
tavola, *f.* 970
tavoletta, *f.* 971
tazza, *f.* 252
tè, *m.* 977
teatro, *m.* 984
telefono, *m.* 979
telegramma, *m.* 978
temperino, *m.* 740
tempesta, *f.* 949
tempo, *m.* 1004
tenaglie, *f. pl.* 1015
tendina, *f.* 253
termometro per la febbre, *m.* **210**
un terzo 992
testa, *f.* 449
tetto, *m.* 822
tigho, *m.* 536
timbro, *m.* 932
topo, *m.* 617

torta, *f.* 154
torta, *f.* 976
tractore, *m.* 1024
translare 1027
tranvai, *m.* 1026
trapane, *m.* 117
tre 997
trédici 994
trenta 995
trifoglio, *m.* 217
triste 829
tristo; affannato **912**
trovare 347
tulipano, *m.* 1037
tuono, *m.* 1000
uccello, *m.* 92
ufficiale, *m.* 671
ufficio, *m.* 670
ufficio cambiavalute, *m.* **317**
ufficio di polizia, *m.* **742**
ufficio postale, *m.* **750**
ufficio informazioni, *m.* **483**
úndici 310
unghia,*f.* 349
uno 678
uomo, *m.* 565
uomo, *m.* 566
uovo, *m.* 303
uovo al tegame, *m.* **846**
uovo cotto, *m.* **107**
uscita, *f.* 322
l'uscita, *f.* 936
uva, *f.* 423
uva spina, *f.* **418**
vacca 245
vaglia postale, *m.* **601**
valle, *f.* 1053
vasca da bagno, *f.* **70**
vecchio 675
velluto, *m.* 1056
vedere 854
vendere 855
verdura, *f.* 1055
venerdi, *m.* 380
venire; arrivare **229**
venti 1039
vento, *m.* 1100
ventre, *m.* 85
verde 426
vero; molto 1057
vespa, *f.* 1078
vestaglia, *f.* 290
vestito, *m.* 288
viaggio 1028
villaggio, *m.* 1060
vino bianco, *m.* 1095
vino rosso, *m.* 792
violetta, *f.* 1062
violetto 1063
violino, *m.* 1064
violoncello, *m.* 1065
vite, *f.* 847
vitello, *m.* 155
volatili, *pl. m.* **754**
volpe, *f.* 378
zaino, *m.* 824
zero, *m.* 1120
zia, *f.* 44
zio, *m.* 1046

zingo, *m.* 1121
zoccolo, *f.* 462

zucca, *f.* 764
zucchero, *m.* 957

diverse cose 1125
Buon giorno 1126
Buona giornata 1127
Buona sera 1128
Buona notte 1129
A rivederci 1130
Come sta? 1131
Cerco un alloggio 1132
Io voglio mangiare 1133
Io voglio bere 1134
Como si chiama Lei? 1135
Avete capito? 1136
Che cosa è (questo)? 1137
Dove è? 1138
Indicate mi ... 1139
Mi dia (Datemi) ... 1140
Quanto costa? 1141
maglia, *f.* 1142
Dove si può trovare? 1143
A destra 1144
A sinistra 1145
lavare i capelli 1146
tagliare i capelli 1147

andare del medico 1148
Che ora è? 1149
le cinque 1150
le cinque ed un quarto 1151
le cinque e mezzo 1152
le sette meno un quarto 1153
troppo presto 1154
troppo tardi 1155
io sono 1156
egli è; lei è; tu sei 1157
egli, lei è 1158
noi siamo 1159
voi siete 1160
loro sono 1161
io ho 1162
voi avete; tu hai 1163
egli, lei ha 1164
noi abbiamo 1165
voi avete 1166
loro hanno 1167
Avete ... ? 1168
Io so 1169
Io non so 1170

CROATIAN

mjesec, *m.* 604
mladi luk, *m.* 523
mlijeko, *m.* 592
mnogo 626
moj 633
molim 732
more, *n.* 849
mornar, *m.* 832
morski rak, *m.* 546
mort, *m.* 606
most, *m.* 130
motocikel, *m.* 613
motor, *m.* 610
možda 579
mreža, *f.* 643
mrkva, *f.* 173
muha, *f.* 362
muskat, *m.* 663
musti 593
muzički instrument, *m.* 631
muž, *m.* 566
nadlaktica, *f.* 1052
nadzor; pregledba, *f.* 234
nakovanj, *m.* 22
nalaziti 347
nalivpero, *n.* 376
naočari, *pl.* 327
naprstak, *m.* 989
naramenice, *pl.* 124
naranča, *f.* 681
narukvica, *f.* 123
naslov, *m.* 4
naušnica, *f.* 299
nažalost; žao mi je 912
ne 654
nečist 279
nedelja, *f.* 962
netočno, netočan 1051
nikel, *m.* 647
niska cipela, *f.* 554
njiva, *f.* 3
noč, *f.* 648
noćna košulja, *f.* 649
noćni ormarić, *m.* 650
noga, *f.* 363
noga, *f.* 524
nogomet, *m.* 364
nokat, *m.* 349
nos, *m.* 658
nosač, *m.* 747
nov 644
novac, *m.* 600
novčanik, m. 767
novine, *pl.* 645
nož. *m.* 504
nožice. *pl.* 845
nož za brijanje, *m.* 785
nula, *f.* 1120
nužnik, *m.* 1012
oblak, *m.* 215
obraz, *m.* 189
obrok; objed, *m.* 581
obruč, *m.* 1043
obućar, *m.* 875
ocat, *m.* 1061
odgovarati 21
odijelo (muško), *n.* 214
odijelo žensko, *n.* 511
odjaviti 659
odjelenje, n. 230

ogrlica, *f.* 224
ogrlica, *f.* 641
ogrozd, *m.* 418
ogrtač, *m.* 165
oko, *n.* 326
oliva, *f.* 676
olovka, *f.* 710
olovo, *n.* 520
omorika, *f.* 725
ondje 985
opasnost, *f.* 258
opeka, *f.* 128
orah, *m.* 1072
orati 736
ormar, *m.* 196
ormar, *m.* 1073
ormar za akta, *m.* 869
ormar za knjige, *m.* 112
osa, *f.* 1078
osam 304
osamdeset 306
osamnaest 305
ostati 796
ostriga, *f.* 687
otac, *m.* 334
otkuda 1092
otputovati 522
otvoren 680
ovca, *f.* 868
ovdje 456
ovnetina, *f.* 632
ovoj, *m.* 289
ožujak, *m.* 569
padobran, *m.* 695
paket, *m.* 696
palac, *m.* 999
palica za šetnju, *f.* 943
palma, *f.* 690
pamuk, *m.* 243
papar, *m.* 711
papir, *m.* 693
paprika, *f.* 694
papuča, *f.* 898
paradajz, *m.* 1013
park, *m.* 699
pas, *m.* 284
pasoš, *m.* 702
pasta za zube, *f.* 1019
pasulj, *m.* 73
patka, *f.* 296
pčela, *f.* 77
pečat, *m.* 932
pečena guska, *f.* 817
pečena kokoš, *f.* 816
pečeni krumpir, *m.* 382
pečena riba, *f.* 381
peć, *f.* 950
pečenka, *f.* 818
peći 56
peći; pržiti 815
pedeset 342
pekar, *m.* 57
pekmez, *m.* 572
perad, *f.* 754
pero, *n.* 709
peršin, *m.* 700
peškir za kupanje, *m.* 69
pet 355
peta, *f.* 453
peta, *f.* 454

sedamdeset 859
sedamnaest 858
sedlo, *n.* 830
sedmica, *f.* 1086
sekretarica, *f.* 853
sekunda, *f.* 852
seljačka kuća, *f.* **333**
seljački posjed, *m.* **332**
seljak, *m.* 707
seljakinja, *f.* 708
selo, *n.* 1060
seoska cesta, *f.* **459**
sestra, *f.* 662
sestra, *f.* 897
sidro, *n.* 17
sijalica, *f.* 308
sijati 917
sijecanj, *m.* 492
sijeno, *n.* 458
sin, *m.* 910
sir, *m.* 190
sirena, *f.* 887
sito, *n.* 881
siv 427
sjediti 888
sjekira, *f.* 460
sjekira, *f.* 48
sjesti 889
sjever, *m.* 657
skare za žicu, *pl.* **1104**
skela, *f.* 338
skela, *f.* 842
sklonište protiv **napadaja iz zraka 10**
skorup 249
skup 323
sladak 966
sladoled, *m.* 474
slama, *f.* 952
slan 835
slanina, *f.* 52
sledj, m. 457
slika, *f.* 689
slobodan (-dno) **379**
služavka, *f.* 562
smedj 136
smokva, *f.* 343
smrt, *f.* 266
smučke, *pl.* 893
snijeg, *m.* 904
so, *f.* 834
soba, *f.* 545
soba na tavanu, *f.* **397**
sobarica, *f.* 185
sofa, *f.* 907
spavaća kola, *pl.* **896**
spavaonica, *f.* 76
spavati 895
spinača, *f.* 921
spis, *m.;* dokument, *m.* **283**
spojka za spise, *f.* **211**
spomenik, *m.* 603
sposoban 1
sportska cipela, *f.* **925**
sportska košulja, *f.* **924**
spremište, *m.* 394
srce, *n.* 452
srieda, *f.* 1085
srna, *f.* 268
srpanj, *m.* 494
stablo, *n.* 1030

staja, *f.* 928
stajati 933
stan, *m.* 356
stanica, *f.* 948
stanica, *f.* 938
stanka, *f.* 805
star 675
stegno, *n.* 988
stepenice, *f.*, *pl.* **930**
stjenica, *f.* 139
sto 470
sto, *m.* 970
stolac, *m.* 31
stolar, *m.* 171
stolica, *f.* 184
stolna crkva, *f.* **179**
stražnja strana, *f.* **51**
stric; ujak 1046
strina; tetka, *f.* **44**
stroj, *m.* 560
strug; blanja, *f.* **728**
studeni, *m.* 660
stvar, *m.;* posao, *n.* **991**
subota, *f.* 838
suknja, *f.* 384
sunce, *n.* 961
šunka, *f.* 437
sutra 1014
svadba, *f.* 1083
sveća, *f.* 161
svibanj, *m.* 578
svila, *f.* 883
svinja, *f.* 720
svinjetina, *f.* 744
svjetijka, *f.* 516
svjetilka na stolu, *f.* **934**
svjetilka na tavanici, *f.* **183**
svjetlo, *n.* 531
svrdlo, *n.;* bušač, *m.* **117**
šah, *m.* 193
šaka, *f.* 354
šal, *m.* 866
šalica, *f.* 252
šalter, *m.* 113
šalter, *m.* 969
šećer, *m.* 957
šef, *m.* 450
šef stanice, *m.* **939**
šesdeset 892
šest 890
šestnaest 891
šešir, m. 446
šibica, *f.* 576
šiljast 741
šivaća mašina, *f.* **860**
škola, *f.* 844
školjka, *f.* 867
šljem, *m.* 942
šljiva, *f.* 738
šmrk, *m.* 763
šofer, *m.* 293
šparoga, *f.* 37
štakor, *m.* 784
štekontakt. *m.* 737
štitnik za uši, *m.* 298
što 1089
šuma, *f.* 1106
taban, *m.;* djon, *m.* **909**
tableta, *m.* 971
talijanski kesten, *m.* **573**

životinja, *f.* 19
žuriti se   445

žut   1116

općenito   1125
Dobro jutro   1126
Dobar dan   1127
Dobro veče   1128
Laku noć   1129
Do vidjenja   1130
Kako ste?   1131
Tražim stan   1132
hoću jesti   1133
Hoću piti   1134
Kako vi zvate se?   1135
Jeste li razumjeli?   1136
Šta je to?   1137
Gdje je to?   1138
Pokažite mi ...   1139
Dajte mi   1140
Što to stoji?   1141
pletena bluza, *f.*   1142
Gdje je?   1143
Desno   1144
Lijevo   1145
prati kosu   1146
šišati kosu   1147

ići liječniku   1148
Koliko je sati?   1149
pet sati   1150
pet i petnaest   1151
pola šest   1152
sedam manje četvrt   1153
prerano   1154
prekasno   1155
ja sam   1156
Vi ste; ti si   1157
on, ona, ono je   1158
mi smo   1159
vi ste   1160
oni su   1161
ja imam   1162
Vi imate; ti imaš   1163
on, ona ono ima   1164
mi imamo   1165
vi imate   1166
oni imaju   167
Imate li ...?   1168
Znam   1169
Ne znam   1170

NORWEGIAN

död, m. 266
dör, f. 286
dårlig 53
eddik, m. 1061
egg, n. 303
eggeröre, f. 846
eik, f. 664
elv, f. 813
ekteskap, n. 574
elleve 310
elske 550
en 678
eng, f. 580
engelsk 312
enkelt; ledig 885
eple, n. 26
ert, f. 706
erts, m. 682
esel, n. 285
ettermiddag, m. 6
fabrikk, m. 329
falleskjerm, m. 695
fange 178
far, c./m. 334
fare, c. 258
farve, m. 226
farvel 416
fat, n. 120
febertermometer, n. 210
februar 336
feie 965
fem 355
femten 341
femti 342
ferje, f. 338
fiellkjede, m. 616
fiken, m. 343
fil, m. 344
film, m. 346
finger, m. 348
fingerböl, n. 989
finne 347
fiol, m. 1062
fiolett 1063
fiolin, m. 1064
fiolinbue 118
fire 377
fisk, m. 353
fiskekrok, m. 18
fjell, n. 615
en fjerdedel, en kvart 769
fjorten 373
flesk, n. 52
flue, f. 362
fly, n. 5
flyplass, m. 8
flyver, m. 47
flöte, m. 249
flöyl, m. 1056
flöyte, f. 361
forbinding, m. 60
forbinding, m. 289
forbudt 758
fore 337
foreldre, pl. 698
forglemmegei 370
i forgärs 264
forklä, n. 30
formular, n. 372
forretning, c. 143

forside, f. 385
forstå 1048
forstoff, n. 538
forsöke 1035
fortau, n. 703
fot, m. 363
fotballspill, n. 364
fotografiapparat, m. 158
frakk, m.; jakke, m. 491
frakk, m. 683
frakk, m.; skjört, n. 384
fredag, m. 380
fri, ledig 379
frimerke, n. 931
frisk 914
frisör, m. 434
frokost, m. 127
frukt, m. 386
fröken, c./f. 597
fugl, m. 92
fugler, pl. 754
furu, f. 265
fyllepenn, m. 376
fyrstikk, f. 576
födsel, m. 93
födselsdag, m. 94
förste etasje, n. 428
förti 374
fårekjött, n. 632
gaffel, m. 371
gammel 675
en gang 677
to ganger 1040
garasje, m. 394
gardin, m.; forheng, n. 253
gass c. 398
gate, f. 814
gave, c./f. 403
geit, f. 412
gemse, m. 186
gewär, n. 810
gi 405
gitar, m. 429
gjenta 798
gjestgiveri, n. 485
glad 406
glass, n. 407
glemme 369
god 415
god 499
gran, f. 352
gran, f. 725
graslök, m. 200
gresskar, n. 764
grew, n.; hakke, f. 460
gris, m. 720
grönn 426
grönnsaker, pl. 1055
gryte, f. 752
grå 427
Gud, c. 414
gul 1116
gulerot, f. 173
gulvteppe, n. 172
gummiring, m. 1043
gutt, m. 121
gå 1070
gås, f. 417
gåsestek, f. 817
ha, eie 447

konge, m. 500
kone; hustru, c.; fru 625
konsulat, m. 232
kontor, f. 670
kontorchef, m. 450
kontortid, m. 233
kontroll, c. 234
kopp, m. 252
kopper, n. 236
korketrekker, m. 237
korsett, m. 240
kort 877
kost, m. 135
kotelett, m. 255
kran, m. 248
krans, m. 1112
krave, m.; snipp, m. 224
kraveknapp, m. 954
krybbe, f. 250
ku, f. 245
kullskuffe, m. 219
kunstsilke, m. 35
kupe, m. 230
kurv, m. 65
kvinne, f. 1105
kvinnelig; arbeider, m. 1110
kvistvärelse, n. 397
kvittering, f. 787
kyss, c./m. 501
kålrabi, m. 505
käpe, m. 512
lage 564
landevei, m. 459
landsby, m. 1060
landskap, n. 515
lang 548
langsom 900
lanterne, f. 516
lasarett, n. 591
lastebil, m. 614
lav sko, c. 554
lebestift, m. 540
legg, m. 156
lege, m. 717
leie; leir, c. 159
leiligheten, c. 356
lenestol, m. 31
leppe, f.; lebe, m. 539
lese 786
lettmetall, n. 532
lever, m. 544
ligge 527
like ut 951
liktorn, m. 238
likör, m. 541
liljekonval, m. 535
lim, klebestoff, c. 410
lin, n. 537
lin, n. 357
lind, m. 536
linjal, m. 825
liten 901
lite 339
liv, n.; underliv, n. 85
loft, n. 42
lokomotiv, n. 311
lommebok, f. 1071
lommekniv, m. 740
lommelykt, f. 71
lommetörklä, n. 441

lommeur, n. 1079
loppe, f. 358
lue, f. 164
luke; billettluke, f. 113
lukket 213
lunge, f. 557
lus, f. 549
lyn, n. 533
lys 530
lys, n. 531
lyspäre, c. 308
lystig 589
laere 521
lök, m. 523
löpe 826
lördag, m. 838
löscher, m. 100
lår, n. 988
lås, c. 547
låve, m. 62
madrass, c. 577
mai 578
mais, m. 563
makkaroni, pl. 559
maleri, n. 689
mandag, m. 599
mandolin, m. 567
mann, m. 566
margarin, m. 570
marone, m. 573
mars 569
maskin, c. 560
maskingevär, n. 561
matros, m. 832
medisin, m. 583
megen; meget 626
meget 1057
meisel, m. 199
mel, n. 359
melk, f. 592
melke 593
melon, m. 585
menneske, n. 565
messing, m. 125
mester, m. 575
metall, n. 590
metermål, n. 975
middag, m. 656
middagsmat, m. 278
militär, pl. 32
min 633
mineralvann, n. 594
minnesmerke, n. 603
minutt. n. 595
mirabelle, m. 596
mor, f./c. 608
morgen, m. 605
motor, m. 610
motorsykkel, m. 613
muldyr, n. 627
mullvarp, m. 598
munn, m. 618
munnspill, n.; harmonikk, m. 619
munnvann, n. 620
murer, m. 129
murkalk, m. 606
mus, f. 617
musikk, c. 629
musikk instrument, m. 631
muskatnött, m. 663

saks, *f.* 845
sal, *m.* 830
salat, *m.* 833
såpe, *f.* 905
salve, *f.* 674
salt, *n.* 834
salt 835
sand, *m.* 836
sardiner i olje, *pl.* 673
sau, *m.* 868
saus, *m.* 424
se 854
sekk, *m.* 828
sekretär, *m.* 853
seks 890
seksten 891
seksti 892
sekt, *m.* 187
sekund, *n.* 852
selge 855
seng, *f.* 75
september 856
sette 889
si 981
sigar, *m.* 203
sigarett, *m.* 204
sigarforretning, *m.* 1009
sikkerhetsnål, *f.* 831
sil, *m.* 881
sild, *f.* 457
silke, *m.* 883
sink, *n.* 1121
sirene, *f.* 887
sitte 888
sjakk, *m.* 193
sjokolade, *m.* 201
sjåför, *m.* 293
skank, *m.* 863
skap, *n.* 1073
ski, *f.* 893
skikket 1
skildpadde, *f.* 1020
skille 254
skinke, *m.* 437
skinneben, *n.* 870
skje, *m.* 923
skjorte, *f.* 871
sko, *c./pl.* 872
skobörste, *m.* 873
skog, *m.* 1106
skole, *c.* 844
skolisse, *m.* 874
skomaker, *m.* 875
skredder, *m.* 972
skrivebord, *n.* 274
skrivemaskin, *m.* 1042
skrue, *m.* 847
skrujern, *n.* 848
skrunökkel, *m.* 1113
skuffe, *c.* 879
skulder, *m.* 878
sky, *m.* 215
skyts, *n.* 162
slakter, *m.* 144
slange, *m.* 903
slede, *m.*; kjelke, *m.* 894
slips, *n.* 1003
slott, *n.* 176
slöyfe, *c., f.* 119
slå 623

slåbrok,*m.*; morgenkjole, *m.* 290
smed, *m.* 902
smerte, *m.* 688
smör, *n.* 145
smult 517
smussig 279
sne, *m.* 904
snekker, *m.* 171
sofa, *m.* 907
sokkeholder, *m.* 964
sokker; herreströmper, *pl.* 906
sol, *f.* 961
soldat, *m.* 908
sommer, *m.* 960
sommerfugl, *m.* 146
sopp, *m.* 628
sorg, *c.* 1031
sove 895
sovevogn, *m.* 896
sovevärelse, *n.* 76
spade, *m.* 918
spaserstokk, *c.* 943
spiker, *m.* 634
spillekort, *n.* 731
spinat, *m.* 921
spise 301
spiseseddel, *m.* 587
spisestue, *m.* 277
spisevogn, *m.* 276
spiss 741
sportssko, *m.* 925
sportsskjorte, *m.* 924
springvann, *n.* 375
spörre 36
stall, *m.*; fjös, *n.* 928
stasjonsmester, *m.* 939
stek, *m.* 818
steke 815
stekepanne, *f.* 387
stekt fisk, *m.* 381
stekt höns 816
stekte poteter 382
stempel, *n.* 932
sten, *m.* 946
stige, *m.* 507
stikke 944
stikkelsbär, *m.* 418
stikkontakt, *m.* 737
stillas, *n.* 842
stjerne, *f.* 935
stoff, *n.* 955
stol, *m.* 184
stoppe 586
stoppested, *n.* 948
stor 518
storfe, *n.*; buskap, *m.* 180
storm, *m.* 949
strupe, *m.* 998
strykefjel, *m.* 490
strykejern, *n.* 489
strömpe, *m.* 945
strömpeholder, *c.* 513
stump 104
stygg 1044
stövel, *m.* 116
stå 933
stål, *n.* 941
stålampe, *f.* 934
stålhjelm, *m.* 942
sukker, *n.* 957

år, n.   1115
åre, f.   665

åtte   304
åtti   306

forskjellig   1125
god morgen   1126
God dag   1127
God aften   1128
God natt   1129
På giensyn   1130
Hvordan har De det?   1131
Jeg söker et sted å bo   1132
Jeg vil pise   1133
Jeg vil drikke   1134
Hva er Deres navn?   1135
Har De forstått?   1136
Hvad er det?   1137
Hvor er det?   1138
Vil De väre så snild å vise meg . . .   1139
Vil De väre så snild å gi meg . . .   1140
Hvad koster det?   1141
jumper, m.; strikkyakke, f.   1142
Hvor får man?   1143
Til hörye   1144
Til venstre   1145
vaske håret   1146
klippe håret   1147

gå til lege   1148
Hvor meget er klokken?   1149
klokken fem   1150
klokke fem en kvart   1151
klokke half seks   1152
klokke kvart i syv   1153
for tidlig   1154
for sent   1155
jeg er   1156
De er; Du er   1157
han, hun, den det er   1158
vi er   1159
dere er   1160
de er   1161
jeg har   1162
De har; du har   1163
han, hun, den, det har   1164
vi har   1165
dere har   1166
de har   1167
Har De . . . ?   1168
Jeg vet   1169
Jeg vet ikke   1170

POLISH

marzec, *m.* 569
maść, *f.* 674
masło, *n.* 145
maszyna, *f.* 560
maszyna do pisania, *f.* 1042
maszyna do szycia, *f.* 860
material, *f.* 955
material na podszwewki, *m.* 538
matka, *f.* 608
matrac, *f.* 577
melon, *m.* 585
metale, *pl.* 590
metrówka, *f.* 975
mężczyzna, *m.* 566
miasto, *n.* 1022
mieć 447
miedź, *f.* 236
miesiąc, *m.* 602
mięso, *n.* 582
mięso cielęce, *n.* 1054
mięso wolowe, *n.* 79
mieszkanie, *n.* 356
minuta, *f.* 595
miód, *m.* 461
miotła, *f.* 135
mirabela, *f.* 596
miska, *f.* 120
mleko, *n.* 592
młot, *m.* 438
moj 633
motor, *m.* 610
motyka, *f.* 460
motyl, *m.* 146
morela, *f.* 28
morze 579
morze, *n.* 849
mosiądz, *m.* 125
most, *m.* 130
mówić 919
mówić; powiedzieć 981
mucha, *f.* 362
muł, *m.* 627
mundur, *m.* 1049
murarz, *m.* 129
muszla, *f.* 867
muzyka, *f.* 629
mydło, *n.* 905
mysz, *f.* 617
naczelnik stacji, *m.* 939
nagniotek, *m.* 238
nalazić 347
naparstek, *m.* 989
narty, *pl.* 893
naszyjnik, *m.* 641
nazvisko, *n.* 636
nerka, *f.* 497
nici do szycia, *pl.* 861
nie 654
niedziela, *f.* 962
niepunktualnie 1051
niezapominajka, *f.* 370
nikel, *m.* 647
noc, *f.* 648
nocna koszula, *f.* 649
nadramię, *n.* 1052
noga, *f.* 524
nos, *m.* 658
nowy 644
nóż, *m.* 504
nożyce, *pl.* 845

nożyce blacharskie, *n. pl.* 1104
numer, *m.* 661
numerowy, *m.* 747
nuty, *pl.* 630
obcas, *m.* 454
obcegi, *pl.* 1015
obiad, *m.* 278
obiad, *m.* 581
obóz, *m.* 159
obręcz 1043
ocet, *m.* 1061
ochraniacze na ucha 298
odjezdzać; odjechać 522
odkrętka, *f.* 1113
odpowiadać 21
odzienie męskie, *n.* 214
odzienie kobiece, *n.* 511
odźwierny, *m.* 746
oficer, *m.* 671
ogień, *m.* 350
ogórek, *m.* 251
ogród, *m.* 395
ojciec, *m.* 334
okienko, *n.* 113
okno, *n.* 1101
oko, *m.*; oczy, *pl.* 326
okręt handlowy, *m.* 588
okulary, *pl.* 327
oliwa, *f.* 672
oliwka, *f.* 676
olów, *m.* 520
olówek, *m.* 710
opaska, *n.* 60
opasnost, *f.* 258
opieka, *f.* 1031
orać 736
orzech laskowy, *m.* 448
orzech włoski, *m.* 1072
osa, *f.* 1078
osiem 304
osiemdziesiąt 306
osiemnascie 305
osiol, *m.* 285
ostać 795
ostry 741
ostryga, *f.* 687
otwarty 680
otwieracz do puszek, *m.* 1006
owca, *f.* 868
owies, *m.* 666
owoc, *m.* 386
pakunek, *m.* 696
palce u nogi, *pl.* 1011
palec, *m.*; palce, *pl.* 348
palec vskazujący, *m.* 366
palma, *f.* 690
pamiętnik, *m.* 603
pan; Pane! 886
pani, *f.* 625
panna; Panno! 597
pantofle, *pl.* 898
papier, *m.* 693
papieros, *m.* 204
papryka, *f.* 694
parasol, *m.* 1045
park, *m.* 699
parter, *n.* 428
pas, *m.* 86
pas ratunkowy, *m.* 528
pasta do zębow 1019

zrobić; czynić 564
zupa, f. 915

zwierzę n. 19
żyto, n. 827

ogólne 1125
Dobry ranek 1126
Dzień dobry 1127
Dobry wieczór 1128
Dobra noc 1129
Do widzenia 1130
Jak się czujesz? 1131
Szukam pomieszkania 1132
Chcę jeść 1133
Chcę pić 1134
Nazwisko poprosze . . . 1135
Czy zrozumieliście? 1136
Co to jest? 1137
Gdzie to jest? 1138
Pokażcie mnie . . . 1139
Dajcie mnie . . . 1140
Co to kosztuje? 1141
żakiet trykotowy, m. 1142
Gdzie to się znajduje? 1143
Na prawo 1144
Na levo 1145
myć włosy 1146
strzyc wlosy 1147

iść do lekarza 1148
Która godzina? 1149
piąta godzina 1150
kwadrans na szósta 1151
pół do szóstej 1152
trzy na siódma 1153
zawcześnie 1154
zapóźno 1155
ja jestem 1156
oni as; ty jestés 1157
on, ona, ono jest 1158
my jesteśmy 1159
wy jesteście 1160
oni sa 1161
ja mam 1162
oni maja; ty masz 1163
on, ona, ono ma 1164
my mamy 1165
wy macie 1166
oni mają 1167
Czy macie . . . ? 1168
Ja wiem 1169
Ja niewiem 1170

PORTUGUESE

bota de cano alto, *a* 116
botão para colarinho, *o* 954
bote, *o* 105
braço, *o* 1052
branco 1094
brinco, *o* 299
broca, *a* 117
broche, *o* 133
burro, *o* 285
bússola, *a* 231
cabaret, *o* 149
cabeça, *a* 449
cabeçâo de peles, *o* 390
cabeleireiro, *o* 434
cabelo, *o* 432
cabra, *a* 412
cabra montesa, *a* 186
cacau, *a* 220
cachimbo, *o* 726
cacho de uvas, *o* 423
cadeado, *o* 547
cadeira, *a* 184
café, *o* 152
café, *o* 221
casa de campo, *a* 333
caixa, *a* 175
caixinha para pó de arroz, *a* 755
calçada, *a* 703
calcanhar, *o* 453
calças, *as* 1032
calo, *o* 238
cama, *a* 75
cámara municipal, *a* 1023
camarote, *o* 151
camelo, *o* 157
caminho, *o* 1082
caminho de ferro, *o* 776
caminhão, *o* 614
camisa, *a* 871
camisa de dormir, *a* 649
camisa de esporte, *a* 924
camisa para senhoras, *a* 191
campo, *o* 3
campo, *m.* 159
campo de aviação, *o* 8
camponês, *o* 707
camponesa, *a* 708
canela, *a* 870
caneta de tinta permanente, *a* 376
canivete, *o* 740
cantar 884
cantin 163
cão, *o* 284
hábil, capaz 1
capacete de aço, *o* 942
capturar 178
carimbo, *o* 932
carne, *a* 582
carne de carneiro, *a* 632
carne de porco, *a* 744
carne de vaca, *a* 79
carne de vitela, *a* 1054
carniceiro, *m.* 144
caro 323
carregador, *o* 747
carro, *o* 174
carro blindado, *m.;* tanque, *o* 974
carpinteiro, *o* 493
carta, *a* 526
carta para jogar, *a* 645

carta para jogar, *a* 731
carteira, *a* 1071
carvalho, *o* 664
a casa 469
casa de câmbio, *a* 317
casaco, *o* 491
casaco de peles, *o* 389
casaco de senhora, *o* 512
casa comercial, *a* 1074
casamento, *o* 1083
casco, *m.* 462
castanha, *a* 573
castanho 136
catedral, *a* 179
cavalo, *o* 463
cave, *a* 64
cebola, *a* 679
cebolinha, *a* 200
ceifar 623
cem 470
cenoura, *a* 173
censurar 98
centeio, *o* 827
cereja, *a* 192
ceroulas, *as* 287
cerveja, *a* 81
cêsto, *o* 65
cevada, *a* 61
chá, *o* 977
chale, *o* 866
chale, *o* 843
chaleira, *a* 109
chale-manta, *o* 165
chamar 153
champanhe, *o* 187
chapéu, *o* 446
chapéu de senhora, *o* 508
charuto, *o* 203
chave, *a* 496
chávena, *a* 252
chefe de estação, *o* 939
chefe do escritório, *o* 450
chave de parafusos, *a* 1113
chinela, *a* 898
chocolate, *o* 201
chouriço, *o* 839
chumbo, *o* 520
chuva, *a* 778
a cidade 1022
cigarro, *o* 204
cinco 355
cinema, *o* 622
cinqüenta 342
cinto, *o* 86
cinzel, *o* 199
cinzento 427
cipreste, *o* 256
cítara, *a* 1122
clarim, *a* 1034
clarinete, *o* 207
claro 530
cobertor, *m.* 99
cobra, *a* 903
cobre, *a* 236
cocheira, *a* 928
cogumelo, *o* 628
coelho, *o* 772
coisa, *f.* 991
cola, *a* 410
colar, *o* 641

fechado 213
feijão, o 73
feio 1044
feno, o 458
ferir; cortar 254
ferradura, a 465
ferreiro, o 902
ferro, m. 488
ferro eléctrico, o 489
fevereiro, m. 336
ficar' 796
fígado, o 544
figo, o 343
filha, f. 261
filho, m. 910
filme, o 346
flauta, a 361
flôr, a 360
floresta, a 1106
fogão, o 950
fogo, o 350
fonte, a 375
fôrças armadas, as 32
formulário, o 372
fôrro, o 538
fósforo, o 576
framboesa, a 783
frango assado, o 816
frigideira, a 387
frio 223
fritar 56
fruta, a 386
funil, o 388
gado bovino, o 180
gaita, a 619
galinha, a 197
galo, o 218
galocha, a 684
gancho, o 211
ganso, o 417
garage, a. 394
garfo, o 371
garganta, a 998
gâs, m. 398
gasolina, a 399
gato, o 177
gordo 987
groselha, a 791
granada de mão, a 440
grande 518
granizo 431
gravata, a 1003
gravata para traje de rigor, a 119
guarda-chuva, o 1045
guarda-fato, o 1073
guarda-livros, o 114
guichet, o 113
guindaste, o 248
guitarra, a 429
habitaçâo, a 356
herdade, a 332
hoje 1010
o homem 565
homem, o 566
hora, a 468
hora de consultas, a 233
hospital, o 466
hospital militar, o 591
hotel, o 467
igreja, a 202

impermeável, o 779
inglés 312
o instrumento de musica 631
intérpretar, m. 487
inverno, o 1102
interruptor, o 969
irmã, f. 897
janeiro, o 492
janela, a 1101
jantar, a 963
jardim, o 395
javali, o 1098
jòelho, o 503
jôgo de futebol, o 364
julho, o 494
junho, o 495
um kilo 498
lã, a 1107
lábio, o 539
lago, o 514
lâmpada de algibeira, a 71
lâmpada de pé alto, a 934
lâmpada eléctrica, f. 308
langosta, a 546
lanterna, a 516
lápis, o 710
laranja, a 681
latão, o 125
lavar 1076
lavatório, o 1077
lebre, a 442
legumes, os 1055
leite, o 592
lenço, o 441
lenço de cabeça, o 451
ler 786
licôr, o 541
liga, a 513
liga, a 964
ligadura, a 289
lilás, o 534
lima, a 344
limão, o 525
lima para as unhas, a 635
limpo 209
língua, a 1016
linha para costura, a 861
linho, o 357
linho, o 537
lírio dos vales, o 535
lista, a 587
livraria, a 115
livre 379
livro, o 111
locomotiva, a 311
loja, a 876
lua, a 604
lustre, o 183
luva, a 409
luz, a 531
maçã, a 26
macarrão, o 559
machado, o 48
magro 990
mãi, f. 608
maillot, o 66
maio, o 578
mal 53
malinha da mão, a 54
mandolim 567

vitela, *a* 155
xadrez, *o* 193

zéro, *o* 1120
zinco, *o* 1121

diversos 1125
Bom dia 1126
Bom dia 1127
Boa noite 1128
Até logo 1130
Como passa 1131
Procurar a habitação **1132**
Quero comer 1133
Quero beber 1134
Como se chama? 1135
O senhor compreenden? **1136**
O que é isso (. . . isto?) **1137**
Onde está isso? 1138
mostre-me . . . 1139
Dê-me . . . 1140
Quanto custa? 1141
casaco de malha, *o* 1142
Onde há isso . . . ? **1143**
À direita 1144
À esquerda 1145
lavar o cabelo 1146
cortar o cabelo 1147
ir o médico 1148

Que horas são? **1149**
cinco horas 1150
cinco (horas) e um quarto **1151**
cinco e trínta 1152
seis (horas) o três quartos **1153**
muito cedo 1154
muito tarde 1155
eu sou; estou 1156
êles (elas) são; tu és **1157**
éle, ela é 1158
nós somos 1159
vós sois 1160
êles são; estão **1161**
eu tenho 1162
o senhor (a senhora) tem; tu tens **1163**
êle, ela tem 1164
nós temos 1165
vós tendes 1166
êles têm 1167
O senhor tem . . . ? **1168**
Eu sei 1169
Eu não sei 1170

RUMANIAN

ploaiă, f. 778
plugul 735
plumbul 520
poartă, f. 400
poate 579
pod, n. 42
podul 130
poftim 732
poimâne 263
poliţia, f. 742
pompă, f. 763
porcul 720
porcul mistret 1098
portarul 436
portarul 746
port-jartiera 513
portocala, f. 681
portofoliul 1071
portul 745
porumbelul 721
porumbul 563
poşeta, f. 54
poste-restante 751
potărniche, f. 701
potcoavă, f. 465
a prăji 815
prăvălia, f. 876
prieten, m. 383
primăria, f. 1023
primăvara, f. 926
a prinde 178
priză, f. 737
projectilul 759
prosopul 1021
prosopul de baie 69
pruna, f. 738
pudingă, f. 761
pudriera, f. 755
puloverul 762
pulpa, f. 156
pulpa, f. 863
pumnul 354
punctual 765
punga de bani 767
puricele, m. 358
puşcă, f. 810
putin 339
rămas bun! 416
raniţă, f. 824
rapiţă, f. 781
a răspunde 21
raţa, f. 296
rău 53
râul 813
rege, m. 500
repede; iute 771
a repeta 798
restaurantul 485
ridichea, f. 775
ridichea de lună, f. 774
rindeă, f. 728
rinichiul, m. 497
roaba 174
rochia, f. 288
roşu 789
roşul de buze 540
sacul 828
şahul 193
şaisprezece 891
salata, f. 833

salcia, f. 1099
saltea, f. 577
a sămăna 917
Sâmbătă, f. 838
şampanie, f. 187
sănătos 914
sania, pl. 894
sapca, f. 164
săptămîna, f. 1086
săpunul 905
şapte 857
şaptesprezece 858
şaptezeci 859
sărat 835
sardeaua, f. 673
sareă, f. 834
şarpele, m. 903
şase 890
sasezeci 892
satul 1060
săturare, f. 501
scândura de frecat 490
scară, f. 507
scară, f. 930
scaunul 184
schelă, f. 842
schiurile, pl. 893
scoală, f. 844
scoica, f. 867
scrinul 196
scrisoareă, f. 526
scrumbia, f. 457
scump 323
scurt 877
a scuza 318
seară, f. 316
şeaua, f. 830
secară, f. 827
secretară, f. 853
secunda, f. 852
a sedea 888
şeful de birou 450
şeful de gară 939
Septembrie 856
servitoareă, f. 562
sfecla roşie 82
un sfert 769
si; iar 14
sirena 887
siretul de ghete 874
sită, f. 881
slănina, f. 52
smeura, f. 783
smochină, f. 343
şoarecele 617
soarele 961
şocolată, f. 201
socoteală, f. 90
sobă, f. 950
şobolanul 784
sofaná, f. 907
şoferul 293
soldat-ul 908
soldatul colonial 225
sopronul 62
soră, f. 897
sora de caritate 662
sorţul 30
soseaua, f. 459
sosul 424

ziarul   645
zidarul   129

zincul   1121
ziuă de naştere, f.   94

DIVERSE   1125
Bună dimineata   1126
Bună ziua   1127
Bună seara   1128
Noapte bună   1129
La revedere   1130
Ce mal faceţi?   1131
Eu căut locuintă   1132
Vreau să   1133
Vreau să beau   1134
Care tău nume?   1135
Aţi înteles?   1136
Ce-i aceasta?   1137
Unde este aceasta?   1138
Arătaţi-mi . . .   1139
Daţi-mi . . .   1140
Cât costă?   1141
Jerseul   1142
Unde se găseşte?   1143
La dreapta   1144
La stînga   1145
a-şi spala părul   1146
a tunde părul   1147

a merge la doctor   1148
Ce oră e?   1149
orele cinci   1150
orele cinci şi un sfert   1151
orele cinci şi jumătate   1152
orele şapte fără un sfert   1153
prea devreme   1154
prea tirziu   1155
eu sunt   1156
Dumnea voastră sunteti; tu esti   1157
el, ea e   1158
noi suntem   1159
voi sunteti   1160
ei sunt   1161
eu am   1162
ei au; tu ai   1163
el, ea, are   1164
noi avem   1165
voi aveti   1166
ei au   1167
Aveţi . . . ?   1168
Nu ştiu   1170
Ştiu   1169

SLOVAK

most, *m.* 130
motocykel, *m.* 613
motor, *m.* 610
motýl', *m.* 146
možno 579
mnoho; vel'a 626
mrkva, *f.* 173
mucha, *f.* 362
múka, *f.* 359
mulica, *f.* 627
murár, *m.* 129
muškátový oriešok, *m.* 663
mušl'a, *f.* 867
muž, *m.* 566
mydlo, *n.* 905
myš, *f.* 617
nadlaktie, *n.* 1052
náhrdelník, *m.* 641
nájst' 347
nákladné auto, *n.* 614
nákova, *f.* 22
námestie, *n.* 927
námorník, *m.* 832
náprsná taška, *f.* 1071
náprstok, *m.* 989
náramkové hodinky, *pl.* 1114
náramok, *m.* 123
narodeniny, *pl.* 94
narodzenie, *n.*; pôrod, *m.* 93
nástupište, *n.* 730
náušnica, *f.* 299
necht, *m.* 349
nebezpečenstvo, *n.* 258
nedel'a, *f.* 962
nemocnica, *f.* 466
nepresne 1051
nezabúdka, *f.* 370
nie 654
nikel, *m.* 647
nit', *f.* 861
noc, *f.* 648
nočná košel'a, *f.* 649
nočný stolík 650
noha, *f.* 524
nohavice, *f. pl.* 1032
nos, *m.* 658
nosič, *m.* 747
noty, *pl.* 630
november 660
noviny, *pl.* 645
nový, nová, nové 644
nôž, *m.* 504
nožnice, *pl.* 845
nožnice na drôt, *pl.* 1104
nula, *f.* 1120
obchod, *m.* 876
obchod, podnik, *m.* 143
obchodná lod', *f.* 588
obchodný dom, *m.* 1074
obed, *m.* 278
oblak, *m.* 215
obličaj, *m.* 328
oblok, *m.* 1101
obraz, *m.* 689
obuvník, *m.*; čizmar, *m.* 875
obväz, *m.* 60
obväz, *m.* 289
obývacia izba, *f.* 545
ocel', *f.* 941
ocot, *m.* 1061

odcestovat' 522
odev (mužský), *m.* 214
odhlásit' 659
odkial' 1092
odpovedat' 21
odpustit' 318
oheň, *m.* 350
okienko, *n.* 113
oko, *n.* 326
október 669
okuliare, *pl.* 327
olej. *m.* 672
oliva, *f.* 676
olovo *n.* 520
omáčka, *f.* 424
opakovat' 798
opasok, *m.* 86
orat' 736
orech, *m.* 1072
orgován, *m.* 534
osa, *f.* 1078
osem 304
osemdesiat 306
osemnást' 305
osobné auto, *n.* 612
ošetrovatel'ka, *f.* 662
otec, *m.* 334
otvarač na konzervy, *m.* 1006
otvorený 680
ovca, *f.* 868
ovocie, *n.* 386
ovos, *m.* 666
padák, *m.* 695
palce (na nohe), *m. pl.* 1011
palec, *m.* 999
palica, *f.* 943
palma, *f.* 690
pančuchy, *f. pl.* 945
pán, *m.*; panei 886
pani, *f.* 625
paňva, *f.* 387
panciernik, *m.* 974
papier, *m.* 693
paprika, *f.* 694
park, *m.* 699
pauza, *f.* 805
pažítka, *f.* 200
pät 355
pätdesiat 342
pätnást' 341
päst, *f.* 354
päta, *f.* 453
pečená hus, *f.* 817
pečená kura, *f.* 816
pečené zemiaky, *pl.* 382
pečiatka, *f.* 932
pečienka, *f.* 818
pekár, *m.* 57
pelerína, *f.* 165
peňaženka *f.* 767
peniaze, *pl.* 600
pera; pery, *pl.* 539
pero, *n.* 709
pes, *m.* 284
pešiak, *m.* 481
petržlen, *m.*; petruška, *f.* 700
pianíno, *n.* 718
piatok, *m.* 380
pichat' 944
piect', smažit' 56

sedemnást' 858
sedieť 888
sedliačka, f. 708
sedliacky dom, m. 333
sedliacky dvor, m. 332
sedliak, m. 707
sedlo, n. 830
sekera, f. 48
sekunda, f. 852
seno, n. 458
september 856
sestra, f. 897
sever, m. 657
schody, pl. 930
schopný 1
siat' 917
sieť, f. 643
šija, f. 638
siréna, f. 887
sito, n. 881
sivý 427
skriňa, f. 1073
skriňa na spisy, f. 869
skrutka, f. 847
skrutkový kľúč, m. 1113
skúsiť 1035
sláčik, m. 118
sladký 966
slama, f. 952
slanina, f. 52
slaný 835
slečna, f. 597
sliepka, f.; kura, f. 197
slivka, f. 738
slnko, n. 961
slúžka, f. 562
smažená ryba, f. 381
smädny 993
smotana, f. 249
smrek, m. 725
smrt, f. 266
smutný 829
sneh, m. 904
snubný prsteň, m. 1084
šnurovačka, f. 240
sobota, f. 838
sol', f. 834
somár, m. 285
spací vozeň, m. 896
spalňa, f. 76
spat' 895
spievat' 884
spínadlo, n. 831
spodné nohavice, pl. 287
sponka na spisy, f. 211
srdce, n. 452
srnec, m. 268
stajňa, f. 928
stanica, f. 938
starosť, f. 1031
starý 675
stát' 933
stehno, n. 988
sto 470
stodola, f. 62
stôl, m. 970
stolička, f. 31
stolička, f. 184
stolná lampa. f. 934
strecha, f. 822

streda, f. 1085
strela, f. 759
stretnút' sa 584
stroj, m. 560
strom, m. 1030
strýc; ujec 1046
studený 223
studňa, f. 1087
sud, m. 63
suchár, m. 95
sukňa, f. 384
svatba, f. 1083
svetlo, n. 531
svieca, f. 161
syn, m. 910
syr, m. 190
šach, m. 193
šál, m. 866
šalát, m. 833
šálka, f. 252
šampaňské, n. 187
šatka na hlavu, f. 451
šatka na hrdlo, f. 843
šaty, pl. 288
šest 890
šesťdesiat 892
šestnásť 891
šijací stroj, m. 860
škaredý 1044
škola, f. 844
šnúrky do topanky, pl. 874
špargľa, f. 37
špenát, m. 921
špendlík, m. 724
špinavý 279
športová košeľa 924
športová topánka, f. 925
štetec, m. 137
štetka na holenie, f. 865
štopkat' 586
štrnást' 373
jedna štvrtina 769
štvrtok, m. 1001
štyri 377
štyridsat' 374
šunka, f. 437
tabak, m. 1008
tabletka, f. 971
ťahacia harmonika, f. 2
tajomníčka, f.; tajomník, m. 853
tam 985
tanec, m. 257
tanier, m. 729
ťava, f. 157
tehla, f. 128
tekvica, f. 764
teľa, n. 155
telefón, m. 979
telacie mäso, n. 1054
telegram, m. 978
telo, n. 85
tenký 990
teplomer, m. 210
teplý 1075
tesár, m. 493
teta, f. 44
tisíc 996
tlmočník, m. 487
tlstý 987
tmavý 259

všeobecné 1125
Dobré ráno 1126
Dobrý deň 1127
Dobrý večer 1128
Dobrú noc 1129
Do videnia 1130
Ako sa mate? 1131
hľadám byt 1132
(ja) chcem jesť 1133
(Ja) chcem piť 1134
Ako sa volate? 1135
Rozumeli ste? 1136
Čo je to? 1137
Kde je to? 1138
Ukážte mi . . . 1139
Dajte mi . . . 1140
Čo to stojí? 1141
pletená vesta, f. 1142
Kde je to . . . ? 1143
Vpravo 1144
vľavo 1145
umývať vlasy 1146
strihat' vlasy 1147

ísť'k lekárovi 1148
Koľko je hodin? 1149
päť hodín 1150
pät hodín patnáct 1151
pol šiestej 1152
tri štvrte na sedem 1153
veľmi zavčasu 1154
veľmi neskoro 1155
ja som 1156
Vy ste; Ty si 1157
on, ona, on je 1158
my sme 1159
vy ste 1160
oni sú 1161
(ja) mám 1162
(vy) máte; (ty) máš 1163
on, ona, ono má 1164
my máme 1165
vy máte 1166
oni majú 1167
Máte . . . ? 1168
Viem 1169
Neviem 1170

SPANISH

bomba de mano **440**
bomba incendiaria, *f.* **477**
bombilla, *f.* 308
bosque, *m.* 1106
bota, *f.* 116
bota deportiva, *f.* **925**
bote, *m.* 105
botón, *m.* 147
botón de cuello, *m.* **954**
brazo, *m.* 1052
brocha, *f.* 137
brocha de afeitar, *f.* **865**
brújula, *f.* 231
bueno 415
buey, *m.* 686
buque mercantil, m. **588**
burro, *m.* 285
cabalgar 809
caballo, *m.* 463
cabaret, *m.* 149
cabello, pelo 432
cabeza, *f.* 449
cabra, *f.* 412
cacao, *n.* 220
cadena, *f.* 641
café, *m.* 152
café, *m.* 221
calabaza, *f.* 764
calcetines, *pl.* 906
caldera, *f.* 109
cálido 1075
calle, *f.* 814
callo, *m.* 238
calzoncillos, *pl.* 287
cama, *f.* 75
cámara, *f.* 158
camarera, *f.* 185
camarote, *m.* 151
camello, *m.* 157
camino, *m.* 1082
camión, *m.* 614
camisa, *f.* 871
camisa de deporte, *f.* **924**
camisa de día para mujeres **191**
camisa de noche, *f.* **649**
campo, *m.* 3
campo, *m.* 159
canasto, *m.* 65
canilla, *f.* 870
cañón, *m.* 162
cantar 884
cantina, *f.* 163
capa, *f.* 165
hábil, capaz 1
capitán, *m.* 166
cara, *f.* 328
carne, *f.* 582
carne de cerdo **744**
carne de vaca 79
carnero, *m.* 632
carnicero, *m.* 144
carpintero, *m.* 493
carretera, *f.* 459
carrera de caballos **464**
carreta, *f.* 174
carta, *f.* 526
cartera, *f.* 1071
casa, *f.* 469
casco, *m.* 462
casco de acero, *m.* **942**

casería, *f.* 333
castaña, *f.* 573
castillo, *m.* 176
catedral, *f.* 179
catorce 373
caza, *f.* 393
cebada, *f.* 61
cebolla, *f.* 679
cena, *f.* 963
centeno, *m.* 827
cepillar 138
cepillo de carpintero, *m.* **728**
cepillo para el cabello **433**
cepillo para los dientes **1018**
cepillo para el calzado *m.* **873**
cerdo, *m.* 720
cerezas, *pl.* 192
cerradura, *f.* 547
cerrado 213
cero, *m.* 1120
cerveza, *f.* 81
cien 470
ciervo, *m.* 929
cigarro, *m.* 203
cincel, *m.* 199
cinco 355
cincuenta 342
cine, *m.* 622
cinta métrica, *f.* **975**
cinturón, *m.* 86
cinturón salvavidas **528**
ciprés, *m.* 256
ciruela, *f.* 738
ciruela amarilla, *f.* **596**
cítara, *f.* 1122
ciudad, *m.* 1022
clarinete, *m.* 207
claro 530
clavel, *m.* 170
clavija de conexión **737**
clavo, *m.* 634
clavo de especia **216**
cobija, *f.* 99
cobre, *m.* 236
cocer (en el horno) **56**
coche-cama **896**
coche-restaurant, *m.* **276**
cocina, *f.* 502
codo, *m.* 307
coger 178
colchón, *m.* 577
coliflor, *m.* 181
colinabo, *m.* 505
color; colorido, *m.* **226**
color violeta 1063
colza, *f.* 781
comedero, *m.* 250
comedor, *m.* 277
comenzar 83
comer 301
comida, *f.* 278
comida, *f.* 581
comino, *m.* 169
la cómoda 196
comprar 148
coñak, *m.* 222
conejo, *m.* 722
consigna, *f.* 556
contento 406
contestar 21

pasaporte, *m.* 702
pasta dentífrica, *f.* 1019
pasteles, *pl.* 154
patata, *f.* 753
patatas fritas, *pl.* 382
pato, *m.* 296
pausa, *f.* 805
pecho, *m.* 194
peine, *m.* 228
peletero, *m.* 391
película, *f.* 346
peligro, *m.* 258
peluquero, *m.* 434
pendiente, *f.* 299
pepino, *m.* 251
pequeño 901
pera, *f.* 705
perdiz, *f.* 701
perejil, *m.* 700
periódico, *m.* 645
permitido 714
perro, *m.* 284
perturbación, *f.*; pena, *f.* 1031
pescado frito, *m.* 381
pescado hervido 108
pez, *m.* 353
piano, *m.* 718
piano de cola, *m.* 422
pie, *m.* 363
piedra, *f.* 946
pierna, *f.* 524
pierna, *f.* 863
pijama, *f.* 768
pimienta, *f.* 711
pimiento picante, *m.* 694
pinchar 944
pino, *m.* 725
pino negro, *m.* 947
pino rodeno, *m.* 265
la pintura 689
pinzas para alambre 1104
piojo, *m.* 549
pipa, *f.* 726
piso bajo, *m.* 428
piso primero 351
pistola, *f.* 727
pitillo, *m.* 204
plancha, *f.* 489
plato, *m.* 729
plaza, *f.* 927
plomo, *m.* 520
pluma, *f.* 709
pluma estilográfica 376
poco puntual 1051
pocos 339
pollo asado 816
polvera *f.* 755
por qué 1096
portal, *m.* 400
portero, *m.* 436
portero, *m.* 746
poste restante 71
pozo, *m.* 1087
prado, *m.* 580
Prefectura de Policía 742
preguntar 36
probar; ensayar 1035
prendedor, *m.* 133
prendedor de escritorio 211
primavera, *f.* 926

prohibido 758
pronto 771
proyectil, *m.* 759
pudín, *m.* 761
puente, *f.* 130
puerta, *f.* 286
puerro, *f.* 200
puerro, *m.* 523
puerto, *m.* 745
puerto aéreo, *m.* 8
pulga, *f.* 358
pulgar, *m.* 999
pullover, *m.* 762
pulmones, *pl.* 557
pulsera, *f.* 123
puño, *m.* 354
puntual 765
que; que cosa 1089
quince 341
queso, *m.* 190
quizás 579
rabanito, *m.* 774
rábano, *m.* 775
ramo de flores, *m.* 141
rastro, *m.* 175
rastro, *m.* 780
rata, *f.* 784
ratón, *m.* 617
red, *f.* 643
refugio antiaéreo, *m.* 10
regla, *f.* 825
relámpago, *m.* 533
el reloj 212
reloj de bolsillo 1079
reloj de pulsera, *m.* 1114
remo, *m.* 665
remolacha, *f.* 82
repetir 798
repollo, *m.* 150
res 180
restar; quedar (se) 796
rey, *m.* 500
rico 807
rienda 794
riñón, *m.* 497
río, *m.* 813
rodilla, *f.* 503
rojo \ 789
rosa, *f.* 821
sábado, *m.* 838
sacacorchos, *m.* 237
saco, *m.* 828
saco de provisiones 824
sal *f.* 834
salado 835
salchichón, *m.* 839
salida, *f.* 936
salida, *f.* 322
salsa, *f.* 424
sano 914
sardina en aceite, *f.* 673
sartén, *f.* 387
sastre, *m.* 972
sauco, *m.* 534
secatintas, *m.* 100
secretaria, *f.* 853
seda, *f.* 883
seda artificial, *f.* 35
sediento 993
segar 623

zinc, *m.* 1121
zorro, *m.* 378

zurcir 586

generalidades 1125
Buenos días 1126
Buen día 1127
Buenas tardes 1128
Buenas noches 1129
Hasta la vista 1130
¿Cómo está? 1131
Busco alojamiento 1132
deseo comer 1133
Deseo beber 1134
¿Cómo se llama? 1135
¿Ha entendido? 1136
¿Qué es esto? 1137
¿Dónde está esto? 1138
Muéstreme usted ... 1139
Deme usted ... 1140
¿Cuánto vale esto? 1141
jubón de punto, *m.* 1142
¿Dónde hay ... ? 1143
A la derecha 1144
A la izquierda 1145
lavar el cabello 1146
cortar el pelo 1147

ir al médico 1148
¿Qué hora es? 1149
las cinco 1150
las cinco y cuarto 1151
las cinco y media 1152
las siete menos cuarto 1153
demasiado temprano 1154
demasiado tarde 1155
soy; estoy 1156
Vd. es, está; eres, estás 1157
él, ella es, está 1158
somos; estamos 1159
sois estáis 1160
son; están 1161
tengo, he 1162
Vd. tiene, ha; tienes, has 1163
él, ella ha 1164
tenemos, hemos 1165
tenéis, habéis 1166
ellos (ellas) tienen, han 1167
¿Ha ... Vd.? (¿Tiene Vd.?) 1168
Yo sé 1169
No sé 1170

SWEDISH

skinka-n   437
skjortan   871
skoborste-n   873
skog-en   1106
skola, f.   844
skomakare-n   875
sko, n.; skon-na, pl.   554
skorpa-n   95
skosnöre-t   874
skosula-n   909
skott-et   759
skottkärra-n   174
skrivbord-et   274
skrivmaskin-en   1042
skruv-en   847
skruvmejsel-en   848
skruvnyckel-n   1113
skräddare-n   972
skuldra-n   878
skyddsrumm-et   10
skynda   445
skål-en   120
skåp-et   1073
skära; hugga   254
sköldpadda-n   1020
skön   74
skörda   444
slaktare-n   144
slips-en   1003
slott-et   176
släde-n   894
smed-en   902
smultron-et   953
smutsig   279
smärta-n   688
smör-et   145
snickare-n   171
snö-n   904
sobrumm-et   76
socker   957
soffa-n   907
sol-en   961
soldat-en   908
sommar-en   960
son, m.   910
sopa   965
soppa-n   915
sorgsen; ledsen   912
sova   895
sovvagn-en   896
spad-en   918
spade-n   879 .
sparris-en   37
spatserkäpp-en   943
spelkort-en   731
spenat-en   921
spets-en   506
spetsig   741
spik-en   634
sportskjorta-n   924
sportskor-na, pl.   925
springa   826
springbrunn-en   375
spårvagn-en   1026
spädbarn   49
späck-et   52
stad-en   1022
stall-et   928
stanna; blive   796
station-en   938

stations-inspektor, m.   939
stege-n   507
stek-en   818
steka   815
stekpanna-n   387
stekt höns   816
stekt fisk   381
stekt potatis   382
sten-en   946
stenget-en   186
sticka   944
stjärnor-na, pl.   935
stol-en   184
stoppa   586
stoppgarn-et   861
stor   518
storm-en   949
stridsvagn-en   974
strumpa-n   513
strumpor-na, pl.   945
strupe-n   998
strykbräde-t   490
strykjärn-et   489
stråke-n   118
stå   933
stål-et   941
stalhjälm-en   942
städ-et   22
stämpel-n   932
stängd   213
stövel-n   116
sur   916
svamp-en   628
svara   21
svart   97
svin-et   720
syd   913
sy fast   862
symaskin-en   860
syren-en   534
syster-n   662
syster, f.   897
så   917
såg-en   840
såll-et   881
sås-en   424
säck-en   828
säkerhetsnål-en   831
sälja   855
säng-en   75
söndagen   962
söt   966
tablett-en   971
tack   983
taga   973
tak-et   822
taklampa-n   183
tala   919
tala; urskilja   981
tall-en   352
tallrik-en   729
tand-en, tänder-na, pl.   1017
tandborste-n   1018
tandkräm-en   1019
tant-en   44
tavia-n   689
té-et   977
teater-n   984
tegelsten-en   128
telefon-en   979

allmänt 1125
God morgon 1126
God dag 1127
God kväll; God afton 1128
God natt 1129
På återseende 1130
Huru mår ni? 1131
Jag söker rum 1132
ag will äta 1133
Jag will dricka 1134
Hvad är din namn? 1135
Har Ni förstått? 1136
Vad är det? 1137
Var är det? 1138
Visa mig ... 1139
giv mig ... 1140
Vad kostar det? 1141
tröja-n 1142
Var finns det? 1143
Till höger 1144
Till vänster 1145
tvätta håret 1146
klippa hår-et 1147

gå till läkaren 1148
Hur myket är klockan? 1149
klockan fem 1150
en kvart över fem 1151
halv sex 1152
en kvart i sju 1153
för tidigt 1154
för sent 1155
jag är 1156
Ni är; du är 1157
han, hon, det är 1158
vi äro 1159
ni är 1160
de äro 1161
jag har 1162
Ni har; du har 1163
han, hon, det ar 1164
vi ha (-va) 1165
Ni ha 1166
de ha 1167
Har Ni ... ? 1168
Jag vet 1169
Jag vet inte 1170

TURKISH

pişmek 106
pişmek 235
pişmiş balık 108
pismis yumurta 107
piyade askeri 481
piyano 718
pôjd, *n.* 42
polis dairesi 742
portakal 681
posta havale senedi 601
postada kalarak 751
postahane 750
potin 554
prasa 523
priz 737
puding 761
pudra kutusu 755
pul 931
pullover 762
pusej; opücük 501
pusula 231
radio 1103
rasgelmek 584
reçel 572
rende728
renkler 226
resim 689
resmen bildirmek 793
rica ederim; lûtfen 732
ringa baligi 457
rüzgâr 1100
saat 212
saat 468
sabah 605
sabah entarisi 290
sabun 905
sac 432
saç fırçasi 433
saglam 914
sağmak 593
sal 338
salata 833
salça 424
sali 1036
salik, ehil 1
saman 952
samanlik 62
sandaliye 184
sandık 175
saniye 852
sapan 735
saplamak 944
saray 176
sarga 1116
sarği 289
sarierik 596
sarki söylemek 884
sarmusak yapraği 200
sarrâf dükkâni 317
sarzmusak 396
satin almak 148
satmak 855
savdalya baligi 673
sayiler 661
sebzevat 1055
sekiz 304
seksen 306
sene 1115
sepet 65
serbest 379

servi ağaci 256
sevmek 550
seyahat 1028
seyahat billeti 1002
seyyar hastane 591
siçak 1075
siçan 784
siçan kulagi 370
sifir 1120
sigar 203
sigara 204
sıginak 10
siğir 180
sigir eti 79
silcim 781
sinek 362
sinema 622
sirke 1061
sitma termometrosi 210
sivri 741
sivri sinek 607
ski 893
soğan 679
soğuk 223
so ihriği 109
sonbahar 46
sonbahar 330
sormak 36
söylemek 919
spor ayak kabi 925
spor gómleği 924
su 1080
subat 336
sucuk 839
sulhen; sevimli 499
suni ipek 35
susamiş 993
suterazisi 922
suyut ağaci 1099
süpurga 135
süpürmek 965
süt 592
süzgeç 881
şampanya şarabi 187
şapka 446
şark 300
şatrenc 193
şäl 866
şehir 1022
şehriye 655
şeker 957
şemsiye 1045
şen; hoş 589
şey; iş 991
şilte; döşek 577
şimal 657
şofer 293
tabak 729
taban 909
tabanca 727
tablet 971
tahta kurusu 139
tank yeri 345
tarak 228
tarak 780
tarla 3
taş 946
tatli 966
tava 387
tavan lambasi 183

umumi şeylar 1125
Gün aydin 1126
Gün aydin 1127
Aksaminiz hayir olsun 1128
Geceniz hayir olsun 1129
Yine görüşelim 1130
Nasilsiniz? 1131
Ikamet ariyorum 1132
Yemek isteyorum 1133
Içmek isteyorum 1134
Isminiz ne? 1135
Aniadiniz mi? 1136
Bu nedir? 1137
Bu nerede? 1138
Bana gösteriniz 1139
Bana veriniz ... 1140
Bu kaçadir? 1141
örgü çaketti 1142
Nerde var ...? 1143
Sağda 1144
Sola 1145
saç yikamak 1146
saç kesmek 1147

doktora gitmek 1148
Saat kaçtir? 1149
saat beş 1150
bes i on beş 1151
beş buçuk 1152
yediye çeyrek var 1153
çok erken 1154
çok gec 1155
benim 1156
onlar dir; sen sin 1157
o (iste) 1158
biz iz 1159
siz siniz 1160
onlar dirler 1161
benim var 1162
Sizin var; senin var 1163
onun var 1164
bizim var 1165
sizin var 1166
onlarin var 1167
Sizde var mi? 1168
Bilirim 1169
Bilmem 1170

RUSSIAN

рынок, *m.* 571
сад, *m.* 395
салат, *m.* 833
сало, *n.* 52
сапяр, *m.* 837
самолет, *m.* 5
самопишущяя **ручка, f. 376**
сани, *pl.* 894
сапог, *pl.* 116
сапожник, *m.* 875
сарай, *m.* 62
сардинка, *f.* 673
сахар, *m.* 957
свеча, *f.* 161
свет, *m.* 531
светло; -ый 530
свинец, *m.* 520
свинина, *f.* 744
свиня, *f.* 720
свободный 379
север, *m.* 657
сегодня 1010
седло, *n.* 830
секретарша, *f.* **853**
секунда, *f.* 852
селедка, *f.* 457
семь 857
семьдесят 859
семнадцать 858
сено, *n.* 458
сентябрь 856
сердце, *n.* 452
серна, *f.* 186
серьга, *f.* 299
серый 427
сестра, *f.* 897
сиделка, *f.* 662
сетка, *f.* 643
сеять 917
сигара, *f.* 203
сидеть 888
синий 102
синяя капуста, *f.* **790**
сирена, *f.* 887
сирень *f.* 534
скамья, *f.* 87
скачки, *pl.* 464
скобки для бумаги, *pl.* **211**
сковорода, *f.* 387
скорняк, *m.* 391
скоро 771
скрипка, *f.* 1064
скотина, *f.* 180
сладкий 966
слива, *f.* 738
слива, *f.* 596
сливки, *pl.* 249
смалец, *m.* 517
смерть, *f.* 266
смородина, *f.* 791
смычек, *m.* 118
снег, *m.* 904
собака, f; пес, *m.* **284**
собор *m.* 179
совок, *m.* 219
солдат, *m.* 908
соль, *f.* 834
соленый 835
солома, *f.* 952
солнце, *n.* 961

сорок 374
сорочка, *f.* 871
сосна, *f.* 265
соус, *m.*; подлива, *f.* **424**
спасательный пояс, *m.* **528**
спальня, *f.* 76
спальный вагон, *m.* **896**
спаржа, *f.* 37
спать 895
спина, *f.* 50
спички, *pl.* 576
спортивная рубашка, *f.* **924**
спортивные ботинки, *pl.* **925**
способний 1
справочное бюро, *n.* **483**
спрашивать 36
среда, *f.* 1085
стакан, *m.* 407
сталь, *f.* 941
стальной шлем, *m.* **942**
старый 675
сто 470
стол, *m.* 970
столовая, *f.* 277
столяр, *m.* 171
стоять 933
стоячая лампа, *f.* **934**
стул, *m.* 184
суббота, *f.* 838
сумочка, *f.* 54
суп, *m.* 915
супружество; брак **574**
сустав ноги, *m.* **20**
сухарь, *m.* 95
счет *m.* 90
сын, *m.* 910
сыр, *m.* 190
табак, *m.* 1008
табачный магазин, *m.* **1009**
тачка, *f.* 174
там 985
танец, *m.* 257
танк, *m.* 974
тарелка, *f.* 729
театр *m.* 984
телеграма, *f.* 978
теленок, *m.* 155
телефон, *m.* 979
телятина, *f.* 1054
темно; -ый 259
тепло; -ый 1075
термометр, *m.* 210
тмин, *m.* 169
толстый 987
томат.; помидор, *m.* **1013**
тонкий 990
топор, *m.* 48
топор, *m.* 460
торговое судно, *n.* **588**
торт, *m.* 976
трактор, *m.* 1024
трамвай, *m.* 1026
треть 992
три 997
тридцать 995
тринадцать 994
трость, *f.* 943
тротуар, *m.* 703
трубка, *f.* 726
тупой 104

Что это такое? 1137
Где это? 1138
покажите мне . . . 1139
дайте мне . . . 1140
Сколько это стоит? 1141
кофта вязанная, *f.* 1142
Где это можно найти? 1143
Направо 1144
Налево 1145
мыть голову 1146
стричь волосы 1147
итти к врачу 1148
Который час? 1149
пять часов 1150
пять часов пятнадцать **минут** **1151**
пол шестого 1152
три четверти седьмого 1153

слишком рано 1154
слишком поздно 1155
я (есьм) 1156
ты (есьм) 1157
он, она, оно (есьм) **1158**
мы (есьм) 1159
вы (есьм) 1160
они (есьм) 1161
я имею 1162
ты имееш 1163
он, она, оно имеет **1164**
мы имеем 1165
вы имеете 1166
они имеют 1167
Имеете ли? 1168
(я) знаю 1169
я не знаю 1170

SERBIAN

мандолина, *f.* 567
маргарина, *f.* 570
Март, *m.* 569
маслац, *m.* 145
маст 517
маст, *f.* 674
мастионица, *f.* 484
мачка, *f.* 177
мед, *m.* 125,
мед, *m.* 461
мењачница, *f.* 317
мерило, *n.* 975
месар, *m.* 144
месец, *m.* 602
месец, *m.* 604
месо, *n.* 582
метак, *m.* 759
метла, *f.* 135
минерална вода. *f.* 594
минђуша, *m.* 299
минута, *f.* 595
мирабела,*f.* 596
митральез, *m.* 561
миш, *m.* 617
млеко, *n.* 592
много 626
можда 579
молим 732
море, *n.* 849
морнар, *m.* 832
морски рак, *m.* 546
морт, *m.* 606
мост, *m.* 130
мотор, *m.* 610
мотоцикл, *m.* 613
мрежа, *f.* 643
мркве, *pl.* 173
музати 593
музицки инструмент, *m.* 631
муж, *m.* 566
муньа, *f.* 533
муха, *f.* 362
надзор, *m.* 234
надлактица, *f.* 1052
нажалост; жао ми је 912
накат, *m.* 349
наковань, *m.* 22
наливперо, *n.* 376
наочари, *pl.* 327
налазити 347
напрстак, *m.* 989
наранча, *f.* 681
наруквица, *f.* 123
наслов, *m.* 4
не 654
недельа, *f.* 962
незаборавак, *m.* 370
непогода, *f.* 949
нечист 279
нивела, *f.* 922
никал, *m.* 647
ниска ципела, *f.* 554
ньива, *f.* 3
нов 644
новац, *m.* 600
Новембар 660
новина, *f.* 645
новчаник, *m.* 767
нога, *f.* 363
нога, *f.* 524

ногомет, *m.* 364
нож, *m.* 504
нож за бријање *m.* 785
нос, *m.* 658
носач, *m.* 747
нота, *f.* 630
ноћ, *f.* 648
ноћна кошульа, *f.* 649
ноћни орманчић, *m.* 650
нужник, *m.* 1012
нула, *f.* 1120
обесак, *m.* 165
облак, *m.* 215
образ, *m.* 189
оброк, *m.* 581
обруч, *m.* 1043
обућар, *m.* 875
овде 456
овнетина, *f.* 632
овца, *f.* 868
ог 14
огрлица, *f.* 641
огртач 512
одговорити 21
оделение, *n.* 230
одело, *n.* 214
одело женско, *n.* 511
одјавити 659
око, *n.* 326
Октобар 669
олива, *f.* 676
оловка, *f.* 710
олово, *n.* 520
оморика, *f.* 725
опасность, *f.* 258
опека, *f.* 128
ораменице, *pl.* 124
орати 736
орах, *m.* 1072
ормар, *m.* 1073
ормар за акта, *m.* 869
ормар за књиге, *m.* 112
оса, *f.* 1078
осам 304
осамнаест 305
осамдесет 306
остати 796
острига, *f.* 687
отач, *m.* 334
отворен 680
Откуда? 1092
отпутовати 522
официр, *m.* 671
падобран, *m.*695
пакет, *m.* 696
палюх 999
палица за шетньу, *f.* 943
палма, *f.* 690
памук, *m.* 243
панталоне, *pl.* 1032
паприка, *f.* 694
папуча, *f.* 898
парадајз, *m.* 1013
парк, *m.* 699
пас. *m.* 284
пасош, *m.* 702
паста за зубе, *f.* 1019
пасуль, *m.* 73
патка, *f.* 296
педесет 342

салата, *f.* 833
сандук, *m.* 175
саонице, *pl.* 894
сапун, *m.* 905
сардина у уљу. *f.* 673
састајати се 584
сат, *m.* 468
сашити 862
свадба, *f.* 1083
светиљка, *f.* 516
светлост, *f.* 531
свила, *f.* 883
свиња, *f.* 720
свињско месо, *n.* 744
свећа, *f.* 161
седам 857
седамнаест 858
седамдесет 859
седети 888
седло, *n.* 830
седмица, *f.* 1086
сејати 917
секира, *f.* 460
секретарица, *f.* 853
сект, *m.* 187
секунда, *f.* 852
сељак, *m.* 707
сељанка, *f.* 708
сељачка кућа, *f.* 333
сељачко газдинство, *n.* 332
село, *n.* 1060
сено, *n.* 458
Септембар 856
сестра, *f.* 662
сестра, *f* 897
сив 427
сидро, *n.* 17
сијалица, *f.* 308
сир, *m.* 190
сирена, *f.* 887
син, *m.* 910
сирће, *n.* 1061
сито, *n.* 881
сјевер, *m.* 657
сјести 889
скела, *f.* 338
скела, *f.* 842
склониште, *n.* 10
скоруп, *m.* 249
скуп 323
слабо 53
сладолед, *m.* 474
сладак 966
слама, *f.* 952
сланина, *f.* 52
слеђ, *m.* 457
слика, *f.* 689
слободан 379
служавка, *f.* 562
слушкиња, *f.* 185
смоква, *f.* 343
смрт, *f.* 266
смучка, *f.* 893
снег, *m.* 904
со, *f.* 834
соба, *f.* 545
соба на табану, *f.* 397
спаваоница, *f.* 76
спавати 895
спаваћа кола, *f.* 896

спаваће одело, *n.* 768
спинача, *f.* 921
спис, *m.* 283
споменик, *m.* 603
спортска кошуља, *f.* 924
спортска обућа, *f.* 925
способан 1
среда, *f.* 1085
срце, *n.* 452
стаја, *f.* 928
стајати 933
стан, *m.* 356
станица, *f.* 938
станица, *f.* 948
станка, *f.* 805
стар 675
стеница, *f.* 139
степенице, *pl.* 930
сто 470
сто, *m.* 970
стојећа лампа, *f.* 934
столар, *m.* 171
столац, *m.* 31
столица, *f.* 184
стрина; тетка, *f.* 44
стриц, *m.* 1046
строј, *m.* 560
струг, *m.* 728
субота, *f.* 838
сукња, *f.* 384
сунце, *n.* 961
сутра 1014
та 973
табан, *m.* 909
таблета, *f.* 971
тачно 765
таман 259
Тамо 985
тањир, *m.* 729
творница, *f.* 329
теле, *n.* 155
телеграм, *m.* 978
мелетина, *f.* 1054
телефон, *m.* 979
тело, *n.* 85
тенк, *m.* 974
теретни ауто, *m.* 614
тесар, *m.* 493
тестера, *f.* 840
тигањ, *f.* 387
топ, *m.* 162
топао 1075
топломер, *m.* 210
торта, *f.* 976
трактор, *m.* 1024
трамвај, *m.* 1026
трафика, *f.* 1009
тгр, *m.* 927
трг; пијаца, *f.* 571
трговачка лађа, *f.* 588
трећина 992
трешња, *f.* 192
три 997
тридесет 995
тринаест 994
тротоар, *m.* 703
трпезарија, *f.* 277
труба, *f.* 1034
трчати 826
туга, *f.* 1031

Шта је то? 1137
Где је то? 1138
покажите ми . . . 1139
дајте ми . . . 1140
шта стаје то? 1141
плетена блуза, ƒ. 1142
Где је то? 1143
Десно 1144
Лево 1145
прати косу 1146
шишати косу 1147
ићи лекару 1148
Колика је сати? 1149
пет сати 1150
пет и четверт 1151
пет и по 1152
шест и тричетврт 1153

прерано 1154
прекасно 1155
ја сам 1156
ти си 1157
он, она, оно је 1158
ми смо 1159
ви сте 1160
они су 1161
ја имам 1162
ти имаш 1163
он, она, оно има 1164
ми имамо 1165
ви имате 1166
они имају 1167
имате ли? 1168
знам 1169
не знам 1170

UKRAINIAN

мати 447
мати, *f.* 608
матрац, *f.* 577
матрос, *m.* 832
машина, *f.* 560
машина до писання, *f.* 1042
машина до шиття, *f.* 860
мед, *m.* 461
мережка, *f.* 506
металі, *pl.* 590
метелик, *m.* 119
метелик, *m.* 146
метер, *m.* 975
мило, *n.* 905
мінерална вода, *f.* 594
миш, *f.* 617
мідь, *f.* 236
мірабеля, *f.* 596
міст, *m.* 130
місто, *n.* 1022
місяць, *m.* 602
мішок, *m.* 828
можливо 579
молоко, *n.* 592
молот. *m.* 438
море, *n.* 849
мореля, *f.* 28
морква, *f.* 173
морозиво, *n.* 474
мосяж, *m.* 125
мотор, *m.* 610
мотуз, *m.* 823
музика, *f.* 629
музикални інструмент, *m.* 631
мука, *f.* 359
мул, *m.* 627
муляр, *m.* 129
мускатний горіх, *m.* 663
муха, *f.* 362
мушля, *f.* 867
мущина, *m.* 566
м'ясо, *n.* 582
нагніток, *m.* 238
накидка; пелзрина, *f.* 165
намисто, *n.*; коралі, *pl.* 641
наперсток, *m.* 989
наплечник, *m.* 824
порід, *m.*; народження, *n.* 93
наручний годинник, *m.* 1114
напятковий сустав, *m.* 20
наушники, *pl.* 298
находити 347
начальник бюра, *m.* 450
начальник станції, *m.* 939
небезпека, *n.* 258
неділя, *f.* 962
незабудька, *f.* 370
немовля, *n.* 49
не точно 1051
нирка, *f.* 497
нитки, *pl.* 861
ні 654
ніготь, *m.* 349
ніж, *m.* 504
нікель, *m.* 647
ніс, *m.* 658
ніч, *f.* 648
нічна сорочка, *f.* 649
нічний столик, *m.* 650
новий 644

нога, *f.* 524
ножик, *m.* 740
ножиці, *pl.* 845
ножиці блягарські, *pl.* 1104
носильник, *m.* 747
ноти, *pl.* 630
обід, *m.* 278
обід, *ж.* 581
обруч, *m.* 1043
обручка; браслет, *m.* 123
овес, *m.* 666
овоч, *m.* 386
огірок, *m.* 251
одна четверта 769
один 678
один; неодружений 885
один раз 677
одинадять 310
одна третя 992
одно кіло, *n.* 498
однострій, *m.* 1049
одяг, *m.* 214
одяг, *m.* 288
одяг жіночий, *m.* 511
озеро, *n.* 514
око 326
оксамит, *m.* 1056
окуляри, *pl.* 327
олень, *m.* 929
олівець, *m.* 710
оливка, *f.* 676
олій, *m.* 672
олово, *n.* 520
опаска, f.; бандаж, *m.* 60
орати 736
оса, *f.* 1078
осел, *m.* 285
оселедець, *m.* 457
орзшрубник, *m.* 848
осінь, *f.* 46
особове авто, *n.* 612
оцет, *m.* 1061
отворений 680
Падолист 660
пакунок, *m.* 555
пакунок; пакет, *m.* 696
палиця, *f.* 943
пальма, *f.* 690
пальці, *pl.* 348
пальці в нозі, *pl.* 1011
палац 999
памятник, *m.* 603
пан, *m.* 886
пані; дама, *f.* 625
підштанці, *pl.*; панталони, *pl.* 287
чулок. *m.* панчохи, *pl.* 945
папір, *m.* 693
паприка, *f.* 694
паросоля, *f.* 1045
пасок; пояс. *m.* 86
паста до зубів, *f.* 1019
пауза, *f.* 805
пашпорт, *m.* 702
пекар, *m.* 57
пекти 56
пекти 815
пендзель до гелення, *m.* 865
перевязь, *f.* 289
передвчора 264
переділ, *m.* 230

сардинка на оливі, *f.* **673**
свердел; сверлик, *m.* **117**
светер, *m.* 762
свиня, *f.* 720
свиняче мясо, *n.* **744**
світло, *n.* 531
свічка, *f.* 161
секретарка, *f.* **853**
секунда, *f.* **852**
село, *n.* 1060
селянин, *m.* 707
селянська хата, *f.* **333**
селянка, *f.* 708
сердце, *n.* 452
середа, *f.* 1085
Серпень, 43
сестра, *f.* 662
сестра, *f.* 897
сидіти 888
син, *m.* 910
сир, *m.* 190
сирена, *f.* 887
сито, *n.* 881
сідати 889
сідло, *n.* 830
сіль, *f.* 834
сім 857
сімдесять 859
сімнадцять 858
сіно, *n.* 458
сірий; сивий 427
сірник, *m.* 576
сітка, *f.* 643
Січень, *m.* 492
сіяти 917
склянка, *f.* 407
склеп з цигарками,   *m.* **1009**
сковородка, *f.* **387**
скриня, *f.* 175
скрипка, *f.* 1064
сливка, *f.* 738
смалець 517
смерека, хвоя, *f.* **725**
смерть, *f.* 266
сметана, *f.* 249
смик; смичок, *m.* **118**
смок, *m.*; помпа, *f.* **763**
сніг, *m.* 904
сніданок, *m.* **127**
собор, *m.* 179
совги; лещети, *pl.* 893
солдат; вояк, *m.* **908**
солодкий 966
солома, *f.* 952
солоний 835
солонина, *f.* 52
сонце, *n.* 961
сорок 374
сорочка, *f.* 871
сосна, *f.* 265
сьогодні; нині 1010
спальня, *f.* 76
спальний вагон, *m.* **896**
спальний одяг, *m.* **768**
спати 895
спинка, *f.* 954
співати 884
спортова сорочка, *f.* **924**
спортовий черевик, *m.* **925**
споювач, *m.* 211

справа; діловитість **143**
стайня, *f.* **928**
сталь, *f.* **941**
старшина, *m.* 671
старий 675
стегно, *n.* 988
хребет, *m.*; спина, *f.* **50**
стіл, *m.* 970
стіл до писання, *m.* **274**
сто 470
столяр, *m.* 171
стопа, *f.* 363
стояти 933
стаяча лямпа, *f.* **934**
стравоспис, *m.* 587
стрільно, *n.* 759
струг, *m.* 728
студня; криниця, *f.* **1087**
тинк, *m.*; ступка, *f.* **606**
субота, *f.* 838
суконка, *f.* 384
сумний 829
суниця; полуница, *f.* **953**
супружиство, *n.*; шлюб, *m.* **574**
сухар, *m.* 95
схід, *m.* 300
сходи, *pl.* 930
табір, *m.* 159
так 1117
Там 985
танець, *m.* 257
танк, *m.* 974
тарілка, *f.* 729
тачка, *f.* 174
театер, *m.* 984
темний 259
телеграма, *f.* 978
телефон, *m.* 979
теля, *n.* 155
теляче мясо, *n.* 1054
теплий 1075
тепломір, *m.* 210
тесля, *m.* 493
тіждень, *m.* 1086
трийцять 995
тисяча 996
тіло, живіт, *m.* 85
тістечко, *n.*; торт, *m.* **154**
тітка, *f.* 44
тонкий 990
топір *m.*; сокира, *f.* **48**
торбинка, *f.* 54
торг; базар, *m.* 571
торговельний дім, *m.* **1074**
торговельний корабель, *m.* **588**
торт, *m.* 976
точно 765
трактор, *m.* 1024
трамвай, *m.* 1026
тринадцять 994
три 997
тримбулька, *f.* 200
труба, *f.* 1034
тульпан, *m.* 1037
тупий 104
тут 456
туфлі, *pl.* 898
тютюн, *m.* 1008
умивальня, *f.* 1077
уродини; день народженна,   *m.* **94**

Де це находитьтя? 1143
Нн право 1144
На ліво 1145
мити волосся 1146
стригти волосся 1147
йти до лікара 1148
Ктора година? 1149
пята година 1150
чверть на шосту 1151
пів до шостої 1152
три чверти на сему 1153
за скоро 1154
за пізно 1155
я е 1156

ти е 1157
він, вона, воно е 1158
ми е 1159
ви е 1160
вони е 1161
я маю 1162
ти маеш 1163
він, вона, воно мае 1164
ми маемо 1165
ви маете 1166
вони мають 1167
Чи ви маете? 1168
я знаю 1169
я не знаю 1170

More Language Books
From Carol Publishing Group